# Reports of Cases in the Court of Chancery in the Time of Queen Anne

## English Law Reports of the Early Modern Period

**Volume One:** *Equity Cases in the Court of Exchequer, 1660–1714*, Edited by W. H. Bryson, 2007. [This volume can be cited as Eq. Cases Exch.]

**Volume Two:** *Robert Paynell's Exchequer Reports (1627–1631),* Edited by W. H. Bryson, 2009. [This volume can be cited as Paynell Exch.]

**Volume Three:** *Robert Paynell's King's Bench Reports (1625–1627),* Edited by W. H. Bryson, 2010. [This volume can be cited as Paynell K.B.]

**Volume Four:** *Reports of Cases in the Court of Exchequer in the Time of King George I (1714–1727),* Edited by W. H. Bryson, 2013. [This volume can be cited as Exch. Cases *temp.* Geo. I.]

**Volume Five:** *Reports of Cases in the Court of Exchequer in the Time of King Charles II,* Edited by W. H. Bryson, 2017. [This volume can be cited as Exch. Cases *temp.* Char. II.]

**Volume Six:** *Reports of Cases in the Court of Chancery in the Time of King George I,* Edited by W. H. Bryson, 2019. [This volume can be cited as Chan. Cases *temp.* Geo. I.]

**Volume Seven:** *Paul Jodrell's Chancery Reports (1737 to 1751),* Edited by W. H. Bryson, 2020. [This volume can be cited as Jodrell.]

Medieval and Renaissance
Texts and Studies

Volume 581

Center for Law Reporting

Volume 8

# Reports of Cases in the Court of Chancery in the Time of Queen Anne

## (1702 to 1714)

EDITED BY

W. H. BRYSON

Arizona Center for Medieval & Renaissance Studies
Tempe, Arizona
2021

Arizona Center
for Medieval &
Renaissance Studies

Published by ACMRS (Arizona Center for Medieval and Renaissance Studies)
Tempe, Arizona


ISBN 978-0-86698-641-0

∞
This book is set in Adobe Caslon Pro.
*Printed in the United States of America.*

# Introduction

The law reports published here include cases from the Court of Chancery from 1702 to 1714, the judicial tenures of Sir Nathan Wright, 1700 to 1705, Lord Cowper, 1705 to 1708, Lord Harcourt, 1710 to 1714, and Lord Cowper again, 1714 to 1718. There were commissioners to hold the great seal and to sit in the Court of Chancery from 1708 to 1710. The majority are reports of cases decided by Sir Simon Harcourt, Lord Harcourt (1661–1727), who was Lord Chancellor from 1710 to 1714.[1]

Only a few of these cases have been reported elsewhere. Thus, the importance of these reports is that they fill a gap in the printed reports from the Court of Chancery during the tenure of Lord Harcourt, about whose decisions not much has been known. From the five-year tenure of Lord Harcourt, only approximately 150 Chancery cases have heretofore been reported in print; there are now more that double than number of cases from these five years in this set of reports printed here. Edward Foss and Lord Campbell had somewhat tepid opinions of Lord Harcourt as a judge,[2] but there were only a few of Harcourt's opinions in print at the time when they were writing. Perhaps, a reassessment is now due.

This is a collection of miscellaneous manuscript reports from the Court of Chancery from 1702 to 1714, the reign of Queen Anne. There can be no pretension to completeness, as there is no way of knowing what manuscripts are lurking in private libraries. A few out of the way cases and some short printed reports are also included. Among the larger manuscript collections used are the following.

## Cases in Chancery

Although the original manuscript of this collection has not been located, three copies have been found.

---

[1] J. Campbell, *Lives of the Lords Chancellors of England* (1874 ed.), vol. 5, pp. 296–351; S. Handley, 'Harcourt, Simon, first Viscount Harcourt', *Oxford Dictionary of National Biography*, vol. 25, pp. 131–134.

[2] E. Foss, *The Judges of England* (1864), vol. 8, p. 40; J. Campbell, *The Lives of the Lords Chancellors, supra.*

### A. Lincoln's Inn MS. Misc. 383

Lincoln's Inn MS. Misc. 383 was owned by Lucius O'Brien of Dublin and later by Lord Chancellor Alexander Wedderburn, earl of Rosslyn (1733–1805). It was bought by Lincoln's Inn in 1848 from the London bookseller, Thomas Rodd (1796–1849).[3] This manuscript ends with an incomplete report of *Pearson v. Rowland* (Ch. 1715).

### B. Lincoln's Inn MSS. Misc. 106 and Misc. 107, ff. 1–66

Lincoln's Inn MSS. Misc. 106 and Misc. 107, ff. 1–66, is another copy of these reports. It includes most, but not all, of the cases printed here. Each case ends with a notation that it came 'from Mr. Cox's notes'. This is not sufficient to know which Cox is being referenced or, since the original is at present unlocated, to know whether Cox reported the cases himself or copied them from someone else or merely owned the manuscript book. This copy is better than the other two that have been located so far; therefore, it has been used to correct silently misreadings in British Library MS. Hargrave 80. These manuscripts are long notebooks; however, the reports are not notes made in court, but, rather, it is a carefully made copy of another manuscript. These books were owned by Charles Abbot, baron Colchester (1757–1829), and were presented to Lincoln's Inn in November 1848.[4]

### C. British Library MS. Hargrave 80

British Library MS. Hargrave 80 has the title 'Cases in Chancery'. It was bought by Francis Hargrave (c. 1741–1821) from Elizabeth Lynch (d. 1794) of Dublin. Hargrave's manuscripts were bought by the British Museum (now the British Library) in 1813.[5] This is a professional copy of the original; corrections have been made in another hand to correct some of the obvious misreadings, such as 'marriage' for 'mortgage'. This manuscript has slightly more cases than Lincoln's Inn MS. Misc. 383, which ends with an incomplete report of *Pearson v. Rowland* (Ch. 1715). The British Library manuscript continues on for another fifteen cases.

## British Library MS. Hargrave 81

British Library MS. Hargrave 81 is an eighteenth-century professional copy. The text was copied on the rectos only, leaving the versos blank except for one case, *Cope v. Futor* (Ch. 1714), which the copyist omitted in the copying and

[3] J. H. Baker, *English Legal Manuscripts* (1978), vol. 2, pp. 108–109.

[4] J. H. Baker, *English Legal Manuscripts* (1978), vol. 2, p. 98.

[5] H. Ellis, *A Catalogue of Manuscripts . . . of Francis Hargrave, Esq.* (1818), pp. [v], 21.

then went back and added at the correct place, but on the facing verso. There is no internal or external evidence of the reporter's identification. The book was bought by Francis Hargrave (d. 1821) from Elizabeth Lynch (d. 1794) of Dublin along with a number of other legal manuscripts. Hargrave's manuscripts were sold to the British Museum (now the British Library) in 1813.[6] This manuscript has 287 folios at the present; the following folios in the original foliation are now missing, 89, 94, 107–124, 193–194. They were missing when the British Museum acquired the book, and most probably also when Hargrave received it. The cases date from 1710 to 1724. They are not in chronological order. These cases all come from the Court of Chancery except for one case from the Court of Exchequer, *Bean v. Lee* (Ex. 1713). This manuscript is a combination of two separate sets of Chancery reports: part 1, ff. 2–163 (1710–1718); part 2, ff. 164–286 (1722–1724). Note that each has a different version of the case of *Duke of Rutland v. Duchess of Rutland* (Ch. 1724).

British Library MS. Hargrave 82 is another copy of the set of reports found in British Library MS. Hargrave 81. The copying is not as careful as British Library MS. Hargrave 81. It also was acquired by Hargrave from Elizabeth Lynch and, no doubt, in the same shipment. It also is a professional copy in a very similar hand, and the versos are left blank. One may suppose that they were both made for Mrs. Lynch for her stock of books for sale.

British Library MS. Hargrave 77, ff. 1–42v, is another copy of the reports that comprise the first part of British Library MS. Hargrave 81, ff. 2–163, and British Library MS. Hargrave 82, ff. 1–173, with some additional cases at ff. 43–55 dating from 1714 to 1716. It came from Mrs. Lynch also.

British Library MS. Hargrave 303, ff. 1–75, is another copy of the cases in British Library MS. Hargrave 77, ff. 1–42v. The same additional cases at the end of Hargrave 77 are at ff. 75v-94 here. This was formerly Lynch MS. 28.

Hargrave 77 and Hargrave 303 are the same. These two collections are very close to Hargrave 81 and Hargrave 82, but there are substantial differences.

Lincoln's Inn MS. Misc. 107, ff. 91–141, includes some of the reports towards the end of this set of cases.

---

[6] H. Ellis, *A Catalogue of Manuscripts . . . of Francis Hargrave, Esq.* (1818), pp. [v], 21; J. H. Baker, 'Hargrave, Francis', *Oxford Dictionary of National Biography*, vol. 25, pp. 270–271.

## Lincoln's Inn MSS. Misc. 10–12

Lincoln's Inn MSS. Misc. 10–12 were compiled and partly written by William Melmoth, Sr. (1665–1743), a bencher of Lincoln's Inn. They cover the period 1695 to 1742. After a contentious will dispute, these books were acquired by Lincoln's Inn in 1835.[7] The cases are not in chronological order.

These reports were originally in English. They have been rendered into modern spelling for this edition, according to the principle of *idem sonans*, which is that a word is the spoken word, not the written word.

[7] J. H. Baker, *English Legal Manuscripts*, vol. 2, pp. 91–92 (1978); E. Major and N. Pohl, 'Melmoth, William, the elder (1665/6–1743)', *Oxford Dictionary of National Biography*, vol. 37, pp. 757–759.

# Table of Cases Reported

[These references are to case numbers, not page numbers.]

# Reports of Cases in the Court of Chancery in the Time of Queen Anne

## 1

### Stokes v. Stokes

(Ch. 1702)

*A mutual and voluntary contract for separate maintenance is valid and specifically enforceable.*

Lincoln's Inn. MS. Misc. 9, p. 23, pl. 1

Easter term 1 *Annae reginae.*

The plaintiff and her husband living in some difference, they agreed to part, and he was to allow her £20 a year for a separate maintenance. Thereupon, he entered into articles with two friends of his wife to pay her £20 a year during so long time as she should live apart from him and should maintain herself at her own charge, and the trustees covenanted to save him harmless against all debts that his wife should contract during the time that they lived asunder. The husband paid the £20 a year for some time. But, afterwards, being sued for a debt of his wife (in which action the plaintiff was nonsuited and paid the usual costs), he refused to pay the £20 a year.

And, thereupon, the wife preferred a bill against her husband and the trustees to have an execution of this agreement, to which the husband put in his answer and, thereby, confessed the agreement. But he said that he was willing to receive his wife and, if she would come home to him, he would provide for her. And, therefore, he prayed that the articles might be set aside.

And it was insisted on on his behalf that to decree a performance of this agreement would be to decree a divorce, which this court would never do. And so My Lord Nottingham refused to do in the case of [ *blank* ].[1]

---

[1] *Mildmay v. Mildmay* (1682), 1 Vernon 53, 23 E.R. 305, 2 Chancery Cases 102, 22 E.R. 866, 1 Eq. Cas. Abr. 67, 21 E.R. 881.

But it was answered by the court [Trevor] that this differs from that case, for there was an elopement, but here is a parting by consent and the husband had put it out of his own power to take his wife, for he has agreed to pay her £20 so long as she will live from him and maintain herself. And, accordingly, it was decreed that the articles were good and that the husband should pay the arrears and the growing rent, out of which should be deducted what the suit had cost him over and above the costs received upon the nonsuit. But the defendant was to pay the costs of this suit.

## 2

## Bruen v. Bruen

(Ch. 1702)

*Where land is charged with raising a portion, it is intended to be for the benefit of the family, and, if the child dies before there is a need for that portion, it shall not be raised for his or her administrator, because the portion was only intended for an advancement of that child.*

Lincoln's Inn MS. Misc. 9, p. 23, pl. 2

Mrs. Bruen, the widow of [ *blank* ] Bruen and administratrix of her daughter, Honora Bruen v. the trustees and encumbrancers of the estate of the said Mr. Bruen.

Mr. Bruen, upon his marriage with the plaintiff, conveys an estate to trustees to the use of himself for life, then to his wife for life, then to his first and other sons in tail, with remainder to the trustees, their executors, etc. for 500 years, with remainder over. And, as for the term, it was declared to be upon trust that, in case he should die without issue male and should have one or more daughters, then the trustees, out of the rents and profits of the premises or by sale or mortgage, should raise £3000 for such daughter or daughters to be paid them within a year after the death of the survivor of Mr. Bruen and his wife.

Afterwards, he makes his will (having one daughter only) and, thereby, devises other land to his wife in the first place to make up her jointure £200 a year and then to raise £3000 portion for his daughter and, when she had secured her £200 a year and the £3000 for her daughter, then, she was to surrender to him to whom he had devised the reversion. Some time after which, Mr. Bruen dies. And, after his death, his daughter dies, being then about five years of age.

The plaintiff takes administration to her daughter and prefers a bill for the £3000. And if it should now be raised was the question.

This cause was heard before the Master of the Rolls [Trevor], who decreed against the plaintiff. And, now, it was heard before My Lord Keeper [Wright] upon an appeal from that decree.

Lord Keeper [Wright]: If it was a personal legacy, there would be no doubt, for if a legacy is given to a child to be paid at twenty-one and the child dies before, it shall go to the administrator of the child.

But where land is charged with raising a portion, it is intended for the benefit of the family, and, if the child dies before there is occasion for that portion, it shall not be raised for the administrator, for the portion was only intended for an advancement of that child. And, when that reason ceases, the inheritance shall not be charged. And so were the cases of Pawlet and Pawlet and Yates and Fettyplace.[1] It began to be so decreed in My Lord Nottingham's time and has continued ever since.

It has been objected that, if a portion should not be raised until the child has occasion for it, why then, where there is no maintenance in the meantime, a child may share. Why pray consider how it would be in the case of a personal legacy where a sum of money is devised to a child to be paid at twenty-one or day of marriage and no provision is made in the meantime for the maintenance of that child, sure, if any *prochein ami* of that child comes into this court, this court will take care that the child be maintained. Indeed, if the profits are devised away in the meantime, we cannot.

Why then, suppose it was where land is charged with raising a portion in the like manner, if no maintenance is directed, this court will compel the trustees to raise a maintenance by the mortgaging of the land.

I think, as this case is, the decree ought to be affirmed. As to the maintenance of the child, the mother must have an allowance for that out of the estate for so long as she maintained her.

[Other reports of this case: 2 Vernon 439, 23 E.R. 881, Precedents in Chancery 195, 24 E.R. 94, 1 Eq. Cas. Abr. 267, 21 E.R. 1036.]

## 3

## Dixie v. Dixie

(Ch. 1702)

*A court of equity will grant relief against a bond made in bad faith where the consideration for it was not performed.*

*A court of equity can prohibit a life tenant from committing bad faith waste.*

---

[1] *Lady Poulet v. Lord Poulet* (1683), 2 Ventris 366, 86 E.R. 489, 1 Vernon 204, 321, 23 E.R. 415, 496, 2 Freeman 93, 22 E.R. 1079, 2 Chancery Reports 286, 21 E.R. 680, 1 Eq. Cas. Abr. 267, 21 E.R. 1036, Chancery Reports *tempore* Jac. II, 85, British Library MS. Lansdowne 1064, f. 338v; *Yates v. Fettyplace* (1701), 2 Vernon 416, 23 E.R. 868, also Precedents in Chancery 140, 24 E.R. 67, 12 Modern 276, 88 E.R. 1319, 2 Freeman 243, 22 E.R. 1185, 1 Lord Raymond 508, 91 E.R. 1239, 2 Eq. Cas. Abr. 541, 559, 653, 654, 22 E.R. 456, 471, 548, 550.

*The certificate of a deposition is amendable.*

Lincoln's Inn MS. Misc. 9, p. 28

Sir Woolston Dixie v. the widow and younger children of Sir Beamont Dixie.

Sir Beamont Dixie, upon the marriage of Sir Woolston, his eldest son, with Mrs. Atkins, makes a settlement upon them, in which was reserved a power to Sir Woolston to make leases for twenty-one years or three lives at the improved rent, to commit waste, and to make a jointure upon a second wife, but all this after Sir Beamont's death.

Sir Beamont, after the marriage, was uneasy that his son had so great a power and, therefore, employed one John Harper to treat with his son about extinguishing those powers and told him, if his son would agree so to do, he would settle Catsby upon him, which was £150 a year. (This was proved in the cause.) In pursuance of this agreement, a deed was executed by Sir Woolston, whereby he covenanted not to make use of those powers of making a second settlement and making leases, and he enters into a bond of £10,000 penalty for the performance.

Sir Beamont, after this, refuses to settle Catsby on his son according to his agreement, but settles it upon his son for life, but that was after the expiration of a term of fifty years, which was not to commence until after the death of a life in being. There was a second bond given by Sir Woolaston to his father of £1000 penalty not to commit waste. But this was given after Sir Beamont refused to make the settlement.

And to be relieved against these bonds and covenants, the bill was brought, it being insisted on that the consideration on which they were founded was not performed and that Sir Beamont had not power to cut timber for repairs, but was threatened to be sued on his bond.

Lord Keeper [Wright]: It is plain not one tittle of the consideration was performed. And, therefore, I am of the opinion that the articles and the first bond ought to be delivered up and a perpetual injunction [made] in the meantime.

As to the second bond, that was given after Sir Beamont refused to make the settlement and so that could not be the consideration but that which seems to be the consideration was that Sir Beamont, being tenant for life with power to commit waste, tells his son, if he would not consent to relinquish his power of committing waste, he would cut down the wood himself, so that I can come up to the same decree as to the delivering up of this bond. But, then, I shall leave the plaintiff at liberty to commit waste which would be contrary to Sir Beamont's intention, which makes me a little at a loss. But I think the best way would be to let the bond be brought into court and not put in suit without leave of the court and that the plaintiff shall not cut any timber nor commit any waste and that commissioners be appointed, three to be nominated by the plaintiff and three by the defendants, and they to be renewed from time [to time] and that nothing be done as to the cutting of the wood but what they shall approve of.

12 Simons 346, 59 E.R. 1164

4 May 1702.

Whereas, upon the plaintiff's humble petition preferred to the Right Honorable the Master of the Rolls [Trevor], the 1st instant, showing that, on Tuesday the 5th day of February last, a commission for examination of witnesses was executed in this cause at the house of Judith Mathews, widow, in Market Bosworth, in the County of Leicester, wherein the defendants joined and examined one witness and cross-examined most of the defendant's (plaintiff's, query) witnesses and the commissioners on both sides signed and certified the commission and the interrogatories and depositions on both sides, and the defendant's commissioners brought the commission up to London and delivered the same into Court, that, upon opening the commission, it appeared that the clerk who took the depositions, through inadvertency, omitted to set down the day of taking the depositions in the title thereof and only mentioned the same to be taken at the house of the same Judith Mathews, which being not taken notice of by the commissioners, the same was with that omission certified and returned into Court, wherefore and for that it appeared by the certificate of the commissioners and affidavit thereto annexed that the execution of the commission was begun on the day aforesaid and continued four days, it was prayed that the said mistake might be rectified and the day of the month and year of our Lord inserted therein and the record amended accordingly, which was ordered accordingly unless cause [be shown] on this day, and the clerks in court on both sides this day attending and the defendant's clerk in court consenting that the said mistake should be rectified, His Lordship, on hearing the said petition read, does order that the said mistake be rectified and amended and that, between the word 'taken' and the words 'at the house of Judith Mathews, widow', in the title of the said depositions be inserted these words, *viz.* 'on Tuesday the 5th day of February, in the 13th year of the reign of our Sovereign Lord William the Third, by the grace of God, King of England, Scotland, France, and Ireland, Defender of the Faith, etc. *anno Domini* 1701', and that the plaintiff's Six Clerk do insert the same and amend the same accordingly.

[Lib. Reg. 1701 A, f. 271.]

4

## Bateman v. Bateman

(Ch. 1702)

*If a father purchases something in the name of a child and there is no declaration of trust, it is taken to be an advancement of that child.*

2 Vernon 436, 23 E.R. 880

7 May [1702].

Joseph Bateman, the father, in 1691, purchased an estate at Erith in Kent in the name of William Bateman, his eldest son, and he was put into possession. And, about a year afterwards, falling sick, his father, Joas, got him to execute a deed, declaring his name was used only in trust for his father. But he, recovering of his sickness, continued the possession as formerly.

And, in 1695, he married the defendant, the widow of Vanackre, she having a jointure of £600 *per annum* and an inheritance of £400 *per annum* more. Upon the marriage, an agreement was made that, in case she survived William Bateman, he would leave her £4000, and he gave a bond to perform covenants. As to dower, nothing was mentioned one way or the other. William Bateman dying without issue, Sir James Bateman, his brother and heir, conveyed to Joas Bateman, the father.

The defendant, the widow of William, brought her writ of her dower.

Joas Bateman, the father, brought his bill to be relieved against it, and he obtained a decree at the Rolls.

Now, upon an appeal to the Lord Keeper [Wright], he dismissed the plaintiff's bill, declaring it to be a secret and fraudulent deed of trust to deceive creditors and purchasers.

Lincoln's Inn MS. Misc. 9, p. 25

Joseph Bateman, the plaintiff and father of the defendant, purchases the rectory of A. in Kent in his son, the defendant husband's name for £6500, £5500 of which were paid by the father and the other £1000 the son had engaged to pay. After this, the father puts his son into possession of this estate, only the father kept the capital messuage for his own convenience to retire to sometimes in the summer. But the son was always looked upon to be the owner of the estate, and so the father declared several times. And being once in the country, he began to blame the ill husbandry of his son for not improving one of the fields, to which the son made answer that it would cost him more money than the field was worth, whereupon the father replied, 'if it was mine, I am sure I would do it'.

It was also proved in the cause that, the rectory being vacant, application was made to the father in the behalf of one B. to be presented, but the father made answer that he would speak to his son about it. And, after that, the father acquainted the person that applied to him that he had spoken to his son and that his son was pre-engaged.

Sometime after this, the son, upon the credit of this estate, makes his address to a lady of a considerable fortune and marries her. And, afterwards, falling ill, the father comes to him and brings him a declaration of trust, which he signed, whereby he acknowledges that his name was only used in trust for his father and that he would convey to the father when requested. And, after this, he dies without issue. The defendant, his widow, brings a writ of dower and has judgment. And to be relieved against that judgment, the plaintiff, who had got a conveyance from his second son, to whom the legal inheritance descended as heir to his brother, prefers his bill to be relieved against that judgment.

It was proved also in the cause that the defendant's husband repaired the premises at his own charges and had laid out £700 in so doing and that he paid the gardener's wages.

This cause was heard before the Master of the Rolls [TREVOR], who set aside the judgment. But, upon an appeal to the Lord Keeper [WRIGHT], he reversed that decree.

Lord Keeper [WRIGHT]: The constant rule of this court is that, if a father purchases in the name of a child and there is no declaration of trust, it is always looked upon as an advancement of that child. It is true in this case here is a declaration of trust, but it is such a trust as has all the marks and badges of fraud and ought to be relieved against within the express words of the [Statute] 27 Hen. VIII.[1]

Suppose the plaintiff had stood by and let his son have mortgaged this estate and had been a witness to the deed. Which think you should have taken place, the deed of trust or the mortgage?

The decree must be reversed and the bill dismissed with costs.

The Master of the Rolls [TREVOR] was present in court and seemed then to be of the same opinion.

Lincoln's Inn MS. Misc. 9, p. 27, pl. 2

12 June 1702.

This cause came on again upon a matter reserved by the Lord Keeper [WRIGHT] for his consideration. Bateman, the defendant, had brought a cross-bill and, therein, set forth that her husband, before marriage, entered into a bond to some friends in trust for her to leave her worth £4000. And, now, the declaration of trust being by His Lordship's decree set aside (*quod vide ante 25*), she moves by her counsel that the deed of trust might be delivered up and the writings of the estate brought before a Master that she might have the benefit of them at a trial at law in an action to be brought against the heir or assignee upon that bond, for it was objected that the plaintiff would set up his deed of trust at law and so she could have no judgment against the heir.

Lord Keeper [WRIGHT]: Cannot you read the answer of the plaintiff, where he admits that the estate descended from his son, the defendant's late husband, to Sir James, his second son, and that Sir James has conveyed to him?

[1] Stat. 27 Hen. VIII, c. 10 (*SR*, III, 539–542).

*Vernon*: If we read the answer at law, they will tell us we must admit all of it to be true or none. Now, though he admits to seisin in the son, yet he swears positively it was in trust for the father.

Lord Keeper [Wright]: I fear I cannot give you any assistance here until you have been at law. The late Act of Parliament in the 4th & 5th years of the king and the late queen[1] has now chalked out a new way how you are to proceed to charge the heir upon the debt of his ancestor. And that Statute being introductive of a new law, you ought to go the way the Act has prescribed.

Then it was objected that there was a mortgage upon the estate and that would be set up at law against them.

Lord Keeper [Wright]: I suppose that is only a mortgage for years, and you will have judgment to charge the redemption, and, then, you will be proper to come here to redeem. I believe you never knew a bond creditor come here for discovery of real assets until he had been at law.

But notwithstanding, it was at last ordered that the deed of trust should be delivered up and the purchase deeds brought before a Master.

Precedents in Chancery 198, 24 E.R. 95

A man binds himself and his heirs. And he dies, leaving a real estate to descend to his heir, subject to a mortgage for years. The heir aliens the real estate before a bill [is] brought. And if the obligee was relievable here against the heir and the purchaser on the Statute for Preventing Fraudulent Devises[2] or if he was to be sent to law to get a judgment first was the question.

My Lord Keeper [Wright] thought that Statute being introductive of a new law, the relief on it must be at law. And he held likewise that a bond creditor could not redeem a mortgage for years without first having a judgment at law against the heir, though it might have been otherwise in the case of a mortgage in fee.

[Other reports of this case: 1 Eq. Cas. Abr. 149, 218, 315, 382, 21 E.R. 949, 1001, 1070, 1118.]

## 5

## Bird v. Major

(Ch. 1702)

*The questions in this case were whether the Bankruptcy Act incorporates the provisions of the older bankruptcy acts and whether a member of the Stationers' Company is covered by the Bankruptcy Act.*

---

[1] Stat. 4 Will. & Mar., c. 16 (*SR*, VI, 404–405), or Stat. 3 Will. & Mar., c. 14 (*SR*, VI, 320–321).

[2] Stat. 3 Will. & Mar., c. 14 (*SR*, VI, 320–321).

2 Lord Raymond 851, 92 E.R. 69

Upon an issue directed in Chancery to be tried before the Lord Chief Justice Holt for his opinion, the case, upon the trial before him at the Guildhall the sitting after this term, appeared to be thus. A scrivener, who was not liable to be a bankrupt before the Statute of 21 Jac. I, c. 19,[1] committed an act, which was made an act of bankruptcy by the Statute of 1 Jac. I, c. 15,[2] *viz.* absconding etc., and he had also a share in the Stationers' Company.

And the question was whether he was not a bankrupt by that.

And Holt, Chief Justice, held that, since the [Stat.] 21 Jac. I, c. 19, had made a scrivener liable to be a bankrupt, it had subjected him to all the old acts, which, by the former statutes made a man a bankrupt, as well as to the acts mentioned in the Statute of 21 Jac. I, c. 19. But as to the share in the Stationers' Company, he seemed to incline that that would not make him a bankrupt. See for that the [Stat.] 13 & 14 Car. II, c. 24,[3] where it enacts that the having a share in the East India Company etc. will not make a man a bankrupt. And a judgment given to the contrary in 1653 was by the said Act declared illegal.

But the Lord Keeper [Wright] held the scrivener to be a bankrupt by both the points.

Upon the importunity of the counsel, it was reserved as a case as to both points for the further consideration of the Chief Justice.

6

## Hollingshead v. Hollingshead

(Ch. 1702–1708)

*An infant can execute a power of appointment, and such execution need not recite the power.*

*An agreement to execute a power of appointment can be specifically enforced.*

2 Peere Williams 229, 24 E.R. 709

4 June 1 Anne, by the Lord Keeper.

One Samuel Mottershead, by will, devised lands to the use of himself in tail, remainder to Francis Hollingshead for life, remainder to his first etc. son in tail male, remainder over, with a power to the several tenants for life, when in possession, to make a jointure, so as such jointure did not exceed a moiety of the estate. And, by the same will, the testator gave a legacy to this Francis Hollingshead.

[1] Stat. 21 Jac. I, c. 19 (*SR*, IV, 1227–1229).

[2] Stat. 1 Jac. I, c. 15 (*SR*, IV, 1031–1034).

[3] Stat. 14 Car. II, c. 24 (*SR*, V, 419–420).

Samuel Mottershead, the first tenant in tail, died without issue, and, during the infancy of Francis Hollingshead, there was a treaty for his marriage, which being agreed, his mother and he, the infant, covenanted with the wife's relations that, within six months after Francis's coming of age, he should settle so much of the land as should amount to £100 *per annum* upon his then intended wife for her life.

The marriage took effect. And they had issue a daughter. And the husband, Francis, dying afterwards without making the jointure, the widow brought her bill against the remainderman for making good the same, in which case it was objected, first, that this covenant was made by an infant who could not covenant; secondly, no land in particular was covenanted to be settled, but only so much as should amount to £100 *per annum*.

But [it was] decreed by Lord Keeper [Wright] that this covenant was in equity a good execution of the power, wherefore a jointure of £100 *per annum* ought to be made good to the wife and that, if a moiety of the premises which the husband had a power to settle would not make up £100 *per annum*, the same should be made good out of the £1000 legacy given to Francis, the husband, by the will, which decree showed that the land, if it might be had, was to be the fund, but, if the land could not be had, then and not otherwise, satisfaction was to be made out of the personal estate.

1 Strange 604, 93 E.R. 727,
Gilbert Rep. 167, 25 E.R. 117

14 June 1708, before Lord Cowper.

A man devises his estate to A. for life, with several remainders over, with a power to the person in possession to limit any part of the premises for a jointure, not exceeding one moiety. The first devisee for life, whilst an infant, marries the plaintiff and, with his mother, enters into articles to settle lands of £100 *per annum* on the plaintiff for her jointure. But, in the articles, no notice was taken of the power. Before any jointure [was] made pursuant to the power, the tenant for life dies. The bill was against the remainderman to have the jointure made good. [It was] decreed accordingly.

Lincoln's Inn MS. Misc. 9, p. 73, pl. 3

14 June 1708.

A man, by his will, devises his estate to A. for life with several remainders over. And he gives a power to the several persons to whom the lands were limited, when in possession, to limit any part not exceeding a moiety for a jointure.

After the testator's death, the first devisee, being then an infant, marries. And, upon his marriage, he and his mother enter into articles and covenants to settle lands of £100 a year for the jointure of the plaintiff, his wife, but there was no notice taken in these articles of the power. And, after his marriage and before any settlement was made, he died. And his wife preferred her bill against the next in remainder to have her jointure made good.

Serjeant *Parker*, for the plaintiff: It has been held a married woman may execute a power; so may an infant. There is nothing of discretion concerned in these cases, which is the reason why the acts of an infant are void. And, here, the testator himself has adjusted that matter.

If, then, an infant may execute a power, the question will be if the covenant of the infant in our case to settle a jointure will be an execution of the power. I think, indeed, we cannot say it is. But, surely, it is such an agreement as this court will carry on to an execution so as to give the wife the benefit of it, notwithstanding the infant died before he came of age.

*Vernon*, for the defendant: The settlement out of which this power arises was purely voluntary. We do not dispute but an infant may execute a power or may act by a letter of attorney. But then, the question will be how far he has executed his power. Now, he has not covenanted to execute his power, but that he would settle lands of £100 a year for a jointure. And it does not appear that he has this power in view at that time.

Lord Chancellor [Lord Cowper]: I think the case is very strong, notwithstanding he took no notice of the power. You remember the Case of My Lord Burlington, in the Temple Hall, before Lord Keeper Wright,[1] where a covenant to execute a power was made good. I presume it was upon a bad consideration. Indeed, I think that case is governed by right reason and upon the reason of parallel cases, as where this court supplies the want of a surrender for the benefit of purchasers; nay, for those that are less meritorious, *viz.*, younger children. I think, indeed, it has been carried to grandchildren.

As to what was offered by Mr. Ward, that the articles might be performed another way, that is that, the infant being a tenant in tail of other lands, the jointure should be made good out of them, we have no precedents in this court where an agreement of a tenant in tail to levy a fine was ever carried on against his issue.

Lincoln's Inn MS. Coxe 89, vol. 3, part 2, p. 12, pl. 1

24 June 7 Anne *coram* Lord Cowper.

Francis Hollingshead, an infant, was seised of certain lands for his life with power to make a jointure out of them not exceeding a moiety of them. And, by articles precedent to marriage, he covenanted within six months after he attained his age of twenty-one years to settle upon his intended wife £100 *per annum* for her jointure. The marriage took effect, and Francis attained the age of twenty-one, but made no jointure pursuant to the articles, and he died.

[1] *Lady Clifford v. Lord Burlington* (1700), 2 Vernon 379, 23 E.R. 841, Lincoln's Inn MS. Misc. 11, p. 51, pl. 2.

The widow of Francis exhibited her bill to have her jointure pursuant to the articles, insisting that her husband being seised and in full power to make a jointure, such covenant ought to be esteemed an appointment in pursuance of the power.

And, accordingly, she had her jointure decreed her so far as a moiety of the lands, which was as much as he had a power to settle, and, if those did not amount to £100 *per annum*, the deficiency was to be made up out of a legacy which was then owing to Francis.

## 7

## Pingle v. Gibbs

(Ch. 1702)

*The sole beneficiary of a trust can destroy the trust by renouncing his interest in it.*

Lincoln's Inn MS. Misc. 9, p. 27, pl. 1

Trinity 1 Anne.

Sir John Pingle settles the manor of A. and the advowson of the church of A., which was appendant to the manor, upon trustees. And, as to the advowson, he limits it to the use of himself, his executors, etc., for forty years and, after the determination of that term, to himself in fee. And he entails the manor upon his heirs male, with remainders over. And, by his will, he devises this term to the late bishop of Worcester and the defendant upon trust that, if the then incumbent should die, that they should present the plaintiff, his second son, to the living, if he was then qualified; if not, that then they should present one Mr. Stringer if he was then living, and, if he was dead, that they should present a fit person and take a bond to resign to his said son when he should be qualified.

The incumbent died and the trustees presented Mr. Stringer, the second son not being qualified. After which, the eldest son died, leaving one daughter, who was made a party here, whereby the estate came to the plaintiff as heir male, and, thereupon, as executor to his father, he brought his bill against the heiress of his brother and the surviving trustee to have the term assigned to him, he never intending to take [Holy] Orders, and, consequently, the trusts were at an end.

And whether the plaintiff should have it or it should result to the heir at law was the question.

And [it was] decreed for the executor.

## 8

## Franklin v. Fisher

(Ch. 1702)

*A will of long standing brought out of a court of probate does not need further proof.*

Lincoln's Inn MS. Misc. 9, p. 30, pl. 1

Michaelmas 1 Anne.

The plaintiff's title was founded on a will made thirty-nine years ago. And they being at liberty to prove it *viva voce*, at the hearing, an old woman was produced as a witness who swore she saw some writing executed and could not remember what. And it was objected that this was not a sufficient proof of the will.

Lord Keeper [Wright]: A will of forty years' standing, if brought out of the Prerogative Office, proves itself, and, if there was no witness to prove it, I would have it read.

## 9

## Anonymous v. Nelthorp

(Ch. 1702)

*In this case, an inter vivos gift was held to be an advancement.*

Lincoln's Inn MS. Misc. 9, p. 30, pl. 2

6 November 1702.

Nelthorp, the grandfather, makes a voluntary settlement of land in moieties upon his two grandsons, their father being dead. And he charges it with the payment of £500 apiece to his three granddaughters at their respective ages of twenty-one or days of marriage. Afterwards, he makes his will, and settles the same land upon his two grandsons in the same manner, and he gives his granddaughters the like sums of £500 apiece to be paid them in like manner, but he takes no notice in his will of the settlements. One of the granddaughters, afterwards, marries in her grandfather's lifetime, who gives with her £200 to make up her fortune £1000, she having £800 of her own. And, after this, the grandfather dies.

The question[s were], first, if the granddaughters should have two £500 apiece; secondly, admitting they should not, whether the £200 given by the grandfather to advance his granddaughter's fortune in his lifetime should not go in discharge of the £500 given her by the deed and the will.

Lord Keeper [Wright]: As to the first, I am of the opinion that the granddaughters shall have but one £500 apiece. It is the same sum both in the deed and in the will and to be paid in the same manner, and there is nothing [that] appears to show his intent to be otherwise. All the difference between the deed and the will is only this, by the deed, he had charged his land with the payment of this money but, by the will, he had charged his personal estate. But the circumstances of this case are to be considered, for Nelthorp, the son, being executed for rebellion in Scotland and having forfeited his estate,[1] the grandfather looked upon himself to stand *in loco parentis*, and, therefore, he made a provision for his grandchildren. But it is not to be thought he would give them a double fortune.

As to the second point, I am of the opinion that the £200 shall only go in discharge of the £500 *pro tanto* and not for the whole, for a lesser sum can never be a satisfaction for a greater. It is a constant rule in this court that, if a man makes a settlement of his estate with a provision therein for raising daughters' portions and he, in his lifetime, advances any one of his daughters with a portion equal to what is charged by the settlement, the lands shall be discharged as to her portion. Why then, sure as this case is, where the grandfather had advanced his daughter with a lesser sum, it can only be a discharge *pro tanto*. She must have her £300 and interest and the other daughters their £500 and interest from their grandfather's death.

## 10

## Haines v. Haines

(Ch. 1702)

*A will that was destroyed after the death of the testator can be established, and the devises ordered by the court to be paid.*

2 Vernon 441, 23 E.R. 883

The uncle having devised his real estate, part to the plaintiff and the other part to other relations, and disinherited his nephew and heir at law, at the funeral of the uncle, a younger brother of the heir at law snatched the will out of the hands of the executor and tore it into many small pieces. And most of them, and particularly such part wherein it was the devise of the land, were picked up and stitched together again.

The bill was to have the will established.

And [it was] decreed that the devisees should hold and enjoy against the heir and he to convey to the devisees, although no direct proof was made that the heir directed the tearing of the will.

[1] R. L. Greaves, 'Nelthorpe, Richard (d. 1685)', *Oxford Dictionary of National Biography*, vol. 40, pp. 420–421.

Dickens 18, 21 E.R. 173

Michaelmas 1702.

A will having been destroyed by the brother of the disinherited heir, the devisee was decreed to hold and enjoy, and a trial was denied.

[Other reports of this case: 1 Eq. Cas. Abr. 402, 21 E.R. 1133.]

## 11

## Anonymous

(Ch. 1702)

*An issue out of Chancery can be ordered in order to determine the existence of a deed of conveyance.*

Lincoln's Inn MS. Misc. 9, p. 31, pl. 1

10 November. Master of the Rolls.

The plaintiff's bill was to have a discovery of an old deed of entail supposed to be made by his ancestor in 1625.

The defendant, by his answer, made a title to the land in question under a deed of settlement made in consideration of marriage and a £300 portion.

The evidence for the plaintiff was, *viz.* one swore he had seen an old deed, another that he had seen a copy of such a deed of entail, and a third that he had seen the deed itself and sets forth the contents itself.

Upon hearing the cause, the court [Trevor] directed an issue at law to try whether there was such a deed of entail as the plaintiff had set forth in his bill.

But it was objected that it would be difficult to settle that issue, the plaintiff not having set forth any deed in particular, but only in general terms.

But, notwithstanding, it was ordered *ut supra.*

## 12

## Boteler v. Boteler

(Ch. 1702)

*The issue in this case was the enforcement of a marriage settlement.*

Lincoln's Inn MS. Misc. 9, p. 31, pl. 2

13 November. Lord Keeper. Sarah Boteler, only daughter of Sir Oliver Boteler, deceased, against Sir Philip Boteler, baronet, son and heir of Sir Oliver by a former wife, and the Lady Boteler, widow of Sir Oliver, defendants.

Sir Oliver Boteler, upon his first marriage, settles the manor of Chatham in Kent to the use of himself for life, remainder to his then Lady for life, with remainders to the first and other sons in tail, with remainders over, with a power reserved to Sir Oliver to revoke the uses, provided he settled other lands of the same value to the same uses. Sir Oliver, upon his marriage with the [ *blank* ][1]

## 13

## Shephard v. Shephard

(Ch. 1702)

*Where a person conveys land to which he has no right, he must refund the purchase price with interest.*

Lincoln's Inn MS. Misc. 9, p. 32

Thomas Shepard, second son of Thomas Shephard, deceased, against John Shephard, eldest son of old Thomas, Richard Paine, and the executors of the lord of the manor of A. and John Shephard against Thomas, the plaintiff, Richard Paine, and the executors of the lord etc. Before the Master of the Rolls.

The case [was] old Thomas [Shepard] had issue, three sons, *viz.* John, the defendant, the plaintiff Thomas, and William. And he was seised in fee of borough English and freehold land and, for his life, of the copyhold in question, of which the defendant Paine was also seised for his life in reversion after the death of old Thomas, being of the yearly value of £10.

Old Thomas, knowing (as was alleged by the plaintiff) that the freehold land would descend to his eldest son and the borough English land to his youngest son, William, and being minded to make some provision for his second son, the plaintiff, agrees with Paine to purchase his interest in the copyhold for £110. And, accordingly, Paine, by the direction of old Thomas, in the year 1688, surrenders the copyhold land to the plaintiff Thomas and his heirs during the life of Paine.

Paine, after this, goes beyond the sea. William, the youngest son, dies. And, in the year 1695, old Thomas dies, having a little before his death made his will and the defendant John his executor and residuary legatee of his personal estate, but takes no notice of his copyhold land.

After the death of old Thomas, the lord of the manor, supposing that Paine was also dead and that the copyhold land was come to himself, sends to the defendant John to renew the lives, telling him, if he would not, he would grant the copyhold to somebody else, whereupon, John agrees to renew and pays a fine to the lord, who grants the premises to him for his own and two other lives, by virtue of which John enters and receives the rents. Sometime after which, Paine returns from beyond the sea, whereupon Thomas prefers his bill, praying he may be admitted to the copyhold during Paine's life.

[1] This report ends here in mid-sentence.

And John prefers his cross-bill, insisting that his father paid the purchase money and that the plaintiff's name was only used in trust for his father. And, therefore, he prays that he may enjoy the copyhold or that the defendants, the executors of the lord, repay him his fine with interest and costs.

The Master of the Rolls [TREVOR]: The plaintiff Thomas must enjoy the copyhold during Paine's life, and the lord must admit him, paying his fine, and he must have his costs. Here is no declaration of trust, neither from the son nor the father, and, therefore, it must be an advancement of the son.

Then, as for the cross-bill, why, in regard the lord has taken upon him to sell an estate he had no right to, he must repay back the fine with interest and costs.

## 14

## Cookley v. Rawlins

(Ch. 1703)

*Part performance of an oral contract will take it out of the Statute of Frauds.*

Lincoln's Inn MS. Misc. 9, p. 33

27 January 1702[/03]. Lord Keeper.

The bill was to have the execution of a parol agreement. The case was this. The plaintiff agrees to let the defendant a malting house and to make him a lease of it for six years, in which lease was to be a proviso that, at the end of three years, the defendant, giving six month's warning, might leave it and the plaintiff was to put the premises into repair. This agreement was put into writing but not signed by either of the parties. The plaintiff delivered the key to the defendant's agent by his order, and put the premises into repair within a month after the time agreed. The three years were expired, and no rent [was] paid.

The plaintiff brought his action at law for the rent, but he could not maintain it, whereupon, his bill now was to have an execution of this agreement.

This was heard before the Master of the Rolls [TREVOR], and decreed for the plaintiff, and now came on before the Lord Keeper [WRIGHT] upon an appeal.

Lord Keeper [WRIGHT]: It is no objection to say this bill is no more than an action of debt for rent, for, though it is so in effect because the time is expired and nothing more remains to be done but to pay the rent, yet the bill may notwithstanding be brought to have an execution of the agreement. And, where part of the agreement is executed by one of the parties, this court will enforce the other to execute his part notwithstanding the agreement is not in writing. And, here, the plaintiff having put the premises into repair, the defendant must perform his part.

Mr. *Vernon* cited the case of Butcher and Butcher, in My Lord Jeffries's time,[1] which was this. A man agrees for the purchase of land and had possession delivered him, and he stocked the land, but the agreement was not in writing. Afterwards, the vendor enters into articles with another, and conveyances were executed accordingly. But, notwithstanding, upon a bill brought, it was decreed for the first purchaser, and, upon an appeal to the Lords, that decree was confirmed.

## 15

## Duke of Hamilton v. Lord Mohun

(Ch. 1703–1710)

*An agreement not to trouble an executor does not bar a suit for an account or for a legacy.*

*An agreement coerced shortly before the obligor's date of marriage is not enforceable in equity.*

Lincoln's Inn MS. Misc. 9, p. 34

*Eodem die* [27 January 1703]. Duke and Duchess of Hamilton v. Lord Mohun.

My Lord Macclesfield, by his will, gave to the duchess of Hamilton a pair of diamond earrings and a diamond necklace upon this condition, *viz.* provided that she 'gives no trouble to any executor'. And to have this legacy, the plaintiffs prefer their bill against My Lord Mohun, who was the executor of the will.

My Lord Mohun, by his answer, confesses the will and the devise *prout supra*. But he says that My Lord Macclesfield was the executor of the Lady Garrard, who was the guardian to the duchess, the plaintiff, and that a suit was depending in My Lord Macclesfield's lifetime, which was brought against him by the plaintiffs for an account of the profits of the duchess's estate and that he did conceive by 'no trouble' in the will was meant that the plaintiffs should not trouble his executor for any matters touching the former suit.

It was said by *Sir Thomas Powys*, for the plaintiffs, that, though this cause came on upon the bill and answer whereby all parties were obliged to admit the matters of fact as they stand upon the bill and the answer, yet it did not thence follow that the plaintiffs must or should be obliged to admit any inferences or conclusions that the defendant should make from his own case.

Then, as to the words of the will, why, all that the Lord Macclesfield could intend by 'no trouble' was that, in regard the plaintiff, the duchess, was one of the co-heirs of the Lord Macclesfield, and if he had died without a will, would have been entitled to part of My Lord's estate, that she should not anyways controvert

[1] *Butcher v. Stapely* (Ch. 1686), 1 Vernon 363, 23 E.R. 524, Chancery Reports *tempore* Jac. II, 210, 1 Eq. Cas. Abr. 21, 21 E.R. 843.

the will, and, accordingly, she had not given the executor any trouble upon that account. And, therefore, it was prayed that the plaintiffs might have the legacy.

On the other side, it was said that the meaning could be no other than what the defendant had insisted on in his answer, and, therefore, he insisted on it, that the plaintiffs ought to give a release before they received the legacy.

Lord Keeper [WRIGHT]: The rule of expounding wills is to construe the testator's meaning from the words of the will and not from any matter *dehors*. I remember My Lord Somers, in the Case of Mr. Cary,[1] would not suffer letters to be read to explain the meaning of a will, though they were relative to the will.

The words in this case are general and indefinite, and I cannot restrain them to a particular limited sense. In common parlance, a man is said to be in trouble when he is involved in suits and by 'no trouble' must be understood no trouble of any sort, that is that his executor, as such, should have no suit brought against him, either in law or equity.

The plaintiffs must have their legacy, but the court cannot decree it without taking care that the plaintiffs shall give the defendant no trouble, which may be done three ways, either by giving security *non molestari* or by a release or by decreeing that the plaintiffs shall give the executor no trouble, which would be a bar to any suit to be brought by the duke in the right of the duchess. But whether a release may be proper, I am not so well satisfied, for, perhaps, that may release more than was intended. And, therefore, as to that, let precedents be searched.

In the meantime, the decree must be that the legacy shall be delivered to the plaintiffs, and the duke must give security to give the executors no trouble. Let it be in the very words of the will.

1 Salkeld 158, 91 E.R. 147

20 May, 9 Anne.

One of the marriage articles was that the intended husband should, within two days after the marriage, for the peace of the family, release the guardian of the young lady, the Lady Gerard, of all accounts of the mesne profits of an estate that belonged to the lady.

*Et per* COWPER, Lord Chancellor: Admitting there was no surprise or concealment, yet this covenant ought to be set aside as extorted from the husband, who could not have the daughter but upon these terms and that, wherever a mother or father or guardian insists upon a private gain or security for it and obtains it of the intended husband, it shall be set aside, for the power of a parent or guardian ought not to be made use of to such purpose, 'you shall not have my daughter unless you do so and so' is to sell children and matches. And he held

[1] *Bertie v. Lord Falkland* (1697–1715), 3 Chancery Cases 129, 22 E.R. 1008, 2 Freeman 220, 22 E.R. 1171, 1 Salkeld 231, 91 E.R. 205, 2 Vernon 333, 23 E.R. 814, 12 Modern 182, 88 E.R. 1248, Holt K.B. 230, 90 E.R. 1026, 1 Eq. Cas. Abr. 110, 21 E.R. 917, Colles 10, 1 E.R. 155, Dickens 25, 21 E.R. 176, Chancery Cases *tempore* Geo. I, 143.

these contracts with the father etc. to be of the same nature with brokage bonds etc. but of more mischievous consequence, as that which would happen more frequently, and that it is now a settled rule that, if the father, on the marriage of his son, take a bond of the son that the son shall pay him so much etc., it is void, being done by coercion while he is under the awe of his father.

Lincoln's Inn MS. Misc. 10, p. 6

The plaintiff married the earl of Macclesfield's daughter, to whom the countess, her mother, was guardian and had received the rents and profits of her daughter's real estate. The countess encouraged the match and, two days before it was to have been consummated, she told the plaintiff that, unless he would give a bond to release all claims and demands against her on account of any moneys she had received as guardian to her daughter [ *blank* ]. Accordingly, the plaintiff enters into such a bond. And now, he comes to be relieved against it.

Lord Chancellor [Lord Cowper]: It is a common case where a man comes to his son just before his marriage and after his affections are settled and tells him, unless he will take a less fortune than he is entitled to, that he will not consent to the marriage. This court always relieves against such practices.

If the release had been given after the marriage and no agreement had been before, this court would not have set it aside though there had been no consideration given for it nor any account stated in order to it.

But here is an agreement just before the marriage at a time when the plaintiff was not free and no account stated to induce him to give such release. It is plain the plaintiff was under a coercion. And therefore, it is highly equitable that such an agreement should be set aside and, therefore, an account must be taken of the rents and profits of the earl of Macclesfield's real estate.

But then a second question did arise, *viz.* whether the countess being entitled to dower and there being a mortgage made by the earl which would bar her at law and she, as guardian to her daughter, having received the profits and paid the interest and the defendant, her representative, being now to account, he shall not retain a third of the profits for her dower or whether the mortgage which would bar her at law shall not now bar her in equity.

Lord Chancellor [Lord Cowper]: This differs from Vandebende's Case,[1] in the House of Lords. There was a purchase and a term kept on foot to protect against encumbrances, but here is neither, only a mortgage standing out and the mortgagee never in possession. If the account is broken into and the defendant is

[1] *Countess of Radnor v. Vandenbendy* (1683–1697), Shower P.C. 69, 1 E.R. 48, *sub nom. Lady Bodmin v. Vandenbendy*, 1 Vernon 179, 356, 23 E.R. 399, 520, 2 Chancery Cases 172, 22 E.R. 899, *sub nom. Lady Radnor v. Rotheram*, 2 Freeman 211, 22 E.R. 1165, Precedents in Chancery 65, 24 E.R. 32, 1 Eq. Cas. Abr. 219, 21 E.R. 1002, 2 Eq. Cas. Abr. 383, 22 E.R. 326, Chancery Reports *tempore* Jac. II, 165, Lincoln's Inn MS. Misc. 559, f. 111.

to do equity, it is but reasonable equity should be done him. And whatever agreement the countess made in relation to her dower, it was upon the consideration of the bond to release, which being now set aside, it is but reasonable to let her in for her dower.

[Other reports of this case: 2 Vernon 652, 23 E.R. 1025, 1 Peere Williams 118, 24 E.R. 319, 1 Eq. Cas. Abr. 90, 21 E.R. 901, 2 Brown P.C. 239, 1 E.R. 916, 2 Eq. Cas. Abr. 387, 652, 22 E.R. 330, 1025.]

## 16

## Dugdale v. Hamersley

(Ch. 1703)

*Copyhold lands pass by general words in a will.*

*The court will not compel a surrender of a copyhold to a donee who is a stranger.*

Lincoln's Inn MS. Misc. 9, p. 36

3 February 1702[/03].

One Baker [was] seised in fee of freehold and copyhold land and having mortgaged his freehold land by lease and release and, by the same deed, covenanted to surrender his copyhold land to the mortgagee under a proviso etc. but no surrender was made. Afterwards, he makes his will. And he devises to the plaintiff all his lands of inheritance for the payment of his debts and legacies, and, then, he gives all the rest and residue of his real and personal estate to the plaintiff.

And to examine witnesses *in perpetuam rei memoriam* to prove the will, the plaintiff preferred his bill against the defendant and his wife, who was the sister and co-heir of the testator.

The first question [was] if the copyhold lands passed by the general words in the will.

[It was] agreed it did.

Secondly, admitting it did, then whether, there being no surrender made by the testator in his lifetime to the use of his will, this court will aid that defect and compel the heir at law to surrender to the devisee.

Lord Keeper [Wright]: The rule of this court is, wherever copyhold land is devised by will, either for the payment of debts or raising portions for children and there has been no precedent surrender to the use of that will, this court will supply that defect, but not where it is a voluntary devise to a stranger.

If freehold and copyhold lands are devised for the payment of debts and a surrender has been made to the use of the will, the lands shall be equally charged in proportion to their value. But, where no surrender has been made, the freehold lands shall be first sold, and, if they are not sufficient, then the copyhold shall be sold. And so it was ordered in this case, there being a bill for that purpose.

## 17

## Box v. Box

(Ch. 1703)

*This case settles a point as to the customary law of the City of London as to decedent's estates.*

King's Inns, Dublin, MS. 92, p. 39

Michaelmas 2 Anne.

In a suit in Chancery between these parties, the two sons of Sir Ralph Box, upon Sir Ralph's will, these questions were sent by My Lord Keeper [Wright] to the Court of Aldermen, who were to give answer to them by the mouth of their Recorder upon the differing in opinion between Sir Salathiel Lovell, Recorder, and Duncan Lee, Esq., the Common Serjeant. The Court of Aldermen required the opinion of the four Common Pleaders, Richard Richardson, William Lightfoot, Joseph Major, and Isaac Ewer, esquires, and the four attorneys of the Outer Court, Mr. James Gibson, Edward Smith, John Andrews, and Thomas Jackson, who all unanimously were of opinion with the Common Serjeant in every question, that is to say:

First question, whether, if a freeman of the City of London dies leaving two sons unadvanced and two daughters advanced in his lifetime and no wife and leaves sufficient assets to pay his debts and legacies and having before his death made his will and thereby expressly by the words of his will debarred his two daughters and not taken notice of or observed the customs of London in dividing his estate but devised the same by way of legacy and thereby devised a legacy to his younger son, such son shall have such legacy over and besides a child's orphanage part of the testator's estate in case the legacy be more than the orphanage part of such child does amount unto.

Second question, in case such legacy given by such will be less than the orphanage part, whether such son shall have such legacy over and besides such orphanage part or shall only have such legacy made up a full orphanage part.

Third question, whether in either of those cases, the orphan shall have both the orphanage part and the legacy also when the testator makes no declaration in his will whether the legacy shall or not be in lieu or satisfaction of the orphanage part or any part thereof.

First answer, that, by the law and customs of this City, if a freeman of this City dies leaving two sons unadvanced and two daughters advanced in his lifetime and no wife and leaves sufficient assets to pay his debts and legacies and do make his will and thereby expressly debars his two daughters but does not take notice of or observe the customs of this City therein in dividing his estate but devises the same by way of legacy and thereby devises a legacy to his youngest son out of his personal estate greater than the orphanage part of such son does amount unto, such son shall not have such legacy over and besides his orphanage part, but his orphanage part shall be deducted out of such legacy and the remainder only accounted as a legacy.

Second answer, in case such legacy given by such will be less than the orphanage part, the same shall be made up a full orphanage part, but such son shall not have such legacy over and above his orphanage part.

Third answer, the orphan shall not in either of the said cases have both the orphanage part and the legacy also when the testator makes no declaration in his will whether such legacy shall or shall not be in lieu or satisfaction of the orphanage part or any part thereof.

[Other reports of this case: 1 Lord Raymond 484, 91 E.R. 1223, Dodd 189, 1 Eq. Cas. Abr. 154, 21 E.R. 953, Brasenose Coll. Oxford MS. 59, p. 22, Yale Beinecke OSB MSS. 184, box 41, Taussig 311, vol. 1, pp. 441, 444, Lincoln's Inn MS. Misc. 10, p. 170.]

## 18

## Anonymous

(Ch. 1703)

*A renewed bishop's lease is subject to a trust on the former lease.*

6 Modern 58, 87 E.R. 818

Michaelmas 2 Anne.

It was said by *Powys*, Serjeant, in Chancery that, if a bishop make a lease for twenty-one years and the lessee create a trust thereupon and, after the bishop die and his successor suppose for a fine, renews the lease, though not compellable to do it and though there be no trust of the second lease, yet equity shall subject it to the former trust.

## 19

## Aston v. Aston

(Ch. 1703)

*In this case, the devise in issue created a vested estate with a condition subsequent.*

*Where there is a gift over, a condition subsequent will be enforced even where it is a harsh one.*

Lincoln's Inn MS. Misc. 13, p. 40

17 December 1703.

The case was [thus]. By a settlement made on the marriage of Sir Willoughby Aston, a term of 500 years was created to raise £6000 for younger children payable at eighteen or marriage to be divided amongst them as Sir Willoughby should appoint and to raise £50 *per annum* for the maintenance of each until their portions became payable.

Sir Willoughby, by his will, appointed the £6000 to his six unmarried daughters equally. And he devised several manors and lands to trustees and their heirs upon trust to sell the same and to make up the moneys given them by his will £4000 apiece and to pay the surplus to his two younger sons, Richard and Robert Aston, equally, and, if they died without issue, then to the said six daughters.

And he added this condition:

Provided and I declare it to be my full intent and meaning that I do give the said £4000 to each daughter upon condition and provided that my said daughters be married with the consent of my wife if living and, if dead, then with the consent of my eldest son, Thomas, in writing in the presence of three witnesses and that the portion of each of them as shall marry without such consent shall go to my said two younger sons.

The two younger sons insisted that they ought to be looked on as tenants in tail of the trust estate and residuary legatees, that the condition of marrying with consent was a condition precedent and the additional legacies [were] not vested, that the trust lands ought not to be sold until the additional portions became payable and then no more to be sold than was necessary, that the daughters ought not to have interest until their portions became payable, and the rather since the settlement had provided £50 *per annum* each for their maintenance, and that the interest ought to increase the surplus.

The Lord Keeper [Wright] and the Master of the Rolls [Trevor] declared that, although the words of the condition, provided they be married etc., imported a condition precedent, yet it is a condition subsequent and the additional legacies are vested legacies.

His Lordship [Wright] decreed a sale to be forthwith made and all the moneys to be brought before a Master and applied to make the shares of the £6000 up £4000 and to be paid at their ages of twenty-one and to be placed out upon securities. And, as touching interest, His Lordship [Wright] declared that, the additional portions being vested, each daughter ought to have the interest of her own share towards her maintenance.

Lincoln's Inn MS. Misc. 13, p. 42

Sir Willoughby Aston, by will, directed that the portions of his then unmarried daughters, being the six plaintiffs, of £6000 provided by his marriage settlement should be made up of £4000 apiece out of his personal estate, and land [were] devised to be sold for that purpose provided that each of his said daughters be married with the consent of his wife if living and, if dead, then with the consent of his eldest son in writing and signed in the presence of three or more witnesses before marriage, 'and, if any of my daughters shall marry without such consent, her portion shall go first to make up the other daughters' portions £4000 apiece' if the fund provided deficient, and if [there were] any surplus, that [was] to go to his younger sons.

The Lord Keeper [Wright] decreed:

First, as to the £6000 provided by the settlement, the father had only a power of appointing portions, that, in case any of them died before payable and unmarried, that the portion would extinguish in the land for the benefit of his heir and could not annex any condition to it or devise it over;

Secondly, that, although the devise be to them if married with consent, yet it is but a condition subsequent, and not precedent, and the portions are vested portions;

Thirdly, that, in the case of marrying without consent, although but a condition subsequent, the court cannot relieve against the forfeiture by reason of the devise over, although it be a hard condition, no time being limited, but it goes to a marriage at any time, even after the age of twenty-one.

But he decreed the portions to be paid but on security to refund in case the condition should be broken.

Lincoln's Inn MS. Misc. 10, p. 3

The Lady Mary Aston, widow, *et al.*, plaintiffs; Sir Thomas Aston, baronet, *et al.*, defendants.

Sir Willoughby Aston, by his will, gave portions to his daughters. And, in the will, was this proviso, that each of his said daughters should marry with the consent of his wife, if alive at the time of such marriage, and, if she should be dead, then with the consent of his eldest son Thomas, such consent to be had and made in writing under the hand of his said wife, if alive, if not, of his said son Thomas, if alive, before their respective marriages and to be signed in the presence of three or more credible witnesses and, if any of his said daughters should marry without such consent and their portions should fall short of £4000 apiece, then the share of such daughter so marrying without consent should be equally divided amongst the rest of the unmarried daughters.

None of these daughters were married but two of them being of age, a bill was brought for the sale of part of the testator's estate for raising their two portions and for other purposes. And the question was whether this proviso was only *in terrorem*.

The cause was heard before the Lord Keeper Wright, who took time to consider upon it, and he said he would take the opinion of the Master of the Rolls [Trevor]. And, for that purpose, he directed that His Honor [Trevor] should be attended with precedents, after which the cause came on again and both declared that the portions were vested and that the proviso was not *in terrorem* only but, if the children married without such consent as is thereby declared, the respective portions of them so marrying were forfeited. And inasmuch as two of them had attained the age of twenty-one, it was ordered that they should receive their shares immediately upon giving their own recognizance to pay back the same to the court in case they should marry during the respective lives of the plaintiff, the Lady Aston, or the defendant, Sir Thomas Aston, without their consent and the Master should place out the fortunes of the other daughters who were under age on security and that they should receive their portions at their marriages with consent as aforesaid or age of twenty-one, which should first happen etc. If they should first attain such age, then they should give their recognizances in like manner.

[Other reports of this case: 2 Vernon 452, 23 E.R. 890, Precedents in Chancery 226, 24 E.R. 110, 1 Eq. Cas. Abr. 111, 336, 21 E.R. 919, 1085.]

## 20

## Popham v. Bamfield

(Ch. 1704)

*A recital in a codicil cannot convert a devise of a life estate into a devise of an entail.*

1 Salkeld 236, 91 E.R. 209

Hilary 2 Anne.

[There was a] devise to A. for life, remainder to the first son of A. in tail male and so on to the tenth son in tail male, and, if the said A. die without issue male of his body, the remainder over. Also, by a codicil annexed, he recited, 'whereas he had given an estate tail to A.' etc.

And it was objected that, by the codicil, the intent of the devisor appeared and that, by the will, A. had an estate tail, for he might have posthumous children and more than ten sons.

*Sed non allocatur*, for, where a particular estate is expressly devised, we will not by any subsequent clause collect a contrary intent inconsistent with the first by implication. And, therefore, they construed dying without issue male, a dying without such issue male. And they said there was a mighty difference between a devise to A. and, if he die without issue, then to B., and a devise to A. for life and, if he die without issue, then to B.

[It was] adjudged, *per* WRIGHT, Lord Keeper, HOLT, Chief Justice, and TREVOR, Chief Justice.

[Other reports of this case: 1 Vernon 79, 167, 344, 23 E.R. 325, 391, 510, 2 Vernon 427, 449, 23 E.R. 873, 888, 2 Freeman 266, 269, 22 E.R. 1201, 1023, 1 Peere Williams 54, 24 E.R. 290, Holt K.B. 233, 90 E.R. 1028, 1 Eq. Cas. Abr. 108, 183, 21 E.R. 916, 975, 2 Eq. Cas. Abr. 308, 22 E.R. 260.]

## 21

## Anonymous

(Ch. 1704)

*The issue in this case was the construction of a will.*

Lincoln's Inn MS. Misc. 9, p. 37, pl. 1

4 May 1704.

Upon an appeal to the Lord Keeper [WRIGHT] from the Master of the Rolls' [TREVOR] decree, the case was this. A man, having a son and three daughters, makes his will, and he gives to each of them £12 apiece, and all the rest and residue of his estate [ *blank* ].[1]

## 22

## Hopkins v. Ellis

(Ch. 1704)

*If a bankrupt pays off all of his debts, he ceases to be a bankrupt.*

1 Salkeld 110, 91 E.R. 101

Trinity [term] 3 Anne *coram* Holt, C.J., at *Nisi Prius* at the Guildhall.

Upon an issue directed out of Chancery, whether bankrupt or not at such a time, it was held by HOLT, Chief Justice, that, if H. commits a plain act of bankruptcy, as keeping house etc., though he after goes abroad and is a great dealer, yet that will not purge the first act of bankruptcy, but he will still remain a bankrupt. But, if the act was not plain but doubtful, then going abroad and dealing etc. will be an evidence to explain the intent of the first act, for, if it was not done to defraud creditors and keep out of the way, it will not be an act of bankruptcy within the Statute.[2] Also, if, after a plain act of bankruptcy, he pays off or compounds with all his creditors, he is become a new man.

Holt K.B. 95, 90 E.R. 951

Trinity [term] 3 Anne.

An issue was directed out of Chancery to try whether the defendant was a bankrupt or not at such a time.

HOLT, Chief Justice: If a man commits a plain act of bankruptcy, as keeping house etc., notwithstanding he afterwards goes abroad and is a great dealer, he will still remain a bankrupt. And that will not purge the first act of bankruptcy.

---

[1] This report ends here in mid-sentence.

[2] Stat. 21 Jac. I, c. 19 (*SR*, IV, 1227–1229).

But, if the act be not plain, but doubtful, then going abroad and dealing etc. will explain the intent of the first act, for, if it was not done to defraud creditors and keep out of the way, it will not be an act of bankruptcy within the Statute. And, if after any plain act of bankruptcy, he pays off or compounds with all his creditors, he thereby becomes a new man.

## 23

## Whitlock v. Warren

(Ch. 1704)

*A bankrupt can sue a creditor to have a debt set aside.*

Lincoln's Inn MS. Misc. 12 p. 103, pl. 1

21 July 1704.

The plaintiff's bill [was] to be relieved against several notes gained from him by imposition.

The defendant pleads that a commission of bankruptcy has been awarded against the plaintiff and that the commissioners have declared him to be a bankrupt.

Lord Chancellor [WRIGHT] overruled the plea. Upon the opening, he said a bankrupt might bring a bill against any of his creditors to be relieved against any imposition that had been put upon him notwithstanding his bankruptcy, for he was entitled to the surplus of his estate after debts paid.

## 24

## Hill v. Atkinson

(Ch. 1704)

*A land owner cannot be compelled to give discovery of his title deeds in order to show a defect in his own title.*

Lincoln's Inn MS. Misc. 9, p. 37, pl. 2

12 November 1704.

The plaintiff is the *cestui que trust* of a term, and the defendant is a mortgagee under the trustee.

The plaintiff's bill is for an account of the rents and profits of the estate and that the defendant may set out his title. And it is suggested therein that the defendant had notice of the trusts at the time of the mortgage and that the trusts are expressed in the lease, which is mortgaged to the defendant.

The defendant in his answer denies expressly that he had notice of any trust. And he says that, in none of the deeds, is any trust expressed.

The plaintiff replies. And the question upon the hearing was whether the defendant should produce his deeds that the court might judge whether any trust appears in them or no.

*Vernon*, for the plaintiff: There is no case where a plaintiff replies to the defendant's answer that he is concluded by that answer. Now, by this means, the defendant makes himself judge. And, at this rate, no man can be safe, for, if a mortgagee, for instance, will be so hardy as to swear there is no proviso in his deed and deny notice, a man may be stripped of his estate.

Lord Keeper [WRIGHT]: By the rules of this court, no honest purchaser without notice shall produce his deeds, and, by this artifice, it is but flinging into the bill that, in some of the deeds, there is a trust declared. And, though the defendant denies it never so expressly, yet, if you reply, you will compel him to lay open all his title. At this rate, no purchaser can be safe.

Master of the Rolls [TREVOR] *e contra*: There are two sorts of notice, one express and the other implied. Express is actual notice and must be proved. Implied [is] where it is in the deed, of which everyone must take notice at his peril. Now, as to the latter, the deeds ought to be produced that the court may judge if the man swears true.

But, notwithstanding, the Lord Keeper [WRIGHT] adhered to his opinion.

## 25

## Needham v. Smith

(Ch. 1704)

*If, after a witness has testified, it is discovered that he was not a competent witness, at a later hearing, his testimony can be impeached and stricken from the record.*

2 Vernon 463, 23 E.R. 897

Upon an appeal from the Rolls, it was objected to the evidence of one Norris, a witness examined in the cause and read at the hearing at the Rolls, that, since that hearing, in answer to a bill exhibited against him, he had confessed that, on the day on which he was examined as a witness, he took a bond of the plaintiff that, if the plaintiff recovered the estate in question, he would convey part of it to the said Norris.

The question now was whether that answer should be now read to take off his evidence.

And the Lord Keeper [WRIGHT], assisted with the Lord Chief Justice HOLT and Justice POWELL, were all of the opinion that the answer ought to be read.

Justice POWELL: The cause upon an appeal from the Rolls is entirely open. And, if the answer had been in then, it might have been read there, and you may now read it here upon the appeal. And, as to the objection that was made, that, after publication, you may examine as to the credibility, but not as to the competency of a witness, it was a difference without color of reason. If you may examine to the credibility, which goes to part, you may certainly examine to the competency, which goes to the whole and totally destroys his evidence. And, as to the objection, that, by taking the advantage of an answer to take off the evidence of a witness, the adverse party looses the opportunity of cross-examining of him, it was answered that it being proved the witness was a party interested, no proof is to be admitted to show him not to be interested.

Lord Chief Justice [Holt]: If, after the hearing, a witness is convicted of perjury, you may take advantage of it upon a re-hearing.

Lord Keeper [Wright]: Though a witness is examined an hour together at law, if, in any part of his evidence, it appears that he was a party interested, the court will direct the jury that he is no witness nor any regard to be had to his evidence.

The answer, thereupon, was read.

[Other copies of this report: Holt K.B. 757, 90 E.R. 1316.]

[Other reports of this case: 1 Eq. Cas. Abr. 224, 21 E.R. 1006.]

## 26

## Clavering v. Clavering

(Ch. 1704)

*Where a person makes two deeds of gift and dies solvent, the earlier gift will stand.*

British Library MS. Hargrave 80, f. 24v

Sir James Clavering made a voluntary conveyance of his estate which he kept privately by him and frequently declared that his estate would go otherwise than it was there conveyed. Sometime after, he made a second voluntary conveyance with the greatest solemnity imaginable and soon after died. The first conveyance was then found amongst some old cancelled writings, it being sixteen years after the date.

And [it was] decreed that, both being voluntary and no purchaser to contend with, the first should stand.

[Other copies of this report: Lincoln's Inn MS. Misc. 383, p. 46.]

Lincoln's Inn MS. Misc. 10, p. 59, pl. 1

Sir William Clavering, by deed, makes some provision out of part of his estate for one of his children. He lives sixteen years afterwards and makes no use of this deed but keeps it by him. And not long before his death, he makes a voluntary settlement of his whole estate and takes no notice of the former deed. After his death, the first deed was found in an old trunk among a parcel of cancelled writings.

And, notwithstanding this deed was revocable in its own nature, yet both being voluntary and no creditors in the case, the LORD COWPER established the first deed.

And, afterwards, upon an appeal, the decree was affirmed.

[Other reports of this case: 2 Vernon 473, 23 E.R. 904, Precedents in Chancery 235, 24 E.R. 114, 7 Brown P.C. 410, 3 E.R. 267, 1 Eq. Cas. Abr. 24, 21 E.R. 845, 2 Eq. Cas. Abr. 351, 22 E.R. 299.]

## 27

## Lamlee v. Hanman

(Ch. 1704–1705)

*A gift in fraud of a marriage settlement will be set aside.*

Lincoln's Inn MS. Misc. 384, p. 50

Michaelmas 1704, reheard 24 May 1705.

The husband having a leasehold estate and his mother, on his marriage, surrendering her jointure, he privately assigns this leasehold estate to her, and gives her a bond as a consideration for the surrender, yet it being a fraud against the wife and her relations, they were both set aside. This is within the same reason as marriage brokage bonds. And the party only who is aggrieved can come to set it aside.

Lincoln's Inn MS. Misc. 506, p. 15

Michaelmas 1704.

The mother, for the advancement of her son, agreed to part with her jointure, and the son, by a private agreement between him and his mother, assigned a leasehold estate to her in lieu thereof. But, in regard there was no mention made of this in the marriage treaty and the son was in possession of the leasehold estate, the wife, who was the representative of the son, did by a decree of this court recover the leasehold estate from the mother.

[Other reports of this case: 2 Vernon 466, 499, 23 E.R. 900, 920.]

## 28

## Ash's Case

(Ch. c. 1704)

*A decree of foreclosure in a court of equity does not affect the common law title, but only destroys the debtor's right of redemption.*

Lincoln's Inn MS. Misc. 9, p. 63

Sir Edward Ash's Case, about four years ago.

There was a decree against him [Sir Edward Ash] to foreclose the equity of redemption of a mortgage and that the mortgagee should hold and enjoy against him and all claiming under him. He, afterwards, appealed to the House of Lords because the mortgage was not good in law, upon which, that part of the decree was reversed, and he was left at liberty to proceed at law. And, accordingly, he did proceed and recovered the land, for this court does not foreclose the legal title, but only the equitable one.

Note this case was cited by Sir Thomas Powys.

Master of the Rolls [TREVOR]: I suppose this mortgage was made by the ancestor of Sir Edward Ash.

It was likewise said by the Master of the Rolls [TREVOR] that, if there is a decree of foreclosure and, afterwards, an appeal to the Lords and that appeal is dismissed, this dismission does not put the decree in a better condition, but leaves it as it found it.

## 29

## Parker v. Lamb

(Ch. 1705)

*A subsequent lease revokes an inconsistent previous devise of a fee, but not a previous devise of an annuity charged upon the income from the land.*

British Library MS. Hargrave 80, f. 12, pl. 1

J.S., being seised in fee of certain land, devises it to his son for 99 years, paying out of it an annuity of £40 a year to his daughter. Afterwards, in his lifetime, he makes a lease of the same land for 99 years, reserving £50 a year rent, and dies.

This lease subsequent to the will shall be a revocation of the devise of the land to his son, but not of the devise of the rent to the daughter, for that shall remain and issue out of the rent reserved upon that lease, ruled Lord Keeper WRIGHT 20 July 1705 by the opinion of HOLT, POWELL, POWYS.

[Other copies of this report: Lincoln's Inn MS. Misc. 383, p. 19, pl. 1.]

[Other reports of this case: 2 Vernon 495, 23 E.R. 917, 2 Freeman 284, 22 E.R. 1213, 3 Brown P.C. 12, 1 E.R. 1145, 1 Eq. Cas. Abr. 410, 21 E.R. 1140, 2 Eq. Cas. Abr. 658, 769, 22 E.R. 553, 654.]

## 30

## Elliot v. Davenport

(Ch. 1705)

*Where a testator directs his executor to release a debtor but the debtor dies before the testator, the release lapses.*

British Library MS. Hargrave 80, f. 83, pl. 1

In the case of Smith and Orma, fol. 142,[1] *Mead* cited the case of Elliot and Davenport. Elliot owed the Defendant's testator £800 by a recognizance. The testator gave the £800 to his executors and directed that they should release to Elliot, his heirs, executors, and administrators. Elliot died before the testator. The Master of the Rolls [Trevor] decreed that the legacy was not lapsed. But Lord Cowper, upon appeal, decreed that it was. [It was] appealed to the House of Lords but, before the hearing, [it was] agreed.

[Other copies of this report: Lincoln's Inn MS. Misc. 383, p. 150, pl. 1.]

[Other reports of this case: 1 Peere Williams 83, 24 E.R. 304, 2 Vernon 521, 23 E.R. 935, 1 Eq. Cas. Abr. 296, 21 E.R. 1057, 2 Eq. Cas. Abr. 540, 22 E.R. 455.]

## 31

## Fawcet v. Fothergill

(Ch. 1705)

*Sequestrators of land may redeem a mortgage thereon.*

Dickens 19, 21 E.R. 173

Francis Calvert and others, claiming a mortgage for £1000 on the estates sequestered, by order dated 18th February 1669[/70] (entered Reg. Lib. A, fol. 396), they were to come in to be examined *pro interesse suo*, and the plaintiff was to exhibit interrogatories for that purpose.

By an order dated the 7th of January 1700[/01] (entered Reg. Lib. A, f. 340), on the petition of the plaintiff, after stating that the claimants had been examined, and the depositions returned, it was referred to the Master to certify what proof the claimants had made of their pretended right.

[1] *Smith v. Orma* (Ch. 1712), see below, Case No. 354.

The Master made his report.

The matter of the said report came on to be heard 8th of April 1703 (entered Reg. Lib. A, fol. 206), when His Lordship [WRIGHT] ordered the plaintiff to reply to the examination and the examinant was to be at liberty to examine witnesses touching his claim and to take out a commission wherein the plaintiff was to join if he thought fit.

Witnesses having been examined, there was an order for setting the matter down to be heard on the report the 26th October 1705, entered (Reg. Lib. A, fol. 101).

The matter of the report, by which the master found the claimant to have really and *bona fide* paid £400 and no more, came on to be argued.

Upon debate of the matter and hearing the exhibits and the proofs taken in relation to the matter aforesaid, His Lordship [COWPER] conceived the sequestrators might redeem the mortgage, and he directed an account as to £400.

## 32

## Toller v. Carteret

(Ch. 1705)

*When a court of equity has personal jurisdiction over the defendant, it can make a personal order to make him do equity in regard to foreign land.*

1 Salkeld 404, 91 E.R. 351

Easter 4 Anne [14 May 1705].

A bill was brought in Chancery to foreclose a mortgage of the Island of Sark.

The defendant pleaded to the jurisdiction of the court, *viz.* that the islands of Sark, Guernsey, Jersey, etc. were four islands governed by the laws of the Duchy of Normandy. And it was objected that bills to redeem were ancient, but bills to foreclose were of a later day, that Serjeant [George] Hutchins [d. 1705] had said he remembered the first of them, that the party ought to sue in the courts of the island and appeal.

On the other side it was said that Chancery *agit in personam*, that, if the person be here, he may be sued in Chancery, though the lands lie in a county palatine or in another kingdom, as Ireland or Barbados.

And WRIGHT, Lord Keeper, overruled the plea, saying the court acted against the person of the party and his conscience, and there might be a failure of justice if the Chancery would not hold plea in such a case, the party being here and the whole island in mortgage.

[Other reports of this case: 2 Vernon 494, 23 E.R. 916, 1 Eq. Cas. Abr. 134, 21 E.R. 938.]

## 33

## Hodges v. Sibley

(Ch. 1705)

*Where a London widow has waived her customary share of a decedent-citizen's estate, the custom of London is silent as to who gets her customary share.*

Yale Beinecke OSB MSS. 184, box 41,
Taussig 311, vol. 1, p. 442

22 May 1705.

In pursuance of an order of 5 December 1704, they certify that, in all cases where a freeman [of London] dies having children, his personal estate by the custom must be divided into three parts. One third, he may devise as he pleases, the second third part belongs to his children unpreferred by him in his lifetime, and the other third belongs to his widow. But when a freeman makes a settlement of lands upon his wife before marriage in lieu of her thirds or customary part of his personal estate, there is not any custom in London which particularly directs to whom in such case that part of his personal estate belongs.

## 34

## Kinsman v. Crooke

(Ch. 1705)

*Where a witness becomes incapacitated to testify in court, his deposition and evidence in a court of equity is admissible de bene esse.*

*A remote interest in the outcome of litigation will not render a person an interested witness and thus not competent to testify.*

2 Lord Raymond 1166, 92 E.R. 271

In a trial at bar on 14 May 1705, of an issue directed out of Chancery to try if a lease was made in pursuance of a power which was to make leases for the best rent that could be got, a witness named Rushley was examined in Chancery concerning the value of the land, having been collector of the rents. And, at the time of his examination in Chancery, he referred to and consulted his rental [book]. But now, at this trial, he was become blind, and, therefore, his examination in Chancery and the depositions there were admitted to be read because, if he had been so ill as that he could not have come to the trial, they had been good evidence, and now he is disabled to consult the rental by the act of God, and, therefore, the same reason holds. He also gave evidence of what he remembered besides.

Secondly, £6000 was devised to A. and B. in trust to purchase lands to be settled on Francis Gofton for life, with remainder to his sons in tail in contingency, remainder to William Gofton for life, with a contingent remainder to his sons in tail, remainder to Harold Kinsman in fee, with power to make leases, *ut supra*, etc. Francis Gofton made a lease to Crooke, rendering £170 *per annum* rent, and he died. And the question was whether the value was £170 *per annum* at the time of the purchase or not.

My Lord Gorges and Mr. Latin, the trustees, were produced as witnesses to prove it. And it was objected that they were not witnesses, because Kinsman, the remainderman, not joining in the purchase and who now contested the lease, if the lands were not of that value, it would be a breach of trust in the trustees, and they would be liable in Chancery to make satisfaction to the *cestui que trust*, and, therefore, they were to give evidence to excuse themselves.

*Sed non allocatur per curiam*, and they were sworn and gave evidence.

## 35

## Best v. Stamford

(Ch. 1705)

*Where the owner of a fee simple receives the beneficial interest of a trust of a lease of it, the leasehold merges into the fee.*

1 Salkeld 154, 91 E.R. 141

Michaelmas 4 Anne.

A *feme sole*, seised in fee, upon her marriage with A., makes a lease to trustees for 100 years in trust for the husband for his life, remainder to herself for life, remainder to the issue of that marriage, remainder to the wife, her executors, and administrators. The husband dies without issue; she marries a second husband and dies. Whether this term should be attendant upon the inheritance or should go to the husband as a term in gross was the question.

*Et per curiam*: It is a term attendant, because the trust for which it was created is at an end, the first husband being dead without issue, as, where a term is created to raise portions and the portions are paid or a termor purchases the inheritance in trust, the term shall be attendant. And, as for the second husband, it cannot be intended that he was then thought of.

[Other reports of this case: 2 Freeman 288, 22 E.R. 1216, 2 Vernon 520, 23 E.R. 934, Precedents in Chancery 252, 24 E.R. 123, 1 Eq. Cas. Abr. 274, 21 E.R. 1042.]

## 36

## Oldham v. Litchford

(Ch. 1705)

*Where a devisee promises his testator that he will honor a particular intended gift, he will be estopped to deny that promise even though the Statute of Frauds would defeat it.*

British Library MS. Hargrave 80, f. 28v, pl. 1

An annuity was decreed against the devisee of the real and personal estates upon the deposition of Mr. Bagshaw, the attorney who drew the will, that the annuity was omitted at the request of the devisee that it might not appear that the estate devised to him was charged with it and this notwithstanding there was nothing in writing and the Statute of Frauds and Perjuries.[1]

[Other copies of this report: Lincoln's Inn MS. Misc. 383, p. 54, pl. 1, Lincoln's Inn MS. Misc. 106, p. 22.]

British Library MS. Hargrave 83, p. 3

The uncle of Oldham had by his will devised to him £40 *per annum* out of certain lands. There were but two witnesses to the will. The uncle, being apprised that this devise was not valid for want of such a number of witnesses as the Statute of Frauds requires, wrote to A. to let him know that he intended for this reason to make a new will. A. wrote back to him and promised by his letter that the devise should be punctually complied with and, therefore, he need not be at the trouble of making a new will. The uncle dies without altering his will. A. refuses to pay the annuity.

Oldham brings his bill.

A. pleads the Statute.

[The plea was] overruled, and [he was] decreed to pay the annuity to Oldham.

[Other reports of this case: 2 Freeman 284, 22 E.R. 1214, 2 Vernon 506, 23 E.R. 923, 1 Eq. Cas. Abr. 231, 21 E.R. 1011, 2 Eq. Cas. Abr. 44, 22 E.R. 39.]

## 37

## Attorney General, ex rel. v. Reynolds

(Ch. 1705)

*A court of equity will not take jurisdiction of a case where the parties have an adequate remedy at common law.*

---

[1] Stat. 29 Car. II, c. 3, s. 5 (*SR*, V, 840).

1 Eq. Cas. Abr. 131, 21 E.R. 936

Michaelmas 1705.

The bill was at the relation of several freemen of the Weavers' Company against the defendants and other bailiffs, wardens, and assistants of the said Company, setting forth their incorporation *tempore* Hen. II but that the freemen, being imposed upon and abused by the governing part of the corporation, had a further charter and rules granted them *tempore* Car. I but that the defendants had been guilty of many breaches and violations of their charters and had oppressed the freemen etc. And they mentioned some particulars. And for a discovery of the rest and that they might be decreed for the future to observe the charters and to have an account of the revenue of the corporation, which the defendants had misspent, etc. was the end of the bill.

To which, the defendants demurred, because, as to part of the bill, it was to subject them to prosecutions at law and to a *quo warranto* and, as to the other parts, the plaintiffs had a remedy by *mandamus*, information, or otherwise, and not here.

And to the same opinion was Lord Keeper [Cowper], who said it would usurp too much on the King's Bench and that he never heard of any precedent for such a case as this. And so he allowed the demurrer.

## 38

## Taylor v. Hill

(Ch. 1705)

*A bill of discovery lies to discover specific things belonging to a judgment debtor that are in the hands of a third party.*

1 Eq. Cas. Abr. 132, 21 E.R. 937

Michaelmas [term] 1705.

The plaintiff, having recovered a judgment against J.S. (but no writ of execution having been sued out), supposing some particular effects of J.S. to be in the defendant's hands, brought a bill to discover them in order to subject them to his judgment.

The defendant demurs, because there is no equity to compel such a discovery and no such bill would lie against the debtor himself, much less against a third person.

The Lord Keeper [Cowper] seemed to agree it would not lie against the debtor himself, nor to have a general discovery from a third person, but only for particular things, as this bill was. And he overruled the demurrer.

## 39

## Pym v. Pym

(Ch. 1705)

*A marriage settlement will be specifically enforced according to the intent of the parties.*

Lincoln's Inn MS. Misc. 9, p. 38

27 October 1705. Lord Keeper.

The defendant, upon his marriage with the plaintiff's mother, in consideration of her portion, enters into a bond to settle lands to such a value upon the heirs of their two bodies begotten. The mother dies. And the plaintiff, who is the eldest son of that marriage, prefers his bill against his father, in which he makes the trustee in the bond a defendant, to have lands settled according to the bond.

[Cowper] decreed that the father should make a settlement which should be to the use of himself for life, remainder to the plaintiff and the heirs of his body, with like remainders to all the other sons in tail if there were any, for, though this is not according to the letter of the condition, yet it seems to be the meaning of the parties, and it is most agreeable to equity.

## 40

## Puckley v. Tippin

(Ch. 1705)

*There can be no remainder over after the gift of a chattel.*

Lincoln's Inn MS. Misc. 9, p. 39

29 October.

A man, by his will, devises to the plaintiff's wife, when unmarried, £400 and the interest of it, and, if she died without issue, then he devised it over.

The plaintiffs prefer their bill to have this legacy paid them. And the question was whether any provision should be made thereout for their issue or, in default of such, for the remainderman.

Lord Keeper [Cowper]: There can be no remainder limited of a chattel. Why then, suppose this was a devise of land; it would have been an estate tail in the devisee by implication, but no immediate devise by the issue. So, by a parity of reason, this must be an absolute devise of the money to the plaintiff's wife, which being a chattel and not to be entailed, she must have it.

But, then, the question was if it should not be some way secured for the wife so that the husband should not spend it, it being the method of the court in such cases to take care of married women.

But, as to that, the woman being in court and desiring it might be paid to her husband, it was ordered accordingly.

## 41

## Skett v. Whitmore

(Ch. 1705)

*The question in this case was whether a trust by implication can be declared by the court where there is no deed in writing.*

Lincoln's Inn MS. Misc. 9, p. 40

20 November 1705.

The reversioner of an estate in fee expectant upon an estate for life mortgages for 1000 years. And, afterwards, he sells the reversion in fee to A.B., who takes a conveyance of the inheritance in his own name and an assignment of the mortgage in his brother's name, which was in consideration of £100 paid the mortgagee by the brother and of £350 more paid, but [it was] not said by whom. And, in this assignment, [there] was no mention of any trust for the purchaser nor that it was to attend the inheritance. Nor was the purchaser's name so much as mentioned in the deed, but the writings were sealed at the same time and drawn by the same person. He to whom the conveyance in fee was made died. And his brother sets up a title to the term, and insisted upon it that he had purchased it absolutely in his own right and that, there being no declaration of trust, those that claimed the inheritance under his brother could set up no title, especially since the Statute of Frauds and Perjuries,[1] says that all declarations of trust must be in writing.

It was proved in the cause that A.B. treated for the purchase and that, afterwards, the tenant in possession wanting to renew his lease, he treated with A. about it and not with the brother.

Lord Keeper [Cowper]: If the Statute was out of the case, there would be no difficulty to declare this a trust considering the circumstances and proof in the case. Now, as to the Statute, that said all declarations of trusts must be in writing except trusts arising by implication of law. But it is not necessary that the trusts arising by implication must be in writing, for, if so, the exception would signify nothing, for, then, it would be no more than to say that all declarations of trust must be in writing, and, therefore, this court has admitted parol proof in order to make out a trust arising by implication, as if a man purchases in another's name and there is no declaration of trust yet, if, upon proof, it appears that the other person paid the purchase money, this is a trust by implication for that person.

---

[1] Stat. 29 Car. II, c. 3, s. 9 (*SR*, V, 840).

If an absolute conveyance is made to a man and he declares at the sealing it is only a mortgage, this court, upon proof of such declaration, will adjudge it a mortgage notwithstanding there was no defeasance in writing. It was said by the counsel that it had been decreed in this court that, where an absolute conveyance is made and the grantee promises to execute a defeasance and does it not, that this court will compel him, because this is a fraud, but that there was a difference between promising to execute a defeasance and declaring the conveyance was only a mortgage. Why, now, is not one as much a fraud as the other? For my part, the difference is above my comprehension.

As to the case before us, it appears that the deeds were all executed at the same time and, in the conveyance of the reversion, there is a covenant for a fine which was to be at the costs of the purchaser and also for further assurance. And there is nothing of all this in the assignment of the term, which it is strange there should not if the brother had purchased the term in his own right. There is likewise an exception in the conveyance of the inheritance of the estate of the tenant for life but no exception of the term, which is another evidence that the term was only in trust. And, therefore, from what appears in the deeds and in the proofs in the cause, but, principally, from what appears in the deeds, I ground my judgment in this case. And I am of the opinion that the assignment to the brother was in the first place to be a security to him for what money he had lent his brother to pay for the purchase and, afterwards, he to stand a trustee for the brother, to whom the reversion was conveyed.

I make use of the proofs in the cause only to satisfy my judgment as to the trust by implication appearing from the deeds.

There had been no immediate possession in this case to A.B., for the tenant for life is yet living, or else that would be another evidence of a trust, for, if A. takes a conveyance in the name of B. and A. enters and receives the profits of the estate and continues quietly in the possession, though there is no declaration of trust, yet this will be a trust by implication in B.

Note it was said by My Lord Keeper [Cowper] that, as to the cases before put of absolute conveyances, where the grantee promises to execute a defeasance or declares the deed was only a mortgage, the grantor must come speedily into this court to have a defeasance executed, for, after some years' acquiescence under it, it will be too late to make such proof.

In the principal case, an issue at law was directed to enquire how much of the purchase money was paid by the brother.

2 Freeman 280, 22 E.R. 1211

The plaintiff and other creditors of William Whitmore, deceased, prefer a bill against the defendant John Whitmore, for a discovery of assets. And the only question was whether a term which was assigned to John Whitmore was in trust for William. The case was [thus].

Sir Samuel Clarke, being seised in fee of the reversion of the lands in question expectant upon the death of Margaret Mumpford, who was tenant for life, made a lease for 500 years by way of mortgage to commence upon the death of Margaret Mumpford. Afterwards, William Whitmore agrees with Sir Samuel Clarke for the purchase of the reversion, and the term was assigned to the defendant William Whitmore 16 May, and the fee was conveyed to William Whitmore 17 May. In the conveyance of the fee, the consideration is mentioned to be paid by John and William, but there was a concurrence of many other circumstances whereby it plainly appeared that John Whitmore was only a trustee for William and that the term was intended to attend the inheritance, but there was no declaration of trust in writing.

And the defendant having denied the trust by his answer, the question was whether any decree could be made by reason of the Statute.

And it was said for the plaintiff that this court had in several cases where there was no writing caused the execution of an agreement, as where an agreement was in part executed, as where a tenant had taken a lease, but no writing was signed, and possession had been delivered, and the tenant had laid out his money in stock, or, where he had laid out money in building, the court has compelled the making of the lease, and so in the Lord Nottingham's time, where the purchase money was paid, and the deeds refused to be sealed, he decreed the sealing of them.[1] And so, if a mortgagee refuse to seal a defeasance, he has been decreed to do it.

The reason in the two first cases is because the agreement was in part executed and in the two last cases there was an apparent fraud. But, in this case, though the Lord Keeper [Cowper] declared he was fully satisfied that it was intended a trust, yet, there being no writing to declare it, he was not satisfied to do it in opposition to the very letter of the Statute, unless they could show him some precedents. And so he took time to consider.

## 42

## City of London v. Garway

(Ch. 1705–1706)

*In this case of a devise to a widow who was the executrix, the decedent's personal estate devised to her was ordered to be used to pay the decedent's debts notwithstanding the devise.*

*In this case, the surplus of the decedent's estate resulted as undisposed of to the heir at law.*

*In order to disinherit an heir at law, there must either be express words or a necessary implication.*

---

[1] *Potts v. Turvin* (Ch. 1681), 79 Selden Soc. 856.

*A devise of lands to the heir after the death of the wife, by a necessary implication, gives an estate for life to the wife.*

Lincoln's Inn MS. Misc. 10, p. 199

27 November 1705.

Thomas Garway devised the profits of all his real estate to Frances, his wife, for life. And, the freehold and inheritance, he devises to his trustees and their heirs in trust to sell for the best price they could get or to lease or mortgage the same and the moneys, rents, and profits arising thereout to pay and distribute in the proportions and manner and for such uses and purposes as the testator should appoint by any paper or papers in writing under his hand to be signed in the presence of two or more witnesses entitled 'Thomas Garway his paper of the money and legacies he would have paid and disposed of by A., B., and C., his trustees named in his last will dated the 18 February 1695[/96]'. And, if any of the persons to whom the money to be appointed should die, he gave their shares to the survivors, and, if they all died, he willed that the money should be for the benefit of the Norrises, his nephews. And, if he left no such paper, he devised his real estate to his trustees and their heirs to the use of his brother for life, then to the use of his nephews and their heirs, and he directed the charges and expenses of his trustees to be first paid or retained out of the said estate.

Then he goes on:

I make and ordain my said dear wife full and sole executrix of this my will, and I do give her all my personal estate whatsoever (not herein or by the said paper or papers disposed of), and I do order that she do pay to my brother William Garway £20 for mourning.

He left a note entitled as in the will, and, under the title, he says only 'I give to my natural son and daughters £1500, to Mrs. Leave £500, to Mr. Milman, I give £25', and so on to the amount of £2333.

Lord Chancellor [Lord Cowper], on the hearing, as to the personal estate devised to Frances, declared that it was plain by the words of the will the same was not thereby devised to her until after the debts and legacies which, by his will and paper instructions were appointed to be paid should be first discharged. And, therefore, he decreed an account of the personal estate and that it should be applied towards the payment of his debts etc. according to the paper instructions and in aid of the reversion of his real estate to which the heirs at law were entitled.

British Library MS. Hargrave 81, f. 122, pl. 1

Christ's Hospital v. Gallway.

[Where there was] a devise to a widow and executrix, there it was decreed the personal estate devised to her shall go to pay the debts notwithstanding the devise.

[Other copies of this report: British Library MS. Hargrave 82, f. 135, British Library MS. Hargrave 77, f. 33, pl. 4, British Library MS. Hargrave 303, f. 61.]

2 Vernon 571, 23 E.R. 972

Thomas Garway devised several lands to his wife for life, she paying £20 *per annum* to A. and B. for their lives, and the life of the longer liver of them, and, if she died before them, his trustees to pay the £20 *per annum* out of the lands devised to them. And therein he devises several lands therein mentioned to three trustees and their heirs upon trust to sell and to dispose of the monies to be raised by such sale to such persons as he should by a paper to be signed by him direct and appoint, provided, if he left no such paper of appointment, then the trustees to stand seised in trust for the benefit of his four nephews and, if any of the appointees died before sale and payment of the money, such share to [result] to his nephews.

Thomas Garway, by a paper signed by him, appointed his trustees to pay several sums of money to several persons therein named, but not near to the value of the land. The question was whether the surplus should pass by the will to the nephews or result as undisposed of to the heir at law.

And [he] decreed it to the heir at law, the Lord Keeper [Lord Cowper] saying this was not so strong a case as that of Sir Caesar Cranmer and the Duke of Southampton[1] and that, to disinherit an heir at law, there must either be express words or a necessary implication, according to the case in the yearbook of Hen. VII.[2] A devise of lands to the heir after the death of the wife, by a necessary implication, gives an estate for life to the wife, because the heir was not to take until after her death; but, if the devise be to a stranger after the death of the wife, that gives no estate for life to the wife by implication, but the estate during her life shall descend and go to the heir at law.

[Other reports of this case: 1 Eq. Cas. Abr. 196, 272, 21 E.R. 985, 1040.]

[Related cases: Christ's Hospital v. Budgin (1712), 2 Vernon 683, 23 E.R. 1043, 1 Eq. Cas. Abr. 70, 21 E.R. 883.]

## 43

## Noyes v. Mordaunt

(Ch. 1706–1707)

*Those who take under a will must abide by all of the terms of the will or renounce it entirely.*

---

[1] *Duke of Southampton v. Cranmer* (1685), 1 Vernon 338, 23 E.R. 506, 2 Freeman 186, 22 E.R. 1151, Shower P.C. 83, 1 E.R. 58, Chancery Repts. *tempore* Jac. II, 122.

[2] YB Hil. 13 Hen. VII, f. 17, pl. 22 (1498).

*A mortgagee can dispose of the mortgage as an equitable estate or as a legal estate.*

British Library MS. Hargrave 80, f. 131

A man intended to provide for his children by his will. He gave an estate to one, which, afterwards, appeared to be entailed, and he made a provision for the other two out of his fee simple lands. The two would have taken advantage of the entail to defeat the third and, as to the fee simple lands, would have had the benefit of the will. But they were obliged to abide entirely by the will or renounce it quite.

[Other copies of this report: Lincoln's Inn MS. Misc. 383, p. 232.]

Lincoln's Inn MS. Misc. 9, pp. 48, 51

6 February 1706[/07].

John Everard, having issue, two daughters, by will, devises all his entailed lands to his oldest daughter and all his fee simple lands to his youngest, provided she released her right in the entailed lands to her eldest sister, and, moreover, he declares that, if he had issue, another daughter, then the fee simple lands were to be divided between the two youngest. And he further devises all his bonds and mortgages between the two youngest (if there was another daughter). And he also devises to them and their heirs all his estate which he had in F., which was a mortgaged estate, which he had been in possession of ten years.

*Resolutio per curiam* [Lord Cowper]: It was a condition implied in the nature of the thing, that the youngest daughter should hold the fee simple lands in case she would permit her eldest sister to hold the entailed lands, admitting there had been no proviso, for, since the testator intended a provision for the eldest in those lands as well as for the youngest in the fee simple ones, a court of equity ought to interpose and help the youngest, and, therefore, if the youngest (as she might) should insist on a share of the entailed lands, the eldest in such case should have a recompense out of the fee simple lands.

Secondly, it was resolved that the lands in Fenlock should go to the daughters and their heirs, for the testator, before, devised all his mortgages to the two daughters and their executors. But, in the other case, he devised all his estate in Fenlock to them and their heirs. And, though, as to the mortgagor, it was a redeemable interest, yet the mortgagee might dispose of it in his own family as he pleased and either consider it as an equitable estate and give it to his daughter and their executors or as a legal estate and give it to them and their heirs.

[Other reports of this case: 2 Vernon 581, 23 E.R. 978, Gilbert Rep. 2, 25 E.R. 2, Precedents in Chancery 265, 24 E.R. 128, 1 Eq. Cas. Abr. 273, 21 E.R. 1041.]

## 44

## Baker v. Holmes

(Ch. 1706)

*Where infant defendants cannot be found to be served with process, the process can be served on their parents.*

Dickens 18, 21 E.R. 173

25 February 1705[/06]. Lord Keeper WRIGHT.

This cause came on to be heard the 16th of May last, when it was ordered to stand over with liberty for the plaintiff to amend his bill by adding parties. The plaintiff did amend his bill by adding the children of one Rudge, but, not being able to find them and the defendant's solicitor refusing to tell where they were to be found, by an order dated the 20th of December last, it was ordered that service of a subpoena for the infants to appear on the defendant Mary Rudge, their mother, should be good service. She was served, and the children not having appeared and the plaintiff not knowing where they were to be found, it was, on the motion of Mr. *Vernon*, ordered that the plaintiff should be at liberty to sue out an attachment against the infants to compel them to appear.

## 45

## Clare v. Wordell

(Ch. 1706)

*An answer to a bill of revivor cannot respond to the merits of the case, but it can only object to the revivor of the lawsuit.*

Dickens 20, 21 E.R. 174

Clare v. Werden.

It was held that a defendant, by his answer to a bill of revivor, is not to contest the justice of a decree, but only to show cause against it.

[Other reports of this case: 2 Vernon 548, 23 E.R. 955, 1 Eq. Cas. Abr. 3, 83, 21 E.R. 829, 895.]

## 46

## Orby v. Lord Mohun

(Ch. 1706)

*By the devise in this case, money was to be paid immediately and not out of the income from land.*

*An ancient rent can be passed generally without specifying a sum certain where it is capable of being reduced to a certainty.*

*A question in this case was whether a single deed of lease can demise separate parcels of land and they will be separate demises if so designated in the deed.*

Lincoln's Inn MS. Coxe 89, vol. 3, part 2, p. 13

5 April 5 Anne, *coram* Lord Keeper, Holt, Chief Justice, and Trevor, Chief Justice.

Charles, late earl of Macclesfield, being seised in fee of divers lands etc. having two sons, Charles, Lord Brandon, and Fitton Gerard, upon the marriage of Charles, Lord Brandon, with Anne, daughter of Sir Richard Mason in pursuance of an agreement for settling the said premises on that occasion by indentures of lease and release dated 23 and 24 April 1683, the said earl and Lord Brandon, in consideration of the intended marriage and other considerations, did convey to Sir Henry Hobart and R. Mason and their heirs all the lands etc. and all other lands which they or any other in trust for them had any right or title to to the use of the said Sir Henry Hobart and R. Mason and their heirs to make them tenants of the freehold for suffering a recovery and, after the recovery suffered, to the use of the said earl of Macclesfield until the marriage and, after, to the intent the said Charles, Lord Brandon, might out of part of the lands receive £1000 *per annum* for his life and, after his decease, that the intended wife might receive annually the like sum for her life in lieu of dower and that, during the life of the said Lord Brandon to the use of the earl and his heirs chargeable, nevertheless, with the said annuities, and as to all other the lands until the marriage and after during the life of the said Lord Brandon to the use of the said earl for ninety-nine years if he so long live and after the determination of that estate to trustees to preserve [contingent remainders], then to Charlton and Harford, the executors for 300 years without impeachment of waste upon trust that they without prejudice to the annuities payable to the said Lord Brandon and his intended wife should after the earl's death raise by sale or mortgage and pay to such persons as the said earl by any writing or will duly attested should direct any sum not exceeding £12,000 after raising the said sum and payment thereof the term to cease and, after the said term of 300 years was determined, to Charles, Lord Brandon, for ninety-nine years if he so ling live with a like provision for preserving contingent remainders and with remainders over to his first and other sons in tail and, for default of such issue, to every other son of the said earl in like manner and, for default of such issue, to the said earl, his heirs, etc. And, in the said indentures was a power for the said Lord Brandon and Fitton Gerard, when each came into possession, to make leases for twenty-one years or three lives in possession at the usual fines and rents or more and, until the recovery suffered, that Hobart and Mason and their heirs should stand seised to such uses as were by the said indenture mentioned and declared.

No recovery was suffered. But the earl, in pursuance of the power reserved thereby for raising £12,000 by his indenture dated 11 December 1685, appointed the said trustees to raise the said £12,000 and to pay £8000, part of it to his daughter, Lady Elizabeth and £4000 to his son, Fitton Gerard. The said earl of Macclesfield died in 1693, leaving only his son, Lord Brandon, and Fitton Gerard, his issue.

The marriage between Lord Brandon and Mrs. Mason took effect, but, in 1897, it was dissolved by an act of Parliament. And the limitation and provisions for her and her issue were declared void. In 1701, Charles, the eldest son of the late earl, died without issue, whereupon Fitton Gerard entered, and, intending to make leases pursuant to the power reserved in the said indenture of 1683, he sent to the lord Mohun, who claims title under same will of the late Earl Charles, brother to the said Fitton, for the books and rent rolls in order to ascertain the fines and rents. But he refusing them to him, he made leases and pursued the powers as near as he could without them.

Fitton Gerard, earl of Macclesfield, died in 1702 without issue, and he made Thomas Orby and two others of the plaintiffs executors, who by virtue thereof became entitled to £4000 which, pursuant to the appointment of his father was to be raised and paid him out of the term of 300 years and to have the benefit of the leases made by Fitton and the £4000.

A bill was exhibited. And the plaintiffs charge that, if the leases were not strictly pursuant to the power, it was occasioned by the lord Mohun's refusing the survey [?] rolls etc.

Lord Mohun admitted that Earl Charles, the father, was seised in fee, that he and his son, Lord Brandon, executed the indentures of lease and release, and that Earl Charles, the father, executed the deed of appointment of £12,000, and claimed title under the will of Charles, the late earl's brother, to Fitton. And he insisted that the power of leasing had never a legal and effectual existence in regard it was to raise out of the recoveries, which were never suffered, and also that the powers were not duly pursued and, therefore, void and, being voluntary, ought not to be favored in equity. And he said he knew nothing of the refusal of the rolls etc. And he insisted that Fitton could have no occasion for them to ascertain the fines and rents, having the counterparts of the old leases in his power and custody.

Lord Mohun's bill was to discover whether Earl Fitton had any part of the £4000 and how much of it and for the trustees to convey.

The defendant's answer to the cross-bill was to the same effect as the original bill.

The causes were heard 28 and 29 January and 1 February. And the court took time to consider until the 15 April and then declared the £4000 to be due to Earl Fitton upon the death of Earl Charles, the father, and that it ought to carry interest from that time during the possession of his brother, Earl Charles, and during the time that Fitton was in possession, no interest, but interest [was] to commence again on his death. And he declared the leases made by Earl Fitton to be void against the remainderman.

British Library MS. Hargrave 80, f. 4v

15 April 1706. Lady Charlotte Orby against Lord Mohun. *Coram* COWPER, HOLT, TREVOR.

Charles, lord Macclesfield [d. 1694], by lease and release dated [ *blank* ] conveys the land in question to Hobart and Mason with covenants that a common recovery should be suffered by them to the use of himself for life, remainder to Charles, lord Brandon [d. 1701], his eldest son, for life, remainder to Fitton Gerard [d. 1702], his second son, for life, with powers to each of the tenants for life as they should respectively come into possession of the land to make leases for twenty-one years or for three lives or for any number of years determinable on three lives of all the lands that had been anciently let, reserving the ancient rent, and of all the lands not formerly in lease, reserving the full improved rent with a clause providing that, upon the making of such leases, counterparts signed by the tenants should be always taken. It was likewise covenanted as to part of the lands that the recovery should be to the use of Hobart and Mason for a long term of years, which term was in trust to raise £12,000 payable in such manner and to such persons as should be directed by the will of Charles, lord Macclesfield, and afterwards to attend the inheritance. Charles, lord Macclesfield, by his will dated [ *blank* ] directs that £8000 of the £12,000 should be paid to the Lady Gerard, his daughter, who is a stranger to this case, and the other £4000 to Fitton Gerard, his younger son, whose executrix the plaintiff, Lady Orby, is, to be raised by a mortgage or sale of the term created for that purpose.

Charles, lord Macclesfield, dies before any common recovery is suffered; so the limitations intended upon it remain to be executed in equity. Upon the death of Charles, lord Macclesfield, the lord Brandon became tenant for life of the lands in question, remainder to Fitton Gerard for life according to the intended limitation of the common recovery, remainder to the lord Brandon in fee as heir to his father. The lord Brandon, being thus seised, devises all his estate and interest in the said lands to My Lord Mohun, whom he makes his executor, and he dies. Upon his death, Fitton Gerard, as next in remainder, came into possession of the land and makes the leases upon which the present question arises in this manner, 'I demise, set, and to farm let' such and such lands, naming all that had been anciently let severally, 'according to my power' reserving therefor respectively the ancient and accustomed rent, not specifying any sum in certain, and, of the other which never had been let before, he made a joint demise reserving a rent of £500 a year and so much more as the land should be worth.

Upon this case, two questions arose, first, whether the £4000 devised by Charles, lord Macclesfield, to Fitton Gerard in the manner aforesaid should be now paid to the lady Orby, his executrix, with interest from the time of the death of Charles, lord Macclesfield, or without interest. It was argued that this money, being charged upon an estate in land, was to be paid not immediately upon the death of the devisor, but as the profits of the land would answer it and that, therefore, there had been no default or delay in payment in the executor in respect whereof he should be charged with interest.

But, as to this, the opinion of the court was clear that the £4000 was to be paid with interest from the death of the devisor, for the direction of the will is that it should be raised not out of the profits but by a mortgage or sale of the lands charged so that it was plainly intended to be raised and paid immediately. And if the executrix, to whose possession the term came liable to the payment of this money, thought fit to retain the land and receive the profits of it instead of mortgaging or selling of it, as the will directed, for the satisfaction of the legacy, that ought not to turn to the loss of the legatee, but the executor shall hold the land himself liable to the same charge, both of principal and interest, as it would have been if mortgaged, as the will directed, to a third person. But it was the opinion of the court that, in computing this interest, there should be a deduction for the time whilst the land itself was in the possession of Fitton Gerard, to whom the interest was due, for, during that time, he received a satisfaction for his interest in the profits of the land which was mortgaged for his principal debt.

The second question was concerning the validity of the leases made by Fitton Gerard in pursuance of the power reserved in his father's settlement and as to the lease of those lands which had not been formerly let in lease reserving £500 *per annum* rent and so much more as the lands were worth that was held to be a lease not pursuant to the power and void in respect of the uncertainty of the reservation as to him who had the inheritance.

But the principal doubt was concerning the other leases made by Fitton Gerard, whether the demise of all the lands formerly in lease reserving therefor respectively the ancient rent without specifying any certain sum was a good execution of the power in respect of those lands.

And the Chief Justice Holt delivered his opinion that the power was in this case well pursued. It has been objected to it that this was one entire and joint demise of several parcels of land that were anciently let distinctly, that the rent reserved thereupon was entire and to be distrained for through all the lands in the lease, whereas the ancient rents were several for each part and every distinct rent only to be recovered by distress upon those lands whereon it was reserved, that, for this reason, the rent reserved upon this lease was not the ancient rent and the power in that circumstance, therefore, not pursued. To this, he said that, though several parcels of land are comprehended in one deed of demise executed at the same time, yet, if the reservations are several of so many distinct rents for each parcel, the rents are thereby as much distinguished and separated as if they had been by several deeds of lease. Now, in the principal case, the premises of the lease do specify by name all the parcels of land which were anciently demisable and the reservation is 'yielding and paying therefor respectively the ancient rent', that is, for every parcel respectively, the ancient rent that had been paid for that parcel. To construe this a joint reservation of one entire rent for all the lands mentioned in the premises of the deed would be to construe it a new rent where an ancient one is expressed and to understand one entire rent where the reservation is of a rent to be respectively distributed and proportioned according to the several parcels of land that were anciently in lease.

Secondly, it was objected that this reservation of the ancient rent generally without specifying a certain sum was void for the uncertainty because the remainderman, for whose benefit the reservation was intended, cannot be able to inform himself what the ancient rent was in order to demand or avow for it.

To this, the Chief Justice [Holt] said the reason was in the respect sufficiently certain because it was capable of being reduced to a certainty. A lease for so many years as J.S. shall name is good because the term, though not defined in the lease itself, may be rendered certain by the nomination of J.S. to which it is referred. A lease reserving 12d. for every acre *per annum* has a sufficient certainty in the reservation because it is capable of being reduced to a certainty by admeasurement. So, if the king makes a grant of a manor with all the profits, franchises, etc. as the former patentee had, this is a good grant even against the king of all such profits as the ancient patentee had, though, perhaps, it was not known to the king or the grantee at the time of the grant that passed by it.

He said that, if this lease had been made by a tenant in fee simple, there had been no question but the reservation had been good and sufficiently certain to bind himself and his heirs, and there is no reason to distinguish such a lease from this, for this is derived and carved out of the fee simple though a tenant for life is the immediate lessor. The tenant for life is only an instrument in conveying to another a more durable estate than he himself has. And he acts by virtue of an authority created out of the inheritance and vested in him by the tenant of the fee simple.

And as to the uncertainty and difficulty that he in the remainder was put under for the recovery of his rent by such a general reservation, he said it was no greater than if a certain sum had been reserved, for, even in that case, upon an action of debt or avowry for such rent, it would be necessary for him to aver that it was the ancient rent and to prove it, for, else, the lease would be void as not pursuant to the power and, consequently, no rent due and his action or avowry groundless. And, by the same averment and proof, he may recover on the present lease. But this difficulty, he said, was not so great as was urged, for, by the ancient rent, he understood no more than the rent that was reserved on the last lease, according to the opinion of My Lord Hale, Hardres 325, 326, Morrice against Antrobus.[1] And this would be no hard matter for the remainderman to know when, together with the possession of the estate, he would have a right to all the old leases and the possessory writings which concern the land.

He cited the Case of Leveson and Pigott, in Chancery 1693, where a power was to make leases for three lives or twenty-one years reserving 12d. *per annum*

[1] *Morrice v. Antrobus* (Ex. 1663), Hardres 325, 145 E.R. 480.

for every Cheshire acre that should be leased. By virtue of this power, a lease was made of a parcel of the lands, reserving generally, according to the words of the power, 12d. for every Cheshire acre. And, by the Lord Chancellor and Chief Justice Trevor and himself [Holt], it was held to be a good lease and the reservation pursuant to the power. So he concluded in the principal case that the lease was good to bind the inheritance.

But, as to this point, the Lord Keeper [Lord Cowper] and Chief Justice Trevor disagreed. They doubted whether the deed of lease, as it was made, could be construed to amount to a lease of the several parcels of land comprehended in the ancient leases with a distinct reservation of respective ancient rents out of each.

But in respect of the difficulty which was laid on the remainderman by so general and uncertain a reservation, they held that the power was not sufficiently pursued. They agreed that a tenant in fee simple making such a lease with such reservations should bind himself, his heirs, and assigns by it and that the interest of the tenant for life himself was bound by the lease in the principal case, for there is a difference between a man's own acts to bind his own estate and interest, which shall ever be taken most strongly against himself, and such as are done in pursuance of a particular power to the prejudice of another man's inheritance. One who makes a lease or grant by virtue of a special power extending beyond his own estate must hold himself strictly to the execution of his power, not only to the substance of it, but to all the circumstances that may possibly be of ease or benefit to him in the remainder upon whose estate such power entrenches. In Montjoy's Case, 5 Coke,[1] it was resolved that the power to make leases reserving the ancient rent was not well pursued by reserving the ancient annual rent payable half yearly which had been before payable quarterly, because that change in the manner of payment was in some degree to the prejudice of him in the remainder, who was to receive the rent. So a reservation of a rent payable in silver which had been before in gold was for the same reason held ill. Now, in the principal case, the reservation is far from having all the beneficial circumstances for the advantage of the remainderman, as the power requires that it is in effect to him only a conditional reservation of any rent at all, for, if he cannot discover what parcels were anciently let together and what rents were reserved on each parcel, he will never be able to make a demand or avow properly for any rent, so the recovery of the rent provided for him in satisfaction of the land which would otherwise have been his must depend upon foreign circumstances and helps an information which may never be in his power to procure, whereas it was certainly intended he should have sufficient means for the recovery of the rent upon the face of the lease itself. And for that purpose, particular care is taken in the qualification of the power that counterparts of the leases should be taken which, upon

[1] *Shephard v. Blackaller* (1589), 5 Coke Rep. 3, 77 E.R. 52, also Moore K.B. 197, 72 E.R. 528.

such a general reservation, would be useless to the remainderman as not directing him what to demand when the rents should become due to him and, though, if the reservation had been of a certain sum, it had been incumbent on the remainderman equally as now to have averred in his action or avowry for it that the rent demanded was the ancient rent, yet the tenant would never have contested that with him or have put him to the proof of it because, if it should not be the ancient rent, his lease would be void and the remainderman would be sure either to have his rent in one action or the land in another.

But in the principal case, upon this general reservation, the remainderman might very probably fail in the demand of his rent and would yet be never the nearer the recovery of the land. As to the Case of Leveson and Pigott, they said it was very different from this case, for the reservation of 12d. yearly for every acre, though it was uncertain in itself, was capable of being reduced to a certainty without difficulty, for it referred only to the measures which might be at any time certainly and easily taken.

They said that, since the statutes of Hen. VIII [and] 4 Queen Elizabeth[1] which first introduces this manner of leasing, no such general reservation had ever been attempted, and, if it should receive a sanction now, it would work a great mischief to the church in general, to all the noble families in England upon the settlement of whose estates these powers were usual, contrary to the policy of these laws and settlements whereby it is intended principally to preserve the inheritance from being dismembered and diminished by the temporary possessors to the prejudice of those who should come after them.

[Other copies of this report: Lincoln's Inn MS. Misc. 383, p. 2.]

Lincoln's Inn MS. Misc. 12, p. 50

Sir Ch. Orby and Lord Mohun.

The earl of Macclesfield [was] tenant for life under a settlement with power to make leases when in possession for any term not exceeding twenty-one [years] or for three lives, so as in every lease, where fines have been usually taken, the old and accustomed rents were reserved and, where no fines have been taken, there should be reserved the best rent that could be gotten.

The earl made a lease of the whole estate to the plaintiff, reserving no particular rents, but in general the old and accustomed rents that had been payable for the respective premises.

The court would not aid this or make it good, for it would be to do a wrong to a third person. Powers annexed to an estate for life go in enlargement of the estate of the tenant for life and shall be taken strictly.

[1] Stat. 32 Hen. VIII, c. 28 (*SR*, III, 784–786); Stat. 1 Eliz. I, c. 19, s. 4 (*SR*, IV, 381–382).

[Other reports of this case: 2 Vernon 531, 542, 23 E.R. 944, 951, 3 Chancery Reports 102, 21 E.R. 741, Gilbert Rep. 45, 25 E.R. 32, Precedents in Chancery 257, 24 E.R. 124, 2 Freeman 291, 22 E.R. 1218, 1 Eq. Cas. Abr. 343, 21 E.R. 1090.]

## 47

## Davison v. Goddard

(Ch. 1706)

*In this case, the rent charge in issue was to be paid as a satisfaction of the ancient rent and not in addition to it.*

British Library MS. Hargrave 80, f. 4, pl. 1

J.S., seised in fee of seventeen houses in London, devises them to his wife for life, remainder to A. in fee paying out of the profits £20 *per annum* to Davison, the plaintiff, for life, and he dies. This estate is afterwards divided into four parts, three of which are devised to the defendant's brother in fee and, by him, settled upon the defendant by deed with a clause rendering it liable to the payment of £20 a year to the plaintiff. And the question in Chancery was whether this charge of £20 a year of the plaintiff's benefit should go in satisfaction of the £15 a year ancient rent issuing out of these three parts to the plaintiff before or whether it should be understood of a distinct and additional rent charge.

And the opinion of My Lord Keeper [Lord Cowper] was that it should go in satisfaction of the old rent and not inure as a new gift. And likewise, if the plaintiff insisted to have this £20 a year according to this settlement, he should take it in the manner it was given subsequent to all encumbrances and debts that affected the land, though contracted by the defendant's brother, who claimed the land subsequent to the rent charge or else he should have his election to have the old rent of £15 a year precedent to all debts and encumbrances contracted since the devise whereby that rent was first created, but that he should not be suffered to divide the £20 a year and take £15 of it as an old rent precedent to all encumbrances and the other £5 as a new gift subsequent to them.

[Other copies of this report: Lincoln's Inn MS. Misc. 383, p. 1, pl. 1.]

[Other reports of this case: Gilbert Rep. 65, 25 E.R. 45, 2 Eq. Cas. Abr. 61, 217, 256, 351, 22 E.R. 54, 185, 217, 299.]

## 48

## Powell v. Bell

(Ch. 1706)

*A husband is liable for his deceased wife's debts only so far as he had received any assets from her.*

Precedents in Chancery 255, 24 E.R. 124

The defendant had married an administratrix to her former husband, to a share of whose personal estate, the plaintiff was entitled. The administratrix was likewise entitled to a third. And, before her second marriage, she had wasted a great part of the estate, and then she died.

This bill was brought against her husband to have an account of the estate and a satisfaction of his share.

And, being heard at the Rolls, an account was decreed to be taken of what of the estate had come to the hands of the administratrix before her second marriage and also what had come to her or her husband's hands since the marriage and the plaintiff [was] to have satisfaction against the defendant absolutely for so far as came to his or his wife's hands after the marriage, and, for what came to her hands before her second marriage, to have a satisfaction against the defendant so far as he had any estate of his wife.

And this was affirmed on appeal to My Lord Keeper [Lord Cowper].

Mr. *Vernon* said it has been several times held that, where a man marries a woman without stipulating for any particular fortune or making any settlement, if, after the death of the wife, debts of her's appear, the husband, not being a purchaser in such case, shall be answerable for the debts of the wife in equity so far as he had any money or other personal estate of her's.

[Other copies of this report: 1 Eq. Cas. Abr. 61, 21 E.R. 874.]

## 49

## Anonymous v. Briscoe

(Ch. 1706)

*A suit in equity can proceed against some members of a large class of defendants although all of the defendants have not been served with process.*

British Library MS. Hargrave 80, f. 7v

[ *blank* ] v. Briscoe and others, undertakers for the establishment of a land bank.

Upon the hearing this cause in Chancery, it was objected that many who were made parties to the bill were not summoned or brought before the court. So it was prayed for that reason that the cause should not be heard.

If these defendants had been omitted in the bill, the rest might have demurred for want of proper parties. But being mentioned in the bill and not summoned, the time for the defendants to take advantage of it was on the hearing.

The case was thus. The plaintiffs had been contributors for the establishment of a land bank and had laid down their money and had borne all the loss that had attended that project. The defendants had all entered into the project, had all subscribed their share, and were under terms to share the gain and bear the loss which might ensue in proportion to what they had subscribed.

The end of the plaintiff's bill was that the defendants might be obliged to pay to them who had borne all the loss such sums of money as should appear to be the defendants' respective proportions.

It was objected that, unless all the parties to that project were brought before the court, it could not appear how much should be due to the plaintiffs, for, perhaps, some of the absent parties may have paid something towards the loss as well and the plaintiffs and then they would be equally entitled and may afterwards demand again and recover against the defendants sums of money which they should now pay.

To this it was answered that the books which contain the public accounts of this project were in the defendants' hands or might be gotten by them, from whence it would appear who had borne the loss and were to be repaid, that this was a case of necessity. All the defendants could not be found, or, if they could, there would be so many of them and the suit would be so often interrupted by the death of parties that it would be without end to proceed against them. They cited the case of Richmond and the City of London,[1] where a lease was made by the City to three persons; these three make under-leases to a vast number of other persons. For the breach of covenants, the City proceeds against these three in Chancery. And it was held that they well might. Another case was cited where some Frenchmen were plaintiffs demanding against an administrator their share of the intestate's estate. It was objected that there were other persons in France in the same relation to the intestate and entitled also to shares in the distribution who ought to have been made parties. But this was overruled because no process could possibly issue, especially in time of war, to bring them before the court.

But My Lord Keeper [Lord Cowper] did not rely upon either of these cases, for, in the first, he said the City of London had taken care to make their contract with such numbers as might be dealt with and the interest was passed by the defendants' own act into a multitude of other hands against whom no suit could be safely and effectually prosecuted, and it was not reasonable that the acts of the defendants should prejudice, much less defeat, the plaintiffs of their legal remedy. In the other case, there was a plain necessity; the parties that were want-

[1] *City of London v. Richmond* (1701), 2 Vernon 421, 23 E.R. 870, Precedents in Chancery 156, 24 E.R. 75, 1 Brown P.C. 516, 1 E.R. 727, 2 Eq. Cas. Abr. 86, 631, 22 E.R. 74, 530.

ing could no more be brought before the court than if they had not been in being; they were in an enemy's country where no civil process could reach them.

But he ruled, however, in this case, that the trial should go on, for, by that, no wrong could ensue. The defendants would pay but their just proportions as if all had appeared; the only mischief would be that the plaintiffs would be put to another suit against the other parties to recover what should be due from them. But, on the other hand, if this objection was suffered to stop the suit, it would put an end to it forever. The plaintiffs would be rather forced to drop their right than prosecute it under such difficulties against so many parties. And there appeared no fraud in the choice of the defendants, who were the principal and most substantial of the parties and unlikely to betray themselves and the rest, and not to defend it to the utmost would be vexatious and endless.

[Other copies of this report: Lincoln's Inn MS. Misc. 383, p. 8.]

## 50

## Earl of Bath v. Sherwin

(Ch. 1706–1709)

*The question in this case was whether a bill of peace lies in equity to prevent a multiplicity of actions of ejectment at common law.*

British Library MS. Hargrave 80, f. 8

For the plaintiff, it was urged that the ancient policy of the common law was to suffer the rights of freehold and inheritance to be tried only in real action which seldom admitted more than two suits; if the plaintiff failed in his first action, he had liberty of resorting to a writ of right, whereon the proceedings were very slow and solemn and the determination perpetually conclusive upon both parties. In this method, the law had some end and men's inheritances came in reasonable time to be settled and ascertained.

But the wisdom of the law in this respect is utterly eluded by introducing another method for the determination of the rights of inheritances by ejectments and personal actions, which is a modern contrivance and received not its establishment until the time of Chief Justice Rolle. By this means, it happens that suits concerning titles to land may be now repeated and renewed without end. And wealthy men have it in their power to wrest their neighbors' rights out of their hands by a multiplicity of suits which they are not able to defend.

This, being a corruption of the common law, is proper for a court of equity to cure, especially where the instances of it are notorious and extraordinary for this reason where a dispute is between the lord of a manor and the tenants concerning a matter wherein all the tenants of the manor are equally interested, as upon enclosure of a common etc. It is common upon a bill of peace preferred in this court to grant an injunction that one action should be brought by one of the tenants whom the rest should choose and that the rights of all should be determined by that one action. And this is in respect to the lord's right and the tenants that the lord might not be wearied by a multitude of suits against every one of his tenants singly and that no one of the tenants singly should be liable to be invaded alone and to be squeezed out of his right by the lord's power and riches.

They said that, in reason, there was no difference between that case and this, for there is the same danger that men may be wearied and oppressed and forced to yield their right by a multitude of actions brought by a wealthy adversary, as by a multitude of actions brought by many; and when it is notorious that suits are renewed and multiplied for no other end but to tire men out of their right, and when the right is settled by several verdicts fairly obtained, equity ought to interpose to quiet men's possessions and inheritances and to restrain vexation. And an injunction is no new thing even at common law, for, in [an action of] debt upon a bond, if the plaintiff has received a great part of his money and will not be satisfied to cease his suit upon payment of the rest, the court before which the action is will grant a perpetual imparlance, which is in the nature and has the effect of a perpetual injunction. And in all cases whatsoever when the Court of Chancery thinks proper to direct a trial at law for the information of the court in any matters of fact in order to found a decree upon [it], the fact is looked upon as sufficiently determined and ascertained by two concurrent verdicts.

To this, it was answered by the defendant's counsel that his liberty to bring new ejectments for the trial of his right was by law plain and clear. Actions of ejectment are as ancient as the Register, wherein this writ is specified among other original writs, beyond which nothing in law is known and though the rules for confessing a lease, entry, and ouster be of modern contrivance invented to render these sorts of trial more commodious, yet the action itself after an entry made and a lease sealed upon the land is an ancient legal remedy, which the law gives to every man indifferently and equity ought not to restrain or take away.

As to the bills of peace which are preferred where questions arise between the lord of a manor and his tenants and which have so far obtained as that injunctions have been granted upon them to oblige all the tenants to submit all their rights to one determination, there is this particular reason for it, that forcible pulling down of enclosures and riots which were common upon occasion of such differences might be prevented and that such questions as were of danger to the public peace might receive speedy determination in the courts of law. And this is the true reason and ground of it. The name of the bill imports as much, though, after this method was once settled, it was extended to all cases of the same kind, though not in the same degree or reason, that is, when it had obtained in those manors where the tenants were very numerous and from whom there might be danger of outrage, it was made an universal rule in all questions between a lord of a manor and his tenants whether they were many or few.

As to the perpetual imparlances granted by courts of law in actions of debt upon a bond, that is because the demand of that action is upon a single duty which appears to be satisfied and for which there is no reason that the plaintiff should be suffered any further to proceed, unless he would go upon that single question whether the debt is satisfied or not.

But titles to land are very various and depend upon a great multiplicity of questions, which a court of equity cannot undertake to determine upon a bill and answer, but ought to leave to the trial of the law in the proper way.

As to the other matter insisted on, that the Court of Chancery did always in the case of trials directed at law conclude itself by two or three verdicts, that makes not at all to this case for, when there is relief asked of a court of equity in a cause that is proper for the jurisdiction of it either in respect of fraud or trust or other matters suggested, it is in the breast of the court to grant it upon such terms as are reasonable and equitable and after so many trials as upon the circumstances may be a sufficient satisfaction to the court of the truth or falsity of the facts suggested. But, in this case, the defendant insists purely upon his legal title, is brought into Chancery against his will, has no want of the assistance of the court, nor has anything to ask but that the benefit of the law should not be taken from him.

The Lord Keeper [Lord Cowper] did upon this argument deliver no opinion. But afterwards, in Trinity term *anno octavo*, 1709, he made his decree against the plaintiff taking it that he had in this case no power to stop the course of law. But on what reasons, I did not hear.

[Other copies of this report: Lincoln's Inn MS. Misc. 383, p. 9.]

Lincoln's Inn MS. Misc. 9, p. 97

28 June 1709.

The earl [of Bath] claimed under a voluntary conveyance, and the defendant as heir at law. The latter had brought five several actions in ejectment upon which trials had been had and the earl had recovered verdicts in all five. And now, he brought his bill for a perpetual injunction to quiet his title.

The question was whether such an injunction was reasonable to be decreed by the court.

After the Lord Chancellor [Lord Cowper] had taken some time to consider of it, he gave his opinion that no injunction ought to be decreed. And the substance of his reasons was as follows.

I think the court of equity has no authority to extend its jurisdiction so far as to restrain the courts at law from proceeding in matters purely within their own cognisance, concerning which no matter of equity does arise. It is going further than this court has ever yet done and extending its jurisdiction beyond what has been done in the same or any parallel case.

It has been urged for the plaintiff that this court has relieved and does constantly relieve against penalties and forfeitures and yet the law says the penalty shall be recovered, and, when this court relieves in such a case, it is saying contrary to what the law says.

It is true this court does relieve in these cases, but, then, it is upon payment of principal, interest, and costs so that the court has a fixed and settled rule to go upon, and it is sure to do right and to give an adequate satisfaction to the party wronged. But now, in the case before us, there is no such rule to go by. If this court should restrain a man from trying his title at law after he has made several essays and failed, they may do him a great wrong, for this court cannot judge upon what reasons a verdict or nonsuit turns. The plaintiff in such a case may fail of that evidence at one time which he may be supplied with at another trial so that I say the court has no certain rule to go by. And, therefore, it is not like the case of relieving against penalties.

Another thing has been urged for the plaintiff, *viz.* that this court allows bills to be brought for settling the boundaries of manors and other things of that nature and, when trials are directed in such cases, they are final.

But neither is this like the present case, for such trials are a great convenience to both sides, for it is a great ease to them to have a right settled in such a manner. It is a convenience for him who is liable to be sued by a great number of persons at the same time to have these join in one suit against him to try their right, and, on the other hand, it is a very great convenience for these persons to be allowed thus to unite and combine together. But no one will say there is any such mutual convenience in the case before me.

A third thing urged for the plaintiff is that, where an issue is directed by this court to be tried at law, the court never allows more then two trials and, therefore, why should they not enjoin a man from trying his cause any more after he has had several trials and failed in every one.

When the court directs an issue to be tried at law, it is only to inform themselves of some matter or doubt in order to pass a right judgment of the case before them. And, as the court, in such cases, have writings, depositions, and all other things relating to the case before them, by that means, they can the better judge of the reasons upon which the verdict is given. And, besides, the matter before the court is purely a matter within its own cognizance. But to restrain the courts of law from proceeding in a cause of which they have the proper and immediate cognizance and which is not before this court would be for this court to take upon itself the legislative authority. The law says you may try your right as often as you please. The court of equity says no; you shall try it but so many times.

Besides, though a decree has been pronounced after one or two trials upon an issue directed out of this court, it is not so final but that, if new matter arises and it is well proved, upon a bill of review, the court will open the former decree.

Upon the whole, it is plain the court has never yet gone so great a length as the plaintiff would have it go. And, though it has been said that the court may now set the precedent, I think it is too hard for me to do it. And what I shall never do in any case but where I am well assured such a precedent cannot afterwards be made use of to the prejudice of men's rights and properties.

The bill must be dismissed with costs.

[Other reports of this case: 10 Modern 1, 88 E.R. 596, Precedents in Chancery 261, 24 E.R. 126, Gilbert Rep. 2, 25 E.R. 2, 2 Eq. Cas. Abr. 171, 243, 522, 22 E.R. 147, 206, 440.]

[Reversed on appeal: 4 Brown P.C. 373, 2 E.R. 253.]

## 51

## Barnard v. Jolliffe

(Ch. 1706)

*A conveyance is presumed to have been made when it was executed.*

*A person is presumed to be bankrupt at the time of the date of the commission of bankruptcy.*

*When mortgages of entailed land are redeemed, the tenant for life pays off one-third of the debt and the remainderman two-thirds.*

British Library MS. Hargrave 80, f. 10v, pl. 2

Bernard and his wife against Jolliffe and My Lord Bernard.

The plaintiffs prefer a bill to have an execution of their marriage articles, which were that My Lord Bernard [d. 1723] should settle upon his son, the plaintiff, £2000 a year upon a marriage then intended with the present plaintiff's wife, the daughter of Jolliffe [d. 1712], in consideration of £500 *per annum* to be settled on My Lord Bernard by the said Joliffe as a marriage portion with his daughter.

To this, an answer was put in that the defendant Jollife was, since the execution of the said articles, become a bankrupt.

And upon the hearing, the commission [of bankruptcy] was produced. And it was insisted that My Lord Bernard should not be obliged to answer until those persons were made defendants who were assignees of the commissioners of bankruptcy of that estate of £500 *per annum*, which was required by the articles to be conveyed to My Lord Bernard as the marriage portion of his son for that it would be unequitable for him to be bound to execute the articles by the settlement on his part without having the proper parties before the court who may be likewise obliged to execute the rest of the agreement which was intended for his benefit and in satisfaction of what he parted with to his son upon the marriage. As, in case A., B., and C. are bound in an obligation jointly and severally for the payment of £200, being the proper debt of A., [and] B. is sued upon that debt alone and judgment is against him and execution, he shall not bring a bill in Chancery against C. to require contribution unless he makes A. a defendant in the bill too, that in case there should be a decree against C. for the payment of his part in the contribution, there might be a decree over against A., the principal, for the satisfaction of both.

In answer to this, a deed was produced importing a conveyance from Jollife to My Lord Bernard of £500 *per annum* pursuant to the articles and bearing date before the *teste* of the commission of bankruptcy. And to prove the execution of this deed, a deposition was read, which was allowed by My Lord Keeper [LORD COWPER] to be a good answer, for it shall be presumed *prima facie* that the conveyance was executed at the time of the date and that Jollife was not a bankrupt until the time the commission bears *teste*, there being no evidence on the part of the defendant to prove the contrary. In Chancery, if there be a fee simple estate mortgaged and the equity of redemption of that estate comes afterwards to be conveyed over to one for life, remainder in tail, the rule is that, in the redemption, the tenant for life pays a third part of the encumbrance and the remainderman in tail two-thirds.

[Other copies of this report: Lincoln's Inn MS. Misc. 383, p. 15, Lincoln's Inn MS. Misc. 106, p. 2.]

[Related cases: Vane v. Lord Barnard, Gilbert Rep. 6, 25 E.R. 5, 2 Eq. Cas. Abr. 17, 514, 22 E.R. 13, 434.]

## 52

## Legat v. Shewell

(Ch. 1706–1710)

*The question in this case was whether the devise in issue created a life estate or an estate tail.*

British Library MS. Hargrave 80, f. 27v

The testator, having a great personal estate, devised the residue of it after to be laid out in the purchase of lands in fee to be settled on his nephew for life and, after his death, upon the heirs male of his body and their heirs male and, for default of such issue, upon his brother Henry in tail. The nephew obtained a decree from the commissioners for the residue of the personal estate upon this ground that, if it was vested in land, he would be tenant in tail and have it in his power to bar the entail at his pleasure. The nephew dies without issue.

And Henry brings his bill.

And the judges, upon its being referred to them whether it would be an estate tail if lands were devised by these words, certifying that it would, Henry's bill was dismissed. This point was thus adjudged in regard to the general precedents of the court at that time.

But My Lord Cowper decreed the money to be vested in land in regard of the possibility of the tenant in tail dying without issue before he comes of age or bar[ring] the entail [so] that he in the remainder might have his chance.

[Other copies of this report: Lincoln's Inn MS. Misc. 383, p. 51, pl. 2.]

Lincoln's Inn MS. Misc. 10, p. 37

24 November 1710. *Coram* Baron Price *in absentia domini custodis sigilli.*

George Legatt, upon his marriage with the plaintiff [Elizabeth Legatt] entered into articles and thereby agreed to settle a rent charge of £100 a year upon the plaintiff for her jointure to be issuing out of lands with a clause of distress.

The marriage was had, and no settlement was ever made, but, by his will, he ratifies the articles and thereby makes Weller and Titchburne executors. And, after some legacies, he bequeaths the residue of his estate to be paid out by his executors in the purchase of lands in fee. And his will was that the same should descend upon the issue of his body, but if he died without issue, then he appointed the said lands should be entailed upon his nephew, William Legat, for life and, after his death, to the heirs male of the body of the said William and the heirs male of the body of every such heir male severally and successively as they should be in priority of birth and seniority of age, every elder of the heirs male of his body to be preferred before all and every the younger and the heirs male of his body and, for want of such issue, unto and upon his brother Henry Legatt for life with remainders over.

The testator died without issue. Titchburne renounced, and Weller proved the will. And, during the minority of William Legatt, a bill was brought in his name against the executors and against the testator's wife, the now plaintiff, for an account of the testator's personal estate. The cause was heard.

And it was decreed that the said rent charge of £100 a year should be settled and secured to the now plaintiff Elizabeth for life and that Weller should account for the testator's personal estate, which, after his debts and legacies paid and the annuity settled, should be laid out in land and settled according to the will. And the Master having afterwards made his report, by a subsequent order, it was ordered that, when lands were bought, the same were to stand charged with the said annuity.

William Legatt coming of age, the cause was reheard, and it was then ordered that Weller should pay over to William Legatt all the moneys in his hands and William Legatt was to give security to perform the trust.

Upon a petition to rectify the minutes, it was ordered that, until the said £100 a year should be purchased for Elizabeth for her life, the interest of a mortgage of £1200 should be applied towards the payment of the annuity and that the security to be given by William Legatt should be to secure the payment thereof and Weller was to pay all the money in his hands to William Legat, who was to purchase an annuity of £100 a year within two years then next for the said Elizabeth for her life.

In pursuance of this order, William Legatt and one Mr. Gore entered into a recognizance to the then Master of the Rolls and the senior Six Clerk conditioned that the said William Legatt should purchase an annuity of £100 a year within two years for the said Elizabeth for her life and, in the meantime, to pay her the same by quarterly payments.

Weller paid the money in his hands to W. Legatt, who, for several years, paid this annuity, and then he died, having never purchased any lands. And, before his death, he made his will and gave his sister Margaret, who afterwards married the defendant, all his real and personal estate subject to the payment of his debts, and he left no personal estate, only an estate in land of £70 a year.

The defendant having neglected payment of the plaintiff's annuity, she got an order to sue Legatt's recognizance and then brought a bill against Sewell and his wife and Mrs. Gore, executrix of the other cognizee, for discovery of assets of their respective testators.

Upon this, Mr. Sewell offered to pay the arrears of the annuity, provided the plaintiff would allow taxes. But she not only refused so to do but insisted upon interest for her arrears.

In order to end this matter amicably, a case was drawn up and signed by the plaintiff and the defendants, and they annexed it to a petition signed by all the parties praying the judgment of the court thereon and that a day might be appointed for that purpose.

But the Lord Chancellor Cowper refused to answer the petition as not being very regular.

This method not succeeding, it was agreed that the defendants should move the court to stay proceedings upon the recognizance and that it might be referred to a Master to see what was due to the plaintiff for her arrears and to state the matter specially to the court touching interest and taxes and the plaintiff was not to oppose this. Accordingly this was done. And such order being [entered], the Master reported the case to be as before [and the case came] on to be heard among the exceptions upon the [Master's report].

And the court declared that, there being no land purchased, the allowing taxes will be allowing what was never paid and the acts of Parliament saying that all payments out of land shall pay taxes in proportion to what the lands out of which the same issues pays and here being no land, the annuity can bear no proportion. And this being only a personal security, the court saw no reason to allow any taxes.

And, as touching interest for the arrears of the annuity, the court declared that, the defendant being to be relieved against a penalty, he ought to pay interest and costs.

Lincoln's Inn MS. Misc. 10, p. 41

This was a bill brought by Henry Legatt, the remainderman named in the will of George Legatt, set forth at large in the preceding case, *quod vide*, and by his sons to have the surplus of the testator's estate laid out in lands and settled upon him and his sons according to the testator's will under the pretense that William Legatt was dead without issue.

The defendants, Mr. Sewell and his wife, put in a plea and answer to this bill. And, as to so much of the bill as seeks a discovery of the personal estate of George Legat, deceased, or of the real or personal estate of William Legat, his nephew, or which seeks to apply any part of the personal estate of the said George Legat or of the real or personal estate of the said William Legat towards the purchase of any lands to be settled upon the plaintiffs or to charge the real or personal estate of the said William Legat with any breach of trust pretended to be committed by Thomas Weller, one other of the defendants, they plead the will of the said George Legat and the decree and proceedings thereon (set forth at large in the preceding case). And, further for plea, they say that Weller paid several sums of money in part of the £3013 15s. 1d. reported to be in his hands to the said William Legat and, afterwards, paid him the remainder. Then they set forth William Legat's will and the marriage of the defendants Sewell and his wife and a settlement made by her before marriage of William Legat's lands devised to her by his will and that, by virtue of the marriage and the said settlement, the defendant John Sewell is entitled to the lands thereby conveyed for his life and that, by virtue of the said marriage, he, in the right of his wife, became entitled to the residue of the personal estate of William Legat subject to the payment of his debts, all which etc. and demand judgment etc.

And as to so much as is not pleaded to, by way of answer, they deny several unfair practices charged in the bill and say the decree was fairly obtained without any collusion.

This plea was argued before Lord Keeper WRIGHT and was overruled in regard the parties not being parties to the decree, it could not be pleaded against them. But the benefit of the plea was saved at the hearing.

The defendants having afterwards put in their answer, the cause came on to be heard before the Lord Chancellor COWPER, who was of opinion that, in regard the plaintiffs were no parties to the first suit, the matter was now open and might be considered as if no suit had been; so that the question now was whether, by the limitations in George Legatt's will, William Legat was tenant for life, with remainder to his first and other sons in tail, with remainder to the plaintiff Henry, or whether William Legat was tenant in tail, with remainder etc., for, if he was tenant in tail, it was proper and according to the course of the court to direct the money to be paid him and not to invest it in a purchase of land and settle it when he might by a recovery bar the entail the next day.

The Lord Chancellor [Cowper] doubting what estate William Legat had by the will, though he had given Mr. Sewell his opinion when he was counsel that it was an estate tail in William Legat, and so did Mr. Vernon, though I [Melmoth] was told Mr. Pooley was of another opinion, directed that a case should be drawn as though it had been a devise of lands and referred to the judges of the Common Pleas.

Accordingly, it was drawn up and settled by Mr. Peere Williams and myself [Melmoth] and was as follows.

> George Legatt, seised in fee of lands, had a wife named Elizabeth. He had no issue of his body but had a nephew named William Legatt, being his elder brother's son, and had a brother named Henry Legat. In September 1685, George Legat, by his will, after many legacies, devises his lands, in default of issue of his own body, to the said William Legatt for the term of his natural life and, after his decease, unto the heirs male of the body of the said William Legat lawfully to be begotten and the heirs male of the body of every such heir male severally and successively as they shall be in priority of birth and seniority of age, every elder and the heirs male of his body to be preferred before all and every younger and the heirs male of his body and, for want of such issue, unto his brother Henry Legat for his life and, after his decease, unto the heirs male of the body of his said brother Henry Legat lawfully begotten or to be begotten and the heirs male of the body of every such heir male severally and successively as they shall be in priority of birth and seniority of age, every elder and the heirs male of his body to be preferred before all and every younger and the heirs male of his body. Soon after the making the will, the testator dies without issue. Query whether William Legat, the nephew has an estate tail vested in him or an estate for his life only in the lands devised to him. /s/ *William Peere Williams, pro querente; William Melmoth, pro defendentibus Sewell et ux.*

The case being thus settled, it was argued at the Lord Chief Justice Trevor's chambers before him and the other judges by Sir Thomas Powis and Mr. Williams, for the plaintiffs, and Serjeant Hooper and myself [Melmoth], for the defendants, after which the Chief Justice and the two judges, Blencowe and Dormer, certified as follows, *viz.*:

> May it please Your Lordship, in pursuance of Your Lordship's order, the parties concerned have attended us with their counsel and, after hearing what was alleged by counsel on both sides and upon consideration of the will of George Legatt, we are humbly of opinion that William Legatt, the nephew, by virtue of the will of his uncle, had an estate tail vested in him, November 15, 1706, which is submitted to Your Lordship's great wisdom. /s/ *T. Trevor, John Blencowe, Robert Dormer.*

But Mr. Justice Tracy being of a contrary opinion, he gave his judgment and his reasons for it by himself, which was as follows, *viz.*:

> I am humbly of opinion that William Legat had only an estate for life and that the words 'heirs male of his body', as this case is, are words of purchase, for so the intent of the devisor seems apparently to be by limiting the estate expressly to William Legat for his life and by the limitation over to the heirs male of the body of every such heir male severally and successively etc., which words must be wholly rejected as idle and void if we make the former words 'heirs male of the body of the said William Legat' to be words of limitation. And this construction I think is warranted by the case of Clerk and Day, 3 Cro. 313, and by Archer's Case, in the first Report,[1] for the reason of Archer's Case is not because the devise is to the heir male of the tenant for life in the singular number, for, if it had gone no farther, it would have been an estate tail executed, because the words 'heir' is *nomen collectivum* and the same with the word 'heirs'. And so it is resolved in the case of Pausey and Lowdall, 1 A. 626, lre. J,[2] and in the Case of Clerk and Day, cited before. But the reason why the heir male there took by purchase was because the estate was limited over to the heirs male of the body of such heir male. And so is the opinion of the court in that Case of Pausey and Lowdall and of My Lord Chief Justice Hale in the Case of King and Melling, Vent. 232,[3] and, if that be the reason of Archer's Case (and these are great opinions I have used for it), then it is a direct authority for me in this case. In the Case of Lisle and Gray, 2 Jo. 114 and 2 Levinz 223,[4] where the limitations were to the same effect as here, it was held not to be an estate tail executed in the father, who had an estate for life limited to him. And the court went upon the same reasons, among others, which I have relied on in this case and yet that was upon the construction of a conveyance, where generally the words shall be taken according to their legal sense and their operation in law shall control the intent and meaning of the party. But we are in the case of a will, where the intent of the party shall control the legal sense and meaning of the words. And it appears by the record of that case of Lisle and Gray that the judgment of the Court of King's Bench was af-

---

[1] *Clerk v. Day* (1594), Croke Eliz. 313, 78 E.R. 564, also Moore K.B. 593, 72 E.R. 779; *Baldwin v. Smith* (1597), 1 Coke Rep. 63, 76 E.R. 139, also Croke Eliz. 453, 78 E.R. 692, 2 Anderson 37, 123 E.R. 533.

[2] *Pawsey v. Lowdall* (1650), 1 Rolle, Abr., *Discent*, pl. I, 4, p. 626, also Style 249, 273, 82 E.R. 685, 704.

[3] *King v. Melling* (1672), 1 Ventris 214, 225, 86 E.R. 144, 151, also 2 Levinz 58, 83 E.R. 448, 3 Keble 42, 52, 95, 84 E.R. 584, 589, 614, Pollexfen 101, 86 E.R. 526, 3 Salkeld 296, 91 E.R. 835, 1 Eq. Cas. Abr. 181, 21 E.R. 973, Lincoln's Inn MS. Misc. 500, f. 209.

[4] *Lisle v. Gray* (1680), T. Jones 114, 84 E.R. 1174, 2 Levinz 223, 83 E.R. 529, also Pollexfen 582, 86 E.R. 653, 1 Freeman 462, 89 E.R. 345, 2 Shower K.B. 6, 89 E.R. 758, T. Raymond 278, 302, 315, 83 E.R. 143, 156, 163, Dodd 34.

firmed in the Exchequer Chamber, although the reports of the case differ in that matter. /s/ *R. Tracy*.

This cause came on again upon the judges' opinion for the judgment of this court. And notwithstanding the opinion of three judges against one, My Lord Chancellor [Cowper] would give no judgment but declared he was not satisfied and, therefore, directed that a trial at law should be had in the Common Pleas in an [action of] ejectment by consent and a special verdict should be found according to this case that the judges might judicially determine the question and, after judgment was given, if either party did not think fit to acquiesce, he might bring a writ of error; if not, they might come back to this court and the court would then give judgment.

Mr. Sewell being apprehensive that this proceeding would be very tedious and expensive, he rather chose to give Mr. Legat £200 to release his pretenses. And so the cause ended without any farther proceedings had therein.

[Other reports of this case: 1 Peere Williams 87, 24 E.R. 306, 2 Vernon 551, 23 E.R. 957, Gilbert Rep. 141, 25 E.R. 99, 1 Eq. Cas. Abr. 394, 21 E.R. 1127, 2 Eq. Cas. Abr. 530, 22 E.R. 447.]

## 53

## Brotherton v. Hatt

(Ch. 1706)

*The beneficiary of a trust is considered to be the owner of the trust property.*

British Library MS. Hargrave 80, f. 219v

March v. Gunter and Williams, before the Master of the Rolls [Trevor].

A second mortgagee without notice procured a prior incumbrance to be assigned to a third person who covenanted to stand seised in trust for him, in which case, it was agreed that, if the prior incumbrance rested in an indifferent hand, equity would give the first mortgagee the redemption of it. But, being in the hands of a trustee for the second mortgagee, who could not dispose of it from him without a breach of covenant, it was decreed to be the same thing as if it were in the hands of the second mortgagee himself.

[Other copies of this report: Lincoln's Inn MS. Misc. 107, f. 64.]

[Other reports of this case: 2 Vernon 574, 23 E.R. 973, 2 Freeman 290, 22 E.R. 1217, 1 Eq. Cas. Abr. 330, 21 E.R. 1081.]

54

## Lechmere v. Blagrave

(Ch. 1706)

*A pecuniary devise will be deducted from the sum payable upon the testator's death pursuant to a marriage settlement.*

Lincoln's Inn MS. Misc. 9, p. 46

10 April 1706. Lord Keeper.

Thomas Blagrave, the defendant's grandfather, upon the marriage of his daughter to the plaintiff's father, by indenture dated in December 1677, covenanted to lay out £1000, part of the fortune, in the purchasing of lands to be settled upon the plaintiff's father for ninety-nine years if he lived so long, remainder to trustees to preserve contingent remainders, remainder to the plaintiff's mother for life, then to the heirs of the body of the plaintiff's father and mother, remainder to their right heirs.

After the marriage, the plaintiff's father wanting money and having contracting some debts, his father-in-law, Mr. Blagrave, applied the £1000 for supplying his son's occasions and, thereupon, by indentures of lease and release dated 6 and 7 January 1680[/81], reciting the marriage agreement and that, since the marriage, Blagrave had at his son-in-law's request and for the discharge of his debts paid his creditors £1000. Lechmere, the son, for securing, saving harmless, and indemnifying Blagrave, his heirs, etc. against the covenants in the said marriage agreement and for securing the said £1000 to be laid out as by the same was agreed, grants a messuage in Friday Street, London, to Blagrave and Gregory and their heirs to the same uses as the £1000 was by the marriage agreement when vested in land [was] to be settled only omitting the limitation to trustees to preserve contingent remainders, in which deed there is a proviso that, if Lechmere should during his life or by will appoint £1000 to be laid out in a purchase to be settled to the same uses, then the indenture to be void.

This house was before this conveyance mortgaged to one Beaumont. But it does not appear that Blagrave had notice of it.

Lechmere and his wife are dead, and the plaintiff is their eldest son. Blagrave died after his daughter, and, by his will, he gave to the plaintiff £400 to be paid him at his age of twenty-one.

The plaintiff received his legacy, and now brings his bill against the executor of Blagrave and against the defendant Blagrave, his daughter, for a specific performance of the covenant for laying out the £1000.

The question was whether the conveyance of The Pelican was a purchase and settlement within the intent of the marriage agreement.

[Lord Cowper] decreed it was not and that the plaintiff be paid the £1000, out of which he must allow the £400 legacy and the value of all lands and personal estate come to him from his father. And, for that purpose, he must be examined on interrogatories.

[Other reports of this case: Gilbert Rep. 64, 25 E.R. 45, 2 Eq. Cas. Abr. 351, 22 E.R. 299.]

## 55

## Montagu v. Ratcliffe

(Ch. 1706)

*An assignee of a mortgagor with notice of a second mortgage cannot turn the unpaid interest into additional debt secured by the first mortgage.*

Lincoln's Inn MS. Misc. 9, p. 42, pl. 1

5 June 1706.

A man takes an assignment of a mortgage and pays the principal and interest due upon it, having notice at the same time of a subsequent mortgage.

Upon a bill brought by the second mortgagee to redeem, it was ordered that the assignee of the first mortgage should not turn interest into principal against the second mortgagee.

## 56

## Thomas v. Freeman

(Ch. 1706)

*A possibility can be released before the contingency happens.*

Lincoln's Inn MS. Misc. 9, p. 42, pl. 2

24 October.

A term was vested in trustees upon trust for the raising of £1000 for a daughter at her age of twenty-one or marriage in case she was living at the death of the survivor of her father and mother. She marries. And, afterwards, she and her husband and the trustees, in the lifetime of the father and mother, for a consideration paid by the father, release and extinguish this term.

And the question was if this possibility might be released before the contingency happened.

[Cowper] decreed it might.

[Other reports of this case: 2 Vernon 563, 23 E.R. 967, 1 Eq. Cas. Abr. 46, 21 E.R. 863.]

# 57

## Bowdler v. Smith

(Ch. 1706)

*In this case, the testator charged his real property with the payment of his debts.*

*Where there is an express devise of copyhold lands for the payment of debts or for a provision for younger children, the lack of a surrender to the use may be supplied in equity.*

*Strictly speaking, the word 'devise' does not include copyhold lands.*

Lincoln's Inn MS. Misc. 9, p. 43, pl. 1

25 October 1706.

'As to all my temporal estate wherewith it has pleased God to bless me, I dispose thereof as follows. First, I will that all the debts that I shall owe at the time of my death shall be in the first place paid. Also, I give unto A.B. all those my lands and' [ *blank* ]. This is a charge of the debts upon the land.

Note, in the Case of Lechmere and Blagrave,[1] it was said that, where copyhold lands [are] devised for the payment of debts and there is no surrender to the use of the will, yet the land shall be charged because it is for the benefit of the creditors and the intent is apparent. But query, if the devise was *ut supra*, whether copyhold land in such case should be charged, for the intent is not so apparent.

British Library MS. Hargrave 80, f. 4, pl. 2

One, seised of copyhold lands and of other lands in fee, makes his will in this manner, 'As to the disposition of all the lands wherewith God has blessed me, I devise, first, that my debts shall be paid' etc. And he dies.

The questions in Chancery was whether his copyhold lands were by this will rendered liable to the payment of debts. It seemed agreed that, where there is an express devise of copyhold lands for the payment of debts or for a provision for younger children, the want of a surrender to the use of that will may be supplied in equity.

And the Lord Keeper [Lord Cowper] was of opinion that, if the words had been 'as to the disposition of my copyhold lands, I devise, first, that my debts shall be paid', such a devise might have rendered the copyhold lands liable to the payment of debts. But, as the principal case is, the devisor dying seised of other lands besides copyhold, whereby the general words of the will are sufficiently answered, there is no reason to make them extend to copyhold lands, which, by law, he had regularly no power to devise.

[Other copies of this report: Lincoln's Inn MS. Misc. 383, p. 1, pl. 2, Lincoln's Inn MS. Misc. 106, p. 1.]

---

[1] *Lechmere v. Blagrave* (Ch. 1706), see above, Case No. 54.

[Other reports of this case: Precedents in Chancery 264, 24 E.R. 128, 2 Eq. Cas. Abr. 371, 504, 22 E.R. 316, 427.]

## 58

## Taylor v. Wheeler

(Ch. 1706–1709)

*A defective conveyance to a creditor to secure the debt will be enforced by a court of equity, even after the debtor has been adjudged a bankrupt.*

Lincoln's Inn MS. Misc. 9, p. 43, pl. 2

11 November 1706.

The bill is to supply the defect of a presentment of a surrender which was made out of court to two tenants of the manor to the use of the plaintiff and his heirs upon condition to be void upon the payment of so much money. And it was not presented within a year, as it ought to have been. And, after five years' time, in which interest was duly paid, Wheeler, the mortgagor, having been all that while in possession, becomes a bankrupt. And the commissioners assign this copyhold estate.

The question was if the plaintiff, who was the mortgagee, or the assignees should have this estate.

*Vernon*, for the plaintiff: I agree, if a man sells his copyhold land and the surrender to the purchase becomes void for want of being duly presented and he continues in possession and then surrenders to a second [person] who had no notice and, then, the second surrender is first presented, the first purchaser is defeated. But this is not our case.

*Pooley*, of the same side: The assignees can be in no better condition than the bankrupt himself. And there is no doubt but, if we had preferred our bill against him, he must have made good this surrender.

*Sir Joseph Jekyll, e contra*: We have the law on our side and as much equity as the plaintiff. And the court will not take away the legal estate, which is vested in us by the Statute of James I.[1]

Here is a fraud intended to the lord, for this secreting of the surrender was with the intent to defeat the lord of his fine. And, therefore, [there is] no reason the plaintiff should have any relief.

Lord Keeper [Lord Cowper]: I very much doubt of the case put by the party's counsel that, where a man is a trustee by writing under hand and seal yet being in possession and the visible owner of an estate [and] sells it for a valuable consideration to a purchaser without notice and receives the money, that the *cestui que trust* shall be relieved. I think that trust ought never to be aided.

---

[1] Stat. 21 Jac. I, c. 19 (*SR*, IV, 1227–1229).

As to the principal case, I think it is plain, by not presenting this surrender, it was not known that the estate was mortgaged and, consequently, by the reputation of this estate, the mortgagor had a greater credit given him than he would have had if it had been known. And I am persuaded, if this surrender had been known, he would never have broken for so much.

Suppose now this man had after this surrender made a second surrender for the payment of other creditors and the first surrender had not been presented. Would this court, after five years' laches in the mortgagee, have taken the estate from the creditors? Now, by the act of bankruptcy, the estate is vested in the commissioners of bankrupts. And shall not the conveyance in law be as much regarded as an actual conveyance? *Fortior est dispositio legis* is the maxim. But we will lay it down that it is as strong.

I will consider of it.

British Library MS. Hargrave 80, f. 17v

A tenant in fee of a copyhold surrenders into the hands of two tenants for the use of J.S. in fee, by way of a mortgage. That surrender is not presented at the next court. The surrenderer becomes bankrupt, and a commission is taken out against him. And the assignees of the commissioners of bankrupts are admitted in court to these copyhold lands whereof the bankrupt was seised at the time of the bankruptcy committed, notwithstanding the surrender which was not presented.

J.S. prefers his bill against the assignees of the commissioners of bankrupts, that they may surrender to him according to the uses of the intended mortgage.

And it was decreed that they should, for, though they had a legal estate and likewise an equitable interest for the satisfaction of creditors, yet these creditors, for whom the assignees had gained that legal estate, had never contracted with the copyholder for this estate in particular, but rested in general upon a personal security and that, therefore, their interest ought to be regarded as subsequent to J.S., who had paid his money upon the security of this very estate and had contracted for the conveyance of it, which was begun though not perfected in time and which, in pursuance of the agreement to convey, the copyholder became seised of from that time in trust only for J.S.

[Other copies of this report: Lincoln's Inn MS. Misc. 383, p. 30.]

Lincoln's Inn MS. Misc. 506, p. 65, pl. 2

Money was advanced at the time of the deed and an inchoation of a legal estate. [There was] a surrender and no admittance, for the assignees must stand in the place of the bankrupt, and take the land subject to the same conditions and charges, not because a surrender is a partial conveyance, for a partial conveyance is no conveyance at all, but it is only evidence of an agreement. What the bankrupt could not do, what he could not honestly do, the assignees cannot do.

2 Salkeld 449, 91 E.R. 388

Michaelmas 8 Anne.

A copyholder in fee surrendered to the use of the mortgagee in fee and became bankrupt before presentment. And there never was any presentment made. And the question was whether the assignee of the commissioners of bankruptcy or the mortgagee should be preferred.

*Et per* Cowper, Lord Chancellor: Though the surrender was void in law for want of a presentment and that might be the laches of the mortgagee in not procuring it, yet the surrender was a lien and bound the land in equity, and the assignee ought not to be in a better case than the bankrupt, who was plainly bound in equity by this defective conveyance. And, as it seems to me, he became a trustee for the purchaser [mortgagee].

[Other reports of this case: 2 Vernon 564, 23 E.R. 968, 1 Eq. Cas. Abr. 122, 312, 21 E.R. 928, 1068.]

59

## Chadwick v. Doleman

(Ch. 1706)

*When an eldest child dies, the next eldest then becomes the eldest in regards to gifts for younger children.*

British Library MS. Hargrave 80, f. 64v, pl. 3

Sir Thomas [Doleman]'s father, having a power to charge his estate with £4000 for younger children, appointed £3000 of it to be for Sir Thomas, who was at that time his second son. I think some of the counsel said that the reason of that appointment was Sir Thomas's having married a lady with a great fortune. After this, Sir Thomas's older brother died, and, then, his father.

And then the rest of the children brought their bill for the whole £4000 in regard the second son was become the eldest and so out of the meaning of the settlement.

And Lord Cowper decreed the £4000 to them.

[Other copies of this report: Lincoln's Inn MS. Misc. 383, p. 121, pl. 3, Lincoln's Inn MS. Misc. 106, p. 70, pl. 2.]

[Other reports of this case: 2 Vernon 528, 23 E.R. 941, 1 Eq. Cas. Abr. 344, 21 E.R. 1091.]

## 60

## Willcocks v. Willcocks

(Ch. 1706)

*An inheritance that satisfies an obligation by a marriage settlement has priority over the decedent's bond creditors.*

British Library MS. Hargrave 80, f. 137

There were articles to settle lands to the value of £2000. And, the party dying before he made a settlement and leaving £100 *per annum* to descend to the same person on whom the settlement was to be made, Lord Cowper decreed that it should be taken as a satisfaction of the £2000 and retained against bond creditors.

[Other reports of this case: 2 Vernon 558, 23 E.R. 961, 1 Eq. Cas. Abr. 26, 156, 21 E.R. 847, 955.]

## 61

## Gunter v. Hungerford

(Ch. c. 1706)

*When borrowers and lenders employ the same person to be their agent, they are bound by the knowledge of their agent, including knowledge of prior encumbrances.*

Lincoln's Inn MS. Misc. 9, p. 45

Margaret Gunter *et al.* v. Sir Edward Hungerford *et al.*

Francis Marsh, in 1699, lent £4000 to Sir Edward Hungerford upon a mortgage of the manor of Broadwater in Sussex. Afterwards, Sir Edward borrows £450 of Mr. Web and conveys the equity of redemption to him and his heirs for his security.

This was done by means of Sir Richard Hawkins, a scrivener. Afterwards, Williams and Ellecker, who were servants to Sir Richard Hawkins and privy to the foregoing transaction, borrow £2400 for Sir Edward of one Gunter. And Web being paid off, he, by the direction of Sir Edward, conveys to Gunter by indenture 1 July 1691, in which deed Sir Edward appoints March, upon the payment of his money, to assign to Gunter.

Afterwards, Sir Edward Hungerford wanting more money, Williams and Ellecker prevail with one Burrell to lend £300, who having taken advice of counsel, the security that was taken for it was this. Sir Edward Hungerford enters into a bond to Burrell and, by indenture, charges Marsh's mortgage with £300 more to him and, by endorsement on that deed dated the same day, March declares the money to be the money of Burrell and that, after he is paid, the premises shall stand a security to Burrell for his £300.

Burrell and March had no notice of Gunter's mortgage nor the counsel that Burrell consulted, but Williams and Ellecker, who transacted that affair and were employed both by the borrower and lender, knew of all the securities. And the question was whether Gunter should be paid before Burrell.

Lord Keeper [Lord Cowper]: Williams and Ellecker were agents for all the lenders as well as the borrower, and, therefore, notice to them is notice to the lenders. And they must be paid as they lent their money.

It is agreed that, if March had had notice of the second mortgage before he lent the £300, the second mortgage would have come in before him. Then, the agent for March having this notice, it is the same thing.

This, indeed, ought to make people cautious how they employ scriveners. But what is more just than when scriveners are employed by the borrower and lender, that they that come first should be first served.

## 62

## Murrell v. Cox and Pitt

(Ch. 1707)

*Where co-executors are under no compulsion to sell an asset of the decedent's estate, they are both liable to the estate for the receipt of the purchase price.*

Lincoln's Inn MS. Misc. 9, p. 44

24 January 1706[/07].

Upon an appeal to the Lord Keeper [Lord Cowper] from the Master of the Rolls' [Trevor] decree, the case was this. The defendants were executors in trust and had sold some East India stock. Both joined in transferring it, but Cox received all the money, and, afterwards, he became insolvent.

The question was if the other executor should be answerable for this money.

Lord Keeper [Lord Cowper]: He must, for there was no necessity of selling and the whole transaction was joint. This is not like the case of Fellows and Owen,[1] lately decreed, where trustees for the sale of an estate sold it and both signed the receipt for the consideration money, but Owen only received it and, afterwards, failed. In this case, the other trustee was not answerable, for they were obliged to sell. But, in the principal case, there was no necessity, but it was all voluntary.

[1] *Fellows v. Owen* (1705), 2 Freeman 283, 286, 22 E.R. 1212, 1215, 1 Peere Williams 81, 24 E.R. 302, 2 Vernon 504, 515, 23 E.R. 922, 929.

[Other reports of this case: 2 Vernon 570, 23 E.R. 971, 1 Eq. Cas. Abr. 247, 399, 21 E.R. 1023, 1131.]

## 63

## French v. Chichester

(Ch. 1707)

*Where a will charges lands with the payment of a daughter's portion and the heir at law pays it, the heir can be reimbursed out of the testator's personal estate.*

Lincoln's Inn MS. Misc. 10, p. 200

Sir John Chichester, by his will, charged his lands with £1000 for his daughter Susanna's portion. And he made his will and John, his son and heir, executor. John, the son, died having settled lands on trustees for the payment of his debts. And he made Dorothy, his wife, executrix, who married Henry Chichester

Susanna brought her bill against Francis, the heir, and Henry and his wife, the executrix. And the question between the heir and the executrix was whether the real or personal estate should bear the burden.

18 February 1690[/91], the Lords Commissioners [to Hold the Great Seal] decreed in favor of the heir and charged John's personal estate with the £1000 portion.

22 July 1693, Susanna reheard the cause against Francis, the heir, singly, without bringing the executrix before the court, and, having a plain demand out of the real estate, she obtained a decree against the heir.

Francis, the heir, having paid £1575 for the portion and interest, carried on the suit for reimbursement out of John's personal estate, and the defense was that John's personal estate was discharged thereof and that it ought to remain on the real estate.

27 and 28 January 1703[/04], the cause was heard before Lord Keeper Wright, who was attended with the deeds, wills, and former decrees. And, 1 February following, he declared he had fully considered the matter, and decreed an account of the personal estate of John Chichester to be applied to reimburse the heir,

18 January 1706[/07], a bill of review was brought to reverse this decree before the present Lord Chancellor [Lord Cowper], and that bill was dismissed.

[Other reports of this case: 2 Vernon 568, 23 E.R. 970, 3 Brown P.C. 16, 1 E.R. 1147, 2 Eq. Cas. Abr. 493, 22 E.R. 419.]

## 64

## Coleman v. Upcot

(Ch. 1707)

*When a conditional offer to sell is accepted, it becomes a binding and enforceable contract, even though a later contract for the same matter was entered into with a third party.*

British Library MS. Hargrave 80, f. 124v

There being a treaty between the plaintiff and defendant about the purchase, which was pretty dear, and the main inducement to the plaintiff was a seat in a church, which his wife had a mind to, the defendant wrote a letter to the plaintiff, in which he told he should have it if he would advance £50 more than he had offered. The plaintiff sent an answer that he would the next day, though a neighbor stepped in and bid more for it.

The plaintiff, following his letter, immediately brought his bill.

The defendant was decreed to perform his offer by his letter.

[Other copies of this report: Lincoln's Inn MS. Misc. 383, p. 219, Lincoln's Inn MS. Misc. 106, p. 176.]

2 Eq. Cas. Abr. 16, 22 E.R. 13

If a man, being in company, makes offers of a bargain and then writes them down and signs them and the other party takes them up and prefers his bill, this shall be a good bargain, and the party shall be compelled to a specific performance of it, said by the Lord Keeper [Lord Cowper].

2 Eq. Cas. Abr. 45, 22 E.R. 39

Hilary 5 Anne.

The Provost and Scholars of King's College, Cambridge, being seised in fee of the tithes of Prior's Quarter in Tiverton in the County of Devon *cum pertinentiis*, by deed, demised the same to D. for twenty-one years, who, afterwards, for £350 consideration, covenanted to convey to the defendant, his executors, and assigns, the said tithes during her interest therein. Then the plaintiff treats with the defendant for these tithes, and the defendant sends his son and two other persons with a letter to the plaintiff, wherein the defendant said that, if he parted with the tithes, it should be on the conditions therein particularly mentioned. The plaintiff accepted of the terms and the next day sent his attorney to acquaint the defendant with it, and the defendant delivered to the attorney a copy of D.'s agreement and appointed a day for executing the same. But, in the meantime, the defendant went to D., who had notice of the defendant's agreement with the plaintiff, and settled a conveyance from her.

Lord Keeper [Lord Cowper] decreed the defendant to perform this agreement, for that it was directly within the Statute of Frauds,[1] as being an agreement signed by the party to be charged with the same, and there was no need of its being signed by both parties, and the plaintiff, by his bill, has submitted to perform his part of the agreement; this, though it was not at first a contract, but conditionally only if the other would accept of it, yet, when the other had accepted of it, it was all one, and the defendant intended it so, by his sending his son with the letter and two persons besides.

## 65

## Jones v. Saunderson

(Ch. 1707)

*A trust that will defeat the custom of the City of London as to the succession to a deceased citizen's goods will not be enforced.*

*Where a London citizen's child has been advanced, the money brought into hotchpot will be added to the orphanage part of his estate only.*

Lincoln's Inn MS. Misc. 11, p. 185

John Jones and Hester, his wife [and] daughter of Edward Nourse, plaintiffs; Robert Saunderson and Catherine, his wife [and] daughter of Anthony Nourse, the said Edward Nourse and Charles Nourse, sons of Anthony Nourse, and others, defendants.

Anthony Nourse, being a brewer and freeman of London, by a deed dated 26 August 1704, assigns over all his stock and debts in trade, household goods, and other things to trustees upon trust to permit the defendant Catherine, his daughter, to receive the profits for her own separate benefit, paying him and his wife £3 a week during their respective lives and, after their death, upon trust to permit the defendant Catherine to take a moiety of the stock to her own separate use and, out of the other moiety, the plaintiff Hester, his granddaughter, was to be paid £1000 at twenty-one or marriage and the remainder of such moiety was to be equally divided between the two sons of the defendant Edward Nourse, who are also defendants in the cause.

Anthony Nourse and his wife being dead and the plaintiff Jones having married Hester, the granddaughter, they brought their bill to be paid her £1000.

The cause was heard before Lord Cowper 27 February 5 Anne [1707], who decreed that the deed of trust was made in fraud of the custom and, therefore, he decreed the profits of the brewing trade from the date of the deed to the death of Anthony and all the personal estate comprised in that deed or which he was possessed of at his death ought to be divided into moieties, one moiety whereof was

[1] Stat. 29 Car. II, c. 3 (*SR*, V, 839–842).

to be divided equally between the two sons and the daughter of Anthony Nourse, but that they must bring into hotchpot what had been paid by their father in his lifetime as a provision or for their advancement.

And, as to the other moiety, being the said Anthony's testamentary part, it was ordered that the same should be divided into moieties and that the defendant should have one moiety and that the other moiety thereof should be applied in the first place to make good the plaintiff Hester's £1000 and interest and the residue of that moiety to be equally divided between the defendants, her two brothers.

Note, when the account before the Master was taken in this cause, a question arose whether the sums to be brought into hotchpot ought to be brought in before the estate was divided into moieties whereby the testamentary part would be increased in favor of the grandchildren or whether it ought to be brought into the orphanage part only after a division of the estate into moieties. And, both sides having agreed to take Mr. Vernon's opinion and abide by it, he gave his opinion that the money to be brought into hotchpot ought to be brought into the orphanage parts only after the division was made of the estate into moieties.

## 66

## Shore's Executor v. Edwards

(Ch. 1707)

*The question in this case was whether an agent who has received funds on behalf of his deceased principal can deduct his own salary and expenses out of those funds where the principal's personal representative sues for them or whether the agent must sue the estate of his principal as a creditor.*

Lincoln's Inn MS. Misc. 9, p. 51, pl. 2

10 February 1706[/07]. Executor of Shore v. Edwards, administrator *cum testamento annexo* of Fane.

Shore was employed by Fane and one Thornton to receive the rents of an estate of which they were jointly seised and to manage suits at law and equity for them. And, afterwards, Shore and Fane both die. And the defendant, being a creditor of Fane, takes administration of his estate *cum testament annexo* and brings an action against the plaintiff for money received to Fane's use.

The plaintiff, thereupon, prefers his bill in this court, praying he may deduct his testator's fees and charges of those suits and also his salary for receiving the rents out of the money in his hands. And the defendant, in his answer, insists there is a defect of assets.

Mr. *Vernon*, for the defendant: You must pay us what you have in your hands, deducting your salary. But, as to the law charges, you must come in as a creditor. This is not like the case where an account is open between two persons, in which case, you shall not take one side of the account and leave the other. But, here, the lawsuits are a distinct matter from the collecting the rents. And, therefore, as to that, you must come in as a creditor and have a satisfaction out of the assets.

Master of the Rolls [TREVOR]: I am very willing to relieve you if I can. Go before a Master and let him state your demands and see what is in your hands and if there is any defect of assets. And I reserve the whole matter until after the report.

## 67

## Wilmot v. Wilson

(Ch. 1707)

*A creditor by an unsecured debt of a decedent's estate who receives the payment of his debt cannot be ordered to refund the payment if the estate is unable to pay a bond debt to another creditor.*

*Where an executor assigns a decedent's estate for the payment of debts and the performance of the will, the assignee becomes a co-executor.*

Lincoln's Inn MS. Misc. 9, p. 52

11 February 1706[/07].

A man dies in November 1703, having made his will and his wife executrix, who, after probate of the will and inventory exhibited, makes an assignment of all her husband's personal estate to a creditor, in which assignment, his debt was recited and, likewise, that he has paid other debts for the testator in his lifetime (but in truth had not). And this assignment was made to the intent that he should pay the testator's debts and perform his will.

The assignee pays a debt on bond and some debts on simple contract. And, about half a year after the assignment, another bond creditor prefers his bill against the executrix and the assignee for a satisfaction of his debt and an account of the testator's personal estate. The defendants by their answer insist they had no notice of this debt.

Lord Keeper [LORD COWPER]: I take it he has officiously and fraudulently thrust himself into an executorship and, therefore, must stand in the room of the executrix and be subject to the same rules as she would have been.

He must account for the estate deducting his own debts, for I cannot fetch that back. If an executor will pay a debt on single contract before a bond, the creditor by simple contract shall not refund, though it is a *devastavit* in the executor. And I cannot help it. But, as to the rest, he must stand in the room of the executrix.

## 68

## Anonymous

(Ch. 1707)

*An equity of redemption is a real asset that descends to the mortgagor's heir at law.*

Lincoln's Inn MS. Misc. 9, p. 53, pl. 1

28 February 1706[/07].

[LORD HARCOURT] decreed that the heir of a mortgagor should pay a bond entered into by the mortgagor to the mortgagee if he would redeem, for the equity of redemption is assets in his hands.

## 69

## Anonymous

(Ch. 1707)

*Where a sum of money is contracted for in a marriage settlement to be used to purchase land for a man's wife and it is not so done, he can be decreed to receive the interest for the money.*

Lincoln's Inn MS. Misc. 9, p. 53, pl. 2

A sum of money was agreed to be laid out in a purchase and settled so that a man would have been tenant by the curtesy of the lands in case a purchase had been made. The money was not laid out. And, thereupon, he brings his bill, praying he may have the interest of the money for his life[time].

And it was decreed accordingly.

## 70

## Anonymous v. Hutchinson

(Ch. 1707)

*The estate of a bona fide purchaser for value will not be set aside because the purchaser's grantor had not paid the purchase price to his own grantor.*

Lincoln's Inn MS. Misc. 9, p. 53, pl. 3

3 March 1706[/07]. Baron Smith.

The plaintiffs claim an estate as heirs at law of Awbrey, who had released all his rights to one, of whom the defendants purchased this estate. And, now, they prefer their bill to set aside this release, and insist upon it that the consideration of the release was never paid. It was proved that Awbrey had £40 paid him after the release and that there was a kind of a promise made him to pay him and his wife an annuity of £5 a year during his life, which was never done.

*Curia* [Baron SMITH]: The bill must be dismissed with costs. Suppose the consideration to Awbrey was never paid. Yet what is that to a purchaser who is not obliged to enquire into the consideration? Besides, if this release had been fraudulent, yet, as to a person who had afterwards purchased without notice, the fraud would have been purged.

If the person that gave the release had come into this court and preferred his bill, setting forth that the consideration was never paid, the court would not have set aside the release, but ordered the consideration to be paid.

## 70a

## Anonymous

(Ch. 1707)

*A gift by a testator to his executor must be proved by greater evidence than the mere oath of the executor.*

G. Gilbert, *Law of Evidence* (1754), p. 39

Hilary vacation 1707.

A bill was brought by creditors against an executor to have an account of the personal estate. The executor sets forth by answer that there was £1100 left by the testator in his hands and that, coming afterwards to make up his accounts with the testator, he gave a bond for £1000 and the other £100 was given him as a gift for his trouble and pains taken in the testator's business. And there was no other evidence in the case. The £1100 was deposited but merely by the executor's own oath.

And it was argued that the answer, though it was put in issue, should be allowed, since there is the same rule of evidence in equity as at law, and, therefore, if a man was so honest as to charge himself when he might roundly have denied it and no testimony could have appeared, he ought to find credit where he swears in his own discharge.

But it was answered and resolved by the Court that, when an answer was put in issue, what was confessed and admitted need not be proved, but it behoved the defendant to make out by proofs what was insisted upon by way of avoidance. But this was held under this distinction, where the defendant admitted a fact and insisted on a distinct fact by way of avoidance, there, he ought to prove the matter of his defence, because it may be probable that he admitted it out of apprehension that it might be proved, and, therefore, such admittance ought not to profit him so far as to pass for truth whatever he says in avoidance, but, if it had been one fact, as if the defendant had said the testator had given him £100, it ought to have been allowed unless disproved, because nothing of the fact charged is admitted and the plaintiff may disprove the whole fact as sworn, if he can do it.

But it was urged that, here, the probability was on the defendant's side, because he did not take a bond for this sum as for the residue.

But the Chancellor [Cowper] said there was some presumption in that, but not enough to carry so large a sum without better attestation.

## 71

## Marmack v. Bishop

(Ch. c. 1707)

*A promise made after the marriage to give a marriage portion is valid and enforceable in equity.*

British Library MS. Hargrave 80, f. 11

Easter Term 6 Anne [1707], King's Bench, in [an action of] covenant, the declaration was on a covenant to pay a certain sum of money to the plaintiff if he should marry the defendant's sister with an averment that he had married the defendant's sister and that he had nevertheless refused to pay the money. The defendant pleads that the plaintiff was married to his sister at the time of the covenant entered into and demands judgment *si actio etc.* Whereupon, there is a demurrer. And it was adjudged for the defendant because this covenant was on a precedent condition which, under the circumstances the parties were in, was impossible ever to be performed, and, therefore, the covenantee was without means at law ever to obtain the benefit of it.

But afterwards, upon a bill in Chancery suggesting the covenant and the marriage and the intention of the parties to accept and give that sum for and as a portion with the wife, the plaintiff was relieved and the defendant was compelled to pay the money.

[Other copies of this report: Lincoln's Inn MS. Misc. 383, p. 16, pl. 1.]

## 72

## Langley v. Baldwin

(Ch. 1707)

*In this case, the devise in issue created an estate tail.*

British Library MS. Hargrave 80, f. 12, pl. 2

Easter 1707.

This was a case sent out of Chancery for the opinion of the judges of the Common Bench; the case was this. John Langley, the grandfather, being seised in fee makes his will and devises his estate to S. Langley, his son, for life, remainder to John Langley, his grandson, for life and, after his death, to his first, second, fourth, sixth son in tail male and, for want of such issue male of his body, remainder to Thomas Langley, second son of the testator, for life and, after his death, to his first, second, fourth, sixth son in tail male and, for want of such issue, remainder over.

The question was, upon this limitation in a will, whether John Langley, the grandson of the testator, took an estate for life according to the express words in the beginning of the sentence or an estate tail by the import of the words in the close of the sentence, whereby the remainder is limited over for want of issue male of his body generally. It was argued that it should be only an estate for life because that appeared to be the intention of the testator by his express limitation, contrary to which no estate ought to arise from an implication of law. It was said that the word 'issue' in the limitation of the remainder over should be taken to mean such issue to whom any estate had been before limited, that is, for want of issue of the first, second, and sixth son, the estate should remain over to the next in limitation, that each of these sons were to take by purchase, as the testator appeared to intend, and so [there was] no necessity to create an estate tail in John, the grandson, to answer the intent of the testator in any of the limitations, that this construction might be reasonably made and [be] agreeable to what had been made and allowed in other cases.

A case was cited between Tuck and Frencham, Dyer 171, pl. 7 and 8, pl. 17; Moor 13, pl. 50,[1] which was this. Clement Frencham, seised in fee, devised to Clement Frencham, junior, and the heirs male of his body and, in case he should die without heirs of his body, remainder over; the question was whether he should have an estate in tail male according to the express limitation in the first clause or in tail generally from the import of the words 'for want of heirs of his body' in the limitation over. And it was adjudged that it was an estate in tail male, for so appeared the intention of the testator to be, and the words 'heirs of his body' in the limitation over should be understood of such heirs as were capable of taking by the first limitation.

Another case, between Popham and Bamfield,[2] ruled lately in Chancery, was cited, which was this; A., being seised in fee, devises to J.S. for life, afterwards to his first, second, third, and every other son, according to their seniority of age in tail and, for want of issue of the body of J.S., remainder over; now it was insisted that this created an estate tail in J.S. for the benefit of a posthumous son, who might be born and could not take by purchase by virtue of this limitation

[1] *Turke v. Frencham* (1559), 2 Dyer 171, 73 E.R. 375, Moore K.B. 13, 72 E.R. 407, also Benloe 68, 123 E.R. 53, 1 Anderson 8, 123 E.R. 325.

[2] *Popham v. Bamfield* (Ch. 1704), see above, Case No. 20.

and whom it was never the testator's design to exclude from the benefit of the next in remainder. But it was ruled by the opinion of the two chief justices and the Lord Keeper Wright that this was an estate for life only in J.S. according to the express and legal limitation which should not be defeated upon a suspicion of a devisor's intent to provide for a mere accident that was very foreign and unlikely ever to happen. To this, it was answered and resolved, by all the four judges unanimously that the words of this will did create an estate tail.

As to the express limitation for life, that availed little, for an estate tail carries in it an estate for life, and the difference of the interest is not understood by many testators who are unlearned and are not presumed to be well advised. Besides, the case of King and Melling, 2 Lev. 58,[1] and many others are full and clear that a person to whom an estate for life is expressly limited in a will may by subsequent words signifying more plainly the intention of the testator take an estate tail. They said they took it to be plainly the intention of the testator that a seventh son of his grandson who might be the heir of the family should take as well as the sixth or the first or any other son, because the limitation over was not to take effect until the grandson 'should be dead without issue male of his body', which words extend equally to every one of his issue, the seventh and eighth, as well as the first, and, since the intention of the testator were that the seventh and eighth and the rest of the sons should take, it is the duty of the judges so to mold the words into a meaning as might render everyone capable by the rules of law of taking in his time that interest which was intended him. Now, it is plain that a seventh son cannot take by purchase upon the implication of those words 'for want of issue male, remainder over' and, since it is necessary he should take some estate to answer the intention of the testator and can take only by descent, his father, the grandson of the testator, must take an estate descendible which, in this case, can be only an estate tail.

The case of Popham and Bamfield, they said, was very unlike this because there was nothing but a posthumous son who could not be defeated by construing the first an estate for life; such a son was a mere contingent thing, very unlikely ever to happen, and it might not be in the intention of the testator and probably was not to take provision against such an accident.

But in this case, there is no reason to exclude one son more than another from that benefit which the words of the will upon a legal and usual construction may well give him. They distinguished this case likewise from Frencham's Case because the construction made in that case did only exclude daughters to whom there was no reason upon the whole will to think the testator intended any estate.

This opinion was certified into Chancery Easter term 1707, *anno Reginae Annae* 6.

---

[1] *King v. Melling* (1672), 2 Levinz 58, 83 E.R. 448, also 1 Ventris 214, 225, 86 E.R. 144, 151, 3 Keble 42, 52, 95, 84 E.R. 584, 589, 614, Pollexfen 101, 86 E.R. 526, 3 Salkeld 296, 91 E.R. 835, 1 Eq. Cas. Abr. 181, 21 E.R. 973.

[Other copies of this report: Lincoln's Inn MS. Misc. 383, p. 19, pl. 2.]

8 Modern 258, 88 E.R. 183

The Case of Langley v. Baldwin, which was referred out of Chancery to the judges of the Common Pleas for their opinion, was thus. The testator devised his lands to Jonathan Langley for life without impeachment of waste, remainder to J.S., his grandchild, for life without impeachment of waste, with a power to him to make a jointure of the same land to any woman he should marry for her life. And, after his [J.S.] death, he devised the lands to the first son of J.S., the grandchild, in tail, and so to the sixth son. And then he devised that, if J.S., the grandchild, should die without issue male, the land should remain to J.B. And the question was what estate J.B. took by the will.

And it was certified by the Court of Common Pleas that he took an estate tail, which was decreed accordingly.

As to the concomitant clauses, if the words in a will are sufficient to raise an estate tail, these clauses, *viz.* with or without impeachment of waste, or any power to raise money by cutting and selling timber or otherwise, shall not control the devise.

[Other copies of this report: 1 Eq. Cas. Abr. 185, 21 E.R. 976.]

## 73

## Hancock v. Hancock

(Ch. 1707)

*Where a wife has been fully advanced upon marriage by a settlement and agreement and so barred of her customary part, her share goes to increase the personal estate, and the orphanage part is a moiety.*

*An election of a wife to receive a settlement in lieu of her customary rights does not bind her children; they must make any elections for themselves.*

*If a father settles freehold lands on a child, that shall not exclude him from his customary orphanage part.*

Yale Beinecke OSB MSS. 184, box 41,
Taussig 311, vol. 1, p. 445

The case [was] Leonard Hancock, a freeman of London, having children by a former wife, Isaac and Thomas Hancock, in 1690 married one Anne Turner. And, by articles before marriage, it was agreed that the said Leonard, the husband, should have £2000 of her fortune and that the said husband should within four years purchase the inheritance of lands of £200 *per annum* within thirty miles of London to be settled to the use of himself for life, remainder to the said Ann for life, remainder to their children in such manner as they or the survivor of them should direct or appoint, and he assigns several leasehold houses as a security for performance of the said articles.

The said Leonard Hancock had issue by the said Anne, two children, Leonard and Mary.

The said Anne Hancock, in her husband's lifetime, exhibits a bill against him for a specific performance of the said articles.

On the hearing of the cause, 19 May 1707, [she] obtains a decree for the performance of the said articles and that the said Leonard Hancock, the husband, should in twelve months purchase messuages and lands of £200 *per annum* to be approved by the Master and, after, settled, the messuages only there by consent to settle £220 *per annum*.

Before the said decree [was] performed, the said Leonard Hancock died having made his will and his sons Thomas and Isaac Hancock by his former wife executors. And, thereby, he declared the settlement he made of the said leasehold premises was by him intended as a full provision and advancement for his said wife and children by her and that, if she accepted the said settlement as a full provision for herself and children, then he willed his executors to make good all covenants and agreements on his part unperformed at his death and that his two sons, Isaac and Thomas, by his former wife should have that part of his personal estate which they were entitled to by the custom of the City of London. But, if his said wife did not accept the said settlement for herself and her children but should claim a third of his personal estate in lieu of the said settlement, then he willed that all his children should have one-third of his personal estate according to the custom of the City. And he devised all the residue of his personal estate as well his own third as what should be coming on his wife's acceptance or refusing the said settlement, after some small legacies therein specified, to his said two sons, Isaac and Thomas, equally.

Afterwards, the said Ann Hancock and her said two children, Leonard and Mary, being infants, exhibit their bill against the said Thomas and Isaac Hancock for a discovery of the assets of the testator for satisfaction of the said articles and praying an account of his personal estate, to which overplus the said plaintiffs Leonard and Mary claimed title by the custom of the City.

And the cause coming to be heard before My Lord Chancellor Cowper, His Lordship declared that the plaintiff Anne could not have the settlement and her thirds both and, she having elected to abide by her settlement, the defendants were entitled to the plaintiff Anne's third part and to the testamentary third and to a moiety of the orphanage third part equally with the plaintiffs Leonard and Mary and to the reversion of the lands after the death of the plaintiff Anne, which was to be taken as part of his personal estate and that a settlement should be made on the plaintiff Anne with a proviso to avoid the uses therein for the benefit of the infants unless they should elect to abide by the same.

The said plaintiffs Leonard and Mary Hancock, being dissatisfied with this decree, obtained an order to rehear before My Lord Harcourt.

His Lordship [Lord Harcourt] declared that, according to the custom of the City of London, the plaintiff Anne, the widow, having been advanced in her marriage, she was not entitled to her thirds of the personal estate, but such thirds ought by the custom to be brought into the whole personal estate and that after the testator's debts [be] paid, the whole personal estate ought by the custom to be divided into equal moieties, one moiety whereof is the testamentary part and that the other moiety is the orphanage part, which ought to be divided between the plaintiffs, the infants, and the defendants equally.

Lincoln's Inn MS. Misc. 10, p. 30, pl. 2

Leonard Hancock, upon his marriage with the plaintiff, enters into articles with her trustees and, thereby, in consideration of a £2000 portion, assigns over some leasehold lands in trust for himself for life, then for the plaintiff for her life for her jointure and in bar of dower, then in trust for all their children in such proportions as he and his wife should appoint by writing and, for want of such appointment, in trust for all the children equally and, if but one child, in trust for such only child. Then, he covenants to purchase freehold lands of such value within four years and settle them to the same uses. He dies without having made any purchase, leaving the plaintiff and several children under age.

This case was heard before the late Lord Chancellor [Wright], who declared that the plaintiff had her election and might either abide by the marriage articles or take her thirds by the custom. And, in regard the election of the wife could not bind the children, he decreed that they should have the like election when they came of age. But, if they elected to take by the custom, they should not have both, and, in that case, the surplus of the leasehold lands and also of the freehold lands to be purchased should be considered as personal estate and be flung into hotchpot and divided into moieties.

This cause was reheard before Lord Keeper [Lord Cowper], who, at first, differed in opinion with Lord Chancellor [Wright], but, upon taking time to consider of the case, affirmed the decree with only some little variation in respect to a matter, which both sides agreed to be a mistake in the Register in drawing up the decree.

In this case, it was said by *Dee*, Common Serjeant, and not contradicted that, if a father settles freehold lands on a child, that shall not exclude him of his orphanage part or, if, by deed executed in his lifetime, he settles any part of his personal estate upon any one of his children, such child shall, notwithstanding, have his [share] by the custom, and no act of the father can bar him.

Lincoln's Inn MS. Misc. 380, pt. 3, p. 145

It was laid down as a rule by the Common Serjeant as the custom of London that a wife should in such a case be excluded even though the jointure was not said to be in bar of her customary part. And, in the case it was [that] the wife's fortune was all in land and there was a covenant in the marriage settlement that all the personal estate, if there was any issue, should go to the issue and, if none, then over.

Lincoln's Inn MS. Misc. 506, p. 21, pl. 3

The wife being fully advanced upon marriage by a settlement and agreement and so barred of her customary part, her share should go to increase the personal estate, and the orphanage part should be a moiety.

[Other reports of this case: 2 Vernon 605, 665, 23 E.R. 995, 1033, 1 Eq. Cas. Abr. 153, 21 E.R. 952.]

## 74

## Attorney General v. Baines

(Ch. 1707)

*The lack of an inter vivos surrender of copyhold lands devised in trust to a charity can be supplied in equity in general, but not against a bona fide purchaser for value.*

*A devise to a charitable use must satisfy the requirements of the Statute of Frauds.*

British Library MS. Hargrave 80, f. 13

One, being seised of copyhold land in fee, does devise it to certain persons in fee in trust for charitable uses. But there was no surrender before his death to the uses of his will, nor was his will published before three witnesses according to the Statute of Frauds and Perjuries.[1] Hereupon were two questions: whether the want of a surrender should be supplied in equity; second, whether the insufficiency of the publication should be helped to support the charity.

To the first, it was held by the Lord Chancellor [Lord Cowper] that the want of a surrender should be supplied, for so it had been before ruled in several cases. And it was reasonable enough upon the 45th of Elizabeth,[2] concerning charitable uses, to take this devise without a surrender to be a sufficient appointment to a charity within that Statute.

As to the second, it was held that the want of a sufficient publication of the will could not be helped in favor of the charity because the Statute of Frauds and Perjuries, which makes all wills void unless published in such a manner, is subsequent to the 45th of Elizabeth, concerning charitable uses, and does repeal and alter it in respect of the appointment of charities made by will.

In Chancery, if one seised of a copyhold estate devises it without a surrender to the use of his will, the court will not make good the want of a surrender or

---

[1] Stat. 29 Car. II, c. 3, s. 5 (*SR*, V, 840).

[2] Stat. 43 Eliz. I, c. 4 (*SR*, IV, 968–970).

supply the loss of it, though the devise be to charity or to children, or so much as direct an issue whether there was a surrender or not if there has been a purchase made of it under the heir for a valuable consideration without notice of the will. But such a purchaser shall have all the advantage that he can by the law to defend himself. But, if the purchase was with notice, then shall the purchaser stand in the place of the heir and be liable in the same manner as he was, for he knew what he bought and gave the less because of the hazard of eviction.

[Other copies of this report: Lincoln's Inn MS. Misc. 383, p. 22, Lincoln's Inn MS. Misc. 106, p. 3.]

[Other reports of this case: 3 Chancery Reports 150, 21 E.R. 753, Precedents in Chancery 270, 24 E.R. 131, *sub nom.* Attorney General v. Barnes, 2 Vernon 597, 23 E.R. 990, Gilbert Rep. 5, 25 E.R. 4, 1 Eq. Cas. Abr. 97, 21 E.R. 908.]

## 75

## Smith v. Goodman

(Ch. 1707)

*Where land is devised in trust to be sold to pay the decedent's debts, this land is the first assets of the estate to be used to pay his debts, and, if such trust assets are not sufficient for that purpose, the legacies will abate proportionally.*

Lincoln's Inn MS. Misc. 10, p. 128

9 May 6 Anne. Warnett v. Goodman.

Edward Warnett, by will, devised to Edward Godman and his heirs his mansion house called Hempsted and several lands in the County of Sussex. And he did also devise to the said Edward Godman and his heirs his farm called Huntingtons and another farm called Masketts upon trust, within twelve months after the death of the testator, to sell the same for the best price that might be had, and he willed that the moneys to be raised by the sale should be equally divided between the defendant, his nephew, and the testator's other nephews, John Smith, Edward Smith, Francis Smith, and his niece Anne Smith, share and share alike, after his debts, legacies, and funeral expenses paid, his mind being that the said Edward Godman, whom he made executor of his will should out of the money raised by the sale of the premises called Huntingtons and Masketts pay his debts, legacies, and funeral expenses and that the residue should be equally shared and divided as aforesaid. And he did therein give several legacies to divers persons therein mentioned.

A bill being brought by the creditors of the testator against the said Edward Godman, the court declared, among other things, that the said Edward Godman was well entitled to the said testator Edward Warnett's personal estate free from the payment of the debts and legacies of the testator and should have the same accordingly and that the testator having devised part of his real estate, which was the said Huntingtons and Masketts, in trust to be sold for the payment of his debts, the principal and interest due on the mortgage in the bill mentioned to John Smith ought to be paid out of the money raised by the sale of the said trust estate. And [the court] decreed the trust estate to be sold to the best purchaser and that the moneys to be raised by the sales together with the rents and profits thereof should be applied to pay what was due to the said Smith for principal, interest, and costs, as aforesaid; after the payment of Smith's mortgage, to pay the said testator's other debts and legacies and, after the said mortgage and the testator's other debts and legacies were paid out of the moneys arising by the sale of the said trust estate and the rents and profits thereof until the sale. [It was] decreed that the surplus be divided according to the said testator's will.

Note, in this case, the moneys raised by the sale of Huntingtons and Maskets was not sufficient to pay the debts and all the legacies, and, therefore, the legatees were to abate in proportion.

[Other reports of this case: 2 Vernon 586, 23 E.R. 982.]

## 76

## Morris v. Bellamy

(Ch. 1707)

*The debts and legacies of a testator can be charged by him upon his real estate.*

Lincoln's Inn MS. Misc. 9, p. 48, pl. 2

18 June 1707.

Sir Solomon Swayle, having by his will taken notice of his second and third sons and that he owed debts, charges his heir and executor to pay those debts. And, then, he gives legacies to his grandchildren. And he makes his eldest son executor, but he gives him no lands, but leaves them to descend to him. And, then, he says 'I charge my heir and executor with the payment of my legacies.' The personal estate was not sufficient to pay the debts and legacies. And the question was if this should charge the lands.

*Dobbyns*: This is only a description of the person.

*Vernon*: In the Case of Dean and Pelham,[1] lands were devised to Pelham for life, remainder to his first and other sons in tail, with divers remainders over, and then the testator says 'I desire the said Mr. Pelham to pay my debts and legacies.' This was heard before Lord Nottingham and decreed by him and, afterwards,

[1] *Clowdsley v. Pelham* (1686), 1 Vernon 411, 23 E.R. 552, 1 Eq. Cas. Abr. 197, 21 E.R. 986, Chancery Repts. *tempore* Jac. II, 279.

affirmed in the House of Lords that the estate was chargeable with the debts etc. and that it should be sold for the payment of them.

Lord Chancellor [LORD COWPER]: This is a charge upon the land, for, otherwise, the word 'heir' is superfluous, for there was a sufficient description of the person without adding the word 'heir'. And, since this construction is to support the intent of the testator, which was to give legacies to his grandchildren, it is the more reasonable.

*Dobbyns*: Suppose the heir had died. Would this have been a charge *in infinitum*?

LORD COWPER: No doubt it must, for it is a charge upon the inheritance and not upon the person of the heir, for that was not in his power.

## 77

## Anonymous

(Ch. 1707)

*A legacy to a bond creditor in the amount of the bond debt is a payment and satisfaction of that debt.*

Lincoln's Inn MS. Misc. 9, p. 49

21 June 1707.

A., being a citizen of London, upon his marriage, in consideration of a £200 portion which his wife had and which was then out upon securities, enters into a bond to trustees to leave his wife £500 by his will or, otherwise, to be paid her within two months after his death.

After the marriage, having never altered the securities, he makes his will and gives her £500, but he takes no notice of the bond nor that the legacy should be in satisfaction of it.

The question was if the legacy should go in satisfaction of the bond.

*Curia* [LORD COWPER] decreed it should, being for the same sum and that the wife should come in for her share of the personal estate by the custom after the payment of the debts, of which this bond is one. I admit, if he had died intestate, what she would have received by the custom would have gone in discharge of the bond by reason of the word 'otherwise'. But, since the husband has made his will and given her £500, it is plain he meant the bond should be paid that way, and, therefore, no part of what she receives by the custom shall be reckoned a part of the bond.

There was another question, which was whether the wife should have the £200 which was out in her name upon the same securities it was when she married, it being a chose in action and not altered in the husband's lifetime.

LORD COWPER: Had the husband made no will, she should have taken that £200 in part, for it is plain the husband kept those securities in that manner like an honest man lest he should not be able to make any other provision for his wife. But, when he found himself able, he then makes his will and gives her £500. And, sure, she must not have both.

*Dobbyns*: Suppose a man takes a mortgage in his own and his wife's name and dies. Shall not she have the money?

LORD COWPER: Whose was the money?

*Dobbyns*: The husband's.

LORD COWPER: Can the wife have it then? She is only a trustee for the executors or administrators.

[It was] decreed *contra* in the Case of Watts v. Goddard[1] by the Master of the Rolls.

## 78

## Anonymous

(Ch. 1707)

*Where a person subjects his land to the payment of his debts, debts barred by the Statute of Limitations will be paid.*

*Where the interest of a bond debt exceeds the penalty for non-payment, no interest is payable greater than the penalty unless the delay in payment was due to negligence.*

1 Salkeld 154, 91 E.R. 142

27 June 1707. At the Lord Chancellor's House.

It was held, first, that, if one, by will or deed, subject his lands to the payment of his debts, debts barred by the Statute of Limitations[2] shall be paid, for they are debts in equity and the duty remains. The Statute has not extinguished that, though it has taken away the remedy.

Second, it was held that, if there be a bond debt and the interest has outrun the penalty, it shall not carry interest beyond the penalty, for the design of the settlement was not to increase the debt beyond what is due, but to give a farther security. However, if the devisee or trustee neglects to pay in a reasonable time, he shall after such neglect pay interest beyond the penalty.

*Per* COWPER, Lord Chancellor.

---

[1] *Watts v. Goddard* (Ch. 1714), see below, Case No. 597.

[2] Stat. 21 Jac. I, c. 16, s. 3 (*SR*, IV, 1222).

## 79

## Slayer v. Bussey

(Ch. 1707)

*A legacy lapses if the legatee dies before the legacy is payable.*

Lincoln's Inn MS. Misc. 10, p. 223

18 July 1707.

A.B., by will, gives lands to his wife for life, with remainders over, and he also gives £50 apiece to his two daughters two years after the death of his wife to be paid out of the lands. The daughters survived their mother, but they died within the two years.

*Curia*: This is a bequest *in futuro*. And the daughters dying before their legacies became payable, the same are lapsed and shall not be raised for the benefit of the executors.

## 80

## Alkin v. Alkin

(Ch. 1707)

*There is no legal duty for a brother to support his sister.*

Lincoln's Inn MS. Misc. 9, p. 54

28 July 1707. Alkin and Alkin v. Alkin and Wareing.

Martha Farrian, the plaintiff's grandmother, in August 1692, conveys her estate to the defendant Wareing and his heirs to the use of Richard Alkin and Margaret, his wife, the plaintiffs' father and mother, for their lives, remainder to the heirs male of their bodies, with remainders over, and, then, there is this proviso, *viz*. 'provided and upon this condition that, notwithstanding the settlement of the premises, the lands shall be chargeable with the payment of £3000 for the portions of the three daughters of Richard and Margaret Alkin to be paid them when they shall attain the age of twenty years in case they shall attain that age'.

Richard and Margaret die leaving a son and three daughters. One of the daughters is paid her portion, and the other two prefer their bill against their brother and the trustee for theirs. And they insist upon a maintenance out of the estate from their father's death to the time their fortunes became payable in regard they were destitute of a maintenance, their father having left no personal estate.

Upon the hearing of the cause, the Master of the Rolls [Trevor] took time to consider of it, whether the parties should have any maintenance allowed them or any interest for their portions from their father's death. And, he, afterwards, decreed they should have neither and, therefore, that what the defendant Wareing had expended towards their maintenance should be deducted out of their fortunes. And he allowed interest from the time the fortunes became payable and gave them £5 costs.

He said the brother, by natural equity, ought to have allowed his sisters maintenance, but he could not compel him to it.

## 81

## Stafford v. Selby

(Ch. 1707)

*A purchaser with notice of a fraud cannot shield himself by purchasing from a bona fide purchaser for value.*

Lincoln's Inn MS. Misc. 9, p. 55

2 November 1707.

The defendant [Serjeant James] Selby [d. 1724] had purchased a considerable estate of one Stafford, upon which there were several mortgages which were transacted by the defendant, the money lent thereon being procured by him, in the management whereof some unfair practices had been used towards Stafford, which looked ill. And the plaintiffs, who claimed under a deed of trust made before the defendant's purchase, for the payment of Stafford's creditors, prefer their bill and pray they may redeem the defendant, who, it was alleged, had not purchased fairly and, besides, had bought the estate much under value.

The defendant pleaded himself a purchaser without notice of the deed of trust, and, moreover, pleaded the Statute of 4 & 5 of King William and Queen Mary, ca. 16,[1] touching the making of a second mortgage without giving notice of the first, whereby such mortgagor is foreclosed of the equity of redemption, which plea was allowed by the Lord Keeper WRIGHT.

And the plaintiffs having replied to that plea, the cause came on now to be heard. And three days were spent in hearing it.

Lord Chancellor [LORD COWPER]: The Statute was not intended to purge any fraud which was committed in transacting a second mortgage, but only to foreclose the equity of redemption of a second mortgage, upon which money is fairly and honestly lent. But, if a second mortgage has been made without any fraud in the lender, but the person who transacted that mortgage was guilty of a fraud in the management of that affair, if, afterwards, this mortgage comes to be assigned to the person who was guilty of this fraud, yet, though the equity of redemption of that mortgage might be barred while it continued in the hands of

[1] Stat. 4 Will. & Mar., c. 16 (*SR*, VI, 404).

the fair mortgagee, yet coming into the hands of such fraudulent person, the redemption shall be revived.

Secondly, I lay it down for a rule that, if a man purchases an estate upon which there are mortgages, one of which is fraudulent, at least to part of it, and the purchaser was privy to the fraud, this court will let in the mortgagor to a redemption notwithstanding his sale.

It is true in the case before us the defendant has purchased of Stafford. But consider how. The defendant, who was Stafford's counsel, stirs up a mortgagee to bring a bill in equity to foreclose. Then, Stafford's goods are taken in execution, and he is stripped of the possession. And then comes the defendant and says sell me the equity of redemption, for, in truth, you are foreclosed of it by the Statute, which was false, for he was not. Why now, shall a man that sells in these circumstances be foreclosed though he has sold the equity of redemption, especially when it does not appear that any account was ever stated and adjusted and more was reckoned to be due upon the mortgages than in truth was due? Surely no.

The defendant must re-convey upon the payment of what is due for principal and interest and must account for the rents and have all usual allowances and, besides, must have a full allowance for lasting improvements.

As to the costs, if the plaintiffs redeem, it must be without costs. If they do not, they must pay costs.

[Other reports of this case: 2 Vernon 589, 23 E.R. 983, 1 Eq. Cas. Abr. 320, 21 E.R. 1074.]

## 82

## Cuthbert v. Peacock

(Ch. 1707)

*In this case, the testator's creditor was given her legacy over and above her bond debt.*

Lincoln's Inn MS. Misc. 9, p. 56

10 November 1707.

A man, being indebted in £200 by bond, makes his will. And he gives the obligee, his niece, a legacy of £300 to be paid her eighteen months after the testator's death.

The legatee prefers her bill for the legacy. And the question was whether the legacy should not go in discharge of the debt.

Lord Chancellor [Lord Cowper]: The general rule is with the defendant, which is that, where a man gives legacy to one to whom he is indebted, if the legacy is greater than the debt, that the legacy shall go in discharge of the debt, for a man is presumed to be just before he is bountiful. But I think this rule is against the intention of the testator in such case and a flat contradiction to the plain sense of his will, for it is manifest a man intends to give another a legacy and, by this means, he is defeated perhaps of one half of it. And, therefore, if a case can be fairly distinguished from the common case, I shall be for doing it.

In the case before us, the legacy is not payable until eighteen months after the testator's death. And, if the debt is to be discharged by the legacy, the interest will run on in the meantime upon the bond, by which means the legatee will not receive £100 for her legacy. Besides, the testator, in this case, was in the nature of a parent, so that, considering the circumstances of this case, it ought not to come within the general rule. And, therefore, the plaintiff must have her legacy and interest at £5 percent. But, as to costs, I think in regard the defendant might well enough insist upon this matter, he ought not to pay costs.

1 Salkeld 155, 91 E.R. 143

Michaelmas 6 Anne [10 November 1707].

H. owed his niece A. £100 by bond and, having two other nieces, B. and C., makes his will and bequeaths £300 to his niece A. and to his two other nieces £200 apiece. After that, he borrowed another £100 of his niece and, being indebted to her in £200, died.

And to prove the £300 should go in satisfaction of the debt, Mr. *Vernon* insisted that it was the rule in equity, and had been often decreed, that, where a testator, being indebted, gives his debtee a legacy greater than his debt, it shall go in satisfaction, for a man shall be intended to be just before he is kind; otherwise, where a legacy is less, for that is neither to be just nor kind and shall not be taken to go in satisfaction of any part.

Cowper, Lord Chancellor, said it might be as good equity to construe him to be both just and kind if he intended to be both, that, if any part of the £300 be applied to the payment of the debt, as for so much, it is not a gift, whereas a legacy must be taken to be a gift or gratuity. And, there being assets and some proofs of the testator's greater kindness to A. than his other nieces, His Lordship [Lord Cowper] decreed her the whole £300 over and above her debt.

[Other reports of this case: 2 Vernon 593, 23 E.R. 986, 1 Eq. Cas. Abr. 204, 232, 21 E.R. 992, 1012.]

## 83

## Anonymous

(Ch. 1707)

*If a trustee or executor make an advantageous bargain, the benefit of it goes to the creditors, legatees, or residuary beneficiaries of the estate.*

1 Salkeld 155, 91 E.R. 143

Michaelmas 6 Anne.

If a trustee or executor compound debts or mortgages and buy them in for less than is due upon them, he shall not take the benefit of it himself, but other creditors and legatees shall have the advantage of it. And, for want of them, the benefit shall go to the party who is entitled to the surplus.

But, if one acts for himself and, being not in the circumstances of a trustee or executor, buy in a mortgage for less than is due or for less than it is worth, he shall be allowed all that is due upon the mortgage, for he stands in the place of him that assigns, *viz.* the mortgagee, who might have given it to him *gratis.* And what is due must be the measure of our allowance, and not what he gave, for that might have been more than it is worth, as well as less. And, since he runs the hazard, if loss happens, he ought to have the benefit in case it turns to advantage.

So [it was] said and admitted *per* COWPER, Lord Chancellor.

## 84

## Smell v. Dee

(Ch. 1707)

*Where a time is annexed to a legacy itself, and not to the payment of it, if the legatee dies before the time of the payment, i.e. the existence of the legacy, the legacy lapses.*

*An infant cannot be guilty of laches.*

2 Salkeld 415, 91 E.R. 360

Michaelmas 6 Anne.

H. bequeathed by his will in these words, *viz.* 'I give £100 apiece to the two children of J.S. at the end of ten years after my decease'. The children died within the ten years.

*Et per* COWPER, Lord Chancellor: This is a lapsed legacy and shall not go to the executors of the children, for the diversity is where the bequest is to take effect at a future time and where the payment is to be made at a future time.

And, though it was objected by *Sir Thomas Powys* that this differed from the case where a man devised £100 to J.S. at his age of twenty-one, because it is a contingency whether he attain to that age, but the expiration of the ten years is inevitable.

Yet the Lord Chancellor [LORD COWPER] answered that, wherever the time is annexed to the legacy itself, and not to the payment of it, if the legatee dies before the time of payment, it is a lapsed legacy in that case. *Vide* Dy. 59b; 2 Vent. 342; Off. Ex. 347; Swinb. 311, 313.[1]

---

[1] *Regina v. Lady Latimer* (1545), 1 Dyer 59, 73 E.R. 131; *Cloberry v. Lamden* (1678), 2 Ventris 342, 86 E.R. 476, also 2 Freeman 24, 22 E.R. 1035, 2 Chancery Cases 155,

If a legacy be devised generally and no time ascertained for the payment and the legatee be an infant, he shall be paid interest from the expiration of the first year after the testator's death. But it seems a year shall be allowed, for so long the Statute of Distribution[1] allows before the distribution be compellable and so long the executor shall have that it may appear whether there be any debts. But, if the legatee be of full age, he shall only have interest from the time of his demand after the year, for, no time of payment being set, it is not payable but upon demand, and he shall not have interest but from the time of his demand. Otherwise it is in the case of an infant, because no laches is imputed to him. But where a certain legacy is left payable at a day certain, it must be paid with interest from that day.

And note the interest allowed is £5 percent, *per* COWPER, Lord Chancellor.

## 85

## Grimston v. Lord Bruce

(Ch. 1707)

*A legatee or heir should have interest where both the sum and time of the payment were certain and past.*

*Where a sum in gross is given secured by a right of entry on lands for non-payment, there is to be no deduction for any taxes.*

1 Salkeld 156, 91 E.R. 144

[11 November 1707.]

H. devised his lands to J.S. and his heirs on condition to pay £20,000 to the heir at law, *viz.* £1000 *per annum* for the first sixteen years and £2000 *per annum* after that until the whole should be paid. The heir entered for non-payment of one of the £1000 *per annum.* And J.S. brought his bill. And it was objected that the condition restores the heir and that Chancery ought not to aid in disherison of him.

But it was resolved by COWPER, Lord Chancellor:

First, that the entry of the heir in this case was only to enforce the payment of his principal, as where a mortgagee enters, and that the court can give him interest for the same from the time it became payable and that, wherever the court can give satisfaction or compensation for a breach of condition, they can relieve;

Secondly, that, for every £1000 from the time it became payable, the legatee or heir should have interest, because both the sum and time of payment were certain and past;

---

22 E.R. 892, 1 Eq. Cas. Abr. 294, 21 E.R. 1055, 2 Eq. Cas. Abr. 539, 22 E.R. 454, 79 Selden Soc. 509, 529; T. Wentworth, *Office and Duty of Executors*; H. Swinburne, *Brief Treatise of Testaments and Last Wills.*

[1] Stat. 22 & 23 Car. II, c. 10, s. 5 (*SR*, V, 720).

Thirdly, that there is to be no deduction of any taxes, because it is not to issue nor arise from the lands, but is given as a sum in gross secured by entry on the lands for non-payment.

[Other reports of this case: 2 Vernon 594, 23 E.R. 986, 1 Eq. Cas. Abr. 108, 21 E.R. 917.]

86

## Perkins v. Micklethwaite

(Ch. 1707–1714)

*A court of equity construes words in favor of younger children, and, therefore, the general words in the will in issue included all the younger children whether born after the will or before.*

*When a condition or clause of survivorship is once performed, it is gone forever.*

*A codicil is a republication of the will.*

Lincoln's Inn MS. Misc. 9, p. 57, pl. 1

12 November 1707.

Upon an objection made for want of parties, the Lord Chancellor [Lord Cowper] decreed that, where a sum of money is chargeable by will upon land only and a demand is made in this court for the money, it is not necessary to have the executor here. But, where a legacy is given and, by the will, lands are charged for the payment of it, if you come into this court and demand the legacy out of the lands only, yet you ought to have the executor here.

Lincoln's Inn MS. Misc. 10, p. 165, pl. 2

11 June 1714.

A.B. gives £1500 to C. by a will and, if C. dies before twenty-one, then he gives it over. C. dies under twenty-one in the lifetime of the testator. And the question is if it should go over.

Mr. *Vernon* insisted it should not in regard it never vested in the first legatee. He argued, where a legacy is given to two and one dies, the survivor shall have the whole, for the whole was given to both.

*Curia* took time to consider of it.

Lincoln's Inn MS. Misc. 384, p. 20, pl. 2

11 June 1714.

Micklethwaite has issue, Joseph, and, by his will, he gives him £1500. Joseph dies. Afterwards, he has issue another son of the same name.

The question was whether the second son Joseph can take, being substituted by a codicil in the place of the other by these words, 'I give to my son Joseph which I had since my former will the sum of £500 more than is given by that will.'

*Jekyll*, for the defendant: The codicil is a republication of the will within the Statute of Frauds[1] and substitutes the second son Joseph in the room of the first.

*Vernon*, for the plaintiff: The devise to the first Joseph is a lapsed legacy. Where there is a bequest of £1000 to three and one dies in the life of the testator, it will survive to the rest. But when it is devised over by way of a remainder, if it does not vest in the first taker, it cannot go over. Lord Bindon's Case.[2] Where a legacy is given to three and if any of them die, then to survive, if one die, the survivorship is at an end, and, when the second dies, it will go in the course of administration.

*Hooper*: If a man give a legacy to one *in ventre sa mere*, it will vest, though it was formerly doubted.

LORD HARCOURT: I will consider of it whether the second Joseph can take as substituted in the room of the first.

*Curia* [LORD HARCOURT]: The testator plainly intended the second Joseph to stand in the place of the first. And the codicil is attested by three witnesses. And so it is sufficient to charge land and is a republication which amounts to the same as a new will.

British Library MS. Hargrave 80, f. 180

The father of the plaintiff and defendant having issue, two sons and two daughters, Ann and Elizabeth, devised his real estate to his eldest son in fee upon condition that he should pay £1500 to Joseph, his younger son, at twenty-one, £1000 apiece to his two daughters, Ann and Elizabeth, at their respective marriages. And he willed that, if Joseph died underage or either of the daughters [died] unmarried, the share and portion of the child so dying should be equally divided among his younger children. After making this will, Joseph died and the testator had another son Joseph born. And, afterwards, he wrote a codicil to his will upon the same paper attested by three subscribing witnesses, in which he confirmed his will to all intents and gave to his son, Joseph, and to his daughters, Ann and Elizabeth, £500 apiece over and besides what he had given them by his will. And he died leaving another daughter, the plaintiff Barbara, born before his death. Elizabeth died after him unmarried, and then Ann died and before marriage too. Upon this case, several questions arose: first, whether, upon the death of the first Joseph in the testator's life, the £1500 given him lapsed [and the] devise of it over became void; secondly, whether 'younger children' should be confined to those who were in being when the will was made; thirdly, whether the share of Elizabeth, which survived to Ann, was carried over by the clause of survivorship

1 Stat. 29 Car. II, c. 3, s. 5 (*SR*, V, 840).

2 *Lord Bindon v. Earl of Suffolk* (1707–1708), 1 Peere Williams 96, 24 E.R. 309, 4 Brown P.C. 574, 2 E.R. 391, 2 Eq. Cas. Abr. 535, 22 E.R. 451.

upon the death of Ann; fourthly, whether the codicil substituted the second Joseph in the place of the first.

To the first, it was insisted by *Vernon*, for the defendant, that the £1500 could not go over to the younger children, but, as it stood upon the will, it was a lapsed legacy. He said that many causes had been ruled upon a distinction between joint and distinct devises that, if a legacy were given to three jointly and one died, the testator living, the devise being entire and joint, the survivors would take the whole. But, if the devises were distinct and one died, his legacy lapsed, that, in this case, they were plainly distinct legacies, and, though upon the death of Joseph under twenty-one, the £1500 was limited over, it was never the intent of the testator that those whom it was to go over to should take it in the first instance and that, if he to whom it was first given never took it, they to whom it was limited over never should.

*Jekyll*, of the same side, [said] that, though a testator might be in health at the time of making his will, his words were to be considered as those of a dying man and that the natural construction of them was, 'if after my death, Joseph should die before twenty-one' and that, in the Case of Lord Bindon, the words were stronger than here and Lord Cowper [was] induced by them to apprehend the testator to be providing for a contingency, which might and did happen in his life, as it did here, but that decree was reversed by the House of Lords.[1]

*Lutwyche*, on the other side, [said] that the devise over could not take effect only in cases it never vested in Joseph, that nothing was to vest in him until twenty-one and, if he attained that age, nothing [was] to go over.

Lord Chancellor [Lord Harcourt] took time to consider.

To the second, *Vernon* said that equity often extended words in favor of younger children, but it did not restrain them to their prejudice, that, the words being general, all the younger children would take by them whether born after the will or before.

To which Lord Chancellor [Lord Harcourt] agreed [and] decreed upon that foundation a proportion of the £1000 of Elizabeth and Ann to Joseph.

To the third, *Vernon* said that equity never entangled devises with conditions or limitations over unnecessarily, that, therefore, when a condition or clause of survivorship is once answered, it is at an end, that, upon the death of Elizabeth, her share went over to Ann and the rest of the younger children, by which the clause of survivorship was satisfied as to that part and the part of Elizabeth's share that vested in Ann became entirely hers and, upon her death, was distributable in a course of administration.

Lord Chancellor [Lord Harcourt] decreed it to be distributed accordingly.

---

[1] *Lord Bindon v. Earl of Suffolk* (1707–1708), *ut supra.*

To the fourth, it was said by *Sir Joseph Jekyll* that, though the second Joseph was not a being *in esse* nor the person meant by the testator at the time of making his will, yet the first Joseph being dead and the second born before, the codicil, being upon the same paper attested as the Statute[1] requires and expressly confirming his will to all intents, amounted to a republication and that the words 'over and besides' etc. were plainly accumulative and showed the apprehensions of the testator to be that this Joseph would take something by his will, that the testator plainly intended to give the first Joseph £500 more than any of his daughters and, if the codicil should be construed by republishing the will to substitute the second Joseph in the place of the first, he would have just £500 more than his sisters but otherwise £1000 less, which could hereby be thought to be the testator's design.

This point Lord Chancellor [Lord Harcourt] took time to consider of.

This was ruled afterwards by Lord Cowper in favor of Joseph.

[Other copies of this report: Lincoln's Inn MS. Misc. 383, p. 300.]

British Library MS. Hargrave 81, f. 163

[11 June 1714].

Upon the will of Mr. Micklethwaite, father of the plaintiff Barbara [Perkins] and the defendant, it was said that, if a legacy be a lapsed legacy, the devise of such legacy over is void because, to support a devise over, there must be first a vesting in the first devisee before the devise over can take, for the intent of the testator is only that he should take secondarily and not originally nor primarily. Here, the will was to pay the daughters £1000 apiece at their age of twenty-one or day of marriage, but, if any of them died before twenty-one or marriage, the respective portion of such child so dying to be divided among the younger children. Elizabeth dies. Her £1000 is decreed to be divided among the rest of the younger children. Amy dies after the decree. The question here is whether [ *blank* ].

[Other copies of this report: British Library MS. Hargrave 82, f. 173.]

Lincoln's Inn MS. Misc. 10, p. 165, pl. 2

11 June 1714.

A.B. gives £1500 to C. by will and, if C. died before twenty-one, then he gives it over. C. died under twenty-one in the lifetime of the testator. And the question is if it should go over.

Mr. *Vernon* insisted it should not in regard it never vested in the first legatee. He agreed, where a legacy is given to two and one dies, the survivor shall have the whole, for the whole was given to both.

[1] Stat. 29 Car. II, c. 3, s. 5 (*SR*, V, 840).

The *Curia* took time to consider of it.

[Other reports of this case: British Library MS. Hargrave 77, f. 42v, pl. 2, British Library MS. Hargrave 303, f. 75, 1 Peere Williams 274, 24 E.R. 386, 2 Eq. Cas. Abr. 542, 22 E.R. 456.]

## 87

## James v. Duchess of Monmouth

(Ch. 1707)

*A debt due to a married woman that was not paid in her husband's lifetime is not assets of the deceased husband's estate.*

Lincoln's Inn MS. Misc. 9, p. 57, pl. 2

*Eodem die* [12 November 1707].

The Lady Duchess had a pension of £4000 a year paid her out of the Exchequer. The plaintiffs are creditors by simple contract for provisions furnished for the family during the Lord Cornwallis', the duchess's late husband's, life. And, after his death, the duchess had received part of the pension which had incurred due in her husband's lifetime. And the question was if this should be assets in her hands.

It was held *per curiam* that nothing should be assets but what she had received in her husband's life and was resting in her hands at his death, and, as to that, though she was neither executor nor administrator, yet she should have all just allowances.

## 88

## Gawler v. Wade

(Ch. 1707)

*A bill for discovery of a decedent's assets must be brought against the heir at law as well as others.*

Lincoln's Inn MS. Misc. 9, p. 58

12 November.

The bill was for discovery of real and personal assets of the defendant's testator, who had entered into a bond to the plaintiff. And it was brought against the executors and others who are charged to be heirs at law. The executor sets out the will, by which the residue of the real and personal estate is devised to him. The other defendants say they are not heirs at law and know not who is.

It was objected at the hearing that there was a want of parties, for that the heir at law was not before the court and there must be the same rule here as at law. Now, by the Statute 3 & 4 of Will. & Mar.,[1] the action is to be brought against the heir and the devisee. Besides, there is this further reason for it, because, if the bill should only be brought against the executor and [one] recover against him, the heir might afterwards come and controvert the will and perhaps set it aside and so recover back again what the executor had paid.

And of this opinion was the Lord Chancellor [Lord Cowper], who said, if you had set forth that you did not know who was heir or could not find him and had made good proof of your inquiry, it might have been a good foundation for a court of equity to break into the rule the Act has prescribed.

Let the bill be amended.

[Other reports of this case: 1 Peere Williams 99, 24 E.R. 312, 2 Eq. Cas. Abr. 165, 22 E.R. 141.]

## 89

## Waterer v. Waterer

(Ch. 1707)

*Land in borough English descends to heirs by representation.*

Lincoln's Inn MS. Misc. 9, p. 59, pl. 1

13 November 1707.

Land was borough English. There were three sons. And, after the death of the father, the youngest entered and was seised. And, during his life, the second son died, leaving a son. Then, the youngest son died without issue. And, upon a bill brought in this court, a trial at law was directed to try whether the land ought to descend to the elder brother or to the son of the second.

A special verdict was found, and judgment thereupon was given that the land ought to descend to the son of the second brother, for he is *in loco parentis* and the custom shall extend to carry it to him.

## 90

## Phillipson v. Fleming

(Ch. 1707)

*A conveyance alleged to be a mortgage will be so taken where the defendant admits it to be so in his answer, regardless of the Statute of Frauds.*

[1] Stat. 3 Will. & Mar., c. 14 (*SR*, VI, 320–321).

Lincoln's Inn MS. Misc. 9, p. 59, pl. 2

21 November.

The bill was to redeem an estate said to be mortgaged, though the conveyance was in fee and was absolute, without any proviso or defeasance and the plaintiff, as he alleged, objected against it when he came to seal, but the mortgagee said that, notwithstanding it was drawn so, yet it should only be a mortgage.

The bill was brought against the heir of the mortgagee, who died two years after the conveyance was made.

There was no proof that the mortgagor ever received any rent after he made the conveyance. But it was proved that he made up an account with the tenant and allowed all the rent in repairs, after which the tenant attourned to the mortgagee. It was also proved that the mortgagee refused to let a lease for more than one year because, said he 'I do not know but the estate may be redeemed.' And it was further proved that the mortgagor paid interest after the conveyance.

Lord Chancellor [Lord Cowper]: They must redeem.

*Vernon*: They have not made any case so as to bring it out of the Statute of Frauds etc.[1] It is true, where a man takes an absolute conveyance and promises to execute a defeasance and, afterwards, refuses to do it and would take advantage of the Statute, it is plainly a fraud. And, in My Lord Nottingham's time,[2] relief was given in such case. But, here now, all that they insist on is that the plaintiff said he would trust the mortgagee and depend upon his honor for a redemption.

Lord Chancellor [Lord Cowper]: The defendant, in his answer, has insisted upon interest for the first nine months, so that that is plainly making it a mortgage by a defeasance in writing. I do not go upon the other matters, but upon what appears by the answer, which is in writing.

N.B. What My Lord [Cowper] went upon was an account which was signed by the mortgagor and an agent of the mortgagee, in which there was an item which reckons interest on the mortgage for nine months from the date, which account being in the defendant's hands was set out in a schedule to his answer. So My Lord [Cowper] said this was plainly a condition in writing.

## 91

## Lord Ossulston v. Lord Yarmouth

(Ch. 1707)

*An agreement for future compound interest is void.*

[1] Stat. 29 Car. II, c. 3 (*SR*, V, 839–842).

[2] *Potts v. Turvin* (Ch. 1681), 79 Selden Soc. 856.

2 Salkeld 449, 91 E.R. 388

December 1707.

The earl of Yarmouth made a mortgage to My Lord Ossulston with a proviso that, if the interest was behind six months, that then that interest should be accounted principal and carry interest.

*Et per* Cowper, Lord Chancellor, this clause was decreed to be vain and of no use, saying no precedent had ever carried the advance of interest so far and that an agreement made at the time of the mortgage will not be sufficient to make future interest principal. But, to make interest principal, it is requisite that interest be first grown due and then an agreement concerning it may make it principal.

92

## Markham v. Markham

(Ch. 1707–1712)

*A decedent's secured debts should be paid off out of his personal property.*

*In a suit that is successful against an executor, the court has the discretion to award costs against the executor out of the assets of the estate or de bonis propriis.*

*The heir of a mortgagee is a trustee for the executor.*

Lincoln's Inn MS. Misc. 10, p. 130, pl. 1

5 December 1707.

Thomas Markham, the plaintiff's father, having mortgaged his real estate and entered into several bonds, in which the plaintiff was bound with him, died in 1703, having first made his will and the defendant, his wife, executrix. And, therein, after several legacies given, [he gives] her the residuum.

The real estate being descended to the plaintiff, he brought his bill against the executrix that the personal estate might be applied in exoneration of the real estate and that the mortgage thereon and also the bonds in which he was bound for his father might be paid off out of the personal estate.

[It was] decreed it should be so, saving that all the legacies were to take place of the plaintiff's demands of exoneration.

British Library MS. Hargrave 80, f. 92

*How*: Where we prevail against an executor, the ordinary justice of the courts gives us costs out of assets. But, in this case, the obstinacy of the defense and the having her answer falsified not only deprives the defendant the benefit of retaining costs out of assets but entitles us to our costs *de bonis propriis*, there not being assets to answer the bare debt.

Lord Keeper [Lord Harcourt], for the badness of the defense, would not let her retain her costs out of assets, which an executor that accounts fairly may do, even out of insufficient assets, but yet he would not charge her with paying the plaintiff's costs *de bonis propriis.*

The bill was by a son against a mother, which had some weight.

*Mead*: I must admit that a judgment is no lien upon a term of years until execution is actually sued out.

Lord Keeper [Lord Harcourt] said that the heir of a mortgagee is but a trustee for the executor, but, if the equity be released or foreclosed in the life of the mortgagee, then it seems to be in the nature of a purchase.

[Other copies of this report: Lincoln's Inn MS. Misc. 383, p. 166, Lincoln's Inn MS. Misc. 106, p. 118.]

93

## Godfrey v. Chadwell

(Ch. 1707–1713)

*A prior mortgagee who sues to foreclose a subsequent mortgagee does not have to pay court costs.*

2 Vernon 601, 23 E.R. 993

18 December [1707].

A bill [was brought] by a second mortgagee to redeem.

The first mortgagee pleaded his mortgage and the decree to foreclose the mortgagor without notice of the second mortgage.

The plea was overruled.

Lincoln's Inn MS. Misc. 384, p. 8, pl. 1

Chadwell v. Godfrey.

*Howe*: If a prior mortgagee come to foreclose a subsequent mortgagee, he ought not to pay costs, any more than a mortgagor.

[Other reports of this case: 1 Eq. Cas. Abr. 318, 21 E.R. 1072.]

94

## Kemp v. Coleman

(Ch. 1707)

*An agreement to return or refund part of a marriage settlement or a portion is fraudulent and void.*

1 Salkeld 156, 91 E.R. 144

Michaelmas vacation, 6 Anne.

*Per eundum Dominum Cancellarium* [Lord Cowper] *inter Kemp et Coleman*, Michaelmas vacation 1707, it was laid down as a rule in equity that, where the son, without the privity of the father or parent treating the match, gives a bond to return or refund any part of the portion, it is void.

## 95

## Higgins v. Derby

(Ch. 1707)

*A remainder after an estate tail is void.*

1 Salkeld 156, 91 E.R. 145

Michaelmas vacation 6 Anne.

A trust of a term of years was declared to the husband for life, remainder to the wife for life, remainder to the first son of their bodies, and the heirs male of the body of such first son, and so on to every other son, and, for want of sons, then, to the daughters of the said husband and wife. The husband and wife died, and there was no son of the marriage, but there was a daughter. And the question was whether she should take by virtue of this limitation, it being after a limitation in tail to the sons.

*Et per* Cowper, Lord Chancellor: Where the limitations to the sons ever took effect and the estate vested, the remainder and limitation to the daughters become void, but, if there never was a son, as it happened in this case, the remainder is good, for the limitation must be construed, if there be a son, then to him; if no son but a daughter, then to her.

But, upon reading the settlement, it appeared to be thus, 'and, in default of issue male of the body of the said husband, then to the daughters'. And, therefore, it was held that the husband took an estate tail, and, for that reason, the limitation to the daughters was held void, being after a plain limitation in tail to the husband.

[Other reports of this case: *sub nom.* Higgins v. Dowler, 1 Peere Williams 98, 24 E.R. 311, 2 Vernon 600, 23 E.R. 992.]

## 96

## Small v. Brackley

(Ch. 1708)

*A person who seeks an equitable remedy must do equity to the defendant.*

*In this case, the plaintiff was ordered to pay his debt to the defendant with interest and costs in order to have the bond in issue cancelled.*

Lincoln's Inn MS. Misc. 9, p. 60

31 January 1707[/08]. Small v. Brackley, widow.

The defendant lent the plaintiff £600 upon bond, who, afterwards, pays her £100 in part. And she then insisting upon further security, he, thereupon, assigns over to her £500 tallies and orders upon salt, after which the interest upon the orders becomes due. And she trusts him with the orders to receive it, which he does and pays it to her. And this he does three times successively. The interest became due a fourth time, and he takes the orders from her to receive it as before, and gives a note to return them again. But he, finding the principal was payable, receives that too. And, soon afterwards, he breaks. And, thereupon, a commission of bankruptcy is taken out against him.

The plaintiff, after this, makes a composition with his creditors to pay them 9s. in the pound, and the defendant was prevailed on to signify agreement upon security given her to pay her £75 above the composition. And, in the agreement, there was a clause that, if all the creditors did not come in by such a day, whose debts amounted to £20 in the whole, the agreement should be void.

Heysham, a creditor, refused to come in. And the plaintiff having obtained a [writ of] *supersedeas* of the commission, Heysham, upon a petition, procures it to be revived. But, he, having afterwards a satisfaction made him of his debt, let the matter fall. And, thereupon, the defendant petitions to have the benefit of the commission, which was ordered accordingly unless the plaintiff should give her security for her debt. But, the plaintiff never complying with the terms of that order, the defendant, thereupon, puts her bond in suit. And to have the bond delivered up and that the defendant might abide by the agreement, the plaintiff came into this court.

Lord Chancellor [Lord Cowper]: The foundation of this matter is as foul a fraud as can well be. The plaintiff was entrusted by the defendant with the orders to receive the interest, and he receives the principal. Why now, shall I relieve him who has acted in this manner and stretch an agreement in his favor?

The woman has done nothing but what was justifiable, for, as the circumstances of the case are, she might very reasonably insist upon a better composition than the other creditors, and, therefore, £75 was given to induce her to execute the agreement. But then, I do not find that there was any particular agreement made that she should deliver up her bond otherwise than what is implied in the deed of composition. And what were the terms of that? Why, that she should accept 9s. in the pound, provided all the creditors whose debts amounted to £20 came in and signed it. Why now, one of them never did. Shall a court of equity then make this good in favor of one who has acted so knavishly? No, sure, if the plaintiff will be relieved, it must be upon payment of the principal, interest, and costs.

[Other reports of this case: 2 Vernon 602, 23 E.R. 993, 1 Eq. Cas. Abr. 28, 21 E.R. 849.]

97

## Cludd v. Prince

(Ch. 1708)

*A power of attorney can be revoked by a will without notice of the power.*

*A jointress can be a bona fide purchaser for value.*

Lincoln's Inn MS. Misc. 10, pp. 174, 176

3 February 1707[/08].

Wrottesley Prince, on his marriage with Beatrice, the plaintiff's [Mary Cludd's] mother, settles lands for her jointure, with remainder to the first and other sons of the marriage, with a power in Wrottesley to revoke the uses by any writing executed in the presence of two witnesses.

Wrottesley, afterwards, makes his will, and, without taking notice of the settlement or the power he had to revoke it, he gives legacies to all his younger children. And, for the raising thereof, he gives to his eldest son and J.O., his sister-in-law, all his messuages and lands he had any power, reservation, or liberty by any deed or settlement for settling or disposing of, for, or towards raising portions for his younger children and also his personal estate, provided, if Richard paid the portions, the estate should be conveyed to him and his heirs. He makes Richard and John executors.

Richard, after the death of his father, marries the defendant Mary [Prince], and settles the lands charged with the portions for the jointure of his wife, who had no notice of the will. And, then, he died intestate.

William, the next brother and heir of Richard, buys the jointure of Mary with part of his own wife's portion and then settles it on her [his own wife], who had no notice of the will.

The bill is to have a satisfaction of two of the legacies.

The court, on hearing this cause, declared the will of Wrottesley was a revocation well executed as to so much as Wrottesley had power by the proviso in the settlement to revoke, and referred it to the Master to see what estate Wrottesley had the power to charge.

And, inasmuch as part of the [lands] settled in jointure by Richard Prince on the defendant Mary [Prince] without notice to her of the will and William's having purchased Mary's estate for life for a valuable consideration and settled the same in jointure on the defendant Frances, his widow, without notice to her of the said will, the court declared that the defendant Frances ought to enjoy Mary's jointure estate during Mary's life discharged of the plaintiff's demands. But, after Mary's death, the same are then to be liable so far as the personal estate of Wrottesley and Richard shall fall short of satisfying the same.

And, inasmuch as Richard Prince, knowing of the will, settled a jointure on his wife, the court declared that the personal estate ought to make good so much of Wrottesley's personal estate as came to his hands and the value of the profits received by Richard and the value of the jointress's estate for life, of which the Master was to estimate the value.

The Master [was] to compute interest for the legacies from the end of the first year after the death of Wrottesley.

Note, by the will, the testator directed the legacies should be raised and paid to the legatees as soon as the same should be raised at the discretion of the executors.

## 98

## Young v. Chandler

(Ch. 1708)

*A court can construe the intent of an instrument, but not the intent of the maker of the instrument.*

Lincoln's Inn MS. Misc. 9, p. 62

9 February 1707[/08].

A man, in consideration of marriage, assigns a dean and chapter lease to trustees upon trust, among others, that, after his death, they should pay his heir male £50 a year during the life of the wife and, after her death, £100 a year until he attained the age of twenty-one and the residue of the profits during his minority should be applied for the increase of such younger children's portions as the father should appoint by his will, and, for want of such appointment, to be equally divided among them and, when the heir male came of age, then upon trust to assign the leases to him, but, if the father died without issue male or such issue male died before twenty-one, then upon trust for the executors or administrators of the father.

It happened that the father died leaving one child only, *viz.* a son, having made a will and the plaintiff executor and residuary legatee. And this will was made three years before the settlement. And now, in regard there were no younger children nor any disposition in the settlement of the surplus of the rent during the minority of the heir male if such contingency happened, the question was to whom the rent should go during the minority of the son, whether to him or to the executor of the father as an interest undisposed of by the settlement.

Those who argued for the plaintiff said it should go to him as a resulting trust. On the other side, it was said that there was plainly a mistake in the settlement, that it was manifest the intent of it was that the executors should have no benefit but in default of issue male and that, therefore, the consideration of marriage and of the portion should not carry it to the son, like the case at common law where a man, in consideration of money, bargains and sells lands to another and it is not said to him and his heirs, yet the consideration will carry the use to him in fee.

Lord Chancellor [Lord Cowper]: The case is somewhat stronger than if it had been in the case of an administrator. As to the surplus of the rents, it is not disposed of, nor can I say it was intended so to be. Had the father been asked what would you have done with the profits in case there should happen to be no younger children, perhaps, he would have said let my son have them. But, as that does not appear by the deed, I cannot supply it. It is one thing to make good what appears to be the intent of a deed and another thing to supply what one may reasonably presume was the intent of the maker of that deed. And, therefore, I am of the opinion that the surplus of the profits, being an interest undisposed of, will consequently result to the executor, who is the representative of the father.

99

## Docksey v. Docksey

(Ch. 1708)

*In this case, the will in issue was explicit, and there could be no implied or resulting trust in favor of the heir.*

2 Eq. Cas. Abr. 506, 22 E.R. 429

Hilary 6 Anne.

J.S., by his will, gives to his son, the plaintiff, certain lands, he paying £100 to the testator's wife, the defendant, and all the rest and residue of his real estate he devises to his wife and her heirs to the intent to pay all his debts and legacies. He further devises that, if his son had a mind, he should exchange lands of the value of £100 *per annum* with the testator's wife for other lands not exceeding that yearly value, and he appointed two persons to settle the matter between them, provided that, if the wife thought fit, she should live in the capital messuage during her life. And he made his wife his executrix, and he died.

Evidence was produced for the defendant, which the Lord Chancellor [Lord Cowper] allowed to be read, to show that the testator's intent was that his son should have no more than what was expressly given him and that the reason of giving his wife so much was because the devisor talking with the witness about the settlement of his affairs and telling him he designed his heir, the plaintiff, the same lands which are given him by the will and that he did design other lands for his younger son, whereupon the witness said that that would be a means to set the two sons at difference and, therefore, he had better give them to the defendant and depend upon her generosity to the younger son, which he then did approve of and said he would do.

The heir's bill was to have what was over and above paying the debts and legacies, which was £2000.

For the plaintiff, it was said that, in all cases, where lands are given to a man for any particular purpose, when that purpose is satisfied, the trust shall result to the benefit of the heir at law.

And *Sir Thomas Powys* cited a case, which was a man devised lands to his executors for the payment of debts and that it should be sold and turned into money, yet the heir at law exhibited his bill and prayed that no more might be sold than would pay the debts and that he might have the overplus, and it was accordingly decreed at the Rolls and after[wards] affirmed in this court.

On the other side was cited North v. Crompton, 1 Chan. Ca. 196 (1 vol., Abr. Eq. 272, ca. 3).[1]

Lord Chancellor [LORD COWPER]: This would at law certainly have been a disinheritance of the heir. Now the question is whether this is not an implied trust for the benefit of the heir. Here would have been an implied trust for the benefit of the heir after the particular purpose satisfied if that implication had not been destroyed. But it is destroyed, as appears from the will itself.

First, he has expressly given lands to the son, which is a much stronger case than if he had only given a rent.

Secondly, he has appointed an exchange to be made, and that is with a most critical exactness, which is £100 *per annum* for £100 *per annum* and no more, and appointed two persons to settle it.

Now, can it be imagined that he would be so nicely exact upon the exchange if he designed him to have £100 *per annum* back again, for there appears to be the value of £2000 over and above paying the debts and legacies, so that, thereby, the implication is destroyed by the other part of the will. But there have been other matters read, which still make it much plainer, which, I think, may be read to explain any implication, although it is a general rule that matter *dehors* ought not to be averred.

And it was decreed accordingly.

[1] *North v. Crompton* (1671), 1 Chancery Cases 196, 22 E.R. 759, 1 Eq. Cas. Abr. 272, 21 E.R. 1040.

Equity Cases Exch. 623

10 February 6 Anne [1708], in Chancery, Ralph Docksey v. Elizabeth Docksey.

[There was a] devise of land to the defendant in fee to be sold for the payment of his debts and legacies and that the defendant and the plaintiff, his heir at law, were to exchange some land by the will.

It was resolved that there was no implied or resulting trust in the defendant, the executrix, for the benefit of the plaintiff, the heir, for that it appears by the words of the will, as also by the proof, that such implication is contradicted and that it was the intention of the testator that this should be a beneficial devise to the defendant. It appeared that the exchanged land should be sold; otherwise, there could be no fee, and, without a fee in the defendant, she could not exchange, that the defendant brought a fortune, had no jointure or dower but £1000 four years after, which could not be a provision, that the testator declared [that] he designed it wholly for her, and that he had given his heir as much as he designed.

[Affirmed on appeal: 3 Brown P.C. 39, 1 E.R. 1163, Lincoln's Inn MS. Misc. 10, p. 121, 2 Eq. Cas. Abr. 415, 430, 22 E.R. 352, 366 (H.L. 1710).]

## 100

## Nelthorp v. Anonymous

(Ch. 1708)

*A husband may dispose of his wife's paraphernalia.*

*In the absence of a will disposing of the testator's wife's paraphernalia, they go to her by operation of the common law.*

Lincoln's Inn MS. Misc. 9, p. 64, pl. 1

28 April 1708.

It was said by the Lord Chancellor [Lord Cowper] in this case that, notwithstanding the Statute of Distributions,[1] which says that all the personal estate of the intestate shall be distributed, yet the wife shall have her paraphernalia, for the Statute does not direct a distribution of anything but what is not actually or legally disposed of. Now, the law disposes of the paraphernalia unless the husband actually disposes of them, as he may do by his will. Yet, if he makes his will and does not give them away, the wife shall have them, though they are not particularly given her by the will.

[1] Stat. 22 & 23 Car. II, c. 10 (*SR*, V, 719–720).

## 101

## Parsons v. Briddick

(Ch. 1708)

*A surety is subrogated to the rights of the person who was paid by him.*

Lincoln's Inn MS. Misc. 9, p. 64, pl. 2

*Eodem die* [28 April 1708].

A. and B. are bound to C. with and for the debt of D., who gives a counter-bond to A. and B.; D. is sued and puts in bail. And, afterwards, the bail are sued, and judgment is recovered against them. Then, C. sues A. and recovers the money. And, thereupon, A. prefers his bill against C. and against the high sheriff and also the bail of D. to have an assignment of the judgment upon the bail bonds.

Lord Chancellor [LORD COWPER]: The judgment must be assigned, for the surety having paid the money stands in the room of the person to whom he paid it. And he and the sheriff, in whose name the judgment was recovered, must assign, being indemnified, unless the defendants, the bail, will agree to pay principal, interest, and costs.

[Other reports of this case: 2 Vernon 608, 23 E.R. 997, 1 Eq. Cas. Abr. 93, 21 E.R. 904.]

## 102

## Draper v. Borlace

(Ch. 1708)

*If a debtor is the beneficiary of a trust that is a cloud on his own title, a court of equity will remove the cloud in favor of his creditors.*

*If a trustee lends money to the beneficiary, he can hold the trust estate as a security for repayment.*

Lincoln's Inn MS. Misc. 9, p. 64, pl. 3

30 April.

It was said by the Lord Chancellor [LORD COWPER] in this case that, if a man has a statute or a mortgage of the freehold of a manor and he comes to extend his statute or to enter upon his mortgage and finds a copyhold or a term for years standing out in his way, if it appears that the copyhold or the term is only kept on foot in trust for the debtor, this court will assist the creditor and remove this obstruction.

It was likewise said by My Lord [COWPER] in the same case that, if the trustee lends money to the *cestui que trust*, he shall hold the trust estate as a security, for it shall be presumed he lent his money upon the credit of that estate.

[Other reports of this case: 2 Vernon 370, 23 E.R. 833.]

## 103

## Anonymous v. Shallet

(Ch. 1708)

*A trustee cannot retain and offset a debt to himself out of the corpus of the trust.*

Lincoln's Inn MS. Misc. 9, p. 65, pl. 1

3 May 1708.

A., B., C., and D. have an equal share in a debenture which is taken out in the name of Donly. A., by his will, bequeaths his share in this debenture to the plaintiff in satisfaction of a debt he owed him. D. sells the debenture.

And the plaintiff brings his bill for a fourth part of the money. And D. insists that the testator owed him money and that he ought to retain his debt.

Master of the Rolls [TREVOR]: A trustee is not like an executor. If you can show any agreement, you say well. Otherwise, I am of the opinion you ought not to retain. And, therefore, you must go before a Master and account for a fourth part of the money and pay it with interest and costs.

## 104

## Mervin v. Cook

(Ch. 1708)

*It is the same thing where an estate is devised subject to the payment of debts and where it is devised in trust for the payment of debts.*

*All co-obligors, including their executors, must be joined as co-defendants to enforce the obligation.*

Lincoln's Inn MS. Misc. 9, p. 65, pl. 2

5 May.

An estate is devised to A., B., and C. and charged with the payment of debts generally. They sell. And a bond creditor prefers his bill.

Mr. *Vernon*: It is true, if an estate is devised to or settled upon trustees to be sold for the payment of debts generally, a purchaser is safe though he does not see the debts paid. But, if there is a schedule of the debts, it lies upon him to see those debts paid. But now, in our case, the land is not devised to trustees to be sold for the payment of debts, but it is devised to three persons and their heirs and made subject to the payment of the testator's debts so that whoever purchases must stand in the room of the devisees.

Lord Chancellor [LORD COWPER]: There is at first view some appearance of a reason between this difference, but, if it is considered, there is really none, why now, if an estate is devised to a man and made subject to the payment of debts, is it not the same as if it had been devised to a man and his heirs in trust for the payment of debts, for is not the devisee in the first case a trustee for the creditors as well as in the latter?

It is true, if a man purchases (where the devise is for the payment of debts generally) immediately after the testator's death and makes no inquiry after the debts, it may bring him within the odium of a court of equity. But, when he purchases some considerate time after and is told that all the debts are paid, it would be hard to affect him.

An objection was made in this case for want of parties, because one of the obligors was not before the court, for all that are liable ought to be here and ought to contribute, not only the devisees who have sold and received the money but the surviving obligor also.

Lord Chancellor [Lord Cowper]: You must amend, and pay the costs of the day, which the Register said was £5 and which was to be divided among all the defendants.

## 105

## Turner v. Metcalf

(Ch. 1708)

*In this case, the court of equity held that the rent in issue was properly contracted for and was not a penalty.*

Lincoln's Inn MS. Misc. 9, p. 66

10 May 1708.

The defendant made a building lease of a piece of ground in Gray's Inn Lane at a ground rent of £5 a year and 1s. per foot more for every square foot of building that he should erect upon the garden, which was designed to be laid to the house agreed to be built, above ten feet high. And there was a covenant not to build in the garden any building above ten feet high.

The plaintiff, being an assignee of this lease, erects a building in the garden contrary to the covenant, by which a further rent accrued due. And, for the nonpayment thereof, the defendant entered. And the plaintiff prefers his bill to be relieved against the extremity of this lease.

Lord Chancellor [Lord Cowper]: Every man may part with his inheritance upon what terms he pleases. I should be glad to know what precedents you have where this court has relieved against a stated damage, as where the parties have agreed what shall be the quantum between them if the lessee breaks his covenant, for this is a common case, it being usual for men to make leases and reserve an increase of rent if he plows pasture and to insist [upon] a covenant not to plow. Now, we must take these two together. There is an agreement not to plow, but then, if the lessee does plow, he agrees to pay so much rent more, so that the damage here is stated.

Mr. *Thornhill* cited the Case of Blake v. The East India Company, where the plaintiff gave the Company a covenant not to trade in such goods; if he did, he was to pay such and such rates, and, he, being sued upon his covenant, preferred his bill, but he could have no relief. 2 Canc. Repts. 198.[1]

Lord Chancellor [Lord Cowper]: I can see no reason to relieve against a stated damage.

*Paunceforth*, for the plaintiff: This is like the case of interest where, upon a mortgage, £5 percent is agreed to be paid and the mortgagor covenants that, if the interest is not paid in such a time after it becomes due, that then he will pay 6 percent. This seems to be a stating the damage, and yet relief has been given in such cases.

Lord Chancellor [Lord Cowper]: That may proceed from an inability to pay, and, therefore, it is very reasonable to give relief.

N.B. It was said the plaintiff had abated the building.

Lord Chancellor [Lord Cowper]: Let the plaintiff have a month's time to take down the building, if he has not done it yet, and, if he does not abate it in that time, the bill must stand dismissed with costs.

As to what is past, let the Master examine when the building was set up, and the plaintiff must pay the increased rent for that time, but not for broken quarters, and also must pay costs.

British Library MS. Hargrave 80, f. 14v

The defendant made a lease to J.S. of a house and yard adjoining, reserving a certain rent with a covenant that he should not erect any building in the yard above ten feet high and, if he should erect any such building above ten feet high, then there was a reservation farther of 12d. a year for every square foot that such building should stand upon. J.S. assigns his lease to the plaintiff, who erects a building in the yard contrary to the said covenant. And, after that building had stood several years, the defendant brings [an action of] covenant against the plaintiff and recovers in damages according to the proportion of a 12d. a foot for every year the building had stood.

Against this, the plaintiff prefers his bill to be relieved. And it was insisted this was in the nature of a penalty which the defendant ought not rigorously to require from the plaintiff but only in proportion to the damage which he had really suffered, as in the case of a feoffment made or waste willfully committed by a copyholder or interest not paid by a mortgagor, all which are forfeitures in

[1] *Blake v. East India Company* (1673–1674), 2 Chancery Cases 198, 22 E.R. 909, also Reports *tempore* Finch 117, 23 E.R. 64.

strictness of law and voluntarily committed, yet are they such against which equity will relieve.

But *per curiam*, relief was denied in this case, for the cases mentioned are not like to this. In the case of a copyholder, relief is granted because the forfeiture incurred is not by the agreement of the parties, but by the provision of law, to which the party does not so expressly consent. And as to the case of a mortgagor, there is a further time indulged to him in equity, for the payment of his interest money in regard to the disability of his circumstances, whereby he was unable to satisfy his agreement. But this case is like to the common case of a lease reserving one rent for grazing and another for plowing.

[Other copies of this report: Lincoln's Inn MS. Misc. 383, p. 25.]

2 Eq. Cas. Abr. 16, 22 E.R. 13

Easter 7 Anne [1708].

A., seised of lands in fee, demised them to B. upon a building lease, B. paying £5 *per annum* and also 12s. yearly for every foot square that he should build above the height of ten feet, which B. covenanted to perform. The reversion of those lands came to C. This lease, being mortgaged, was afterwards assigned by B. to D., who building above the height and, upon demand, refusing to pay the increased rent, the reversioner brought an action of covenant and recovered.

Then D. brings his bill to have a mitigation of the increased rent, alleging that he had done little or no damage to C. and that he was ignorant of any such covenant. The first allegation appeared to be true, but the other false.

Lord Chancellor [Lord Cowper] decreed D. to pay the increased rent from the time he exceeded the height until the abatement of so much as he has transgressed, but no broken quarters to be paid for. And, if he had paid rent to C. without deducting the taxes, they were to be allowed him before the Master.

## 106

## Herne v. Humphreys

(Ch. 1708–1713)

*A person who pays money to someone who has been adjudicated a bankrupt but not discharged loses that money, but, if the money is paid to the bankrupt's creditor, he is subrogated to the creditor's claim.*

Lincoln's Inn MS. Misc. 9, p. 68, pl. 1

11 May 1708. Herne *et al.*, assignees of the commissioners of bankrupts agent, Shephard, plaintiffs and Sir William Humfreys *et ux.*, executors of Lancashire, Shephard, *et al.*, defendants.

In this case, Shephard's books were produced as evidence against the defendant's testator to prove him indebted to the bankrupt. And this was supported by the oath of the bookkeeper, who swore he made some of the entries and believes he account to be true and the testator indebted. And it was objected that this was no good evidence.

Lord Chancellor [Lord Cowper]: At law, a man's books are evidence in an action for goods sold and delivered where a servant comes and swears that he entered the going out of the goods and believes the account to be true.

Then, it was said that Shephard had by an answer put in to a bill brought against him in another cause confessed that he had made erasures and alterations in his books, and so, in some measure, he has destroyed the evidence of those books.

Lord Chancellor [Lord Cowper]: Was this done before or since his bankruptcy?

It was answered, since.

Lord Chancellor [Lord Cowper]: Why then, what he says signifies nothing. The law says he has no credit. And, as to any facts done since his bankruptcy, they are a mere nullity and signify nothing.

British Library MS. Hargrave 80, f. 169v

In this cause, a distinction was taken and allowed *per curiam* that, where Colonel Lancashire, being indebted to Shepherd, had paid several sums to him after he became a bankrupt, the colonel could have no benefit of those payments, but those sums were entirely lost to him, but, where he paid sums to creditors of Shepherd after the bankruptcy, he might stand in their places *pro tanto* and come in among the other creditors under the commission, paying his contribution.

[Other copies of this report: Lincoln's Inn MS. Misc. 383, p. 291, pl. 1, Lincoln's Inn MS. Misc. 107, p. 13, pl. 1.]

## 107

## Litten v. Lady Falkland

(Ch. 1708)

*A devise of 'lands, tenements, and hereditaments' passes reversions thereto.*

*A will is not valid if the witnesses do not subscribe their names to it in the presence of the testator.*

*A court of equity will supply the lack of a surrender of copyhold lands for the benefit of younger children and charitable uses.*

Lincoln's Inn MS. Misc. 9, p. 68, pl. 2

14 May 1708. Litton v. Dame Frances Russell *et al.* Lord Chancellor [Lord Cowper], assisted by the Chief Justice Trevor, Mr. Justice Tracy, and the Master of the Rolls [Trevor].

Sir William Lytton, having a real estate of £3000 a year, which was entailed by his father by two settlements, one in 1665 and the other in 1672, by which he was tenant in tail, with remainder to himself in fee of part of the lands and, of the other part, the limitations were determined and he was seised in fee, and having also a considerable personal estate, makes his will dated 25 March 1700, whereby he makes the plaintiff, who was the grandson of Philippa Strode, one of the sisters of Sir William Litton, and the defendant, the Lady Russell, executors. And, after some legacies, he gives them his personal estate upon condition as to the plaintiff that he should change his name from Strode to Litton. He likewise gives him all his messuages, lands, and hereditaments out of settlement to hold to him and his heirs upon the same condition of changing his name.

Part of these lands were copyhold, but there was no surrender to the use of the will. Another part of the lands at the time of the will was only a mortgage, but, after the will, Sir William purchased the equity of redemption, but he made no new publication of his will, only he executed a codicil afterwards. But there was no notice taken nor any devise of those lands. Nor was that codicil annexed to the will, nor the will upon the table when the codicil was executed.

The bill was brought against the rest of the co-heirs of Sir William Litton to prove the will. And the questions that arose were three:

First, whether any of the lands in the two settlements passed by this will;

Secondly, whether this court would supply the want of a surrender as to the copyhold;

Thirdly, whether the lands in mortgage purchased after the will passed or no and if the codicil was a new publication of the will.

Serjeant *Hooper*, for the plaintiff: As to the words 'out of settlement', it must be understood lands that were not so tied up by any settlement but that he had the power to devise them. It is plain his intent was to continue his estate in his name and the personal estate which he gave him does not seem to be a sufficient reason to oblige the plaintiff to change his name. Besides, it is plain Sir William Litton has broken in upon those settlements, for he has charged part of those lands with a rent charge to his wife.

He insisted that the codicil was a republication of the will and that the defect of a surrender ought to be supplied for the benefit of a grandson.

Then, the will was read, and a question arose whether parol evidence should be read to explain the testator's meaning.

The Lord Chancellor [Lord Cowper], the two judges [Trevor and Tracy], and the Master of the Rolls [Trevor] agreed the evidence should be read, and they declared that, in case the testator's meaning could be collected from the words of the will, no parol proof should weigh with them to explain the will in any other sense, but, if the words, upon the most mature consideration were so uncertain that it was extremely doubtful what the testator's meaning was, then they would consider how far parol proof should be of force to determine their judgment.

Lord Chancellor [Lord Cowper] cited a case where a man had two sons, both named John, and he gives his lands by his will to his son John. In this case, it is perfectly uncertain which son he meant. And, therefore, rather than the will should be void for uncertainty, parol proof was admitted. Why then, suppose there are words in a will upon which two distinct notions arise in the mind and the judgment is perfectly in an *aequilibrio* and [one] knows not which side to incline to. In such a case, I see no reason why parol proof should not be read. And, if from thence, the judgment may be determined, it seems to be very just and righteous to take such proof in order to bring the judgment to a right determination.

Then, the depositions were read. And the witnesses swore that Sir William Litton had declared that he intended his lands should go as his father had settled them and that he never designed to alter those settlements, for My Lady Falkland was as much his father's daughter as the rest.

Serjeant *Parker*, for the defendant: If the matter should come to an equilibrium, we think our being heirs at law will weight down, for the presumption ought to carry it to the heir at law and no uncertain words shall disinherit him.

*Vernon*, of the same side: Suppose it had been a devise of all the lands under settlement; in that case, the devisee could have had no lands new[ly] purchased. Why then, suppose it had been all the lands not under settlement; the devise could not have extended to any lands comprised in the settlement. And this I take to be the same as out of settlement.

The settlements were not wholly determined at the time of the making of the will, but at the testator's death. And it lies upon the other side to show that the testator plainly intended to give them the lands in the settlements.

As to the copyhold, there is no pretense for that land, for it never was carried so far, even for a child, as to supply the want of a surrender where it was not plain that the testator intended to give away such copyhold, as where he devises the land in particular, and not where there are only general words.

As to the mortgages, at the time of the will, they were only personal estate and, by buying in the equity of redemption afterwards, it was plainly a new purchase, and the will could no more pass those lands than it could any other lands that he had afterwards purchased. But then they tell us he executed a codicil. The codicil had no relation to the lands. I must own, if he had taken notice in that codicil of any purchase made after the will and had declared that such new purchased lands should pass by the general words of his will, it would have been sufficient even though he had not his will then by him. But that is not the case here.

The court took time to consider upon the case and, upon the 16th of June following, gave their judgment, *viz.*:

Mr. Justice TRACY: I am of the opinion that the depositions read in this case ought to be rejected.

I very much doubt whether any uncertainty in a will ought to be set right by collateral proof, for, if such proof is admitted, then I must judge upon parol evidence and not upon the written will, which I think ought not to be. But the words of the will is what the judgment must be upon.

And, therefore, as to the case before us, I am to consider what the testator meant by 'lands out of settlement'. Now, if, by this, you will understand lands not comprised in any settlement, to what time will you go back? It is plain Sir William had no prospect of issue at the time of making his will. And the condition in his will that the plaintiff was to change his name is a plain evidence to me that he intended to give him the bulk of his estate.

Besides, that he intended to give him the Hertfordshire estate, which is in the settlement in 1665, is further evidence, because he has broken into that settlement and given part of those lands to his wife for life and that the reversion thereof passed by the general words in the will. He cited Wheeler and Walrond, Allen 28, and 2 Vent. 285.[1] So that I am of the opinion that all the lands comprised in those settlements in 1665 and 1672 passed by this devise.

As to the other three points, he was of opinion against the plaintiff.

And of the same opinion as to all the points and also as to the parol evidence were the Chief Justice TREVOR, the Master of the Rolls [TREVOR], and the Chancellor [LORD COWPER].

British Library MS. Hargrave 80, f. 13v

[Stroud] Litten, being seised of certain lands in fee, makes a settlement of them upon himself for life, remainder to his wife for life, remainder to his first, second, etc. sons in tail, remainder to himself in fee. And being so seised by virtue of this settlement, he makes his will whereby he devises all his lands, tenements, and hereditaments out of settlement to one Stroud upon condition that he should take upon him the name of Litten and, after due publication of this will, his wife dies without issue, and then he dies.

And it was held that, by this will, passed to the plaintiff not only those lands which were not comprehended in the settlement but also all the estate in those settled which was in the power of the devisor to dispose of by his will, *viz.* his own reversion in fee which, by the failure of the intermediate limitations, was at the time of his death the only interest subsisting; so there passed to the plaintiff a clear fee simple in all those lands.

---

[1] *Wheeler v. Walroone* (1642), Aleyn 28, 82 E.R. 898; *Willows v. Lydcot* (1689), 2 Ventris 285, 86 E.R. 443, also 3 Modern 229, 87 E.R. 148, Carthew 50, 90 E.R. 633, 1 Eq. Cas. Abr. 210, 21 E.R. 996.

The reason was principally because, by the devise of all his lands, tenements, and hereditaments without more, the reversion in these lands would have passed and the following words, which restrain the former to such lands etc. as were out of settlement, do not certainly exclude this reversion which was then out of settlement and was perfectly and absolutely in the power of the devisor by an interest not created by the deed of settlement but resulting by implication and act of law on the settling the precedent estates.

It was insisted pretty much that, because the devisor had required the plaintiff to take his name upon him, that it was therefore to be presumed his intention to give him the bulk of his estate, whereas, if nothing passed but those lands which were not mentioned in the deed of settlement, there would pass but a small estate loaded with half the value.

But how they could come at this reason, *quaere* because it is founded in foreign facts and circumstances that do not appear nor are to be collected from the will itself and they all agreed in this case that as foreign depositions or evidences of facts were to be admitted to explain a will, 5 Co., Cheyney's Case,[1] much less now than before the Statute of Frauds and Perjuries,[2] which provides so strongly and particularly against the mischief of a parol will, for to give a new sense to a will different from what the natural and common acceptation of the words of it are because of collateral circumstances proved by witnesses is in effect to make a new will on parol evidence and to introduce the mischief intended to be remedied by that Statute by rendering men's estates liable to be disposed of contrary to their minds by fraud and perjury.

The authorities cited were 2 Vent. 285, Willows and Lydcot,[3] where the case was this. J.S., being seised in fee of Black Acre and White Acre, devises Black Acre to A. for life and all the rest of his lands, tenements, and hereditaments not above so disposed to B. And [it was] adjudged, by these words, not only White Acre but the reversion of Black Acre passed to B. And Allen 28, Wheeler and Walrond; J.S., being seised in fee of two manors in Somersetshire, devises one to A. for life and then makes other devises and, in the end, devises all the rest of his lands in Somersetshire to B.; by this devise, B. shall take the reversion of the manor devised to A. as well as the other manor.

Another point in this case was this. Litten, being seised of lands by way of mortgage in fee, makes his will in writing whereby he devises all of his lands, tenements, and hereditaments as above and then he purchases the equity of redemption of that mortgage and after[wards] he makes a codicil whereby he ratifies and confirms his will and devises in it £500 and declares that it should be taken as annexed to and part of his will. This codicil he publishes and signs in the presence of three witnesses but at a place where the will was not. The questions were, first, whether

1 *Lord Cheyney's Case* (1591), 5 Coke Rep. 68, 77 E.R. 158, also Moore K.B. 727, 72 E.R. 867.

2 Stat. 29 Car. II, c. 3, s. 5 (*SR*, V, 840).

3 *Willows v. Lydcot* (1689), *ut supra*.

these mortgaged lands whereof the equity of redemption was purchased by the devisor after the publication of his will should pass to the devisee. And [it was] held that they should not but descend to the heir, for, at the time of making this will, he had not any estate in those lands which a court of equity regards, but he had only a right to his money which was a chattel and, if it had continued in that right until his death, [it] should have gone to his executors. But, by his purchase of the equity of redemption, he parted with the right he had before to his money and instead thereof he became seised of an absolute estate in the lands, both in law and equity, perfectly different from what he had when he made his will and such as it could not be in his intention to pass when he had it not.

The second question was whether the publication of the codicil in the manner as above should amount to a republication of the will so as to make this equity of redemption pass which was purchased before that time. And it was held it should not amount to such a republication because, by the words of the Statute of Frauds and Perjuries, a will to pass lands and tenements must be attested and subscribed by three or four witnesses in the presence of the devisor and it cannot be said that the subscribing of this codicil by the witnesses was within the meaning of the Statute a subscribing of the will which was then in another place.

How far the publication of a codicil expressed in the aforesaid words, which is the usual form, may amount to a republication of a will if that be really annexed to it may be a question; it seems that it would.

All these points were unanimously resolved by the Lord Chancellor LORD COWPER, the Master of the Rolls [TREVOR], Chief Justice TREVOR, and Justice TRACY, who assisted the Lord Chancellor in this case.

There was another point in this case, which was whether copyhold lands which he was seised of at the time of making this will should pass by it. But [it was] resolved by the Lord Chancellor, that, though he had gone so far as to supply the want of a surrender to the use of a will for the benefit of younger children and charitable uses, yet he would not extend it any farther.

[Other copies of this report: Lincoln's Inn MS. Misc. 383, p. 23.]

[Other reports of this case: 3 Chancery Reports 169, 21 E.R. 758, 2 Vernon 621, 23 E.R. 1008, 3 Brown P.C. 24, 1 E.R. 1152, 1 Eq. Cas. Abr. 210, 21 E.R. 996.]

## 108

## Ledsome v. Hickman

(Ch. 1708)

*In this case, the devise in issue granted a vested right that survived the death of the legatee in the lifetime of the testator.*

Lincoln's Inn MS. Misc. 11, p. 169

5 June 7 Anne.

William Hickman, by will, gives £300 apiece to the three children of one Henry Strode to be paid them at twenty-one or marriage and, if either of them [die] under twenty-one or unmarried, then the £300 was to go to the survivors.

One of the three children died in the lifetime of the testator. And the question was if the £300 of the child that died should go to the two surviving children or should be looked on as a lapsed legacy.

Lord Cowper decreed the £300 to the survivors. It was a contingent devise, *viz.* that, if either of the three children died before the devise took effect, the legacy of such child shall go amongst the rest.

The survivors shall take it as an original and immediate devise to them, as where lands are devised to one for life, remainder to another in tail or in fee, and the devisee for life dies in the lifetime of the testator, the remainderman shall take as an original devise to him, according to Brett and Rigden's Case in Plowden.[1]

[Other reports of this case: 2 Vernon 611, 23 E.R. 999.]

## 109

## Ingleby v. March

(Ch. 1708)

*Where a Master in Chancery approves an investment of an infant's money, notice of a prior mortgage by the scrivener only does not bind the infant.*

Lincoln's Inn MS. Misc. 9, p. 73, pl. 1

9 June 1708.

There were two mortgages. The first mortgagee, after the second mortgage was made, lends more money, part of which was an infant's money and lent out with the approbation of a Master. And it was proved that Ellecker, the scrivener, who transacted that affair and helped the mortgagor to the money, had notice of the second mortgage.

Lord Chancellor [Lord Cowper]: Notice to the scrivener in this case is not sufficient. It ought to have been given before the Master, who put out the money.

---

[1] *Brett v. Rigden* (1568), 1 Plowden 340, 75 E.R. 516.

## 110

## Holder v. Barker

(Ch. 1708)

*The devise in this case passed only an estate for life, the words of the devise being purely local.*

Lincoln's Inn MS. Misc. 9, p. 73, pl. 2

11 June 1708.

A man, by his will, gives the estate of Moulsgreen to J.S. And the question was if this was an estate for life or in fee.

Lord Chancellor [Lord Cowper]: I think it can be but for life. All the estate of Moulsgreen must be all the estate at Moulsgreen or lying at Moulsgreen. The words are purely local and have not any respect to the estate.

However, let it be tried at law upon a feigned issue.

## 111

## Bishop of Oxford v. Wise

(Ch. 1708)

*A court of equity can order a forged document to be brought into court and be cancelled.*

Lincoln's Inn MS. Misc. 9, p. 75

18 June 1708.

An issue at law was directed to try the validity of a deed which was set up by the defendant and supposed to be made by the bishop's predecessors in Queen Elizabeth's days for a long term of years. And, upon the trial, the deed was found to be forged. And, now, they came back to the court upon the equity reserved and, likewise, upon a petition for a new trial.

Lord Chancellor [Lord Cowper]: I think it is as bold and confident a forgery as ever I saw. And, since the verdict falls in with my judgment, I can never be brought to grant a new trial.

I think the deed ought to be brought into court and cancelled, and let it afterwards remain with the Register as a standing memorial to justify the verdict and the decree of this court.

As to decreeing possession to the plaintiff, which is insisted on, I am in some doubt how far this court has gone in giving possession. And, therefore, I will consider of it.

Then, it was prayed since the decree was pronounced that the deed might forthwith be brought into court and cancelled. And, accordingly, *eo instante*, it was brought into court and cut cross and cross by the Register with a pen knife in whose hands it was then left.

## 112

## Hyde v. Hyde

(Ch. 1708)

*A cancellation of a will must be done with an intent to cancel it.*

*A will that is imperfect to pass real estate may be valid to pass personalty.*

3 Chancery Reports 155, 21 E.R. 755

A man makes his will in writing, and he thereby gives all his real and personal estate to his wife, her heirs, executors, etc. in trust to pay his debts and legacies, and he devises several legacies to his children and other persons, and concludes 'in witness whereof I have to this my last will and testament, containing nine sheets of paper, and to a duplicate thereof, to be left in the hands of [such a one], set my seal in the presence of three witnesses', who all subscribed their names in due form of law. Afterwards, the testator being minded to add other trustees to his wife and make some little alterations in his will, sends for a scrivener, and he gives him directions to prepare a draught of instructions for another will, which the scrivener did accordingly. And he brings the paper of instructions to the testator, which he read over and approved very well, and he set his hand to it.

And, being at a tavern, thinking he now had made a new will, he pulls out of his pocket the first will, and tears off the seals from the first eight sheets, which the scrivener seeing asked him, what he was doing. 'Why', says he, 'I am cancelling my first will.' 'Pray', says the scrivener, 'hold your hand; the other will is not perfected; it will not pass your real estate for want of being subscribed and executed pursuant to the Statute of Frauds and Perjuries.'[1] 'Say you so', says the testator, 'I am sorry for that.' And he, immediately, desisted from tearing off any more of the seals. And, in some short time after, he dies without having done any further act to perfect the second will or cancel the first.

After his death, on application to the spiritual court by the wife, who was made executrix of this last will, they sentenced it a good will, as to the personal estate, and admitted her to prove it.

And, now, this bill was brought by the legatees against the wife and other trustees to have a specific performance of the trust in the first will and that the estate might be sold pursuant to the directions of that will and their legacies be paid them.

1 Stat. 29 Car. II, c. 3, s. 6 (*SR*, V, 840).

It was insisted that that will was revoked by making the other and that the other, though there were the same legacies given out of the lands thereby demised to be sold, was not sufficient to pass the real estate or make any charge upon it, for want of the circumstances required by the Statute of Frauds and Perjuries.

*Sir Joseph Jekyll* urged that the last sheet of the first will was avoided by the tearing off the seals from the eight first sheets, for, when, in the last sheets, he refers the execution of it as his will to his sealing of every sheet as the signal or testimonial of its being his last will, if any of these signals fail or are destroyed, the whole will becomes void. And, here, he has torn off eight of the seals. Besides, the Statute of Frauds and Perjuries having four words, *viz.* burning, cancelling, tearing, or obliterating, and that, by any of these, the first will is to be avoided, here are two of those acts, for here is tearing and cancelling. And so the first will is defeated and avoided.

Mr. *Cowper*, on the other side, insisted that, though the original will shall by this act be supposed to be cancelled, yet here being no *animus cancellandi* or *revocandi* and that, as soon as he was told of it, he desisted and went no farther, that the duplicate thereof, which he took notice of in his will, remaining entire and un-defaced in the hands of the party to whom it was delivered shall be sufficient to pass the real estate.

Mr. *Williams*, on the same side, insisted, that it should be only a revocation *pro tanto*, for so much as the seals were torn off from and no more and that, for the last sheet, it should remain a good will, for a man may revoke part of his will if he pleases and yet the rest stand good.

And Mr. *Gilbert* said that sealing of all the sheets was not essentially necessary to the perfection of the will, but only to the last sheet, and that it remains entire and absolutely perfect and executed, and that he had not any intention of cancelling the will, for that, when he was told of the consequence, he desisted. And the last sheet was only essential for the making the will remain entire. And, therefore, it cannot be said to be cancelled, but it shall be good and essential to all intents and purposes, the essential part which makes a will still remaining.

Serjeant *Hooper* cited a case in the [Court of] Common Bench since the Revolution, where a man made his will in due form and afterwards made another will, whereby he revoked the first will. But the last will had but two witnesses, and it was adjudged no revocation, for that Statute was made on purpose to take away all constructions of a man's intentions, where the form of the Statute was not exactly pursued.

But my Lord Chancellor [Lord Cowper] wondered how that could come to be the question, and he thought he was mistaken, since the Statute is express, that no will shall be revoked by a subsequent will unless such subsequent will be signed and attested by three or more witnesses. And, in the principal case, he decreed this tearing off the eight sheets the seals to be no cancelling of his first will, not being done *animo cancellandi*. As soon as he was told of it that the other would not be sufficient to pass his real estate, he immediately desisted, and left the last sheet entire and uncancelled. And he took this difference, that, for the whole personal estate, this making of the second will was a sufficient revocation of the first *in toto* and that it should not be taken to be a good will as to part of the personal estate and no will or revocation as to the other part of the personal estate, for his intention should not be taken by halves. And, since the spiritual court has sentenced it a good will of the personal estate, it must be good for the whole. And such legatees of the personalties in the first will as are left out in the second must lose their legacies, but, for those that had legacies by the first will chargeable upon the real estate, if the same legacies were devised to them by the second will, that they should still continue chargeable on the real estate and should be raised out of it. And so he said it would be, whether their legacies were increased or diminished, they being by the second will made chargeable upon and to be raised out of the real estate likewise, which, though it was not sufficient to charge the real estate in itself, yet, since the real estate remained well devised by the first will, they should be still secured by that real estate, for they were not out of lands like a rent, but only secured by land, which, he said, was well devised. But, for other new absolute personal legacies devised by the last will, they should be chargeable only upon the personal estate, and should have the preference to be first paid out of the personal estate before the other legacies in the first will upon the real estate, because they had their several funds out of which they were to be paid, the personal legacies in the last will out of the personal estate, which was well devised by that will and the legacies charged upon or secured upon the real estate, which was well devised by the first will, out of the real estate.

And all agreed that the second will, though not sealed and subscribed, as the Statute of Frauds and Perjuries directs, yet it is good for the personal estate, it being *casus omissus* out of the Statute and then it was good at common law.

[Other copies of this report: 1 Eq. Cas. Abr. 409, 21 E.R. 1139.]

2 Comyns 455, 92 E.R. 1157

A man, having made and duly executed a will of his real and personal estate, had a mind to change a trustee and make some alterations. And, for that intent, he sent for a scrivener, gave him instructions for a new will, who drew up another will pursuant to them, read it over to the testator, by whom it was approved and signed, and who then took the old will out of his pocket, tore the seal from off eight sheets of it. But, before he had torn off the seal from the ninth and last sheet, the scrivener asked what he did; the second was not yet perfected. And he died before it was so.

And it was held that the last not being executed according to the Statute 29 Car. II and, consequently, not sufficient to pass his real estate, was no revocation of the former will, and, though the seals were torn off from eight of the sheets of the first will in order to cancel it, yet that not being done with the intent of cancelling, unless the second will was good, should not amount to a cancelling.

## 113

## Turner v. Jennings

(Ch. 1708)

*An assignment made in fraud of a local custom is void and will be set aside.*

British Library MS. Hargrave 80, f. 130v

A freeman of London, having but one child, a daughter, and grandchildren by a son, who was dead, made an assignment of a leasehold estate in trust for himself during his life, then, in trust for his grandchildren.

And this assignment, though for a provision for his grandchildren by his son, who could not come in with his daughter on the foot of the custom, was set aside as made in fraud of the custom.

[Other copies of this report: Lincoln's Inn MS. Misc. 383, p. 230, Lincoln's Inn MS. Misc. 106, p. 194.]

[Other reports of this case: 2 Vernon 612, 685, 23 E.R. 1000, 1044, 1 Eq. Cas. Abr. 152, 21 E.R. 952.]

## 114

## Webster v. Mitford

(Ch. 1708)

*A contract to make a bequest of a personal estate includes the personalty owned at the time of the contract as well as what is owned at the time of the testator's death.*

*A fund forfeited by an election to take against the will will be sequestered for the compensation of those legatees whom that election disappointed.*

2 Eq. Cas. Abr. 362, 22 E.R. 308

Trinity 7 Ann. [1708].

A., by marriage articles, engages himself to leave his wife a moiety of his personal estate at his death and, being possessed of an annuity in the Exchequer, disposed of it by deed poll in his lifetime. Afterwards, he made his will and, thereby, devised to his wife certain lands for life upon condition that she should not make any demand upon the articles against his executor, and, after her decease, he devised the lands to B. and gives several legacies. And he dies. The wife waives the devise, and insists upon the articles.

The question was whether the wife should have one moiety of the personal estate which the husband had at the time he entered into the articles or only a moiety of the personal estate he died possessed of.

Lord Chancellor [Lord Cowper]: The annuity must be accounted a part of the personal estate the wife is to have a moiety of, for, were she to have but a moiety of the personal estate the husband should leave at his death, it would be in the power of him to defeat the articles by alienation or gift. The reason of inserting 'at his death', was to explain he meant only a moiety of his estate at his death which has escaped misfortunes and losses.

The wife's waiving the devise and being let in upon the personal estate, wrought a deficiency, in the legacy.

Lord Chancellor [LORD COWPER] thought it the highest equity that B., who had by the waiver gained the possession of an estate of which he would have had but a reversion if the wife had accepted the devise, should contribute what he was benefited by the waiver towards raising a fund for payment of the legacies. And His Lordship [LORD COWPER] thought £4000 in reversion worth but £3000 in possession. And he decreed that, according to this estimate, the value of the lands being settled by the Master should be charged if the legacies require it.

1 Swanston 445, 36 E.R. 454

June 1708.

The testator directed the sum of £4000 to be invested in the purchase of lands, one moiety of the rents of which was to be paid to his widow and the other moiety to Elizabeth Webster and Jane Richardson, during their lives, with remainder, after the determination of those estates, to Mary Harrison and Winifred Webster and an express proviso that, if his widow insisted on her marriage agreement, the bequest to her should be void, and, in such case, the moiety originally devised to her was limited to Elizabeth Webster and Jane Richardson and, after their death, to descend as the other moiety.

The widow electing to take a moiety of her husband's personal estate, to which she was entitled under her marriage settlement and that demand having caused a deficiency in the funds for the payment of legacies, the court directed that such part of the profits of the sum of £4000 as by the will was intended for the widow should be applied during her life towards supplying the deficiency. In this case, the widow's election, by the express words of the will, operated a forfeiture.

Yet the court assumed jurisdiction to qualify the effect of that forfeiture and, instead of permitting it, by determining her interest, to accelerate the enjoyment of the estates in remainder, sequestered her interest for compensation to those whom her election disappointed and assumed that jurisdiction, according to the only printed note[1] of the judgment, on general principles of equity.

This decision, therefore, established the principle that the fund forfeited, though under an express proviso, by an election to take against the will, should be sequestered for compensation to those whom that election disappointed.

[1] The report at 2 Eq. Cas. Abr. 362, 22 E.R. 308, which was copied here.

1 Swanston 449, 36 E.R. 460

22 June 1708. Elizabeth Webster, widow, Jane Richardson, widow, and others, plaintiffs; Margaret Mitford and others, defendants.

Upon the hearing etc., the substance of the plaintiffs' bill appeared to be that Michael Mitford, late brother of the plaintiffs, Elizabeth Webster, and Jane Richardson, and the defendant Margaret Mitford's late husband, did in February 1706 make his will in writing, and, reciting that, upon his marriage with the defendant, Margaret, he did make some articles or agreement for securing £1200 which he had in portion with her or leaving her some other consideration in lieu thereof. Therefore, in full performance of the said articles of agreement, he did devise unto the said defendant, Margaret, his wife, the lease of his house at Clapham and all his estate and interest in the said house and all his plate, rings, linen, bedding, and other household goods whatsoever and also £100 *per annum* issuing out of the Exchequer, which he purchased for the said defendant, Margaret's, life upon the Act of Parliament for tonnage[1] with the order and tally. And he devised unto his executors, George Mertins, Thomas Nisbett, and William Mitford, whom he also appointed trustees, the sum of £4000 upon trust that his said executors should with all convenient speed after his decease purchase lands of inheritance in fee simple of the yearly value of £200 or thereabout in some northern county within sixty miles of Newcastle upon Tyne, where he was born, to be settled in such manner as might best answer his will and that the interest and proceeds of the said £4000 until such purchase made should be paid to such persons and in such manner as the rents and profits of the lands, when purchased, were devised and were made payable.

And he did devise one moiety of the rents and profits of the lands so to be purchased unto the defendant, Margaret, his wife, for her life, subject, nevertheless, to the proviso in the will and hereafter mentioned and the other moiety to the plaintiffs, Elizabeth Webster and Jane Richardson, his two sisters, for life, equally to be divided between them and to be by them held and enjoyed severally as tenants in common without benefit of survivorship and from the determination of the said several estates and as the same should severally drop by the deaths of the said parties, such part immediately to descend and come to the plaintiffs, Mary Harrison and Winifred Webster, his two nieces, to be equally received and enjoyed between them. But, in case the plaintiff, Mary Harrison, should marry any person, who, by his family, should be a gentleman of the name of Mitford or Midford by birth then all and singular the said premises so to be purchased as aforesaid, should after the respective deaths of the defendant, Margaret, and of the plaintiffs, Elizabeth and Jane, descend and come to and be enjoyed by the said Mary and such husband for and during their natural lives and the life of the longer liver of them and, from and after their decease, to the first son of the body

[1] Stat. 5 & 6 Will. & Mar., c. 20 (*SR*, VI, 483–495).

of the said Mary by such husband, which first son he desired might be christened by the name of Michael, and to the heirs male of the body of such first son, and, for default of such issue, to the second and every other son and sons of the body of the said Mary by such husband and the heirs male of the body of such sons successively in tail male, provided that, if the said Plaintiff, Mary, should not by her first marriage intermarry with one of the name and family aforesaid or, in case she should and such husband should happen to die without such issue male as aforesaid, then the said premises so to be purchased as aforesaid should descend and come to the plaintiff, Winifred, upon the same terms, and, in case neither of his said nieces should by their first marriage intermarry with one of the name and family aforesaid or if they should both happen to die without such issue male as aforesaid, then the said premises so to be purchased should descend and come to his cousin, the plaintiff, Michael Mitford, for life and to the first, second, and every other son and sons of the said plaintiff, Michael Mitford, and the heirs male of the body of such sons successively in tail male, and, for want of such issue, to his own right heirs forever.

And the testator, by his said will, declared that the said bequests thereby given to his wife should be in full recompense of what she might or could claim by virtue of the said articles or agreement or otherwise howsoever, and that, if she refused to accept the same, then all and every the devises and bequests aforesaid should become absolutely void as to his said wife. And, in such case, he devised the moiety of the rents and profits of the premises to be purchased and devised as aforesaid to his wife to the plaintiffs, Elizabeth Webster and Jane Richardson, in such manner as the other moiety is devised to them and, after their deaths, to descend and go in such manner as the said other moiety is limited. And, as to the other legacies devised to his wife (in case the same became void as aforesaid), the same to go to the plaintiffs, his two sisters and two nieces, equally among them. And he gave to his said two sisters and the survivor of them the £25 *per annum*, which he purchased in their names and for their lives upon the Act of Parliament for tonnage with the tally and order for the same and £50 apiece to buy them mourning and to the plaintiff, Mary Harrison, £600 and to the plaintiff, Winifred Webster, £400, to be paid at their respective ages of twenty-one years or marriage, which should first happen, and, if either of them should die before marriage, her legacy to go to the survivor, and, if either of them should marry without the consent of her mother, if living, to forfeit and lose one-half of her legacy, which was to go and be paid to her sister, and that the said several sums should be put out at interest upon good security to be approved by the executors until the same should become payable and, the interest thereof, in the meantime, to be applied for their maintenance. And, after several other legacies given to other persons in the bill named, he gave all the rest and residue of his real and personal estate unto his said wife, two sisters, and two nieces, equally among them, share and share alike, and to the minister and churchwardens of the parish where he should die £50 to be laid out in such manner and for such uses as in the will is particularly directed.

And, in August 1707, the said Michael Mitford died without issue. The defendants, Mertins and Nisbett, two of the executors, proved his will and took upon them the execution thereof. In September 1694, the said testator paid into the Exchequer as a contribution the sum of £208 6s. 8d. upon an Act of Parliament then lately passed for granting several rates and duties for tonnage of ships and vessels, for which said sum of £208 6s. 8d., the said testator had a tally and order out of the Exchequer to entitle him to receive the annual sum of £25 during the lives of the plaintiffs, Elizabeth Webster and Jane Richardson, his two sisters, and the life of the longer liver of them, who were nominees for him in the said order. And the said testator, designing the benefit of the said annuity for them after his decease, did by deed poll under his hand and seal, dated the 30th of May 1695, declare and agree that the said annuity should be to the use and benefit of himself for life and, after his decease, to the use and benefit of his mother, Mary Mitford, and the plaintiff, Elizabeth Webster, equally, and, after the death of his said mother, then to the use and benefit of his said two sisters, Elizabeth Webster and Jane Richardson, equally between them.

The said Mary Mitford, the mother, died in the lifetime of the testator. And, the said testator being also dead, the plaintiffs, Elizabeth Webster and Jane Richardson, are advised that they are entitled to the said £25 annuity in their own right, by virtue of the said deed poll. The defendants, the executors, having possessed themselves of the said testator's personal estate and of the said tally and order, the plaintiffs expected that they would have applied the same according to the testator's will. But the defendants, by contrivance together, pretend that the said will cannot be performed, in regard, by an agreement made by the testator on his marriage with the defendant, Margaret, he did agree to leave her one full moiety of his estate, and that the said will cannot bind the said defendant, Margaret, or exclude her from the benefit of the said marriage agreement, whereas, if any such agreement was made, the same was voluntary and subsequent to the testator's marriage and unfairly obtained. And, therefore, the defendants, the executors, may deliver to the plaintiffs, Elizabeth Webster and Jane Richardson, the aforesaid tally and order and to have a discovery and an account of the said testator's personal estate and that the same may be applied according to the directions of the said will and to be delivered in the premises is the scope of the plaintiffs' bill.

Whereupon, it was insisted by the defendant's counsel that the defendant, Margaret Mitford, by her answer, says she believes that the said Michael Mitford, her late husband, was at the time of his death possessed of a plentiful personal estate and that, before his death, he made his will in writing to the effect in the bill set forth, but insists that the said will ought not in anywise to affect this Defendant, for that, before her intermarriage with the said testator, *viz.* in or about the 6th of December 1686, the testator did enter into an agreement by deed poll, whereby, in consideration of the intended marriage with this defendant and of her marriage portion, he did covenant and agree with this defendant and with P.W. and J.O. that he, the said Michael Mitford, should and would in and by his last will and testament or by good and sufficient assurances and conveyances in the law or otherwise, before his death, if this defendant should him survive, give, grant, convey, assure, and leave for the use of the defendant the one full and clear moiety or half part of all his estate in lands, houses, hereditaments, goods, chattels, money, and estate whatsoever as he, the said Michael Mitford, or any other person or persons whatsoever for him or to his use should stand or be seised or possessed by any ways or means whatsoever and that in such ample and beneficial manner as that this defendant, her heirs, executors, administrators, or assigns, at all times after the death of the said Michael Mitford, should and might quietly hold and enjoy and dispose of the same as her and their own proper estate without any let or molestation whatsoever, and she says that the said deed poll or marriage agreement was precedent to the said marriage and in consideration of a marriage portion and to the intent as is expressed in and by the said marriage settlement. And, therefore, she hopes she shall not be compelled to accept the provision made her by the will or be excluded from the benefit of the said marriage agreement. And she says that she is willing to come to a fair account with the plaintiffs, touching her late husband's personal estate, and is willing that the same shall be applied according to his will, deducting first a moiety, according to the said marriage agreement, and that the said will should be performed as to the other moiety as far as may be and the plaintiffs have the benefit thereof.

And the defendants, Mertins and Nisbett, by their answer, do say that they believe that the said Michael Mitford did make his will as in the bill is set forth and appoint these defendants and the defendant, William Mitford, executors thereof and that the said defendant, William Mitford, the other executor, being at the time of the testator's death in the north of England, at a great distance from London, these defendants did, therefore, prove the said will without him and did possess themselves of such part of the testator's personal estate as they could come by. And they have defrayed the charges of the testator's funeral and paid several debts owing by the said testator. And they say that, in a schedule annexed to their answer, they have set forth a true account of the goods, chattels, and personal estate of the said testator, which has any way come to their hands, as also an account of what debts they have paid, and what debts are still owing by the testator, and, likewise, an account of the funeral charges and that, among the debts owing, they have inserted a bond entered into by the testator to Her Majesty of £2000 penalty conditioned for Mr. C.C. faithfully demeaning himself in his employment of commissioner of prizes at Leghorn. And these defendants do insist to retain so much of the testator's assets in their hands as shall be sufficient to answer that demand in case the crown shall have occasion to resort to them for the same or otherwise, that these defendants may be effectually indemnified against the said demand as also against another bond of £300 penalty to M.C.

And they say that they were willing to have performed the said will as far as was in their power, but the defendant, Margaret Mitford, has produced and does insist on her marriage agreement in her answer before set forth, whereby she claims a moiety of the said testator's estate, wherefore these defendants crave the direction and judgment of this court touching the construction of the said will and the application of the said testator's personal estate. And these defendants believe that the said testator did pay into the Exchequer, as a contribution, £208 6s. 8d. upon security of the Act of Parliament in the bill mentioned, and that he had an order and tally for receiving £25 *per annum* during the lives of the plaintiffs, Elizabeth Webster and Jane Richardson, as nominees for the testator, which said tally and order are in these defendants' custody, and that the said testator did execute such deed poll, concerning the said annuity as in the bill is set forth, and that, therefore, these defendants submit to the judgment of this court whether the plaintiffs, Elizabeth Webster and Jane Richardson, are become entitled in their own right to the said annuity or whether the same is to be esteemed part of the said testator's estate.

And the defendant, William Mitford, by his answer says that, being named one of the executors of the said Michael Mitford's will, he has proved the said will and intends to act as an executor so far as to see the said will performed, according to the directions and true meaning thereof and pursuant to the trust reposed in him for the benefit of all parties concerned therein. But he says that he has not hitherto at any time possessed himself of any part of the said testator's personal estate or of any of the rents or profits of the real estate or any way intermeddled therewith otherwise than by proving the will as aforesaid and that he is ready to do as this court shall direct, being indemnified by the decree of this court.

Whereupon and upon reading the will of the said testator, Michael Mitford, the agreement or deed poll made by the said testator before his marriage with the defendant, Margaret Mitford, dated the 6th of December 1686, and the deed executed by the said testator concerning the annuity of £25 *per annum* issuing out of the Exchequer, as also the proofs taken in this cause, and hearing what was alleged by the counsel for all the said parties, this court declared that, inasmuch as the defendant, Margaret Mitford, has renounced all benefit by the testator's will and does insist upon the agreement or articles made by the said testator before and in consideration of his marriage with her, the said defendant, Margaret Mitford, ought to have one full moiety of the said testator's estate after his debts and funeral charges and the £50 to the parish of Clapham, hereafter mentioned, paid according to the said agreement, and does, therefore, order and decree that it be referred to Samuel Kerb, Esq., to take an account of the estate whereof the said testator, Michael Mitford, died seised or possessed and that the defendants, the executors, do severally account before the said Master for what thereof has in any way come to their respective hands or possession or to the hands or possession of any other person or persons to or for their or either of their use or in trust for them to their knowledge by their procurement or with their privity, in the taking of which account, the said Master is to make to the said executors all just allowances, and the said defendants, the executors, and also the defendant, Margaret Mitford, the widow, are to be examined upon interrogatories before the said Master for the better discovery thereof and of other the personal estate of the said testator, in the taking of which account, the said Master is to make unto the said other defendant all just allowances, and the said defendant, William Mitford, one of the said executors, is to have notice from time to time to the end that he may attend the Master upon the said account if he shall think fit.

And this court now declared that the two annuities of £100 and £25 *per annum* issuing out of the Exchequer are to be looked upon and taken as part of the said testator's personal estate and are to be brought into the account thereof. And the said Master is to examine and certify what the said testator's debts and funeral charges with the legacy to Clapham parish do amount unto and to make a deduction thereof and what the said testator's whole estate, after a deduction of the said debts and legacies and funeral charges, shall amount unto.

It is ordered and decreed that the defendant, Margaret Mitford, shall receive and enjoy one full moiety thereof according to the said marriage agreement, and, in case the said defendant, Margaret Mitford, should desire to have any part of the said personal estate, which was specifically devised to her by the will, she is to have the same at the appraised value in part of her said moiety. And, as to the other moiety, it is ordered and decreed that £4000 thereof or so much as the other moiety shall amount to of such £4000 be laid out by the defendants, the executors and trustees, in the purchase of lands to be settled according to the uses and limitations in the will in all respects, which purchase is to be approved of by the said Master. And the said executors are hereby indemnified in the making thereof, except as to that part of the said £4000 to be laid out by the said will, which, by the said will, was to be enjoyed by the defendant, Margaret Mitford, for her life and, in case the moiety of the said testator's estate, which the said testator had power to dispose of by will, shall not be sufficient to answer and make good the said £4000, then the several legatees in the will, whose legacies are above £10, are to defalk in proportion out of their respective legacies to make up the said £4000, but there is to be no defalcation out of any legacy of the value of £10 or under already paid or hereafter to be paid.

And, as to such part of the profits and benefit of the said £4000, which, by the said will, was intended for the defendant, Margaret Mitford, during her life, it is ordered and decreed that the same do go and be applied during the said defendant, Margaret's life towards making good to the several legatees what shall be so defalked out of their legacies for the making up the said £4000.

And, as to the £2000 bond entered into by the testator to the crown upon the account and as security for C.C. in the pleadings named, it is ordered and decreed that the defendant, Margaret Mitford, do give security to be approved by the said Master to indemnify the defendants, the executors, as to the moiety of the said bond or demand and that the plaintiffs, Elizabeth Webster, Jane Richardson, Mary Harrison, and Winifred Webster do give security also to be approved of by the said Master to indemnify the said defendants, the executors, as to the other moiety thereof. The said securities are to be also against any dormant debts of the said testator.

And it is hereby referred to the said Master to approve and take the security so to be given for the said parties. And, as to the £50 legacy given by the will to the parish where the testator died, it is ordered and decreed that the same be paid out of the said testator's personal estate unto the minister and churchwardens of the parish of Clapham to be by them laid out in the purchase of lands for the uses and purposes directed by the said will.

And it is further ordered that the Master do tax all parties their costs of this suit which are to be paid to them respectively out of the estate in question as also the costs of the said account, and, for what the executors shall act or do in pursuance of this decree, they are hereby indemnified.

[Reg. Lib. B 1707, f. 352.]

## 115

## Baile v. Coleman

(Ch. 1708–1711)

*In this case, the devise in issue created an estate tail and not a life estate.*

Lincoln's Inn MS. Misc. 177, p. 148

26 July 1708, by Lord Cowper and, afterwards, on rehearing, by Lord Harcourt on 28 April 1711. Register's Book 1710 Lib. A, 309.

William Stawell, by will, on 2nd June 1702, devised to four trustees and their heirs all his manors and lands to the intent they should by sale or leasing pay his debts and the residue of the premises to the same four persons, their heirs, and assigns equally to be divided between them. By codicil of the same 10th June 1702, the testator declared his will to be, after his debts be paid and a dividend made of the remainder of the premises, that notwithstanding the express words of the will to 'Elizabeth Bale [one of the four trustees], her heirs, and assigns forever', his meaning was that such part as should fall to the share of the said Elizabeth should be and remain to the said Elizabeth for her life with a power to make leases for 99 years determinable on three lives and, after her death, to the plaintiff, Christopher Bale, her son, for life, with like power to make leases, remainder 'to the heirs male of his body' lawfully to be begotten and, for default of such issue, to Coleman and Bogan and their heirs equally to be divided between them.

Christopher Bale, the son of Elizabeth, was plaintiff in the cause.

And the defendant Coleman insisted that he ought only to have by the conveyance to be executed an estate for life limited to him with remainder to his first etc. sons and the heirs male of the body of such sons successively, with remainder to the defendants Coleman and Bogan and their heirs.

Upon the hearing of the cause by my Lord Cowper in 1708, he was of that opinion and decreed that there should be a partition of the residue of the estate and that the shares should be conveyed in this manner, *viz.* one-fourth to the defendant Coleman, two-fourths to Bogan, and the remaining fourth to Elizabeth Bale, the plaintiff's mother, that this last fourth part should be settled to the use of Elizabeth Bale for life with the power of leasing and, after her decease, to the plaintiff, Christopher, her son, for life with like power of leasing and, after his decease, to the first and every other son of his body and the heirs male of the body of every such son successively and, for default of such issue, to the defendants Coleman and Bogan and their heirs as tenants in common.

April 1711. Reheard by Lord Harcourt.

[It was] ordered that Lord Cowper's decree, so far as it directed a conveyance of the last fourth part to the first and every other son of Christopher Bale, should be reversed and instead thereof it should be conveyed after the death of Christopher to the use of the 'heirs male of the body' of the said Christopher and, for default of such issue, to the use of Coleman and Bogan and their heirs as tenants in common. In this decree, my Lord Harcourt has caused his reasons to be very minutely entered, and, from these, the plaintiff's counsel have argued more than from the judgment itself. The declarations are these.

> His Lordship declared that this case arising upon the words of a will was much different from the several cases decreed in this court upon marriage articles, that such articles are always intended to be carried into a farther and more perfect execution, that the parties to such articles are to be considered as purchasers, and, in a court of equity, ought to have their contracts executed according to the intent and the nature and course of marriage articles and settlements, in making whereof the issue male of the marriage are particularly regarded and generally taken as purchasers, that, when, by the careless penning of marriage articles, the contract is expressed in consideration of an intended marriage and portion to settle the husband's estate to the use of him and his intended wife and the heirs male of their bodies or the like, that generally limitation has been restrained in this court when an execution of the marriage of the marriage articles and agreement has been decreed to an estate to the [ *blank* ] for life, with a remainder to his first and other sons in tail male, for that it could not reasonably be supposed a valuable consideration was agreed to be given to have an estate so settled, that the husband might destroy or bar the settlement as soon as he should make it, but that no one case had been cited where the like decree had been made upon the words of a will under which the devisees claimed voluntarily, that,

in this case, the question arose upon the words of a codicil, and that all wills ought to be construed according to the intent of the testator, so as such intent appears with certainty and be consistent with the rules of law, but such intent could be no otherwise considered in a court of equity than in the courts of law, and that the same words of limitation in a will ought to receive the same construction in a court of equity as they have at law, that the same words in a will which at law would create a legal entail ought to be so construed by this court when they fall under a trust and are to be carried into farther execution, as in the present case, by the words of the codicil, according to the known rule of construction of law, the testator has given the plaintiff an estate tail in Elizabeth Bale's share, after her decease and subject to her power of leasing, and that, in this case, it could not be inferred with any certainty from the power of leasing given by the Statute 30 Hen. VIII[1] to tenants in tail, and, it being admitted that the debts and legacies are paid, therefore, the same construction ought to be made as if no trust had been, and, then, in construction of law, it will be an estate tail executed.

Lincoln's Inn MS. Misc. 10, p. 60

26 April 1711; Coleman v. Baile.

A., by his will, gave lands to trustees and their heirs subject to the payment of his debts and legacies. And, after payment thereof, he directs that they shall convey to his four children and their heirs equally as tenants in common. And then, by a codicil, he takes notice of this devise and declares his intent to be that, as to the share of one of them, it should be conveyed to her for life with a power to make leases and, after his death, to her son for life with the like power, then to the heirs male of the body of the son, with remainders over.

The Lord Chancellor Cowper, upon hearing this case, was of opinion that the intention of the testator was that the son should be only a tenant for life, with a remainder to his first and other sons in tail, and he decreed the conveyance to be made accordingly in that manner, for he considered it as if it had been upon marriage articles.

But, upon a petition for a rehearing, the Lord Keeper [Lord Harcourt] now reversed that decree and declared that a trust estate in a will must be construed in the same manner as a legal estate would be construed at common law. And there is no doubt but such a limitation of an estate at law would be an estate tail.

The intention of the testator ought to be considered in the exposition of a will. But then, this intent must be plain and manifest and must be governed by the rules of law.

---

[1] Stat. 32 Hen. VIII, c. 28 (*SR*, III, 784–786).

In this case was cited the Case of Legatt and Sewell, *quod vide ante* 41, as also Sir John Hobart's Case upon Serjeant Maynard's will,[1] wherein there was a direction that lands should be conveyed to A. for ninety-nine years if he etc., remainder to the heirs male of his body with remainders over, they came into this court to have an execution of the trust, and the court considered what was the intent of the testator, and, in regard that, if a settlement had been made according to the letter of the will, the limitation to the heirs male would have been void, there being no freehold to support that remainder, the court directed that there should be a limitation to trustees and their heirs during the life of the tenant for life to support the contingent remainders. This went up into the House of Lords and was there affirmed.

British Library MS. Hargrave 80, f. 27v, pl. 2

This case came before the court upon a rehearing and was thus. Stowel devised all his real and personal estate to four and their heirs in trust to lease or sell for the payment of debts and the surplus to them and their heirs equally to be divided. Afterwards, by a codicil, taking notice of his will, he appoints the share of the first of the four to be to her for her life, with a power to make leases for 99 years, remainder to the plaintiff for life with like power, remainder to the heirs male of the plaintiff etc.

One of the four being an infant, an Act of Parliament was obtained to enable him to join in sale or leases. The tenant for life and the plaintiff joined in a fine to make a tenant to the *praecipe* and suffered a common recovery. The tenant for life died, and the plaintiff now brings this bill to ascertain the surplus and have a division. The single point in question was whether the plaintiff took an estate tail by the will or for life only, remainder in tail for his first son etc.

Serjeant *Hooper*, for the defendant: No lawyer ever made a question where an estate is limited to a man for life, remainder to his heirs male, but that it is an estate tail in him, and there is nobody who is not a lawyer but thinks otherwise. Now, the testator was not a lawyer. This, he said, was an executory trust and that it was the constant course of that court to direct the execution of executory trusts according to the intention of the parties, that, in the Case of Pym and Pym,[2] when a bond was conditioned for settling an estate upon a marriage and, in several other cases of marriage articles, this court had always directed the conveyance to be made pursuant to the intention of the parties. The power of leasing was urged as a proof of the devisor's intention that the plaintiff should have but an estates for life etc.

---

[1] *Legat v. Shewell* (Ch. 1706–1710), see above, Case No. 52; *Hobart v. Earl of Stamford* (1709), see below, Case No. 161.

[2] *Pym v. Pym* (Ch. 1705), see above, Case No. 39.

*Sir Thomas Powys*, for the plaintiff: He said that, in the case of King v. Melling,[1] there was a devise to Melling for life, remainder to the issues of his body etc. and there [it was] insisted that it was but an estate for life, the word 'issue' not necessarily implying an estate tail, and Hale was overruled by the other three judges in the King's Bench, but, in the Exchequer Chamber, it was adjudged an estate tail as to executory trusts. He cited the case of Legal and Shewin,[2] where the testator, having a great personal estate, devised the residue of it after to be laid out in the purchase of lands in fee to be settled on his nephew for life and, after his death, upon the heirs male of his body and their heirs male and, for default of such issue, upon his brother Henry in tail; the nephew obtained a decree from the commissioners for the residue of the personal estate upon this ground that, if it was vested in land, he would be tenant in tail and have it in his power to bar the entail at his pleasure. The nephew dies without issue, and Henry brings his bill, and the judges, upon its being referred to them whether it would be an estate tail if lands were devised by these words, certifying that it would, Henry's bill was dismissed. This point was thus adjudged in regard to the general precedents of the court at that time. But My Lord Cowper decreed the money to be vested in land in regard of the possibility of the tenant in tail dying without issue before he comes of age or bar[ring] the entail [so] that he in the remainder might have his chance.

*Sir Thomas Powys* further urged the inconveniences that would necessarily ensue if the same words in a will should have different constructions in law and equity and that the devise of a term and the limitation of the trust of a term were guided by the same rules.

Mr. *Vernon* argued from the words of the will 'I give and bequeath' that it was an immediate and not an executory devise and admitted that, in the cases of marriage articles, when the intention of the parties for the benefit of the issue was apparent, equity had taken a latitude in directing the conveyances in such manner that the remainder may be preserved to them. But that, he said, arose from its being a contract and the issue purchasers, that the will was but of one side and the devise voluntary, and that it was true that no words in that will ought to be rejected and that those which gave the power of leasing would have their effect if this was construed an estate tail since a tenant in tail could not make such leases without such particular power.

Lord Keeper [Lord Harcourt]: I have as great a deference to the judgment of my predecessor as any man living, but, while I sit here, I must be guided by my own judgment.

---

[1] *King v. Melling* (1672), 1 Ventris 214, 225, 86 E.R. 144, 151, 2 Levinz 58, 83 E.R. 448, 3 Keble 42, 52, 95, 84 E.R. 584, 589, 614, Pollexfen 101, 86 E.R. 526, 3 Salkeld 296, 91 E.R. 835, 1 Eq. Cas. Abr. 181, 21 E.R. 973.

[2] *Legat v. Shewell* (1706–1710), see above, Case No. 52.

The cases of marriage articles do not come up to this. There, there is a contract and the issue purchasers and, where the intention of the parties appears, equity will not decree the settlement to be made in such manner as that they may be defeated the next minute.

You cannot show me one case where it has been adjudged an estate for life. The case of Legal and Shewin is much stronger; that is executory as well as this; the limitation to the heirs male of the body of his nephew and their heirs male express more fully the intent of the testator that the heirs male of his body should take by purchase, and their heirs male seems added to express the quantity of the estate. It is true that, in devises, the intent should guide, but that must not be arbitrary, but certain and agreeable to the rules of law.

His Lordship seemed to think this case the same as if there were no precedent trusts and that the words should have the same construction here as at law and decreed it an estate tail and that the trustees should convey to the plaintiff in tail, which Mr. Vernon chose, rather than in fee. Lord Cowper had decreed it an estate for life upon the intention of the parties and its being executory and on the cases of marriage articles.

[Other copies of this report: Lincoln's Inn MS. Misc. 383, p. 51, pl. 2.]

[Other reports of this case: 2 Vernon 670, 23 E.R. 1036, 1 Peere Williams 142, 24 E.R. 330, 2 Eq. Cas. Abr. 309, 472, 717, 22 E.R. 261, 402, 603.]

## 116

## Clare v. Almuty

(Ch. 1708–1709)

*Where all of the children of a London citizen have been fully advanced in his lifetime, his widow takes one-half of his estate by the custom of London upon his death after having deducted his funeral expenses and her widow's chamber.*

2 Eq. Cas. Abr. 420, 22 E.R. 358

Trinity, 7 Anne.

An executor is a person entrusted by the law with the testator's personal estate, and, therefore, if there does not appear to be some insolvency in the executor or some gross design to waste the testator's effects or to go into another kingdom, equity will not take the securities out of his hands, *per* Lord Chancellor [Lord Cowper].

But the executrix in this case having married and so put herself under the power of her husband, His Lordship [Lord Cowper] said he would hear any affidavit against him.

And, accordingly, an affidavit was produced to this effect, that the husband was the younger son of a man of a small estate in Ireland and no visible substance and that they feared he might waste the testator's effects and go over into Ireland.

But His Lordship [Lord Cowper] held that this was not sufficient.

Note: The Master of the Rolls [Trevor] having ordered upon an interlocutory decree that the testator's securities should be lodged in a Master's hands, now, upon an appeal, His Lordship [Lord Cowper] reversed that part of the decree.

Yale Beinecke OSB MSS. 184, box 41,
Taussig 311, vol. 1, p. 443, pl. 1

24 May 1709. Clare *et al. contra* Anchurnby.

In pursuance of an order of the 9th July 1709,[1] they certify that, by the custom [of London] time out of mind used, the testator's personal estate, after his debts and expenses about his funeral and the allowance of the widow's chamber deducted, is to be divided into two equal parts, one his relict is entitled to, *viz.* the plaintiff Mary, and the defendant Elizabeth, being barred absolutely from all claims by the custom to demand any share of the testator's personal estate by reason they had marriage portions and were fully advanced by him in his lifetime, and the other moiety the said testator had power to dispose of by his will according to the said custom.

Lincoln's Inn MS. Misc. 12, p. 199, pl. 1

24 May 1709.

In a cause depending in the Court of Chancery between Clare and others against Acmooty and his wife, the case was that Henry Clare, a freeman of London, died leaving a wife and two children, both fully advanced in the testator's lifetime.

The question referred to the City was what share of the testator's estate the freeman's widow was entitled to by the custom, whether a moiety or a third, and what part the testator had a power to dispose of.

It was certified that the testator's personal estate was to be divided into two moieties whereof the widow of the freeman (the children being excluded by their advancement) was to have one moiety and the other the freeman had a power to dispose of by his will.

From this last case, it may be inferred that, as the widow is entitled to a part of the advanced children's share, so the children ought to be entitled to a part of the widow's share when she is advanced by a settlement.

---

[1] Sic in MS.

Lincoln's Inn MS. Misc. 380, pt. 3, p. 216

The children were all advanced in full. And it was held that, in that case, the father was to be considered as dying without children and the estate was to be divided into moieties: the one moiety to go to the wife, the other to be the testamentary share of the father. And [it was] not at all considered what the nature of the estate was, whether real or personal, out of which the children were advanced. Though, in law, the bond can bind no farther than the penalty, yet, in equity, the bond and articles make but one agreement, and, therefore, [it is] not in the liberty of the wife, by incurring the penalty of the bond, to free herself from the agreement.

## 117

## Crane v. Drake

(Ch. 1708)

*A bona fide purchaser for value is not liable to the decedent's unpaid creditors.*

*In this case, the purchaser was not in good faith and was an aider and abettor of the waste of the decedent's estate.*

Lincoln's Inn MS. Misc. 9, p. 76

30 October 1708.

Francis Hopper, being indebted to several persons, by his will, gives the residue of his estate to his sister, whom he makes his executrix, subject to the payment of his debts. The residuum was a leasehold estate, which the defendant purchased of the executrix for £700 but paid no more than £100 in money. The rest of the purchase money was made up with debts that the executrix owed the defendant on her own account and with debts owing him from the testator.

The plaintiff was likewise a creditor of the testator. But no part of the purchase money was applied for the payment of his debt, though the defendant had notice of it at the time of his purchase. Two years after the purchase, the executrix broke. And, then, the plaintiff brought his bill to have a satisfaction out of the defendant's purchase.

This cause was heard before the Master of the Rolls [Trevor], and he decreed for the plaintiff with costs. And now, it came on upon an appeal to Lord Chancellor [Lord Cowper].

*Dobbins*, for the defendant: If the defendant is to be affected in this case, no one can be safe in purchasing of an executor, for, by the same rule, that you may follow the real assets, you may follow any of the personal assets, as a horse, for instance, or a suit of hangings. And, at this rate, an executor can never sell part of the assets to pay part of the testator's debts unless he sells enough to pay the whole, nor can anyone be safe in buying if he knows there are any debts of the testator which remain unpaid.

Lord Chancellor [LORD COWPER]: The decree must be affirmed. There seems to have been a great deal of art and contrivance used by the defendant to hedge on his own debt and to get an application of the assets for the payment of a debt owing from the executrix on her own account, which ought to be applied towards satisfaction of the testator's debts. And, therefore, the defendant having assisted the executrix to commit a *devastavit*, he has made himself *particeps criminis* and ought to pay the plaintiff's debt. And there is no inconvenience in this, as the defendant's counsel would argue, as if a man could never be safe in purchasing real assets of an executor until he was satisfied all the testator's debts were paid, for I do not say that a fair and honest purchaser that pays his money must do so. But that is not the case here, for the defendant has not paid his money, but set off a great part of it with debts owing him from the executrix on her own account, which was not fair, for the assets ought to be applied in the first place for the payment of the testator's debts.

Lord Chancellor [LORD COWPER] seemed to be of the opinion that, if he had been a fair and honest purchaser, notice would not have affected him.

Lincoln's Inn MS. Misc. 384, p. 227, pl. 2

The plaintiff was a creditor of the testator for £100. Hooper's wife was executrix and residuary legatee. Hooper wasted the assets. Drake, a creditor of Hooper, bought a term of him, which was part of the testator's estate for £950, which he discovered, having notice of the plaintiff's debt. Hooper *et ux*. were bankrupt. A bill [was brought] for the £100. It was decreed against Drake because he was a party and privy to the *devastavit*.

[Other reports of this case: 2 Vernon 616, 23 E.R. 1004, 1 Eq. Cas. Abr. 240, 21 E.R. 1018.]

## 118

## Davison v. Rainsford

(Ch. 1708)

*A court of equity will grant relief against fraud and misrepresentation.*

Lincoln's Inn MS. Misc. 9, p. 77

8 November 1708.

The plaintiff and another were joint tenants under a will of the lands in question. The other joint tenant dying, leaving issue, the defendant came to the plaintiff and desired to purchase his share of the lands, and he offered him £500 for them. And, afterwards, he told him, if he would sell him all his share of the lands and the benefit of the contingency, *viz.* that, if the issue of the other joint tenant should happen to die without age whereby, as he pretended, the other part would come to the plaintiff, that he, the purchaser, should have the benefit of it, he would then give him £670, upon which they came to an agreement. And the plaintiff, thereupon, conveyed all his right in the whole estate to the defendant, not apprehending he was then entitled to the whole by survivorship, but taking the case to be as the defendant had represented it. And now, he came to be relieved.

And he was relieved accordingly with costs.

## 119

## Boulter v. Levet

(Ch. 1708)

*A lien of lis pendens dates from the teste of the original writ.*

Lincoln's Inn MS. Misc. 9, p. 78, pl. 1

10 November 1708. Boulter *et al.* v. Sir Richard Levet *et al.* Lord Chancellor.

In this case, it was agreed by the court and counsel that, if a man files an original against an heir to whom real assets are descended and, afterwards, obtains a judgment against him upon a bond of his ancestor, this judgment shall relate to the *teste* of the original so that, though the heir aliens the assets between the *teste* of the original and the judgment, yet the lands shall be bound in the hands of a purchaser.

But, in this case, it happened that the original was not filed. However, upon a motion to the Court of Common Pleas, it was ordered that it should be filed *nunc pro tunc.*

## 120

## Vincent v. Fry

(Ch. 1708)

*A court of equity will order specific performance of an oral land sales contract where there has been a part performance of it.*

Lincoln's Inn MS. Misc. 9, p. 78, pl. 2

12 November 1708.

The defendant, being possessed of a lease in the right of his wife of a lease for ninety-nine years if she should so long live held of the duke of Devonshire, borrows £10 of the plaintiff's father. And, for the securing thereof, he gives a penal bill and deposits this lease in his hands as a pledge. Sometime after this, the plaintiff's father and the defendant came to an agreement together that the former should have this lease outright for £15, and this money was made up part by the principal and interest due on the bill. And the remainder was paid in money. And, thereupon, the bill was delivered up, but no actual assignment was made of this lease. Upon this, the plaintiff's father goes to the duke's steward, desiring to renew this lease. But he being told that the duke would never grant any lease in reversion without the consent of the tenant in possession and it did not appear that he had a right to the lease, there being no assignment made to him thereof and, thereupon, he brought the defendant to the steward, who declared he had sold all his right in this lease to the plaintiff's father, which satisfied the steward, who, accordingly, agreed that the plaintiff's father should surrender his old lease and should have a new one for ninety-nine years, determinable on the death of the defendant's wife and of the plaintiff and his sister. Sometime after this, the plaintiff's father entered on the premises, and he died. And, after his death, the defendant entered and got possession, against whom the plaintiff brought his bill to have an account of the profits and possession delivered him. And the defendant denied the agreement, but it [was] fully proved against him.

The court [Lord Cowper] declared that, notwithstanding the agreement was not in writing, yet possession being delivered and the purchase deed given up, it should be carried on to an execution. And, therefore, he decreed the defendant should assign his interest, deliver possession, and account for the rents and should pay costs.

## 121

## Woodman v. Skuse

(Ch. 1708)

*In this case, the court refused to set aside a bargain on the ground of harshness, particularly as the plaintiff had ratified it twice and was not in a position of good faith.*

Lincoln's Inn MS. Misc. 9, p. 79

17 November 1708.

The plaintiff, coming home from Blechingley Fair, by the way, called in at the defendant's house and stayed there some time, the defendant himself not being then at home. But, afterwards, coming home late, he went directly upstairs and found his wife in bed and the defendant with his clothes off in the same room just going into bed with her. Upon this, the defendant took up the plaintiff's clothes and was going to turn him out of the house naked. But the plaintiff to pacify him, told him he would make him what satisfaction he desired, and, accordingly, gave him a note to pay him £500 and interest. This was in June. In August following, the defendant met the plaintiff, and, insisting upon better security, the plaintiff gave him a bond to pay him £500 and interest and a warrant of attorney to confess judgment upon the bond. And, in November following, for better securing this money, he surrenders a copyhold estate to him of £20 a year.

And now comes the plaintiff to be relieved against these securities and to have them delivered up, pretending that he was terrified into those securities, the defendant, when he came upstairs, taking up an axe and threatening to kill him if he did not give him satisfaction. But nothing of this was proved. And the case, as sworn by the defendant's answer, appeared to be as is before mentioned.

Lord Chancellor [Lord Cowper]: I see no cause to relieve the plaintiff. He has done the defendant an injury and has three several times successively agreed to make him satisfaction. Suppose a jury in this case had given damages. Would this court have relieved against them? No, sure. Why then, since the plaintiff has freely and voluntarily assessed damages upon himself? There is as little reason to relieve against them.

The plaintiff's bill must be dismissed, but, I think, without costs. It is a hard bargain. Or, if he will be relieved against the penalty of the judgment, it must be upon payment of the principal and interest without costs.

[Other reports of this case: Gilbert Rep. 9, 25 E.R. 7, Precedents in Chancery 266, 24 E.R. 128, 2 Eq. Cas. Abr. 183, 22 E.R. 157.]

## 122

## Haley v. Haley

(Ch. 1708)

*A gift to an heir goes to the common law heir, not to an heir by any customary law.*

Lincoln's Inn MS. Misc. 9, p. 82, pl. 1

27 November 1708.

The Lord Chancellor [Lord Cowper] declared that he took it that, if a copyhold estate is surrendered to a man and his heirs, who declares it to be in trust for J.S. and his heirs, this trust shall go to the heir at common law and not to the heir by the custom [of the manor], as if the land is borough English, the heir at common law shall have the estate.

Mr. *Vernon* seemed to doubt it.

## 123

## Moor v. Godfrey

(Ch. 1708)

*Marriage does not defeat survivorship.*

Lincoln's Inn MS. Misc. 9, p. 82, pl. 2

*Eodem die* [27 November 1708].

A man, by his will gives a sum of money to each of this three daughters to be paid them with interest when married and not before. And, if either of them happened to die unmarried, then her portion was to go to the survivors or survivor.

One of them marries and has her portion paid her. Another of them dies. And the question was if the married daughter should have a share with the other sister unmarried.

[It was] decreed she should.

[Other reports of this case: 2 Vernon 620, 23 E.R. 1007.]

## 124

## Crofts v. Pyle

(Ch. 1708)

*A trust that is uncertain cannot be enforced.*

British Library MS. Hargrave 80, f. 15v

Crofts v. Sir Seymour Pile *et al.*, 8 December 1708.

The father of the defendant and of the plaintiff's wife, in pursuance of articles made before marriage with their mother, did settle part of his estate upon himself for life, remainder to his wife for life, remainder to trustees for twenty-one years, remainder over; and the trust of the term for twenty-one years was declared to be for raising such a sum as should be appointed by deed or will not exceeding £2000 for the portions of younger children who should not be provided for in his lifetime, provided if there should be no younger children or if there should be nobody entitled within the meaning of this clause to the sum intended to be raised by it or to any part thereof, that then the term should not arise.

The father dies leaving younger children, but without making any appointment, either by deed or will. And the plaintiff, in behalf of his wife, who was one of the younger children, prefers his bill that the trustees, for the benefit of his wife and the rest of the younger children, should enter and execute their trust, whom he makes parties with Sir Seymour Pile as heir to his father and likewise several others as purchasers under the title of the father subsequent to this settlement.

It was urged for the plaintiff that this case was different from the case of a naked power of making a jointure or charging an estate for portions, in which case, if nothing be done by the person who is vested with the power, it seemed to be agreed that the Court of Chancery would not execute it for him, though, to help a defective execution of such a power, there have been instances of relief in equity.

But in this case, it was said that, since the term must arise in law and vest in the trustees according to the limitation of the settlement, the trust of it was in equity to be directed and applied for the maintenance of the younger children of that marriage in the proportion intended according to the purpose of the parties, which was to make some provision for their children.

But by the Lord Chancellor [Lord Cowper], the plaintiffs can have no relief because the trust of the term is for raising such sums as shall be appointed by the father not exceeding £2000 and there being no sum appointed by the father to be raised, the trust of the term remains perfectly uncertain and nobody is entitled to the benefit of it. This limitation for the benefit of younger children is of itself perfectly uncertain and void and capable of being reduced to a certainty and a possibility of execution only by the act of the father to which it referred, and, this never happening, that clause can never have any effect as being imperfect. And as to what was said that the term must arise at law and consequently remain liable to the discretion of the court, that is a mistake, for the term is by the proviso that follows the limitation of it never to arise in case nobody shall be entitled to the benefit of it, which, as the matter has happened, nobody is. He distinguished this case from that of Dr. Garth and Lady Blanfrey, *coram* Somers,[1] for there, the father of the plaintiff's lady had by his marriage settlement, whereby he was made tenant for life, a power of charging his estate to a certain value for the portions of younger children and did covenant to charge it with such a certain sum but died without doing it. And there, upon a bill exhibited that the sum, which the father had covenanted to charge upon the estate according to his power, should be charged for the benefit of younger children who were otherwise unprovided for, it was accordingly decreed in regard to the father's covenant. But, if the matter had stood barely upon that power without any act done towards the execution of it, the court seemed to think the daughters had been without any relief, which, he said, was the present case.

Another case was cited, which was the Case of the Lady Clifford,[2] and it was thus. A tenant for life with a power to make a jointure of £1000 *per annum* marries the Lady Clifford, having first covenanted to make a settlement according to his power of £1000 a year for her jointure; after marriage, he makes a settlement of lands in Ireland, which were taken to be of that value, and he dies, and the lands proving to be of much less value than appearing by the settlement, the lady preferred her bill to have her settlement according to her husband's power made £1000 a year which he had covenanted to execute to the full. And this was accordingly decreed in regard to the husband's covenant, which being made for a valuable consideration, the execution of it was supported in equity even under a

[1] *Garth v. Lady Blanfrey* (1695), Gilbert Rep. 166, 25 E.R. 117, 2 Eq. Cas. Abr. 659, 22 E.R. 554.

[2] *Lady Clifford v. Lord Burlington* (1700), 2 Vernon 379, 23 E.R. 841, Lincoln's Inn MS. Misc. 11, p. 51, pl. 2.

naked power to the prejudice of a stranger's estate. But otherwise it had certainly been if there had not been such a covenant.

[Other copies of this report: Lincoln's Inn MS. Misc. 383, p. 27, Lincoln's Inn MS. Misc. 106, p. 4.]

Lincoln's Inn MS. Misc. 9, p. 82, pl. 3

11 December 1708.

Upon a marriage settlement, a term for twenty-one years was vested in trustees upon trust that they should raise such a sum not exceeding £2000 and to be paid at such times and in such proportions to the younger children of the marriage as the father, by his last will or other writing should appoint and, in case there should be no younger children or, there being such, all of them should die before twenty-one or should be otherwise provided for by the father, the term should cease.

The father dies intestate, leaving a son and two daughters, having made no appointment nor any manner of provision for his younger children. And if the £2000 could be raised for the benefit of the two younger children was the question.

It was said for the children that the father died suddenly and had not time to make his will and, in all probability, if he had, he would have made an appointment pursuant to the power and that, by this means, it had fallen out that they were destitute of a provision. And the Case of Dr. Garth and his wife was cited in Lord Somers's time, where an express provision was made for younger children's portions as Dr. Beaufoy should appoint by will or writing and Dr. Beaufoy died without making any appointment, and yet the court decreed the portion to be raised.

*Sir Simon Harcourt*: What the court went upon in that case was an agreement of Dr. Beaufoy, a covenant with Dr. Garth, that he would execute the power. Defective executions of powers this court has aided, but never that I know of the non-execution of them. And, therefore, how compassionate soever this case may be, it is too hard for a court of equity.

Mr. *Vernon*: There was a case where a man had a power to limit a jointure and, upon his marriage, he agreed to settle a jointure of £1000 a year. And, in order thereunto, he executed his power upon part of his lands. But it happened not to be sufficient, and this court supplied that deficiency.[1]

Lord Chancellor [Lord Cowper]: [There is] no doubt of it. But to make the present case before us parallel to that, you must show that the father has done something which does not come up to a full execution of the power. The bill must be dismissed.

---

[1] *Lady Clifford v. Lord Burlington* (1700), *ut supra*.

The Lord Chancellor [LORD COWPER] was of the opinion that, if the land had been charged with a fixed and determinate sum and the father was only to appoint the time of the payment and the proportioning of it, the court might have supplied that. But, here, the father is to appoint the sum itself with which the land is to be charged though he is limited, for it is such a sum not exceeding £2000 as the father shall appoint.

## 125

## Banks v. Banks

(Ch. 1708–1712)

*Where a jointress enforces her jointure rights against a decedent's personal estate, the decedent's particular and residuary legatees are subrogated to the rights of the jointress.*

Lincoln's Inn MS. Misc. 9, p. 84

12 December 1708. Sarah Banckes and her daughter, and infant v. Rebecca Banckes, executrix of John Banckes *et al. et e contra.*

John Banckes, upon the marriage of Richard, his son, with the plaintiff Sarah, in consideration of a portion of £3000, which Richard received, enters into articles before the marriage and, thereby, covenants to pay his son £200 a year during the joint lives of John and his wife and Richard. And, by the same articles, John and Richard covenant that John shall pay the plaintiff Sara, if she survived her intended husband, during her life an annuity of £300 a year quarterly and that John shall settle the manor of Pollislo in Devon[shire] to the use of John for life, then to Rebecca, his wife, for life, then to Richard for life, remainder to trustees for £500 years in trust and for the further and better securing the said annuity of £300 a year, with a remainders over.

The marriage took effect. And by lease and release dated 5 and 6 June 1692, in consideration of the marriage and the portion and for raising and assuring an annuity of £300 a year for the plaintiff Sara in lieu of dower and for settling the said manor to the several uses therein according to and in pursuance and execution of certain articles made, John and Richard convey the said manor to the uses before mentioned as to John, Rebecca, and Richard, then to trustees for 500 years, as before, with a remainder to the first and every other son of that marriage in tail male, then to John and the heir male of his body, remainder to the right heirs of John.

The trusts of the term are declared to be that, if the person to whom the freehold or inheritance of the premises expectant upon the term shall pay the annuity, in case Sara survives her husband, as therein is mentioned, then the trustees shall permit such person to enjoy the premises for the payment of the said annuity, for which end, the said 500 years term is therein limited. But, on failure, the trustees are to raise and pay the said annuity out of the rents etc. by making, renewing, or filling up of leases or other disposition thereof as to them shall seem meet and to pay the overplus to the person next in remainder. Then, there is a proviso that Richard, during his life, after the death of John, by writing under hand and seal, may grant, dispose, limit, or appoint, to be raised out of the premises, any sum not exceeding £3000 for younger children's portions to be paid at such times and in such proportions with such reasonable provision for maintenance until such portions become payable as to Richard shall seem meet, subject always to the said term of 500 years.

John Banckes, afterwards, died, *viz.* in September 1700, having made his will, dated 15 May 1699. And, thereby, he bequeathed to his wife and children and other relations several specific legacies amounting to £6967. And, as to the residue of his personal estate not therein before disposed of, after his debts, funeral expenses, and legacies paid, he disposes as follows, *viz.* he gives all his plate, jewels, household goods, corn, stock, etc. to his wife and gives all the residue to his wife, his son Richard, and his two daughters, Alitia [?] and Rebecca, equally between them. And he makes his wife executrix and releases his son Richard, to whom he had before given a legacy of £500, and £100 apiece to his two children, the whole to the survivor, from all sums of money which he owed him.

Rebecca proves the will. And she pays her son his £500 and £200 for his daughter, the other child being dead. And she also pays the other legacies and then divides the residue according to the will, which amounted to about £2860.

11 December 1700, Richard, by a writing under his hand and seal, reciting the power, by virtue thereof, grants, limits, and appoints that the sum of £3000 should, as soon after his death as conveniently might be, be raised and paid out of the rents of the premises to his daughter, the plaintiff, in case he had no other daughter or younger sons, but, if he had, then he declares the same should go in such proportions as he should appoint, if no appointment, equally, and that the interest of the £3000 until the same could be raised should be applied for the maintenance of his said younger children according to their proportions of the money.

Richard died in August 1706, having made his will a little before, whereby he earnestly requests his mother to discharge such of his debts as his personal estate would not answer on the kind condition she had offered. But, to secure his creditors in all events, he devises all his estate in the premises to A. and B. and their heirs, which, if his debts should be paid, he declares to be to the use of his daughter for life with remainder over, but, if his debts should not be paid by his executors within a year after his death, then the trustees should sell the premises and therewith pay his debts with interest from his death and should keep the overplus in his hands for the indemnification of his mother from any trouble which might be given her on account of the said annuity until his wife should release her from all demands touching the same, but, after such release, then to pay the overplus to his wife for the benefit of his daughter. And he makes his wife executrix.

Richard died much in debt, leaving one child only, *viz.* the plaintiff, the infant. His wife renounces the executorship, and the defendant Northleigh, as principal creditor, takes administration.

And now, the plaintiff Sara and her daughter prefer their bill that the annuity might be paid her and the £3000 raised for the benefit of the infant. And Rebecca brings her cross-bill that, if she should be liable to the payment of this annuity, she might be reimbursed out of the term.

And upon the hearing, the points were three, *viz.*:

First, if John's covenant by the articles was not discharged by the settlement;

Second, if it was not, then whether his executrix should not be reimbursed out of the term what she should pay by virtue of her husband's covenant;

Third, how the £3000 should be raised and from what time interest should commence.

[Lord Cowper] decreed that the settlement was in the nature of a mortgage for securing the annuity and no discharge of John's covenant. And, therefore, it was in the power of the plaintiff Sara to resort to both or either of them at her election.

John having charged both his real and personal estate with the payment of this annuity, according to the constant method of this court, the heir, whether *natus* or *factus haeres*, it matters not, shall be preferred before the executor and the personal estate applied to exonerate the real in favor of the heir unless his ancestor has some way declared his intention otherwise.

Now, as to this, John Bancks has by his will given away several specific legacies. And, as to so much of his personal estate, it is manifest he never intended his real estate should be exonerated by his personal. But, as to the residuum, which he has bequeathed after the payment of his debts etc., it is a question whether that shall not be applied in discharge of the real estate, for, though the covenant was not broken at John's death, yet it was in the nature of a debt upon him.

And, this being a matter vigorously opposed by the defendant's counsel, the Lord Chancellor [Lord Cowper] took time to consider of it, though he seemed to be of an opinion against the defendants, and also whether the defendant Rebecca should be reimbursed all that she should pay in the performance of this covenant or only so much as she should happen to pay over and above the residuum.

The Lord Chancellor [Lord Cowper], likewise, took time to consider upon the last point and how far the term should stand in the daughter's way as to the raising of her portion, whether she must wait until after her mother's death or whether the term shall only be kept on foot as a security for her mother's annuity, it being insisted on by her counsel that, as to her, the case was as where a man makes two mortgages and pays off the first, he cannot keep that on foot to prejudice the second mortgagee, but, as to him, when paid, it is as if no mortgage had been. So here, the real estate being to be discharged by the personal [estate] in favor of the daughter, who, in respect of the settlement is *haeres factus*, though not *natus*, she ought to be let in to a present satisfaction and the term, as to her, is as if no such had ever been.

In the arguing this case, the Case of Chichester and French[1] was cited to be decreed by Lord Keeper Wright that the personal estate should go in aid of the real [estate], though a man had by his will charged his real estate with the payment of his debts, there being no negative words that his personal estate should not be charged.

Lincoln's Inn MS. Misc. 10, p. 153

11 November 1712.

This court declared that the personal estate of the said John Bancks was by virtue of his covenant in the said marriage articles become liable to make good the annuity of £300 to the plaintiff, Sarah Bancks, his mother, from the time of the death of the said Richard Bancks so that the plaintiff Sarah had two securities for her said annuity, *viz.* the said John Bancks's covenant and the said term of 500 years, and that she was at liberty to resort to both or either of the said securities for her annuity and the arrears thereof and she having elected to come on the personal estate of the said John Bancks by virtue of the said covenant and the defendant Rebecca Bancks having by her answer admitted assets of the said testator, John Bancks, it was ordered that it should be referred to examine what was due to the plaintiff Sarah for her annuity of £300 since the death of the said Richard Bancks. And what should be found to be remaining due for the arrears of the said annuity, it was ordered that the defendant Sarah Bancks should pay the same to the plaintiff Sarah together with costs and that the defendant Rebecca should also pay to the plaintiff Sarah the said annuity of £300 for the future during her life as the same should grow due in case the person next in remainder should fail to pay the same.

But, as to what security should be made by and out of the assets of the said John Bancks for the future payment of the said annuity, the consideration thereof as also interest of what should be found in arrear of the said annuity, was thereby reserved until further order. And, in case the payment of the said annuity of £300 unto the plaintiff Sarah out of the personal estate as before directed should affect any of the legatees of the said John Bancks who had any particular legacies devised to them by his will, the court declared that such particular legatees ought to have and receive a satisfaction for the same with respect to such their particular legacies out of the said term of 500 years and did order the same accordingly.

But whether the devisees of the residue part of the said John Bancks's estate should receive a satisfaction out of the said 500 years term, the consideration

[1] *French v. Chichester* (Ch. 1707), see above, Case No. 63.

thereof and of all other points in these causes not being determined were thereby reserved until after the report, when the court, after being attended with precedents, would make such further order as should be just. And the further consideration of costs was thereby likewise referred.

A report being made dated 6 July 1710, these causes came on 3 July 1713 to be further heard as to matters reserved on the said former hearing before the Lord Keeper. And it was then ordered *ex parte* that the defendant Rebecca should bring so much money before the Master as would be sufficient to answer the £300 *per annum* to the plaintiff Sarah and that the money when brought should be placed out at interest on government securities to be approved by the said Master and that the same should be subject to answer and pay the said £300 to the plaintiff Sarah for life and the Master to compute interest for the arrears of said annuity at the end of every six months until the same was paid to the said plaintiff Sarah. And what the Master should certify to be due for the interest of such arrears, it was ordered that the defendant Rebecca should pay the same as also that the defendant Rebecca should join with the defendant Archer, the surviving trustee, in said 500 years term in granting leases and filling up lives in the premises within that term in order to raise the £300 for the plaintiff Sarah, the daughter, in such manner as the said Master should direct and that the money arising thereby should be brought before him and be by him placed out at interest on security for the benefit of the plaintiff Sarah, the daughter, until twenty-one and then paid her and the said Master to examine what was fit to be allowed for her maintenance and state the same to the court, whereupon such further order should be made touching the same as should be just.

And, as to the residuary legatees of John Bancks, His Lordship [LORD HARCOURT] did not think fit to make any order relating to them.

And the Master was to tax the plaintiffs Sarah, the mother, and Sarah, the daughter, and the defendants, the trustees, their costs of these suits, which were to be paid them out of the said estate.

With which decree, the defendant Sarah being dissatisfied, for that provision ought to have been made out of the said 500 years term for raising and reimbursing her such sums as she had or should pay in respect of the said annuity or costs of these suits together with interest for the same and that such reimbursements ought to take place of the plaintiff's, the infant's, portions, who could have no right but subject to the 500 years term, which ought to make good the said annuity in the first place before any part of the said portion is raised, and that such provision was the more reasonable in regard, by the order on the first hearing, the like provision was made for the particular legatees in the said John's will, it being thereby decreed that, in case the payment of the said annuity should affect the particular legatees of John, such legatees were to have satisfaction out of the said 500 years term and the defendant Rebecca, who had really paid and applied all the assets of her testator in the payment of his debts and legacies (not expecting to be anyways affected with the said annuity) ought not to be in a worse condition than the legatees, who ought to be decreed to refund to Rebecca in proportion to the legacies they have received so much as the said Rebecca should be obliged to pay towards the said annuity and costs.

And the said first order having provided for reimbursing the said legatees yet giving no direction for their refunding, the said Rebecca, therefore, petitioned the Lord Keeper to have the cause reheard, which being granted and the plaintiffs Sarah, the mother, and Sarah, the daughter, being also dissatisfied with the said decree also, petitioned to have those causes reheard, which being granted, both causes came on to be re-heard accordingly before His Lordship. His Lordship [Lord Harcourt] did order that the plaintiffs, Sarah, the mother's, and Sarah, the daughter's, petition for re-hearing be dismissed. And, upon the defendant Rebecca's petition, His Lordship declared that he saw no reason to distinguish between the residuary legatees of the said John and his particular legatees, and, therefore, as far as the residuary legatees should be affected by applying the personal estate of the said John in payment of the £300 *per annum* annuity, the former order of the 3d July 1711 should be varied and with such variation be as follows, *viz.* that the defendant Rebecca do either by the first day of Easter term next bring before the Master so much money as will be sufficient to answer the £300 *per annum* to the plaintiff Sarah during her life or give security in the meantime to be approved by the said Master for the payment thereof during the life of the plaintiff Sarah, the mother, and, if the defendant Rebecca should not think fit to give such securities but bring before the Master sufficient [assets] to answer the same such money when brought to be put out at interest on government or other real security to be subject to answer and pay the said £300 to the plaintiff Sarah, the mother, for life and the Master to compute interest at £5 percent *per annum* for the arrears of the said annuity from the end of every six months, the same was payable until it was paid. And what the Master should certify due for interest of such arrears, it is ordered the defendant Rebecca do pay the same to the plaintiff Sarah, the mother, accordingly.

And it was further ordered that the defendant Rebecca and Archer, the surviving trustee in the 500 years term, do join in granting leases and filling up lives in the premises within that term and that the money raised thereby do go in the first place to make good what the defendant Rebecca has paid or shall pay for arrears and growing payments of the said annuity to the plaintiff Sarah, the mother. And, if more [be] raised by granting leases and filling up lives than will make good the said arrears and growing payments, the surplus [is] to be brought before the Master and put out at interest on government or real security to make a fund for answering the further growing payments of the said £300 *per annum* and, afterwards, for raising the said £300 for the plaintiff Sarah, the daughter, as the said Master should direct.

And it was further ordered that the estate be sold to the best purchaser to be approved by the said Master, subject to the estate of the defendant Rebecca for life and the said 500 years term, in which sale, all parties are to join as the Master directs and moneys arising thereby to be applied to pay the plaintiff Sarah, the daughter's, said £300 with interest at £4 percent from her father's death during her minority or until marriage, which[ever] should first happen. And, after the plaintiff Sarah, the daughter, should be paid, then, the surplus is to be applied towards satisfaction of the creditors of the said Richard Bancks. And, if such surplus should not be sufficient to pay the said creditors their whole debts, then they are to abate in proportion to their demands. And the Master is to examine what is fit to be allowed for the maintenance of the plaintiff Sarah, the daughter, and state the same to the court, whereupon such further order shall be made touching the same as shall be just.

And, as to the residuary legatees and the particular legatees, His Lordship [Lord Harcourt] did not see fit to make any distinction between them. And he ordered that, so far as the residuary legatees should be affected by applying the personal estate of the said John Bancks in paying the said £300 *per annum* to the plaintiff Sarah, the mother, the said residuary legatees are to be let in to receive a satisfaction out of the said 500 years term in the same manner as the particular legatees with this difference only, that the particular legatees be first satisfied and, if the defendant Rebecca has paid any particular legatees their legacies or the residuary legatees any part of their residuary share or if she herself be entitled to any particular or residuary legacy, she is to be let in to receive a satisfaction for what shall appear she has so paid or is entitled to out of the said 500 years estate. But what she or the other particular or residuary legatees are so entitled unto is not to affect or be charged upon the said 500 years term further than they shall be affected by applying the said personal estate in the payment of the said £300 *per annum* to the plaintiff Sarah, the mother. The Master is to tax the plaintiffs Sarah, mother and daughter, and the trustees their costs in both causes to be paid them by the defendant Rebecca, and, what costs should be so paid by her, she is to be reimbursed again together with her own costs of these suits to be taxed by the said Master out of the said 500 years term.

British Library MS. Hargrave 80, f. 123v

Pursuant to articles entered into by John Banks and Richard, his son, upon the marriage of Richard, by which John covenanted, *inter alia*, to settle an annuity of £300 *per annum* upon the wife of Richard for her jointure, a settlement was made to the use of John for life, remainder to his wife for life, remainder to Richard for life, remainder to trustees for five hundred years in trust only as a further security for the raising the annuity of £300 *per annum* for the jointure of the wife of Richard, remainder to the first and every other son of the marriage in tail, remainder to the right heirs of the said John with a power to Richard with consent of the trustees to charge the estate with any sum not exceeding £3000 for a younger child or children or for a daughter or daughters but subsequent to the term of five hundred years. John and Richard both died and left widows, John having first appointed £3000 to be raised for his daughter. And the wife of John being living and entitled to the whole estate for life, the wife of Richard resorted to the personal estate of John for a satisfaction of her jointure of £300 *per annum* pursuant to her covenant. The executrix of John had paid away all the assets in debts and particular legacies and distributed the surplus pursuant to the will before any demand by the wife of Richard.

And the question now was whether the particular and residuary legatees of John would not stand in the place of the wife of Richard to have satisfaction so far out of the term for five hundred years, as the fund for their legacies was exhausted by her resorting to the personal estate.

Lord Cowper decreed that the particular legatees should, but he reserved the consideration of the residuary legatees.

And upon rehearing, Lord Keeper [Lord Harcourt] affirmed the decree to the first and decreed the residuary legatees should likewise come in, there being no difference in reason between their cases and that, as the executrix had paid them and was to make a fund out of her own pocket for securing £300 *per annum* to the wife of Richard, she should stand in their places.

It was strongly insisted on by the counsel for the daughter that she was a purchaser of her £3000 and that the legatees being volunteers ought not to be let in upon the real estate to have a satisfaction antecedent to her, though the mother, who had a liberty to resort to either fund, had taken the personal for her satisfaction and that the words of the trust of the term being for a further security was an evidence that she intended only to come in aid of the personal estate to make her satisfaction for her £300 *per annum.*

On the other hand, it was insisted that the land was the principal debtor and the personal estate only auxiliary, the land being the most proper fund for it to issue out of, a grant of an annuity charges the person but the land principally, that the daughter was no purchaser, it being left purely to the father's will to charge the lands with £3000 or not and, if she was a purchaser, it was only upon reversion subject to the term and the jointress having taken away the fund for the legatees, it was the common justice of the court to let them stand in her place though not to load the term farther than £300 *per annum* and that the words for a farther security were added only that the £300 *per annum* might not be raised instead of one.

[Other copies of this report: Lincoln's Inn MS. Misc. 383, p. 218, Lincoln's Inn MS. Misc. 106, p. 174.]

## 126

# Whitlock v. Waltham

(Ch. 1709)

*The question in this case was whether the creditor or the debtor bears the risk of loss where an agent appointed to receive the interest on the loan becomes insolvent.*

1 Salkeld 157, 91 E.R. 146

27 January Hilary 7 Anne; at the Rolls.

The interest of a mortgage was paid to and received by the scrivener that put out the money; the scrivener proved insolvent. And the question was who should bear the loss? And it was admitted in this case:

First, that, if the scrivener be entrusted with the custody of the bond, he may receive the interest, and, though he fails, yet the mortgagee shall bear the loss and that so it is also in such case if he receive the principal and deliver up the bond, for, being entrusted with the security itself, it shall be presumed he is entrusted with a power over it and with a power to receive the principal and interest, and the rather because the giving up of the bond upon the payment of the money is a discharge thereof; [it is] otherwise if the obligee take away the bond, for then he has no authority to receive any money;

Secondly, if a scrivener be entrusted with the mortgage deed, not the bond, he has only authority to receive the interest, but not the principal, because the giving up the deed is not sufficient to restore the estate, but there must be a reconveyance, whereas the giving up a bond is in law an extinguishment of the debt;

Thirdly, that, though the scrivener has neither the custody of the mortgage nor the bond, yet, if the mortgagee agrees that the mortgagor shall pay the interest to the scrivener, the interest may be well paid to the scrivener as long as the mortgagee lives;

Fourthly, that, if the mortgagee dies and his executor comes to the scrivener and receives the interest of him and at his hands that became due after the death of the mortgagee, this is a good payment; and, if, after such receipt, the scrivener breaks, the mortgagor shall not bear the loss, for it was the mortgagee that trusted the scrivener and the executor came into the agreement and thereby renewed it, supposing it was determined by the death of the mortgagee, but it was rather an agreement than an authority and could not die with the party.

Note this was the principal case, and [it was] affirmed by Cowper, Lord Chancellor.

## 127

## Green v. Wood

(Ch. 1709)

*A court of equity can dismiss a lawsuit that has lain dormant for a long period of time.*

Lincoln's Inn MS. Misc. 9, p. 89

27 January 1708[/09].

Green enters into articles with Wood for the purchase of the reversion of an estate in fee expectant upon an estate for life. And, in the year 1704, he brings a bill to have a specific performance of these articles, having paid £100, part of his purchase money to a third hand. After this, he lies still until 1707, and, in all that time, he never brought his adversary into contempt. He declares he is weary of the suit and endeavors to get back his £100 and actually receives it.

And now, the tenant for life being dead, Green brings his cause on to a hearing and insists upon his bargain.

Lord Chancellor [Lord Cowper]: If a reversion is agreed to be purchased and the man proceeds quickly to have an execution of his agreement, I cannot say but this court ought to carry it on, though it should have fallen out that, by the tenant's for life dying soon after the bargain was made, it has proved very advantageous to the purchaser. But, if a man will lie still and make no steps for some time and when he sees his bargain is become a very good one, he then begins to stir, it may alter the case. I cannot say but the parties' agreement was honest at first and that nothing has been done by him absolutely to vacate it, but, however, take all the circumstances together, I think it is an agreement I cannot now carry on to an execution. The bill must be dismissed, but without costs.

[Other reports of this case: 2 Vernon 632, 23 E.R. 1013, 1 Eq. Cas. Abr. 18, 21 E.R. 840.]

## 128

## Kirke v. Clerke

(Ch. 1709)

*In a suit to enforce marriage articles, the wife must be a party to the litigation.*

*Marriage is a good and valuable consideration for a contract.*

Lincoln's Inn MS. Misc. 9, p. 90, pl. 1

Same day [27 January 1709].

The defendant Clarke, upon his son's marriage, entered into articles with trustees to settle a copyhold estate upon his son and his then intended wife and their issue. The marriage took effect. And, sometime afterwards, the son and the trustees prefer a bill against the father and some others who claimed an interest in this copyhold estate to have a specific performance of these articles.

It was objected at the hearing that the wife was no party, neither plaintiff nor defendant, as she ought to have been, for, otherwise, the matter in question may sometime or other be brought over again, the decree that will now be made not being conclusive to her.

Lord Chancellor [Lord Cowper]: It is a good objection. Let the cause stand over, and make her a party. The plaintiff must pay the costs of the day.

Note Mr. *How* said she could not be made a plaintiff, for then the proofs would not be in the same clause in which they were taken, but she ought to be a defendant.

British Library MS. Hargrave 80, f. 16v

The defendant, being seised in fee of a copyhold according to the custom of the manor, makes a voluntary surrender of it to the use of himself for life, remainder to his son in tail. Afterwards, on his son's marriage, he offers to settle other lands upon his son and to retract this voluntary conveyance. But it being insisted on that, in consideration of his son's marriage portion, he should settle other lands proposed and likewise suffer the first settlement to remain, that was agreed to. The other settlement, being of lands of inheritance, was made by deed, and this remained unaltered. Afterwards, the father, in order to [have] the marriage of a second wife, agrees to surrender these copyhold lands to himself for life, remainder to her for a jointure, remainder to the first and other sons of that marriage. The marriage ensues, and the wife prefers her bill to have the execution of these articles.

It was insisted that the settlement was merely voluntary and, therefore, fraudulent and not to prevail against the second wife, who was a purchaser, that, though it was agreed on the son's marriage that the settlement should stand in consideration of the marriage portion, yet that agreement, being by parol only, cannot aid the settlement against a purchaser by deed.

But [it was] decreed the first surrender should stand, for, though it was voluntary at the first, yet, afterwards, when it became a consideration of marriage, it was a settlement upon a good and valuable consideration and, though there is only a parol evidence of that agreement, yet that is enough to destroy the presumption of fraud which the law does *prima facie* induce. So it was decreed that the son's settlement should stand and that the father should make good his articles by settling some other estate of equal value.

[Other copies of this report: Lincoln's Inn MS. Misc. 383, p. 29.]

[Other reports of this case: Precedents in Chancery 275, 24 E.R. 133, 2 Eq. Cas. Abr. 144, 165, 479, 22 E.R. 123, 141, 407.]

## 129

## Gibbs v. Gibbs

(Ch. 1709)

*Money payable to a married woman for her separate use must be paid or demanded during her lifetime; if it was not, her personal representative cannot sue for the arrears.*

Lincoln's Inn MS. Misc. 9, p. 90, pl. 2

1 February.

By articles made upon marriage, it was agreed that the wife should have the power to dispose of £500, part of her portion, by her will as she should think fit and that the interest of £1000, the other part thereof, should be paid her for her separate use. The wife survived her husband and disposed of this £500 by her will. The bill was brought not only for this £500 but for the arrears of the interest of the £1000 which became due in the husband's lifetime.

Lord Chancellor [Lord Cowper]: If the wife has not received the whole interest of the £1000 during the coverture, it may well be presumed it was upon some private agreement between her and her husband. And it not appearing to me that either she or her trustees ever demanded it during her husband's lifetime, I think it would be too hard for me to say that a satisfaction shall now be made to her estate for these arrears out of the husband's estate.

As to the £500, I think, when articles are made touching the disposition of the wife's portion, whatever part thereof is not there disposed of will go to the husband, notwithstanding it is a chose in action. And, if he dies before his wife, his executors shall have it and not the wife, for the articles are the measure of what was and was not to go to the wife.

Now here, the wife has a power to dispose of £500 by her will, and, though there is no time limited as to her making her will, for it is indefinite, I cannot (as they of the other side would have it) restrain it to the coverture. The plaintiff must be paid the £500 with interest from the wife's death.

## 130

## Phillips v. Wilcocks

(Ch. 1709)

*A person who has an interest in the outcome of a lawsuit is not competent to testify in it as a witness.*

Lincoln's Inn MS. Misc. 10, p. 18

8 February 7 Anne.

At the hearing of this cause, a question arose whether Hunt, the bankrupt, should be allowed to be a good witness to prove a fraud in which he was a party himself and which, if true, would increase the bankrupt's estate and consequently be an advantage to the bankrupt.

But it appearing that he had released to the assignees of the creditors etc. all his right to his own estate, My Lord Chancellor [Lord Cowper] was of opinion that he was a good witness. However, he did not think fit to give an entire credit to his evidence. But he directed an issue at law to try this fraud.

And, upon the trial before My Lord Chief Justice Trevor, the like objection was made. But, upon producing the release, the Chief Justice was of the opinion that he was a good witness. But then, it appearing upon reading the release that the bankrupt had released to the assignees in trust for the creditors, the Chief Justice [Trevor] said the release signified nothing, for, if there was a surplus, the bankrupt would have it notwithstanding, whereupon a juror was ordered to be withdrawn, after which the bankrupt executed a general release. And the case came on again to be tried, and he was then allowed to be a good evidence.

In this case was cited the Case of Newton and Hare, which was heard before Baron Price the 22nd June 1710, where the like objection was made and there was a release. But the judge said that, in this case, the bankrupt swore to discharge himself of a debt, which is said to be owing from him, for, though he is a bankrupt, yet he may be sued by the creditors. However, at last, the court agreed to read his evidence.

[Other reports of this case: 2 Vernon 637, 23 E.R. 1016.]

## 131

## Dodson v. Dodson

(Ch. 1709)

*Where a person who has a power of appointment exercises it in a very unequal manner for no very good reason, a court of equity will set the distribution aside.*

Lincoln's Inn MS. Misc. 9, p. 91

9 February 1708[/09]. Mary Dodson and five of her children v. Thomas and John Dodson, her two sons, *et al.*

J. Dodson, the plaintiff Mary's husband, upon his marriage, settles lands to the use of himself for life; then he charges the whole with a rent charge of £150 a year for a jointure for his wife; then a term of 500 years is limited to trustees, remainder to the first and other sons in tail male, with a remainder to his own right heirs. The trusts of the term are declared to be for raising £2000 for younger children to be equally divided between them unless the father should otherwise appoint by his will or any other writing executed etc.

The father, having five daughters and two sons, by a writing, appoints £1998 15s. to be paid to his youngest son at twenty-one or day of marriage, and he appoints 5s. apiece to his five daughters, the plaintiffs.

The plaintiff Mary prefers her bill for a satisfaction of the arrears of her rent charge, suggesting that her eldest son suffered the land to lie unmanured on purpose to defeat her of her rent charge so that she can have no distress nor any remedy for her rent charge. And the daughters come for portions and maintenance out of the £2000, suggesting that this appointment was fraudulent.

Lord Chancellor [Lord Cowper]: Had the words been clear to have given him [the father] a discretionary power and he had executed this power and made a distribution somewhat unequal, I think this court would not have interposed. But, when a man that has such a power will come and limit almost the whole to one child and give only 1s. or 5s. apiece to his other children, surely, this court will consider such a disposition as fraudulent. Besides, it is clear to me that the plaintiff Mary's husband had a power by the settlement to distribute this money otherwise than equally. And, therefore, the words being uncertain and it appearing to me by the proofs that he had no very good design in what he did, I am of the opinion the appointment is void as to all but the sum to be raised.

As to the rent charge, it is charged upon the term, and, since the plaintiff Mary has had no remedy by way of distress, it must be raised out of the term. And the Master must see what is in arrears and allow interest from the end of every half year it became due. It is a debt upon land, which shall carry interest.

## 132

## Hipsley v. Hyde

(Ch. 1709)

*In this case, the legacy to 'the next heir' was not a contingent bequest but a vested one.*

Lincoln's Inn MS. Misc. 9, p. 92

*Eodem die* [9 February 1709].

Humphry, the grandfather, devises land to Humphrey, his grandson, and to the heirs male of his body and, if he died in his minority, then he gave it to his son Humphry's next heir male. Humphry, the grandson, died in his minority and John, his next brother, entered during the life of Humphry, his father.

And the question was whether the limitation to the 'next heir male of Humphry, my son,' was a contingent remainder, for, if so, it was void, for he could not be the heir male of his father during his father's lifetime, and, therefore, the contingent remainder not vesting when the particular estate determined, it must be void according to Archer's Case.[1]

This was sent out of Chancery for a trial at law, though not upon this point directly, yet upon a point that brought this in question. And the judge that tried the cause was of the opinion that it was not a contingent remainder, but a *descriptio personae*, according to Burchet and Durdant's Case, in Ventris,[2] and that John might enter and take in his father's lifetime.

This came back into this court. And it was very much labored to have a new trial. But, it being in the case of creditors, the court would not grant it.

## 133

## Massey v. Craven

(Ch. 1709)

*A gambling debt is void and unenforceable.*

Lincoln's Inn MS. Misc. 9, p. 93

5 March 1708[/09]. Massey v. Craven, Killigrew, and John and Morgan Whitley. Master of the Rolls.

Killigrew owed Craven £500 on a note, being for money won at play. The plaintiff owed Killigrew money, who, thereupon, desired Craven to take the plaintiff's bond for £300 in part [payment] of the £500 note, which Craven consenting to, the plaintiff gave him a bond for the payment of £300 by installments and, at the same time, Craven discharged Killigrew of £300, part of the £500.

Sometime after this, Craven being indebted to the defendant John Whitley in the sum of £400, he desires him to take the bond the plaintiff had entered into in part of payment, which he agreed to. And, thereupon, he gave a letter of attorney to the defendant Morgan Whitley to empower him to receive the £300 due on the plaintiff's bond. (This was in trust for John Whitley, but no trust was declared.)

---

[1] *Baldwin v. Smith* (1597), 1 Coke Rep. 63, 76 E.R. 139, Croke Eliz. 453, 78 E.R. 692, 2 Anderson 37, 123 E.R. 533.

[2] *Durdant v. Burchett* (1685–1690), 1 Ventris 334, 86 E.R. 216, 2 Ventris 311, 86 E.R. 458, also *sub nom. James v. Richardson*, Pollexfen 457, 86 E.R. 610, T. Raymond 330, 83 E.R. 172, 2 Levinz 232, 83 E.R. 533, 3 Keble 832, 84 E.R. 1039, T. Jones 99, 84 E.R. 1166, 1 Freeman 458, 472, 89 E.R. 343, 353, 1 Eq. Cas. Abr. 214, 21 E.R. 998, Lincoln's Inn MS. Misc. 557, f. 94, pl. 2, Skinner 205, 90 E.R. 95, Comberbach 153, 90 E.R. 400, Carthew 154, 90 E.R. 694, Holt K.B. 223, 224, 90 E.R. 1022, 1023, 1 Eq. Cas. Abr. 214, 21 E.R. 999, Dodd 60.

Afterwards, Craven and John Whitley stated accounts together, and Craven appeared to be indebted to John Whitley in £100, for which he gave a bond and, in some time, paid it. And then, general releases were given on each side.

This bond was put in suit at law by the defendant John Whitley against the plaintiff in Craven's name. And judgment being recovered thereon and execution taken out for part, the plaintiff came here to be relieved and, accordingly, was relieved, it appearing the money for which the bond was given was won at play and the defendant Whitley having not made good proof of the consideration of the letter of attorney, which, if he had done and it had appeared the bond was assigned over in satisfaction of a just debt to one who had no notice, it might, perhaps, have been otherwise. The bond was decreed to be delivered up and satisfaction to be acknowledged on the judgment and restitution to be made the plaintiff of what things had been taken of value of any execution upon the judgment.

## 134

## Anonymous v. Stone

(Ch. 1709)

*The question in this case was how far co-trustees are liable for the actions of each other.*

Harvard Law Sch. MS. 537, pt. 2, p. 120, pl. 1

Easter term 8 Anne.

The bill was by creditors against Turner Stone *et al.*, trustees of a real estate to be disposed of to the payment of their debts.

And a question being made how far the trustees should be charged jointly for the purchase money, it was said by My Lord Chancellor [Lord Cowper], if, upon the sale and receipt of the purchase money, it was agreed among them that one shall have so much and the others so much to such and such uses, that they are only answerable for so much as they, each of them, had. But it seemed by him, if the rest let the one have the money and repose a trust of their own in him, they may be charged jointly, there having been a joint receipt. And it seemed likewise by him, upon putting cases by the counsel for the plaintiff that, if one only acts as much as necessary for him in order to make a sale and meddles no further, [he is] not liable for anything.

Query of these differences because the case was not determined, but adjourned.

And *Sir Joseph Jekyll*, a counsel for the plaintiff, cited for him a case, Hilary, four years, one Pitt's Case, about a joint stock in the East India Company, and one Fellows and Owen's Case, Michaelmas, three years ago.[1]

And it appeared likewise that, if he who trusted interposed in the agreement, it would make it much firmer to discharge those not meddling in the pursuance of that agreement. *Vide* Hard. 314.[2]

## 135

## Lord Anglesey v. Lord Altham

(Ch. 1709)

*A foreign deposition is admissible in evidence de bene esse.*

*A conusee is a tenant to the* praecipe, *and a tenant in tail coming in as vouchee admits him as such.*

*The Statute of Frauds does not apply to uses (unless to a third person) and not to a conusee.*

Holt K.B. 736, 90 E.R. 1305

Easter 8 Anne.

Upon an issue directed out of Chancery to be tried at common law, this cause came before the court.

The two questions reserved upon the trial for the opinion of the court were, first, whether a copy of a fine and recovery in Ireland proved by a witness that was and is still in Ireland, who was examined by a commission out of the Chancery, may be allowed as evidence here.

The second is whether there be a good tenant to the *praecipe*. And this depends upon the Statute of Frauds,[3] *viz.* whether the use of a fine does not result to the conusor, there being no deed to declare the uses thereof, and, if so, the common recovery is void.

Holt, Chief Justice: As to the first point, these depositions ought to be allowed to be evidence. It is true the law requires the best evidence that can be had, but, when no other proof can be had, the law will allow such as may be.

It is objected that there might have been better proof had, this being a matter of record, for there might have been one sent over to examine it. In answer to this, there is no legal compulsion to send a man into Ireland to inform himself in

---

[1] *Murrell v. Cox* (1707), see above, Case No. 62; *Fellows v. Owen* (1705), 2 Freeman 283, 286, 22 E.R. 1212, 1215, 1 Peere Williams 81, 24 E.R. 302, 2 Vernon 504, 515, 23 E.R. 922, 929.

[2] *Gill v. Attorney General* (Ex. 1662), Hardres 314, 145 E.R. 474.

[3] Stat. 29 Car. II, c. 3 (*SR*, V, 839–842).

order to be made capable of giving evidence. Indeed, if that witness was in England, you might have had him at the trial.

If it be in the same cause and between the same parties upon an issue directed out of Chancery, we allow of the depositions being read every day if the party be sick or beyond the sea. And, though this is a record, yet it makes no difference, since there is no legal course to compel any man to go over to examine it. The certificate of a minister of a marriage beyond the sea was allowed to be evidence. 2 Cro. 541, 542.[1]

As to the second point, the first clause in the Statute of Frauds is general, that all uses must be manifested by writing, and, if it had stopped here, a fine or feoffment had cut off all resulting uses, though there had been no consideration.

But the second clause excepts all trusts and confidences that arise or result in construction of law. And I take it that the conusee is in at common law. Was he a feoffee, it need not to be averred to the use of the feoffee, as appears by the form of pleading. Coke's Entr. 414, 273; Com. 477.[2] But it must be averred that it is to the use of the feoffor and that intent must be proved, as, if there is no consideration, it shows that the use was not intended to the feoffee.

The intent here is manifest, for the conusee being tenant to the *praecipe*, a tenant in tail coming in as vouchee admits him as such.

I take it that the Statute of Frauds does not extend to uses unless to a third person and not to the conusee. The conusee has the use by operation of law, and, so, here is a tenant to the *praecipe*. The law knows no difference between uses and trusts.

Judgment for the plaintiff [was given] by the whole court.

[Other reports of this case: Gilbert Rep. 16, 25 E.R. 12, 11 Modern 210, 88 E.R. 994.]

[Related cases: Lord Anglesea v. Lord Altham (K.B. 1696), Holt K.B. 733, 90 E.R. 1303, 2 Salkeld 676, 91 E.R. 574.]

## 136

## Honeywood v. Hards

(Ch. 1709)

*Generally, where a committee keeps a stated sum for several years in his hands and never applies to the court for an order to put it out, he will be charged with interest.*

---

[1] *Alsop v. Bowtrell* (1619), Croke Jac. 541, 79 E.R. 464.

[2] *Jackson v. Darcy* (1573), E. Coke, *A Booke of Entries* (1614), 'Partition', pl. 6, f. 414; *Tavener v. Crumwell* (1598), E. Coke, *A Booke of Entries* (1614), 'Error', pl. 15, f. 272; *Nichols v. Nichols* (1575), 2 Plowden 477, 75 E.R. 711, also Benloe 245, 123 E.R. 173.

Lincoln's Inn MS. Misc. 9, p. 94

14 May 1709. Honeywood and Dr. South v. Sir William Hards *et ux.*

A committee of a lunatic states her accounts before a Master, upon which it appears there is a sum of money resting in her hands. This report is confirmed, and the balance remained several years in the hands of the committee, after whose death it came to be a question whether her estate should answer interest for this money.

Lord Chancellor [LORD COWPER]: I think, in a common case, it is the constant course of the court that, when a sum is liquidated by a Master's report and that is confirmed, it shall carry interest.

Why now, when a committee, who is a guardian of a lunatic, keeps a stated sum of money in his hands for several years and never applies to the court for direction to put this money out at interest, I think it is so great a breach of trust that he ought to pay interest. He is more than a receiver; he is a trustee and a guardian appointed by the court.

But, as to the case before us, I think no interest ought to be allowed. Generally speaking, there is a beneficial allowance made by the court for keeping the lunatic to the intent the committee may have some compensation for his care and trouble, and, if the lunatic is provided with common necessaries, no farther enquiries are made. Now, in the case before us, the committee has been so kind as to charge the lunatic's estate with no more than barely what she has expended for him and has demanded no allowance for her own trouble, and, therefore, I think there ought to be no allowance of interest for money in her hands.

But, I say, as long as I sit here, I shall in a common and ordinary case, where a committee keeps a stated sum for several years in his hands and never applied to the court for an order to put it out, charge him with interest.

## 137

## Thompson v. South

(Ch. 1709)

*In this case, a legacy by a debtor to his creditor was not intended to be a satisfaction of the debt.*

Lincoln's Inn MS. Misc. 9, p. 95

17 May 1709. Thompson v. South *et al.*, executors of Grey.

The plaintiff, residing at Jamaica, in the year 1699, consigned three bags of pieces of eight to his uncle, the testator, who employed the defendants, the Souths to dispose of them. They sell them at 5s. 8d. per ounce, which, clear of freight, came to £463 16s. 11d. And, in April 1700, they account with Grey and give him credit for that sum. Gray puts the money out at interest with his own money. And, in a letter, he tells him that he might have his money when he pleases.

Afterwards, Gray makes his will and gives the plaintiff £200 to be paid him in Barbados money within twelve months after his death. And he makes the defendants executors, against whom the plaintiff prefers his bill for the £463 16s. 11d. and interest. And the defendants insist that the legacy ought to go towards satisfaction of the debt.

Lord Chancellor [Lord Cowper]: The plaintiff must be paid his debt with interest. It is plain the testator intended a kindness to his nephew by the legacy he gave him. This is not a debt for money borrowed, and he would never have it in his view, when he made this will, to discharge any part of this debt, which was owing in England by a legacy to be paid in Barbados twelve months after his death.

## 138

## Sibthorpe v. Anonymous

(Ch. 1709)

*In this case, the contract provision in issue was a valid liquidated damages clause and not an invalid penalty.*

Lincoln's Inn MS. Misc. 9, p. 96

19 May 1709.

The plaintiff and the defendants entered into articles of co-partnership for three years. And, for that time, they had taken a lease of a house in Lombard Street, where they carried on their trade. And, in the articles, there was an agreement that neither of the partners should at the three years' end renew the lease without the other joined with him and, if either of them should renew or endeavor to renew without the other two, he should forfeit £300 to the two other partners. There were other covenants, and mutual bonds of £500 penalty each were given for the performance of these covenants.

The plaintiff and the defendants, at the three year's end, not agreeing to renew the partnership, the plaintiff renewed the lease in his own name, upon which the defendants put their bonds in suit against the plaintiff, who now came to be relieved, suggesting the defendants had first broken their covenants, they having endeavored to take a new lease before the plaintiff attempted to renew. And, besides, it was insisted that the defendants were not damaged by the plaintiff's taking a new lease and that the £300 was only in the nature of a penalty.

Lord Chancellor [Lord Cowper]: The £300 is a liquidated and stated damage and not a penalty. It is what the parties agreed should be the measure of the damage in case either party broke the covenant in renewing without the other.

As to the defendants' endeavoring to renew the lease before the plaintiff went about to take a new lease, I do not find they did more than enquire whether the landlord would grant them a separate lease if they were minded to take it, that is they were seeing whether, if they were minded to break their covenant and pay the £300, it was in their power or no. I do not think a jury would look on this as a breach. However, the plaintiff, if he pleases, may bring his action. I will not hinder him. But, if he will be relieved against the penalty of the bond, it must be upon the payment of the principal, interest, and costs.

## 139

## East v. Coggs

(Ch. 1709)

*In this case, the widow was not allowed to receive both a marriage settlement and her customary share of the London decedent's estate.*

Lincoln's Inn MS. Misc. 9, p. 99

29 June 1709. East, widow and relict of Thomas East v. Coggs *et al.*, executors of [ *blank* ] East, who was the executor of the said Thomas East, upon a bill of revivor.

Thomas East, upon his marriage with the plaintiff, entered into articles with her father and agreed to give a bond to leave the plaintiff £500 at his death. And the father covenanted to settle an estate upon the husband and his wife to take effect after the death of the father and his wife.

Thomas East neglects to give this bond. And, thereupon, the plaintiff's father prefers a bill against him, upon which he was decreed to give such a bond and the plaintiff's father was to make a settlement pursuant to the articles. Accordingly, East gives a bond to trustees to leave his wife £500, and the father makes a settlement. The father dies. And the plaintiff's husband enjoyed the estate for several years, which had been settled on him by his wife's father. And, afterwards, he died having made his will and given away all his estate from his wife.

The plaintiff, after her husband's death, brought a bill against his executor for a satisfaction of the bond and for a moiety of her husband's personal estate, he being a citizen of London and having left no issue.

The executor of Thomas East put in his answer and said the plaintiff eloped from her husband and had delivered up the bond to him to be cancelled and that, during the time she lived [apart] from her husband, her mother left her a chattel lease. And he brought a cross-bill to have an account of this estate.

To this cross-bill, the plaintiff put in her answer. And she says her husband used her very ill and went away from her first, that she did what in her lay towards a reconcilement and, in order thereunto, made him several visits, at one of which he upbraided her with the bond and told her that was what she relied upon. And, thereupon, she admits that she flung down the bond and believes she might tear off the seal. But what she did was upon condition that he would be reconciled to her, which he never would.

As to the lease her mother left her, she says it was given to trustees upon trust to pay the rents to her for her separate use, she having no allowance from her husband and must have starved had it not been for what her mother left her.

Serjeant *Hooper*, for the plaintiff: The bond being given to trustees for the benefit of a married woman, she could not divest herself of the interest of it during the marriage. And, therefore, the debt remained though the bond was cancelled by her inadvertency. Besides, it was upon a condition of reconciliation, which the husband would not come into.

Note there was no marriage articles produced, and it was supposed the agreement was parol.

And My Lord Chancellor [Lord Cowper] said it was uncertain whether, by the agreement, the bond was to be in satisfaction of what she might claim by the custom.

So they read a proof that the husband declared his wife would be entitled to a moiety of his personal estate by the custom.

But My Lord Chancellor [Lord Cowper] said this was after the bond was cancelled and, perhaps, that might be the ground of his opinion.

Lord Chancellor [Lord Cowper]: I am of the opinion the bond is in force and that the plaintiff is at liberty either to take the moiety of her husband's personal estate by the custom or the £500 due on the bond. And, therefore, there must be an account taken. And, if the moiety is more than the bond, then she is to have that; if less, she may abide by the bond. But she ought not to have both.

As to the pearl necklace given her by her mother and what she has saved out of her separate estate, she ought to retain it. The husband's estate is sufficiently recompensed by not having maintained her in all that time.

*Sir Thomas Powys* insisted that the plaintiff ought to have the bond and her share by the custom too, for, suppose a citizen makes a settlement of land on his wife, this will not defeat her of the benefit of the custom.

Lord Chancellor [Lord Cowper]: The construction that is to be made of this bond must be that the wife shall have £500 paid her at her husband's death, that is that he shall leave such an estate that shall be sufficient to pay her £500; so that, if she has £500 out of his estate, whether it is by the custom or any other way, it is a satisfaction of the bond.

The plaintiff's counsel elected to abide by the bond rather than enter into an account. So it was decreed that the £500 should be paid her with interest from her husband's death and costs.

2 Eq. Cas. Abr. 275, 22 E.R. 232

Easter 8 Ann. [1709].

A citizen of London entered into a bond to a trustee to leave his wife at his death £500. He dies and leaves her nothing.

She brings her bill for the £500 and to have a moiety of the residue of her husband's personal estate.

[It was] decreed that she cannot have both, but she may have her election. The £500 is to be left her at all events, although, at his death, she was entitled unto a moiety of his personal estate, yet the husband might have converted that moiety into a real estate.

## 140

## Finney v. Finney

(Ch. 1709)

*An eldest son must bring into hotchpot upon an intestacy any portion he had received out of his father's personal estate.*

Lincoln's Inn MS. Misc. 10, p. 130, pl. 2

Trinity 1709.

[It was] decreed by Lord Cowper (as Mr. Peere Williams informed me) that the eldest son should bring into hotchpot upon the Statute of Distributions[1] the portion he had received out of his father's personal estate. And so Mr. *Vernon* said in this case it had been decreed before.

## 141

## Pye v. George

(Ch. 1709–1710)

*The issue of a tenant in tail is entitled to revive a decree obtained by his ancestor.*

*The question in this case was whether an entail of lands within a manor was barred by a fine of the manor.*

*It is a breach of trust for trustees appointed to preserve contingent remainders to join in a conveyance to destroy the remainder.*

[1] Stat. 22 & 23 Car. II, c. 10 (*SR*, V, 719–720).

Lincoln's Inn MS. Misc. 9, p. 101

1 July 1709.

The issue of the tenant in tail brings a bill to revive a decree obtained by his father, to which the defendants plead and demur.

As to so much of the bill as demands an account of the rents and profits of the lands in question and a discovery of encumbrances, the defendants [Gorge *et ux.*] plead the Statute of 11 & 12 King William,[1] for disabling Roman Catholics from taking by descent, limitation, or remainder any lands etc. unless he conforms as the Act directs.

Lord Chancellor [Lord Cowper]: By this Act, the fee is not put in abeyance. The inheritance is in the Popish heir, and the next Protestant heir shall take the profits. But then that is only temporary until the death of the Popish heir or until he conforms so that, surely, if there should be any encumbrances on his estate, he may for the benefit of his family bring a bill for an account and discovery of these encumbrances.

Serjeant *Hooper*: As to our demurrer, we say the issue of the tenant in tail does not claim from his father, but *per formam doni* paramount to his father. And, as no decree obtained against a tenant in tail can bind his issue, so neither can the issue take advantage of any decree made in favor of a tenant in tail. It is true, I think, if a tenant in tail brings a bill to perpetuate the testimony of his witnesses, the issue may have the benefit of those depositions. But that is the only case I know of, and the reason of that is because the issue was not then born. But, in our case, it appears the plaintiff was born when his father's bill was brought.

In next place, the plaintiff is wrong as to form, for the bill prays to revive and yet, when they come in the close [of the bill] to pray process, they pray a *subpoena tam ad respondendum quam revidendum* instead of *revivendum*.

Lord Chancellor [Lord Cowper]: I am of the opinion the issue of a tenant in tail is entitled to revive a decree obtained by his ancestor. He claims by descent from him. And there is so far a privity between them as that I think he ought to have the benefit a decree made in favor of his ancestor.

As to the mistake about the prayer of process, I think there is nothing in that.

British Library MS. Hargrave 80, f. 191, pl. 2

The question was whether an entail of lands in Trivil was barred by a fine of the manor of Trivil.

[It was argued] by Serjeant *Hooper*, *Chesshyre*, and *Pratt*: M. Finch's Case, 6 Reports,[2] was cited that a manor in reputation will pass by a grant of a manor.

---

[1] Stat. 11 Will. III, c. 4, s. 4 (*SR*, VII, 587).

[2] *Moon v. Crat (Henry Finch's Case)* (1606), 6 Coke Rep. 39, 77 E.R. 310, also Yelverton 82, 80 E.R. 56, 1 Brownlow & Goldesborough 184, 123 E.R. 744.

Thyne and Thyne, Syderfin 191,[1] that lands used with a manor but found not to be really parcel, yet passed. Foreman and Botham, Moor 190,[2] that a rent reserved on a limitation in fee of a parcel of the manor passed though not parcel by the words *cum pertinentiis* and therewith used etc., and 2 Rolle, Abr., 712, Vines and Durham,[3] cited in Sir Michael Finch's Case, *manerium* [was] allowed in pleading though it was only a reputed manor, there being no freeholders to prove the land to be reputed parcel of the manor of Trivil, inquisitions *post mortem*, attendance of the tenants at leets, and the court baron being held together and unity[4] of ownership alleged that a little time is sufficient to gain reputation. 3 Cro. 6, ten years is sufficient, and 2 Rolle 347,[5] two years [is] enough to gain a name from occupation or use, that, in case of a house, and it is the same with respect to a manor, lastly that the number of acres in the fine was sufficient to pass the whole and though the deed and fine make but one conveyance and, where a man is selling (as here the tenant in tail was making a mortgage), the deed will control the general words of the fine so that no more shall pass to the mortgagee than what is in the deed, yet it does not restrain the tenant in tail from comprising more lands in the fine of which he may afterwards declare the use (if he does not, that will result) and that he did here a few years after for a jointure which was enjoyed forty years against the heirs in tail.

*Jekyll* agreed that a manor in reputation will pass by a grant of a manor though it was otherwise adjudged in Mallett's Case, Cro. El.,[6] but that is controlled by Sir M. Finch's Case. But there is a great difference between that case of a reputed manor and this. There, the reputed manor must pass or the grant be void. Here is a real manor which is sufficient to satisfy the words and no necessity therefore that land reputed only parcel should pass by a fine of the manor. Thynns's Case is the only one that a reputed parcel will pass by a grant of the manor. And it is said there to have been the constant opinion since Sir M. Finch's Case that a reputed parcel would pass. But the case in 2 Rolle 347 is contrary and that was since Sir M. Finch's Case.

(*Chesshyre*: That is an opinion *obiter*.)

Nor is there here sufficient evidence of the reputation. Unity of occupation is a ground but not an evidence of a reputation. But here is only unity of ownership. Leets are derived out of the sheriff's tourn and be more extensive than the manor. The tenants' appearance, therefore, at the leets is no evidence of their holding the

---

[1] *Thin v. Thin* (1664), 1 Siderfin 190, 82 E.R. 1050, also 1 Ventris 51, 86 E.R. 37, 1 Levinz 27, 82 E.R. 280, 1 Keble 26, 591, 691, 716, 83 E.R. 790, 1129, 1188, 1203.

[2] *Foreman v. Bobham* (1584), Moore K.B. 190, 72 E.R. 524.

[3] *Vines v. Durham* (1580), 2 Rolle, Abr., *Triall*, p. 712, pl. D, 7.

[4] sembly *MS.*

[5] *Loft v. Baker* (1623), 2 Rolle Rep. 347, 81 E.R. 843, also Palmer 375, 81 E.R. 1131, Benloe 127, 73 E.R. 987.

[6] *Mallet v. Mallet* (1596), Croke Eliz. 524, 707, 78 E.R. 772, 942.

manor. Inquisitions *post mortem* are the weakest evidence. Things are thrown in here carelessly, especially in this case, where the heir was above age and nothing to be gotten.

[Other copies of this report: Lincoln's Inn MS. Misc. 383, p. 310, Lincoln's Inn MS. Misc. 107, f. 31, pl. 3.]

2 Salkeld 680, 91 E.R. 578

Michaelmas 9 Anne.

Trustees appointed to preserve contingent remainders did join in a conveyance to destroy the remainder before a son was born. And this was decreed a plain breach of trust and that whoever claimed under this conveyance, having notice of the trust or by a voluntary settlement, should be liable to make good the estates. *Per* HARCOURT, Lord Keeper.

[Other reports of this case: 1 Peere Williams 128, 24 E.R. 323, Precedents in Chancery 308, 24 E.R. 146, 1 Eq. Cas. Abr. 384, 21 E.R. 1120.]

## 142

## Mason v. Lake

(Ch. 1709)

*A party cannot have discovery of anything that might subject a person to a statutory penalty, and the person asserting the privilege need not state in particular what statute might be applicable.*

Lincoln's Inn MS. Misc. 9, p. 103, pl. 1

*Eodem die* [1 July 1709].

Lake [of the Middle Temple] lent Newell £5000, and the plaintiff gave Lake a mortgage as a collateral security. Newell failing and the plaintiff being called upon to pay the money, he brings a bill suggesting that Lake received £200 as a premium for advancing. And, therefore, it is prayed that he may discover what premium he received and that such premium be discounted out of the money due on the mortgage.

As to so much of the bill as prays a discovery of what the defendant had received for premium and gratuities for advancing the £5000 to Newell, the defendant demurs. And he shows for cause that such a discovery would subject him to the penalties of several statutes, but he does not particularize the Statute of Usury[1] or any other statute.

And yet the demurrer was allowed, for such a discovery might bring him within the Statute of Usury.

[1] Stat. 12 Car. II, c. 13 (*SR*, V, 236–237).

[Other reports of this case: 2 Eq. Cas. Abr. 481, 22 E.R. 409, 2 Brown P.C. 495, 1 E.R. 1088.]

[Related cases: Lake v. Mason (Ch. 1713), see below, Case No. 543.]

## 143

## Onslow v. South

(Ch. 1709–1710)

*In this case, the legacy in issue lapsed upon the death of the legatee.*

Lincoln's Inn. MS. Misc. 13, p. 38, pl. 1

5 July 8 Anne. Onslow v. South.

Charles Knight, by his will, gave £2000 to his kinsman Phillip Knight at his age of twenty-one years. He gave the surplus of his estate, which was vastly great, to his only daughter, Elizabeth Knight, who married Mr. Onslow. And he made South and others executors in trust etc.

Mr. Onslow and his wife brought a bill to have an account etc.

Upon the hearing, Lord Chancellor Cowper decreed that the £2000 should carry interest at £5 percent *per annum* and that the £2000 and interest should be kept in the hands of South, the executor, until Phillip Knight attained twenty-one. But what was then to be done with the interest, the decree is silent.

It seems as if the court intended Phillip should have it.

Phillip Knight died under age, *viz.* at eighteen, having by his will given the £2000 and interest to Draper.

Lincoln's Inn. MS. Misc. 13, p. 38, pl. 2

5 July 8 Anne. Onslow v. Draper and South.

Mr. Inslow brought his second bill to have the £2000 and interest as a legacy not vested in Phillip [Knight], but lapsed by his death.

Lord Cowper: And it was decreed to him as a legacy not vested, but lapsed, allowing particular sums for the maintenance of Philip [Knight].

1 Eq. Cas. Abr. 295, 21 E.R. 1056

Trinity 1710.

So, where one, being possessed of a very considerable personal estate, part in Jamaica and part in England, and being himself residing in Jamaica, made his will and thereof several executors, some for his estate in Jamaica and others residing in England for his estate here. And, amongst other things, he devised in these words, *viz.*: 'I give and bequeath to J.S., now under the custody of R.D., the sum of £2000 at the age of twenty-one years to be paid by my executors in

England.' And he devised all the rest and residue of his estate to the plaintiff. And he died.

J.S., having attained his age of eighteen, made his will, and, thereby, he devised this legacy and all his estate to the defendant.

And Lord Chancellor [Lord Cowper] held this a lapsed legacy and that it was a vain endeavor in the defendant's counsel to construe it a present legacy and, therefore, vested by the word 'now', because it was a plain description of the condition of the legatee, *viz.* 'now under the custody of' etc., for, otherwise, they must stop at 'now', which would be playing with the words. And, though the word 'paid' was made use of, yet it was plainly intended a designation of the persons by whom the legacy was to be paid, *viz.* by his executors in England, which was proper, he having two sets of them.

## 144

## Whitcombe v. Whitcombe

(Ch. 1709)

*The question in this case was whether a court of equity will aid a remote heir at law, an uncle of the decedent, against the decedent's half-sisters.*

Lincoln's Inn MS. Misc. 9, p. 103, pl. 2

8 July 1709.

Peter Whitcombe, being seised in fee of certain lands and having two daughters by his first wife, dies, leaving his second wife secretly pregnant of a son, who was born alive. His mother, who had a right of dower and was guardian to her son, enters generally, after which the son dies.

And the plaintiff, being cousin and heir to him by several descents, brings a bill against the mother and the two daughters to discover what leases and encumbrances were on the estate.

The defendants answer and refuse to make that discovery. And the answer being reported insufficient, upon exceptions to that report, My Lord Chancellor [Lord Cowper] was of the opinion that the plaintiff was not entitled to that discovery until he had made out his title at law.

The plaintiff, upon this, brought an [action of] ejectment. And a trial at the bar being had, he was nonsuited, the defendant having set up a lease for years, after which the plaintiff amends his bill. And now, he comes to have the assistance of this court to set these leases and encumbrances out of the way that he might go on at law to try his title.

It was insisted on for the daughters that they were in the nature of purchasers or creditors, having no provision made them by their father. And, therefore, they ought to be regarded in a court of equity more than a remote relation.

My Lord Chancellor [LORD COWPER] inclined to think that, as to the mother's entry, it shall be presumed she entered as to one-third in her own right and, as to the other two-thirds, in the right of and as the guardian to her son, for an entry ought to follow the right and no one shall be presumed to do a wrong until it appears.

But then, as to what the plaintiff insisted on by his bill, he seemed to think that the daughters stood fairer in the eyes of equity than the plaintiff. But suppose they stood in an *equilibrio*. Is there any reason that the court should assist an heir who claims by descent from the son against an heir who claims from the father? He inclined to think equity should not.

But no decree was made, the cause being ordered to stand over for a reason which I [Melmoth] do not remember.

British Library MS. Hargrave 80, f. 128v, pl. 2

A man left two daughters by a first wife, the second wife pregnant with a son, who lived a year. And the uncle, as heir to him, brought an [action of] ejectment but was nonsuited by terms being set up by the daughters.

He then brought his bill for a discovery of deeds etc. and, particularly, of the leases of the estate to enable him to prove a possession in the infant.

And, upon exceptions to a report of the insufficiency of the answer for not setting them forth, the report was overruled.

And, at the hearing, LORD COWPER would not compel the defendant to discover and declared that this court would not in all cases help a person to deeds that he has a right to at law, that it would not help a first purchaser against a second without notice, nor, where there is a very hard bargain made between two, this court will not help the person that would take an advantage of it to enable him to do so at law.

[Other copies of this report: Lincoln's Inn MS. Misc. 383, p. 227, pl. 4, Lincoln's Inn MS. Misc. 106, p. 189, pl. 3.]

Lincoln's Inn MS. Misc. 506, p. 69

One had purchased a considerable estate in Essex and had by his first wife two daughters and, afterwards, married a second. He made no disposition of his real estate, but, as he lay sick, being asked what he would do with it, he said it should go to his children as by law it ought. The second wife was pregnant and, after his death, was brought to bed of a son, who afterwards died at nine years of age. The daughters were but half-blood.

A poor remote heir to the son brought a bill for a discovery [so] that he might bring an [action of] ejectment.

But the court discouraged it, which prevailed on the heir to take a sum of money.

This was mentioned to show how far the court will be influenced by the nearness of the relation.

[Other reports of this case: Precedents in Chancery 280, 24 E.R. 135.]

## 145

## Weeks v. Weeks

(Ch. 1709)

*In this case, the devise in issue was an executory devise, and a remainder passed to the devisee.*

Lincoln's Inn MS. Misc. 9, p. 104, pl. 1

12 July 1709.

A man bequeaths a term to one for life, then to another for life, and, after his death, to his children. And he declares that, if the second tenant for life died without issue then living, that it should go over. He died without issue. And the question was if it should go over.

[Lord Cowper] decreed it to be an executory devise and that the remainderman should have it, the dying without issue being confined to one life that was then in being.

## 146

## Anonymous

(Ch. 1709)

*Where a legacy is given in trust payable at a date certain, no interest is payable thereon by the trustees before the date of payment.*

Lincoln's Inn MS. Misc. 9, p. 104, pl. 2

A man, by his will, gives lands to trustees and charges them with the payment of £500 to one of his children when he came to the age of twenty-four, and directs his trustees to educate this child in some honest employment. The child was three years old at his father's death. And when he grew up, they put him out apprentice, and gave £60 with him. And the question was when he came of age whether he should have interest for his £500 or any allowance for maintenance.

[Trevor] decreed that no interest or maintenance should be allowed, but the £60 should be reckoned as a gift beyond the £500. And the trustees having expended that sum in putting him out, their determination shall fix the quantum of what the testator intended they should lay out in putting his son out apprentice.

## 147

## Hellier v. Fishweek

(Ch. 1709–1714)

*A contract obligation can be satisfied by the obligor's allowing land to descend to the obligee.*

*A creditor who refuses to join in an assignment for the benefit of creditors can nevertheless receive his share of the proportional settlement if he later joins in before the distribution.*

*The costs of administration of an assignment for the benefit of creditors are payable out of the debtor's estate.*

Lincoln's Inn MS. Misc. 9, p. 105, pl. 1

16 July 1709.

It was said by the counsel and agreed by the Master of the Rolls [TREVOR] that, if a man upon his marriage agrees to settle lands of such a value upon his wife and her issue and she dies in his lifetime and, afterwards, he dies, having made no settlement, but gives or leaves lands to descend upon his eldest son, this shall be a satisfaction *pro tanto* of what he agreed to settle.

Lincoln's Inn MS. Misc. 11, p. 66, pl. 2

24 April 1714. William Hellier, plaintiff; Caleb Fishweek and Sarah, his wife, which said Caleb is administrator of Andrew Wilmer, deceased, Sarah Wilmer, relict of the said Andrew, William Wilmer, and William Boxall, defendants.

Andrew Wilmer, the intestate, before his marriage with Catherine Boxall, entered into a bond to the defendant Boxall dated 17 November 1683 of the penalty of £800 conditioned that he, the said Andrew Wilmer, would within one year after the said marriage settle freehold lands of the yearly value of £20 upon himself and the said Catherine for their lives and, after their decease, to the heirs of their two bodies begotten over and above all such lands as were settled by deed or deeds bearing even date with the said bond.

Katherine died, leaving issue by the said Andrew Wilmer, one child only, *viz.* the defendant William Wilmer, after which, the said Andrew Wilmer intermarried with the defendant Sarah Wilmer, having never settled any lands pursuant to the said bond. And, about August 1705, the said Andrew Wilmer died intestate and indebted to several persons by bond and simple contract, but not leaving assets sufficient to satisfy his bond debts.

And the defendant, his wife, refusing to take out administration, a meeting was had of the greatest part of the bond creditors, who agreed to remit the interest due on their respective bonds and to take their respective principal sums in equal proportions so far as the assets would extend. And in order for the getting in of the same, it was agreed that the defendant Fishweek, a bond creditor, should take out administration to the intestate. Pursuant to which agreement, articles were prepared between the bond creditors of the one part and defendants Fishweek and Wilmer of the other part, which were to the purport and effect of the said agreement and were executed by most of the bond creditors, except the plaintiff, who was a creditor by bond for £90 and was present at the said meeting of the said creditors and made a party to the said articles and was pressed and importuned to execute the same but would not, he insisting upon having his whole debt paid him.

The plaintiff refusing to execute the articles and threatening to sue the defendant Fishweek, other articles were executed wherein it was agreed by the creditors who executed the first articles that, in order to prevent the said bond debts being unequally paid and that an equal division might be made of the said intestate's estate and for the legal protecting of the defendant Fishweek, an attorney for the bond creditors should file originals in their names and deliver declarations and proceed therein to recover judgments against the defendant Fishweek as administrator of the said intestate.

After executing the articles, the plaintiff was requested to agree with the rest of the said bond creditors, but he still persisted in his refusal so to do. Whereupon, the defendant Fishweek got in the said intestate's estate and thereout paid 15s. in the pound of all the said bond debts except the plaintiff's and the said bond entered into to the defendant Boxall, most of the said bond creditors, except the plaintiff, having pursuant to the last mentioned articles recovered judgments on their respective bonds against the administrator.

The plaintiff brought an action at law against the administrator. And, afterwards, he exhibited his bill for a discovery of assets and to be relieved against the said judgments and to set aside the said Boxall's bond and that he might be paid his whole debt and interest.

Upon hearing the cause before the Master of the Rolls [Trevor] on 16 July 1709, it was referred to the Master to take an account of the said intestate's personal estate and the Master was to see whether any and what lands were settled on the said intestate's former wife or, since his death, had descended on the defendant Wilmer and whether the condition of the bond entered into to the defendant Boxal was anyways performed.

The Master made his report 5 April 1712, and stated what had been received and paid by the defendant, the administrator. And the Master further certified that the defendant, the administrator, insisted to retain in his hands the sum of £50 for a debt due to himself upon bond and £20 due to him on bond as executor of the widow Mansfield and that the defendant Boxall had obtained a judgment on his said bond, but that no lands had descended to the defendant William Wilmer as heir at law to the said intestate.

The matter of the Master's report coming on to be heard before His Honor [Trevor] 22 June 1713, His Honor declared the defendant, the administrator, was a trustee for all of the intestate's creditors and that the plaintiff ought not to be excluded from having his proportion of the intestate's estate according to the debt with the other bond creditors and ordered it should be referred back to the Master to tax the plaintiff and the defendants their costs which were to be paid out of the intestate's estate in the first place. And the Master was to settle what the proportion of the said estate after the costs of suit deducted did amount to and the said bond entered into by the intestate to the defendant Boxall was to be paid in proportion after the said costs and what the Master should certify due to the plaintiff for his proportion out of the intestate's estate after the costs deducted was ordered to be paid the plaintiff by the defendant, the administrator, and that such of the intestate's creditors who were already paid more than their proportion of their debt were to refund such overplus to the defendant Fishweek.

The defendant Fishweek appealed from this order to the Lord Cowper for the reasons following:

First, for that he ought to have been decreed to retain his own debt out of the intestate's assets before anything should be paid to the plaintiff, for, though, as to the bond creditors, who came into the agreement to receive their debts in proportion and executed articles for that purpose, the defendant Fishweek might be esteemed in the nature of a trustee and had no right to a retainer against them, yet, as to the plaintiff, who never executed those articles but obstinately persisted in demanding his whole debt, the case was as if no such articles had been made and, therefore, as against him, the administrator was entitled to the same privileges as other executors or administrators are in ordinary cases;

Second, supposing the administrator was not justified to retain his own debt against the plaintiff, yet the plaintiff ought not to have been decreed his proportion with the other creditors out of the whole assets, not only because this was to give him the benefit of those articles, which he refused to come into and be bound by, but because, by this means, the administrator would be forced to pay money out of his own pocket to make good the plaintiff's proportion of the whole assets, notwithstanding the administrator had been guilty of no *devastavit* but administered the assets of his intestate in a legal course of administration. And, though the other bond creditors are ordered to refund what they have received above their proportions, yet, they being no parties to this suit, the administrator had no way to compel them to such a refunding but by commencing a new suit against a great number of persons, many of whom are perhaps dead [or] insolvent, which must be carried on at the administrator's costs and would not only be very chargeable and expensive, but, in all likelihood, ineffectual;

Third, for that the plaintiff ought not to have been decreed any costs in regard he has not prevailed in what he has attempted by his bill, which was to set aside the said bond entered into by the defendant Boxall and to be paid his whole debt with interest and what he has obtained is no more than what he might have had and was pressed to accept long before the commencement of this suit, but, instead thereof, he has put the intestate's estate to an unreasonable expense by his vexations proceedings.

However, if it should be thought reasonable to decree the plaintiff his costs, neither such costs nor the other defendants' costs ought to be deducted out of the whole assets in the first place, as is directed, for that, in effect, is to decree the administrator to pay the costs of all parties out of his own pocket, though he has been guilty of no maladministration of his intestate's estate and at first took out administration to the intestate at the request and importunity of the other creditors after the same had been offered to and refused by the plaintiff.

Upon this appeal, the Lord Chancellor [Lord Harcourt] declared the defendant Fishweek, the administrator, was a trustee for all the intestate's bond creditors to distribute the intestate's assets among them equally in proportion to their debts, that the plaintiff was entitled to receive his proportion with the other bond creditors, and that it was his own fault he did not receive the same. And, therefore, so far as the administrator appears by the Master's report to have applied the assets towards making a proportionable satisfaction amongst the creditors, such assets have been well applied, and the creditors ought not to refund the same. And the defendant Fishweek ought to retain out of the assets in his hands towards satisfaction of the debt owing to him on bond from the intestate in proportion to what he has paid to the other creditors.

But, inasmuch as further assets have been since discovered, there is room for the plaintiff to come in for some satisfaction out of the assets which remain unapplied in pursuance of the agreement between the defendant Fishweek and the other bond creditors.

Therefore, let it be referred back to the Master to tax the defendant Fishweek's costs to be paid out of such unapplied assets in the first place. And the Master is also to tax the plaintiff's costs, which are to be paid out of such unapplied assets in the next place. And, as far as the other creditors appear by the Master's report to have received a satisfaction out of the assets for their respective debts, the plaintiff is to receive a like satisfaction for his debt out of such unapplied assets as aforesaid (the said costs first being deducted thereout) before any other creditors to whom a proportionable satisfaction for his debt has been made by the administrator be let in to receive a further satisfaction of his debt.

And, as to the bond of £400 entered into by the intestate to Boxall, the former directions are to stand, all parties acquiescing therein.

## 148

## Shorter v. Shorter

(Ch. 1709)

*An inter vivos gift in the form of an apprenticeship to a son is not an ademption of a legacy to him.*

Lincoln's Inn MS. Misc. 9, p. 105, pl. 2

Arthur Shorter v. John Shorter and Sir John Philips, executors of John Shorter.

The testator, by his will, gives his real estate to the defendants and their heirs upon trust that they should sell or mortgage the same and, thereout, pay £1500 to the plaintiff and another of his younger sons and £2000 to his daughter. And he directs his executors to apply any part of his sons' portions, not exceeding £300, in putting them out apprentice. After his will and before his death, he puts the plaintiff out apprentice and gives £150 with him, who, after his father's death, sues out his indentures and has £90 of the money paid him back. The question was if this £150 should be deducted out of the plaintiff's legacy.

Master of the Rolls [Trevor]: I remember a case where a man had given £1000 apiece to his daughters by his will and, afterwards, marries [off] one of them and gives her £1000 for a portion. After his death, the husband sues for the £1000 legacy by virtue of the will. But the court decreed the marriage portion was a revocation of the legacy. I do not know the court has ever gone farther than this. The plaintiff must have his whole £1500 paid him with interest from his father's death and costs.

## 149

## Oxwith v. Plummer

(Ch. 1709)

*A creditor who knows that his security is defective and fails to perfect it cannot later go against it after a later lien has been perfected against it.*

*One who has equity and law too will be preferred before one who has only equity where both equities are of the same nature.*

British Library MS. Hargrave 80, f. 17

Oxwick v. Plommer.

One, seised in fee of several parcels of land, copyhold and freehold, makes a mortgage thereof by a deed, specifying all the parcels and mentioning that which was copyhold to be copyhold. The mortgagor, without making any surrender to the use of the first mortgagee, surrenders the copyhold to a second mortgagee upon a valuable consideration, and there is an admission pursuant to the surrender. The first mortgagee, not finding a sufficient security in the freehold lands to answer his debt, prefers his bill against the mortgagor and the second mortgagee to the end that they may concur in making the copyhold liable to his mortgage as it was intended. But the bill was dismissed, for the first mortgagee having notice by the very deed of mortgage that parcel of the lands was copyhold and was not liable by the law to be thus conveyed as freehold lands, it is to be presumed that he did not intend to have that for his security since he neglected that proper means of making it liable.

In the argument of this case, were cited two others, which the court agreed to be good equity. The first was this. One, seised in fee, makes a feoffment by way of a mortgage but the feoffment is never executed any otherwise than by the delivery of the deed; no livery is made upon it; the mortgagor does afterward contract debts and acknowledge judgments to other persons and dies. The lands descend to the heir and, in his hands, are taken in execution for the satisfaction of the judgments; the first mortgagee prefers his bill against the heir and against the conusees of the judgment that he might have livery and seisin made to him upon his feoffment and his lands effectually secured to him in preference to the judgments which were subsequent to his intended mortgage. For the defendant in this case, it was said that the legal estates being in the conusees of the judgment and they, being in the nature of purchasers for a valuable consideration and in that respect entitled to the equity of this court as well as the plaintiff, ought not to be deprived of their estate at law for the plaintiff, who has a bare equity. To this it was answered and so ruled *per curiam* that the common rule, which is that one who has equity and law too should be preferred before one who has only equity, is certainly true where both equities are of the same nature. But, in this case, the first mortgagee, from the time of the feoffment made to him, had the trust of the estate though not an effectual conveyance until livery; he depended upon the land for the security of his debt, and the tenant at law was seised in trust for him. But the defendants never meddled with the estate by the contract, but relied upon a personal security for their debts, and, therefore, it is not reason nor equity that the estate should be made liable for their satisfaction in preference to another who contracted expressly for it. So it was decreed that the defendants should complete the plaintiff's conveyance. If the defendants had distrusted their security and desired a better from their debtor by way of a mortgage and he had actually conveyed his lands to them without notice of the precedent trust, their title should in that case have been preferred to the first mortgagee who relied upon an imperfect conveyance. And this the Lord Chancellor [Lord Cowper] now allowed.

The other case cited was this.[1] A tenant in fee of a copyhold surrenders into the hands of two tenants for the use of J.S. in fee, by way of a mortgage; that surrender is not presented at the next court. The surrenderor becomes bankrupt, and a commission is taken out against him, and the assignees of the commissioners of bankrupts are admitted in court to these copyhold lands whereof the bankrupt was seised at the time of the bankruptcy committed notwithstanding the surrender which was not presented. J.S. prefers his bill against the assignees of the commissioners of bankrupts, that they may surrender to him according to the uses

[1] *Taylor v. Wheeler* (1709), see above, Case No. 58.

of the intended mortgage. And it was decreed that they should, for, though they had a legal estate and likewise and equitable interest for the satisfaction of creditors, yet these creditors, for whom that assignees had gained that legal estate, had never contracted with the copyholder for this estate in particular, but rested in general upon a personal security and that, therefore, their interest ought to be regarded as subsequent to J.S., who had paid his money upon the security of this very estate and had contracted for the conveyance of it, which was begun though not perfected in time and which, in pursuance of the agreement to convey, the copyholder became seised of from that time in trust only for J.S.

[Other copies of this report: Lincoln's Inn MS. Misc. 383, p. 30.]

[Other reports of this case: Gilbert Rep. 13, 25 E.R. 10, 2 Vernon 636, 23 E.R. 1016, 2 Eq. Cas. Abr. 226, 577, 22 E.R. 192, 486.]

## 150

## Anonymous

(Ch. 1709)

*A lease will merge into an inheritance of the same estate.*

*When a term of years attends upon the inheritance, it attends upon the whole and every part of the inheritance and every estate that is derived out of the inheritance, including tenancies by the curtesy.*

Lincoln's Inn MS. Misc. 9, p. 106

4 November 1709.

A man settles his estate, upon a marriage, upon himself for life, then to his wife for a jointure, remainder to his first and other sons in tail male, remainder to trustees for 500 years to raise daughters' portions, upon failer of issue male, remainder to his own right heirs. He dies leaving two daughters and no sons, after which the daughters join with their mother in making a mortgage, which they do by demise for 1000 years. And this term, as also the 500 years term after payment of the money and performing some trusts, is declared to attend the inheritance.

After this, one of the daughters marries and dies, leaving a child. The husband prefers his bill. And the points are two:

First, if the husband should have the benefit of the term created by the settlement so as to come in for the portion provided for her by that settlement;

Second, if he should not, then whether the term should be made use of against him to deprive him of the right the law gives him of being tenant by the curtesy.

Lord Chancellor [Lord Cowper]: There is no reason the husband should have the benefit of this term to raise the portion. The trusts of the term and the inheritance uniting in one and the same persons and they having considered themselves as having the inheritances by making a mortgage, there is no reason now to separate them, and the rather because it is plain the husband looked on his wife as an inheritrix when he married her and did not consider the portion provided for her by the settlement, for he made her no jointure.

As to the second point, I think it would be very hard the term should not be of any avail for the husband in one case and yet be made use of against him in the other.

When it is descended, that a term of years shall attend upon the inheritance, the natural meaning and import of those words is that it shall attend upon the whole and every part of the inheritance, that is upon every estate that is derived out of the inheritance, whether it be for years or for life. If this is the intent of the parties, as it is plain it is, is it not against all sense and reason to say that this term, which was declared should protect every part of the inheritance, shall now be made use of to defeat an estate which is derived out of the inheritance?

As to the case of dower, this court has gone a great way already in denying to set aside mortgages and other terms for years which have been set up at law to defeat a woman of her dower. For my own part, I see no reason to go any farther, and, indeed, I am not fully satisfied of the Case of Lord Radnor and VanderBende.[1] But there was a purchaser, and he is always favored. And, as to Serjeant Maynard's making a lease to his man Bradford the day before his marriage to prevent his wife's dower, which is mentioned in that case, it might perhaps be reasonable so to do, that she who brought but a small fortune should not be endowed of so large an estate. However, I think I am not borne down with the weight of the authority of that case. And, therefore, I am of the opinion the plaintiff is to be relieved as to the last point. But then, he must do, as is done in all cases where there is a mortgage upon the estate of a tenant for life, that is he must pay off a third of the mortgage and, in the meantime, pay a third of the profits towards the discharge of that encumbrance.

## 151

## Ingram v. Kersteman

(Ch. 1709–1713)

*The cancelling of a mortgage does not take away the underlying obligation.*
*In a suit for mutual accounts, either party can bring a bill of revivor.*

[1] *Countess of Radnor v. Vandebendy* (1683–1697), Shower P.C. 69, 1 E.R. 48, *sub nom. Lady Bodmin v. Vandenbendy*, 1 Vernon 179, 356, 23 E.R. 399, 520, 2 Chancery Cases 172, 22 E.R. 899, *sub nom. Lady Radnor v. Rotheram*, 2 Freeman 211, 22 E.R. 1165, Precedents in Chancery 65, 24 E.R. 32, 1 Eq. Cas. Abr. 219, 21 E.R. 1002, 2 Eq. Cas. Abr. 383, 22 E.R. 326, Lincoln's Inn MS. Misc. 559, f. 111, Chancery Repts. *tempore* Jac. II, 156.

Lincoln's Inn MS. Misc. 10, p. 132, pl. 2

8 November 1709. Master of the Rolls.

Stephen Egerton, possessed of a leasehold estate, borrows £120 of the defendant and assigns his lease for a security on the 17 February 1699[/1700]. Afterwards, the defendant lends him £380 more. And, in June 1701, the defendant takes a second mortgage, which, being made for both sums, the first mortgage was thereupon cancelled. And, sometime after, he buys in the equity of redemption for £230.

In 1704, Egerton failed, and a commission of bankruptcy was taken out against him, and he was found a bankrupt before the making of the second mortgage. And the commissioners having assigned this lease to the plaintiff, he brought his [action of] ejectment. And, thereupon, the now defendant brought his bill to be relieved. And the cause being heard, an issue at law was directed to enquire when Egerton became a bankrupt. And, upon the trial of that issue, it was found that Egerton became a bankrupt before the second mortgage, upon which, the plaintiff's bill was dismissed with costs.

The plaintiff then recovered possession in his [action of] ejectment and sold the lease. But not having the original lease, for that was in the defendant's custody, who would not part with it, he was forced to give the purchaser a covenant that he would get up the original lease.

In pursuance of this covenant, the plaintiff Kersteman brought his bill to set aside the cancelled mortgage and to have up the original leases.

And, upon the hearing, the court declared that the £120 lent by the defendant on the cancelled mortgage was a subsisting debt, and ordered the Master to compute what was due for principal and interest, discounting what the defendant had received for the rents of the premises, upon payment whereof, the defendant was to deliver up the leases and assign to the plaintiff. And costs were reserved until after the account.

17 February 1712[/13]. Ingram v. James Kersteman, executor of William Kersteman, Phillips, and Withers.

The plaintiff in the preceding cause dying soon after the hearing of that cause, the now plaintiff, who was the defendant in the other cause, brought his bill to revive the former decree and that he might be paid the £120 and interest due upon his cancelled mortgage.

It was insisted on for the plaintiff that, though he was a defendant in the former suit, yet he might bring a bill to revive, for, where there are mutual accounts decreed, as there were in this case, either party may revive (and so the court agreed) upon the death of the other, that, by the former decree, it was declared the £120 was a subsisting debt and that the defendant Withers having purchased of the defendant Phillips after that decree, he was a purchaser *pendente lite* and, besides, was a purchaser with notice of the plaintiff's title, for, he having purchased of Phillips and Phillips of William Kersteman and there being a covenant in the assignment to Phillips to indemnify him against the plaintiff's cancelled mortgage, he shall be presumed to have notice, it being incumbent on everyone who purchases a leasehold estate to look into all the assignments which bring down the title and, whatever is contained in any of them, he shall be affected with; so that the plaintiff was now proper to pray that the defendant Withers might stand in the room of William Kersteman and might pay what upon the account was directed by the former decree shall appear to be due to the plaintiff. And this it was said was the more reasonable in regard the plaintiff had both law and equity of his side, for he was an honest mortgagee and the cancelling of his deed did not destroy his title at law. It is true the erasing of a deed after it is executed vitiates the deed because of the supposed fraud, but cancelling the deed does not divest the estate, which still remains in the party notwithstanding.

On the other side, it was said that the cancelling of the deed had destroyed the plaintiff's title at law, it being done by himself or with his consent, and the rather because he had accepted of another security, that notice in this case was not material, the defendant having only notice of a deed which was not subsisting, and, as to the decree, that was made in favor of Kersteman, who came to redeem. And, therefore, whatever the court might think fit to do as between the plaintiff Ingram and Kersteman, who was the assignee of the commissioners of bankrupts against Edgerton, yet the case was now altered as to the defendant, who was a fair purchaser for a valuable consideration. And, therefore, it was prayed the bill might be dismissed. And, if the plaintiff thought he had a good title at law, he might try it if he pleased.

The Master of the Rolls [Trevor] seemed to make a great doubt whether the cancelling of the deed had not destroyed the plaintiff's title at law. And he said the case was very different now from what it was at the former hearing in respect of the defendant Wither's being a purchaser. And, therefore, he was inclinable to dismiss the bill and leave the plaintiff to [the common] law.

But, upon the plaintiff's discerning that the bill might be continued for a twelve month that he might have an opportunity of trying his title upon an [action of] ejectment in the meantime, it was granted, and the court was of the opinion that, if he could make good his title at law, they should decree the defendant Withers to pay him the money.

Lincoln's Inn MS. Misc. 10, p. 172

Ingram v. Kersteman, executor of Kersteman and John Phillips.

Stephen Egerton, possessed of some houses and ground in Camberwell under two leases made by Mr. Bowyer, mortgages the premises to the plaintiff for £120 by indenture 17th February 1699[/1700].

Upon the 9 June 1701, Egerton borrows more money of the plaintiff and makes another mortgage of the premises to the plaintiff for £380, in which sum the £120 being included, the first mortgage was cancelled, but not delivered up.

Upon the 18th December 1702, the plaintiff buys in the equity of redemption for £230, and, Egerton afterwards absconding, a commission of bankruptcy is taken out against him, and all his estate and effects are assigned to the defendant Kersteman's testator, who, thereupon, brings [an action of] ejectment to recover possession of the premises, and Ingram, the now plaintiff, brings his bill to stay the proceedings upon that [action of] ejectment.

17 June 1707, the cause was heard, and an issue was directed to try whether Egerton became a bankrupt before the 9 June 1701, the date of the second mortgage, which being found against the plaintiff, his bill was afterwards dismissed with costs.

Upon this, Kersteman, the assignee, exhibits his bill against the plaintiff to compel him to deliver up the original leases, who, by answer, insisted upon his cancelled mortgage, which he had not put in issue in the former cause, he relying on his second mortgage.

This cause was heard 8 November 1709 at the Rolls. And the court declared the £120 lent on the cancelled deed was a subsisting debt and referred it to a Master to compute what was due to the plaintiff for the £120 and interest, discounting what he had received by the perception of the profits and, upon the payment of what should be formerly due, the now plaintiff was to deliver up the leases and all his securities and assign the premises to Kersteman.

Before any account was taken, Kersteman died, having, before the bringing of the last bill, sold the premises to the defendant Phillips and covenanted to indemnify him against the plaintiff, and that was the reason of bringing that bill.

After Kersteman's death, the plaintiff brings his bill to carry on the former decree against the executor of Kersteman and that the defendants may pay what is due for the principal and interest or be foreclosed.

This cause was heard the [ *blank* ] day of [ *blank* ]. And an issue was directed to try whether the complainant had any title under the cancelled deed. And this issue being tried and found for the plaintiff, it came on before the Master of the Rolls upon the equity reserved. And it was then decreed that the Master should compute what was due for principal, interest, and costs on the cancelled mortgage and, on the payment thereof, the plaintiff was to assign his mortgage to the defendant Withers, but, in default of payment within six months after the Master's report, the defendant was to stand foreclosed.

## 152

## Rock v. Dade

(Ch. 1709)

*In a suit to set aside a fraudulent transaction, the transferee is a necessary party.*

Lincoln's Inn MS. Misc. 9, p. 108

15 November 1709.

A woman, being seised in fee of lands, marries a second husband. And, before her marriage, she conveys this estate to him and his heirs, and he covenants to charge it with £1000 for the children of the wife by her first husband. Accordingly, after the marriage, he settles this estate and charges it with £1000 pursuant to his marriage agreement, and, then, he entails it upon his own children. After this, he borrows money upon bond, and dies. And the question was if this settlement was fraudulent against a bond creditor.

*Sir Simon Harcourt*, for the defendant: In this case, the husband was not indebted at the time of the settlement. And I never knew it said that, when a man makes a settlement as a provision for his family and is in good circumstances at that time, that this was fraudulent. The circumstances of the party is a matter that the judges, upon trials in such cases, do always direct to be enquired into.

Mr. *Vernon*: This is a matter purely at law and triable there. Besides, they have not the proper parties before the court, for they have only the widow, who has an estate for life, and not the heir, whose estate they would charge.

Lord Chancellor [Lord Cowper]: They have not the proper parties here, and, therefore, no decree can be made. But this much I may say, that it is a case very proper for this court, for it is certain that the settlement is good as to the £1000, and, therefore, it is very proper for the plaintiff to come here to redeem that mortgage in case the settlement does not stand in their way. And, truly, I cannot but declare so much of my opinion as to say that, when a man makes a voluntary settlement to provide for his family and keeps in possession of his estate and, upon the credit of that, contracts debts, it will be hard I think to make this a good settlement against creditors and to say than an inquiry shall be made what the circumstances of the man were at the time of the settlement is a great fineness and cannot be supported on solid reason, for may not a man make a settlement to secure his estate against future creditors as well as present. But now, in the case before us, there are two powers of revocation, which makes it still the stronger, first, a power for the man and his wife jointly during the marriage to revoke, so that he had in effect the power in himself, for the wife is *sub potestate viri*, second, there is a power for him to revoke if he survived his wife, paying £1000 to his wife's children. But I give no opinion.

Serjeant *Hooper*, for the plaintiff: We may have a decree to enquire into the personal estate, and, if it appears the £1000 has been paid out of that, we may stand in the room of the mortgagee and have a satisfaction out of the real estate, which was agreed.

But, afterwards, they thought it more proper to pay the costs of the day and pray no decree and so bring the heir before the court.

## 153

## York v. Stone

(Ch. 1709)

*The question in this case was whether a mortgage of an undivided interest in a joint tenancy severs the joint ownership.*

1 Salkeld 158, 91 E.R. 146

16 November Michaelmas 8 Anne.

Three persons being jointly interested in the trust of a term of years, one of them mortgaged his third part. And the question was whether the joint tenancy was severed in this case.

It was admitted to be a settled point in Chancery that, if H. makes his will and devises his land to one in fee and after[wards] mortgages his land to another in fee, this is no total revocation, but the equity of redemption shall pass by the devise.

But Cowper, Lord Chancellor, held that a joint tenancy is an odious thing in equity, that, as to the case of the will, it might be for the benefit of the mortgagor, that this will should not be revoked, but that it is to the disadvantage of the mortgagor that the joint tenancy should continue, because, if he happen to die first, all his estate and interest goes from his representatives to the survivor unless it be construed a severance.

## 154

## Lamplugh v. Lamplugh

(Ch. 1709)

*Where a father purchases land in the name of a son, the son is considered the owner of it where the son is not otherwise provided for.*

Lincoln's Inn MS. Misc. 9, p. 109

16 November.

A man purchases an estate in the name of his younger son and another person. The son was then but eight years of age. The father lives until the son came to twenty-one and receives the rents all along. And then, he dies, having made his will and thereby given an estate to his wife with a recommendation to her to take care of this son.

The eldest son brings a bill against his brother and the trustee to have a conveyance of this estate, it being, as he insisted, a trust for the father. There was never any declaration of trust executed.

Lord Chancellor [Lord Cowper]: The son is unprovided for. And, therefore, it is plain the father intended this estate for him. And, therefore, it shall be considered as a provision. And, although there is another person joined with the son, that will not vary it from the common case where a man purchases in the name of a son who is unprovided for, which has been always looked upon as a provision for that son.

[Other copies of this report: 1 Eq. Cas. Abr. 293, 21 E.R. 1055.]

[Other reports of this case: 1 Peere Williams 111, 24 E.R. 316, 2 Eq. Cas. Abr. 415, 744, 22 E.R. 352, 632.]

## 155

## Robinson v. Stephens

(Ch. 1709)

*There can be no deduction for taxes out of the payment of an annuity charged on land.*

2 Salkeld 616, 91 E.R. 522

Michaelmas 8 Anne.

If one covenants to pay an annuity to J.S., the covenantor shall not deduct for taxes, for the charge is on the person of the covenantor, and not the land. So, if H., having a term for years, devises an annuity to J.S. and his heirs, there can be no deduction for taxes, for the term for years is not otherwise chargeable with it than as it is part of the personal estate, for it cannot be said to issue out of the term when in point of duration it may continue much longer. So, if H. grants an annuity to J.S. and, afterwards, secures it out of a real estate, there shall be no deduction for taxes, for the subsequent security cannot lessen the effect of his former grant, which, in its creation, was tax free. *Per* Cowper, Lord Chancellor, at his house.

## 156

## Anonymous

(Ch. 1709)

*A feme sole trader in London can sue and be sued for matters arising from her own business affairs.*

10 Modern 6, 88 E.R. 599

Michaelmas 8 Anne.

By a return to a [writ of] *habeas corpus*, it appeared that, in the City of London, there is a custom that, if a married woman exercise a trade in which her husband does not at all concern himself (*intromitteret*), she may be sued as a *feme sole* for debts contracted in the carrying on of that trade. And, if she has not goods that are not her husband's, she must be imprisoned until she pay them, and, as she may be sued, so she may sue as a *feme sole* for debts owing her in her way of trade and within the City. She has a special and separate interest in the profit of her trade or else it were an unreasonable custom.

## 157

## Ackworth v. Mew

(Ch. 1709)

*In this case, the negotiations for a contract were not completed, and no contractual obligation was entered into by the parties.*

Lincoln's Inn MS. Misc. 9, p. 110

21 November 1709.

A.B., having a lease for three lives held of the bishop of Winchester, two of which were dead, enters into a treaty for filling up the lives. In August, the defendant [Mew, chancellor of Winchester,] writes a letter to the lessee and insists on £500 as a fine, which the lessee would not agree to. But, in February following, West, a scrivener, goes to one Andrews, who was the agent for the defendant and, after some treaty, agrees on the behalf on the lessee that he shall give £500, which Andrews consents to and promises the lease should be forthwith made. Upon this, West delivers him the old lease. And, afterwards, the lessee executes a letter of attorney to a person to take livery of seisin.

At this time, the lessee was dangerously ill, but the bishop or his agents knew nothing of it then, but, having notice of it afterwards, refused to make the lease. And shortly afterwards, the lessee died. And, thereupon, the bishop grants a lease for three lives to the defendant in satisfaction of a debt of £1000 which he owed him.

And now, it was insisted that the agreement was in part executed in the lifetime of the lessee. And, therefore, it was attempted to make the defendant a trustee for the plaintiff, who was the executor of the lessee as to two of the lives in the lease granted to him by the bishop, who was likewise dead.

Lord Chancellor [LORD COWPER]: I think the delivering up the lease is too slight a circumstance to be called an execution of the agreement on one part, for it was not delivered up absolutely to be cancelled, but only *sub modo*. Had it been so, it might have been otherwise. But here, it was only delivered up to be cancelled when a new lease should be made.

As to the offer in the letter written by the defendant, I think it is out of the case, for there was no closing with that offer. Now, all the cases which have been cited where agreements have been carried on upon offers in letters have been where those offers have been presently closed with.

But then, it is said that here was an acceptance of Andrews afterwards and so that shall have a relation. I think it would be hard to say that, when that offer was become as a nullity, Andrews' acceptance afterwards when the lessee was at the point of death, which he did not know of, shall make it binding. To be sure, if Andrews had known what condition the lessee was then in, he would never have agreed to take the £500.

In the next place, as to the letter of attorney, the bishop could never have made use of it to compel the payment of the £500. And, therefore, I think it would be hard of the other hand to say that it should bind the bishop. Besides, it was a writing for another purpose and not for any memorandum of an agreement or so much as a minute of it.

Upon the whole, here is a great difficulty to say what agreement shall be executed. Other agreements are in part executed, and it is plain what remains. But there is such a difficulty in this case that I know not how to extricate myself so that I see no reason to carry it on. And, indeed, what I principally go upon is that here was a sordid selfishness in the lessee. He knew the bishop was very old, and he was fencing from time to time, and, when he found he was in danger of dying himself, then he sends and strikes the bargain.

The bill must be dismissed with costs.

## 158

## Alford v. Alford

(Ch. 1709)

*A contract to make a marriage settlement is specifically enforceable against the obligor's devisee.*

*A contract to make a marriage settlement can be a valid execution of a power of appointment.*

Lincoln's Inn MS. Coxe 89, vol. 3, part 2, p. 12, pl. 2

5 December 1709; at the Rolls.

Gregory Alford made a deed of settlement, whereby, after several limitations to himself for life and his first and other sons, he limited his estate to Francis Alford for life with divers remainders over with a power to Francis to make a jointure out of it not exceeding £100 *per annum*. During a treaty of marriage, between Francis and the plaintiff, this deed was shown to the friends of the plaintiff and the power approved of and, accordingly, Francis articled to settle so much of the lands contained in the said deed on the plaintiff, his intended wife, for her jointure. The marriage took effect. Gregory Alford died without issue, and the lands vested in Francis pursuant to the limitation, who died without settling any jointure in pursuance of the articles. And so the lands came to the next remainderman, who entered.

The plaintiff exhibited her bill against the person in possession to have a jointure made to her according to the articles and for an account of the rents and profits from the death of her husband.

And [it was] decreed that she was entitled to £100 *per annum* from the death of her husband and that the defendant should pay the £100 *per annum* or the plaintiff be put into possession of so much of the lands as were of the value of £100 *per annum*.

1 Strange 604, 93 E.R. 727,
Gilbert Rep. 167, 25 E.R. 117

5 December 1709; at the Rolls.

Gregory Alford [was] tenant for life, remainder to his first and other sons in tail, remainder to Francis for life, to his first and other sons in tail, remainder to the defendant, with a power for Francis, after the death of Gregory without issue, to make a jointure. Francis marries in the lifetime of Gregory, and, before marriage, he covenants to make a jointure on the plaintiff and to execute this power when he should come into possession. Gregory dies without issue male, and Francis survives him, but he dies without making a jointure or executing this power.

The bill [was] against the remainderman to have a jointure made, because Francis, surviving Gregory, might have executed this power, and had covenanted so to do.

[It was] decreed accordingly.

2 Peere Williams 230, 24 E.R. 710

5 December 8 Anne, by Sir John Trevor, Master of the Rolls.

One Gregory Alford settled land on himself for life, remainder to his wife for life, remainder to his first etc. son in tail male, remainder to Francis Alford for life, remainder to his first etc. son in tail male successively, remainder to Edward Alford in like manner, with a power to Francis Alford, after the death of Gregory Alford and Anne, his wife, or any after-taken wife of Gregory, to settle so much of the premises not exceeding £100 *per annum* in jointure to a wife.

Francis Alford, in the lifetime of Gregory, covenants in consideration of marriage to settle lands of £100 *per annum* upon his then intended wife, and, afterwards, Gregory Alford and his wife died without issue. And, then, Francis Alford, who gave this covenant for a jointure, died without issue, whereby the premises came to the remainderman, Edward Alford.

And the widow of Francis Alford having brought her bill against the remainderman to make good her jointure, it was decreed on considering many precedents (as it is there expressed) that the covenant to make this jointure was a good execution of the power and that the wife was well entitled to this £100 *per annum* and to all the arrears from her husband's death.

[Other reports of this case: 2 Eq. Cas. Abr. 659, 22 E.R. 554.]

## 159

## Stationers' Company v. Partridge

(Ch. 1709)

*A patent for the exclusive printing of almanacs is valid and enforceable.*

Lincoln's Inn MS. Misc. 9, p. 112

6 December 1709. The Company of Stationers v. Partherich, the almanac maker, and Darby, a printer.

The plaintiffs set forth by their bill that they were incorporated by King Philip and Queen Mary and that King James, by his letters patent, granted them the sole printing of psalters, primers, almanacs, and prognostications, except some therein particularly mentioned, so as such almanacs and prognostications were licensed by the archbishop of Canterbury and the bishop of London, and prohibits all others etc. that, by virtue of these letters patent, they have the sole power of printing almanacs, and that they have applied £200 a year of the profits for a charitable purpose, and that the defendant Partherich has compiled an almanac and the defendant Darby has printed great numbers of it without licence from the plaintiffs, and, therefore, it is prayed by the bill that the defendants may be enjoined from printing and selling this almanac and may account for what profits they have made.

*Sir Edward Northey*, for the defendants: The patent is a void patent. I do not know it was ever yet established for almanacs. Making almanacs is a common trade and, therefore, cannot be restrained. And it is taken notice of as such by the [Statute] 13 Car. II, ca. [ *blank* ].[1]

Mod. Rep. 256; the Company brought an action against a printer for printing Gadbury's Almanack,[2] and I confess the court was of the opinion that the action was maintainable, but this was at a time when the prerogative was carried higher than it has been since. And several resolutions which were then given as to monopolies have been exploded since, particularly that of the East India and African companies, which were then allowed upon a supposition that the crown might prohibit the subject from trading with infidels for fear they should turn infidels. But no one will open his mouth now to maintain these opinions.

[1] Stat. 14 Car. II, c. 33, s. 7 (*SR*, V, 431).

[2] *Company of Stationers v. Seymour* (1677), 1 Modern 256, 86 E.R. 865, also 3 Keble 792, 84 E.R. 1015.

*Sir John Hawles*, on the same side: The patent for printing the yearbooks has been allowed to be good, for the crown has an interest in them. And that of the Bible may be so too, for I believe the crown was at the charge of the translation. But, as the law now stands, I do not see but that, if anyone writes a new law book, he may print it as he pleases.

*Sir Thomas Powys*, for the plaintiffs: The law patent has been established in the House of Lords by a judgment there and, notwithstanding what Sir John [Hawles] has been pleased to say, will extend to all law books, though I think the patent is now expired.

As to prognostications, it is very reasonable the government should take care of the printing of them, for what mischief might not a man do under the pretense of prognostications if care was not taken about the printing of them.

*Sir Peter King*, of the same side: As to what they insist about the license of the archbishop and the bishop of London as if the patent extended only to prohibit others from printing almanacs that were so licensed and that anyone might print almanacs unlicensed as they pleased, sure, there is nothing in that. All that is meant by giving the plaintiffs a license to print almanacs, so as they were licensed in such manner as is there mentioned, is to be a guard upon the Company that even they should not print almanacs unless licensed and not to give a license to others to print almanacs not so licensed.

Lord Chancellor [Lord Cowper]: [There is] no doubt but that was the meaning of it.

It was further said for the plaintiffs that they were in quiet possession of this right and that, whenever any attempts had been made to break in upon it, it has been always maintained, either by judgments at law or injunctions out of this court, that in the almanac is printed the calendar, in which every subject is concerned, for there are the return [days] of the [law court] terms, which concerns every man's property. In Leo. 242, it was held that the judges might judicially take notice of almanacs.[1]

Lord Chancellor [Lord Cowper]: I think it cannot be expected from me that I should upon a demurrer take upon me to shake that which has been established upon so many authorities to which I ought to give a great regard. The demurrer must be overruled.

4 Burrow 2402, 98 E.R. 254

It came on in the year 1709 before Lord Cowper on continuing the injunction. (There is no report of it, I [Lord Mansfield] believe, in print. At least, I have not seen any. I have read the bill and answer.)

The bill puts it upon all the prerogative notions of power, and insists that the king's patentee had a sole exclusive right of printing almanacs.

---

[1] *Page v. Fawcet* (1587), 1 Leonard 242, 74 E.R. 221, also Croke Eliz. 227, 78 E.R. 482.

The answer insists that these were extravagant illegal notions, that they were taken up at times when the prerogative ran high and when the dispensing power was allowed. And it insists that the question ought since the Revolution to be argued upon proper principles consistent with the rights and privileges of the subject.

The defendants denied the authority of all the cases stated by the bill as far as they went upon prerogative right.

Lord Cowper continued the injunction until the hearing.

(I [Lord Mansfield] have office copies of all the orders and pleas that were cited. I dare say I have thirty or forty of them. It appears that these decrees were all read and that the judgment of the House of Lords was read and gone through.)

Lord Harcourt, afterwards, heard the cause. He did not choose in a case about almanacs to decide upon the prerogative. He, therefore, made a case of it, for the opinion of this Court [of King's Bench], Lord Parker being then Chief Justice.

This Court, so far as it went, inclined against the right of the Crown in almanacs. But, to this hour, it has never been determined. And the injunction granted by Lord Cowper still continues.

(I have Salkeld's manuscript report, and I have had it many years,[1] of what passed in this court in the course of the argument of this case of The Company of Stationers against Partridge. I do not know whether it is got into print. I have not seen it in print. Mr. Yorke had a copy of it when he argued the Case of The University of Cambridge and Baskett.[2] Mr. *Salkeld* argued for the defendant Partridge; *Sir Peter King*, for the plaintiffs. I will state to you, so far as is material to the argument, how they put it and the only grounds that they thought tenable.)

Mr. *Salkeld*, after positively and expressly denying any prerogative in the Crown over the press or any power to grant any exclusive privilege, says 'I take the rule, in all these cases, to be that, where the Crown has a property or right of copy, the king may grant it. The Crown may grant the sole printing of Bibles in the English translation, because it was made at the king's charge. The same reason holds as to the statutes, year books, and Common Prayer Books.'

*Sir Peter King*, for the plaintiffs, argues thus (throwing out at the same time the things that I have already mentioned; though he does not seem to be very serious in it): 'I argue that, if the Crown has a right to the Common Prayer Book, it has a right to every part of it. And the Calendar is a part of the Common Prayer Book. And an almanac is the same thing with the Calendar' etc.

Parker, Chief Justice, speaks to nothing said at the bar, but only whether the calendar is part of the Common Prayer Book. And, as to that, he goes back

[1] This manuscript was destroyed by the Gordon rioters on 6 June 1780.

[2] *Baskett v. Chancellor of Cambridge University* (1758), 2 Burrow 661, 97 E.R. 499.

as far as to the Council of Nice[1] and doubts whether it is, or, rather indeed, he thinks that it is not part of it. He says it may be an index, but it is no part of it.

Mr. Justice POWELL says 'you must distinguish this from the common cases of monopolies by showing some property in the Crown and bringing it within the case of the Common Prayer Book.' And he rather inclined to think that almanacs might be the king's, because there is a trial by almanacs.

To which, LORD PARKER replied that he never heard of such a thing as a trial by almanac.

They leave it upon this. It stood over for another argument to see if they could make it like the case of the Common Prayer Book.

(I do not know what happened afterwards, but there never was any judgment. And though I have made strict inquiry, I do not find that there was ever any opinion given.)

[Other reports of this case: 10 Modern 105, 88 E.R. 647.]

## 160

## Saintsbury v. Grammer

(Ch. 1709)

*A lessee's judgment creditor who has executed his judgment by attaching the lease can afterwards release the lease to the lessor, and thereby terminate the covenants therein.*

Lincoln's Inn MS. Misc. 9, p. 114

7 December 1709.

The lessee of a term becomes indebted, and a judgment is recovered against him. And, thereupon, a [writ of] *fieri facias* being taken out, the sheriff makes a bill of sale to the defendants Grammer and Loveday, who enter and pay about £20 for ground rent. But the houses being out of repair at the time of their entry and, afterwards, finding they were likely to make little of them, they assign the term to a poor almsman, who appeared to be the landlord, but carried it so to the tenants that they left the houses.

And, now, the lessor brings a bill against the defendants, Grammer and Loveday, and the administrator of the almsman, he being now dead, for the arrears of the rent and a specific performance of the covenants in the lease. And if the vendees of the sheriff should be charged after the assignment was the question.

The Case of Cass and Freeman was cited, where the assignee of a term assigns over to an almswoman and was decreed to pay the arrears and put the premises in repair.

[1] The Council of Nicaea in 325.

Lord Chancellor [Lord Cowper]: The question before me does not come up to the case that has been cited, for there, the assignee enjoyed the lease for several years and had the profits of it and, within half a year of the end of the lease, assigns it over to an almswoman and promises to indemnify her against the last half-year's rent. But, here, a man has it but half a year and was in hopes to have been paid his debt, but finds it would not answer and, therefore, endeavors to get rid of it; besides, he offered to surrender it to the plaintiff before he assigned it, and he would not accept it, which makes it very different from the case that has been cited. The bill must be dismissed.

## 161

## Hobart v. Earl of Stamford

(Ch. 1709)

*A court of equity can amend the strict words of a will by adding trustees to preserve contingent remainders in order to effectuate the clear intent of the testator.*

Lincoln's Inn MS. Misc. 177, p. 134

19 December 1709, by Lord Cowper, and affirmed in the House of Lords.

Mr. Serjeant Maynard,[1] by his will, devised his estate to trustees and their heirs to the use of them and their heirs upon several trusts, *viz.* that the trustees, after the death of his wife, should convey part thereof to the use of, or in trust for, Sir Henry Hobart and Elizabeth, his wife, the testator's granddaughter, for their lives and the life of the survivor, the remainder to the first son of the said Elizabeth for ninety-nine years if he should so long live, remainder to the heirs male of the body of such first son, remainder to all and every the sons of Elizabeth for 99 years if they respectively so long should live, remainder to the heirs male of every of them to take not jointly but successively, the son and sons to take the term of 99 years in the immediate remainder to his and their said heirs male, remainder to Mary Maynard, his other granddaughter, afterwards countess of Stamford, for her life with remainders to all and every her sons for such like term of ninety-nine years with remainders to the heirs male of the body of every such son. He farther willed that the other part of his estate should (by the advice of counsel) be conveyed to, or to the use of, Mary Maynard for life without impeachment of waste, remainder to all and every her son and sons for 99 years if such son or sons should so long live with several remainders to the heirs male of the body of every such son, they and all the heirs male of their bodies to take successively, each son to take the said term with remainder 'immediately' to his said heirs male and, after the determination of the said estates and failure of such heirs male of their

[1] P. D. Halliday, 'Maynard, Sir John (1604–1690)', *Oxford Dictionary of National Biography*, vol. 37, pp. 598–602.

respective bodies, the remainder thereof to his other granddaughter, the Lady Hobart, and her sons with the like terms and remainders, the remainder of all the estate to trustees and their heirs during the life and lives of Sir Henry Hobart and Dame Elizabeth, his wife, and of the countess of Stamford to preserve contingent estates 'and to no other use or purpose'.

Mr. Serjeant Maynard died. Several suits arose about his will, and, in 1694, a private Act of Parliament was made directing that his real estate should go to and be enjoyed by such persons for such estates and under such limitations as were mentioned in the will. This Act was not otherwise material than as it let in two terms of 99 years for the benefit of the earl of Stamford and Sir Henry Hobart if they should so long live (in case they should survive their wives) in the respective parts of the estate. Sir Henry Hobart and his lady died, leaving Sir John Hobart, now earl of Buckingham, their only son, an infant, who brought his bill to have a conveyance executed by the trustees pursuant to the will and Act of Parliament. Lord Cowper, on 24th January 1707, decreed the trustees should execute conveyances according to the will and the words of the Act of Parliament, and referred it to a Master to settle the conveyances.

The Master made his report, whereby he allowed the draught of a conveyance in general words referring to the will and Act of Parliament thus, 'to convey the premises to Clayton and Carter and their heirs *habendum* to them and their heirs to the several uses, intents, and purposes in the plaintiff's will and Act limited, expressed, and declared.' To this report and draught, Sir John Hobart excepted that the premises ought at least to have been limited to the use of Carter and Clayton and their heirs only, in trust for such person and persons, and for such estate and estates as are in and by the said will and Act of Parliament limited whereby the legal estate might be vested in the said trustees for the better preservation of the contingent estates and limitations, which, otherwise, as the draught was prepared, were liable to be destroyed and the testator's intention plainly defeated.

The matter of this exception was argued on 19th December 1709 before Lord Cowper, who declared that, in matters executory, as in the case of articles or a will, directing a conveyance where the words of the articles or will are improper or informal, the court will not direct the conveyance according to the improper or informal expressions of the will or articles, but will order the conveyance or settlement to be made in a proper and legal manner so as may best answer the intent of the parties. He conceived the intent of the will to be that the estates should be secured as far as the rules of law would admit to the issue male of the respective devises before the cross-remainders should take place and that it was designed to be as strict a settlement as possible by law. His Lordship did, therefore, order that, in the said conveyance, where any part of the estate was limited in use to the plaintiff, Sir John Hobart, for ninety-nine years if he should so long live, there should be a limitation over to trustees and their heirs during his life to preserve the contingent uses in remainder and, then, to the first and other sons of the said Sir John Hobart in tail male successively, and, where any part of the estate was limited to the countess of Stamford for life, and then to the earl of Stamford for 99 years if he should so long live, that there should be a limitation also to trustees and their heirs during the lives of the said earl and countess and the survivor of them to preserve the contingent uses in remainder and, then, to the first and every other son of the said countess of Stamford and the heirs male of the body of such first and every other son and, then, to the right heirs of Sir John Maynard which right heirs were the countess of Stamford and Sir John Hobart. This was the order which was affirmed by the House of Lords.

(It may be worthwhile to stop a little and observe upon this case.[1])

First, both this court and the House of Lords construed the words 'heirs male of the body of the first son of Lady Hobart' in the sense of the first and every other son of such first son.

Secondly, taking the limitation as it stood in the will and reducing the words or even the strict legal operation of those words in a conveyance by a deed, the limitation 'to the heirs male of the body of such first son' was void in law, for the estate limited to such first son was for 99 years only and was not a freehold, and, consequently, it could not, within the doctrine of Shelley's Case,[2] unite with the limitation 'to the heirs male of his body'. And by way of a contingent remainder, it could not be good because there was no estate of freehold to support it. Hence, it followed necessarily that, had those words been inserted in a conveyance, the freehold and inheritance must at law have vested in the co-heirs of Sir John Maynard and yet the court made good the whole by inserting an estate to trustees to preserve contingent remainders.

Thirdly, the private Act of Parliament did not direct any limitation to trustees to preserve contingent remainders after the estate to the earl of Stamford for 99 years if he should so long live, and yet that was also directed.

Fourthly, Mr. Serjeant Maynard had inserted an express clause in his will directing trustees to support contingent remainders after the devises for life to Sir Henry Hobart, Lady Hobart, and the countess of Stamford and, therefore, it might have been argued, and undoubtedly was so, that, where the testator intended such an estate to preserve contingent remainders, he had inserted it, and, consequently, where he had omitted it, he did not intend it should be done. Farther, the will concluded with negative words 'and to no other use or purpose whatsoever'.

[Other reports of this case: *sub nom.* Hobart v. Countess of Suffolk, 2 Vernon 644, 23 E.R. 1020, 1 Eq. Cas. Abr. 272, 21 E.R. 1040, *sub nom.* Earl of Stamford v. Hobart, 3 Brown P.C. 31, 1 E.R. 1157, note also *In re* Maynard's Will (1691), Dodd 101.]

---

[1] These are Lord Hardwicke's observations.

[2] *Wolfe v. Shelley* (1581), 1 Coke Rep. 88, 76 E.R. 199, 1 Anderson 69, 123 E.R. 358, Moore K.B. 136, 72 E.R. 490, Jenkins 249, 145 E.R. 176, 3 Dyer 373, 73 E.R. 838.

# 161a

## Rawley v. Holland

(Ch. 1709–1712)

*The question in this case was the disposition of two remainders in land.*

22 Viner, Abr., *Uses*, p. 189

A., seised in fee of Blackacre and Whiteacre, had two sisters, E. and F., and had B., a son by a former wife. And, on his marriage with M., a second wife, he conveyed the whole to W.R. and W.S. and their heirs to the uses following, *viz.* Blackacre to A., himself, for ninety-nine years if he so long live, and, after the expiration, to the use of the said M. for a jointure, and, after her death, to the use of the heirs male of the body of the said A., remainder to the right heirs of A., and, as to Whiteacre, to the use of A. for ninety-nine years if etc., and, after[wards], to the trustees and their executors for two hundred years in trust to raise portions for his children by M., remainder to the heirs male of the body of A., remainder to his right heirs. The marriage took effect. And, after[wards], A. died, leaving B., his son by his first wife, and H. and I., daughters by M., his second wife.

M. entered into Blackacre. B. entered into Whiteacre, and caused part of the rents to be paid to the trustees towards raising portions pursuant to the settlement and granted leases etc. And he died without issue in the lifetime of M. Afterwards, M. died. The Master of the Rolls [Trevor] was of opinion that the limitation of Whiteacre was void. And, as to what had been urged, that a use arose by operation and construction of law, His Honor said that to talk of raising a use by implication was a mystery in law which he did not understand, and would have decreed Whiteacre to the sisters of B.

But, upon the importunity of the defendant's counsel, a case was stated, and sent to the judges of the Common Bench, who certified November 26, 1712, that, as to Blackacre, nothing but a reversion expectant on M.'s estate for life descended to B. so that, by her enjoying the land and surviving B., there was no *possessio fratris* to exclude H. and I., the sisters by the second wife from inheriting as heirs to A., their father. But, as to Whiteacre, they held the limitation to the heirs male of the body of A. void, no freehold being limited to any person precedent to that estate, and that no estate of freehold could result to A. for his life by implication, because another estate, *viz.* for ninety-nine years if etc. was expressly limited to him, which would be inconsistent with a freehold in him by implication and that a freehold either expressed or implied was necessary to support such a limitation, and, consequently, the freehold and inheritance in fee simple of Whiteacre descended to B., expectant only on a term for years to the trustees of which there was such a *possessio fratris* as entitles E. and F., the plaintiff's aunts and heirs of the whole blood to B., the son, to that land.

[Other copies of this report: 2 Eq. Cas. Abr. 753, 22 E.R. 638.]

## 162

## Benoist v. Gascoigne

(Ch. 1710)

*The beneficial interest that a married woman had in a lease, upon her death, passes to her widower or to his personal representative.*

Lincoln's Inn MS. Misc. 9, p. 115, pl. 1

1 February 1709[/10].

A man marries a woman who has the trust of a term for years. She dies. And, before he had taken administration, he dies, having made his will. And he gives this term to his executors. And, between them and the administrator of the wife, the question was who should have the term.

[LORD COWPER] decreed to the executor *contra* to 1 Ins. 351a.[1]

## 163

## Tournay v. Tournay

(Ch. 1710)

*A marriage portion does not vest before it is demandable.*

Lincoln's Inn MS. Misc. 9, p. 115, pl. 2

11 February 1709[/10].

Upon a marriage settlement, a term is created to commence at the death of the father upon trust that, if there are no sons and the father dies, leaving issue female, the trustees, by the rents and profits or by sale or mortgage, shall raise £400 apiece for such daughters to be paid them respectively within a year after the father's death with interest. The father dies, leaving daughters, one of which died within a year after her father's death. And the question was if her portion should be paid to her administrator.

Lord Chancellor [LORD COWPER]: Though the portions are to be paid within a year after the father's death so that the trustees, if they had pleased, might have paid it before the end of the year, yet it was not demandable before that time and, consequently, nothing vested in the daughter that died. And, therefore, there is no reason the inheritance should be charged with that sum in favor of the administrator.

[Other reports of this case: Precedents in Chancery 290, 24 E.R. 139, 2 Eq. Cas. Abr. 655, 22 E.R. 550.]

---

[1] E. Coke, *First Institute* (1628), f. 351.

# 164

## Dean v. Lord Delaware

(Ch. 1710–1720)

*Where a daughter of a London freeman has received a marriage portion from her father that is less than her orphanage share, upon his death, she can claim her orphanage share in full.*

Yale Beinecke OSB MSS. 184, box 41,
Taussig 311, vol. 1, p. 443, pl. 2

9 May 1710.

In pursuance of an order of 16 December 1709, they certify that, if a freeman [of London] dies leaving a wife and one daughter married in his lifetime and it appears by his books that he had paid several sums in part of her portion unto her husband and, afterwards, several other sums which ought to be taken as paid on account of the portion, but not expressly entered in such freeman's books as paid in part thereof, all which entries of the testator's own handwriting and such sums altogether do not amount to a third of his estate put together with what he left at his death, such daughter ought not to be taken as fully advanced, but in part advanced. And, by the custom, such child and her husband are to have a third of what the testator left at his death without regard had to what was received in the father's life and without putting what has been so received to the estate left at his death.

British Library MS. Hargrave 81, f. 21

20 July 1710.

The custom of London was certified to be that, if a freeman leave a wife and one daughter married in his lifetime and it appears by the books of such freeman that he had paid several sums of money in part of such daughter's portion unto her husband, afterwards several other sums which ought to be taken as paid on account of the portion but not expressly so entered, and all such entries are of the freeman's own handwriting, if such sum taken together does not amount to a third of such freeman's estate put together with what he left at his death, such daughter ought not to be looked upon as fully advanced, but in part advanced only. And, in such case, by the custom of the City, such child and her husband are to have one-third of what such freeman left at the time of his decease without regard to what was received in his lifetime and without putting what has been so received to the estate left. And the Lord Chancellor [HARCOURT] ordered it to be referred back to the Master to state the account accordingly.

[Other copies of this report: British Library MS. Hargrave 82, f. 17, British Library MS. Hargrave 77, f. 8v, pl. 1, British Library MS. Hargrave 303, f. 12v.]

Yale Beinecke OSB MSS. 184, box 41,
Taussig 311, vol. 1, p. 449

20 July 1720.

Upon hearing that cause on the said certificate, *vide* before us 12 [Anne], it was ordered that it be referred back to the Master to examine and certify whether the several sums paid by the said testator in his lifetime and determined by the court to be paid to the defendants upon the account of his wife's portion put together with the estate of the testator left at his death do or do not amount to a full third part of the said estate so put together and, for that purpose, the Master to state the whole account directed in the cause and, upon his report, such further order shall be made as shall be just, *vide* the order. But no further order [is] to be found.

[Other reports of this case: 2 Vernon 628, 23 E.R. 1011, 1 Eq. Cas. Abr. 156, 21 E.R. 955.]

## 165

## Horne v. Baker

(Ch. 1710)

*Damages for the violation of a copyright do not include the infringer's profits that resulted therefrom.*

*A court of equity will allow a bill of discovery so as to entitle the plaintiff to an action at law, but not to discover the full extent of his damages.*

Lincoln's Inn MS. Misc. 10, p. 1, pl. 1

9 May 1710.

The plaintiff, as executor of her husband, makes a title to the copy of *Hudibras*[1] and sets forth by her bill that the defendant has printed a new edition of that book, having no right or property in the copy. And, therefore, it is prayed that the defendant may discover and account for the profits of what he has sold off and may be enjoined from selling any more.

The defendant demurs generally.

Lord Chancellor [Lord Cowper]: To make the defendant account for the profits of what he has sold is going too far, for the injury that the plaintiff has sustained ought to be the measure of the damage and not the profit which the defendant has made.

Then, as to the discovery of what books the defendant has sold and what he has done in respect to his printing of this book is in order to enable you to recover greater damages at law. I do not know that this court ever went so far. Suppose a

[1] Samuel Butler, *Hudibras, Written in the time of the late Wars* (1st ed., London, 1663).

trespass was done. Would you come here against the trespasser to discover how many cattle he put into the land and what damage he has done? I am not willing to carry this matter so far, especially now the late Act of Parliament[1] has given another remedy in respect of the property in copies of books.

Harvard Law Sch. MS. 537, pt. 2, p. 154

The bill was that, whereas the plaintiff had the copy and sole printing of *Hudibras*, that the defendant, with several others in the bill named did confederate to deprive the plaintiff of the benefit of it and printed without the plaintiff's leave an edition of it. And the bill was to discover what books they had printed of them and the benefit they had made of them and likewise to have an inquisition upon them.

And, upon a demurrer, *Spencer Cowper* argued that the booksellers had no such right to copies as to call to an account any for the printing of them before this Act of Parliament this session and before which this was. And though injunctions had indeed been granted in some cases of this nature, as in the case of almanacs and law books, yet that because the public had an interest in those books in respect of the law, return days, and the law itself that are in them and, besides, they had them by a patent, but this is a book of no such nature etc.

*Sir Joseph Jekyll* affirmed *e contra* that, before the Act, they had a right to their copies. And he conceived the bill very proper, for he took it that this court would relieve where the law does give an action and yet not an adequate remedy, as, in this case, the books were sold privately by mean and unknown people in coffee houses. And so, if [we sued] an action, we should not be able to prove the sale of two or three, which would not yield damages adequate to the damages sustained.

Lord Chancellor [Lord Cowper]: He never knew a discovery extended so far as this. This court will oblige a discovery so far as what will entitle the plaintiff to an action at law, but not a discovery to entitle him to the full extent of his damages. And he mentions a case to a bill to discover how often and what fish and how many the defendant took in the plaintiff's piscary there; the defendant having discovered the taking of two or three, it was ruled a sufficient discovery without more because [it was] sufficient to entitle the plaintiff to an action. And he said he does not know that, where a man has put a great many cattle into another's land, but gets them off before the owner comes and the owner seeing a great deal of damages and ever a bill was brought against them to discover what cattle were put in.

As to Sir John Fleet's Case,[2] which had been mentioned a little by *Sir Joseph* [*Jekyll*], he said there was a combination and confederacy by thirty or forty of the greatest merchants who had got all the wharves about town (as I took it)

[1] Stat. 8 Ann., c. 21 (*SR*, IX, 256–258).

[2] *Heathcote v. Fleete* (1702), 2 Vernon 442, 23 E.R. 883, 1 Eq. Cas. Abr. 76, 21 E.R. 889.

into their hands and people [were] forced to give what they pleased for the use of the lighters. That was only to discover the persons to entitle them to an action because the confederation [was] so private that, though it was known, yet they did not know the persons, so that [it was] only to fix the persons, but, however, if they could maintain themselves by precedents, he would stay it to see how they had gone.

*Sir Joseph* [*Jekyll*] *arguendo*: In case a man lends money where [there is] no witness, there, the plaintiff shall put the defendant upon his discovery.

[Order of 10 May 1710: Public Record Office, C.37/853.]

[Note H. T. Gomez-Arostegui, 'The Untold Story of the First Copyright Suit Under the Statute of Anne in 1710', *Berkeley Technology Law Journal*, vol. 25, pp. 1299–1309 (2010).]

## 166

## Roberts v. Gray

(Ch. 1710)

*A final judgment at common law is res judicata in equity.*

Lincoln's Inn MS. Misc. 10, p. 1, pl. 2

The bill is to be relieved against a judgment recovered at law by the defendant against the plaintiff as executor. The defendant was a creditor of the testator by a note and brings an action at law against the plaintiff, who pleaded *plene administravit*. The plaintiff in the action replies that he had assets at the time of the original brought. The defendant rejoins and takes issue that he had not assets etc. This is tried and found against him. And now, he brings his bill to be relieved against this judgment, suggesting that there were bond debts which he paid with the assets of his testator after the original brought and before the judgment was obtained, which, being an application of the assets as the law directs, he ought to be protected against this judgment.

The defendant pleads these proceedings at law in bar to any relief.

Lord Chancellor [Lord Cowper]: If this court should relieve in such cases as this, I doubt we should draw all the business out of the courts at law into this court and make the business of pleading much more neglected than it is.

We all know there are many cases which are very hard upon executors and administrators at law, but, as the law now stands, this court cannot help them though it is a pity it cannot. I doubt this is one of them.

It would be of ill consequence to allow this bill, for everyone that has a judgment at law recovered against him upon a demurrer at law would come hither and suggest he was ill advised.

The plea must be allowed.

## 167

## Strode v. Strode

(Ch. 1710)

*A contract must be construed according to the intent of the parties.*

Lincoln's Inn MS. Misc. 10, p. 2

12 May 1710.

Edward Strode, upon his marriage with the plaintiff, settles lands for a jointure on her and covenants to levy a fine of those and other lands, which is declared to be, as to the jointure lands, to the uses in the settlement and, as to the other lands, to the use of himself and his heirs. And, in the same deed, he covenants that the said lands are of the yearly value of £400.

The question was whether the words 'said lands' should extend to all the lands in the fine or should be restrained only to the jointure lands.

Lord Chancellor [Lord Cowper]: The covenant must be restrained to the jointure lands. It cannot be supposed that it was intended to include the whole lands when he might have sold part of them the next day and defeated the whole covenant.

The Master must enquire what the value of the jointure lands were at Mr. Strode's death. And the plaintiff must come in as a creditor for so much as they fall short of £400. But the personal estate is not to make good what contingent defects there may be during the plaintiff's life but only so much as they were short of that value at her husband's death.

## 168

## Holt v. Burley

(Ch. 1710)

*In this case, the intent of the settlement in issue was that, if the wife survived her husband, she might execute her power of appointment whenever there was a failer of issue, not that there must be a failer of issue at the time of the husband's death.*

Lincoln's Inn MS. Misc. 10, p. 5

Trinity term 1710.

William Bullock, being seised of lands in the right of Sarah, his wife, they settle the same upon their issue, and, in the settlement, there was a proviso that, in case Sarah should die before her husband, not having issue of her body by him begotten, then she, by writing under her hand and seal executed etc., should have power to dispose of the premises for any estate or term of years. And, in case she should survive her said husband, they not having issue between them, then she should have a like power to dispose etc.

The husband died having one son who afterwards died without issue. And then Sarah, the wife, a year after her son's death, by indentures of lease and release, executed her power, under which the defendants purchased the estate.

The wife being dead, the plaintiffs, as heirs at law to her prefer their bill, suggesting that the husband's leaving issue at his death, the contingency, upon which the wife's power to dispose did arise, never happened and, consequently, the defendants have no title and this being the estate of the wife and the settlement made by her, it ought to have a liberal construction in favor of her heirs.

Lord Chancellor [Lord Cowper]: There is no need of a liberal construction where the sense of the parties and the literal import of the words run the same way.

It cannot be supposed that the intention of the parties was to let in collateral heirs in case the father left a son at his death and that son died without issue in his mother's lifetime, but the intention must be that, if the wife survived her husband, she might execute her power whenever there was a failer of issue.

The words 'that, if the wife survived her husband, they not having issue between them' must not be confined to the precise time of the husband's death but to all the lifetime of the wife so that, when the son died without issue, the contingency happened, for, then, it was that the wife might be said to have survived her husband without issue between them.

The bill must be dismissed with costs.

[Other reports of this case: 2 Vernon 651, 23 E.R. 1024, Precedents in Chancery 293, 24 E.R. 140, 1 Eq. Cas. Abr. 342, 21 E.R. 1089.]

## 169

## Hickman v. Anderson

(Ch. 1710)

*Where marriage portions are to be paid upon the death of a father, they cannot be sued for before he dies.*

Lincoln's Inn MS. Misc. 10, p. 8

Sir Willoughby Hickman v. Sir Stephen Anderson.

Sir Stephen Anderson, the defendant's father, upon his marriage with Sir William Glyn's daughter, settles land to the use of himself for life, then to trustees to preserve contingent remainders, than to his intended wife for life, remainder to his first and other sons in tail male, remainder to trustees for 99 years, remainder to his own right heirs.

The trusts of the term were for raising portions if no sons, *viz.* £7000 if but one daughter, if more, then, other sums, to be paid at eighteen or marriage and maintenance in the meantime, provided that, if Sir Stephen Anderson, having such daughters, should at any time during his natural life dispose any of them in marriage and give a portion with such daughter, such portion to be taken as part of the portion intended thereby to be raised.

Then comes a proviso upon which the question did arise, *viz.* that the said term so limited to the trustees upon condition that, if the said Stephen Anderson shall have no issue female begotten on his said wife that shall survive him or if the said Mary, his intended wife, shall not be pregnant of a daughter which shall be after born and live until eighteen or marriage, that then the said several uses, estates, and terms so limited to the trustees shall cease and be void.

The wife died without issue male, leaving one daughter only, who was married in her father's lifetime before she was eighteen to the plaintiff, to whom Sir Stephen Anderson gave a portion of £5000. The plaintiff's wife died after the marriage, and her father, who survived her, is also dead.

The plaintiff, who had no notice of the settlement until after the death of Sir Stephen Anderson, brings his bill against the defendant, son and heir of Sir Stephen by a second marriage, upon whom the lands are settled, to have his wife's portion made up to £7000.

It was insisted on for him that, by the general intent of the settlement, portions were to be raised if there were daughters and no son, that the term was vested in the trustees, though not in point of profit until after the death of the father, and that the trustees, after the death of the wife, might have sold this term to raise the daughter's portion, even in the lifetime of the father, and it would be very hard if, after they had done so, that a purchaser should be defeated if the term by the last proviso was void.

On the other side, it was said that the daughter dying in the life of her father, the term was void by the last clause in the settlement, the contingency having never happened, *viz.* there being no daughter that survived the father, and, therefore, the term being determined at law, equity ought not to revive it.

Lord Chancellor [Lord Cowper]: The trusts of the term are defeated at law by a clause of defeasance made at the same time that the term was created and not by anything happening afterwards and to say that this court shall now revive it is going a great way.

As to what was said, that, suppose the daughter had married, her husband might have brought a bill to have the portion raised, even in the father's lifetime, if he had, no doubt, the court would have gone as far as ever they had done, that is, to have decreed the reversion of the term to be sold, for it is a vested term. But then, if you had gone before a Master upon such a decree to have sold this reversionary term and a purchaser seeing this clause had objected against it as being subject to a contingency and you had come to the court and prayed that an absolute term might be sold, would the court have decreed it? No, surely; the court would have told you 'sell your term with its contingency; we will not better it'.

Now, the plaintiff comes here to have that done now, which he could not have had if the daughter and father were both living.

The bill must be dismissed with costs.

Lincoln's Inn MS. Misc. 380, pt. 2, p. 15, pl. 2

Sir Willoughby Hickman v. Sir Stephen Anderson.

The plaintiff having married the daughter of the defendant and it having been provided in the marriage settlement of the defendant that portions for daughters should be raised by trustees payable at the age of eighteen or day of marriage in case the father died leaving one or more daughters, the plaintiff brought his bill against the defendant, the father, and the trustees in order to have the portion of his wife raised.

But Lord Cowper decreed that, though there was a time limited for the payment of the portions, to wit at the age of eighteen or marriage, yet the trust being declared to raise the portion for the daughters in case the father died leaving one or more daughters, it could not be raised until the father's death, it being uncertain whether the plaintiffs would be entitled to it or no.

[Other reports of this case: 2 Vernon 655, 23 E.R. 1027.]

## 170

## Coles v. Robinson

(Ch. 1710)

*In this case, a devise was intended to be in lieu of an undelivered inter vivos gift, and the devisee was allowed to elect which one she would take.*

Lincoln's Inn MS. Misc. 10, p. 11

James Coles, the plaintiff's father, by an indenture dated 4 May 3 Will. & Mar. [1691] made between him of the one part and the plaintiff of the other, reciting that he had agreed with one Harris to let him a lease of the Katherine Wheel in Northampton for seven years at £10 a year, in consideration of fatherly love to the plaintiff and, for her preferment, he grants, gives, and assigns to her all the residue of the said term of seven years with the rent to be due for the premises. And he covenants that, after the seven years, the plaintiff might make any lease of the premises with his consent and might receive the rent during her life. In which indenture was a proviso that the father might revoke that deed by any writing under his hand and seal executed in the presence of two witnesses.

Afterwards, he makes his will, which is signed but not sealed, and he thereby directs his debts to be paid on the sale of his houses and closes in Northampton and that his house there, wherein one Wilson lived, should remain unto the plaintiff if she married and had issue male. Otherwise, she should have thereout £10 a year for her life. And all the rest of his lands and tenements he gave to the defendant's wife, another of his daughters.

The testator outlived Harris's lease, and made another lease without his daughter of the same house, and received the rent himself during his life, and never paid it to his daughter. And the reason that he gave why he did not was because he maintained her.

The questions were two, first, if the will was a revocation of the indenture, secondly, if the inheritance passes to the defendant's wife by the devise of the residuum.

Lord Chancellor [Lord Cowper]: If this deed stood by itself, it would have amounted to a voluntary gift of the rents and profits to the plaintiff during her life with a power of revocation. The father has not formally revoked it, nor is his will a revocation of it, not being sealed. But then, he has given her another house by his will if she marries, and, if she does not, she is to have £10 a year out of it for her life, so that he that had made an equitable agreement with his daughter, which he might have revoked, has now given by his will that which is an adequate satisfaction. I think she ought not to have both, but she may make her election either to take the profits of the Katherine Wheel by the deed or the £10 a year by the will.

As to the second point, it is plainly a question of law. However, I am free enough to declare my opinion that the testator has by the first part of his will given all his houses and lands in Northampton to be sold for the payment of his debts, then he gives one of his houses to the plaintiff, his daughter and gives all the rest of his lands and houses to another daughter. Now, I find he had no other estate but what lay in Northampton and, therefore, when he had given the whole in the first place for the payment of his debts, the word 'residue' must be understood the residue that shall remain after payment of the debts, not the residue with respect only to that house in Wilson's possession, so that the whole must be sold, and, if anything remains after the payment of the debts and the plaintiff's £10 a year, if she elects that, the defendants must have it.

## 171

## Corbet v. Maidwell

(Ch. 1710)

*A contingent interest cannot be enforced before it vests, even though it may create a hardship to the donee.*

Lincoln's Inn MS. Misc. 10, p. 13

John Corbet and Margaret, his wife, the only child of Thomas Maidwell by Margaret, his late wife, plaintiffs; the said Thomas Maidwell and Ann, his wife, Ann Maidwell, and Thomas Maidwell and others, their children, Richard Cutts, and Martha Ekins, executrix of Alexander Ekins, defendants.

The defendant, Thomas Maidwell, in consideration of a marriage with his first wife and of £700 portion, by indenture dated 24 March 1680, settles lands, as to part of which, the uses were to himself for life, remainder to trustees to preserve etc., then to Collins and Orlebar for 500 years upon the trusts following, remainder to himself in tail male, remainder to his own right heirs.

The trusts of the term were that, in case the said defendant should die without issue male by his said wife, Margaret, or that such issue should die without issue male before the age of twenty-one and there should be one or more daughters between which should be unmarried or unprovided for at the time of his death as thereinafter is mentioned, then such daughter, if but one, should have £2000, if more than one, the £2000 was to be equally divided.

In case the said portions should not be paid according to the purport of the indentures, then the trustees or the survivor should out of the rents and profits of the premises or by sale or mortgage thereof for all or any part of the term raise the said portions for such daughter or daughters and in the meantime out of the rents and profits should raise a convenient maintenance for such daughter or daughters not exceeding £30 a year apiece, if three, nor £20 a year, if more, and should permit such person to whom the freehold of the premises immediately expectant on the term did belong to receive the overplus of the rents until the said portions should be payable etc. after the same should be raised, the term to attend the inheritance, proviso that, if Thomas Maidwell, in his lifetime either before or after the death of his intended wife or if, after his decease, the person to whom the reversion etc. should belong should pay or secure to the said daughter or daughters which should be unmarried at the time of his death the said portions and maintenance of if there should be no such issue female or they should die before eighteen, then the term to cease.

In July 1688, Margaret, the wife, died leaving issue only the plaintiff's wife, who was married to him in May 1708 and now prefers this bill against her father and his second wife and the children of that marriage, upon whom the premises are settled, to have the £2000 raised and the arrears of maintenance until it became payable.

The court took time to inspect precedents and consider of it. And now the Lord Chancellor [Lord Cowper] delivered his opinion as follows. This happens to be one of those ill penned settlements which occasions difficulties, not so much from a want of skill in the drawer as from using too many words and too great prolixity in it.

There is a great regard to be had to former judgments that so there may be a fixed and settled rule as near as may be, for, otherwise, counsel can never tell how to advise their clients. I think none of the former precedents come up to this case.

There is no question but the term is absolutely vested in the trustees, there being no condition precedent to the vesting of it, so that the question does not arise upon that, but upon the trusts of the term.

Had there been no condition precedent in the trusts, I am clear, though it is a term in remainder, yet it might be sold, for this is agreeable to the rule and practice of this court, the reason of which is because everything that was contingent in the case has happened. The wife is dead without issue male, and, though the father is living, yet it is now become impossible that he should have a son by her so that I say nothing that was contingent remains but the father's death, which it is certain must happen sometime or other. And it is contingent only as to the time. And, therefore, for the sake of children and that they may have their portions at a time when they most need them, that is when they marry, this court has gone so far as to direct them to be raised in the father's lifetime, though I must confess for my own part, were it *res integra*, I think I should not go so far, for it may be a great detriment to an estate to have such terms in remainder sold. However, was there nothing more in this case, I should have followed the former precedents of the court and have decreed the term to be sold for raising the plaintiff's wife's portion. But I am of opinion that none of the precedents come up to this case.

The condition precedent here is not only that the father is to die without issue male (for so far the precedents have gone) but that, if there are daughters, such daughters must be unmarried or unprovided for at the death of the father. Now, this is in none of the other cases and is a contingency which has not yet happened.

Now, who is the portion to be raised for? Why, for such a daughter that shall be unmarried or unprovided for at the death of the father. It is true indeed the plaintiff's wife is married, but yet it is still contingent whether she will be unprovided for at the death of her father, in whose power it is to provide for her in his lifetime if he thinks fit, so that I say that contingency has not yet happened, for she cannot be said to be a daughter unprovided for at the death of the father while he is living.

Besides, what you ask is in the power of the father to determine and defeat as soon as he pleases, for there is a proviso that, if the father shall pay or secure to be paid the portions for such daughters, the term is to cease. Now, you would have a term to be sold, which it is in the father's power to determine by paying or securing to be paid his daughter's portions at his death, for, if he does so, the term itself, by the express words of the proviso is to be void.

Upon the whole, I cannot in my reason direct a sale in the father's lifetime.

Note the precedents cited were:

First, the Case of Jones and Hilyard, in the Commissioners' time,[1] which My Lord said was nothing to the purpose;

Second, the Case of Gerrard, daughter of Sir Charles Gerrard, in Lord Keeper Wright's time;[2] in that case, there was a condition precedent to the vesting of the term itself, that is, if the father died without issue male, then a term was limited to trustees for raising daughters' portions; the mother was dead without issue male, and the father still living so that the term itself was not really vested in the trustees; however, for the reasons aforesaid, the court directed the term to be sold;

Third, the Case of Staneport and Staneport, 3 Anne, at the Rolls;[3] there was a condition precedent as to the vesting of the term, for it was, if the father and mother died without issue male and leave daughters, then to the trustees for 500 years; here, the father was dead and the mother was living;

Fourth, the Case of Greaves and Mattison, Sir Thomas Jones's reports 201.[4]

Lincoln's Inn MS. Misc. 506, p. 89

Trinity, 9 Anne.

Lord Cowper admitted that, if the term did not vest but on a condition or was absolutely vested and the like condition annexed to the payment, there, when the condition for the payment had happened, the term might be sold to raise the portion. But then, he went on and said, 'If this were *res integra*, I should not adjudge it so. And I go into this only by way of concession because one of the cases produced was so. I do not see why the father cannot agree to charge his estate in such manner as shall not take place until after his death. And, if he does, I know no reason why this court should overrule it.' He said that, in that case, the deed went on and made it plainer, for the maintenance is to be raised out of the profits, which profits cannot arise until the death of the father and, therefore, must postpone the payment of the portion, for the maintenance must precede the portion.

Yale Beinecke OSB MSS. 184, box 41,
Taussig 311, vol. 1, p. 457

Trinity, 9 Anne.

The cause having been heard sometime before and the Lord Chancellor having been attended with precedents insisted upon by either side, this term, he

---

1 *Hellier v. Jones* (1689), 1 Eq. Cas. Abr. 337, 21 E.R. 1085.

2 *Gerrard v. Gerrard* (1704), 2 Vernon 458, 23 E.R. 894, 2 Freeman 271, 22 E.R. 1204, 1 Eq. Cas. Abr. 337, 21 E.R. 1086.

3 *Staniforth v. Staniforth* (1703–1719), 2 Vernon 460, 23 E.R. 895, 1 Eq. Cas. Abr. 337, 21 E.R. 1086, 2 Cooper *tempore* Cottenham 432, 47 E.R. 1234, Chancery Cases *tempore* Geo. I, 555.

4 *Greaves v. Mattison* (1682), T. Jones 201, 84 E.R. 1216, also Skinner 38, 90 E.R. 19, 1 Eq. Cas. Abr. 336, 21 E.R. 1085.

gives his judgment. The case arises on the penning of the settlement made on the marriage of Thomas Maidwell. It happens to be one of those ill penned settlements where the difficulty of construing it arises not so much from an ignorance of the law as from an ill modern custom of using a multiplicity of words. These sort of conveyances often create trouble and particularly on this head, whether the portion shall be raised in the lifetime of the father or not. There is no obscurity in the law in this matter, but it depends only on the penning of the settlement so as to express the meaning of the parties clearly.

I own this is a point of some difficulty, not so much from the nature of the case as to judge it agreeable to reason and at the same time agreeably to the judgments that have been already given. And there is a great reason the judgment of the courts in Westminster Hall, especially in the same court, should agree where the cases agree.

Those lands that are subject to this portion were settled by this deed to the use of Thomas Maidwell for life without impeachment of waste, to the use of trustees during his life to support contingent remainders, then for 500 years to trustees for raising portions, which is a term in remainder without any condition precedent for the vesting that term but is absolutely vested, remainder to Thomas Maidwell in tail male special, then to the right heirs of Thomas Maidwell.

These are the uses of the land charged with this portion. Then comes the declaration of the trust of this term, and the question arises on the declaration of the trust of the term and not of the vesting of the term. In case Thomas Maidwell shall happen to die without issue male of his body on the body of Margaret, his intended wife, and there shall be issue, one or more daughter or daughters of the body of the said Thomas on the body of the said Margaret, which shall be unmarried and not provided for at the time of the decease of the said Thomas Maidwell, that then such daughter or daughters shall have such portions as are therein mentioned, *viz.*, if only one daughter, then she shall have £2000, and the said portions to be paid at their ages of eighteen or days of marriage or as soon after as they can be conveniently raised.

Then there is a clause that, in case the portion be not paid, the trustees shall out of the rents, issues, and profits raise convenient maintenance for the daughters not exceeding £30 *per annum* apiece and permit him to whom the inheritance shall belong to receive the remainder, provided that, if Thomas Maidwell, in his lifetime, either before or after the decease of his wife, do pay or sufficiently secure to the good liking of the trustees to such daughter as shall be unmarried at the time of his decease the portion before charged, then the said term of 500 years to cease.

These being material parts of the deed, the facts stand thus. The mother is dead without issue male, and the father is living. There is one daughter, who is the plaintiff's wife, and she desires to have the portion raised in the lifetime of the father. And this is made colorable by several cases that have been in this court, which, when considered, none of them will come up to this case.

I have observed that the question does not arise on the vesting of the term, but on the declaration of the trust of the term in this case. The term is plainly vested in trustees, and there is no condition precedent to the vesting of it; so, no doubt, it is a saleable estate. But the question is whether this court shall decree a sale.

To come at this question the right way is to begin with cases less doubtful and then come to them that are more doubtful and to show how they differ from the present.

The plainest case is this. If a trust directs a portion to be raised at eighteen or day of marriage, as in this case, and that declaration of a trust depends on a term vested, in that case, I make no doubt the daughter is not to stay for her portion until the death of her father, but the term shall be sold, though it be a term in remainder. In the next place, suppose a trust be limited upon a term that is not absolutely vested, but there is a condition precedent to the vesting of the term, as if it be to the father for life and he shall happen to die without issue male of his body on the body of his wife, then to trustees for a term of years to raise portions for daughters at eighteen or marriage, the wife dies without male issue; though there is a condition precedent to the vesting of the term, yet the term may be sold in the lifetime of the father. One of the precedents goes so far, though if I were to adjudge it as *res integra*, I should not adjudge it so. I go into this only by way of concession because it has been done in one of the precedents before me and there is some reason to solve this case, because the court has in this case supposed the contingency in effect to have happened; the contingency is the father's dying without issue male of that woman, and, when she is dead, all that is contingent has happened, for there can be no issue male of that marriage and it is certain the man must die and that, when he dies, it will be without issue male by that woman. And that brings the case to this. He is tenant for life with remainder to trustees for a term of years. And can anyone say it is a contingency whether a tenant for life shall die? If the term were absolutely settled and the condition were annexed to the execution of the trust and it had run thus in the declaration of the trust, in case the father shall die without issue male of his body on the body of his wife, then the trustees shall raise such portions and the mother dies in the lifetime of the father, in that case, according to the precedents, the term shall be sold. And it depends upon the reason of the former case that all that is contingent has happened.

This court has gone so far in order to encourage suitable matches and to make provisions for daughters when there was most occasion for it. And, as this court does sometimes prolong the payment of money beyond the agreement of the parties, it may seem by the same reason that they may in some cases hasten it, and, if the case in question had come up to this, I should have decreed a sale, though, if it had been *res integra*, I should not have gone so far, for I do not see why the father may not charge his estate only after the time of his decease. And why this court should overrule that agreement of the father, I cannot see. But finding it has been done and that the judges of the common law have done it, I have that difference to those authorities that I should have come up to them if this case had been the same.

But this case is materially different from the other cases I have mentioned, for, in this case, in directing the execution of the trust, after it is said in case he shall happen to die without issue male of his body on the body of Margaret and there should be a daughter or daughters, then follow these words, which are not in any of the other cases, 'which shall be unmarried and not provided for as hereinafter mentioned at the time of the decease of the said Thomas Maidwell, then the trustees are to raise portions for such daughters' so that the parties have agreed that portions shall not be raised unless the father die without issue male by Margaret and there be a daughter or daughters unmarried or unprovided for at the time of his decease. These words describe the person entitled to the portion and, though this woman cannot be unmarried at the time of her father's death, yet she may be unprovided for so that this differs from all those cases I came into by way of concession, for it is not contingent whether any daughter will be unprovided for at the death of her father to the amount of this portion. The deed goes on and makes it plainer, for the clause that goes to raising the maintenance says that, if the portion is not paid, it shall be raised by sale or mortgage, but the maintenance is to be raised only out of the profits, which being in contradistinction to sale or mortgage, the word 'profits' cannot there be construed a sale. Therefore, the maintenance before the portion becomes payable and is actually paid is by that deed to be raised out of the profits. But no one can think that the maintenance is to run in the lifetime of Mr. Maidwell. And yet, if this doctrine is true, she may as well demand a maintenance out of the rent as to raise a portion in his lifetime. Then comes a clause that, if Mr. Maidwell do in his lifetime, before or after the death of his wife, pay or secure to such daughter as shall be unmarried at the time of his decease such portion, then the term is to cease, which you would now sell, which shows that he has all his lifetime either to pay or secure this portion. Deeds will be of no avail if the argument of convenience will overrule so plain a declaration of the intention of the parties.

The authorities that have been insisted on are these.

Jones v. Hilliard; but that is nothing to the purpose of this case, for, there, the plaintiff, who had paid part of his sister's portion and secured the rest and, thereupon, had an abatement, thought he had overpaid it and that he was not bound by his agreement and that the term was not vested, but that decree was that he was bound by his agreement and that the term was vested, there being no condition precedent in that case.

Gerrard and Gerrard, 3 Ch. Rep. 200; this settlement was to Sir Charles Gerrard for life, then to Honoria, his wife, for life for her jointure, and, in case of failure of issue male of that marriage and, there being issue female, then to the use of trustees for 200 years. In this case, the condition precedent to the vesting of the term is only on the failure of issue male and not in the case of the father's dying without issue male. Then the trust is to raise portions or the daughters to be paid at their ages of twenty-one or marriage. And then come in these words, 'which shall next happen after the decease of the said Charles and Honoria', so that it was insisted in that case that, in case the daughter did not come to age or marry after the death both of the father and the mother, she should by that accident lose her portion and it should not be raised even after the death of the father and mother. But the court thought that could never be the meaning of the parties than what term was sold a term vested, on which the words directing the raising the portions is only in case of failure of issue male, and nothing was said of the death of the father.

Stanyforth and Stanyforth, 3 Ch. Rep. 201; the settlement is to Jonathan Stanyforth for life, then to Christian for life for her jointure, then to the heirs male of Jonathan and Christian; then comes in a condition precedent to the vesting of the term, if it shall happen that Jonathan and Christian depart this life bearing no issue male and shall have issue, one or more daughters, then to the use of trustees for 500 years. This is made a condition precedent to the vesting of the term, and the trust of the term is absolute without any precedent condition. In this case, the father was dead and the mother living. And the question was whether the term should be vested for raising the portion in the life of the mother so that, in that case, all parts of the contingency had happened. And that case comes to the terms I mentioned before. The woman is tenant for life; the remainder for years is absolutely vested, and the direction of the trust is without any contingency whatsoever.

Greaves and Mattison, 2 Jones 201; Sir Edward Greaves conveys to himself for life, then to the first and other sons of the marriage in tail male and, in case he should happen to die without issue male of his body on the body of his then wife, then to trustees for raising daughters' portions to be paid at their day of marriage or age of twenty-one years. The wife died without issue male, leaving two daughters. It was adjudged that the trustees, after the death of the mother and in the lifetime of the father, may sell the term. Had this case and the other case of Stanyforth been *res integra*, I could not come up to them:

1 Salkeld 159, 91 E.R. 147

Trinity 9 Anne.

A bill was brought for raising the wife's portion out of a reversionary term expectant on her father's death. The case was Thomas Maidwell, the father of the plaintiff's wife, upon his marriage, settled to the use of himself for life, remainder to trustees for 500 years, remainder to the heirs male of his body by his intended wife, and, if he should happen to die without issue male of his body by his wife and there should be one or more daughters of their two bodies which should be unmarried or not provided for at the time of his death, such daughter (if but one) should have £2000 and £30 *per annum* issuing out of the profits until the portion should become due, the portion to be payable at the age of eighteen or day of marriage and a power for the trustees to raise it by sale or mortgage of the term or perception of profits.

There being but one daughter of this marriage, and no son, the wife died, and the daughter being above the age of twenty-one and married to the plaintiff, the question was whether the trustees could raise her portion in the life of her father.

And on great consideration, it was held by the LORD COWPER, Lord Chancellor:

First, that, though a term is limited in remainder to commence after the death of the father, yet, if the trust is to raise a portion payable at the age of eighteen or day of marriage, without question, the daughter shall not wait the death of her father but, at the age of eighteen or marriage, may compel a sale of the term;

Secondly, so it is if the trust of a term for raising daughters' portions be limited to take effect in case the father dies without issue male by his wife and the wife die without issue male, leaving a daughter, in such case, the term is saleable in the life of the father;

That, so far, it had been carried already, but he doubted whether he could have gone so far in case the matter were *res integra*, but that the reasoning upon which it had been founded was that, by the death of the mother, the possibility of issue male was extinct, that all that was contingent in the case has happened, it is become impossible that there should he issue male, and, as to the father's death, that is not contingent, for all men must die, and it is now the same thing to say when the father shall die without issue male by his wife as to say when the father shall die.

And, if this case had gone no farther, it had been no more than that the father is tenant for life, remainder to trustees for 500 years for raising daughters' portions payable at the age of eighteen or marriage. And now, all contingencies having happened and being out of the case, it should seem within the reason of the first resolution.

The Case of Greaves and Mattison, 2 Jo. 201, comes fully up to this resolution. Sir Edward Greaves made a settlement to the use of himself for life, remainder to the use of his first son in tail male, remainder to trustees for forty years, remainder to himself in fee, the term is declared to be in trust that, in case it should happen that the said Sir Edward should die without issue male of his body, then the trustees should raise £5000 for daughters' portions payable at the age of twenty-one or marriage with a provision for maintenance in the meantime. The wife died, leaving two daughters and no issue male, and, by Pemberton, Dolben, and Raymond, it was resolved that the right to the portion was vested by the mother's death without issue male in the life of the father, for, otherwise, the father might live so long that the portions might be of little service. Thus far, the court has gone for convenience that young women may have their portions when they most want them.

But, in the principal case, the daughter, who is the subject of this provision, must be a daughter unmarried or unprovided for at the time of the father's death, which is a contingency not yet happened. And, therefore, it comes not within the reason of either of the rules.

As to the £30 *per annum* for maintenance, he held that must be intended in case the father die without issue male, leaving a daughter under the age of eighteen or not married, because, otherwise, this absurdity must follow, that the daughter must be paid maintenance money in the life of the father out of the profits of a term that is not to commence until after the father's death.

This case was too strong for the court to attempt to get over, and to do it would create great confusion, and it would be to no purpose for anyone to make deeds if the argument of convenience or inconvenience should prevail to overrule them. The bill was dismissed.

[Other reports of this case: 3 Chancery Reports 190, 21 E.R. 764, 2 Vernon 640, 655, 23 E.R. 1019, 1027, 1 Eq. Cas. Abr. 337, 21 E.R. 1086.]

## 172

## Conway v. Shrimpton

(Ch. 1710)

*Married women and infants cannot be guilty of laches.*

Harvard Law Sch. MS. 537, pt. 2, p. 152, pl. 2

Easter term 9 Anne.

A mortgage had been made to [ *blank* ] about thirty-eight years ago, and it had been assigned and gone through several hands until it came to the defendant's.

And now, a bill was exhibited to redeem and to have an account of the mesne profits. And, though [it was] objected that it was of an old date and that it had gone through several hands, of which most [were] dead and consequ[ently] the impossibility to account, yet a redemption was decreed because the delay was answ[ered] because of coverture and infancy and such like.

And it was agreed by the counsel of the defendant that there was no time limited either by statute law or the rules of court, but that it was entirely [in] the discretion of the court.

Then, another question was whether, from a certain time wherein the accounts between them were stated by the guardian of the infant mortgagor and the mortgagees, the interest should be turned into principal.

And *Vernon* etc. urged that it should because, had it been assigned for principal and interest really and *bona fide* paid, then interest would have run upon it in assignees' hands as upon the whole sum that was paid; so this account was for the satisfaction of the mortgagees and to prevent an assignment and though in the case of infancy. And [it was said] by him, when [there is] a bill to redeem against an infant, though there shall not be a foreclosure against the infant until [he be] of age, yet they go upon that bill to an account, and, from that time, the interest runs upon the balance. But [it was said] by him, where [there are] assignments every half year in order to make principal interest, there, the apparent fraud will disappoint them. But, where there has been a rest at any time, there [ . . . ] a conversion of interest into principal.

*Sed quid inde venit nescio.*

[Other reports of this case: 5 Brown P.C. 187, 2 E.R. 617, 2 Eq. Cas. Abr. 596, 738, 22 E.R. 501, 627.]

## 173

## Taylor v. Smith

(Ch. 1710)

*An arbitrator must be as disinterested and impartial as a judge.*

Lincoln's Inn MS. Misc. 10, p. 34

13 June 1710.

The bill was to set aside an award. And it was accordingly decreed so to be for these reasons.

Lord Chancellor [Lord Cowper]: I am always inclined to support awards, for the arbitrators are judges of the parties' own choosing. And it is a good and easy way of ending suits. And, besides, an Act of Parliament[1] had now put matters under a determination in that way. But, notwithstanding my inclination this way, I think the award ought to be set aside for these reasons, first, because one of the arbitrators refused to hear one of the plaintiff's witnesses, alleging that he was not a creditable witness, though it is agreed that the witness was not wholly unexceptionable, yet he being a good witness in the eye of the law, the arbitrators ought to have heard him.

Second, when the plaintiff came to this arbitrator and asked him whether he had read her papers for sure, says she, 'if you had, you would not have made so hard an award as this', he made answer, 'no, I have neither read them nor will and, therefore, pray, take them'. Now, this is sworn by two witnesses and yet I confess I do question whether what the arbitrator said himself was true, for I am inclined to believe he had read them, however, admitting he had, yet I think these are words of heat and passion and too plainly show he was not so impartial as a judge ought to be.

It is plain he has made a great mistake in that account.

1 Stat. 9 Will. III, c. 15 (*SR*, VII, 369–370).

## 174

## Whitcomb v. Jacobs

(Ch. 1710)

*The goods of a principal and the debts due to the principal from third parties that are in the possession of a factor are not the property of the factor and do not pass to the factor's estate upon his death.*

British Library MS. Hargrave 81, f. 22

16 June 1710.

Hobson, who had been employed by the defendant in Turkey, being greatly indebted to the defendant and not able to pay him and having a house and ground at [ *blank* ] in Greece, signs a writing the 25th of April 1694, by which he declared that he had that day finished and settled all accounts between him and the defendant Jacobs and that he was debtor to the defendant by balance the sum of 5,000 dollars, which he was not then able to pay, and did thereby, for security of said balance when capable, transfer and make over the said house and ground to the defendant together with all his proper effects, present and future, until such time as the said balance should be fully satisfied and discharged and, for the true performance, binds himself, his heirs, and assigns under hand and seal. After this, the plaintiff employs him as his factor and consigns him goods, some of which the said Hobson sells for ready money, some upon credit, and some remained undisposed and under the plaintiff's mark and the said Hobson insisted [was] the produce of the said goods, which he had invested, received in other goods, which remained in his warehouse at the time of his death unmarked. And, after his death, the defendant takes out letters of administration as chief creditor and gets the most part of the money and effects of the said Hobson into his hands.

And the plaintiff brings his bill to have an account of the said Hobson's estate and satisfaction for his effects in the hands of the said Hobson at the time of his death and suggests that the debts stand out for his goods sold and that the investitures and also the other goods, which were in his custody at the time of his decease, were the plaintiff's and insists that the defendant was not to have a satisfaction for his debt but out of the said house etc. unless the said Hobson had acquired an estate of his own to satisfy it otherwise.

Curia: If a factor sells his principal's goods and receives the money and dies, the money is to be looked upon as part of his estate because it has no earmark and cannot be distinguished to be another person's. But if the debt be standing out, it belongs to the principal. And, if, in such case, the factor die, such debt shall not be reckoned part of his estate because, in that case, it appears to be the immediate produce of the principal's goods, the property of which is not altered by the consignment.

If a factor sells his principal's goods and gives credit for the money, he must be answerable for it unless he had authority to sell upon trust or give such credit only as is usual and customary in that place and such as probably his principal would have done himself had he been there, for, when he is to dispose of his principal's effects, it must be upon such terms as he is directed or is customary, which sometimes is for three or four months credit.

And the court decreed an account of such of the plaintiff's goods as were remaining with Hobson in specie or under his, the plaintiff's, mark at the time of Hobson's death and also for such debts as were due to Hobson for the plaintiff's goods and received by the defendant, his agent, or factors since the said Hobson's decease as also of all such goods as were purchased by Hobson with the money arising by the sale of the plaintiff's effects and consigned by him and the defendant to have an allowance for factorage and charges on account of the said goods. But interest and costs [were] reserved on both sides until the report.

[Other copies of this report: British Library MS. Hargrave 82, f. 18, British Library MS. Hargrave 77, f. 8v, pl. 2, British Library MS. Hargrave 303, f. 13.]

1 Salkeld 160, 91 E.R. 149

Trinity 9 Anne.

If one employs a factor and entrusts him with the disposal of merchandize and the factor receives the money and dies indebted [in] debts of a higher nature and it appears by evidence that this money was vested in other goods and remains unpaid, those goods shall be taken as part of the merchant's estate, and not the factor's. But, if the factor have the money, it shall be looked upon as the factor's estate and must first answer the debts of a superior creditor etc., for, in regard that money has no earmark, equity cannot follow that in behalf of him that employed the factor.

## 175

## Elwaies v. Kelwish

(Ch. 1710)

*Where a person pays money into court in satisfaction of a debt, he is not liable for interest on the debt after the payment into court.*

Lincoln's Inn MS. Misc. 10, p. 17

16 June 1710.

The plaintiff made a mortgage to the defendant for £500. Sometime after which, it was agreed between them that the money should be paid in and a time and place was appointed, *viz.* at Norwich on the 21st September and that interest should be carried on for five weeks beyond that time. Accordingly, when the time came, the plaintiff brought his money, £200 of which were in guineas, which about that time went at 22s. apiece and, at that rule, the plaintiff paid them to the defendant, who tells over the money, puts it up into bags, but says he would not take the guineas at 22s. unless the drovers at Norwich would take them so. Thereupon, the plaintiff and defendant go to a goldsmith's house at Norwich where the defendant was told that guineas were fallen, upon which he refuses to take the money.

The plaintiff, upon this, prefers his bill, which was in the year 1698, to redeem. And about a month after, he gives notice to move for an injunction and obtains an order for an injunction and that he should bring the money into court.

The defendant never defended the motion nor, as he pretends, had he notice of this order until about November afterwards.

The plaintiff brought his money into court where it has lain ever since. And the question now was who should lose the interest.

Lord Chancellor [Lord Cowper]: The money was paid into court not as a deposit to wait the event of the suit, but as so much due at all events. And it was the defendant's fault he did not apply to take it out. But they say he did not know of the order. There was notice given of the motion. And can you suppose the defendant's clerk would not enquire what was done upon that motion?

The interest must cease from the end of March [?] after the money was paid into court. But, in regard the plaintiff did not make a legal tender, he must pay costs. The defendant must take the money out of court, and, upon his receiving his principal, interests, and costs, he is to reassign his mortgage.

## 176

## Wilson v. Pack

(Ch. 1710)

*If an agreement is made before marriage for a separate maintenance and the wife saves money out of it, this court will preserve that money and the produce of it for her.*

Lincoln's Inn MS. Misc. 10, p. 19

26 June 1710. Wilson v. Penelope Pack, relict of Clifton Pack, Busby, administrator of Clifton, and Bates.

The plaintiff is a creditor upon simple contract of the defendant Pack's husband, and, having brought an action against the defendant Busby as his administrator, who, thereupon, pleaded *plene administravit*, and the plaintiff took judgment *quando* assets *acciderint*. And now, he prefers his bill to have satisfaction of his debt, which was £80, out of some jewels of the defendant Penelope Pack.

She, by her answer, confesses that she has a diamond necklace, buckle, etc., but she says that, upon her marriage, her late husband gave a bond to the defendant Bates, her father, with a condition to allow her £100 a year for pin money and to settle an annuity out of lands to secure it and that, after the marriage, *viz.* 4 July 1698, he, accordingly, in pursuance of that bond, granted an annuity of £100 out of certain lands to the defendant Bates during his own and the defendant, his wife's, lives upon trust that Bates should pay this annuity to the wife for her separate maintenance and peculiar expenses, with which the husband was not to meddle.

She having by her good housewifery laid up money out of this annuity, she did at several times lay out the same in the purchase of these jewels and, being willing to secure the same for her children after her death, by indenture dated [ *blank* ] 1706, between her husband and herself of the one part and the defendant Bates of the other part, reciting the grant of the annuity and that she had bought these jewels with the money she had laid up out of her annuity, her husband and she bargained and sold these jewels to the defendant Bates upon trust that he should permit her to use the same during her life and, afterwards, that the same should be divided between her two daughters in such proportions as therein are mentioned and she insists that these jewels are not subject to her husband's debts. And if they were or no was the question.

The lands out of which this annuity was granted proved to be but £80 a year, and the defendant received the rents and took them in satisfaction of her annuity. Some of the jewels were bought in the year 1699, some in 1702, some in 1703, and some in the years 1705 and 1706.

The bond was not produced, nor was there any positive proof that such a bond was ever executed. Only Mr. Carter, who was concerned in drawing the marriage writings, swears that, to the best of his remembrance, there was a bond executed and that the defendant Penelope refused to marry unless her husband would agree to give such bond.

Mr. *Vernon*: The defendant has made no proof that any bond was executed, only the deed, whereby the annuity was granted, recites that such an agreement was made before the marriage, which, surely, is no proof. Why then taking it to be a conveyance after marriage, it is voluntary and, therefore, fraudulent against creditors by the Statute of Queen Elizabeth.[1]

Lord Chancellor [Lord Cowper]: The plaintiff has a strong equity on his side which goes upon this reason, that it is not reasonable the relict of a man should go splendid when his just debts are not paid.

However, if an agreement is made before marriage for a separate maintenance and the wife saves money out of it, this court will preserve that money and the produce of it for her. But, here, the defendant has not made this to be her case, for she has failed in her proof that any bond was ever executed. And, therefore, she must be decreed either to pay the plaintiff his debt with costs or be examined upon interrogatories for discovery of what is come to her hands.

[1] Stat. 13 Eliz. I, c. 5 (*SR*, IV, 537–538).

[Other reports of this case: Precedents in Chancery 295, 24 E.R. 141, 2 Eq. Cas. Abr. 155, 22 E.R. 133.]

## 176a

## Perkins v. Mansell

(Ch. 1710)

*Whether an infant is liable for court costs on an issue out of Chancery is to be decided by the Court of Chancery not the common law court.*

Lincoln's Inn MS. Misc. 538, f. [130]

Trinity term 1710. Perkins, lessee in ejectment of Dr. Bentham *versus* Mansell, an infant, by a guardian.

There was a suit in Chancery for discovery of writings. The court thought fit that the matter should be tried at law touching the title, and left the plaintiff to bring his [action of] ejectment, which he did in the Exchequer, the lands lying in Wales.

And, upon a trial at the bar by a Herefordshire jury, a verdict passed for the plaintiff upon a point of law by the opinion by the whole court. Upon which, a bill of exceptions was prayed. But, that prayer being out of time and wholly irregular and not drawn up nor duly tendered, it was not allowed. But the plaintiff had his judgment, the Chancery wholly refusing to meddle about the bill of exceptions.

Upon the defendant's appearance by his guardian, there was not a rule entered, as usual, for the guardian's payment of costs if the verdict and judgment were for the plaintiff, which being so, the court was moved for a rule that costs might be paid by the guardian, which, for want of such rule upon entry of an appearance, the court refused to make. And, therefore, the Clerk of the Pleas, entered up judgment with costs against the infant defendant, against which it was moved by *Powys*, the Queen's Serjeant, and *Harcourt* that the suit in this Court [of Exchequer] proceeded by the direction of the Chancery and that, after the trial, resort was to be had to Chancery and the defendant was by order there to deliver possession and an account of the profits to be taken there. And so the costs in the Exchequer, if any should be allowed, should be under the direction of the Chancery. Besides, an infant, by law, is not liable to costs in [an action of] ejectment. And, therefore, he ought not so to be made without a special rule, which is not in this case.

But, on the contrary, it was insisted upon by *Jekyll*, Queen's Serjeant, and *Dodd*, for this plaintiff, that the [action of] ejectment in this case was not directed by the Chancery but the plaintiff was to take his course at law for making out his title, which he has done by this [action of] ejectment, which is a suit not under the governance of the Chancery, but a pure common law proceeding, and to take its success according to the rules of common law. And, though this court would make no rule after the trial for the guardian to pay costs, as upon entry of the appearance is usual, no more would they make a rule that the infant defendant should not pay costs, being in a case wherein he shall not have his age, being a tort [?].

And, thereupon, the court would make no rule about the costs, for, if the defendant can by the Chancery be excused from [paying] costs by what is left to that court, he may resort thither, nothing of that appearing to this court. And, if the defendant, as an infant, is not by law liable to costs and the judgment is entered against him for costs, he may have his remedy upon a writ of error. And so the court would make no rule in the case.

## 177

## Anonymous

(Ch. 1710)

*The commissioners and assignees of a bankrupt succeed to the rights and duties of the bankrupt.*

Lincoln's Inn MS. Misc. 10, p. 22

1 August 1710.

Upon a petition, the case was thus. A.B., upon his marriage, gives a bond to a friend of his wife of £400 penalty conditioned to settle some land of his upon his wife for a jointure within two years after the marriage or, if he did not, that he would leave her £200 at this death. The marriage took effect, and the husband, afterwards, became a bankrupt.

And, now, the wife petitions the Lord Chancellor [Lord Cowper] that, in regard her husband had not made this settlement, that she might come in as a creditor and that £200 might be reserved out of his estate by the commissioners that so, if she happened to survive her husband, she might have it, the creditors receiving the interest of it in the meantime.

Lord Chancellor [Lord Cowper]: If the husband had not become bankrupt, the wife might have come into this court even in his lifetime for a specific performance of this agreement, either to have this settlement made or the £200 secured for her. Now, the commissioners and the assignees stand in the place of the bankrupt and ought to do whatever this court would have compelled the husband to have done. And, therefore, let them either pay off the mortgage (for you say the estate which the husband was to settle is mortgaged) and settle it for the jointure of the wife or, if they do not think fit to do that, the wife must come in as a creditor. And the Master is to see her proportion (as to the £200) secured so as she may receive it if she survives her husband.

## 178

## Davies v. Davenport

(Ch. 1710)

*Where a creditor of a decedent sues to have his debt paid out of the decedent's real property, the executors, heirs, and devisees must be made parties to the suit.*

Lincoln's Inn MS. Misc. 10, p. 23

25 October 1710.

The plaintiff sued the defendant Davenport at law upon a bond entered into by A.B., his testator, for payment of £165 and interest. Upon *non est factum* pleaded, the cause was tried and found for the plaintiff, though not without some suspicion of its being a forged bond. And, there being no personal assets, the plaintiff now brought his bill against the defendant, the executor, and his wife and their son to have a satisfaction out of the real assets, the testator having devised his estate to the defendant and his wife for their lives, remainder to their son in tail, with remainders over. And, in this bill, the plaintiff had made his wife, who was one of the co-heirs at law of the testator, and J.S. and his wife, who was the other co-heir, parties. The Act of Parliament in the 3rd & 4th year of King William,[1] which makes lands in the hands of the devisee assets, directs that the action must be brought both against the heir and the devisee.

## 179

## Cox v. Higford

(Ch. 1710)

*A copyhold can be forfeited for waste in not maintaining the premises in good repair.*

*A court of equity will not give a remedy to a person who delays in bringing his suit.*

Lincoln's Inn MS. Misc. 10, p. 27

27 October 1710.

The plaintiff was presented and amerced five several times by the homage for not repairing his copyhold tenement, after which the homage present the tenement forfeited to his lord, who, thereupon, enters and grants it to the defendant for three lives. The plaintiff brings an [action of] ejectment, and it is found against him. And now he comes to be relieved.

Lord Keeper [Lord Harcourt]: As this case stands, the plaintiff ought to have no relief. Here is a voluntary waste. But I do not go upon that only. It appears that he has not only incurred a willful forfeiture but that he has very much

[1] Stat. 3 Will. & Mar., c. 14 (*SR*, VI, 320–321).

misbehaved himself. Surely, a tenant, after a forfeiture, ought to have come and offered to repair. But now, if, instead of doing so, he will go to law and waive that relief he might have had in this court and when it is found against him at law will come for relief here, it seems to me a good cause to deny it him.

Besides, it is plain he has lain still for eight years since the verdict and, sure, if he is relieved, it must be when he comes recently.

The bill must be dismissed with costs.

Note, in this case was cited the case of Cudmore and Raven,[1] which was thus. The plaintiff was a Quaker and was summoned to appear at the lord's court and take the oath of fealty and, after three proclamations, refusing to come, the homage presented that he had forfeited his copyhold estate and coming afterwards into this court, he was relieved upon the payment of costs.

[Other reports of this case: 2 Vernon 664, 23 E.R. 1032, 1 Eq. Cas. Abr. 121, 21 E.R. 927.]

## 180

## Colthard v. Harrard

(Ch. 1710)

*A mortgage can be redeemed even after a long period of time has elapsed.*

Harvard Law Sch. MS. 537, pt. 2, p. 174, pl. 1

Michaelmas [term], 9 Anne, Master of the Rolls.

Thomas Colthard's father, whose heir and administrator the plaintiff was, being seised in fee of lands about the value of between £15 and £20 a year in the parish of Plymphee in Devonshire, for £280, conveyed them to the defendant's grandfather 18 February 1656 for a term of 3000 years, Richard Harrard, the defendant's grandfather. He, by a deed bearing date the 17th February, but executed at the same time with the other, reconveyed to the plaintiff's father for 2999 years but determined upon non-payment of £280 8s. at the half-year's end. The money was not paid. The mortgagee dies, and leaves the defendant's father executor, who, about twenty-four years ago, died leaving the defendant executor about ten months old. The plaintiff's father lived about thirty-one years after the mortgage. The mortgagees had demised for ninety-nine years determinable upon three lives and had got £320 fines.

And, upon a bill to redeem, a redemption [was] decreed, the leases to be established, but the rents and profits of the unleased premises to be accounted for.

[ . . . ] objected that the father lived thirty-one years after, that the rule never to allow a redemption after twenty years where no interest was paid and a pos-

[1] *Cudmore v. Raven*, 1 Rolle, Abr., *Copihold*, p. 509.

session in the mortgagee, that, though there was an infancy, yet the defendant claimed as executor and there must have been an administrator *durante minore* in the meantime, and that a bill would have been as effectual against him, and never carried further than twenty years, but only when the civil wars [was] some part of the time.

But the Master [of the Rolls, TREVOR] instanced in Sir John Leather's Case a redemption against him where there was so long a possession, even sixty years and under all these circumstances. He did not seem to take notice of the infancy. But query if it is not the same with an infant heir, for, there is a guardian in the meantime.

And another case of fifty [years was] cited by Mr. *How*. And [it was said] by Mr. *How*, if we had brought a bill sooner, we must have stayed until the heir came of age to show cause why there should not be a redemption.

N.B. The bill was exhibited three or four years ago.

*How* and myself [*Eden*] were for the plaintiff; Serjeant *Hooper* [and] Mr. *Fortescue* were for the defendant.

## 181

## Trowell v. Evance

(Ch. 1710)

*Where a promissory note made payable to order is accepted as payment of a debt, the holder of the note bears the risk of the maker's insolvency.*

Lincoln's Inn MS. Misc. 10, p. 28

28 October 1710.

The defendant Ayree gives a note payable to the defendant Beckley or order for £150. Beckley pays it to the plaintiff on the 7th December and, upon the next day, the plaintiff gives it to Sir Stephen Evance,[1] who, thereupon, gives a note to the plaintiff in this manner, 'Received of Mr. Trowell £150 on demand'. Sir Stephen Evance sends his man several times to Ayree for the money, but was put off from time to time, and, upon the 21st of December, he fails. And, in all this time, Sir Stephen never gave any notice to the plaintiff that the money was not paid until after Ayree failed.

The question was upon whom the loss should fall. And, upon the hearing before the Master of the Rolls [TREVOR], it was decreed that Sir Stephen Evance should be the loser and should have his satisfaction over against the defendant Ayree.

[1] H. Lancaster, 'Evance, Sir Stephen (1654/5–1712)', *Oxford Dictionary of National Biography*, vol. 18, p. 660.

And now, it came before My Lord Keeper [Lord Harcourt] upon the appeal of Sir Stephen Evance.

Lord Keeper [Lord Harcourt]: I shall not vary the decree. If the defendant Sir Stephen Evance had only taken the note as a servant to receive the money and he had happened to have been a little negligent and, in the meantime, the party fails, it might have been another matter. But here was an agreement to take this note as money and Ayree paid several sums of money afterwards and did not break until thirteen days after Sir Stephen received the note, and, therefore, I think he ought to bear the loss.

In this case was cited the case of Ward and Sir Stephen Evance, in the Queen's Bench,[1] where it was adjudged that a note on a man, though taken for the money, who failed the next day was no payment.

1 Eq. Cas. Abr. 376, 21 E.R. 1113

Michaelmas, 1710.

One Agris, a goldsmith, having £150 of Berkley's money in his hands, gives him a note, whereby he promises to pay to him or order on demand the sum of £150. Berkley, being indebted in the same sum to the plaintiff, delivers over that note to the plaintiff, but without making any endorsement. The plaintiff, presently, carries this note and likewise another bill for £80 which he had upon one Jackson to Sir Stephen Evans and Hales, goldsmiths in Lombard Street, who were his bankers or cashiers. And they gave him a note to this effect, *viz.* received of Mr. Trowell (the plaintiff) £230 upon account. And, on the margin, it was written thus, Berkley £150, Jackson £80, and his note was signed by Sir Stephen and Hales. They presently sent their dunner to Agris to demand the money, but he put them off from time to time for about thirteen or fourteen days, though the dunner had been several times with him for the money. And, afterwards, Agris fails.

It was proved in the cause that Agris was solvent after the note given by Sir Stephen Evans and had paid above £800 to several people. Upon Agris's failing, the plaintiff applies to the defendants, Sir Stephen Evans and Hales, for payment of the £150. Sir Stephen, not thinking himself obliged to pay it, sends the plaintiff to Berkley, to whom the note was first given.

And, he likewise refusing payment, the plaintiff brought his bill against them for a satisfaction, and he had a decree at the Rolls to charge Sir Stephen Evans and Hales, from which decree, they appealed to My Lord Keeper [Lord Harcourt].

[1] *Ward v. Evans* (1704), 2 Salkeld 442, 91 E.R. 382, 2 Lord Raymond 928, 92 E.R. 120, 1 Comyns 138, 92 E.R. 1002, 2 Salkeld 442, 91 E.R. 383, 3 Salkeld 118, 91 E.R. 726, 6 Modern 36, 87 E.R. 799, 12 Modern 521, 88 E.R. 1492, Holt K.B. 120, 90 E.R. 965.

And they insisted they were not chargeable with this money, that they took Agris's note only as servants to the plaintiff, and had several times sent their dunner to demand the money, that his promising them payment was the reason they did not give notice nor return the note to the plaintiff, that their manner of giving notes in Lombard Street was different from those given by goldsmiths at Temple Bar, yet, in substance, they were the same and amounted to no more than a receipt for the two notes from such persons for so much money, which, when they received, they promise to be accountable for, that this bill was but in the nature of an action of account against them as bailiffs or receivers of so much money and, at common law, if such action had been brought and, upon the trial, it appeared they had received no money, the jury would have found against the plaintiff, that the reason that led Sir Stephen to give a note in such a form was a case Michaelmas 2 Anne, between Ward and him, where the case was that the plaintiff Ward being indebted to one Fellows in the sum of £60 and having a note from Sir Stephen Evans for £100, when Fellows came for his money, Ward sends a servant with him to Sir Stephen with a bill of £100, and ordered him to pay Fellows the £60, and endorse it off the £100 note, but Sir Stephen, having a note on one Wallis for £60 10s. gives that note to Fellows, who pays him the 10s. overplus and goes away with the note; the next day, Wallis fails, and, upon an action brought by Ward for the £100, the Court of Queen's Bench was of opinion that the delivery of the note upon Wallis for £60 10s. was no payment, and, therefore, Ward recovered the whole £100, and, therefore, Sir Stephen now only gave a note for so much received on account, and the note in the margin, showing from whom it was due, made it plain he only acknowledged the receipt of such notes, but had no design to charge himself with the money until it was received.

But My Lord Keeper [Lord Harcourt] was clear of opinion that the note imported an acknowledgment of so much money received on the plaintiff's account, that the entry on the margin could at most only show how it was received, and that the note spoke itself, whatever the forms and meaning of such notes were. And, therefore, he affirmed the decree.

## 182

## Davy v. Hooper

## Hooper v. Pollexten and Davy

(Ch. 1710)

*In this case, the marriage settlement trust fund in issue was payable to the beneficiary, and it was not satisfied by an inheritance from the other parent.*

British Library MS. Hargrave 77, f. 16v, pl. 3

17 November 1710.

Mr. William Davy, afterwards Sir William, in the lifetime of his eldest brother, Sir John, marries Mary Stidman, an infant, who was seised in fee of lands in Somersetshire of £250 *per annum* and the greatest part in jointure to her mother-in-law. Previous to his marriage, William Davy, with his mother and brother, by articles, agree with the infant's trustees to settle £2000 for the benefit of the intended wife if William Davy died in her lifetime without issue by her, if living issue, then but £1500, she to have the interest thereof during her life, the principal to go to the issue and also, upon request, to settle £25 to and for the issue of the marriage in such proportion as the said William Davy should by writing appoint. The marriage was had. They had issue only Mary, wife of Hooper, who is an infant. After the marriage, William Davy and his wife, by a fine and recovery of an estate in the County of Somerset, settle the same to the use of Davy for life, remainder to the wife for life, remainder to the sons of that marriage, remainder to the daughters of that marriage in such proportions as the said William Davy should limit, remainder to the right heirs of William Davy.

Afterwards, the wife dies. Sir John Davy dies without issue, whereby a great estate comes to William Davy as heir male to Sir John. Afterwards, he marries Abig[ail], daughter of the plaintiff, Polexten, has £5000 portion with her, and has issue by her, the plaintiffs, the infants. He, afterwards, purchases £1400 and then settles the same charged with £5000 apiece to his said three daughters by the first wife, *viz.* the plaintiffs, the infants, and, subject to this charge, to the use of himself in tail male, remainder to all his daughters by any other wife. In 1706, he makes his will and devises some small legacies to his daughters by Mary and greater to his other daughters. And he dies.

[ . . . ] after, the daughters of the second wife, by their grandfather Pollexten, bring their bill against the defendants Mary and their father, trustees and executors, for a discovery of the articles of the first marriage and of the settlement of the Somersetshire estate.

Mary also brings her bill against the said plaintiffs, her father's executors, the trustees, for the £2500 and the £1500 mentioned in the articles and for a discovery of her father's real and personal estate.

For the original plaintiffs, it was insisted that the covenant in the marriage [articles] to the defendant Mary by the settlement of the Somersetshire estate upon the fine and recovery which might have been settled or given away from her and, therefore, it ought to be taken in satisfaction for those articles as to the said defendant Mary or however that the settlement of the new purchased estate in the County of Devonshire and the legacies given Mary by her father's will ought to be given in satisfaction of those articles.

For the defendant Mary, it was said, if the Somersetshire estate came only from her mother whose estate that was, and that her father, at the time of the settlement, had no interest of that estate vested in him, she claimed it not as the gift of her father but the gift and settlement of her mother, and it never was expressed or designed as a satisfaction to the issue for the debt by the articles, secondly, if it were to be considered as a satisfaction, [it] must have been so at the time of making the settlement and could not be deemed such, that then whatever was had by the settlement was but a contingent interest by way of remainder after the estate tail, which contingency might not have happened and which interest the tenant in tail might have barred and destroyed.

As to the Devonshire estate, that is charged with the £15,000 for the plaintiffs subject as to £220 of it to their mother's jointure and the defendant had no interest in it by the settlement but a remainder after an estate tail, which her father might have barred when he pleased. And this settlement was never declared by him to be intended as a satisfaction of the articles.

*Curia*: The £2500 is well vested by the articles in the defendant. But she is not entitled to the £1500 also. He dismissed her bill as to this. I decree her £2000 with interest at £5 percent from Sir William Davy's death.

The infants, afterwards, appeal to the Lords from this decree. On 14 February 1711[/12]. It was heard, and the former decree was affirmed.

N.B. The appellants set forth by the appeal that the father often declared his intent to make all his daughters equal fortunes. He, by his will, therefore, had in October 1706 made that settlement of his Devonshire estate and, by his will 10 February following [1707], takes notice of the settlement of his Somerset estate and devises to her his copyhold and leasehold in Somerset, which was her mother's and the arrears of the rent of her mother and household goods of her, and the whole [was] worth £500. And he gave to each of the appellants £500. He also makes the same persons executors as were his trustees.

[Other reports of this case: 2 Vernon 665, 23 E.R. 1032, 1 Eq. Cas. Abr. 336, 344, 21 E.R. 1085, 1091.]

## 183

## Woodward v. Champton and Jones

(Ch. 1710)

*The lord of a manor cannot refuse to admit a copyholder on the ground of a defect of title, but that issue is to be tried in the common law courts.*

British Library MS. Hargrave 81, f. 62

18 November.

The defendant was the steward of a manor and, afterwards, devisee in trust of the same manor and the steward. And, while he was the steward only, the plaintiff desired to be admitted to a copyhold part of the manor, of which another person was in possession and duly admitted. And the steward, upon searching into the rolls and court books, not finding that anyone under whom the plaintiff claimed had ever been admitted, though the petitioner insisted there had been such admittance, both he and the lord of the manor did refuse to admit the plaintiff. And now this bill was brought to compel an admittance of the plaintiff that he may be enabled to maintain an [action of] ejectment and try his title, which otherwise, not being heir at law, he could not do.

And it was decreed accordingly without costs, paying the lord his usual fine and court fees, and that the lord should appoint a court for that purpose and, if not admitted in a month, the lord to pay costs.

[Other copies of this report: British Library MS. Hargrave 82, f. 60, British Library MS. Hargrave 77, f. 17v, pl. 1, British Library MS. Hargrave 303, f. 33.]

## 184

## Moresco v. Leken

(Ch. 1710)

*Where a will is express as to the amount of interest that is to be paid to infant legatees, the court will enforce the testator's intent.*

British Library MS. Hargrave 81, f. 63

*Eodem die* [18 November].

The plaintiffs are infants. Moresco, their grandfather, devises to the plaintiffs certain lands and, when they attain their full age, equally to be divided between them as tenants in common and, if any of them died before that age, that part to go to the survivors and, if they all died before their full age, then the whole to their mother. Then he gives legacies to the defendant Leken, who was his son-in-law and a considerable silk weaver, and to the other defendant Jones, who was his daughter, and he makes them his executors. And he devises all the residue of his personal estate to the plaintiffs in the same manner as he had done the lands and that the executors, until their respective full ages or days of marriage, should pay interest after the rate of £4 percent and no more, and the interest should go and be paid with the principal unless the executors should find it necessary to take part of the interest to increase the maintenance. And this bill was brought by the plaintiffs by their *prochein ami* against the executors, first, to have a security for the residue and, secondly, to have a greater interest than £4 percent, it being a case of infants and for their benefit, who are always favored and protected by this court.

*Sir Joseph Jekyll* and Mr. *Vernon*, for the defendants, said that the executors were persons of the testator's, the donor's, own appointing, whose circumstances and characters he knew and was best judge of the confidence proper to be reposed in them and, as being nearly related to him, designed them a benefit by paying but an easy interest, that, therefore, to take this money from them would be directly contradicting and defeating of the will and the testator's plain intention and as it were making a new one for him which he never designed, that courts of equity had never gone so far, especially where the executors had not misbehaved themselves nor the estate was in danger of being wasted.

*Curia*: This case is very plain. The testator intended the executors a benefit, for there are negative words that they shall pay £4 percent and no more. And I cannot make them pay more. But, as the testator did equally intend that the plaintiffs should have the principal and interest effectually answered to them, it is the duty of the court to take care of infants' estates. The testator did not intend the executors should hazard the principal in order to make a greater interest, yet, if this money were to be employed in merchandise or in the defendant's trade, it might be hazarding the principal and so prejudice the infants and defeat the testator's will. Therefore, let the whole residue be brought before the Master and put out at interest and the £4 percent *per annum* be employed according to the will and the surplus of the interest be ordered equally in moieties between the two defendants.

[Other copies of this report: British Library MS. Hargrave 82, f. 61, British Library MS. Hargrave 77, f. 17v, pl. 2, British Library MS. Hargrave 303, f. 33v.]

## 185

## Dimock v. Bodington

(Ch. 1710)

*The issue in this case was the construction of a marriage settlement.*

Lincoln's Inn MS. Misc. 10, p. 32

20 November 1710.

Lands are settled upon marriage. And there is a term of years created, the trusts whereof are declared to be as follows, *viz.* that, if there shall be no issue male living at the death of the father or such issue male should die without issue male and there shall be then living one or more daughters, then the trustees should by the rents and profits of the premises or, by lease or mortgage thereof, raise for the portions and maintenance of such daughters the following sums, *viz.*, if but one daughter, £1500 to be paid at twenty-one or marriage if she should so long live and, if there should be two or more daughters, then £2000 to be equally divided between them and paid at the same time.

The father died and left a son and two daughters only. One died in her infancy. The other is married to the plaintiff, and he and his wife come now to have her portion raised. And the question was whether the words 'then living' should relate to the death of the father.

[ *blank* ].

## 186

## Dighton v. Dighton

(Ch. c. 1710)

*Where a devise is a charge on land, the land can be sold in order to pay it.*

Lincoln's Inn MS. Misc. 10, p. 33

A man, by his will, gives lands to the defendant, his wife, for her life, subject to the trusts and conditions thereinafter limited and then entails those lands after the death of the defendant upon the plaintiff. And then, there is a clause taking notice that he owed his daughter £100, which was given her by a relation. And, thereupon, he gives her £100 more and charges these lands with the payment of the £200 to his daughters within a year after his death. And then, he goes on and says that, if the £200 is not paid within that time, he orders that A. and B. shall enter upon the premises and, by mortgage or sale, raise money to pay the £200.

The plaintiff prefers his bill against the defendant and insists that she ought to pay the whole £200.

Mr. *Vernon*, for the defendant: All that can be required of the defendant is that, in regard she is tenant for life, she shall either keep down the interest during her life or, if the money is to be paid, that then she shall pay one-third and the plaintiff, who is the remainderman, shall pay the other two-thirds, for that is the constant course of the court.

This £200 is a charge upon the inheritance and was not intended to be paid out of the rents, for it is directed to be paid in a twelve-month and the estate is but £50 a year.

[It was] decreed that a part of the estate be sold for raising the £200 and that it be referred to a Master to see what part was most proper for that purpose.

## 187

## Attorney General, ex rel. v. Atmore

(Ch. 1710)

*In this case, the conveyances in issue were construed to be mortgages which should be redeemed in order to establish a charity created by the will.*

*Trustees who hold land must be made parties to any litigation concerning that land.*

Lincoln's Inn MS. Misc. 10, p. 35

25 November 1710. The Attorney General at the relation of the minister and churchwardens and overseers of the poor of the parish of Cunsby in Lincolnshire, plaintiffs, against William Atmore and John [Moore], Lord Bishop of Ely, defendants.

George Metham, by his will, gave several messuages in W. in Cambridgeshire to his wife for life and, after her death, to the two ancientest and poorest widows belonging to and living of Cunsby aforesaid for their lives and, when either of them should die, then the same should remain to two other poor, ancient widows of the said town forever. And he willed that the same should be done by the appointment of the minister, churchwardens, and overseers of the poor of the same parish when the said devise should take effect and, after that, successively, by the ordering of the minister, churchwardens, and overseers of the poor of the said parish for the time being. And he made his wife executrix. And he died without issue or any heir that could be found.

And the wife being now dead, the relators brought a bill against the defendant Atmore, who had a mortgage of the premises made by the testator for a redemption and to establish the charity, to which bill it was thought proper to make the defendant the bishop of Ely a party, he being lord of the manor of Wisbech Barton in the right of his bishopric of which manor the premises were held and, had there been no will, the premises would have escheated to him for want of an heir.

The defendant Atmore, who was the son of the testator's wife by a former husband, insisted by his answer that the premises were the inheritance of his mother and that, before her marriage with the testator and in consequence thereof, by a settlement dated 8th of January 1675, she covenanted with A. and B. to stand seised of part thereof to the use of her husband and herself for their lives, remainder to the heirs of their two bodies, remainder to the right heirs of the husband, upon condition that, in case they died without issue of their bodies, that then the right heirs of the husband should pay to the defendant and his heirs £20 within three months next after the remainder should happen and, in case of non-payment, the uses limited to the right heirs should cease and that all persons then seised of the premises should stand seised thereof to the use of the defendant and his heirs.

By another indenture dated 27th September 1679, the testator granted other parts of the premises to other trustees for 1000 years on condition to be void on the payment of £20 on the 29th of September 1689 to the use of the defendant. And he insisted that, the first £20 not being paid him, he was entitled to the premises in the first settlement and also was entitled to the £20 secured for him by the last settlement with interest.

The court [Lord Cowper] was of opinion that the first settlement was in the nature of a mortgage and that the plaintiffs ought to redeem that as well as the premises in the other settlement upon payment of both the two sums of £20 and interest. And he decreed the defendant, upon payment of the interest and costs within six months, to convey to the plaintiffs or as they should appoint for the benefit of the charity, which was decreed to be performed according to the will.

Note the trustees in the last settlement were not parties as they ought to have been. However, it being in the case of a charity, the court ordered the defendant should procure them to join in the conveyance at the plaintiffs' charge.

## 188

## Goodford v. Barnes

(Ch. 1710)

*In this case, the devise in issue created a joint tenancy.*

British Library MS. Hargrave 81, f. 66

5 December.

John Pittman, being seised in fee of certain lands, by his will, devises them to Mary Pittman and Rebecca Barnes, equally between them, and, after the death of Rebecca, the whole to Mary Pittman and the heirs of her body with remainder to his own right heirs. Mary dies without heirs of her body. And the plaintiffs, the co-heirs of John, the devisor, bring this bill and allege that this was a tenancy in common and that, therefore, on the death of Mary, one moiety ought to come to them in possession and the reversion of the other after the death of Rebecca, the other tenant in common. The cause was heard and a trial in ejectment was directed to try whether there was a joint tenancy or a tenancy in common. On the trial, a special verdict was found with the words of the will as before set forth, and the Court of King's Bench gave judgment that it was a joint tenancy.

And, in the argument of this case in the King's Bench, *Fortescue*, for the defendants, quoted the Case of Turton and Jefferies; lands were devised to two, equally to be divided between them, and, after their decease, the whole to the heirs of one of them; this was adjudged *per totam curiam* a joint tenancy not a tenancy in common because, by the word 'whole', the intent of the party plainly appeared to be that there should be no partition or division of the estate.

If lands were given to two equally between them, this is a joint tenancy, but, generally speaking, in a will, those words 'equally to be divided between them' creates a tenancy in common because the intent appears that there should be a division of the lands between the parties, but the word 'whole' added shows the intention here is the contrary.

[Other copies of this report: British Library MS. Hargrave 82, f. 63, British Library MS. Hargrave 77, f. 18, British Library MS. Hargrave 303, f. 35, pl. 1.]

## 189

## Musgrave v. Musgrave

(Ch. 1710)

*Upon an action for a bond debt against an infant heir, execution will be stayed until the heir comes of age.*

British Library MS. Hargrave 81, f. 67

5 December.

[An action of] debt upon a bond was brought according to the Statute of 3 & 4 W. & M., cap. 14,[1] against the heir at law and against the devisee. The first prayed the parol might demur in respect to her infancy. And the devisee demurred because he had no interest, the Act of Parliament having made the devise void.

Upon the same bond, an action was brought against the executrix, to be relieved against which, she brought her bill in regard that the testator had by his will devised a term of eleven years to trustees for payment of debts, within which time the infant heir would be of age. An injunction was prayed until hearing judgment was ordered to be given by the plaintiff, the executrix, but that no execution should be made out upon it until the heir came of full age without the leave of the court.

[Other copies of this report: British Library MS. Hargrave 82, f. 64, British Library MS. Hargrave 77, f. 18v, pl. 2, British Library MS. Hargrave 303, f. 35, pl. 3.]

## 190

## Miller v. Thomas

(Ch. 1710)

*A fraudulent conveyance can be set aside and an accounting can be ordered.*

British Library MS. Hargrave 77, f. 18v, pl. 1

5 December. Rehearing.

The plaintiff had a decree against the defendant to be relieved against a fraud in obtaining a conveyance of his lands. This conveyance was set aside, and the defendants Thomas [and] Cooper should account for £958, for which the other defendant, Gifford, had given his note in part of £1500 lent the plaintiff on a mortgage and that note the plaintiff had delivered to Thomas and he to Cooper to receive for him. Cooper, afterwards, received the money and accounted for it to Thomas.

---

[1] Stat. 3 Will. & Mar., c. 14 (*SR*, VI, 320–321).

## 191

## Launt v. Spencer

(Ch. 1710)

*An agreement for the payment of a debt out of the proceeds of a sale of land is an equitable lien on the land, and such a lien is superior to a judgment lien.*

British Library MS. Hargrave 81, f. 24, pl. 1

December 1710.

If a person, a debtor, gives a note whereby he agrees that, out of money which shall arise by sale of a certain estate, his creditors shall be paid, this is a lien in equity upon the estate. And where a man has law and equity, he shall be preferred to one who has equity only.

*Curia* [said] that a note in equity is an appointment to the purchaser to pay so much out of the purchase money and, if the estate be a term for years, such a note in equity amounts to an assignment of the term. [Where] the plaintiff is the creditor to a termor by a judgment [and] the defendant claims by a note, *ut supra*, the note shall be paid out of the purchase money before the judgment, for the judgment before the execution did not affect the term.

[Other copies of this report: British Library MS. Hargrave 82, f. 20, pl. 1, British Library MS. Hargrave 77, f. 9, pl. 1, British Library MS. Hargrave 303, f. 14, pl. 1.]

## 192

## Greenfield v. Goodier

(Ch. 1710–1714)

*The doctrine of equitable conversion creates an estate that can be devised.*

Lincoln's Inn MS. Misc. 10, p. 132, pl. 1

In Lord Keeper Harcourt's time.

A.B. articles for the purchase of lands in the name of C.D. He pays part of the purchase money and is put into possession. And, before a conveyance was made, he makes his will and devises these lands to J.S. and his heirs. And, after this, the vendor conveys the lands to A.B., who dies without making any new publication of his will.

[It was] decreed the lands did pass by the will.

## 193

## Moreton v. Moreton

(Ch. 1711)

*A commission can be executed in the late afternoon.*

Dickens 21, 21 E.R. 174

12 January 1710[/11]. Lord Harcourt.

A commission executed after four in the afternoon of the day on which it was returnable [was] held to be regular.

## 194

## Anonymous

(Ch. 1711)

*A tenant in common of a house may live in all or any part of the house.*

*Where there are no profits or income from a tenancy in common, there is nothing to account for.*

British Library MS. Hargrave 80, f. 18, pl. 1

Hilary term 1710[/11].

A bill was preferred to compel a tenant in common of a fourth part of a cottage, which he had built and lived in alone, to account with the lord of three parts of the manor in common, who was thereby tenant in common of the other three parts, for the profits of the said cottage.

*Sir Thomas Powys*: This is the proper place to compel a tenant in common of land to account for the profits and, if two co-partners be of a house in London and one lives in the whole, she ought to account for the profits with the other.

Lord Keeper [Lord Harcourt]: The case of lands that yield a yearly profit and of such cottage that yields no profit is very different. A tenant in common may live in all or any part of the house. You have the law open to recover your three parts by [an action of] ejectment. I will dismiss your bill with costs unless you agree.

[Other copies of this report: Lincoln's Inn MS. Misc. 383, p. 33, pl. 1.]

## 195

## Cowper v. Cowper

(Ch. 1711)

*In this case, the court of equity enforced a devise for the raising of portions and for the payment of maintenance in the meantime.*

British Library MS. Hargrave 80, f. 18, pl. 2

A bill [was exhibited] by four creditors in the names of themselves and the other creditors and by the younger children of the testator against the executor and heir of the testator and others for an account of the personal estate and of the profits of the real estate of the testator subjected by his will to payment of debts that the creditors might have their debts paid and the younger children the benefit of two leasehold estates bequeathed to them.

Lord Keeper [LORD HARCOURT]: Do the creditors waive all claim to these leasehold estates? Unless it is by consent, I cannot decree the leases to the children and the payment of their debts together. How do they know there are assets besides?

The testator in this case had an interest in a manor for 99 years, and he devised it for raising £1800 apiece for each of his daughters payable at twenty-one or at marriage and for maintenance in the meantime.

Lord Keeper [LORD HARCOURT]: I might decree the reversionary interest of this manor after the death of the executor (on whom it was settled for life) to be sold and the money to be placed out by a master for their present maintenance and subject to the farther directions of the will. But, in regard to the heir, who is residuary legatee and a minor, it may be for his advantage to pay the maintenance and portions and thereby redeem. And I shall only declare the manor to stand charged with £50 a year to each of the daughters for their maintenance, of which the value of the manor (being £100 *per annum*) is the measure, and £1800 at twenty-one or day of marriage redeemable of his payment of such maintenances and portions.

[Other copies of this report: Lincoln's Inn MS. Misc. 383, p. 33, pl. 2, Lincoln's Inn MS. Misc. 106, p. 6.]

## 196

## May v. Vavasor

(Ch. 1711)

*The estate of a deceased principal debtor is liable for his debts and must reimburse any surety for any payments made to the creditor.*

British Library MS. Hargrave 80, f. 18v, pl. 1

May was bound jointly with Vavasor's testator for payment of £30 and interest, which money was borrowed by Vavasor's testator, and May was only a security.

[It was] decreed he should be indemnified against the bond still standing out and be reimbursed the interest he had paid out of the [decedent's] assets.

[Other copies of this report: Lincoln's Inn MS. Misc. 383, p. 34, pl. 1, Lincoln's Inn MS. Misc. 106, p. 7.]

## 197

## Newton v. Walpole

(Ch. 1711)

*General words in a release are limited by the intention of the parties thereto.*

British Library MS. Hargrave 80, f. 18v, pl. 2

Robert Cooke, tenant in tail with a power to make a jointure not exceeding £1000 *per annum*, marries the Lady Anne [1657–1722], daughter to the duke of Leeds [1631–1712], and settles divers manors upon her for a jointure, which he covenants to be above £900 *per annum* and not £1000. He dies leaving issue, only one son, an infant. And Lady Anne receives the whole profits of her husband's estate, being about £8000 a year and marries the defendant Walpole. The son, as soon as he comes of age, gives his mother, the Lady Ann, a general release, then marries, and dies, leaving his wife executrix and residuary legatee. Soon after, she dies, leaving the residue of his estate to the younger children which were between them. These children being infants, Newton, as their trustee, bring this bill against the defendant to have an account of the profits of the jointure lands since the date of the release, reserving the validity of that to be controverted by the infants at their full age, over and above £1000 *per annum*, the rents and profits having been much increased by the falling in of estates which were out upon lives and by several fines for the renewing of copyholds. The defendants admit to account from the date of the release but demand £2400 for jewels sold by the Lady Anne to her son and such damages to be allowed on account as the defendant had sustained by a breach of a covenant in a lease of a house and lands from the infants' father to the defendant for his life, in which he covenanted for himself, his heirs, executors, and administrators that he had power to make such lease, which he had not, being a bare tenant for life.

Lord Keeper [Lord Harcourt]: I cannot make bargains for infants. That release seems to extend only to the profit of the estate which she had received and not to the surplus of the jointure lands. It does not appear there was any demand made at that time for that surplus or that it was so much as thought of. I have known the common law restrain the general words of a release to the matter within view and the intention of the parties.

It was objected that there was no bill for an account before the release and, therefore, the court cannot decree such account.

Lord Keeper [Lord Harcourt]: They may amend their bill or bring a supplemental bill and so bring all the accounts before the court.

It was answered that this was in some measure an amicable cause and that the defendant had been drawn in to admit an account for the surplus since the release which perhaps in strictness they were not bound to do, the lands not being let for £1000 a year at the time of the making the jointure and the improvement since being casual.

The Lord Keeper [Lord Harcourt] seemed to agree that they were not compellable to account for a casual surplus and, the person that drew the release alleging in court that the surplus of the jointure lands was intended to be released to the time of the execution of the release. He ordered an account from that time, reserving a power to the infants to controvert the release, and directed an issue on a *quantum damnificatus* to ascertain the defendants' damages on the breach of covenant.

Interest and costs were reserved etc.

[Other copies of this report: Lincoln's Inn MS. Misc. 383, p. 34, pl. 2, Lincoln's Inn MS. Misc. 106, p. 8.]

## 198

## Allen v. Rouch

(Ch. 1711)

*Interest is due and payable for money received but not used for the benefit of another person.*

British Library MS. Hargrave 80, f. 19v, pl. 1

Upon a rehearing for interest of a sum decreed to the petitioner, the case was the other party had employed him to buy lands in his own name in trust for him and to go into the country and spend money freely to further an election. The sum, for which interest was demanded, was chiefly laid out in retinue and equipage.

It was objected in regard that the money was laid out for the petitioner's grandeur etc. and that there was a running account between the parties and none closed nor the balance stated and £200 in one item allowed the petitioner for his trouble that he ought not to have interest.

To this, it was answered that the money was laid out in those things by order of the other side, and, if he had received several sums from the other party, it was only in discharge of what he had expended.

And interest was decreed. Lord Keeper [Lord Harcourt] cited a case between [ *blank* ] and [ *blank* ]; two coparceners or tenants in common; a suit had depended between them for a great number of years by reason of infancy etc. and, upon finishing the account three years ago, £100 appeared due on the foot of it from one to the other, which was decreed with interest.

[Other copies of this report: Lincoln's Inn MS. Misc. 383, p. 35, Lincoln's Inn MS. Misc. 106, p. 9.]

199

## Collet v. Butler

(Ch. 1711)

*Marriage is a good and valuable consideration.*

*The question in this case was whether there should be specific performance of an agreement to make a settlement or whether there should be a re-conveyance of certain land.*

Lincoln's Inn MS. Misc. 10, p. 50

7 February 1710[/11].

Edmund Butler made courtship to the plaintiff Ann, and, assuring her and her friends that he was the only son of his father, the defendant Butler, and that his father had a considerable real and personal estate, they harkened to the match proposed and a treaty was entered upon.

Afterwards, Edmund Butler writes to his father, who was then in the country, for his consent, who, thereupon, writes a letter directed to the plaintiffs, Ann and her father, and tells them that his son had both his and his wife's consent in what he was come to London about and what he said to his son he would make good when they came into the country and wished he was but one hour with them, it should make all things easy, but all that he had should be for him and his.

Upon this encouragement, the plaintiff Ann's grandmother and father settled several freehold houses upon her and her intended husband for their lives and, afterwards, upon their issue and, for want of such, upon him in fee. They, likewise, assigned over some leasehold houses, which, upon failer of issue between the plaintiff Ann and her husband were to be in trust for him and his executors etc.

The marriage took effect. And the next day afterwards, the plaintiff Ann fell ill of the small pox, and her husband, having never had them, went into the country to his father, where he fell ill of the same distemper and died. But, before his death, he made his will and gave the reversion of these estates to his father and mother.

And now, the plaintiff Ann and her father and grandmother prefer their bill either to fetch back these estates or that a reasonable settlement may be made upon the plaintiff Ann by the defendant Butler.

I did not hear what was said for the plaintiff.

But Mr. *Vernon*, for the defendant, urged that this case was not like the cases of Dr. Hart and of Wangford and Fotherleys,[1] for, though, in both those cases, the marriage proceeded upon the encouragement of letter, yet there was a certain sum fixed; in one of them, the father says that £1500 was the utmost that he would give so that there was a writing under the hand of the party to be bound by it, which put it out of the Statute. It is true, in our case, here is a letter, but then it is wholly uncertain what is meant by it. And this court never went so far as to allow a parol proof to explain so loose an offer.

This case, how compassionate soever, is too hard for this court and is one of those cases that is only relievable by the legislature.

Lord Keeper [LORD HARCOURT]: I think this is a case very proper to be compromised between the parties, and, therefore, let it stand over and see if they cannot end it between themselves. I am sure I would go as far in this case as possibly I could. And, if you can show me any precedent where this court has relieved upon any writing so loose as this is, I would relieve the plaintiffs. And thus much I think fit to declare at present.

British Library MS. Hargrave 80, f. 19v, pl. 2

On a marriage between the son of the defendant and the granddaughter of the plaintiff, the plaintiff settles lands of inheritance and leasehold lands to the use of the son of the defendant, the intended husband, for life, remainder to the wife for life, remainder to the issue of their two bodies in tail, remainder to the husband in fee. Immediately after marriage, the husband dies without issue and devises all his reversionary interest to his father, the defendant.

The plaintiff exhibited her bill to compel the defendant to make a settlement on his son's widow pursuant to an agreement on his part or else re-convey the reversionary interest devised to him by his son.

The evidence of the agreement was a letter written by the father in which were words to this effect: 'All that I have promised, I will make good' and after 'all that I have is for him and his', i.e. the son. This letter was written in answer to one from the son to his father, which was suppressed. The contents and occasion of the son's letter was to acquaint his father that his proposals would not be accepted until they could hear from him.

It was insisted that the words of the father's letter referred to proposals which he had given the son authority to make and which the son's letter would probably

[1] *Moore v. Hart* (1682–1683), 1 Vernon 110, 201, 23 E.R. 352, 412, 2 Chancery Reports 284, 21 E.R. 680, 1 Eq. Cas. Abr. 22, 21 E.R. 844; *Wankford v. Fotherley* (1694), 2 Vernon 322, 23 E.R. 807, 2 Freeman 201, 22 E.R. 1159, 1 Eq. Cas. Abr. 22, 21 E.R. 844.

have disclosed and that, being suppressed by the defendant, ought to be taken most strongly against him and that the words 'all that I have' included both real and personal estate; 'to him and his' his wife and children.

It was said by *How* that, if the court should be against the plaintiff as to making a settlement, that then the defendant ought to re-convey the estate devised to him, the consideration, *viz.* the settlement on the husband's side, not being executed, as, in case lands are sold and conveyed and the purchase money never paid, Chancery will compel the vendee to re-convey.

To this, it was answered that the settlement made by the plaintiff mentioned no consideration of any other settlement to be made by the defendant nor any other consideration at all but marriage, which was executed, and, therefore, no reason for a re-conveyance.

Lord Keeper [Lord Harcourt] told that defendant's counsel that they need not labor that point.

As to the other, the defendant's counsel admitted it to be a case of great compassion but not within the power of the court to relieve. They agreed that a bare memorandum of an agreement put in writing and subscribed was not within the Statute of Frauds[1] provided it to be of a thing in certain; but this was utterly uncertain in itself and not capable of being reduced to a certainty, there being no evidence of the proposals to which it referred. And as to the suppressing of a letter, they thought it very different from suppressing a deed and hard that a man should suffer for not keeping all his letters by him.

*Vernon* cited two cases where the court compelled the execution of proposals made by letters. In one, the father said he would give his daughter £3000; in the other case, the father said he would not give his daughter above £1500. But he distinguished this case from both because, in them, there is a sum certain named, but not in this. He cited likewise several cases of great compassion where Chancery could give no relief; the case of the present earl of Lincoln,[2] which was thus. The last earl of Lincoln, by several successive wills gave his estate to the present earl of Lincoln, to whom the honor was to descend, but, after the date of the last of those wills, he settled his estate in consideration of an intended marriage; now though that marriage never took effect, nor consequently the settlement, yet this being in law a revocation of the will, Chancery would not relieve. Another case was this. Trustees, out of the profits of the trust lands, purchased other lands and, though the proof was very full that they purchased those very lands with the same money that they had received from the trust lands, yet Chancery could not make the purchased lands liable to the trust money having (as it was said)

[1] Stat. 29 Car. II, c. 3 (*SR*, V, 839–842).

[2] *Earl of Lincoln v. Roll* (1696), Shower P.C. 154, 1 E.R. 105.

no earmark.[1] The like case [was] of a miller at Uxbridge,[2] who had hid £500 in a hole of a wall; the person that found it purchased lands with it and died leaving no assets; the court could not decree those lands to the miller.

Lord Keeper [Lord Harcourt]: I will go as far as I can for the plaintiff. Let the plaintiff search for precedents where Chancery has decreed re-conveyances and the defendant attend me that I may see what he will propose.

Afterward, the defendant agreed to settle all the estate he had to the widow of his son for life, and so the matter was compounded.

[Other copies of this report: 3 Swanston 482, 36 E.R. 924, Lincoln's Inn MS. Misc. 383, p. 36, Lincoln's Inn MS. Misc. 106, p. 10.]

## 200

## Bradshaw v. Astley

(Ch. 1711–1714)

*In this case, an account for the profits of an estate was ordered even though it went back several decades.*

*In the case of a purchase made by trustees who had paid off encumbrances, compound interest will be ordered by the court.*

British Library MS. Hargrave 80, f. 20v

Bradshaw, in the year 1665, conveyed his estate to Sir Richard Astley, father of the defendant [Sir John Astley], and two more and their heirs in trust for payment of debts and encumbrances by profits or sale and the residue to his sisters, under whom the plaintiff claims. And the petitioner exhibits his bill for an account of the profits of the estate from 1665.

It was objected that the encumbrances at the time of the conveyance of the estate were £100 *per annum* payable to A. for seventeen years, £5 a year perpetual encumbrance and divers mortgages etc. and that Sir Richard Astley paid debts and mortgages to the value of £1600 and was a purchaser, and that, after so long quiet possession, it would be hard to oblige his heir to account, his vouchers not having been preserved.

The purchase deeds were not produced, but suggested to be gotten away by one, who was formerly the solicitor for the defendant and, at present, for the plaintiff.

[1] Perhaps *Kirk v. Webb* (1698), Precedents in Chancery 84, 24 E.R. 41, 2 Freeman 229, 22 E.R. 1177, 2 Eq. Cas. Abr. 743, 22 E.R. 631.

[2] *Kendar v. Milward* (1702), 2 Vernon 440, 23 E.R. 882, Precedents in Chancery 171, 24 E.R. 83, 2 Eq. Cas. Abr. 365, 744, 22 E.R. 430, 631.

To that, it was answered that, as to the length of time, the residuum was very small and not worth looking after the first seventeen years and that the infancy of the defendant had prevented any inquiry the twenty last years; besides, another reason of their sitting still was their poverty.

It was replied by *Vernon* that the Statute of Limitations[1] extends to all accounts except merchants' and that, though the trust be not within the Statute, yet the reason of the Act extends to all accounts and should guide and direct this court.

No mortgagor [was] ever suffered to redeem after forty-five years without some particular reason which covers the whole estate or where the surplus is very great.

That, as to the objection of the encumbrance for the first seventeen years, he said, it was common to sell estates liable to such annuities and, as to the infancy of the defendant, that could be no objection to the plaintiff's bringing this bill for an account.

The Lord Keeper [Lord Harcourt] directed an account from 1665 of the profits of the estate, and, on the other hand, that what Sir Richard Ashly had paid of debts and encumbrances should be allowed, and an annual rest in the account upon which, if it should appear that his disbursements were greater than his receipts, interest should be allowed him.

There were no deeds, though some presumptive evidence of a sale.

But My Lord Keeper [Lord Harcourt] said that, though there had been proof of a sale, he would have directed an account; it can be no harm to the defendant if it appears on the account that his father has disbursed to the value of the estate.

[Other copies of this report: Lincoln's Inn MS. Misc. 383, p. 38, Lincoln's Inn MS. Misc. 106, p. 13.]

British Library MS. Hargrave 81, f. 130, pl. 1

12 June 1714.

On exceptions to a Master's report after a decree, by which the master was directed in taking the account to make an annual rent and compute interest, the exception was for that this being in the case of a purchase made by trustees who had taken in encumbrances and which were decreed to be for the benefit of the *cestui que trust*, the Master had carried on the account of principal and interest and interest for that and then making an annual rest gives interest for the balance.

*Curia* [Lord Harcourt]: It is usual so to do in this court.

[Other copies of this report: British Library MS. Hargrave 82, f. 143, pl. 1, British Library MS. Hargrave 77, f. 35, British Library MS. Hargrave 303, f. 63.]

[Affirmed on appeal: 4 Brown P.C. 505, 2 E.R. 345.]

---

[1] Stat. 21 Jac. I, c. 16, s. 3 (*SR*, IV, 1222).

## 201

## Higgens v. Anonymous

(Ch. 1711)

*A bill to enforce a contract whereby a debtor agrees to pay one of his creditors his full debt if that creditor will join in an assignment for the benefit of creditors and encourage the other creditors to join also will not be allowed, and the court of equity will prohibit its enforcement at common law.*

British Library MS. Hargrave 80, f. 21

A bill [was exhibited] by a debtor to have advantage of a composition which the defendant had executed with the rest of his creditors, *viz*. 5s. in the pound. It was objected that there was a private agreement between the plaintiff and defendant that, if the defendant would sign the composition deed and endeavor to procure others to do so, that he should have his whole debt and that there was an acquittance given by the defendant to the plaintiff for £30 received since the composition in part [payment] of his debt. It was answered that the composition money and interest came to £30 and that deeds would be entirely useless if they were to be set aside by such private agreements.

And a difference was taken by *Vernon*, where a bankrupt makes such a private agreement with one creditor to draw in the rest to a moderate composition and, after the composition, gives a fresh assurance to him for his debt by bond or otherwise, in which case, perhaps equity would not relieve the bankrupt because they are both equally concerned in the fraud.

But in this case, he laid the stress on the deed's not being avoidable by a parol agreement.

Lord Keeper [Lord Harcourt] decreed all the specialties whereby the plaintiff's debt was secured to the defendant and which were antecedent to the composition to be delivered up and a perpetual injunction to stay proceedings at law.

[Other copies of this report: Lincoln's Inn MS. Misc. 383, p. 39, pl. 1, Lincoln's Inn MS. Misc. 106, p. 14.]

## 202

## Anonymous

(Ch. 1711)

*A mortgage can be foreclosed against a jointress and against an infant, but an infant has the right to re-open the case upon coming of age.*

British Library MS. Hargrave 80, f. 21v, pl. 1

[There was] a decree for a jointress to redeem within six months and hold over and, if she failed, six months were allowed to the heir and, if he did not redeem within those six months, to be foreclosed notwithstanding his infancy. But a day was allowed him after his full age to show cause.

[Other copies of this report: Lincoln's Inn MS. Misc. 383, p. 39, pl. 2, Lincoln's Inn MS. Misc. 106, p. 15, pl. 1.]

## 203

## Anonymous v. Slatterford

(Ch. 1711)

*The words 'equally to be divided' in a will create a tenancy in common, but not where they are in a deed.*

*An annuity that is redeemable is personal property, not real property.*

British Library MS. Hargrave 80, f. 21v, pl. 2

An annuity of £20 a year was granted in fee for the consideration of £400, redeemable on the paying of that sum. The grantee devises it to A. for life, remainder to B., C., D., and E., to be equally divided, B. and C. were married, and D. and E. were not, and, if D. or E. die without issue before the annuity or money came to them, their share to the survivors.

It was resolved that those words 'equally to be divided' make a tenancy in common in a will, but otherwise in a deed, and that, 'if D. and E. die' etc. made a survivorship only as to their shares. Lord Keeper [Lord Harcourt] said that this annuity though in fee was to be looked upon as personal estate because it was redeemable.

[Other copies of this report: Lincoln's Inn MS. Misc. 383, p. 39, pl. 3, Lincoln's Inn MS. Misc. 106, p. 15, pl. 2.]

## 204

## Malberett v. Howett

(Ch. 1711)

*The question in this case was the survivorship of a legacy among the legatees.*

Lincoln's Inn MS. Misc. 10, p. 53

10 February 1710[/11].

A man purchased a rent charge, but there was a clause in the deed of purchase which made it redeemable by the vendor upon payment of £400. The vendee, by his will, devises this rent charge to his four nephews, A., B., C., and D., equally to be divided between them. And then he goes on and says that, if C. and D. or either of them should die without issue, then his will was that those that survive should have the said money if the rent charge was redeemed or, if not, then the rent charge was equally to be divided between them and their heirs.

A. and B. were married at the time of the will. C. and D. were unmarried. D. died, and A., B., and C. survived. Afterwards, A. and B. died.

The bill was to redeem. So the question was between the defendants who should have the money.

Lord Keeper [Lord Harcourt]: The clause of survivorship can extend only to the shares of C. and D. so that, when D. died, his share was to be equally divided between the three survivors and, when the other two died, then that share of D. came to C. as survivor, for the words 'those that survive' must extend to the survivor, though it is not said to the survivors or survivor.

## 205

## Webb v. Webb

(Ch. 1711)

*A condition of a legacy not to disturb trustees is valid and enforceable.*

Lincoln's Inn MS. Misc. 10, p. 54

21 February 1710[/11]. Katherine Web, John Hellier, Edward Foyle, Trustees of Thomas Web and John Baker, Stephen Seagar, William Lockyer, and Edward Web, executors of the said Thomas Web, plaintiffs; Lieutenant General Web, eldest son of the said Thomas Web, defendant.

Edward Web, the defendant's grandfather, and his trustees, in consequence of a marriage between Thomas, his son, and Ann, his then wife, and £350 portion, did assign divers lands in Horsley in Gloucestershire to trustees for the remainder of a term of 1000 years upon trust to permit the son to enjoy the same during so long as he should live and, after his decease, then to Ann, his wife, so long as she should live and, after their decease, to permit the heirs of the said Thomas, the son, on the body of the said Ann, his wife, to be begotten to hold the premises during the remainder of the term and, for want of such issue, to be enjoyed by the right heirs of the said Thomas, the son.

Thomas and Ann had seven or eight children, and, he having survived his wife and settled about two-thirds of his estate on the defendant, his eldest son, to the value of about £1100. And, being indebted above £300, he makes a mortgage of the premises for securing that money. And, in order thereunto, he took administration to the surviving trustee, they being all dead, and, afterwards, he assigns this term to the plaintiffs, the trustees, upon trust that they should sell the same and, in the first place, pay off the mortgage and then pay the remainder to his executors to be disposed of by them for his younger children as he should appoint by his will.

After this, he made his will and the plaintiffs Baker and Seagar etc. executors, and, shortly after, he died.

The plaintiffs, the trustees and executors, being disturbed by the defendant, brought their bill for the execution of the said trust and will.

The defendant, by his answer, set forth the first deed of trust and will and insisted that he, as eldest son and heir of his said father and mother, was entitled to the premises by virtue of the settlement and that he ought to have the same notwithstanding his father's mortgage, assignment, and will.

This case was heard before the Master of the Rolls [Trevor], who dismissed the plaintiffs' bill.

And, upon a petition to the Lord Keeper [Lord Harcourt], it was reheard by him, who took time to consider of it.

And this day being appointed for judgment, Mr. *Vernon* (who was absent at the rehearing by reason of sickness) was heard for the defendant. And it was insisted on by Mr. *Vernon* that this case was exactly the same as that of Peacock and Spooner,[1] where a term for years was assigned in trust for one for life, remainder to the heirs of his body; the cause was heard before Jeffreys in 1688, who was of the opinion that a tenant for life had the whole term and decreed accordingly; afterwards, this cause was reheard before the Commissioners [to Hold the Great Seal], who were of the opinion that the words 'heirs of the body' were a *descriptio personae*, who was intended to take, and reversed Jeffreys' decree, and, upon an appeal to the House of Lords, the Commissioner's decree was affirmed.

In the Case of Ward and Bradley,[2] the trusts of a term were limited to Cole for ninety-nine years, if he should so long live, remainder to the heirs of his body begotten on his wife. Cole disposed of the whole term. And, he dying and leaving children, a bill was brought and decreed for them.

*Sir Joseph Jekyll*, for the plaintiffs: The rule in equity is the same as to the trusts of terms as it is at law in cases of freeholds. Wherever, upon a limitation of a freehold, a man, by a fine or recovery, can bar his issue, if there is the same limitation of the trusts of a term, in that case, the party may dispose of the whole term.

There is a great difference between our case and that of Peacock and Spooner. In that case, the limitation was for so many years as the man should live, then to his wife in the same manner, then to the heirs of the body of the wife begotten by the husband. Now, this was the estate of the husband and was a settlement made by him, and, therefore, it was considered as in the case of a freehold upon

---

[1] *Peacock v. Spooner* (1688–1690), 2 Vernon 43, 195, 23 E.R. 638, 727, 2 Freeman 114, 22 E.R. 1094, Chancery Repts. *tempore* Jac. II, 429.

[2] *Ward v. Bradley* (Ch. 1687), 2 Vernon 23, 23 E.R. 626, Chancery Repts. *tempore* Jac. II, 399.

the Statute of Hen. VII, ca. 20,[1] for preventing women's aliening the estates of their husbands after their deaths, for, in that case, the wife with a second husband was endeavoring to defeat the children of the first husband. And this was a great ingredient in the case to induce the Lords to go so far.

Lord Keeper [Lord Harcourt]: I never heard it said that, before the Case of Peacock and Spooner, the limitation of a term in equity differed from the case of a freehold at common law. That case is the only case which, in any manner, comes up to this. But I think it does not come up to this case, and, therefore, I do not think myself tied up by it. And, for my own part, I shall not go beyond that case.

Now, that case differs from this in several material circumstances.

First, the limitation was to the heirs of the body of the wife; here, to the heirs of the body of the husband.

Second, there, the party had not the legal estate, but the second husband took administration to the first husband, and, imagining that he had a right to the whole term, brought his bill against the trustees to compel them to assign. In the case before me, the party aliening had the legal estate.

Third, in that case, there was no disposition; here is a mortgage and a disposition for younger children which must be defeated.

And, therefore, there being these material variations between the one case and the other, I think I am at liberty to determine as if the Case of Peacock and Spooner was out of the way.

I am sure I have often heard it said by this court as to the Case of Radnor and Vandebembee[2] that that was in the case of a purchaser and that, in any case which varied from it, as if there was no purchaser, they would vary too.

The decree at the Rolls must be reversed, and the trustees ought to have a redemption of the mortgage, and they must be decreed to perform the trusts.

There was £40 given the defendant by his father's will on condition that he did not disturb the trustees. And they come now to have a quiet execution of the trust and that he may either join with them in a sale or be deprived of his legacy. If he will join with them, he shall have the £40; if not, then he shall forfeit his legacy.

The Case of Clavering v. Clavering,[3] heard before Lord Chancellor Cowper and cited by Lord Keeper Harcourt to be thus, [was as follows]. Sir William Cla-

---

[1] Stat. 11 Hen. VII, c. 20 (*SR*, II, 583).

[2] *Countess of Radnor v. Vandebendy* (1683–1697), Shower P.C. 69, 1 E.R. 48, Lincoln's Inn MS. Misc. 559, f. 111, *sub nom. Lady Bodmin v. Vandenbendy*, 1 Vernon 179, 356, 23 E.R. 399, 520, 2 Chancery Cases 172, 22 E.R. 899, Chancery Repts. *tempore* Jac. II, 156, *sub nom. Lady Radnor v. Rotheram*, 2 Freeman 211, 22 E.R. 1165, Precedents in Chancery 65, 24 E.R. 32, 1 Eq. Cas. Abr. 219, 21 E.R. 1002, 2 Eq. Cas. Abr. 383, 22 E.R. 326.

[3] *Clavering v. Clavering* (1704), see above, Case No. 26.

vering, by deed, makes some provision out of part of his estate for one of his children. He lives sixteen years afterwards and makes no use of this deed but keeps it by him. And not long before his death, he makes a voluntary settlement of his whole estate, and takes no notice of the former deed. After his death, the first deed was found in an old trunk among a parcel of cancelled writings. And, notwithstanding this deed was revocable in its own nature, yet both being voluntary and [there being] no creditors in the case, the Lord Cowper established the first deed. And, afterwards, upon an appeal, the decree was affirmed.

## 206

## Anonymous

(Ch. 1711)

*An examination of witnesses upon a bill to perpetuate testimony cannot be opposed.*

Harvard Law Sch. MS. 537, pt. 2, p. 183, pl. 2

5 March, Easter [term], 10 Anne, at the seal.

Upon a motion for a commission to examine upon a bill *in perpetuam* and opposed, the Lord Keeper [Harcourt] doubted whether it could be opposed, but it was [a matter of] of course. And it seemed to be taken as a motion of course.

Mr. *Vernon*: The ground and suggestion of their bill is they could not have the benefit of their evidence without that, and we, by an affidavit, have disproved that.

*Sir Joseph Jekyll*: It is as well because they cannot preserve their evidence alive. If they can come to the trial, they may be cross-examined and must come notwithstanding. And, in this case, an answer was put in, and, upon such a commission, the youngest may be examined.

Lord Keeper [Harcourt]: The bill is besides to have an account of the rents and profits, to ascertain them in case he recovers at law. And here, there has been a demurrer, and the bill was dismissed as to everything but rents and profits. And an answer was put [in], and they may examine the youngest upon this. And [it was] granted.

## 207

## Anonymous

(Ch. 1711)

*A demurrer lies to object to impertinent interrogatories where all of them are impertinent.*

Harvard Law Sch. MS. 537, pt. 2, p. 183, pl. 4

6 March, Easter [term], 10 Anne.

When an order to be examined upon interrogatories as to such and such things, in case any interrogatory is impertinent and no ways touching such and such points, in such a case, a demurrer is good by the Rules of Court.

But [it was said] by Lord Keeper [Harcourt] in case there be some proper questions and some improper and impertinent in the same interrogatory and the demurrer is to the whole, it must be overruled.

## 208

## Jenison v. Pocklington

(Ch. 1711)

*A legacy to younger grandchildren includes those born after the testator's death.*

Lincoln's Inn MS. Misc. 13, p. 113, pl. 1

12 March 10 Anne.

Richard Bradford, by will dated 10 October 1699, amongst other legacies, gave to his son Richard's younger children £800 equally amongst them.

[Trevor] decreed that a child born after the testator's death should have a share of the legacy with the other younger children who were living at his death.

## 209

## Anonymous

(Ch. 1711)

*Where land is devised for the purpose of paying the testator's debts, a purchaser for value is not liable for the discharging of the debts unless the devise is specific as to a particular debt.*

British Library MS. Hargrave 81, f. 20

19 April 1711.

*Curia* [Lord Harcourt]: Where lands are devised or settled in trust for payment of debts generally, if the devisees or trustees sell the estate fairly and the purchaser pays them the money, he is not concerned how they dispose of it nor affected with any misapplication by them, because he is not presumed to have any notice of or to be able to know what these debts are or to whom due. But, where it is for payment of particular debts mentioning them and to whom due, there the purchaser has a particular notice, both of the sums and persons, and, at his peril, he must see them discharged or else, notwithstanding his payment to the devisees or trustees, he shall be liable to the particular creditors unsatisfied.

*Curia* [Lord Harcourt]: Where an injunction is granted until hearing, though the cause be heard unless there be then a complete and final decree, the injunction continues if there be not an express direction in the decree to dissolve it.

[Other copies of this report: British Library MS. Hargrave 82, f. 16, British Library MS. Hargrave 77, f. 8, British Library MS. Hargrave 303, f. 12.]

## 210

## Brown v. Litton

(Ch. 1711)

*Where a person uses another's money for trade, he is a trustee and must account for the profits of the use of the money.*

British Library MS. Hargrave 80, f. 21v, pl. 3

Easter [term] 1711.

The plaintiff is executor of one Brown, captain of an East Indiaman. His testator, having carried out several goods and a great quantity of ducats to trade with pursuant to the liberty allowed captains of East Indiamen, died in the voyage.

The defendant, being appointed by the factor to command the ship, made an inventory of the testator's goods and effects in the presence of all the officers, which he and they subscribed. Afterwards, he takes part of the goods and some of the money to trade with and sends a bottomry bond to the plaintiff for repayment of so much of the money as he had taken and interest at the rate of 50 percent if the ship came home safe.

The plaintiff exhibits her bill now to have an account of the testator's personal estate and of the improvements of it by trade. It was objected that, if the testator's goods had miscarried by the defendant's trading with them, he must have made them good and, therefore, as he was answerable for that loss, so he ought to be entitled to the advantage made of them and that, if the defendant had put them on board any other ship that was going for London and consigned them to the plaintiff, they had not been more secure nor had the defendant been answerable for them if they had been lost; besides, he might have brought them home in specie, and then they had run as great a hazard as the contingency of the bottomry bond and that, if a trustee makes use of the trust money in the way of trade, he shall pay interest for it, but not be accountable for this product of it in trade and that, for these reasons, he had done more than was necessary in giving a bottomry bond for the payment of the principal taken and £50 percent interest.

For the plaintiff, it was said that this case differed from that of a common trustee, that the money and goods were carried out on purpose to trade with, and that the defendant did but what was incumbent on him in pursuing the original intent of the testator. This case was compared to partners in trade, between whom there is no survivorship, and, if one die and the other employ the joint stock in trade, as he ought to do unless he immediately divide it with the executor of his partner, he shall be answerable for the real produce of it to the representatives of the other partner. And it was said that the captain of a ship is a trustee for all the effects of those that die in the ship and answerable if they perish through his management and that, when men venture their lives for the benefit of their country and families in this way, there ought to be the greatest encouragement given them and the greatest advantage that can be to their families.

It was insisted by some of the plaintiff's counsel that the defendant was a wrong-doer in intermeddling with the testator's effects and, therefore, accountable.

But My Lord Keeper [Lord Harcourt] overruled that and said it was what he was bound to do.

Lord Keeper [Lord Harcourt]: If an executor in trust for an infant puts out the trust money at interest, it was formerly held that he should not account for the interest because he must have answered [for] the principal if it had been lost, but the ill use that executors have made of this has given occasion to different resolutions of late in that case. But I shall not at present deliver my opinion upon it. They might have the assistance of the Court of Chancery in placing out such money.

But suppose the testator in his will orders the money to be placed out at interest, there, undoubtedly, the executors are bound to put it out and are accountable for the interest whether they do or not because they may do it securely with the aid of this court. The case that comes nearest to that in question is that of two partners in trade where, if the survivor employs the joint stock in carrying on the trade, he shall account to the representatives of the other partner for the produce. It was objected that, if the defendant had lost the money and goods in trading with them, he would have been accountable for them to the plaintiff, but it was said that neither he nor the partner in the case before would be answerable for any loss, unless it happened through mismanagement or negligence.

Lord Keeper [Lord Harcourt]: Let there be an account taken of the testator's effects and of the product of them in trade and the defendant examined upon interrogatories and the bottomry bond delivered up and all reasonable allowances to the defendant.

The consideration of costs was reserved.

It was insisted that the bottomry bond was never accepted by the plaintiff or that it was not in her power to prevent a letter coming to her.

[Other copies of this report: Lincoln's Inn MS. Misc. 383, p. 41.]

[Other reports of this case: 1 Peere Williams 140, 24 E.R. 329, 10 Modern 20, 88 E.R. 606, 2 Eq. Cas. Abr. 5, 452, 722, 740, 22 E.R. 4, 385, 608, 628.]

## 211

## Anonymous

(Ch. 1711)

*A supplemental bill of complaint incorporates the original bill.*

*In this case where mortgaged lands were redeemed, the occupier of the lands was allowed a credit for repairs, improvements, and interest.*

British Library MS. Hargrave 80, f. 22v

A bill [was exhibited] for the account for the personal estate of an intestate and of the profits of the real estate received during the infancy of the plaintiff M. and since. The defendant pleaded in bar of the account until 1696 that there was an account stated between the defendant and the plaintiff A., husband of plaintiff M. in 1696 and that plaintiff A. gave the defendant a general release and, as to the account of the profits of the real estate since, he pleaded that the plaintiff A., having a freehold in the right of his wife and being likewise entitled to be tenant by the curtesy, became a bankrupt and that he and the assignees of the commissioners of bankrupt, at the request of the other creditors, made an absolute conveyance of the estate of A. to the defendant in consideration of £473 and averred that there was no trust etc. intended.

The plaintiff brought a supplemental bill, in which the account until 1696 was not taken notice of, but a deed of defeasance is set forth dated three weeks after the conveyance but never executed, to which the defendant answered that he never gave any directions for preparing such deed.

It was insisted on by *How*, that, although they might have waived the account until 1696 by express words in their supplemental or amended bill, yet their bare omitting of it was no waiver of it, for the original and supplemental bills make but one record, which was admitted by Lord Keeper [Lord Harcourt]. And it was further urged by him that the plaintiff having replied to their plea had thereby allowed it to be a good plea and that the only thing incumbent on them was to prove their plea and it being said on the other side that their plea went in bar of an account only and not of the redemption, he replied that it was impossible to have a redemption without an account.

The defendant in this case could not prove the account stated before the release. And their counsel said it was not necessary because the stating the account was only laid as an inducement to the release.

But Lord Keeper [Lord Harcourt] seemed to be of a different opinion.

However, the account until 1696 was waived by consent. As to a proof of an absolute purchase, it was said that the premises were worth but £104 a year and that they were mills and often out of repair and that the defendant, immediately after his purchase, laid out £300 in repairing them and that there was an antecedent mortgage on them for £200 and that, if the *cestui que vie* had died the next day, the purchaser had lost all his money and that the interest he purchased and the possibility of the *cestui que vie*'s death were to be considered and that, though he had lived several years, by which means the bargain was made tolerably good, yet that did not alter the case and that the deeds of purchase were an absolute conveyance and that there was no legal evidence to prove it a mortgage, no agreement in writing as the Statute of Frauds and Perjuries[1] requires, that the pretended defeasance was never executed and not so much as bears date until three weeks after the purchase deed.

On the other side, it was proved that there was a land tax tally for £200 and debts due to the bankrupt to the amount of £400 assigned together with the mills etc. to when he advanced the £473. And two or three witnesses deposed that it was agreed at the time of executing that deed that it should be in the nature of a security for the repayment of principal and interest and then in trust for the separate use of the plaintiff M.

And *Sir Joseph Jekyll* insisted that, if there be an agreement to mortgage land by way of absolute conveyance and defeasance and the mortgagee after the execution of the absolute conveyance refuses to execute the defeasance, that it was a fraud and, though nothing be subscribed, yet the Statute of Frauds and Perjuries will not bar the mortgagor's proving it a mortgage, which Lord Keeper [Lord Harcourt] seemed to allow.

Lord Keeper [Lord Harcourt]: The tally sinks the principal £200 and £150. If it should be allowed that the other debts assigned to the purchaser were desperate, yet the remaining principal is but little more than two years' purchase. And, as to the £200 mortgage, it did not appear that he had any notice of it when he purchased; so that will not alter the case and that the most he was compellable to do was to pay the interest and that, if the mortgagee should enter, he might redeem and hold over until he was satisfied.

The Lord Keeper [Lord Harcourt] decreed that an account should be taken of the tally and debts received and that the mills should stand charged with the repayment of the residue of the purchase money and then in trust *ut supra*, that the defendant should have allowance for what he had expended in repairs and lasting improvements and interest for the gross sum of £300 so employed and that £500 laid out by him in the maintenance of the plaintiff M. and lent her during her coverture should be allowed likewise and the defendant was a creditor of the bankrupt, and, by the purport of the intended defeasance, was to have 5s. in the pound allowed him. And that was decreed also.

[Other copies of this report: Lincoln's Inn MS. Misc. 383, p. 43, Lincoln's Inn MS. Misc. 106, p. 16.]

[1] Stat. 29 Car. II, c. 3 (*SR*, V, 839–842).

## 212

## Anonymous

(Ch. 1711)

*Where a bequest to a creditor is not in the exact same amount as the debt, it will not be considered to be a payment or discharge of the debt.*

*A decedent's debts will be marshalled so as to satisfy all of the creditors of the estate.*

*Where mortgaged lands are devised to repay the creditor, the creditor will be fully satisfied and then the widow will receive as her dower a third of the interest of the residue of the purchase money.*

British Library MS. Hargrave 80, f. 24, pl. 1

If a testator be indebted £100 to A. and devises £100 to A. by his will, it shall go in discharge of the debt.

But Lord Keeper [LORD HARCOURT] resolved in the Case of [ *blank* ] and Pollexfen[1] that, if the bequest be not equal or of a greater value, it shall not discharge the debt.

In the principal case, A. bequeathed £1000 apiece to his two daughters and created a term for that purpose and left that inheritance to descend to B., in whom, I think, also the term vested. B. devised two annuities of £500 *per annum* to his two sisters, the daughters of A. for their lives, remainders to their first and other sons in tail.

*Sir Thomas Powys* insisted that they were not to be looked on as bare devisees for life, the remainder being limited to their sons in tail, which would advance them in marriage.

But it was held clearly by Lord Keeper [LORD HARCOURT] that this was intended as a beneficial devise and not in satisfaction of £2000, which was of greater value than the annuities and which they were entitled to from another person.

The Lord Keeper [LORD HARCOURT] and *Vernon* seemed to agree that, if A. mortgages part of his estate and then devises the rest for payment of debts generally, equity will so marshal the debts that all shall be satisfied if possible, and, therefore, if the lands devised be not sufficient to pay all the debts and the mortgage too, the other debts shall be paid in the first place and the mortgagee driven to his security on which he relied, and, where, in this case, the lands devised were liable to payment of debts, it was decreed that the several voluntary devisees shall contribute ratably and, where the devise of part was for life, remainder over in tail, that the devisee for life should pay the whole proportion charged on her lands and hold over for two-thirds of what she so disbursed.

A. mortgages his lands; then he devises them for the payment of debts and the widow insists on dower. The mortgagee shall be first paid and the widow

[1] *Hooper v. Pollexten and Davy* (Ch. 1710), see above, Case No. 182.

shall have a third of the interest of the residue of the purchase money or a ninth of the whole.

[This was] ordered on an equity reserved.

[Other copies of this report: Lincoln's Inn MS. Misc. 383, p. 45, pl. 1, Lincoln's Inn MS. Misc. 106, p. 19.]

## 213

## Anonymous

(Ch. 1711)

*Where an executrix makes a contract and then marries, the woman and her husband are bound in equity not to defeat the contract.*

British Library MS. Hargrave 80, f. 24, pl. 2

A bill [was exhibited] for a specific performance of an agreement. The case was a lessee for years mortgaged his term for years and died. The mortgagee leased the lands to A. for the residue of the term. A. was at a great expense for necessary and unforeseen repairs. And in consideration thereof and of £10, the executrix of the mortgagor agreed that A. should be at full liberty to procure himself a new lease of part of the premises, reserving a rent *pro rata*, when this should expire.

But afterwards, the executrix marries, and she and her husband take a new lease from the lessor and bring [an action of] ejectment against A. An injunction [was] decreed, and, since the new lease prevented a specific execution of the agreement, the husband and wife should assign.

It was said that these bills were in lieu of damages which were recoverable at the common law for breach of covenant, and, therefore, if an action of covenant would not lie at common law, in such case, such a bill is not maintainable here. *Quaere.*

[Other copies of this report: Lincoln's Inn MS. Misc. 383, p. 45, pl. 2, Lincoln's Inn MS. Misc. 106, p. 20.]

## 214

## Jackson v. Evans

(Ch. 1711)

*The bond in issue in this case was held to be a donatio causa mortis.*

*The words 'all my worldly estate' include both real and personal property.*

British Library MS. Hargrave 80, f. 24v

A. makes a bond for the payment of £700 within two months to his sister B. and keeps it by him until near his death and then delivers it over to C., who gave it to B. A. makes his will and his sisters, B. and E., executrices, which began thus, 'as to all my worldly estate, first, I will that my debts be paid' etc. and then he devises his real estate of £60 *per annum* to his son, an infant, in tail, remainder in fee to his sister E. His son dies within three months after him. And B. exhibits her bill for this £700 *inter alia*.

Lord Keeper [LORD HARCOURT]: The objections against B. are first that this bond being without consideration is a trust in B. for A. But that is very absurd to suppose one man should acknowledge himself indebted to another in trust for himself.

I shall not determine this case on the foot of fraudulent devises, though, possibly, it might come within that. This rather seem to be a *donatio causa mortis*. It was never intended to take effect in the lifetime of A. against himself.

I will put you in mind of a case in this court in Lord Cowper's time, which was afterwards affirmed upon appeal in the House of Lords, which was that of Clavering and Clavering.[1] Sir James Clavering made a voluntary conveyance of his estate which he kept privately by him and frequently declared that his estate would go otherwise than it was there conveyed; some time after, he made a second voluntary conveyance with the greatest solemnity imaginable and soon after died. The first conveyance was then found amongst some old cancelled writings, it being sixteen years after the date; and [it was] decreed that both being voluntary and no purchaser to contend with, the first should stand. In this case, there is no creditor. The estate, which, by the will, is made liable to the payment of debts, is in the hands of a voluntary devisee.

It was agreed that the words 'all my worldly estate' include both real and personal [property] and then willing in the manner that his debts should be paid subject both to the payment of them.

Interest of the £700 was decreed from the time of filing of the bill only because [there was] no demand of that sum until fourteen years after the death of A.

This was reheard in Michaelmas Term following by the Lord Keeper [LORD HARCOURT], and the was decree was affirmed.

[Other copies of this report: Lincoln's Inn MS. Misc. 383, p. 46.]

---

[1] *Clavering v. Clavering* (1704), see above, Case No. 26.

## 215

## Anonymous

(Ch. 1711)

*A person need not give discovery of that which will result in a forfeiture.*

*A bill of discovery lies to determine what lands are copyhold and whether they are in the defendant's possession.*

British Library MS. Hargrave 80, f. 25

A. surrenders several acres of copyhold land in mortgage. And, afterwards, in consideration of marriage, he settles all his freehold lands. The boundaries of the freehold lands and copyhold lands by unity of possession were confused. A. dies; his wife and heir enter under the settlement. The mortgagee prefers his bill against them and the lord of the manor to have a discovery of the copyhold lands.

Lord Keeper [Lord Harcourt]: If a man mortgages his copyhold lands and then sells both copyhold and freehold as freehold, shall the purchaser be obliged to discover what is copyhold? Or suppose the purchase deed were not duly executed, is the purchaser obliged to discover that or anything else that might make a title to another?

I think he answered both in the negative and distinguished this case from that because the copyhold lands here were not settled at all in marriage.

He said it was usual in marshes etc, where boundaries were lost, by a commission or a jury, to enquire of the number and value of the acres demanded and to decree a ratable quantity.

An issue was directed in this case, *viz.* how many acres of copyhold and of what value were mortgaged and whether any and what were in the possession of the defendants.

[Other copies of this report: Lincoln's Inn MS. Misc. 383, f. 47, Lincoln's Inn MS. Misc. 106, p. 21.]

## 216

## Anonymous

(Ch. 1711)

*Generally, a debtor can direct which debt he intends to pay, and, if he does not, the creditor can elect to which debt the payment will be applied. But, if the payment is in the exact amount of a particular debt, it will be applied to pay that debt.*

British Library MS. Hargrave 80, f. 27v, pl. 1

It was said that, if a man owes another money on a note that carries interest and book debts too and pays a sum of money, he may direct it to go in discharge of which he pleases, but, if he pays it generally, then it is at the election of the creditor to apply it to either debt. But, in this case, though the payment was made generally, yet, in regard the sum paid amounted to that due on the note and no more, My Lord [Harcourt] decreed it to go in discharge of the note.

[Other copies of this report: Lincoln's Inn MS. Misc. 383, p. 51, pl. 1, Lincoln's Inn MS. Misc. 106, p. 21.]

## 217

## Dunckley v. Caswell

(Ch. 1711)

*Where a bankrupt has released his rights to the assignees in bankruptcy, he is not a party to any proceedings concerning his former estate.*

Lincoln's Inn MS. Misc. 10, p. 59, pl. 2

25 April 1711.

The bill was to set aside a stated account which was made up by the defendants, Caswell and Vaus, two of the assignees of the commissioners of bankruptcy, with the defendant Perrin, to which account the plaintiffs [Sir Robert Dunckley *et al.*], who were the other assignees, were not privy, and Arch and Robinson, the two bankrupts, were made parties but not brought to hearing.

And it was objected there was a want of parties, for, in a bill by the assignees against any of the debtors to the bankrupt's estate for an account, the bankrupt ought to be a party, he being entitled to the surplus, if any, after the creditors are paid and, unless he is a party, he may call over this account again.

To this it was answered that the bankrupts had released to the assignees.

And a release, which was proved in the cause, was produced and read.

And though it did not appear in any of the pleadings that there was such a release, yet it was agreed by the court to be sufficient to excuse the plaintiffs from bringing the bankrupts to hearing.

## 218

## Higford v. Higford

(Ch. 1711)

*In this case, the court enforced a marriage settlement in favor of a widow's right to a life estate in certain lands.*

Lincoln's Inn MS. Misc. 10, p. 64

27 April 1711. Hickford v. Hickford.

The plaintiff recovered a judgment in [an action of] dower and now comes to set aside two terms which she apprehended would be set up at law if she brought her [writ of] ejectment. And she prays that the terms may not stand in her way, the end for which they were created being satisfied.

Lord Keeper [Lord Harcourt]: As to the term which was created for securing a sum of money which is now agreed to be satisfied and the term kept on foot to attend the inheritance, the plaintiff must hold and enjoy against the trustees of that term.

And, as to the term which was created for securing an annuity of £60 a year, she must pay a third part of that annuity and must hold and enjoy against the trustees paying that proportion.

And he decreed that the plaintiff should have an account of the rents from the time of her recovery at law.

It was said by Mr. *Vernon* that Lord Cowper had decreed that, where a sum of money was to be laid out in a purchase and to be conveyed to a man and his heirs, the wife should have dower though the purchase was not made in the husband's lifetime and that the like was done by him in favor of a tenant by the curtesy where land was to be purchased and to be conveyed to a woman and her heirs.

British Library MS. Hargrave 80, f. 25v

The plaintiff had recovered in a writ of dower and had seisin delivered by the plaintiff. [Actions of] ejectment were brought against her by the termors. And she prefers her bill setting forth that, by articles made between her and her husband before marriage, it was agreed that her estate both real and personal should be settled to her sole and separate use. It was endorsed on those articles before the execution that, if the husband's father should convey two estates therein named to the husband and his heirs, that then she should pay the father £2000 and that the husband should settle £300 *per annum* out of those lands upon her for life in case of issue and, if no issue, £400 *per annum.*

The husband received all the profits of the wife's estate, and she joined with him in mortgaging her estate for £1500. In the deed of mortgage, there was a proviso of redemption by the husband or wife or her heirs and a covenant whereby the husband agreed for himself and his heirs to pay the £1500.

After this, the father, in consideration of £800 paid by the son and for continuing the lands in his name etc., conveys those lands to the use of himself for life, remainder to trustees for 500 years to raise £1200 for daughters, remainder in fee to the husband. The father dies; the husband pays the £1200.

Afterwards, the husband purchases Alvington Court, and, at the time of the purchase, there were two terms in being. The trust of one was satisfied; the other was made for securing the payment of an annuity of £60 *per annum* for life and the purchaser, in consideration of this annuity, by agreement, was to retain £1500 of the purchase money without interest during the continuance of the annuity and for repayment of the £1500 when the annuity should cease. The husband created a term by indenture executed the same day but after the purchase deeds.

The husband purchases another estate of £32 a year to himself for life, remainder to the wife for life, remainder to the issue of their bodies in tail etc. The husband dies without issue having devised the lands settled by the father and Alvington Court to his younger brother for twenty-one years; the inheritance descended to the heir. The plaintiff recovered dower of those lands and had seisin delivered to her by the plaintiff and then ejectments were brought against her by the trustees of the term.

The bill was for relief in the premises which implied a demand of performance of the endorsement and for an account of the rents and profits of her estate received during the coverture and to have her estate exonerated of the £1500 mortgage and to have and enjoy her dower against the termors.

As to the performance of the endorsement, it was said that, though the wife had not literally paid the £2000, yet that the husband, by perception of the rents and profits of her real estate and by receipts of her personal estate, had received considerably more before the settlement made upon him by his father and that he was thereby enabled to pay the father £800 and £1200 to his sisters and that, this being an equitable performance of her part of the agreement, she was entitled to a performance of her husband's part.

But, as to this and the receipts of the profits during coverture, she having lived with her husband on the profits of both their estates, the bill was dismissed.

As to the exonerating of her estate of the £1500 mortgage, [it was] decreed that an account be taken of the husband's personal estate and that applied to exonerate her estate and, if the personal estate prove deficient, then an account of the real assets against the devisee and heir.

In My Lord Huntington's Case, it was resolved by the House of Lords on an appeal from this court that both the personal and real assets of the husband should be applied to exonerate the wife's estate though, in that case, there was no covenant on the husband's part for payment of the mortgage money.

The devise in this case, My Lord [Keeper] [Lord Harcourt] said, was within the Statute of Fraudulent Devises.[1]

Mr. *Vernon* said on this head that an heir should not have the benefit of the personal estate to discharge a mortgage on the lands descended until all other debts, and even legacies, were satisfied.

---

[1] Stat. 3 Will. & Mar., c. 14 (*SR*, VI, 320–321).

As to the holding and enjoying against termors, it was urged for the defendant by *Sir Thomas Powys* that it was the common practice to create terms before marriage on purpose to defeat wives of their dower or for a husband to purchase lands to himself and another jointly and that, in the Case of My Lord Radnor, Vanderbendy purchased the inheritance of him and took an assignment of a term in trust that had been created for payment of debts and legacies not then satisfied, knowing at the same time that the vendor was married; the vendor dies, and then his widow prefers her bill to be relieved against the term, she contributing to the discharge of the trusts; the bill was dismissed, and this dismission was confirmed on appeal.[1] Afterwards, the debts and legacies being satisfied, she brought another bill for relief, but [it was] dismissed again in both places.

*Sir Joseph Jekyll* seemed to say that the reason which induced this judgment was the common opinion of the conveyancers at that time that such terms should protect the inheritance from dower.

Lord Keeper [LORD HARCOURT] said that My Lord Cowper was brought with great difficulty to make the decree and would not have done it had he not thought himself tied down by the judgment of the House of Lords. And His Lordship distinguished that case of a purchaser from this, where the defendants are voluntary devisees and an heir.

*Sir Edward Northey* and *Vernon* said that terms which attend the inheritance shall attend and protect all estates growing out of the inheritance.

The Lord Keeper [LORD HARCOURT] decreed that, the trust of the term for 500 years being satisfied, she should hold and enjoy against the trustees of the term and, as to Alvington Court, she should hold and enjoy against the trustees of the first term created out of that estate for the same reason and also against the trustees of the second, she paying one-third of the annuity, and, as to the term for the securing the payment of £1500 in case it should become payable during her life, the consideration was reserved how far she should be charged and what remedy she should have over.

*Sir Edward Northey* said that the term being created after the purchase, though the same day, would not affect her title of dower.

But My Lord Keeper [LORD HARCOURT] seemed to differ from him, but said he would not deliver his opinion as to that then. My Lord [LORD HARCOURT] cited the cases of Bawd Fletcher and Worthington and My Lady Dudly

---

[1] *Countess of Radnor v. Vandebendy* (1683–1697), Shower P.C. 69, 1 E.R. 48, *sub nom. Lady Bodmin v. Vandenbendy*, 1 Vernon 179, 356, 23 E.R. 399, 520, 2 Chancery Cases 172, 22 E.R. 899, *sub nom. Lady Radnor v. Rotheram*, 2 Freeman 211, 22 E.R. 1165, Precedents in Chancery 65, 24 E.R. 32, 1 Eq. Cas. Abr. 219, 21 E.R. 1002, 2 Eq. Cas. Abr. 383, 22 E.R. 326, Chancery Repts. *tempore* Jac. II, 156, Lincoln's Inn MS. Misc. 559, f. 111.

and Clay and Snell,[1] as adjudged in point where tenancy by the curtesy and dower had been decreed against satisfied terms.

My Lord [LORD HARCOURT] decreed the plaintiff her costs in regard the defendants had made the trustees bring ejectments on these satisfied terms and that the defendants should confirm her estate for life in the lands of £32 *per annum* or bring the deeds into court to be made use of by her as she should have occasion.

Mr. *Vernon* said in this case that My Lord Cowper had decreed dower and tenancy by the curtesy where money was vested in trust to be laid out in lands.

*Sir Edward Northey* and Mr. *Vernon* seemed to say that, where terms were created upon special trusts as payment of debts etc., that such terms should attend the inheritance when those trusts were satisfied.

[Other copies of this report: Lincoln's Inn MS. Misc. 383, p. 48.]

## 219

## Clift v. Clift

(Ch. 1711)

*In this case, there was no proof of an allegation that the trust in question was procured through fraud.*

Lincoln's Inn MS. Misc. 10, p. 62

28 April 1711.

Mr. Cliff, by his will, gives £100 to the defendant, his eldest son, upon condition that he should not disturb his wife or give her any trouble in respect of the estate thereinafter given her. And, after some legacies, he gives all his manors, messuages, lands, goods, and chattels to the plaintiff, who was his second wife, and to her heirs, executors, and administrators. And he makes her executrix.

She now prefers a bill to establish the will against the defendant as heir at law, who insists by answer that this was only a trust in the plaintiff for the payment of the debts and legacies and that the surplus belonged to him. And he makes very strong proof that the testator declared his intention so to be.

But the proofs were no read, the court being of the opinion they could not enter into that examination against a written will and it being mentioned by the defendant's counsel that it was proved by the witnesses that the plaintiff declared that the testator had given her his estate upon that trust and that she would perform it.

---

[1] *Lord Dudley v. Lady Dudley* (1705), Precedents in Chancery 241, 24 E.R. 118; *Snell v. Clay* (1695), 2 Vernon 324, 23 E.R. 809.

The Lord Keeper [LORD HARCOURT] cited the case of Horwell and Harris,[1] which was a man gave all his lands which he should die seised of to his nephew, and, after he had made his will, he tells his heir at law that he had given his estate to his nephew and that he had purchased an estate since the making his will and hoped he would not disturb his nephew, upon which he answers 'God forbid I should.' And this being fully proved, though the heir at law had recovered the land purchased after the will, yet this declaration afterwards fetched it back again.

However, the court, in the principal case, did not enter into the proof and decreed the heir to be paid his legacy and to join in a sale of so much as was necessary to pay the debts and to have his costs, except for his proofs.

Note the court, at first, directed the heir should join in a sale of so much as should be necessary for the payment of the debts and legacies, but Mr. *Vernon* desired to take the decree that he should join only for the payment of the debts, for, if we take it for the legacies, it may be they will complain and say the decree is erroneous.

*Vide* 1 Canc. Reports 262.[2]

British Library MS. Hargrave 80, f. 28v, pl. 1

The case was the testator devised £100 to his heir and a bond of his for £200 to be delivered to him and the residue of his real and personal estate to his wife and her heirs. The heir pretended that the devise to the wife was in trust for him, but [there was] no proof of that but a slight parol one.

Lord Keeper [LORD HARCOURT]: Here is no proof of fraud or that the wife procured this devise to herself etc., for which reason he decreed it no trust.

In this, Serjeant *Hooper* cited that of Abel Lichford[3] where an annuity was decreed against the devisee of the real and personal estates upon the deposition of Mr. Bagshaw, the attorney who drew the will, that the annuity was omitted at the request of the devisee that it might not appear that the estate devised to him was charged with it and this notwithstanding there was nothing in writing and the Statute of Frauds and Perjuries.[4] And the like decree, he said, was in the case of Horwell and Harris.

In another case, Serjeant *Hooper* said that a parol agreement executed was always supported in equity notwithstanding the Statute of Frauds and Perjuries.

[1] *Harris v. Horwell* (1708), Gilbert Rep. 11, 25 E.R. 8, 2 Eq. Cas. Abr. 494, 591, 22 E.R. 419, 497.

[2] *Fowle v. Green* (1675), 1 Chancery Cases 262, 22 E.R. 791, also 1 Eq. Cas. Abr. 265, 21 E.R. 1034.

[3] *Oldham v. Litchford* (1705), 2 Vernon 506, 23 E.R. 923, 2 Freeman 284, 22 E.R. 1214, 1 Eq. Cas. Abr. 231, 21 E.R. 1011, 2 Eq. Cas. Abr. 44, 22 E.R. 39.

[4] Stat. 29 Car. II, c. 3, s. 5 (*SR*, V, 840).

[Other copies of this report: Lincoln's Inn MS. Misc. 383, p. 54, pl. 1, Lincoln's Inn MS. Misc. 106, p. 22.]

## 220

## Middleton v. Winn

(Ch. 1711)

*Where a person contracts to receive a portion, this contract is enforceable even though all of the parties concerned in the portion are dead without heirs.*

Lincoln's Inn MS. Misc. 10, p. 65

30 April 1711.

The father, by his will, pursuant to a power in his marriage settlement, charges his estate with the payment of £3500 to his two daughters for their portions. And he directs his executor to give his daughters a bond for the payment of this money. The executor accordingly gives two bonds to a person in trust for each of the daughters. One of them afterwards marries the plaintiff's intestate, and, before the marriage, there were articles made, wherein, taking notice of the bond, it was agreed that the money, when received, should be applied to pay off a mortgage which was upon the husband's estate and that he should then settle £10 a year for every £100 that should be paid upon the bond as a jointure upon the wife and, afterwards, on the issue of that marriage.

The wife died in six months after the marriage, no part of her portion being paid nor any settlement made. The husband takes administration to his wife and, afterwards, dies intestate. And administration of his estate was granted to the plaintiff, who also takes administration *de bonis non* of the wife.

And now he prefers his bill for the portion. And if it should be raised for the benefit of the administrator was the question.

Lord Keeper [Lord Harcourt]: The husband, by the articles, was a purchaser of the wife's portion for a valuable consideration, which distinguishes this case from those cases which have been cited. The plaintiff must be paid it with interest and costs.

## 221

## Meredith v. Wynne

(Ch. 1711)

*The question in this case was whether, where a marriage contract is not executed before the wife dies, the husband is a purchaser of his deceased wife's chose in action that was the subject of the contract.*

*If a decedent's personal estate is exhausted in paying off real encumbrances, a legatee is subrogated to those encumbrances and can have satisfaction over.*

British Library MS. Hargrave 80, f. 28v, pl. 2

The chief point of this case was whether the administrator *de bonis non* of the wife or the representatives of the husband, who survived her, were entitled to a chose in action of the wife not recovered nor the securities altered during the coverture, which were decreed to those who claimed under the husband, for this reason, *viz.* because the husband was a purchaser of them, articles having been made before marriage by which the husband covenanted to sell £70 *per annum* of his estate to exonerate the residue and to settle £10 a year for every £100 he should receive of the wife's fortune and also to settle within a time limited his whole estate on the issue of that marriage. The wife died quickly after the marriage without issue and before any settlement made or fortune received but within the time for making the settlement.

It was insisted by *Vernon* that the husband was bound by the articles and, therefore, a purchaser though prevented by the act of God from being carried into execution. And he seemed to think there would have been no difference though he had lived until after the time limited for making such a settlement.

He said that the case of Martin Lister and My Lord Hereford[1] was much stronger, where a settlement was made in consideration of a sum of money of the wife received and no notice taken of bonds standing out. And yet [it was] decreed that the husband was a purchaser of those bonds. And, in this case, if the articles had been only to settle £10 *per annum* for every £100 that he should receive, there, in regard he could not be compelled to make a settlement until he had received the money, perhaps, he could not be said to be a purchaser of the goods in controversy, but he was also to settle all his estate upon the issues of that marriage.

He distinguished this case from that of Kynaston and Burnett[2] which was a mere voluntary disposition of a chose in action of the wife and was, as I think, said to be in this manner, the husband agrees by articles to settle a mortgage in fee of the wife for £5000 on the issue of that marriage without settling anything of his own.

It was decreed further in this case that, if the personal estate had been exhausted in paying real encumbrances, a legatee should stand in the place of those encumbrances and have satisfaction over.

[1] *Lister v. Lister* (1688), 2 Vernon 68, 23 E.R. 654, 2 Freeman 102, 22 E.R. 1085, 1 Eq. Cas. Abr. 68, 21 E.R. 881, or *Blois v. Viscountess Hereford* (1705), 2 Vernon 510, 23 E.R. 921, 1 Eq. Cas. Abr. 68, 21 E.R. 882.

[2] *Burnett v. Kinaston* (1700), 2 Freeman 239, 22 E.R. 1183, Precedents in Chancery 118, 24 E.R. 57, 2 Vernon 401, 23 E.R. 860, 1 Eq. Cas. Abr. 69, 21 E.R. 882.

[Other copies of this report: Lincoln's Inn MS. Misc. 383, p. 54, pl. 2.]

[Other reports of this case: Gilbert Rep. 70, 25 E.R. 49, Precedents in Chancery 312, 24 E.R. 147, 1 Eq. Cas. Abr. 70, 21 E.R. 883, 2 Eq. Cas. Abr. 352, 22 E.R. 299.]

## 222

## Hutchison v. Hutchison

(Ch. 1711)

*The question in this case was whether a settlement of real estate upon the wife of a freeman of a city is a bar of her customary part of the personal estate.*

British Library MS. Hargrave 80, f. 31

Hutchison, a lunatic, by her committees, and her committees against Huchison.

The bill was for a discovery and account of the personal estate of her deceased husband. She had formerly a decree for a third upon the Statute of Distributions,[1] but that being never enrolled, the defendants, her husband's children by a former wife, brought another bill to bring the matter in question again. And since her lunacy, her committees found a certificate among her papers by which they discovered that her husband was a freeman of London and she was thereby entitled to a third as her customary part and likewise to a third of the dead man's third on the Statute of Distribution.

*Sir Joseph Jekyll*: If either there is no wife or no child or if the wife be not provided for by her husband in his lifetime, the custom [of London] divides the husband's personal estate into moieties and but one moiety is liable to distribution. And that is our case. The husband, before marriage, in consideration of £309 *per annum* to be settled by the wife to the use of them two for their lives, remainder to the heirs of their bodies, remainder to the right heirs of the husband, covenanted to purchase £91 *per annum* and settle it to the same uses, that, as she relied on that covenant, it was the same thing as if he had actually made the settlement (which point the court seemed to admit), and that the value of a jointure was what no court took upon them to inquire into, that this agreement was in the City language a compounding for her customary part. And, for this, he cited a case between Hancock and Hancock decreed by Lord Cowper and varied by My Lord Keeper.[2]

But it was said by My Lord Keeper [Lord Harcourt] that, there, by the agreement, the settlement was expressly mentioned to be in bar of her customary part, that she had an election given her to accept of the recompense or her customary part, and the only question was whether the accepting the settlement

[1] Stat. 22 & 23 Car. II, c. 10, s. 3 (*SR*, V, 720).

[2] *Hancock v. Hancock* (1707), see above, Case No. 73.

should bar her only for her customary part or the issue's too. And [it was] decreed it should bar both, the benefit of the settlement extending to them.

Query whether the issue did in that case make the same election.

He said further that, in this case, the wife was rather a purchaser of the £91 a year for her life by giving the inheritance of the £309 a year to her husband and that if it should be admitted to be a jointure.

Yet My Lord [Harcourt] seemed to think that a settlement of the real estate upon her would be no bar of her customary part of the personal estate.

It was urged by the counsel that the estate would be no bar of her dower and *a fortiori* not of a thing of a different nature. However, at the instance of *Sir J. Jekyll*, it was referred to be certified whether a jointure actually paid before marriage is a bar of a customary part and whether the agreement upon those articles is [a jointure].

It was insisted by the defendants that it was not proper to bring an original bill after a decree upon the same matter.

But it was answered by *Vernon* that, then, they should have pleaded and demurred, but, when they had answered, it was too late to ask whether they should answer or no, that, when new matter arose after a decree and before enrollment, a supplemental bill (I think he said original too) was proper and that a rehearing could be only on the same matter and that, after an enrollment, a bill of review was only fit.

[Other copies of this report: Lincoln's Inn MS. Misc. 383, f. 59, Lincoln's Inn MS. Misc. 106, p. 25.]

## 223

## Anonymous

(Ch. 1711)

*The payment of an annuity accrues when it is payable, even though the payor has a grace period after that date.*

Harvard Law Sch. MS. 537, pt. 2, p. 183, pl. 5

1 May, Easter [term], 10 Anne, before Sir John Trevor, Master of the Rolls.

The case was A. devised lands to his eldest son and likewise an annuity out of them to his younger son payable 25 March and 29 September or within twenty days after. The son dies after one of the days and within the twentieth. And the question was upon Barwick and Foster's Case, Yelverton [ *blank* ]; Clun's Case,

10 Co.; Duppa and Baskervil, in Saunders,[1] whether the executor should have the half-year's annuity or rent charge.

And by the Master [of the Rolls, TREVOR, it was] decreed for him because, in this case, it was intended the younger son should have it and a trust in the other during these twenty days. And it may differ when the dispute is between an heir and executor because the heir is more favored because of the rule of the rents being incident to the reversion, which holds not here.

N.B. There was the like case between Shaftoe, administrator of My Lady Cole and Sir Henry Ballasyse;[2] this was about 1703, when Mr. Justice Tracy, upon a point being made of it at the trial and hearing counsel at his chamber, gave it to the administrator, which must be, as he thought, upon the difference between an annuity or rent charge and a rent incident to a reversion. But query.

## 224

## Johnson v. Johnson

(Ch. 1711)

*A general clause in a will will be limited by a subsequent particular clause.*

*A court cannot give a decree against legatees who are not parties before the court.*

*A question in this case was whether, where a person is entitled to both the equity of an inheritance and also to a charge upon it and both being of the same nature, the charge is merged.*

Lincoln's Inn MS. Misc. 10, p. 66

2 May 1711.

The plaintiff's father, by his will, gives all his freehold, leasehold, and personal estate to his executors, their heirs, executors, etc., upon trust that, out of the rents etc. by sale or mortgage, they should raise money to pay his debts and legacies. And, after payment thereof, he directs his executors to assign the leasehold estate to his second son, the defendant at his age of twenty-four if he paid £1000 towards the debts and legacies, and, if he refused so to do, then they were to assign to the next son if he would pay £1000. And all the residue of his estate, he directs to be settled on another of his sons for life, remainder to his first and other sons in tail, with remainder over.

---

1 *Barwick v. Foster* (1609), Yelverton 167, 80 E.R. 111, also Croke Jac. 227, 233, 79 E.R. 197, 201, 1 Bulstrode 1, 80 E.R. 707, 1 Brownlow & Goldesborough 105, 123 E.R. 695, 2 Brownlow & Goldesborough 220, 123 E.R. 908; *Clun v. Archer* (1613), 10 Coke Rep. 127, 77 E.R. 1117, also Croke Jac. 309, 79 E.R. 265, 4 Leonard 247, 74 E.R. 850; *Duppa v. Mayo* (1670), 1 Williams Saunders 275, 85 E.R. 336, also 2 Keble 576, 84 E.R. 362, Lincoln's Inn MS. Misc. 500, f. 45v.

2 *Southern v. Bellasis* (1707), 1 Peere Williams 179, note, 24 E.R. 346, note.

The plaintiffs are some of the children that had portions given them by the will, and they now come for a satisfaction thereof out of the leasehold estate, which had been assigned to the defendant William by his mother, who was the only acting executrix, one of the executors being dead and the other two having released to her pursuant to a decree. And it was agreed that this estate was the only fund that was left for paying the plaintiffs.

And whether this estate should answer more than £1000 was the question, for, though it was given him after payment of the debts and legacies, yet it was insisted on for the defendant that his father's intention was that he should have this estate at all adventures when he came to the age of twenty-four, only paying £1000, so that he was to be in the nature of a purchaser and the will has fixed the quantum of what he was to pay. And nothing is more common than to restrain general words in a will by particular subsequent words.

And of this opinion was the court, and [it was] decreed that the defendant should pay no more than £1000.

Note there was some proof that the defendant had paid £1000 when the leasehold estate was assigned to him but it not appearing whether that money, if paid, was applied towards the legacies or in discharge of a mortgage which was upon that estate at the testator's death. The court directed the Master should enquire whether the £1000 was paid and how it was applied and, if it appeared that the £1000 was applied in discharge of the mortgage and not of the legacies, the defendant was then to answer £1000 to the plaintiffs and to be reimbursed the money he had paid towards clearing the mortgage out of the surplus of his father's personal estate, and, if he does not pay what shall appear due to the plaintiffs of the £1000, the estate must be sold and all parties to join in a sale.

Note I take the reason why the defendant was to be reimbursed out of the personal estate what was paid by him towards the mortgage was because there was a fund set apart for the payment of the debts, for, otherwise, I conceive the estate would have passed to him *cum onere*.

British Library MS. Hargrave 80, f. 32

Johnson devised his freehold lands to his executors or their heirs and his leasehold for years to them, their executors, and administrators in trust to pay debts and legacies by perception of the profits or sale, and then he gave £4000 to his four daughters and that, after his debts and legacies were paid, the residue of his freehold estate should be conveyed to his eldest son when he attained the age of twenty-four and the leasehold to his youngest son at the like age if he should pay £1000 toward his legacies. The question was whether the leasehold estate could be liable to pay more than the £1000.

*Vernon*: By the devise to the trustees, it appears to have been the intent of the testator to provide a sufficient fund for the payment of his debts and legacies in all events and the devise after to his oldest son of the freehold and to the youngest of the leasehold can only be intended of such part of each as should remain after his debts and legacies [were] paid.

It was answered that the devise to the youngest was not a devise of a residuum but of a specific legacy.

Lord Keeper [LORD HARCOURT]: Nothing is more common in wills than for a general clause to be controlled by a subsequent particular clause; the last clause explains the testator's mind, how much should be charged on his leasehold estates. In all events, they are made liable to the payment of £1000 and no more. But it appearing that they should be charged with a mortgage of £1000 at the time of the testator's death, His Lordship decreed that the land should *transire cum onere.*

In this case, the legatees not being brought before the court, who had received their full proportions, My Lord [HARCOURT] said, and *Vernon* agreed, that the other legatees, who had received but part, could pray nothing against them for to make them refund nor, therefore, against the executors as to those full payments.

The Case of Kemys and Thomas[1] was cited, which was this; a term was created and vested in trustees for raising £1000 for an infant; then the inheritance descended to the infant; the infant, after seventeen and before twenty-one, bequeathed the benefit of this term to J.S., and it was resolved that the bequest was good though it was insisted that it was incongruous that the same person should have the inheritance of the land and a charge upon the land and that, therefore, the term should be looked upon as merged. In the principal case, the same person was entitled to the equity of the inheritance and of the charge and both being of the same nature, it was urged that the charge ought to merge.

But *Vernon* insisted, and the court seemed to agree, that equity never makes a merger, but, on the other hand, sometimes revives terms merged at law for the benefit of younger children and creditors.

[Other copies of this report: Lincoln's Inn MS. Misc. 383, p. 61.]

## 225

## Berkeley v. Clarges

(Ch. 1711)

*A marriage contract entered into before marriage and executed after marriage is enforceable against the parties thereto and their heirs but not against creditors.*

*Deeds cancelled through duress remain in force uncancelled.*

[1] *Thomas v. Kemeys* (1696), 2 Vernon 348, 23 E.R. 821, 2 Freeman 207, 22 E.R. 1163, 1 Eq. Cas. Abr. 269, 21 E.R. 1037, Colles 112, 1 E.R. 206.

Lincoln's Inn MS. Misc. 10, p. 68

4 May 1711.

The plaintiff's husband settled a jointure upon her which was subject to a mortgage of £1600. He, afterwards, uses her very unkindly and, by means of his severity towards her, got her to cancel her settlement and to deliver it up. And he being dead, she now prefers her bill to re-establish her settlement and to redeem the mortgage.

[It was] decreed that the plaintiff should redeem and that it should be referred to a Master to consider what part of the estate in the mortgage should be sold to reimburse her what she should pay, with interest. And [it was] decreed that the heir should make a settlement of the jointure lands on the plaintiff for life and she to have her costs out of the estate to be sold.

British Library MS. Hargrave 80, f. 30v

The plaintiff having several leases for years of houses and other personal estate to the value of £1000 and a treaty of marriage being set on foot between her and Mr. Berkley of Shrewsbury, it was agreed that her leasehold estate should be vested in trustees to her sole and separate use and that Mr. Berkley should make her a jointure of lands in Shropshire. And settlements were drawn accordingly. But, before the deeds were executed, Berkley prevails with her to marry him, and, five days after[wards], the deeds were executed. Sometime after, he obliged her by ill usage to cancel those deeds, which, by the direction of one Wright, an attorney, she did by cutting off the seals. Then, the husband and Wright burned the deeds and all the draughts of it, which were in Wright's chamber, who drew the deeds.

The Lady Clargis took an assignment of a mortgage for £2000, which lay on the Shropshire estate precedent to the marriage agreement, which there was some proof the Lady Clargis had notice of at the time. Afterwards, the husband assigns some of the wife's houses to Lady Clargis, either as a further security or for an additional sum and then assigns the residue to Wright and another in trust for payment of his debts generally, one of which was £300 to this Wright. After this, the husband obliges the plaintiff to join with him in a bill to compel the first trustees to assign. But Lord Cowper would make no decree in it. The husband dies. The plaintiff administers and brings this bill against the mortgagee and trustees to have a reconveyance of the leasehold houses and against the co-heirs of her husband to have the benefit of the marriage agreement.

*How* insisted that, the legal estate remaining in the wife's trustees, nothing passed by the conveyance to Wright but a trust and that, as to his own debt, his title to equity being founded on a fraud, several instances of which notoriously appeared in the case, he could have no relief and that, he having acted as an agent for the other creditors, they came in as creditors with notice.

As to the Lady Clargis's mortgage, the counsel on both sides agreed that nothing could be prayed against it but a redemption.

It was insisted that the settlement being made after marriage was fraudulent against creditors notwithstanding it was reduced into writing before because [it was] not signed by the parties or any other by their direction.

Lord Keeper [Lord Harcourt]: I look upon the deed as uncancelled and think the agreement and execution sufficiently proved. I think the proofs of the marriage deed were the bill of the husband and wife and a brief of it drawn by Wright and two witnesses that deposed to what effect the deed was. As against Mr. Berkley and his heirs, the plaintiff ought to have the benefit of it, but not against creditors, and that, upon her redeeming Lady Clargis's mortgage, it should be assigned to whom she should direct, and that the co-heirs and their husbands should join in a fine to make her a jointure, that her leases were liable to the creditor's and Wright's debt too so far as it appeared to be a just one, and that, for what she suffered on that head or by the mortgage, she should hold over etc.

[Other copies of this report: Lincoln's Inn MS. Misc. 383, p. 58.]

## 226

## Anonymous

(Ch. 1711)

*Where a devise of two-thirds of an estate is made 'to sister B. and sister C. and cousins', one sister and her children take one-third and the other sister and her children the other third and the word 'cousins' does not extend to any other children of any other brother or sister.*

*Where the heir of a mortgagor remains in possession of the encumbered land and receives the profits after the mortgage is forfeited, he shall not account for them.*

*Equity will not aid a volunteer though it will aid a purchaser.*

British Library MS. Hargrave 80, f. 32v

A. devises that his estate shall be divided into thirds and then devises two-thirds to his sister B. and sister C. and cousins.

Lord Keeper [Lord Harcourt]: I think it the most natural construction that one sister and her children should have one-third and the other sister and her children the other third and the word 'cousins' should not extend to any other children of any other brother or sister.

Lord Keeper [Lord Harcourt]: If the heir of a mortgagor continue in possession and receive the profits after the mortgage be forfeited, he shall not account for them.

*Vernon*: I take it to be a rule almost without exception that, where a settlement is merely voluntary, equity will not supply a defect in point of law, as in cases of a voluntary feoffment without livery; otherwise, in the case of a purchaser.

The Lord Keeper [LORD HARCOURT] seemed to say that, if I covenant to settle one-third of the lands that I am seised of upon J.S. etc. without taking notice of any encumbrances, I must settle it clear from all encumbrances, but, if I covenant to settle one-third of the lands I shall die seised of, there, he seemed to think it would be otherwise, possibly because, in the latter case, it is in my power to alienate what I please before my death and consequently to encumber.

[Other copies of this report: Lincoln's Inn MS. Misc. 383, p. 62, Lincoln's Inn MS. Misc. 106, p. 27.]

## 227

## Pewrrin v. Robinson

(Ch. 1711)

*The holder of a bill of exchange can enforce it against an endorser or the drawer at his pleasure.*

British Library MS. Hargrave 80, f. 33, pl. 1

Pewrrin having indorsed a bill payable at a future day, Robinson discounted it. And some considerable time after it became payable, he brought an action upon it against Pewrrin, all the endorsers except Pewrrin and the drawer being then bankrupts.

Pewrrin exhibits his bill to be relieved on this ground, that the drawer was solvent until very lately and that it was the defendant's fault that he neglected bringing his action against the drawer while he was so or against Pewrrin while he might have recovered over and that he should not take advantage of his own negligence.

It was urged on the other side that all the endorsers were liable as well as the drawer, the drawer principally and they as his security, and that the plaintiff might resort to which of them he pleased.

And it appearing that Pewrrin was arrested on this bill four months before the drawer became bankrupt, his bill was dismissed with costs.

[Other copies of this report: Lincoln's Inn MS. Misc. 383, p. 63, pl. 1, Lincoln's Inn MS. Misc. 106, p. 28.]

## 228

## Anonymous

(Ch. 1711)

*Where the executors of a will live in a foreign country and send a pecuniary legacy to their agent for payment, interest on the legacy is not due until the agent receives the money.*

British Library MS. Hargrave 80, f. 33, pl. 2

A legacy was bequeathed payable out of the first money that should come to the hands of the executors. The executors, being in the Indies, receive more money than enough to pay the legacies and remit it to their agents here.

It was decreed it should be paid to the legatees here with interest from the time that the money came to the agents' hands and, as I remember, with costs both to the legatees and agents out of that money.

I think the executors in the Indies were not made parties.

[Other copies of this report: Lincoln's Inn MS. Misc. 383, p. 63, pl. 2, Lincoln's Inn MS. Misc. 106, p. 29, pl. 1.]

## 229

## Anonymous

(Ch. 1711)

*Where a contingent devisee dies, the condition not happening, the devise goes to the next devisee; there is no difference in this case between a chattel real and a chattel personal.*

British Library MS. Hargrave 80, f. 33v, pl. 1

A. devises his goods and chattels to B. and, if B. die without issue and before twenty-one, then to C. and upon like contingency of C.'s dying without issue and under twenty-one, then to D.; B. devises all his personal estate to J.S. and dies without issue and under twenty-one.

*Vernon* agreed that such a limitation of a chattel real would be good, but he took a difference between a term and a personal chattel that is perishable.

*How* insisted that a limitation of a chattel upon a contingency that was to happen during the lives of any persons in being was good.

Lord Keeper [Lord Harcourt] seemed to think there was no difference between a chattel real and a chattel personal in this case and decreed for C. against the devisee etc.

Where a dispute arises necessarily upon the words or circumstances of a will, the costs must come out of the personal estate of the testator, who occasioned that doubt.

[Other copies of this report: Lincoln's Inn MS. Misc. 383, p. 63, pl. 3, Lincoln's Inn MS. Misc. 106, p. 29, pl. 2.]

## 230

## Younger v. Welham

(Ch. 1711)

*Where several persons hold a power of appointment, the power can be exercised by a majority of them, unanimity not being required.*

British Library MS. Hargrave 80, f. 33v, pl. 2

Trinity term 1711.

[There being] four *cestui que trust*s of the office of the Register of the Prerogative Court, the trustees covenanted not to appoint any under-officer etc. without the direction of the *cestui que trust*s. But afterwards, the defendant Norris was made assistant without the privity of three of the *cestui que trust*s but with the consent of the fourth.

Norris was enjoined not to act any longer, but, as he came in without notice of the covenant, he was to have his costs against the plaintiff and the plaintiff to have them over against Welham, who put Norris in.

*Peere Williams* said the four *cestui que trust*s made but one assignee of the office and that, therefore, they ought all to agree in nominating or else nobody could be nominated and the rather because the place was within the Statute[1] and, therefore, could not be sold or the nomination [made for] any profit, but, in cases of profit, he allowed that a majority should bind.

Lord Keeper [Lord Harcourt]: Shall three lose their right because a fourth will not agree? A majority is sufficient.

[Other copies of this report: 3 Swanston 180, 36 E.R. 822, Lincoln's Inn MS. Misc. 383, p. 65, pl. 1, Lincoln's Inn MS. Misc. 106, p. 30, pl. 1.]

## 231

## Anonymous

(Ch. 1711)

*A marriage contract can be specifically enforced by a court of equity after the marriage has taken place.*

---

[1] Stat. 5 & 6 Edw. VI, c. 16 (*SR*, IV, 151–152).

British Library MS. Hargrave 80, f. 34, pl. 1

A bill [was exhibited] for a specific performance of marriage articles. *Inter alia*, it was surmised that the husband had gotten the articles into his hands a month after the marriage and destroyed them and that there was no copy. And [it was] urged that a lease and release drawn by the same hand and after the articles and intended to be executed, which it never was, should rather be looked upon as the measure and evidence of the estate to be settled by the articles than the husband's answer.

And this My Lord Keeper [Lord Harcourt] agreed to if the facts were so, *in odium spoliatoris*.

[Other copies of this report: Lincoln's Inn MS. Misc. 383, p. 65, pl. 2, Lincoln's Inn MS. Misc. 106, p. 30, pl. 2.]

## 232

## Rainsborough v. Seaman

(Ch. 1711)

*Where the third mortgagee paid off the first mortgage without notice of the second mortgage and the mortgagor becomes bankrupt, the second mortgagee can redeem both the first and second mortgages and then have the security sold to pay off his debt, and, if that is insufficient, he can join the bankruptcy proceedings as a creditor for the deficiency.*

British Library MS. Hargrave 80, f. 34, pl. 2

In this case, a third mortgagee, without notice of a second mortgage, bought in a mortgage antecedent to both. (I think he had a judgment too from the mortgagor for another debt.) The mortgagor becomes bankrupt, and the second mortgagee exhibits his bill against the third and the commissioners of bankrupts for a sale of the mortgaged lands and, if they proved deficient, to come in as a creditor for the residue under the commission.

[It was] decreed he should redeem the defendant upon paying what was due to him on both mortgages, that then, unless the commissioners redeemed him, the estate should be sold and that the plaintiff should come in as a creditor for what should appear due to him over and above what arose by the sale.

I think the third mortgagee did not insist on tacking his judgment to the mortgagor's, but submitted to come in as a creditor on that head under the commission.

[Other copies of this report: Lincoln's Inn MS. Misc. 383, p. 65, pl. 3, Lincoln's Inn MS. Misc. 106, p. 31.]

## 233

## Attorney General v. Anonymous

(Ch. 1711)

*An outstanding writ of sequestration is notice to a purchaser that the title is in issue.*

*There cannot be a decree for a sale of land if the heir is not a party to the suit, but there can be a decree if the suit is only to declare that the land stands charged with a charitable trust.*

*Where a deed is produced in court, it will be presumed that there was livery.*

British Library MS. Hargrave 80, f. 34, pl. 3

In this case, there were lands charged with a rent of £15 *per annum* to maintain three exhibitioners at Christ's College in Cambridge. The defendant insisted that they were settled on her by her father in consideration of an intended marriage which took effect and that she was a purchaser without notice.

*Vernon*: If there was no notice, that would be a bar to the charity. But here, at the time of the settlement, the father was under a sequestration for not answering to an information touching this charity.

And [it was] ruled to be notice.

It was objected that they had not brought the heir of the surviving trustee before the court.

Lord Keeper [LORD HARCOURT]: You cannot have a decree for a sale without the heir but only to declare that the lands stand charged with the trust.

It was further objected that this answer was put in by a woman while she was married.

*Vernon*: A married woman has no other privilege than that, if there be an improvident defense made for her or a gross neglect or mistake, she may, when she becomes *sole*, apply herself to the court to amend her answer, but here she has gone on to examine witnesses since she became *sole*.

There was a deed produced made in the time of Charles I without the word 'enfeoff' or livery endorsed.

But the Lord Keeper [LORD HARCOURT] said he would presume livery.

[Other copies of this report: Lincoln's Inn MS. Misc. 383, p. 66, pl. 1, Lincoln's Inn MS. Misc. 106, p. 32.]

## 234

## Gardiner v. Rogers

(Ch. 1711)

*Parol evidence is admissible to explain a doubtful will or against an implication, but not against an express devise.*

*In this case, the intention of the testatrix was clear that the executors should be trustees and not residuary legatees.*

British Library MS. Hargrave 80, f. 34v

Gardiner, committee of an idiot, brought his bill for an account against the executors of the idiot's mother, who, by her will, devised thus. 'I give to A. £10. Item, I give all my goods to A., B., C., and D., whom I make executors and appoint to be guardians of my child earnestly beseeching the Court of Chancery to commit the custody of her to them.' And then she devises all that she had as administratrix to her husband to the same four to have and to hold to them etc. to their own proper use. The legacy to one of the executors and the naming them guardians, which is an office of trust, and the want of any provision by the will for the idiot were urged to prove the devise to the executors to be only in trust.

This was enforced by parol evidence, *viz.* that the testatrix had little or no acquaintance with the executors, that they were recommended to her as honest men, which was an inducement to make them trustees, that she had frequently said that she had made them executors and guardians for her child and, at other times, trustees for her child, and that it was proved one of the trustees had been so honest as to renounce.

Lord Keeper [Lord Harcourt] seemed to say that parol evidence might be admitted to explain a doubtful will or against an implication, but not against an express devise. And he suffered it to be read in this case.

*Vernon*: It has been held that a particular devise to an executor shall exclude him from taking the whole as executor and, from thence, it has been inferred that he was intended only to be a trustee but, certainly, a particular devise to one shall not exclude the rest.

Query, for *Hooper* seemed to say that point had been adjudged otherwise.

He said that that doctrine had grown daily, but now it seemed to be declining again. But it had been admitted in the House of Lords that an executor should be permitted to show that it was the intention of the testator that he should take to his own use though there was no express devise to him, that, if they went into parol proof, those which are consistent with the will must prevail, and that, though the word 'guardian' implies a trust, it was hard to say that it should imply a trust in another clause and of a distinct thing and that the other executor had renounced the executorship not the devise.

The depositions of the attorney who drew the will were read to prove that he drew it according to his instructions and that he believed it was the intention of the testatrix that the executors should have the benefit of the will.

Lord Keeper [Lord Harcourt]: There must be a distinct account taken of the personal estate of the testatrix and of what she had as administratrix to her husband. It is manifest from the face of the will as well as the proofs and circumstances of the child that she intended they should be executors in trust. The character of their honesty that was given her and her having no personal knowledge of them are evidence of it; besides, her earnestly beseeching this court in her will to commit etc. to the executors, though probably inserted to get the child into their hands, yet I must now look upon it as a proof of her concern for her daughter, and yet there is nothing given her by the will. The distinction in the devises enforces this construction. She gives all her personal estate to her executors, then names them guardians, and beseeches them *ut supra*, which seems to be complete. Then she devises to them all that she has as administratrix to hold to their own proper use. Besides her daughter being incapable to take, it was reasonable to devise it in trust for her, that what she had as administratrix should be accounted for to the executors.

My Lord seemed to think he went a little too far in this point, but that it seemed to be admitted on both sides that the three executors should pay costs for their unreasonable demands and the fourth have his costs and the plaintiff to have them over.

The idiot had an estate of £200 a year descended to her besides. And it was said in this case by the Attorney General [*Northey*] and *Sir Thomas Powys* that a committee of an idiot shall have no benefit of the principal money of the idiot but only of the interest.

It was said, in Stroud Litton and Lady Falkland's Case,[1] the Lords blamed the Lord Chancellor for admitting parol evidence but that, since, in that of Docksy v. Docksy,[2] that they had admitted such as stands with the will.

[Other copies of this report: Lincoln's Inn MS. Misc. 383, p. 66, pl. 2, Lincoln's Inn MS. Misc. 106, p. 33.]

## 235

## Anonymous

(Ch. 1711)

*Executors of a decedent's will have a reasonable time within which to pay legacies in order to see what debts are payable.*

*Where the legacy is payable out of the personal estate, no interest is payable, but, where it is payable out of the profits of realty, interest is due and payable from the death of the testator.*

---

1 *Viscountess Falkland v. Lytton* (1709), 3 Brown P.C. 24, 1 E.R. 1152, see also above, Case No. 107.

2 *Docksey v. Docksey* (Ch. 1708), see above, Case No. 99.

British Library MS. Hargrave 80, f. 35v, pl. 1

There was a difference taken by *How* and allowed by the court that, where a legacy is devised payable out of the personal estate and no time of payment is fixed, that the executors shall have a reasonable time for payment in order to see what debts etc. are outstanding and that it shall not carry interest.

Query if he said not in the meantime.

But, where it is payable out of lands without fixing any certain time of payment, [he said] that it shall carry interest from the death of the testator in respect of the growing profits of the land.

[Other copies of this report: Lincoln's Inn MS. Misc. 383, p. 68.]

## 236

## Anonymous

(Ch. 1711)

*Where something is to be done with someone's assent and that person refuses to give any assent, a court of equity can supply it.*

British Library MS. Hargrave 80, f. 35v, pl. 2

If a purchase is to be made with the consent of A. and A. refuses to agree to any purchase, the Court of Chancery will overrule A.

[Other copies of this report: Lincoln's Inn MS. Misc. 383, p. 69, pl. 1.]

## 237

## Claridge v. Owen

(Ch. 1711)

*A devise of a copyhold to two daughters gives them a joint tenancy and not successive estates according to the custom of the manor.*

*If an ancestor devises land of inheritance to his daughters, it destroys the coparcenaries and makes them joint tenants.*

British Library MS. Hargrave 80, f. 35v, pl. 3

J. Owen, seised in fee of lands of £200 a year and possessed of a term for years of £30 *per annum* and of a copyhold estate for life about the same value and having three daughters, devised that his trustees should put his two eldest daughters' lives into the copyhold, A. and M. And in case his personal estate fell short in paying the fine to the lord, he created a term of four years in his fee simple lands to supply the defect and devised that his leasehold lands should go along with his copyhold and that his three daughters should have £150 and left his fee simple lands to descend. And, by a codicil, he devises that, in case he should have a son born, that he should have all his lands and the two eldest daughters £300 apiece.

The trustees put in the three daughters lives. And the question was whether the two eldest should take successively according to the custom of the manor or jointly.

*Jekyll* and *Page*: The devise that the two eldest daughters lives A. and M. should be put into the copy is as full as if he had expressly said they should take successively for, when they were in the copy, the custom of the manor, which he knew, operates upon them to make them take successively, nor does this construction leave the two daughters unprovided for, the fee simple lands are descending upon all.

They read some slight parol proof that the intent of the testator was that they should take successively.

*Vernon*: There is no ground to think that the testator intended an estate for life in possession to one daughter and only a reversion which possibly may never take effect in possession to the other. The leasehold is to go along with the copyhold, and it cannot be thought that he designed to give all to one and strip the other of everything, at least during the term of four years in fee simple lands. That would put the second daughter in a worse condition than the third, who had a certain provision of £150, and yet, by the codicil, in case he should have a son, he leaves his second daughter double what he gives his third by the will and as much as his eldest. And, from their being to have an equal recompense in case they lost the land by the birth of a son, he inferred that what they were to lose was equal.

Lord Keeper [Lord Harcourt] observed there was no direction in the will which should be named first in the copy.

And the Master of the Rolls [Trevor] decreed according to what seemed to be the Lord Keeper's opinion that they should take jointly and equally and also that the third daughter's name being into the copy, she should take after the other two to her own use paying the fine for putting in her life.

The Lord Keeper [Lord Harcourt] put a case that, if the ancestor devised his lands of inheritance to his daughters, it would destroy the coparcenaries and make them joint tenants.

[Other copies of this report: Lincoln's Inn MS. Misc. 383, p. 69, pl. 2, Lincoln's Inn MS. Misc. 106, p. 36.]

## 238

## Gibson v. Albert

(Ch. 1711)

*Co-defendants are not disqualified as witnesses inter se.*

*Where a plaintiff is forced to join a trustee as a co-defendant, the trustee is not disqualified as a witness for the plaintiff.*

10 Modern 19, 88 E.R. 606

Easter 10 Anne.

*Obiter*: If a man unnecessarily make anyone a defendant, he thereby cuts himself off from the benefit of his evidence, for it is his own fault. But, where several are made defendants, it will not hinder any one of the defendants from the benefit of the evidence of any others that are made so.

Indeed, in the case of trustees, it is necessary that they be made defendants, and, therefore, there, the plaintiff may have the benefit of their evidence.

[Other reports of this case: 2 Eq. Cas. Abr. 396, 22 E.R. 338.]

## 239

## Drew v. Walker

(Ch. 1711)

*A legacy to 'executors or administrators' sinks into the residuum of the decedent's estate.*

Lincoln's Inn MS. Misc. 10, p. 113

A man, by his will, gives £300 to his niece A. and, if she died before twenty-one, then he gives this £300 to his niece B. and, if she died before twenty-one, then says he 'I give it to my executors or administrators.' And he makes C. his executor, who proves the will and dies. And, afterwards, the two nieces die, neither of them attaining the age of twenty-one.

After the death of the executor, administration of his estate is granted to one person and administration *de bonis non* of the testator *cum testamento annexo* is granted to another person. And to which of them this legacy belonged was the question.

Upon hearing this cause, the Lord Keeper [Lord Harcourt] was of the opinion that the legacy vested in the executor and should go to his administrator, and he decreed accordingly. But, somewhat afterwards, he said he had considered further of the case, and he decreed it to be a legacy sunk into the testator's personal estate.

## 240

### Harris v. Fewtrell

(Ch. 1711)

*In this case, the court held the transaction in issue to be a loan with the conveyance as a security for repayment.*

British Library MS. Hargrave 80, f. 36v

Fewtrell settled his lands in trust to the use of his son for life, remainder to his grandson in tail, and with a power for his son to charge them with any sum not exceeding £400 for payment of debts or portions. The son, by lease and release, reciting the power, mortgaged the lands to his father and his heirs for £400. There was no proof of the payment of the money, but some of his son's having paid interest. The plaintiff claimed the money under the executor of old Fewtrell. The defendant was his heir and claimed under that settlement and had docked the entail by a fine and recovery.

*Vernon*: The heir is only a trustee to the executor, who is entitled to the mortgage money. The covenant in the deed was to pay to the heirs or executors. He seemed to agree that the power was not well pursued at law, though it is a good execution of it in equity.

*How*: If a tenant for life with such power makes a lease for 99 years determinable on his own life, this is a suspension of the power, which the lease for a year is in this case, and then the release could not execute it.

Lord Keeper [LORD HARCOURT]: They are both but one conveyance.

*Vernon*: He that has a power to raise money for payment of debts or portions is the best judge when he wants it and the lender was never thought to be bound to see how it is applied.

Lord Keeper [LORD HARCOURT]: This conveyance was made twenty-five years ago. The father and son are both since dead. I ought to intend it was raised for payment of debts and the conveyance is a sufficient charge upon the lands.

[Other copies of this report: Lincoln's Inn MS. Misc. 383, p. 70, Lincoln's Inn MS. Misc. 106, p. 38.]

## 241

### Anonymous

(Ch. 1711)

*The question in this case was whether a deceased trader's administrator can take bankruptcy.*

British Library MS. Hargrave 80, f. 37, pl. 1

*Vernon* cited the case of Hitchcock v. Sedgewick,[1] which was this. One Lane mortgaged his lands to Sedgewick and then committed an act of bankruptcy, and then Sedgwick made an absolute purchase of the equity of redemption. It was decreed against Sedgewick in Chancery, and that decree was reversed in the House of Lords. And an issue was directed upon the single point which the Lords made any doubt of, *viz.* whether [there was] notice of the act of bankruptcy or not at the time of the purchase, and [it was] at last settled after three or four hearings in both places that the purchase without notice should not be impeached.

In the principal case, a mortgagee of a bankrupt without notice of the act of bankruptcy took in a mortgage afterwards, which was alleged to be precedent, and an issue was directed to settle the time when he became a bankrupt. And there being a doubt whether ever he was a trader, it was agreed that the point would come within the issue. The person alleged to be a bankrupt had married a milliner's daughter and taken administration to the milliner.

Attorney General [*Northey*]: If an administrator sells the goods in the shop or if, in order to advance their sale, he makes one contract for goods to the value of £100, that will not make him a trader. He cited the case of Sir Thomas Littleton, Commissioner of the Victualing Office in Charles II's time,[2] who, in pursuance of his office, had many contracts with several persons, and yet, in regard they were all directed to one end, [it was] adjudged he was no trader nor could he be a bankrupt.

[Other copies of this report: Lincoln's Inn MS. Misc. 383, p. 71, Lincoln's Inn MS. Misc. 106, p. 39.]

## 242

## Anonymous

(Ch. 1711)

*Unless it is expressly contracted for, a mortgage is not security for a subsequent debt vis-a-vis the mortgagor, but vis-a-vis the mortgagor's heir it is.*

British Library MS. Hargrave 80, f. 38, pl. 1

*Hooper*: If a mortgagor be indebted to the mortgagee by a bond and there is no covenant in the mortgage deed that it shall stand as a further security for such other sums as shall be advanced nor any endorsement on the mortgage, the mort-

---

[1] *Hitchcock v. Sedgwick* (1690), 2 Vernon 156, 23 E.R. 707, 1 Eq. Cas. Abr. 53, 54, 323, 332, 21 E.R. 868, 869, 1076, 1083.

[2] *Gibson v. Thomson* (1675), 1 Freeman 391, 89 E.R. 290, 1 Ventris 270, 86 E.R. 180, 3 Keble 451, 84 E.R. 817.

gagee cannot pray against the mortgagor himself that he may pay him the debt due on the bond as well as the principal, interest, and costs upon the mortgage or be foreclosed. But he may against the heir of the mortgagor because the bond is a lien upon the land, which seemed to be allowed *per curiam*.

[Other copies of this report: Lincoln's Inn MS. Misc. 383, p. 73, pl. 1.]

## 243

## Anonymous

(Ch. 1711)

*Where a party, in his answer, states an account and the other party does not reply, the first party can be examined only as to what occurred after the filing of the answer [the account being deemed admitted by the failure to reply].*

*A defendant may be examined without an order if he has not answered the process that has been prayed against him.*

British Library MS. Hargrave 80, f. 38, pl. 2

The plaintiff having, in his answer to the defendant's cross-bill, stated an account depending, to which the defendant had not replied, [it was] ruled and that the plaintiff should be examined upon interrogatories only to what passed since the filing of that answer. Articles must first be exhibited and then an order obtained before you can examine to the credit of a witness.

And [it was] urged by *Vernon* that the defendants ought to pay costs for having examined to the character of the plaintiff without an order.

But [it was] ruled by Lord Keeper [Lord Harcourt] that they were proper to examine to the character of the plaintiff in this case, it being a case of forgery.

A defendant may be examined without an order if he has not answered the process that has been prayed against him.

[Other copies of this report: Lincoln's Inn MS. Misc. 383, p. 73, pl. 2.]

## 244

## Anonymous

(Ch. 1711)

*The fees allowed to be charged by a sequestrator must be reasonable.*

British Library MS. Hargrave 80, f. 38, pl. 3

A serjeant at arms is an officer of the court (if of the Crown); it is reasonable he should have his daily stated fee. But sequestrators are named by the party, and he is not tied down to any certain number; if, therefore, sequestrators should be allowed 6s. 8d. per day without any regard to his necessary expense or trouble, the defendant might be put to the expense of £5 or £10 a day and soon ruined by a sequestration.

Lord Keeper [Harcourt] seemed much displeased at a report that had admitted such an allowance. And I think he overruled the report.

[Other copies of this report: Lincoln's Inn MS. Misc. 383, p. 74, pl. 1.]

## 245

## East v. Slaney

(Ch. c. 1711)

*To properly plead a fine and recovery, the pleader should set forth the deed and show to whom it was suffered and who was the vouchee.*

Lincoln's Inn MS. Misc. 10, p. 69

The plaintiff, suggesting himself to be the issue in tail, brings a bill for a discovery of a settlement under which he pretended to claim.

The defendant pleads that the plaintiff's father was a tenant in tail and that he mortgaged the lands in question to the defendant for £500 and that he, afterwards, bought the equity of redemption for £500 more. And, then, he sets forth a deed wherein the father had covenanted that a fine and recovery should be had, and then he says that he levied a fine and that a recovery was suffered. But he does not say by whom it was suffered nor who was vouched.

And, for this reason, it was objected that the fine and recovery was not well pleaded. If he had said, after setting forth the deed, that a fine and recovery were thereupon or accordingly levied, it was agreed that it would have been well enough, but, as it was here pleaded, it was insisted on not to be well pleaded.

The court agreed it was not very well pleaded. However, [they] said they would intend it to be a fine and recovery pursuant to the deed and allowed the plea and said the plaintiff might reply to it if he thought fit, and, if there was not a good fine and recovery, it would not hurt him.

## 246

## Soper v. Metham

(Ch. 1711)

*In this case, the portion for a younger son did not merge into the inheritance, and the devise of the portion was valid.*

Lincoln's Inn MS. Misc. 10, p. 71

5 May 1711. William Soper and Alice, his wife, plaintiffs, and Metham *et al.*, defendants.

A man, upon his marriage, settles land upon trustees to the use of himself for life, remainder to the heirs male of his body, remainder to his heirs female, with a remainder to his own right heirs. And he reserves to himself a power to charge this land with £700 for younger children's portions. And, by his will, he charges this estate with £700 for portions for his younger sons.

He dies leaving three sons. The eldest enters and dies before twenty-one without issue. Then, the second brother, who was entitled to £200 of this £700, enters and dies without issue, having first made his will and, thereby, gives the residue of his personal estate to his executor. And the question now was between the executor and the third brother whether this £200 should be raised, it being insisted on for the defendant, the heir, that the £200 was extinguished, in regard his brother, who had this equitable demand on the land had likewise the inheritance in him at the same time.

On the other side, it was said that this equitable demand was still subsisting. And for this was cited the case of Keymish and Thomas,[1] which was decreed by Lord Somers and, afterwards, affirmed in the House of Lords, which was a term for years was created for raising £5000 for a daughter, upon whom the equitable estate of the inheritance did afterwards descend, and then she married and died without issue. It was decreed that this £5000 should be raised notwithstanding she had the equitable interest in the money and in the land at the same time, for, otherwise, the husband would have had no portion at all with his wife.

But, to this, it was said that the case cited did not come up to the present case, for there was a legal term standing out in the trustees and no merger of the estate at law, and, therefore, the court of equity would not go to make a merger of two equities. But, in the case in question, there is no legal estate subsisting for raising this £200, but he that had the equitable demand on the land had likewise the legal estate of the inheritance in him at the same time so that the equitable demand was extinguished and cannot now be revived, as where a man has an easement in land as a way, for instance, and he, afterwards, purchases this land or it descends upon him, by this means, the easement is extinguished, and, if he should sell the land afterwards, the vendee would hold the land discharged of this easement.

This cause was heard before the Master of the Rolls [TREVOR] 29 October 1710, who declared that the £200 was not merged, but vested in Robert, the second son, by the settlement and was well devised by him to the plaintiff Alice, and he decreed the same to be paid her without interest and that the land should

[1] *Thomas v. Kemeys* (1696), 2 Vernon 348, 23 E.R. 821, 2 Freeman 207, 22 E.R. 1163, Colles 112, 1 E.R. 206, 1 Eq. Cas. Abr. 269, 21 E.R. 1037.

stand charged therewith and that the plaintiff should hold and enjoy the land until the £200 should be raised and paid.

The defendant appealed from this decree to the Lord Keeper [Lord Harcourt], and he affirmed the decree.

## 247

## Stanley v. Bennett

(Ch. 1711)

*A judgment creditor who has both law and equity on his side has priority over other creditors who have only equity on their side.*

*A debtor, before he becomes a bankrupt, may give a preference to some of his creditors by making a provision for them.*

*Where property is conveyed in trust to pay a creditor, that creditor has priority over the other creditors in a bankruptcy proceeding against the debtor.*

Lincoln's Inn MS. Misc. 10, p. 73

7 May 1711.

A man makes a mortgage of his estate for 500 years and then confesses a judgment. After this, he conveys the equity of redemption to trustees and their heirs, taking notice that his son was bound for him in several bonds, upon trust to sell the same for the payment of the said debts which his son was bound with him for. After this, he becomes a bankrupt.

The first question was if the judgment creditor should have a preference before the creditors who were to be paid by virtue of this deed of trust.

[It was] decreed he should, for the judgment creditor having both law and equity, there is no reason to put him upon a level with the other creditors who have only equity on their side.

The second question was if this deed was fraudulent against the other creditors.

[It was] decreed it was not, for a man, before he becomes a bankrupt, may give a preference if he pleases to some of his creditors by making a provision for them.

British Library MS. Hargrave 80, f. 29

The bill was brought by a judgment creditor of one that became a bankrupt after the judgment. And it was for the discovery of a deed by which the bankrupt, a little before the act of bankruptcy, had, in consideration that his son had been bound for him, conveyed his lands to his son in trust to satisfy those debts and the other debts of the bankrupt except such as he owed as surety and to have an execution of the trust and to be relieved etc. The trustee in the deed and the assignees of the commissioners of bankrupts were made defendants.

Upon the proof, it appeared that the lands so conveyed were mortgaged before the judgment.

It was agreed that, by 21 Jac. I,[1] a judgment creditor has no preference in the distribution of a bankrupt's estate and, on the other hand, that a judgment would affect lands aliened by the bankrupt after the judgment and before he became a bankrupt. And the question was what would be the effect of this deed, whether this would mend the plaintiff's case since, if there had been no such deed, the lands had come to the assignee and had been equally liable to all creditors.

Lord Keeper [Lord Harcourt] said that the deed being made for payment of debts without giving a preference to any did no more than the act of bankruptcy.

*Vernon* answered: Surely debts were excepted which would come in with the rest in case of bankruptcy.

Lord Keeper [Lord Harcourt]: I look upon this deed as a mortgage and, then it stands thus; here is a mortgage first, then a judgment, then a mortgage, then an act of bankruptcy.

*Vernon*: Just debts have the same preference in equity against the equity of redemption as at law against the legal estate in all cases except that of a purchaser without notice. In the Case of Hungerford and My Lord Bristol,[2] it was strongly urged that all debts were equal in conscience and equity, but [it was] decreed that the trusts and equity of redemption should be liable to the mortgages and judgments according to their priority. Equity following the law in this case, the legal estate vested in the first mortgagee; then, our judgment bound the equity of redemption etc.

Lord Keeper [Lord Harcourt]: Could you redeem without bringing the assignee before the court?

*Vernon*: No, not without bringing all the parties concerned in interest. But the assignee can take it in no other plight than it was in the hands of the bankrupt.

It was objected that the bill was improper and that, if the plaintiff's right was good at law, he ought not to come into equity and that it was unreasonable to desire the assistance of a court of equity to give preference to debts which in conscience are equal and that in opposition to the statutes of bankrupts.[3] Besides, the prayer of the bill is to have an execution of the trusts of the deed, which is to come in but in equal degree with the rest of the creditors, the deed giving no preference.

---

[1] Stat. 21 Jac. I, c. 19 (*SR*, IV, 1227–1229).

[2] *Earl of Bristol v. Hungerford* (1705), 2 Vernon 524, 23 E.R. 938, 1 Eq. Cas. Abr. 44, 142, 21 E.R. 862, 944.

[3] Stat. 1 Jac. I, c. 15 (*SR*, IV, 1031–1034); Stat. 21 Jac. I, c. 19 (*SR*, IV, 1227–1229).

In answer to this, it was said that they could not proceed at law without a discovery of this deed and that a creditor has a right against an heir or any other except a purchaser without notice.

They seemed to waive that part of the prayer and said that, if a bill asks too much or too little, yet when relief is prayed, the court will give such as shall be proper for the case.

There was another judgment entered quickly after the act of bankruptcy, which entry, by fiction of law, had relation to the Grand Sessions, which was before the act of bankruptcy.

The Lord Keeper took time to consider. And, at another day, he said that he could not take away the law from Sir John Stanley, his judgment being before the bankruptcy and the lands not in the hands of the bankrupt at the time of the bankruptcy and that whether the deed to the son was fraudulent or no was triable at law but that there appeared [to be] no fraud. He decreed Sir John Stanley's debt to be paid first with interest and costs. And, as to the deed to the heir, he said that, had the words been only to satisfy what was due to him and other creditors, there, possibly, the heir could come only upon an equal foot with the rest of the creditors, the naming him first giving him no precedence because it was impossible to name or write all at the same instant, but the intent of the deed seems to be to give the son a preference, the consideration of it being for his indemnity and there being a power to him to sell and let the same as he should think meet and, for this reason, the son must be satisfied next after Sir John Stanley and then the trust executed for the rest of the creditors. And, as to the judgment confessed by warrant of attorney, which was entered on a Sunday and had relation to the Grand Sessions before the bankruptcy, he decreed it fraudulent.

[Other copies of this report: Lincoln's Inn MS. Misc. 383, p. 55, Lincoln's Inn MS. Misc. 106, p. 23.]

## 248

## Andrews v. Pendlebury

(Ch. 1711)

*An irrevocable power of attorney cannot be revoked by a later will.*

Lincoln's Inn MS.Misc. 10, p. 74

The same day [7 May 1711]. Andrews, administrator of Andrews, plaintiff; Pendlebury and Lightfoot, defendants.

Brigadier Bloud,[1] by his will, after some legacies, gives the residue of his estate to Mrs. Andrews, the plaintiff's intestate, who was his mistress.

After this, he makes a letter of attorney to the defendant Lightfoot, whereby he empowers Lightfoot to receive all his pay out of the ordinance and all debts then due or which should be due to him for seven years to the use of the brigadier for his life and, afterwards, in trust for Mrs. Andrews and covenants not to revoke this letter of attorney.

Ten years after this, he makes another will and makes the defendant Pendlebury executor and residuary legatee in trust for Holcroft Blood, his natural son by another woman. The question was if this letter of attorney was revoked by the last will.

[It was] decreed it was not. It is plain the intention of this deed was to fix and ascertain what he intended to give Mrs. Andrews and to restrain the general disposition he had made to her of his estate by his first will.

[It was] decreed that Lightfoot should account with the plaintiff for what had been received by him and not accounted for to the brigadier in his lifetime, for it was agreed on all hands that what had been paid over to him was well paid and for such debts as were due at the making of the letter of attorney and not yet received.

## 249

## Havers v. Dormer

(Ch. c. 1711)

*The question in this case was whether the trust of the lease in issue was a void remainder or not.*

Lincoln's Inn MS. Misc. 10, p. 75

Havers and others, creditors of William Dormer, plaintiffs; Robert Dormer and John Web, defendants.

The earl of Carnarvon, by indenture dated 19 October 1677, reciting that he had agreed to settle £100 a year on Ch. Dormer, Esq., and his younger children, in consideration thereof and for other consideration, demises the manor of H. to the defendant Web, now the surviving trustee, and others upon trust to pay William Dormer and his assigns £100 a year if the same could be raised out of the rents of the premises during the term and, in case the said William Dormer should happen to die without issue during the term, then upon trust to pay the said £100 a year to the defendant, Robert Dormer, his brother, and his assigns

[1] J. Spain, 'Blood, Holcroft', *Oxford Dictionary of National Biography*, vol. 6, pp. 268–270.

during the residue of the term, and, if he died without issue during the term, then in trust to pay the said £100 a year to Margaret and Elizabeth Dormer.

William Dormer attained twenty-one before the earl's death and died in September last, having made his will and Robert, his brother, executor and residuary legatee. Robert renounced the executorship, and the plaintiff Havers took administration *cum testamento etc.* And he insists that the term is assets. And if the trust of the term belonged to the administrator of William Dormer or to the defendant Robert Dormer, the remainderman, was the question.

Lord Keeper [Lord Harcourt]: I think it would be hard to make this a void remainder. You agree that, if the limitation had been to Richard Dormer if he be then living, it had been good. Let it be referred to the judges for their opinion as supposing it to be a limitation of a term at law.

## 250

## Granger v. Brett

(Ch. 1711)

*Where no time is set for the payment of a legacy charged on land, the legacy does not carry interest until a year after the testator's death.*

Lincoln's Inn MS. Misc. 10, p. 76

7 June 1711.

A.B. gives several legacies by his will and charges them upon his real estate, but he mentions no time when they shall be paid.

It was said by Mr. *How* that the rule was that, when a legacy is to be paid out of the personal estate and no time is fixed for the payment of it, the executor shall have a reasonable time, *i.e.* a year, to look about him to see what debts there are and to get in the assets and the legacy shall not carry interest from the testator's death. But otherwise it is where the legacy is charged upon land, because, in that case, the profits are applicable to the legacies from the testator's death.

But, notwithstanding this, it was decreed by the Master of the Rolls [Trevor] that the plaintiff's legacy should not carry interest but from a year after the testator's death.

## 251

## Anonymous

(Ch. 1711)

*A power of appointment can be exercised by the creation of a trust to the same purposes for which the power was created.*

Lincoln's Inn MS. Misc. 10, p. 77

11 June 1711.

A tenant for life with a power to charge the lands with any sum of money not exceeding £400 for the payment of his debts and for younger children's portions, by lease and release, conveys the premises to trustees to raise a sum of £400 for the payment of his debts and the overplus for his younger children's portions.

[It was] decreed that it was a good execution of the power though it was insisted on that, by this conveyance, the tenant for life had suspended the execution of his power, as if a tenant for life with such a power makes a lease for ninety-nine years if he shall so long live, this is a suspension of his power.

It was objected that the plaintiffs had made no proof of any debts nor that any part of the £400 was applied for that purpose.

But the court said, after twenty-seven years, they would presume there were debts and that the money was applied to pay them.

## 252

## Maynard v. Maynard

(Ch. 1711)

*Where a child is advanced in the lifetime of the father by him and a sum certain does not appear by a writing under the father's hand, it shall be taken for a full advancement, but not where he mentions a certain sum.*

British Library MS. Hargrave 80, f. 37, pl. 2

A bill [was exhibited] by the youngest against the eldest son, who was executor of the father, a freeman of London, for an account of the personal estate etc.

A difference was taken in this case by *Sir Peter King* and agreed by Solicitor General [*Raymond*] and *Vernon*, of the other side, that, where a child is advanced in the lifetime of the father by him and the certainty, *viz.* the certain sum of that advancement does not appear by any writing under the father's hand, it shall be taken for a full advancement, but not where he mentions a certain sum. To prove the last, *Vernon* cited the cases of Jeffries and Stirt and Box v. Box.[1]

Lord Keeper [LORD HARCOURT]: I take the reason to be of the last because, in that case, there is a certainty to bring into hotchpot.

In the principal case, the father left two children, the plaintiff and defendant, and no wife; he had given several sums of money to the plaintiff in his lifetime, a memorandum of part of which was found under the testator's own hand, besides which he had given him seven years maintenance and a parcel of clothes and, by his will, devised to him £20 *per annum* or £140, at his election, in full sat-

[1] *Box v. Box* (Ch. 1703), see above, Case No. 17.

isfaction of his customary part and that security should be given for the payment of £20 *per annum* in case he elected that, which he did and had received several payments; the residue was devised over.

The defendant had been advanced in the life[time] of his father. And the certainty did not appear in writing under his father's hand, which being a full advancement on his part and the seven years maintenance and clothing being of an uncertain value and, therefore, not to be brought into hotchpot, and so he likewise [was] fully advanced. It was decreed that the defendant should secure the £20 a year to the plaintiff and the residue of the personal estate should go according to the will.

It was urged that the acceptance of the £20 *per annum* was a bar to the plaintiff and the testator's saying that that should be a full satisfaction. But it seemed to be allowed that the father's declaring that he has or has not fully advanced a child signifies nothing.

*Sir Peter King* cited The Lord Delaware's Case,[1] where the question referred to the City was this, if a freeman dies having a wife and daughter married and has given the daughter several sums, the certainty of which appears under his hand, and that is not a full third, what share the daughter shall come in for. (I think that answer was an entire third of what the father left.)

Lord Keeper [LORD HARCOURT] asked whether that opinion was founded on any precedent.

And *Sir Peter King* answered that it was upon one in the time of Charles I.

Query whether the reason be because the wife and daughter cannot put into hotchpot.

[Other copies of this report: Lincoln's Inn MS. Misc. 383, p. 72, Lincoln's Inn MS. Misc. 106, p. 40.]

Lincoln's Inn MS. Misc. 10, p. 78

*Eodem die* [11 June 1711].

The bill was to have a share of the plaintiff's father's personal estate as one of his children by virtue of the custom of London.

It appeared that the father, by his will, had declared that he had fully advanced his son. It likewise appeared by several receipts that the father had paid for seven years' board for his son and also for a parcel of cloth for him.

And it was insisted on by *Sir Peter King* that, by this, the plaintiff was excluded from any share of his father's estate by the custom, for, he said, the custom was that, if a man [ *blank* ].[2]

---

[1] *Dean v. Lord Delaware* (1710), see above, Case No. 164.

[2] This report end here in mid-sentence.

## 253

## Massingberd v. Empson

(Ch. 1711)

*A defendant, who is a bona fide purchaser for value, must plead his title by a proper averment and not by a mere recital.*

Lincoln's Inn MS. Misc. 10, p. 79

The bill is for discovery of the defendant's title. The defendant pleads that, by an indenture dated etc. and made between A.B. of the one part and himself of the other part, reciting that the premises were vested in trustees by an act of Parliament, and that they demised to J.S., who assigned to A.B., and that he, being in possession, did by the said indenture for a valuable consideration assign to the defendant. And he denies notice of the plaintiff's title at or before the time of the assignment.

The plea was overruled because the defendant did not aver that the assignment to A.B. was really made nor set forth that assignment otherwise than by way of a recital.

British Library MS. Hargrave 80, f. 38v, pl. 1

[There was a] plea of a purchaser without notice antecedent to the agreement, conveyance, or payment of the purchase money, and then he sets forth a conveyance under which he claimed which recited the title to the time of conveyance all which he avers etc.

It was objected that, in the case of The Lord Conningsby and Bradshaw, the plea of a purchaser of a term without notice was overruled by Lord Cowper because he did not set forth all the mesne assignments to the person under whom he claimed by purchase. To this it was answered that the plea of a purchaser without notice was the most favored of any plea and, therefore, it was generally that J.S. being or pretending to be seised or possessed etc. conveyed etc. and that that was sufficient, that, in the case of Conningsby v. Bradshaw, there was an assignment of the term by one who was neither executor nor administrator of the lessee. And yet, I think, [it was] allowed that the *que* estate of a term had been allowed by the House of Lords upon a writ of error in respect of long building leases etc.

Lord Keeper [Harcourt]: The averment in this case is no more than that there was a conveyance with such a recital; he should have averred the matters recited. And he overruled the plea.

I think the plaintiffs came in as creditors.

[Other copies of this report: Lincoln's Inn MS. Misc. 383, p. 74, pl. 2, Lincoln's Inn MS. Misc. 106, p. 42.]

## 254

### Anonymous

(Ch. 1711)

*A question in this case was whether a defendant can plead for the first time a matter in abatement to an amended or supplemental bill.*

*A contempt of court can be pardoned, but not a final judgment.*

British Library MS. Hargrave 80, f. 38v, pl. 2

There was an original bill and answer and then a supplemental or amended bill charging a great deal of the same matter. The plea to the amended bill was that there was another suit depending for the same thing.

*Vernon*: A former suit depending was never pleaded in bar of an amended or supplemental bill, that being but one suit with the original bill, that he might have answered to the facts charged a second time in the amended bill, that he could make no other answer than he had made to the original bill.

Query whether the plea was not allowed because of the endless trouble and expense the defendant might be put to by answering to the same things several times.

The plea [was that he was] neither an executor nor administrator but [he] does not deny that he had possessed himself of any of the personal estate nor does [he] discover who is the executor or administrator, both which were prayed in the bill. The plea [was] overruled.

Lord Keeper [Lord Harcourt]: He may be an executor *de son tort*.

It was objected to a plea of excommunication that it was pardoned by the Act of Grace.[1] It was answered that it was *res judicata* and, therefore, not pardoned. But the plea was overruled because [it was] for contumacy only.

[Other copies of this report: Lincoln's Inn MS. Misc. 383, f. 75, pl. 1, Lincoln's Inn MS. Misc. 106, p. 43.]

## 255

### Anonymous

(Ch. 1711)

*A person cannot be compelled to accuse himself of a crime, but he can be compelled to accuse a third person.*

1 Stat. 7 Ann., c. 22 (*SR*, IX, 95–101).

British Library MS. Hargrave 80, f. 39, pl. 1

A bill [was exhibited] for the discovery of the drawing etc. of a lottery and whether the plaintiff was not entitled to the cost of £1000. The plea [was] that, by the [ *blank* ] of King William,[1] it was made penal to exercise, draw, etc. any private lottery and that no man was obliged to accuse himself of criminal matters. The plea was allowed.

But the same plea by two others against whom the bill was to discover what they knew in this case of a third person was overruled.

[Other copies of this report: Lincoln's Inn MS. Misc. 383, p. 75, pl. 2, Lincoln's Inn MS. Misc. 106, p. 44, pl. 1.]

## 256

## Bridges v. Rowe

(Ch. 1711)

*A cross-bill does not have to be officially served on the original plaintiff.*

British Library MS. Hargrave 80, f. 39, pl. 2

It was surmised that two of the plaintiffs in the original bill being made defendants to the cross-bill and being members in Parliament, the defendant had not been able to serve them.

*Vernon*: Our agents have been more cautious than they need have been in this case, for a cross-bill is but a kind of a defense.

[Other copies of this report: Lincoln's Inn MS. Misc. 383, p. 76, pl. 1.]

## 257

## Seymour v. Seymour

(Ch. 1711)

*Conditions to destroy estates must be taken strictly.*

*In this case, and heir was allowed to redeem against a second wife.*

Lincoln's Inn MS. Misc. 10, p. 111

Lady Seymour, widow of old Sir Edward Seymour v. Sir Edward Seymour, son and heir of old Sir Edward *et al.*

[1] Stat. 10 Will. III, c. 23 (*SR*, VII, 532–533).

Old Sir Edward Seymour,[1] in 1661, makes a settlement after marriage pursuant to marriage articles (recited in that settlement but not produced) whereby Sir Edward is made tenant in tail with remainders over. And he covenants with his wife's father that the estate was free from all encumbrances made or to be made by him. He, afterwards, suffers a common recovery and destroys this settlement. And now, the defendant insists that he ought to have a satisfaction out of his father's personal estate by virtue of the covenant to recompense him for being defeated of this estate, for, though a proviso that a tenant in tail shall not suffer a recovery is void, yet he may restrain himself by a covenant from suffering a recovery.

This was agreed to by the other side. But then it was said this was not the case. Old Sir Edward had not covenanted that he would not suffer a recovery but had only entered into the common covenant that the estate was free from encumbrances. Suppose he had limited the remainder in fee to his own right heirs and, afterwards, had devised away the reversion from his heir; might not the heir with as good a pretense have come and said that this was a breach of my father's covenant? No doubt but he might.

Lord Keeper [Lord Harcourt was] of the opinion that the suffering a recovery was no breach of the covenant.

There were other questions and resolutions in this case and, particularly, these two, *viz.* that, if a man, before marriage, articles to settle lands to the use of himself and his intended wife for their lives and, after, to the heirs male of their two bodies, this court will direct the settlement to be made so as to prevent the husband from defeating his issue, i.e., to the first and other sons in tail.

Where a man makes a voluntary settlement and, afterwards, sells for a valuable consideration and dies, the heir who claims under this settlement is entirely defeated at law and without a remedy there, neither can he have any assistance in this court to have a compensation out of his father's estate, even though the settlement had been left in the son's custody.

Note it was said by *Sir Thomas Powys* in this case that, if a man is a tenant in tail of a trust estate, even a feoffment or a bargain and sale enrolled, nay a lease and release by him, has been held by him to be a bar to the issue.

It was also said by Serjeant *Hooper* that, where a tenant for life joins with the remainderman in a fine or recovery and the remainderman only declares the uses, in this case, there will be a resulting use to the tenant for life.

So, if a woman joins with her husband in suffering a recovery, it is true the husband may declare the uses without his wife and it shall bind her unless she does some act to show her dissent, according to Beckwith's Case, 2 Co.[2]

---

[1] D. W. Hayton, 'Seymour, Sir Edward, fourth baronet (1633–1708)', *Dictionary of National Biography*, vol. 49, pp. 871–875.

[2] *Colgate v. Blithe* (1589), 2 Coke Rep. 56, 76 E.R. 541, also 4 Leonard 88, 74 E.R. 749, Moore K.B. 196, 72 E.R. 528, 1 Anderson 164, 123 E.R. 409, Gouldsborough 12,

British Library MS. Hargrave 80, f. 39, pl. 3

Sir Edward Seymour, in consideration of marriage and a £15,000 marriage portion, conveyed the manor of Mayden Bradly to the use of himself for life, remainder to his lady for life, remainder to the heirs male of Sir Edward on her body begotten etc. Afterwards, he prevails with his lady and the trustees to join in a fine and recovery to bar this settlement in order to mortgage it for £4000 upon a promise to resettle it to the uses in the first settlement mentioned, which was accordingly done.

On the death of his lady, Sir Edward, before marriage with his second, by lease and release, conveys the same manor to the use of himself for life, remainder to his lady for life, remainder to the heirs male of the body of Sir Edward on her begotten etc., whereby Sir Edward became tenant in tail. In this settlement, there was a power to make leases for three lives etc. and that, if Sir Edward or his heirs should within [ *blank* ] years, settle £1200 a year hereby agreed to be purchased *prout supra*, only £200 a year was to come immediately to the heir male of that marriage upon the death of Sir Edward, that upon such purchase and settlement, it should be lawful for Sir Edward to revoke etc. by any deed under his hand and seal and to limit other uses. Then he covenants that he has not encumbered, that the trustees stand lawfully seised in fee, that he has full power to make such settlement, and for quiet enjoyment, and further assurance within seven years, and that the £5000 portion should be paid to Lord Pawlet, the trustee, and by him applied towards purchasing the £1200 a year and the interest in the meantime to be paid Sir Edward and his assigns. The £5000 was afterwards paid to Sir Edward by Lord Pawlet. Sir Edward lived about thirty-two years after this settlement and died intestate possessed of a personal estate to the amount of £50,000. £2000 a year descended to the plaintiff, Sir Edward, under an old settlement and £1000 a year as heir to Sir Edward, his father, who purchased. The deed of settlement fell into the defendant's, the Lady Seymour's, hands.

And the plaintiff filed his bill two months after his father's death against the defendant and the children of the first and second marriages and the administrator of Sir Edward for a discovery and delivery of the deeds and to be admitted to redeem Mayden Bradly by selling £1200 a year and to have the £5000 and such further sum as would be necessary to purchase £1200 a year out of the personal estate to have the breaches of covenant in the resettlement satisfied and to have an account and distribution of the personal estate after debts paid etc.

As to the discovery and delivery of the deed after resettlement, the defendant, the Lady Seymour, pleaded that she was a purchaser without notice and for a valuable consideration, which plea was allowed. And, now, at the hearing, they proved their plea by producing and reading the second marriage settlement.

---

67, 75 E.R. 963, 999.

*Vernon*: There is no proof of notice. We are, therefore, to have the benefit of this settlement and, if any equity arises from any clause in that settlement, the plaintiff is entitled to it.

*Sir Joseph Jekyll*: The plaintiff is entitled to redeem both as heir and under his mother's marriage settlement in which there was a power of revocation, but it was with the consent of the plaintiff's mother, that it was necessary for the plaintiff's mother to join with Sir Edward in the fine and recovery, though Sir Edward was tenant in tail, she being entitled to a jointure under the first settlement, that she consenting upon a promise to resettle, and, the resettlement being made in pursuance of it, the resettlement was upon a valuable consideration, that Sir Edward having encumbered our estate by conveying to a purchaser without notice, satisfaction ought to be made out of his personal estate.

In Cherry's Case,[1] it was decreed that he that conveyed to a purchaser without notice should make satisfaction. A copy of the deed of resettlement was offered to be read, which was found amongst Sir Robert Clayton's papers, who was trustee to the first settlement and resettlement, corrected by his own hand. But the reading of it was opposed because the second marriage settlement was pleaded in bar of any former settlement, and that plea was allowed.

Lord Keeper [Lord Harcourt]: If the copy be allowed to be read, I am to have the same regard to it as to the deed itself, and that being on valuable consideration would defeat the second marriage settlement. But he said that the plea was a bar to the discovery only.

The other side urged that they might read it as against the administrator to prove themselves injured and entitled to satisfaction from the personal estate, though not as against the Lady, that the trustee was not before the court, therefore, they could have no decree for the land.

Lord Keeper [Lord Harcourt]: I will not receive any evidence of this kind. There is no proof that this is a true copy etc. Go to the point of redemption first; then, perhaps, you may ask for what is now prayed upon a legal evidence, whether there is not a redemption; the redemption is in Sir Edward or his heirs. And he being dead without having done any act to discharge that power, it is now in the heir. The cancelling his will in which he had devised this estate with the rest to his lady is a proof that he did not intend to hinder his eldest son of anything, the words of the deed and the intent of the parties let us into a redemption, and [there is] no prejudice to the defendant, the use being to Sir Edward for life, he not making a settlement in his lifetime is no prejudice to the defendant, and the heir comes immediately to redeem; so, [there is] no argument from the length of time. And Sir Edward received the £5000 subject to the trust; so that is no bar to the redemption.

---

[1] *Ferrars v. Cherry* (1700), 2 Vernon 383, 23 E.R. 845, 1 Eq. Cas. Abr. 3, 331, 21 E.R. 830, 1081, British Library MS. Hargrave 80, f. 89.

*How*: By the proviso, the estate is expressly redeemable, and an interest redeemable is always so until the equity of redemption is released or foreclosed.

*Mead*: The Lady Seymour might have had a bill to foreclose, and the vesting £5000 in trustees for purchasing etc. and reserving the interest only to Sir Edward and that only until a purchase made is a proof of a redeemable interest.

*Sir Thomas Powys* insisted, on the other side, that this was no equity of redemption, but a legal limitation, the old uses to cease and the new ones to rise as they may do by law, that springing uses to arise upon a contingency must be within a reasonable time, otherwise a perpetuity would ensue, that it must not go beyond lives in being, and that within [ *blank* ] years was within two years, and that it was entirely a legal question whether the uses in this case should arise and when and upon what terms.

*Hooper*: The power ought not to be perpetual nor the settlement always ambulatory what number fit to fill the blanks.

The Lord Keeper [Lord Harcourt]: A 'reasonable time' that conditions to destroy estates should be taken strictly, that, if all the former uses were to be void, then leases would be void, that Sir Edward having received the £5000 was a proof that he did not intend to purchase. The plaintiff pretends to an equitable lien on the estate. But where is the equity to take away the personal estate out of which the younger children are to be provided for in favor of the heir to whom £3000 *per annum* is descended?

*Ward*: The blank makes the time uncertain, therefore, void of [common] law, but that equity makes it a reasonable time, for that the clause of further assurance ought to be the measure, that this may carry it beyond the son born, and that the word 'agreed' did not make it compulsory.

*Vernon*: The term redemption is improper because [there was] no over-value nor penalty. But a power to settle an equivalent [is] no positive agreement to do it, nor could Sir Edward have been compelled to do it if his lady had exhibited her bill for that purpose. Sir Edward might have answered that he or his heirs might do it. Therefore, [it is] not compulsory for the benefit of the wife or the issue of that marriage, much less for that son of a former [marriage] and a stranger to that settlement. [He said] that, if Sir Edward had purchased, he had taken back an estate in fee or, if it had been in tail, he might have barred it, that the receipt of £5000 was a plain evidence he never designed to make a purchase, as well as the length of time. The heir now strives to make his ancestor a debtor for it, which he could not do if there was a covenant, and that, if he came in under the consideration of the settlement, it would be hard for an heir who has an equivalent by descent in fee to make his ancestor a debtor, and that here he was a mere volunteer.

*Cooper*: Whether it was a covenant or a power, it ought to be performed strictly and that neither was pursued, that the £5000 which ought to have remained with the trustees as a deposit until the purchase was not suffered to do so and that the receipt of it by Sir Edward was a determination of his power, that the power to Sir Edward to revoke by deed etc. and the limitation to Sir Edward for life was a plain evidence that the purchase was to be made during Sir Edward's life[time], that £200 *per annum* if there had been a purchase was to come immediately to Lord Conway on Sir Edward's death and that cannot now be done.

*Sir Joseph Jekyll* replied that the time for the execution of the deed was the time the parties first intended, that the blank left in the deed was an instance that the parties first designed to circumscribe and limit the time, but the not filling it at the time of the executing the deed was a waiver of that design, that a lease for years had been adjudged a lease for two years *ut res magis valeat* [*quam pereat*], but that the proviso here was good though no time [was] limited, that what was deposed by Hungerford, an evidence on the other side, *viz.* that Sir Edward said My Lady should piss in the parlour at Mayden Bradley as long as she lived, and his taking upon him to devise that estate by the will that he cancelled a little before his death was an evidence that he thought he had a power to control that settlement. But, however, this power arising from the settlement was not to be controlled by parol evidence nor destroyed by inferences from his receiving the £5000. To the length of time, he cited the case of Lloyd and Carew,[1] in the House of Lords; Sir Evan Lloyd, seised in fee, conveyed to the use of himself for life, remainder to his first son in tail male etc., remainder over, provided, if his heir should within two years after his dying without issue male pay the remainderman £2000, that then etc. And I think [it was] decreed for the heirs.

Lord Keeper [Lord Harcourt]: The defendants have proved their plea and ought to have the benefit of the marriage settlement. But there is a beneficial power in it of revoking in respect of Sir Edward and his heirs, for I cannot reject the word 'heirs'. The first question is whether that power is waived or not, the taking the £5000 goes the nearest to the waiving of it. But that does not seem to be a sufficient waiver. And what can be collected from the parol evidence is much less so. And, if [it is] not waived, the next question will be whether it was forfeited by so long a neglect. And, for that, the uses of the settlement are to be considered and when the heir came to redeem, that no time being limited, a reasonable time ought to be intended, and that that depended upon the uses and contingencies, since, had Sir Edward died quickly and a twenty years' neglect ensued, equity would not interpose, that, here, the heir came immediately after his father's death and the interest accrued to My Lady and though the marriage settlement intended an immediate provision, he came soon enough and was entitled to redeem.

It will make this more beneficial for My Lady. The settlement limits neither time nor place. Let the £1200 a year be purchased in as good a county as Mayden Bradly lies in and the purchase approved of by the Master and made within twelve months and upon those terms to redeem on payment of costs the common terms of a redemption. Otherwise, the bill is to be dismissed with costs.

---

[1] *Lloyd v. Carew* (1697), Shower P.C. 137, 1 E.R. 93, 1 Comyns 20, 92 E.R. 938, Precedents in Chancery 72, 106, 24 E.R. 35, 51, 1 Eq. Cas. Abr. 260, 21 E.R. 1032.

The plaintiff is not entitled to the surplus profits until he makes such conveyances. Let the lessees be quieted. And upon making such settlement, let My Lady produce upon oath all deeds and writing relating to the estate. I will reserve the consideration of what satisfaction the plaintiff shall have over from the personal estate otherwise than as heir until after the settlement.

*Pratt* insisted very much that the words 'hereby agreed to be purchased' imported a covenant and that that was a lien upon the personal estate, and, therefore, the heir, who, by Sir Edward's not having performed that covenant was now compellable to it, ought to have satisfaction for it out of the personal estate.

*How* said, if Mayden Bradly had fallen short in value and My Lady had exhibited her bill to compel the heir to settle £1200 a year, he would have been compelled to do it.

Lord Keeper [Lord Harcourt]: This is no obligation on Sir Edward or his heirs, but a beneficial power.

Upon an appeal to the House of Lords 2nd January 1711[/12],[1] Sir Edward Seymour's counsel insisted strongly to have the depositions of witnesses read who were present when the resettlement was read in the presence of Lady Seymour and swore to the uses of it and, likewise, to have the drafts of the resettlement read. They said that, in cases where a deed was got into the adversaries' hands, the courts of law allowed of parol evidence to prove the uses of that deed, that, in this very case, upon an ejectment brought by Sir Edward Seymour in the King's Bench,[2] the whole court allowed of this parol proof, but that the reason of their being nonsuited there was because the witnesses had forgotten the names of the trustees under whom they derived their legal title, though they remembered the uses of the deed, that what was evidence at law was so in equity.

The Lords were inclined to read the parol evidence and the draft if there should appear anything in their evidence that should lead them to it. But this was prevented by a proposal made by the House of Lords to Sir Edward Seymour which was [ *blank* ].

[Other copies of this report: Lincoln's Inn MS. Misc. 383, p. 76, pl. 2.]

2 Comyns 453, 92 E.R. 1156

Sir Edward Seymour died on the 18th of February 1708. A little before his death, he sent for his will out of his scrutoire [and], in the presence of several persons, cancelled it, and said 'I cancel my will', and desired them to bear witness of it. And, on the next day, he told his physician that he was hot in his body, but easy at his heart. And this was looked upon as a sufficient cancelling of the other duplicate that he had not by him.

[Other reports of this case: 5 Brown P.C. 106, 2 E.R. 563.]

---

1 *Seymour v. Seymour* (1712), 5 Brown P.C. 105, 2 E.R. 563.

2 *Seymour's Case* (1710), 10 Modern 8, 88 E.R. 600.

## 258

## Anonymous v. Richardson

(Ch. 1711)

*Where a purchaser with notice of an equity of redemption redeems the mortgage, he must also pay a rent charge on the land that was made subsequent to the mortgage.*

British Library MS. Hargrave 80, f. 43, pl. 1

A mortgagor devises £10 *per annum* out of the mortgaged premises to J.S. The mortgagee purchases the rent in the name of trustees. This rent is an equitable charge remediless at law. But a purchaser of the equity of redemption under the will and consequently with notice shall not redeem without payment of this rent.

[Other copies of this report: Lincoln's Inn MS. Misc. 383, p. 84, pl. 1, Lincoln's Inn MS. Misc. 106, p. 44, pl. 1.]

## 259

## Rawlinson v. Storeby

(Ch. 1711)

*A court of equity will not enforce a devise upon a condition precedent without evidence that the condition has been performed.*

British Library MS. Hargrave 80, f. 43, pl. 2

[There was a] devise to A. and B. in trust for C. and D. 'until some one of my nephew E.'s sons shall within seven years conform to and profess the Protestant religion according to the usage of the Church of England and shall be confirmed by the bishop and that then the trustees should convey to such son and the heirs of his body, remainder etc., so as my estate come not to the hands of a dissenter.' The testator died in 1699, the plaintiff's nephew's eldest son being nine years old. The plaintiff was christened in 1704 and confirmed in 1705 but did not receive the Sacrament within the seven years. The bill was for a conveyance. And it was decreed for the plaintiff by Lord Cowper. But it was directed by the decree that the plaintiff should bring proof of his having received the Sacrament since he came of age.

Upon a rehearing, it was urged that this was supplying evidence after the hearing, contrary to the course of the court. But it was replied that this was only for the greater satisfaction of the court and not absolutely necessary.

It was urged for the defendant that the estate was devised on a condition precedent, which, though in a case of infancy, must be strictly performed and that the plaintiff not having received the Sacrament within the seven years had not properly conformed etc. and, consequently, had not performed the condition.

On the other side, it was said that equity often relieved against forfeitures and dispensed with time and that the plaintiff had conformed as far as any do at his age and, therefore, as far as the testator could intend he should within the seven years.

Lord Keeper [LORD HARCOURT] declared his opinion that he had sufficiently conformed within the seven years in respect of his age. But, in regard of the clause 'so as' etc., it being the intent of the testator that his estate should never come into the hands of a dissenter, he directed a commission to examine whether he had constantly continued to conform since the seven years and received the Sacrament when it could be expected from him and never returned to the Quakers or any other meeting before he would decree the conveyance to be made.

[Other copies of this report: Lincoln's Inn MS. Misc. 383, p. 84, pl. 2, Lincoln's Inn MS. Misc. 106, p. 44, pl. 2.]

## 260

## Grammar v. Grammar

(Ch. 1711)

*Where a husband receives money or timber that belongs to his wife for her separate use, he must account for it to her or to her executor.*

British Library MS. Hargrave 80, f. 43v, pl. 1

*Vernon*: If a wife that has a power to have annual profits to her separate use cohabits with her husband and they live upon their joint stock, equity will oblige the husband to account. [It is] otherwise where there is a covenant that she shall receive a gross sum etc.

In this case, the wife had a power to cut wood upon her jointure lands by her first husband and covenanted upon her second marriage to have that *inter alia* to her separate use during coverture. The husband cut the wood with her privity and without opposition from her.

And [it was] urged by *Sir Thomas Powys* that she might assign by parol.

*Vernon*: Had you but a parol gift, it would be good. But her standing by and seeing her husband cut the wood is no waiver of it. She might consent to the sale. But did she consent that her husband should have the money?

An account for the wood was decreed and that the assets in the executor's hands should be accounted for according to the real value, not according to inventory.

[Other copies of this report: Lincoln's Inn MS. Misc. 383, f. 85, pl. 1, Lincoln's Inn MS. Misc. 106, p. 46, pl. 1.]

## 261

## Anonymous

(Ch. 1711)

*Upon an account, a mortgagee in possession shall be credited with repairs and improvements and debited for profits received.*

British Library MS. Hargrave 80, f. 44v, pl. 1

A mortgagee, upon an account, shall have all just allowances within which are included repairs and lasting improvements and interest for gross sums laid out on such improvements. On the other hand, he shall account for all profits received or which he might have received without his own willful default.

[Other copies of this report: Lincoln's Inn MS. Misc. 383, p. 86, Lincoln's Inn MS. Misc. 106, p. 46, pl. 2.]

## 262

## Anonymous

(Ch. 1711)

*In this case, it was argued that a plaintiff can dismiss his own case upon paying costs unless the defendant shows that the evidence will confirm his, the defendant's, title.*

British Library MS. Hargrave 80, f. 44v, pl. 2

[It was] urged by *Vernon* that a plaintiff may at any time dismiss his own bill with costs before or after issue joined or publication passed, unless where the defendant apprehends that something will arise on the evidence which will corroborate his title. And, if the plaintiff makes default at the hearing, there can be no more than a dismission with costs decreed.

[Other copies of this report: Lincoln's Inn MS. Misc. 383, p. 87, pl. 1, Lincoln's Inn MS. Misc. 106, p. 47, pl. 1.]

## 263

## Lord Portland's Case

(Ch. 1711)

*The question in this case was whether a court of equity can make a personal order to enforce a right according to foreign law.*

British Library MS. Hargrave 80, f. 44v, pl. 3

A motion was [made] for an injunction to stay the younger children's proceedings in Holland for part of their father's personal estate, which they claimed under his marriage settlement by the laws of Holland, upon a surmise that he had given them £10,000 by his will, which was intended in satisfaction of that claim and not as an additional provision.

*Sir Joseph Jekyll* cited a case where it was ruled that this court may take cognizance of contracts made in Holland and of the laws there.

Lord Keeper [Lord Harcourt] put him in mind of the Case of Sir John Grey, in the House of Lords, to the same purpose, which point seemed to be agreed.

*Sir Joseph Jekyll* said that, the parties' living here, it was proper to bind their consciences by an injunction.

I think it was denied in this case, the defendants' not being in contempt nor having prayed time to answer and, therefore, the motion was too early though the whole matter had arisen within the jurisdiction of the court.

[Other copies of this report: Lincoln's Inn MS. Misc. 383, p. 87, pl. 2, Lincoln's Inn MS. Misc. 106, p. 47, pl. 2.]

## 264

## Anonymous

(Ch. 1711)

*In this case, the court of equity gave directions to the executor of a decedent's estate as to its proper administration.*

British Library MS. Hargrave 80, f. 45

J.S., seised of freehold and copyhold lands, surrenders part of the copyhold lands to the use of his will. The residue descends to the defendant as heir at law for want of a surrender. And being also possessed of a great personal estate, he devised £100 *per annum* to his wife in satisfaction of her jointure to be paid by his executors provided she surrendered etc. and that, in default of payment etc., all his lands should be liable to be entered upon to raise it. He devised part of his lands to the defendant, amongst which were the jointure lands. He devised likewise £7 a year to charitable uses forever and that the devisees of the charity, upon failure of payment by his executors or their heirs, might enter upon all the lands except those devised to the defendant. And he made the plaintiffs his executors and residuary legatees of his real and personal estate after all his debts and legacies [be] paid.

It was urged that the personal estate was perishable and, therefore, not a proper fund for the payment of the annuity for life, much less of the charity, which was to endure forever, and that, in case of a charity, equity would supply the defect of a surrender and that the clause of entry made the annuity a charge on this land.

It was decreed that the personal estate should first be applied and, if that proved insufficient, the freehold devised to the executors to come in aid and, if that was likewise deficient, then the defendant's lands [are] to be liable to the £100 a year in regard of the general clause of the entry.

As to the charity, if the personal and real estate devised to the executors proved insufficient, such copyhold as was not surrendered [is] to come in aid, but in the last place. All parties [are] to have their costs out of this personal estate.

[Other copies of this report: Lincoln's Inn MS. Misc. 383, p. 87, pl. 3, Lincoln's Inn MS. Misc. 106, p. 48.]

## 265

## Anonymous

(Ch. 1711)

*A devise of the profits of land is the same thing as a devise of the land itself.*

*A legacy of a sum certain in gold must be paid in gold even though the testator did not have so much gold in his possession at his death.*

British Library MS. Hargrave 80, f. 45v, pl. 1

A. devised the produce of £200 East India stock to B. for life, remainder to C. in tail, and, for want of such issue, the stock to the plaintiff. B. died; C. died without issue, and the plaintiff procured a transfer of the stock to himself from the person that had the legal interest.

*How*: In common cases, the limitation of a chattel in tail with remainder over, the remainder over is void. But, here, the interest only is devised, which may vary it from those cases.

*Hooper*: Such an invention would make a perpetuity.

Lord Keeper [Lord Harcourt]: The devise of land or the profits of land is the same thing. And that point was decreed clearly against the plaintiff.

In the same case, there was £100 in gold devised to the husband and wife for the life of the wife and, after her death, £50 of it to the plaintiff and the other £50 after the death of the husband; the wife was dead.

Lord Keeper [Lord Harcourt] decreed 50 guineas to the plaintiff immediately and another 50 after her husband's death.

*Cowper*: If a tender was to be made of the £100 in gold, it must be of 100 guineas; otherwise, it would not be good.

But there not being so much among the testator's effects, *Hooper* insisted that the legatees could have no more than was found.

But that was overruled, and it was said the executors must pay it in gold.

[Other copies of this report: Lincoln's Inn MS. Misc. 383, p. 88, Lincoln's Inn MS. Misc. 106, p. 49.]

## 266

## Anonymous

(Ch. 1711)

*A bill in equity to decide a right to enclose a common lies in order to prevent a multiplicity of actions a common law.*

British Library MS. Hargrave 80, f. 45v, pl. 2

A bill [was exhibited] by commoners to be quieted in the enjoyment of their right of common and to prevent the enclosure of it. And [there was] a cross-bill by the terre tenants to be permitted to make up the fences and to be quieted in their separate right in that part of the waste exclusive of the commoners.

Lord Keeper [Lord Harcourt] seemed inclinable to dismiss both bills for want of equity, right of common being properly triable at law.

But it was said that they came here to prevent multiplicity of suits. And by the agreement of both parties, proper issues were directed to try the right of common.

[Other copies of this report: Lincoln's Inn MS. Misc. 383, p. 89, pl. 1, Lincoln's Inn MS. Misc. 106, p. 50, pl. 1.]

## 267

## Countess of Derby v. Earl of Derby

(Ch. 1711)

*In this case, following an issue out of Chancery to a jury, the court of equity decreed quiet possession to the plaintiff of her jointure lands.*

British Library MS. Hargrave 80, f. 46

Lady Derby v. Lord Derby and the heirs general of Lord Derby, her husband.

The case was Lord Derby had brought an [action of] ejectment against Lady Derby for several lands comprised in her jointure and had a verdict in the country.

My Lady brought her bill to be quieted in the possession of her jointure lands and to have satisfaction for such lands as were legally evicted from her out of other lands whereof she was dowable according to the 27th Hen. VIII.[1] And

[1] Stat. 27 Hen. VIII, c. 10, s. 5 (*SR*, III, 541).

the court having directed an issue [to] the Common Bench for a trial of the power of the late Lord Darby to make a jointure of part of the land recovered by the present Lord Darby in the ejectment and that being found for My Lady, she now moved the court upon the equity reserved for an injunction to put her into possession and to be quieted therein.

*Hooper*: In the case of My Lord Bath v. Sherwin,[1] this court would not decree possession after five verdicts, though, upon an appeal to the House of Lords, they did, that there was no trust but a title merely triable at law, that here was no lease to cover the estate, in which case, Chancery would only remove the impediment and leave them to their remedy by [an action of] ejectment with directions that the lease should not be insisted on, that the common law would not hinder any man from bringing as many ejectments as he pleased, and that this court never interposed, that, if it should be decreed that My Lady should be quieted in possession, that would not give her a power to enter; she must bring her action.

*Sir Thomas Powys* replied that none of the issues in the case of the Lord Bath and Sherwin were directed by this court and that, in the case of the Town of New Castle and the Church of Durham,[2] possession was decreed; the question was merely at law, that, in My Lord Gerrard's Case, the court allowed one trial more but upon a proviso it should be had within a year, that My Lady having a power to make leases and My Lord having deterred the tenants from taking any was a proper ground of equity in this case.

Lord Keeper [Lord Harcourt] decreed possession to My Lady and that the tenants should attorn and that My Lord should account for the profits from the time of his entry. He cited the case of Sir Harry Parker and Mr. Stillingfleet,[3] where Mr. Stillingfleet obtained a verdict, brought an action of trespass for that mesne profits, and, afterwards, Sir Harry getting a verdict, brought [an action of] trespass for the mesne profits since Mr. Stillingfleet's recovery and for the profits recovered by him in his action of trespass, and, though he did not prevail below, he did upon an appeal to the House of Lords.

Serjeant *Hooper*: No action will lie at law for mesne profits but from the time of entry or delivery of a declaration in ejectment.

My Lord [Lord Harcourt] decreed further that My Lady should be quieted in possession against everything but actions and that, if any action was brought, My Lady should have liberty to apply to the court in what manner that trial should be directed. And My Lord declared he would never derogate so far from a trial at bar as to have the same tried again at the assizes.

My Lord Keeper [Lord Harcourt] varied the last part of this decree, a precedent in Queen Elizabeth's time being produced, where possession was decreed, as here, by the then Lord Keeper or Chancellor assisted by Wray and

---

1 *Earl of Bath v. Sherwin* (1706–1709), see above, Case No. 50.

2 *Dean etc. of Durham v. Town of Newcastle* (1698), Colles 18, 1 E.R. 159.

3 *Parker v. Stillingfleet* (1703), Colles 337, 1 E.R. 314, 6 Modern 248, 87 E.R. 995.

Gawdy, and, agreeable to that precedent, he ordered that My Lord should apply to the court before he brought any action or made any entry or distress.

[Other copies of this report: Lincoln's Inn MS. Misc. 383, p. 89, pl. 2, Lincoln's Inn MS. Misc. 106, p. 50, pl. 2.]

[Other reports of this case: 2 Vernon 666, 23 E.R. 1034.]

## 268

## Norwich v. Adams

(Ch. 1711)

*In this case, the court of equity ordered the redemption of a mortgage and reserved judgment as to the distribution of the redemption money to await further developments.*

*A party who acts in bad faith during the course of the litigation will not be awarded court costs.*

British Library MS. Hargrave 80, f. 46v

Sir Erasmus Norwich *et ux.* v. Sir Charles Adams *et ux. et al.*

A bill was [exhibited] to redeem and to have the several defendants set forth their titles and to have the direction of the court to whom the redemption money was to be paid etc.

Adams, grandfather of My Lady Norwich, mortgaged the estate in question for £4000, and, after his death, Sir Thomas, his son, joined with the mortgagee in an assignment of the mortgaged term to Chief Baron Atkyns and Chief Baron Ward as a security for £6000 and conveyed the inheritance to trustees as a further security. Upon his death, Sir Charles, his younger brother, entered upon the mortgaged lands under pretense of an entail and continued in the receipt of the profits four years and a half, the Lady Norwich being heir to Sir Thomas and all that time an infant. The mortgaged term came by mesne assignments to My Lady Rolls, and the inheritance came to her trustees.

It was pretended that it was assigned to her as a security for £6500 and that Sir Charles, who was then in possession, joined in the assignment.

On the other hand, it was suggested that there was an endorsement of defeasance in that deed that, upon payment of £6000 and interest, etc.

After this, Sir Charles, marrying a daughter of My Lady Rolls, made a settlement of the lands in question to the use of himself for life etc. and created a term for raising £100 *per annum* for his intended wife's separate use during coverture and £500 a year for her jointure with remainders to the issues of that marriage and, in consideration of that settlement and of the marriage, Lady Rolls conveyed the mortgaged term to trustees in trust as to £5000 to the several uses in the settlement. A year and a half after Sir Charles' marriage, he, discovering his want of title, went beyond the sea, where he now is. And Lady Norwich was let into possession and now came to redeem. There were strong presumptions of Sir Charles' forging deeds to make out his title, but no positive proof.

The chief question was whether, since Sir Charles Adams was become entitled to the mortgage as to £5000, the profits received by him both before he was entitled to the mortgage money as a wrong-doer and after, when he was in possession by the consent of the mortgagee, should go in discharge of the £5000 principal and the interest due for the same *pro tanto.*

It was strongly insisted by *Sir Thomas Powys, How,* and *Mead* that, since the £5000 was not assigned to Sir Charles Adams but to trustees and had not yet been received by him, [it] was under the power of the court and, since Sir Charles had made a fraudulent settlement, which proved void, and the assignment of the £5000 was made in consideration of that settlement, that the equity of it would result to the Lady, who was thus defrauded, and, though the heir had a right to defeat her of her jointure, that this court would not suffer the heir to have any benefit of her portion, that, if one who had a mortgaged term contracted for the purchase of the inheritance and assigned his term to trustees in part of the purchase money and then the purchase was defeated, equity would give him back his term again.

*Vernon*: A purchaser without notice may fence against a latent encumbrance and get in a prior title to protect him[self] but not against heirship when an heir has been beyond the seas several years and a stranger who knows nothing of him purchases of the person in possession and then the heir returns, he cannot defend himself against the heir as purchasing without notice (*caveat emptor*); he ought to have informed himself better.

[He said] that, in many cases, an assignment to trustees was the same thing as to the party himself because the trustees cannot part with it without a breach of trust, that it was decreed by Wright that an old term taken in by a purchaser in the name of trustees should defend him, that, therefore, in this case, the assignment to trustees was the same as to Charles himself.

It was decreed that all the profits received by Sir Charles should go in discount of the £5000 and interest and that the rest should be brought before a Master to be put out for My Lady Adams' separate use during coverture etc.

It was reserved to the court what should be done with it after the death of Sir Charles or My Lady, when it would appear to the court who survived and whether there was any issue which were intended to be provided for by the settlement.

Lady Adams had no costs, she having confessed by her answer that she had destroyed the deeds supposed to be forged by her husband, being not obliged to discover anything to the prejudice of her husband.

Lady Rolls, though a mortgagee, had none because she did not produce the assignment of the mortgaged term to her, upon which it was suggested there was endorsed a defeasance to My Lady's disadvantage and which was necessary in the chain of the title, though she swore by her answer she did not know where to find it. She had put in four or five answers before they could get a sufficient one.

[Other copies of this report: Lincoln's Inn MS. Misc. 383, p. 91, Lincoln's Inn MS. Misc. 106, p. 53.]

## 269

## Copley v. Copley

(Ch. 1711)

*In this case, a daughter was not allowed to have both provisions for her portion, but she was required to elect one.*

*Where only a house is devised and the use of the goods and furniture, the words 'good and furniture' refer only to such goods and furniture as are necessary for the house and do not refer to farm implements.*

*By a bequest of 'household goods and furniture', prints will pass as part of the furniture, but prints in boxes which had never been hung up and books will not.*

British Library MS. Hargrave 80, f. 48

Lionel Copley *et al.* v. Lady Copley and the daughter and heir of Sir Godfrey Copley.

G. Copley, the grandfather, conveyed divers lands to the use of himself in tail, remainder to his son, Sir Godfrey, for life, remainder to himself in fee, provided that both he and all other persons who should be seised under that settlement should stand seised in trust to raise £5000 for the daughter or daughters of Sir Godfrey payable a year after age or marriage in case of failure of issue male who was not then married. This settlement was made in pursuance of the grandfather's marriage settlement that had been accidentally burned. After the grandfather's death, the estate tail descended on Sir Godfrey, who levied a fine and settled the same with other lands upon and in consideration of an intended marriage in trust *inter alia* upon default of issue male to raise £8000 for the daughter or daughters of that marriage payable at eighteen or day of marriage and, in the meantime, £40 *per annum* for maintenance until twelve and, afterwards, £100 a year until the portion became payable. And he covenanted that his estate was free from encumbrances. That lady died, and only one daughter of six of that marriage survived.

Sir Godfrey made another settlement on a second marriage with the defendant, the Lady Copley, and died without any issue by her. And, by his will drawn and written by himself, speaking honorably of his first lady and expressing himself very affectionately as to her children and reciting that there was but one of them left alive, he devised his estate to trustees in trust for the plaintiff, who was a very remote, if any, relation, in tail, remainder to this daughter for life, remainder to her first and every other son in tail, with several remainders over, and that she should have £8000 for her portion, £4000 to be paid at eighteen or her marriage and the other £4000 a year after marriage and, at furthest, the whole

£8000 at twenty-one and, for her maintenance, he gave £80 *per annum* until twelve, £100 from thence until fifteen, and £150 from then until eighteen, and then £200 for life. He gave My Lady likewise several bequests by his will. And Mr. Copley and the trustees brought this bill to have the direction of the court in the execution of the trusts etc.

The daughter sets forth the several settlements and the will in her answer and brought a cross-bill to have the benefit of the three provisions.

*Sir Joseph Jekyll*: The £5000 was an equitable lien on the estate not barred by the fine, that the second settlement was not voluntary, and that the daughter, being a purchaser under the settlement, there is no ground to say that the £8000 should go in satisfaction of the £5000, that they were given by different ancestors and payable at different times, that one was certain, the other contingent, the £8000 being payable at eighteen if married but not until twenty-one if not married, that the will ought to have the most beneficial construction for the young lady, she being an infant and a disinherited heir and the estate given to one who was scarce a relation, that the honorable mention of the first lady's merit and the concern he expressed that her children were reduced to one was an idle apparatus if he intended to give her nothing more than she had before, that of £8000 given her by the will, there was £4000 of it payable at eighteen if married.

*Hooper*: What the law gives us equity will not take away. The £5000 is a lien upon the estate, the proviso extending to all the limitations. The first settlement extended to daughters of any marriage, the second to daughters only of the first marriage and it could not, therefore, be any bar to daughters of the former, for the daughters of the second lady would come in for a share of the £5000. And, if the first settlement were admitted to be voluntary, yet, he that made it being dead, his heir could not avoid it.

*Peere Williams*: Where one that is indebted for £100 to another gives him £100 by his will, it has been held that the £100 devised should be in satisfaction of the debt, though it seems unreasonable to interpret giving £100 so as to make it the same thing as giving nothing. However, there is no reason to extend that case.

In this, it is hard that the will should be good against the heir and signify nothing for her. The fine is so far from being a bar to the £5000 that it amends our case. It was adjudged in the King's Bench, in the case of Symmons and Cudmen,[1] that, if a tenant in tail, remainder to a tenant in tail in fee, levies a fine, that bars the estate tail and brings the remainder in fee into possession for, as it was termed by others, [it] consolidates the estate, but that a recovery has a

[1] *Symons v. Cudmore* (1691–1693), 1 Salkeld 338, 91 E.R. 296, 2 Salkeld 619, 91 E.R. 524, 3 Salkeld 335, 91 E.R. 857, 1 Shower K.B. 370, 89 E.R. 646, 12 Modern 32, 88 E.R. 1145, 1 Freeman 503, 89 E.R. 379, Skinner 284, 317, 328, 90 E.R. 128, 142, 146, 4 Modern 1, 87 E.R. 226, Carthew 257, 90 E.R. 753, Holt K.B. 666, 90 E.R. 1268, Dodd 100, 127.

different effect, for that bars the remainders and reversions and derives a new fee out of the estate tail. If the son be a tenant in tail and the reversion in fee [is] in the father and he encumbers the reversion in fee by judgments and die and the reversion descends to the son and he levies a fine, this lets the reversioner into possession and lets in all encumbrances immediately.

There were some endeavors to read parol evidence that Sir Godfrey Copley intended what he gave by his will as an additional provision. And it was insisted that they were in the nature of a construction and that it was not to prove what should or should not pass by the will but whether that which did pass should be a bar or not to a former provision.

But the reading of the parol proof was overruled.

The word 'portion' is carried through the settlements and wills. They all speak *ad idem*. This case, therefore, is stronger than that of the £100 debt and the devise of £100 to the creditor. And were there no will in this case, the young lady would only have an election which of the settlements she would abide by.

Solicitor General [*Raymond*]: The second settlement comprised the same lands among others with the first. There is no notice taken in the second of the £5000 charged by the first, and the covenant that the estate was free from encumbrances is an evidence that it was the intention of the parties to the second settlement that the £8000 should be a satisfaction for the £5000.

*Vernon*: The young lady may elect which of the portions she pleases. But it was equally the intention of the parties to the second settlement that they to whom the estate is there limited should take it chargeable with the £8000 only, as it was that she should have £8000 and they equally purchasers with her. The case of Kemys and Thomas[1] was much stronger than this here. The same lands are included in both settlements, but, there, £5000 was secured by the settlement of lands in one county for a daughter's portion and afterwards by a second settlement of lands in another county, £5000 was likewise provided to be raised for a daughter's portion. The portions were made payable at different times, one at sixteen, the other at eighteen, and the maintenance provided by the settlements [were] different, but it was decreed that she should have her election only, and that was confirmed upon an appeal.

*Mead*: The engagement to pay £5000 is sufficiently answered by the second settlement. The will has provided an equivalent for the Lady Copley's jointure and likewise for the £8000 portion.

*Sir Joseph Jekyll*: They do not say that the £8000 is a bar to the £5000, but that she shall be driven to her election. There is not the same latitude for intendment in a deed as there is in a will. Is there anything expressed in the deed to support the intendment they labor for? Not a word. Suppose Sir Godfrey had a daughter to his second lady, should she have taken the £5000 and have driven this young

[1] *Thomas v. Kemeys* (1696–1700), 2 Vernon 348, 23 E.R. 821, 2 Freeman 207, 22 E.R. 1163, Colles 112, 1 E.R. 206, 1 Eq. Cas. Abr. 269, 21 E.R. 1038.

lady to have resorted to this £8000 or should there have been fractions? Here is nobody that contends with us who could claim under the second settlement. The plaintiff's title is under the old reversion in fee. In the Case of Kemys and Thomas, the second settlement was voluntary. Here, we are purchasers; there, both settlements were made by one person; here by different. And he concluded with showing the danger of intendments.

Lord Keeper [Lord Harcourt]: There are three provisions. She shall have the best, but, however, but one. And it is yet uncertain which will prove the best. The £5000 cannot be raised without the aid of this court. I must, therefore, consider the intention of the parties and how far it has been answered. The intent of the first settlement was to provide for daughters; the second betters the provision. It might, indeed, have happened that the £5000 might have been the best. But shall a daughter of that marriage so much advanced by the second settlement come here to demand both? She cannot have both without the assistance of this court. Shall I give my assistance contrary to the intention of the parties? It is most apparent that what Sir Godfrey gave in his will was designed to be an entire provision. And since that is the best, if she live until twenty-one, I decree that to her unless cause [be shown]. If she die before twenty-one, her representatives may apply to the court for either of the other two provisions.

Sir Godfrey had purchased some lands after making his will and, by a codicil, in which he took notice of his will and appointed it should be taken as part of his will, he revoked a legacy given to his lady by the will and gave her another in lieu of it. Rolle 618[1] was cited to prove this a republication of the will. And it seemed to be agreed that, even since the Statute of Frauds and Perjuries,[2] if he had used the words 'ratify and confirm' or 'republish my will' in the codicil, that this had been a sufficient republication.

But it was said by *Sir Joseph Jekyll* that, in this case, the appointing the codicil to be part of the will was idle, it being no more than the law would have said and, therefore, of no effect, that the reason why, where a codicil is annexed to a will and published, the publication of that is a publication of the will is because the one cannot be published without it. (*Quaere.*) He relied upon Litton's Case[3] as a case directly in point, and it was decreed accordingly that this was no republication of the will and that neither the purchased lands nor some copyhold lands which were not surrendered to the use of the will could pass by the will.

Sir Godfrey devised all his lands etc. to trustees in trust that they should permit his lady to receive all the rents, issues, and profits and all the royalties and chief rents of all his lands and tenements in or belonging to Sprodborough or Newton. Sprodborough was a vill, a manor, and a parish, and Newton and Lately were likewise vills and a part of the manor and parish of Sprodborough. And the

1 *Beckford v. Parnacott* (1596), 1 Rolle, Abr., *Devise*, p. 618, pl. Z, 8.

2 Stat..29 Car. II, c. 3, ss. 5, 6 (*SR*, V, 840).

3 *Litten v. Lady Falkland* (Ch. 1708), see above, Case No. 107.

question was whether lands in Lately should pass by this devise. And it was insisted that they should, chiefly upon account of the words 'royalties' and 'belonging to Sprodborough' and that this being in the case of a will and of a declaration of a trust ought to have a beneficial construction.

But [it was] ruled by Lord Keeper [Lord Harcourt] that they did not pass. The lands in Sprodborough and Newton, which did pass, were £1000 *per annum*, and the jointure they were given in satisfaction of was but £600 a year.

It was likewise decreed that she should have the corn growing on the lands at the death of Sir Godfrey.

Attorney General [*Northey*] said it had been often adjudged that an executor shall have the growing corn against an heir but not against a devisee of the land, for, in that case, the land is given in the state it is in.

It was further decreed that, by a devise of all the goods and furniture at Sprodborough to the lady, implements of husbandry should pass because the lands there were bequeathed to her with a restriction not to fell timber except for husbandry. But, where a house only is devised and the use of the goods and furniture, there those words carry no more than such goods and furniture as are necessary for the house.

It was directed that a schedule and appraisement should be made of all the goods and furniture there and that My Lady should enter into a covenant to restore them without any other damage than by the reasonable use thereof, wear and tear, and inevitable accidents only excepted, and that the schedule should be annexed to the covenant and that, in case the executors refused to make such an inventory, it should be done by two to be named by My Lady and as many by the plaintiff.

Manure also remaining in the yard at the testator's death was allowed to pass.

It was further decreed that, by the devise of all his household goods, plate, jewels, and furniture at, in, or belonging to his house in Red Lion Square, plate that had been formerly used there and had lain in Mr. Mead's, the goldsmith's, hands for three years before the testator's death, during which time Sir Godfrey had often lived in town, should not pass, but, if it had been sent there for securing it at Sir Godfrey's going out of town and been there at this death on that account, the court seemed to hold that it should have passed and that is the same thing as being in the house. Prints were ruled to pass as part of the furniture, but prints in boxes which had never been hung up and books were not allowed to pass, and some five pieces that Sir Godfrey had presented My Lady in his lifetime were ruled to belong to the executors, a married woman having nothing of her own not [ . . . ] her dowry.

It was further decreed that the personal estate devised to Lady Copley for life and which was in suspense during her life should after her death go to the person to whom the inheritance should then belong in regard the land was devised to come in aid of the personal estate if that proved deficient for the purposes of the will. The reversion, therefore, of the personal estate ought first to be sold and applied before any part of the land comes in and but, that reversion being more beneficial to be kept than sold, it was reasonable that benefit should accrue to the owner of the land, whose burden was increased by keeping it unsold.

*Sir Joseph Jekyll* said in this case that, where, by the will, the land was devised to A.B. in trust for the plaintiff and the heirs male of his body, remainder in trust for the young lady for life, remainder in trust for her first etc. sons in tail, that the whole legal estate being in trustees would preserve the contingent remainders though there was not a particular limitation for that purpose after the estate for life but that, however, the plaintiff being tenant in tail might bar the estate tail and remainders.

Lord Keeper Wright said that, if a trustee for the preserving contingent remainders joined with the tenant for life to destroy those remainders, that he would make no scruple to set aside such a conveyance. And the Lord Keeper [was] much to the purpose. But no case has yet been adjudged in point.

Note that, in the case of Kemys and Thomas, the lands on which the £5000 were secured were different, that they were made payable at different times, and that the maintenances were different.

In Copley's Case, the ancestors who made the settlement were different, the persons to whom [it was] payable might have been different, the £5000 to daughters of any marriage, the £8000 to the daughters of the first marriage, the £5000 was payable a year after age at farthest, sooner if married, the £8000 [was] not payable at all until marriage and the £8000 was also payable by the will in a different manner from either, *viz.* £4000 at eighteen and marriage, the other £4000 a year after marriage, and the whole £8000 at twenty-one at farthest. The maintenance also given by the second settlement and by the will were different and yet, in both cases, but one fortune [was] decreed.

[Other copies of this report: Lincoln's Inn MS. Misc. 383, p. 94.]

[Other reports of this case: 1 Peere Williams 147, 24 E.R. 333, 2 Eq. Cas. Abr. 639, 22 E.R. 536.]

## 270

## Anonymous

(Ch. 1711)

*A sheriff is liable for an excessive levy upon an execution, but not the judgment creditor.*

*An undervaluing of goods taken in execution must be proved by clear and convincing evidence.*

British Library MS. Hargrave 80, f. 53

If a sheriff or his officers take several goods in execution and make a bill of sale of part to the person at whose suit etc. and thereby satisfy his debt, the party whose goods are taken may maintain [actions of] trover or trespass for the residue against the sheriff, but can have no remedy for them against the person at whose suit etc., they never coming to his hand.

In a case of manifest oppression in undervaluing the goods, equity will let in the party aggrieved to prove the real value. In a case of that nature, on positive evidence of the price at which the goods were sold and of how much he believed them to be the worse for wearing was allowed by the master as a sufficient proof of the value against appraisement and an exception taken to the report on that head was disallowed, the plaintiff, after the goods were taken in execution not having any means to come at them and show them to anybody to prove the value and the defendant at whose suit they were taken and to whom sold not having produced one witness to prove the value or support the appraisement on which he relied.

But My Lord Keeper [Lord Harcourt] said, unless it were in cases of manifest oppression, an appraisement by the sheriff's appraisers ought not to be broken into without very plain proof of the goods' being of a greater value.

[Other copies of this report: Lincoln's Inn MS. Misc. 383, p. 102, Lincoln's Inn MS. Misc. 106, p. 56.]

## 271

## Anonymous

(Ch. 1711)

*If a pauper is granted relief against a penalty, he must pay court costs, but he does not pay court costs if the court does not grant relief.*

British Library MS. Hargrave 80, f. 53v, pl. 1

[It was] agreed by Lord Keeper [Lord Harcourt], *Sir Joseph Jekyll*, and the Register that, if a pauper seeks to be relieved against the penalty of a bond, it must be on the common terms of payment of principal, interest, and costs. But, if his bill be dismissed for not complying with those terms, that dismission shall be without costs.

[Other copies of this report: Lincoln's Inn MS. Misc. 383, p. 103, pl. 1, Lincoln's Inn MS. Misc. 106, p. 57, pl. 1.]

## 272

### Anonymous

(Ch. 1711)

*Substituted service of process can be made only at a party's usual place of abode.*

British Library MS. Hargrave 80, f. 53v, pl. 2

Notice left at the house or chambers of the adverse party's clerk in court is not good for it ought to be at his seat.

[Other copies of this report: Lincoln's Inn MS. Misc. 383, p. 103, p. 2, Lincoln's Inn MS. Misc. 106, p. 57, pl. 2.]

## 273

### Anonymous

(Ch. 1711)

*Notice must be given to all parties before an order nisi causa can be granted.*

British Library MS. Hargrave 80, f. 53v, pl. 3

Lord Keeper [LORD HARCOURT] seemed resolved never to make any orders *nisi causa* unless notice was before given of the motion.

[Other copies of this report: Lincoln's Inn MS. Misc. 383, p. 103, pl. 3, Lincoln's Inn MS. Misc. 106, p. 57, pl. 3.]

## 274

### Anonymous

(Ch. 1711)

*A reversion expectant cannot constitute a jointure in bar of dower at common law, but it can in equity.*

British Library MS. Hargrave 80, f. 54, pl. 1

If a reversion expectant on an estate for life be settled for a jointure and it is expressly agreed that it shall be in bar of dower, yet this is not a bar at the common law, though the reversion falls into possession immediately. But [it was] held to be a good bar in equity.

[Other copies of this report: Lincoln's Inn MS. Misc. 383, p. 103, pl. 4, Lincoln's Inn MS. Misc. 106, p. 58, pl. 1.]

## 275

## Westcombe v. Jones

(Ch. 1711)

*An executor is not liable to account for personal chattels after a great length of time.*

*In this case, the court of equity held that the limitation over in the will in issue was good.*

*A question in this case was whether a specific legacy to an executor excludes the executor from taking anything as an executor.*

*A specific legacy does not exclude the legatee from his or her share of the residue on a distribution of the estate.*

*A question in this case was whether a devise for life excludes the devisee from coming in for a distributive share of the very same leases.*

Lincoln's Inn MS. Misc. 10, p. 82

31 October 1711.

A man, by his will, in the year 1686, gives legacies to the plaintiffs, who were sisters, and also he gives a legacy to the defendant, his wife. And then he gives all the rest of his lands, tenements, goods, and chattels to his wife for her life and, after her death, to the child that his wife should be pregnant of and to the heirs of such child, but, if such child should die without issue before twenty-one, then he appointed that one-third of his estate should go to his wife, another third to one of his said sisters, and the other third to the other of his sisters. And he makes his wife executrix.

The wife proves the will and pays the plaintiffs their legacies, and, not being pregnant of a child, she takes it for granted that she had the whole interest in the personal estate, which consisted of long leases for years and other personal assets, not only for her life, but after her death as executrix. And so it was thought by the plaintiffs, who had acquiesced under that opinion above twenty years. And now they brought their bill for an account of the personal estate, they insisting that they were entitled to one moiety thereof by the Statute of Distributions[1] etc., the testator having made no disposition of it after his wife's death.

The questions were two: first, whether the wife, as executrix, had not the whole interest in the personal estate; second, to whom the reversion of the freehold lands did belong after the death of the wife.

It was insisted on for the defendant that, notwithstanding she had a legacy given her by the will, yet that did not exclude her from taking what remained

[1] Stat. 22 & 23 Car. II, c. 10 (*SR*, V, 719–720).

undisposed of by the will as executrix and that this will being made before the resolution in Foster and Monk's Case,[1] this case could not be governed by that.

The devise over to the plaintiffs as to two-thirds was in case there was a child and that child happened to die without issue before twenty-one, which contingencies having never happened, the plaintiffs could not take.

The Lord Keeper [LORD HARCOURT] did not think it reasonable that there should be any account of the personal assets taken after so long an acquiescence, and, therefore, he dismissed the bill as to them.

But, as to the leasehold estate, of which it was easy to know what the yearly value was and so an account might be easily be taken, he seemed to think that the reversion of them did not belong to the wife as executrix, they being expressly given her but for life by the will, and that they ought to be distributed according to the Statute.

But, then, he doubted whether the wife could come in for a share by the Statute, for he inclined to think that the giving them to her for life by the will did exclude her from all interest that she might claim in these leases any other way. And, therefore, he asked Mr. Vernon if he had ever known any case where an executor, having part of a thing given him by the will, was let in to have a share of the remaining part of the same thing by the Statute.

Mr. *Vernon* could not mention any case, but he said that, where the court has been of opinion that the executor by having a legacy given him was excluded of the residuum when it was not expressly given him by the will, he has, however, come in for his share of that surplus by the Statute if he was next of kin to the testator.

The plaintiff's counsel gave up that question at first and seemed to allow that the executrix ought to come in for her share by the Statute, but, finding the court to doubt, then they insisted upon excluding her.

As to the second point, it was insisted on that the testator's wife not being pregnant at his death, the remainder over vested immediately and did not depend upon the testator's having a child and that child's dying without issue before twenty-one, according to Holcroft's Case, Moo. 486,[2] which was thus. Sir John Holcroft settled lands to the use of Sir John, his son, for life, then to the first son of the body of Sir John, the son, in tail male and so in like manner to the second, third, fourth son of the same Sir John in tail male and, if it fortuned the said fourth son to die without heirs male of his body, that then and from thenceforth to the use of A.B. in tail male with remainders over. Sir John, the son, had one son only, who died without issue, and, afterwards, Sir John, the son, died. And it was adjudged that the use limited to A.B. vested in him notwithstanding there

[1] *Foster v. Munt* (1689), 1 Vernon 473, 23 E.R. 598, 1 Eq. Cas. Abr. 243, 21 E.R. 1020, 2 Eq. Cas. Abr. 433, 443, 22 E.R. 368, 378, Dodd 78, Chancery Repts. *tempore* Jac. II, 368.

[2] *Holcroft's Case* (1596), Moore K.B. 486, 72 E.R. 712.

was not a fourth son and that the having a fourth son was not a condition precedent to the vesting of the remainder in A.B.

The court took time to consider of both points. And, afterwards, *viz.* on the 31st October 1711, the court gave judgment that, the wife not being pregnant at the husband's death, the remainder both of the leasehold and freehold estates vested immediately and, accordingly, decreed one-third of the reversion of both estates to the wife and the other two-thirds to the plaintiffs, which determination including both questions, no judgment was given on the first point.

Note, in the arguing of this case was cited the Duchess of Beaufort's Case, which was lately decreed in the House of Lords,[1] where the old duke of Beaufort had devised the use of all his plate to the duchess for life and made her executrix, not having disposed of the residuum of his estate, and My Lord Cowper, who thought himself tied up by the Case of Foster and Monk, decreed that the surplus did not belong to her as executrix and that she was excluded to claim it as executrix by reason of the devise of the plate to her for life. But this decree was reversed by the House of Lords.

Buckley v. Littlebury, decreed since in the House of Lords,[2] was also cited, where they decreed the surplus to the executor notwithstanding he had a specific legacy bequeathed to him by the will. But this case was much governed by proofs of the testator's intent, which were admitted to be read.

British Library MS. Hargrave 80, f. 54, pl. 2

Michaelmas 1711.

The bill, so far as it sought an account of chattels personal after twenty-four years, was dismissed for length of time. The executor had all along not thought himself not liable to an account.

The testator devised his leasehold lands and lands of inheritance to his wife for life, remainder to the child which he then supposed his wife was enceinte with and his heirs and, if such child as shall happen to be born shall die under twenty-one and without issue, that then it shall be to his wife and B. and C. and their heirs, and he made his wife executrix, and he died, his wife not being enceinte nor any child born of her.

*Sir Thomas Powys* argued that the limitation to his wife and B. and C. and their heirs was on a condition precedent and, as that never happened, that limitation never could arise, that, in the Case of Sir Harry Wood's Will,[3] it was decreed and the decree affirmed in the House of Lords on these words, *viz.* 'if the

[1] *Duke of Beaufort v. Lord Dundonald* (1716), 2 Vernon 739, 23 E.R. 1083, 1 Eq. Cas. Abr. 201, 21 E.R. 989.

[2] *Buckley v. Littlebury* (1711), 3 Brown P.C. 43, 1 E.R. 1165, 2 Vernon 677, 23 E.R. 104,, 1 Eq. Cas. Abr. 245, 21 E.R. 1021, Lincoln's Inn MS. Misc. 10, p. 86.

[3] *Wood v. Duke of Southampton* (1692), Shower P.C. 83, 1 E.R. 58, 2 Freeman 186, 22 E.R. 1151, 1 Vernon 338, 23 E.R. 506, Chancery Repts. *tempore* Jac. II, 122.

duke of Southampton should die without issue by my daughter, then I devise it to' [ *blank* ]. The daughter died without issue. And though it was then certain that the duke must die without issue by her that the devise could not however take place until after the duke's death, that, until the Statute of Hen. VIII,[1] no heir could be disinherited by a will, nor since but by a will in writing, and that the words for that purpose ought to be direct, not uncertain, and the implication necessary.

On the other side, it was said that this was only a limitation of the estate devised to the supposed child and, that being annexed to that estate, it fell to the ground with it and did not make the limitation over conditional. And a case in Moore [was] cited to that purpose with this difference only, that, there, it was annexed to an estate tail where there was room for a limitation over by way of remainder, but, here, to an estate in fee. The case of Scattergood and Edge[2] was likewise cited, which was a devise to trustees for eleven years, remainder to the first and every other son of J.S. in tail, provided that, if they do not take his name, that then it should remain over to J.N.; J.S. never had any son, and yet this was adjudged a good devise to J.N. in the Common Bench though the first devise was but for years and not capable of supporting a remainder and consequently J.N. could not take by way of remainder. There was a writ of error brought in the [Court of] King's Bench, and the case [was] argued there, but never determined, the parties agreeing and J.N. still enjoying the estate.

Lord Keeper [Lord Harcourt], after taking time to consider, decreed the limitation over to his wife and B. and C. and their heirs to be good.

The next question was whether the devise to the wife of the leasehold for life should prevent her taking anything more as executrix. And as to this, the Lord Keeper [Harcourt] seemed to think there would be a difference between those wills, which were made before the case of Foster and Monk, which was, I think, about 1687, where that notion was first introduced, that a specific legacy to an executor excluded the executor from taking anything as an executor and those wills which were made since. This will was made before the Case of Littlebury was distinguished from this, for, in that case, proof was admitted of the intention of the testator to give the surplus to the executor. And, in this case, there was no such proof. On the contrary, the limitation of the leasehold estate over after the devise to her for life was made use of as an argument that he intended her no more than the estate for life. It seems no proof that she should not take as executrix if the limitation over did not take effect, though, if it did, it is some proof.

There was another thing stirred in this case, which was in case the wife should be excluded from taking as executrix and the surplus of the leasehold es-

[1] Stat. 27 Hen. VIII, c. 10 (*SR*, III, 539–542).

[2] *Scattergood v. Edge* (1699), 12 Modern 278, 88 E.R. 1320, 1 Salkeld 229, 91 E.R. 203, 1 Eq. Cas. Abr. 189, 21 E.R. 980, 2 Eq. Cas. Abr. 337, 22 E.R. 287.

tate by that means be liable to a distribution whether she should be admitted to come in for her distributive share of it.

*Vernon*: The specific legatees in the case of Foster and Monk and in all the cases since were never excluded by their legacies from coming in for their distributive share, except in the case of Vachell and Vachell;[1] there, the testator, looking on two of his sons not to be his own, gave them £10 apiece by his will and no more; they were, notwithstanding, decreed by this court to be let into a distribution. But the decree, indeed, was reversed in the House of Lords on account of the negative words and the apparent intention of the testator to exclude them, against which they were not to be let in by construction.

But, in this case, there were no such negative words nor intention to exclude, but, on the contrary, the greatest affection for his wife [was shown].

Lord Keeper [Lord Harcourt]: Though a specific legacy does not exclude the legatee from his share of the residue on a distribution, yet will not the devise for life to the wife exclude her in this case from coming in for a share of the very same leases? His Lordship seemed to think it would. But the bar held not, for, in cases of a distribution, all parties come in upon the foot of that Statute.

[Other copies of this report: Lincoln's Inn MS. Misc. 383, p. 104.]

[Other reports of this case: Gilbert Rep. 74, 25 E.R. 52, Precedents in Chancery 316, 24 E.R. 149, 1 Eq. Cas. Abr. 245, 21 E.R. 1022.]

## 276

## Atkinson v. Smith

(Ch. c. 1711)

*A legacy to a creditor will be paid in satisfaction of a liquidated debt that the testator owed to the creditor.*

*If the debt be not liquidated, the court of equity will not enjoin an action at common law on the debt.*

Lincoln's Inn MS. Misc. 10, p. 89

The plaintiff's testator, being indebted to the defendant, his sister, for diet and lodging touching which no agreement was made in his lifetime, by his will, gives the defendant a legacy of £100 and makes the plaintiff executor, who pays the legacy.

The defendant sues the plaintiff at law upon a *quantum meruit* for his testator's diet and board, upon which the plaintiff brings his bill and obtains an in-

[1] *Vachel v. Vachel* (1669), 1 Chancery Cases 129, 22 E.R. 727, 1 Eq. Cas. Abr. 361, 21 E.R. 1103.

junction. And, at the hearing, he insists that, if anything was due for the testator's board, it was satisfied by the legacy.

Mr. *Vernon*, for the defendant: I agree that, if a legacy is given to a man to whom the testator is indebted in a sum certain and the legacy exceeds the debt, it shall go in satisfaction of that debt. But it never was pretended that, where the debt exceeded the legacy, that then the legacy shall be a satisfaction *pro tanto*. Now, here is no debt ascertained. It may be more or it may be less than the legacy, and, therefore, surely, this does not come within the rule that has been observed in this court.

Master of the Rolls [TREVOR]: This bill was brought too soon. The plaintiff ought to have stayed until the debt had been ascertained at law, for the rule in this court is that, where the legacy is less than the debt, it shall not be looked upon as a satisfaction of any part of the debt.

However, it appearing by the defendant's answer that she insisted upon no more than £90 for the testator's board, which was less than the legacy, His Honor [TREVOR] decreed a perpetual injunction against the defendant's action at law.

## 277

## Anonymous

(Ch. c. 1711)

*A defendant who is in contempt of court for failing to respond to a writ of process will not be arrested until a writ of arrest has been issued by the court.*

*A party can object to an interrogatory on the ground of discharge of the obligation, release, or retainer.*

Lincoln's Inn MS. Misc. 10, p. 90, pl. 1

Upon a *subpoena scire facias* to revive a decree against an administrator and the heir at law, it was moved that the infant might be brought into court by a Messenger, he not having appeared. But, there being no [writ of] attachment taken out, the court would not order a Messenger until then.

It was also prayed that, the administrator having appeared, the decree might be revived as to him, which was ordered.

Then, it was prayed that the defendant, the administrator, might be examined on interrogatories for discovery of assets.

But this was opposed by Mr. *Vernon*, who said the plaintiff ought to exhibit a new bill for this purpose, for the administrator might have something to say in discharge of the assets, as a release or retainer or that there are debts of a higher nature.

But the court said he might insist on anything of this nature upon his examination and, therefore, ordered he should be examined on interrogatories.

## 278

## Haron v. Pullney

(Ch. 1711)

*In a suit by a widow to enforce a trust pursuant to marriage articles, her deceased husband's personal representative is a necessary party.*

British Library MS. Hargrave 80, f. 55v

A bill was [exhibited] for the execution of a trust pursuant to marriage articles and to have £800 paid My Lady by the defendants, who were executors of the trustee. But an exception was taken and allowed for want of proper parties, the husband, Sir Charles Haron's representatives not being brought before the court. And, Sir Charles having died much in debt, nobody had taken out letters of administration, but the plaintiff was forced to set up an administration before she could bring the cause to a hearing.

[Other copies of this report: Lincoln's Inn MS. Misc. 383, p. 106, Lincoln's Inn MS. Misc. 106, p. 58, pl. 2.]

## 279

## Jeoffry v. Dixon

(Ch. 1711)

*A contingent interest of a personal estate must vest within the same rule against perpetuities as a chattels real and real property.*

Harvard Law Sch. MS. 537, pt. 2, p. 185, pl. 1

Easter term 10 Anne.

The case was A. devised his personal estate to B. and, if B. died before twenty-one and without issue, then to C. and his children. B. did die before twenty-one and without issue.

And [it was] decreed that such contingent interest is good and C. is well entitled to the personal estate, for the contingency being become in so short a time as that was and such conv[eyance] of the personal estate was resembled to a devise of chattels real, and such devises were put under the same rules and upon the same foot with chattels real, which note well.

And note well The Duke of Norfolk's Case, 3 Chanc. Case, *ex relatione Magistri Gilby*, [who was] concerned in that case.[1]

[1] *Howard v. Duke of Norfolk* (1681), 3 Chancery Cases 1, 22 E.R. 931, also 1 Vernon 163, 23 E.R. 388, 2 Swanston 454, 36 E.R. 690, Pollexfen 223, 86 E.R. 568, 2 Chancery

## 280

## Anonymous

(Ch. 1711)

*The contents of a lost deed can be proved by other evidence, such as subsequent acts in reliance and recitals in other deeds.*

British Library MS. Hargrave 80, f. 56

In the Case of Sir John Ellis in the King's Bench, a surrender of a monastery to Henry VIII could not be produced, and, upon showing that there was not one in twenty of those surrenders to be found, the court, in regard that the possession had gone pursuant to the surrender for a long time, directed the jury to find it without any difficulty.

If one deed recites another, it is good evidence of that deed against the party that recites it.

In the Case of St. Bartholomew's Hospital, the deed by which the City of London covenanted with Henry VIII to pay that hospital 500 marks a year was lost, but the notice that was taken of that covenant in subsequent acts of the Common Council seemed to be admitted *per curiam* to be sufficient evidence of it.

[Other copies of this report: Lincoln's Inn MS. Misc. 383, p. 107, pl. 1, Lincoln's Inn MS. Misc. 106, p. 58, pl. 3.]

## 281

## Hale v. Hale

(Ch. 1711)

*In this case, the question was whether the debts of a testator should be paid out of lands devised to be sold for the payment of his debts or out of the bequest of the residuum of his personal estate made to a person who was not his executor.*

British Library MS. Hargrave 80, f. 56v

Mr. Matthew Hale, grandson of the Chief Justice,[1] devised all his lands in Gloucester to his wife for life, remainder etc., and gave her a power to lease and then devised his books to such of his nephews as should study the law and his

---

Reports 229, 21 E.R. 665, 2 Freeman 72, 80, 22 E.R. 1066, 1070, 79 Selden Soc. 904, 922, 999, Dodd 42, Oxford Bodleian Library MS. Rawlinson C.347.

[1] Sir Matthew Hale (1609–1676) was Chief Justice of the King's Bench from 1671 to 1676 and Chief Baron of the Exchequer from 1660 to 1671. A. Cromartie, 'Hale, Sir Matthew (1609–1676)', *Oxford Dictionary of National Biography*, vol. 24, pp. 533–540.

mathematical instruments as an heirloom and the rest and residue of his personal estate to his wife, and then he gave her a power to alter the mortgages on his estate and made her executrix. He likewise devised a particular estate of inheritance to be sold and the purchase money and what should arise by the leasing (*ut supra*) to be applied to the payment of debts.

The single question was whether the residuum devised to the wife should be first applied to pay debts in exoneration of the land devised to be sold for that purpose.

*Powys*: Where a man devises his lands to be sold for payment of debts and is wholly silent as to his personal estate, the personal estate shall be first applied, for it cannot be imagined he intended his executor should retain it, but, in case the personal estate be devised, the real shall be first applied.

*Jekyll*: If a man devises his personal estate to his executor, it is no more than the law says and, therefore, there ought to be negative words to protect it from debts and, if the devise be to a stranger, it is all one, for the law has charged it and the testator has not discharged it. And when a man is providing a fund by his will for payment of his debts which is not otherwise liable, he is providing for his creditors, not his legatees. In the case of the City of London v. Garraway,[1] there was a devise of all the personal estate and yet that was decreed to exonerate the real estate by being first applied to pay debts that affected both. He cited the cases of Lady Gainesborough and of French v. Chichester,[2] that, when a man devises the residue of his personal estate, it is the residue after debts and legacies. The cases of Coxeter v. Cutler[3] was cited, where all the personal estate was devised to Cutler, who was made executor, yet the real estate was decreed to be exonerated, and Wilkinson's Case,[4] where the devise was to a brother, who was made executor, after[wards], by a codicil, that executor was changed, and [it was] resolved that [ *blank* ]. And the case of Cook v. Gwavis[5] and Brickinshaw's Case [was cited].

*Vernon*: The testator in this case first gives his wife his real estate for her life, then a power to lease, then he comes to his personal estate and disposes of his books and mathematical instruments, 'and, as to all the rest of my personal estate, I give it to my wife,' i.e. the rest after books and mathematical instruments. It does not yet appear that he intended to make her executrix. Then he gives di-

---

[1] *City of London v. Garway* (1705–1706), see above, Case No. 42.

[2] *Countess of Gainsborough v. Earl of Gainsborough* (1692), 2 Vernon 252, 23 E.R. 764, 2 Freeman 188, 22 E.R. 1152, 1 Eq. Cas. Abr. 230, 21 E.R. 1010; *French v. Chichester* (1707), see above, Case No. 63.

[3] *Cutler v. Coxeter* (1693), 2 Vernon 302, 23 E.R. 794, Lincoln's Inn MS. Misc. 10, p. 198.

[4] *Wilkinson v. Wilkinson* (1681), 1 Vernon 23, 23 E.R. 277, 1 Eq. Cas. Abr. 413, 21 E.R. 1142.

[5] *Coke v. Gwavas* (Ex. 1683), Exch. Repts. *tempore* Car. II, 528.

rections touching the mortgages; then at last, he makes her executrix. And he endeavored to establish a difference where the devise and naming him executor is in one clause and where in different.

He said that this seems as much intended as a provision for her out of the personal [estate] as the other out of the real estate and the exoneration aimed at is directly opposite to the will. He cited the case of Moor v. the Countess of Meath, where the testator made two wills, one of his English, the other of his Irish estate. In the first, he devised all the residue after debts paid to J.S.; in the second, he devised an estate to be sold for payment of debts. In that case, the personal estate was decreed to exonerate the real. But it was because it was devised expressly after debts paid. And that decree was affirmed in the House of Lords. He said that this was a beneficial devise to his wife and that the heir shall never have the aid of the personal estate to exonerate the real so as to disappoint creditors or even legatees, that this court has always marshalled, that there was no color for what Sir Joseph Jekyll said, that, if the whole was devised to a stranger, that yet it should be first applied for payment of debts in exoneration of the real estate, which the court seemed to admit, and that the residue here was not devised to the executrix taking notice of her being executrix.

Lord Keeper [Lord Harcourt]: Can you show me any case to support that difference?

*Vernon* said that, if a specific legacy had been devised to her, that would not be liable to exonerate etc., which was agreed, from whence he inferred that the reason being the same where the whole was devised to her that ought as little to be liable to exonerate.

Lord Keeper [Lord Harcourt] desired to be attended with precedents that his decree in this case might be agreeable to others in the like cases, but he seemed to think there was a difference between a devise of the whole to an executor and to a stranger.

[Other copies of this report: Lincoln's Inn MS. Misc. 383, p. 107, pl. 2, Lincoln's Inn MS. Misc. 106, p. 59.]

Lincoln's Inn MS. Misc. 10, p. 90, pl. 2

31 October 1711.

Matthew Hale, grandson of the Chief Justice, by his will, gives several legacies. And, as for all the rest of his estate, real or mixed, and all his manors of etc. and all his lands in the County of Gloucester, he gives the same to his dear wife and her heirs upon trust that, sometime during her widowhood, she should convey the premises to his brother Gabriel Hale, Edward, or Matthew Hale, or some other son of the said Gabriel that should be born with and under such limitations as she should appoint so that an estate of inheritance should be conveyed by her to the said Gabriel or one of his sons with remainder to the testator and his heirs.

He declares further that it should be lawful for his wife, at any time during the continuance of her estate therein, to make leases of any part of the premises which were leased out at the death of Sir Matthew Hale for one, two, or three lives and that all such money as should be raised by such leases should be applied to the payment of such debts as he should owe at his death.

All his books he gives to such of his nephews as should practice the law.

And, as for the residue of his personal estate, he gives the same to his wife, except some mathematical instruments. And he appoints that his wife, out of the rents of the premises, should pay the interest of the mortgages which should be thereon at his death. And he makes her executrix.

By a codicil, he declares that, though he had directed by his will that a settlement should be made by his wife during her widowhood, yet his intent was that the estate should not commence in possession until after his wife's death and that she should enjoy the same during her life. And then he directs that an estate which his grandmother purchased for him at Hilsley should be sold and the money arising thereby be applied to the payment of his debts.

There were mortgages at the death of the testator upon his real estate. And Gabriel, the brother, exhibits his bill to have those encumbrances paid off out of the real estate.

The cause was heard before LORD COWPER, who declared that it did not appear that the lands directed to be sold were a sufficient provision for the payment of the debts, and, therefore, he decreed that the residuum of the personal estate should be applied to exonerate the real estate.

The cause was now reheard.

*Sir Thomas Powys*, for the defendant: When an executor claims the residue as executor, I agree the court will not suffer him to run away with the personal estate if there are debts which charge the real estate. But, when the residuum is expressly devised, it is otherwise. The court, in that case, where there is another fund provided for the debts, will not take away the residuum from the devisee in favor of the heir.

Mr. *Vernon*: All the rest and residue is not all the rest after payment of the debts, but all the residue except what he had before given away.

If the dispute here was between the executor and creditors, no doubt but they might come upon the personal estate if they pleased. But, here, the dispute is between the heir and the executor.

It is agreed on all hands that a specific legatee shall hold against the heir. Now, what reason can there be why the executor to whom the residuum is given should not do so too?

It is plain the testator in our case intended this should be a beneficial devise to his wife and, since, if this had been the case of anyone that had not been made executor, he should have held the residuum against the heir, it will be hard that the wife, by being made executrix in the close of the will, should be put into a worse condition than she would have been in case she had not been executrix.

*Sir Joseph Jekyll*, on the other side: The law has made the personal estate the fund for the payment of the debts. And, since the testator has not by any words of the will exempted the residuum from the payment of his debts, surely, in favor of the heir, it shall be applied to exonerate the real estate.

I take this to be the distinction that has always prevailed where the residuum has been by express words exempted from the debts and where it has not.

Garraway and Garraway's Case, in Lord Cowper's time, [and] Chichester and French, in Lord Keeper Wright's time [were] decreed upon that difference.

The court took time to consider of it.

Lincoln's Inn MS. Misc. 10, p. 201

Matthew Hale, by his will, gives all his lands in Gloucestershire to Mary, his wife, and her heirs on trust that she should sometime during her widowhood convey an estate of inheritance to his brother, Gabriel Hale, or some of his sons. Then, he declares it lawful for his wife, during the continuance of her estate, to lease in possession or reversion any lands that were leased in Sir Matthew Hale's time for one, two, or three lives and willed that all such money as should arise by the said leases should be applied to the payment of such of his debts as should be unpaid at the time of his death. And, after disposing of his books, he goes on:

and, as for all the rest of my personal estate, I give the same to my wife Mary Hale [and he goes on] and I further declare that it shall be lawful for my wife and she shall have full power to mortgage any estate now in mortgage for any sum or sums of principal and interest that shall be due at the time of my death, paying the sums so due by the former mortgage with the money taken upon the said security. And my further desire is that my wife shall continue out of the rents and profits of the manors etc. to her devised to pay the interest due on the mortgages and securities and do hereby appoint my dear wife Mary Hale sole executrix of this my last will and testament.

Here was no creditor before the court, but only the widow and persons interested under the will.

And the present Lord Chancellor [Lord Harcourt] was pleased to declare that there was not a full and complete provision for the payment of debts out of the real estate and that the personal estate, notwithstanding the devise, ought to exonerate the real estate, except the mortgages and what was by the will particularly directed to be charged thereon. And he decreed an account of the personal estate accordingly.

## 282

## Anonymous

(Ch. 1711)

*A mortgagee in possession is entitled to reimbursement for capital improvements.*

British Library MS. Hargrave 80, f. 58, pl. 1

Rebuilding ruinous houses is a lasting improvement, which a mortgagee will be allowed for upon his accounts.

[Other copies of this report: Lincoln's Inn MS. Misc. 383, p. 109.]

## 283

## Anonymous

(Ch. 1711)

*Interest does not accrue on a demand note before payment is demanded.*

British Library MS. Hargrave 80, f. 58, pl. 2

A note payable on demand carries no interest until demanded.

[Other copies of this report: Lincoln's Inn MS. Misc. 383, p. 110, pl. 1.]

## 284

## Anonymous

(Ch. 1711)

*An ex parte preliminary injunction can be granted upon affidavits that support the bill of complaint.*

British Library MS. Hargrave 80, f. 58, pl. 3

Mr. *Vernon* moved for and obtained an injunction to stay execution until answer or further order. Though the bill was filed the same day he moved, he had an affidavit to support the allegations of the bill, which proved a great oppression against the defendant.

[Other copies of this report: Lincoln's Inn MS. Misc. 383, p. 110, pl. 2.]

## 285

## Anonymous

(Ch. 1711)

*A copy of a letter is inadmissible in evidence unless it is proved that the letter was received by the addressee.*

British Library MS. Hargrave 80, f. 58v, pl. 1

A copy of a letter sent by A. to B. is no evidence for A. unless he can prove it came to the hands of B.

[Other copies of this report: Lincoln's Inn MS. Misc. 383, p. 110, pl. 3.]

## 286

## Wise v. Rowe

(Ch. 1711)

*Where a bill for an account is revived against the executor of the deceased defendant, the plaintiff can only reach the decedent's personal assets, not the real estate.*

*An executor can retain the assets of the estate, but a trustee cannot.*

British Library MS. Hargrave 80, f. 58v, pl. 2

Wise had a decree against Rowe *quod computet* in 1698. Though there had been an account stated and a bond for the balance, there was a report on that decree, but that report was never confirmed. And now, upon a rehearing of the original bill and arguing the exceptions to the report, the report was in most things confirmed. And, upon two bills of revivor for discovery of assets against Rowe's representatives, the question was what kind of assets should be affected by the sum now reported due and the costs. There was an attempt to affect the real assets because [they were] settled after the decree and report and for that reason fraudulently.

*Vernon*: You would not have them in a worse condition than if they had never been settled. A decree for a personal duty would not have affected them in the last case, much less *ad computandum*. In the case of University College in Oxford (in Lord Nottingham's time, as I think),[1] the decree was carried to a sequestration. And yet, even there, it was ruled that the lands sequestered would not be liable after the death of the party. And that decree has never been shaken since.

It was ruled accordingly that the real assets were not liable but that the personal were, most of which were leases and mortgages taken in the name of trust-

[1] *University College, Oxford v. Foxcroft* (1683), 1 Vernon 166, 23 E.R. 390, 2 Chancery Reports 244, 21 E.R. 669.

ees and the trust of some of them had been declared by the trustees at the request of Rowe to be since the report to be for the benefit of his wife.

And Mr. *Vernon* cited a case where a lease of a house was taken in the name of Sir Francis Winnington in trust, I think, for Sir Charles Sidney, and, after a decree for a personal duty, as this was; Sir Charles procured the trust to be declared for the benefit of a lady and it was ruled that the lease was not liable to make the plaintiff satisfaction.

Lord Keeper [LORD HARCOURT]: But you thought that a hard decree, to which *Vernon* made no reply.

A trustee in this case desired to retain part of the trust money for payment of a debt due from Rowe to him.

Lord Keeper [LORD HARCOURT]: An executor may retain because he cannot sue himself nor anybody else, but a trustee cannot retain; that reason ceases in him.

[Other copies of this report: Lincoln's Inn MS. Misc. 383, p. 110, pl. 4, Lincoln's Inn MS. Misc. 106, p. 62.]

## 287

## Stapleton v. Cheele

(Ch. 1711)

*If a legacy is given to a person when he attains a certain age and the legatee die beforehand, the legacy lapses, but, if the legacy vests by the death of the testator or the legatee's attaining that age, then the legacy goes to the legatee's personal representative.*

*One legatee may sue the executor without making the other legatees parties.*

Lincoln's Inn MS. Misc. 10, p. 96

12 November 1711. John Stapleton, administrator of Mary Stapleton, his daughter, and Mary, his wife, administratrix of Mary Andrew, her daughter by a former husband, plaintiff; Elizabeth Cheals, executrix of Richard Cheals, executor of William Cheals, defendant.

Richard Cheals, by will, gives to Mary Andrew £50 to be paid when she should attain the age of sixteen years with interest to be paid her quarterly every year after his death. And, to Mary Stapleton, he gave £30 when she should attain the age of sixteen years with interest likewise to be paid quarterly after his decease.

Mary Andrew died at fifteen and Mary Stapleton at six years of age. And the plaintiffs, as their respective administrators, prefer their bill for a satisfaction of those legacies.

The defendant, by answer, insisted that the legacies were lapsed or, however, if they were not, that she had no assets. And, by the account that she had set forth in her answer, it appeared that her testator had given bonds to two of the legatees for their legacies and that the defendant had paid those bonds out of the assets of the testator.

It was insisted on for the plaintiff that these legacies vested in the respective legatees and, consequently, did now belong to the plaintiffs as their representatives. The constant difference that had been always taken was where a legacy was given to one at twenty-one and where it was given to be paid at twenty-one. In the latter case, it is a *debitum in praesenti* but *solvendum in futuro*. And, even in the first case, where interest has been directed to be paid in the meantime, it has been decreed to the administrator. And this was Cloberrie's Case, 2 Vent. 342.[1]

*Sir Joseph Jekyll*, for the defendant, admitted that the first legacy vested, but not the latter.

But the Master of the Rolls [Trevor] was of the opinion that both vested in regard of the interest that was to be paid in the meantime, according to Cloberrie's Case. He also declared that it was a misapplication of the assets in Richard Cheele to prefer one legatee before another. He ought to have paid them all equally.

Then, it was insisted that we ought to have made the other legatees parties.

Mr. *Vernon*: There is no need of that. One legatee may prefer a bill against the executor without bringing the other legatees before the court.

And of that opinion was the Master of the Rolls [Trevor]. And he decreed that there should be an account taken of the assets of William Cheele, and, if it appeared there was sufficient assets of William to pay all the legacies, then the plaintiffs were to be paid their whole legacies with interest and costs, but, if not, then to be paid in proportion with the other legatees and that an account should be also taken of the assets of Richard Cheele that the plaintiffs may have a satisfaction out of his assets of what should appear to be due to them out of the assets of William.

British Library MS. Hargrave 80, f. 59

It was ruled clearly in this case by the Master of the Rolls [Trevor] according to the difference taken in Cloberry's Case, 2 Vent., and several others that, if I give a legacy to J.S. when or if he attains his age of sixteen or at his age of sixteen, there, this time being inserted in the body of the devise, if J.S. dies before sixteen, the legacy is quite lost. But, if the testator directs the interest of the legacy to be paid to J.S., as in this case, from his own death, that is an evidence that the testator intended that the legacy should vest in J.S. immediately, which it shall therefore do and go to the executors of J.S. If a legacy be given to J.S. to be paid

[1] *Cloberry v. Lamden* (1678), 2 Ventris 342, 86 E.R. 476, also 2 Freeman 24, 22 E.R. 1035, 2 Chancery Cases 155, 22 E.R. 892, 1 Eq. Cas. Abr. 294, 21 E.R. 1055, 2 Eq. Cas. Abr. 539, 22 E.R. 454, 79 Selden Soc. 509, 529.

him at the age of sixteen, in that case, it vests in him immediately and shall go to his executors upon the old difference, *debitum in praesenti solvendum in futuro.*

[Other copies of this report: Lincoln's Inn MS. Misc. 383, p. 111.]

[Other reports of this case: 2 Vernon 673, 23 E.R. 1038, Precedents in Chancery 317, 24 E.R. 150, Gilbert Rep. 76, 25 E.R. 53, 1 Eq. Cas. Abr. 294, 295, 21 E.R. 1055, 1056.]

## 288

## Anonymous

(Ch. 1711)

*One legatee may bring a bill against the executor without making the other legatees parties.*

*If the executor gives one legatee a bond for payment of his legacy, that gives him no preference against the assets of the estate.*

British Library MS. Hargrave 80, f. 59v, pl. 1

In another case, Mr. *Vernon* held clearly that one legatee may bring a bill against an executor without making the other legatees parties and that, if the executor gives the other legatees a bond for payment of their legacies, that gives them no preference against the assets of the first testator, but it does against the assets of that executor in case he dies and he had wasted the others assets, for, as against them, the bond debt is a debt by specialty, the other only by simple contract.

[Other copies of this report: Lincoln's Inn MS. Misc. 383, p. 112, pl. 1.]

## 289

## Rich v. Bedoe

(Ch. 1711)

*The question in this case was whether one co-executor is liable for the receipt of money by the other co-executor.*

Lincoln's Inn MS. Misc. 10, p. 94, pl. 1

7 November 1711. Pirke v. Biddowes.

A. devised lands to the defendant and one B. to be sold for the payment of his legacies. The executors sell, and both receive the money. Afterwards, the defendant permits B. to take the whole money, and B. gives the defendant security to pay it to the legatees and then becomes insolvent.

[It was] decreed that the defendant should answer the money to the legatees and should have the benefit of the security to reimburse himself.

Fellows and Owen's Case,[1] before Lord Cowper soon after he had the seal, was cited, which was this. Two executors joined in a sale, and both gave a receipt for the money, and one of them took one-half of it, and the other took the other half. One failed. And [it was] decreed that the other should not be charged with any more than the moiety which he received.

British Library MS. Hargrave 80, f. 60v, pl. 2

Fellows v. Owen, before Lord Cowper; two trustees, in the presence of the *cestui que trust*, joined in a sale and in the acquittance, and the one received the one moiety and the other the other moiety, and it was decreed that each should be answerable but for a moiety. But that case was so ruled chiefly upon the presence of the *cestui que trust*.

This case was cited in the case of Rich and Bedoe, where two executors joined in a sale, Rich received the greatest part of the money, and Bedoe took his security for it, and he was decreed to pay it. But it was agreed that there were several cases [where there were] two executors and they take care of two estates, one in one county and another in another county, each shall answer for himself only.

[Other copies of this report: Lincoln's Inn MS. Misc. 383, p. 113, pl. 2.]

## 290

## Minshall v. Lord Mohun

(Ch. 1711)

*Laches is a good defense to an original bill in the nature of a bill of revivor.*

Lincoln's Inn MS. Misc. 10, p. 94, pl. 2

10 November 1711.

A decree was had for the plaintiff several years ago, and, after some proceedings were had thereon, the then defendant died and devised the lands, touching which the decree was made, to the defendant, the lord Mohun. And the plaintiff brought an original bill in the nature of a bill of revivor to revive the decree and all proceedings thereon.

The defendant, by the answer, insisted that the plaintiff could not revive against him, who was only a devisee. And, at the hearing, he endeavored to go into the merits of the cause and to bring the whole matter in question over again.

But, for the plaintiff, it was said this could not be, for, if the heir himself was here, he could not have unravelled the decree, and, therefore, a devisee, who is

[1] *Fellows v. Owen* (1705), 2 Vernon 504, 515, 23 E.R. 922, 929, 1 Peere Williams 81, 24 E.R. 302, 2 Freeman 283, 286, 22 E.R. 1212, 1215.

*haeres factus*, shall not be in a better condition than the *haeres natus* would have been.

The Lord Keeper [Lord Harcourt] would not suffer them to enter into the merits of the cause, but he ordered that all things should go on upon the foot of the old decree. To say you cannot revive against a devisee is only a nicety of form. However, there is no question but an original bill in the nature of a bill of revivor may be brought.

N.B. In this case, it was said that, where a man purchases after a decree, while the matter is recent and before things are carried on to an execution, though he has no notice, yet he shall be affected with the decree and shall not be let in to contest the decree. But, where the matter has lain still some time and a man comes in without notice, he shall defend himself by all the ways he can.

British Library MS. Hargrave 80, f. 59v, pl. 2

Minshall brought an original bill in the nature of a bill of revivor against Lord Mohun, devisee and executor of [ *blank* ] and against several others, to revive and execute a decree. The cause had depended a great many years.

*Vernon*: My Lord coming in as a devisee and, therefore, not in privity, a bill of revivor could not be brought against him, but an original bill in the nature of a bill of revivor might. And, in this case, he shall not be in a better condition than an heir or executor if a bill was brought against them, and he shall not be allowed to show anything against the decree unless it be new matter since the decree, such as a purchaser without notice while the decree slept. This matter was determined by My Lord Cowper in the case of Clare and Worden.[1] On the other hand, an assignee may bring an original bill in the nature of a bill of review if the decree is enrolled; if it is not, he may enroll it. But he seemed to think he could not petition for a rehearing. And he said there was a difference between a purely original bill to carry a decree into execution and an original bill in the nature of a bill of revivor.

*Powys*: An heir cannot enter into the examination of the justice of a decree upon a bill of revivor against him to revive and execute it. But he may petition for a rehearing. A *lis pendens* must be carried on with a recent prosecution and then a purchaser who comes in, though without notice, can have no aid in this court, but, where it is not so carried on, he will.

*Pratt*: Lord Mohun has never been heard to the justice of this decree. He has never until now been before the court. The cause is open. The decree is not enrolled. And it is fit he should be heard against it before it has the sanction of the court. And he said the precedents were generally against the case of Clare and Worden.

[1] *Clare v. Werdell* (Ch. 1706), see above, Case No. 45.

Lord Keeper [Lord Harcourt] decreed against Lord Mohun chiefly for the length of time and in some measure because he did not think the cause [was] open enough for him. But, however, he altered the other decree in some small things, as where one was charged to answer *de bonis propriis*, which should have been *testatoris*. He said Lord Mohun was not without a remedy.

[Other copies of this report: Lincoln's Inn MS. Misc. 383, p. 112, pl. 2.]

[Other reports of this case: 2 Vernon 672, 23 E.R. 1038, 1 Eq. Cas. Abr. 3, 21 E.R. 829.]

[Affirmed on appeal: Mordaunt v. Minshull (1724), 6 Brown P.C. 32, 2 E.R. 914.]

## 291

## Anonymous

(Ch. 1711)

*Notice to affect the good faith of a purchaser must be positive and certain.*

British Library MS. Hargrave 80, f. 60v, pl. 1

Notice to affect a purchaser ought to be positive and certain, not a common rumor only. If it comes before he has paid his money, it is soon enough. When a defendant is charged with particular circumstances which amount to notice, especially if it be a deed, he ought to answer to that, for to say that he did not know the right and title of the plaintiff is too general, for that is no more than that he is not acquainted with all the deeds which make out his title.

[Other copies of this report: Lincoln's Inn MS. Misc. 383, p. 113, pl. 1.]

## 292

## World v. Henly

(Ch. 1711)

*A submission to arbitration should be made a rule of court before the arbitration is made. An ultra vires arbitral award is void only pro tanto.*

British Library MS. Hargrave 80, f. 61, pl. 1

[It was] ruled that the submission to arbitration ought to be made a rule of court before the arbitration [is made]. The plea was overruled because the submission was made a rule of court after the award. The award was 29th of September of all etc. until January following.

*Mead*: It exceeds the submission and is therefore void.

Lord Keeper [Lord Harcourt]: That was the law 100 years ago. It is good certainly for so much as is within the submission.

[Other copies of this report: Lincoln's Inn MS. Misc. 383, p. 114, pl. 1, Lincoln's Inn MS. Misc. 106, p. 63.]

## 293

## Anonymous

(Ch. 1711)

*Where a person surrenders a lease and takes a new one of the same land, the new lease is a different estate from the first one.*

British Library MS. Hargrave 80, f. 61, pl. 2

The archbishop of York granted lands to J.S. and his heirs for three lives; the trust of the lease was to J.N. and her heirs. J.N. died leaving an infant, who thereby became entitled to the benefit of the trust. One life dropping during the minority of the infant, the trustee surrendered and took a new lease for the lives in trust for the infant and his heirs.

*Vernon*: The trustee has done no more than he was compellable by a decree of this court.

And [it was] ruled clearly, the infant being dead, the benefit of this new lease should go to his heirs by his father's side and not by his mother's, it being a new purchase in him and not a continuance of his old estate, as was urged of the other side.

[Other copies of this report: Lincoln's Inn MS. Misc. 383, p. 114, pl. 2.]

## 294

## Harris v. Brent

(Ch. 1711)

*The question in this case was whether a Roman Catholic can receive an interest in land by a devise.*

Lincoln's Inn MS. Misc. 10, p. 98

13 November 1711.

A Roman Catholic devised his lands to Gilbert Whitehall and his heirs, who was also a Roman Catholic. Gilbert Whitehall, afterwards, devised these lands to be sold for the payment of his debts, and he gives the surplus to the defendant, who was also a Papist. And if this could be done since the Disabling Statute of King William[1] was the question.

[1] Stat. 11 Will. III, c. 4, s. 4 (*SR*, VII, 587).

Lord Keeper [Lord Harcourt]: There are three clauses in this Act. The first respects the act of another person and does not make the devise void, but only puts the person under a temporary disability. The second respects his own person and disables a Roman Catholic from purchasing. And the last clause makes all estates and interests created 'for such persons' void, so that 'such' must relate to persons in the second clause, that is to persons purchasing. What sticks with me is the first clause. Now, according to the construction the plaintiff's counsel would put on this Act, the last clause is inconsistent with the first, for, if the last clause extends to devises, it makes them void, and then it cannot consist with the first, which does not make devises void; it only puts the party under a temporary incapacity.

The devise to Gilbert Whitehall is not within the first clause, which extends only to persons under eighteen. Now, he was above eighteen at the time of the first testator's death. And, therefore, he could not qualify himself within six months after he attained the age of eighteen, for that time was past before the testator's death, so that the devise to him must be considered upon the last clause.

*Adjornatur.*

British Library MS. Hargrave 80, f. 61v

The question was whether a Papist of full age was capable of taking an interest in land by devise since the 11th of William, for it was held clearly that that Act does not extend to things merely personal.

It was insisted that he was not capable from the words of the latter part of the disabling clause, *viz.* that, 'from the 10th of April 1700, every Papist or person making profession of the Popish religion shall be disabled . . . to purchase'.

It seemed to be agreed that they need not be Papists convict to bring them within this clause.

Now, it was said that whosoever does not take by descent takes by purchase and that the following words made it still clearer, *viz.* 'that all estates . . . to be made, suffered, or done to or for the use . . . of such person etc. shall be void' etc.

On the other hand, it was argued that the word 'purchase' extended only to acquisitions by the person's own act and that was the common acceptation of the word and that this, being a penal act, must be construed strictly though it be in favor of religion and that the following words 'made, done, or suffered' etc. were the usual words in conveyances and only a confirmation of the preceding, that, if this part of the clause should be extended to one who takes by devise, it would be a repugnancy in the Act, for, this making the devise void, it would descend to the heir, whereas, by the beginning of the clause which renders Papists etc. incapable of taking by descent, limitation, or devise, it is limited to the next of kin, that the first part of the clause related to those who claim under others, the second to those who claim by the Act.

*Sir Joseph Jekyll*: The first part of the clause relates to those under eighteen or six months after; the second to others. If the defendant had been under that age, there might have been a repugnancy, but, as he was not, there is none.

It was urged against the plaintiff that this equity was founded on a forfeiture.

Lord Keeper [LORD HARCOURT]: I will give him relief notwithstanding if I was convinced that it was a forfeiture.

It was urged that the second part not extending to the case of descent, it was, therefore, not intended by the word 'purchase' to mean anything but buying.

The cause depending in some measure on the determination of another point, the court reserved the determination of this until that should be determined.

[Other copies of this report: Lincoln's Inn MS. Misc. 383, p. 115, Lincoln's Inn MS. Misc. 106, p. 64.]

## 295

## Anonymous

(Ch. 1711)

*The lack of a surrender of a copyhold to the use of a will will be supplied in equity in favor of younger children unless it would completely disinherit the heir at law.*

British Library MS. Hargrave 80, f. 62, pl. 1

*Vernon*: The want of a surrender of a copyhold estate to the use of a will is generally supplied in equity in favor of younger children. But the court refused to do it in the case of Barker and Jenny[1] because, if it had been supplied there, the heir would have been wholly disinherited by it.

[Other copies of this report: Lincoln's Inn MS. Misc. 383, p. 116, pl. 1.]

## 296

## Osborne v. Mingay

(Ch. 1711)

*The income of an estate belonging to a woman before marriage is her property, while the income during the marriage is her husband's property.*

[1] *Baker v. Jennings* (1699), 2 Freeman 234, 22 E.R. 1180, 2 Eq. Cas. Abr. 230, 22 E.R. 195.

British Library MS. Hargrave 80, f. 62, pl. 2

The administrator of the wife, and not the husband, was decreed to account for the profits of an estate received by the wife before coverture and the husband only for those received during coverture. And the court directed that there should be no greater allowance made in respect of the children's maintenance than the annual product of their estate.

[Other copies of this report: Lincoln's Inn MS. Misc. 383, p. 116, pl. 2, Lincoln's Inn MS. Misc. 106, p. 65.]

## 297

## Attorney General v. Hastings

(Ch. 1711)

*A trustee of a hospital who is under a disability will have a trustee appointed by a court of equity or a deputy appointed by the crown to exercise the office.*

British Library MS. Hargrave 80, f. 62, pl. 3

Three and their heirs were trustees for the government of a hospital; one was a Roman Catholic, another a minor.

And upon an information to settle the government of it, it was decreed that a trustee should be named by the Master in the place of the minor during his nonage and that the Roman Catholic should pursuant to 25 Car II, c. 2,[1] name a deputy to be approved by the crown.

The Attorney General [*Northey*] insisted that this was an office within that Statute. *Sed quaere*. The Attorney General held that a foundership with all its consequences was assignable and that this trust was so too.

But of the last, Lord Keeper [Lord Harcourt] seemed to doubt.

[Other copies of this report: Lincoln's Inn MS. Misc. 383, p. 116, pl. 3, Lincoln's Inn MS. Misc. 106, p. 66, pl. 1.]

1 Stat. 25 Car. II, c. 2, s. 9 (*SR*, V, 784).

## 298

## Anonymous

(Ch. 1711)

*Court costs cannot be awarded to one co-defendant against another.*

British Library MS. Hargrave 80, f. 62v, pl. 1

One defendant cannot have costs against another defendant.

[Other copies of this report: Lincoln's Inn MS. Misc. 383, p. 117, pl. 1.]

## 299

## Anonymous

(Ch. 1711)

*Where executors who have acted improperly have been forbidden to act further, others can act in their names to administer the decedent's estate.*

British Library MS. Hargrave 80, f. 62v, pl. 2

Executors in trust misbehaved themselves after probate.

And the court decreed in regard an execution was not assignable that they should be enjoined from intermeddling any farther and that they should permit others to make use of their names in getting in debts etc. giving them security to indemnify them.

[Other copies of this report: Lincoln's Inn MS. Misc. 383, p. 117, pl. 2.]

## 300

## Lord Ashburnham v. Briscoe

(Ch. 1711)

*In this case, a debtor was given further time to redeem a mortgage after having been already given further time several times before, he having repaid part of the debt and he acting in good faith to repay in full, but the part payment was to be forfeited in the case of failure to repay in full.*

British Library MS. Hargrave 80, f. 62v, pl. 3

Sir J. Briscoe had his time to redeem enlarged four times, and the last was upon condition that he signed the Registers' Book to stand absolutely foreclosed in case he did not redeem within the time limited, which he did not. But, in the meantime, he raised some of the money and had made contracts for selling almost as much as would raise all the rest.

Lord Keeper [Lord Harcourt], upon his having made such good use of his time and upon his paying £1000, enlarged his time again notwithstanding his having signed etc. the £1000 to go as part of the principal and interest in case he redeemed by the time now fixed, otherwise to be lost and he to stand absolutely foreclosed. Dr. Woodroff's Case was cited to prove that such deposits are not only *in terrorem*, for his was forfeited and, upon his appeal to the House [of Lords], he could get no relief.

In Lord Somers's time, Sir John Turner had his time to redeem enlarged four times after signing the Book. The estate in Sir John Briscoe's case was of a much greater value than the principal and interest due on the mortgage.

[Other copies of this report: Lincoln's Inn MS. Misc. 383, p. 117, pl. 3, Lincoln's Inn MS. Misc. 106, p. 66, pl. 2.]

## 301

## Ward v. Audley

(Ch. 1711)

*A settlement of land made ex turpi causa, such as adultery, will not be enforced.*

British Library MS. Hargrave 80, f. 62v, pl. 4

Ward's wife, while sole, was kept by Audley, a married man, and she drew him in to make several settlements upon her until she had stripped him of almost all his estate. It was sworn by Audley in his answer that, though there was £1000 consideration money paid at the time of the first conveyance, it was only colorable, the money being Audley's and delivered by him to her to pay over to him before witnesses at the execution of the deeds.

Lord Keeper [Lord Harcourt] directed an enquiry by a master into that reality of the consideration and declared that, if it appeared to be *ex turpi causa*, he would make such a decree as should most discourage these practices without regard to precedents. He said that, in Baudely's Case,[1] who gave a bond for payment of £500 to a mistress, Lord Nottingham would not relieve him upon a bill brought for that purpose, and he thought it was a proper punishment for his lewdness and folly. Pegtoe's Case was cited to the same purpose. But he said he thought there was a great difference between that case and this, where a whole estate was swept away and a family ruined.

*Vernon* insisted strongly that, admitting there was no consideration, yet Audley himself could have no pretense to relief, that there were several years

[1] *Bodley v. Anonymous* (1672), 2 Chancery Cases 15, 22 E.R. 824.

between the several conveyances and no room for suspicion of fraud or surprise, that, if they had creditors or even the children of Audley to contend with, that might have varied the case, but that it would be of very ill consequence if a man could at any time unravel a settlement that he had made, though a voluntary one. He said upon the head of *ex turpis causa* that Lord Nottingham always laid the burden upon the tempter.

[Other copies of this report: Lincoln's Inn MS. Misc. 383, f. 117, pl. 4.]

302

## Anonymous

(Ch. 1711)

*After the publication of the depositions, further depositions cannot be taken, even upon a supplemental bill of complaint.*

British Library MS. Hargrave 80, f. 63, pl. 1

You cannot examine on a supplemental bill brought after publication.

[Other copies of this report: Lincoln's Inn MS. Misc. 383, p. 118, pl. 1.]

303

## Meers v. Lord Stourton

(Ch. 1711)

*Specific performance of a contract for the sale of land will not be ordered if the seller's title is defective.*

*In this case, compound interest on a debt was disallowed.*

*A peer answers upon his honor, but, otherwise, he responds under oath.*

Lincoln's Inn MS. Misc. 10, p. 80

18 June 1711.

The defendant made a mortgage to the plaintiff for £15,000, and, in the mortgage, there was an agreement that, if the interest was at any time in arrear for the space of twelve months, that, from that time, such interest should be turned into principal and should carry interest at £6 *per centum*. And, if the plaintiff, by virtue of this clause in the mortgage, should be allowed to turn interest into principal was one question upon a bill brought by the plaintiff to foreclose.

*Sir Joseph Jekyll*, for the defendant: There have been several attempts made of this kind, but they have been always disallowed in this court, and, particularly in the Case of Lord Ossulston and Grey,[1] where there was just such another clause as this.

It is true, in Sir John Cutler's Case,[2] interest was allowed to be turned into principal, but there was an account stated and a subsequent agreement to make the interest principal.

Mr. *Vernon*, on the same side: Even an agreement in a mortgage that, if the money is not paid at the day, that then, upon payment of a further sum, the mortgagor shall release the equity of redemption has been set aside in this court, for, where there is a communication about lending money, the court will not allow a person upon any agreement to make an advantage beyond what the law allows.

It was a great while before the court would allow that, where a mortgage was made at £5 *per centum* and an agreement that, if the interest is not paid at such a time, that then the mortgage should carry 5½ or 6 *per centum*, that such agreements should bind. And there have been several redemptions decreed where such agreements have been set aside. But, at last, I must agree the court did come into it and it has been settled that such agreements are good. But I never knew an agreement in a mortgage to turn interest into principal has ever been allowed.

Why even where an account has been stated and it has appeared by the account that interest upon interest has been computed, the court has set aside the stated account, it being an error appearing upon the face of the account.

The counsel on the other side insisted strongly that the agreement was good.

But the court would not hear of it.

It was said by the Attorney General [*Northey*] that, if Sir Thomas Meers, at the year's end, had assigned over his mortgage, the assignee should have had interest for the interest he had paid, and, therefore, there is the same reason for it in the present case.

But My Lord Keeper [Lord Harcourt] said that an assignee should not turn interest into principal in such a case, but he seemed to allow it might be done where there is a large arrear of interest and there have been frequent applications to the mortgagor, if, in that case, the mortgagee assigns his mortgage, the assignee shall have interest for what interest he has paid the mortgagee.

Lincoln's Inn MS. Misc. 10, p. 99, pl. 2

15 December 1711.

Lord Sturton was ordered at the hearing to produce before the Master upon oath all deeds, writings, etc. He accordingly produces the writings and affirms upon his honor that they were all.

And now, Mr. *How* moves he might do it upon oath, for, though a peer, when he puts in his answer to a bill, is to do it upon his honor, yet, when he is to

---

[1] *Lord Ossulston v. Grey* (Ch. 1711), see below, Case No. 324.

[2] *Lord Delaware v. Cutler* (Ch. 1693 x 1700).

make an affidavit or be examined as a witness, he is to do it upon his oath. And of that opinion he said was the court in Lord Craven's Case,[1] who had brought a bill for discovery of a deed which was lost and had annexed the usual affidavit, and, because he had only made that affidavit upon his honor, the defendant demurred, and the demurrer was allowed by the Lord Cowper.

*Sir Joseph Jekyll* said this differed from Lord Craven's Case, for what My Lord Sturton is to do is only in the nature of a further answer and supplying the defect of his former answer. And, therefore, it ought only to be done upon his honor.

The Master of the Rolls [TREVOR] would make no order in it, but he directed Mr. How to move My Lord Keeper [LORD HARCOURT]. However, he declared he was of the opinion the writings ought to be brought in upon oath.

My Lord Keeper [LORD HARCOURT], being afterwards moved, was of the same opinion.

Dickens 21, 21 E.R. 174

20 December 1711.

On a bill for a partition, there is no occasion to examine witnesses previously to the hearing.

The commissioners named in the commission may examine witnesses under the commission *ore tenus* or take their depositions in writing as they think fit and found their partition on such evidence. This was affirmed by Mr. *Vernon* to be the practice.

Where a peer is to perfect an answer by being examined on interrogatories before a Master after hearing and the like, in such cases, it is to be upon honor. But, where a peer comes himself and is to make satisfaction to a party or the bill is for discovery of deeds or the like, it must be upon his oath.

And so it was held on motion the above day [20 December 1711], Lord Stourton insisting it ought to be upon honor.

Lincoln's Inn MS. Misc. 10, p. 141, pl. 3

21 December 1711.

The decree was, *inter alia*, that the defendant, the Lord Sturton, should produce writings before the Master upon oath.

The question afterwards upon a motion was whether this should be done upon oath or upon the defendant's attestation upon his honor in regard, as it was said for him, this was only the carrying on of his answer and, therefore, ought to be attested in the same manner.

But, to this, it was said that, in all cases where a peer is to be examined as a witness either in this court or in any civil or criminal matter or was to make an

---

[1] *Lord Craven v. Lady Craven* (Ch. 1712–1713), see below, Case No. 347.

affidavit, he must be sworn. And, therefore, it was insisted that My Lord Sturton ought to bring the writings before the Master upon oath.

And of that opinion was the court.

Note Mr. *How* cited My Lord Craven's Case, who brought a bill to discover a deed and annexed the usual affidavit, but he put it in upon his honor. The defendant demurred, and the demurrer was allowed by My Lord Cowper.

2 Salkeld 512, 91 E.R. 437

Sir Thomas Meers exhibited a bill against the Lord Stourton. And it was ordered that the Lord Stourton should be examined upon interrogatories touching his title.

And it was objected that he, being a peer of the realm, ought to answer upon his honor only.

And it was ruled by Harcourt, Lord Keeper, that, where a peer is to answer to a bill, his answer put in upon his honor is sufficient, but, where a peer is to answer interrogatories, to make an affidavit, or be examined as a witness, he must be upon his oath.

British Library MS. Hargrave 80, f. 43v, pl. 2

Sir Thomas Meers created two terms for payment of £15,000 and then conveyed the inheritance to others in trust for the same purpose and, as a further security, gave a recognizance for £30,000.

The bill was to redeem or stand foreclosed and, in case of foreclosure, to have a value set upon the mortgaged premises in order to be let in to have the benefit of the recognizance. There had been some agreement a little before between the parties to purchase these lands at £19,400 and short minutes of it were produced signed by Thomas Meers. But after that agreement, Sir Thomas Meers, discovering that these lands were entailed, the reversion in fee to a tenant in tail and that, he being attainted of felony, the reversion escheated to the Crown, of whom they were held and that, though the entail was barred, that crated but a base fee, refused to purchase. And the defendant brought a cross-bill for the specific performance of these articles.

[It was] urged for Sir Thomas Meers that equity would not compel anyone to purchase an ill title.

Lord Keeper [Lord Harcourt] decreed that agreement to be good if the title was so and referred it to a master to examine it.

There was a covenant in the mortgage deed that, if interest was behind for the space of a year, that then the interest should be turned into principal and carry interest.

*Sir Joseph Jekyll*: The case of Lords Ossulston and Yarmouth[1] was much stronger than this. There, the mortgagor had an absolute fee but in part of the mortgaged premises and that not above £100 a year, which was not sufficient to pay the mortgage. The rest was subject to a jointure and yet, in that case, a covenant to turn interest into principal upon default of payment for half a year was set aside upon argument here. In Sir John Cutler's Case, there was an account constantly stated at set times, and it was on that reason that interest was allowed to be turned into principal there.

*Vernon*: This court has always been so careful to prevent interest upon interest that an agreement, if the money was not paid at such a day, that then, upon payment of a further sum, it should be an absolute purchase has been disallowed.

It was with difficulty that an agreement for interest at 5% and that upon failure of payment, it should be 5½ or 6% plus costs was admitted to be good, which it was at length in regard it kept within legal interest.

Interest upon interest was disallowed in the principal case.

[Other copies of this report: Lincoln's Inn MS. Misc. 383, f. 85, pl. 2.]

Lincoln's Inn MS. Misc. 380, pt. 2, p. 1

My Lord Harcourt held and decreed that, where there was a covenant in the mortgaged deed, that, if interest should not be paid from time to time within three months after it became due, such interest should be made principal and from that time carry interest, that such covenant was void and such interest should not carry interest according to that agreement.

Cases *tempore* Talbot 40, 25 E.R. 649

Sir Thomas Meers had in some mortgages inserted a covenant that, if the interest was not paid punctually at the day, it should from that time, and so from time to time, be turned into principal and bear interest.

Upon a bill filed, the Lord Chancellor [Lord Harcourt] relieved the mortgagors against this covenant, as unjust and oppressive.

[Other reports of this case: 1 Peere Williams 146, 24 E.R. 332, 2 Eq. Cas. Abr. 14, 46, 22 E.R. 11, 209.]

## 304

## Hyde v. Hyde

(Ch. 1711–1713)

*An infant male of fourteen years and a female of twelve years may make a will of any personal estate.*

[1] *Lord Ossulston v. Lord Yarmouth* (Ch. 1707), see above, Case No. 91.

*A party who is in willful contempt of court will not be allowed to make a petition or a motion in court, but he may do so where the issue is bona fide in dispute.*

Lincoln's Inn MS. Misc. 11, p. 142

30 October 1711. William Hyde, son and heir of William Hyde, plaintiff; Humfry Hyde, William Walcot, Ann Hyde, and others, defendants.

William Hyde, the father, by his will dated 20 September 1702, gave to the defendants, Humfry and Ann, and to Rachel Hyde, since deceased, his younger children, the sum of £4500 to be divided among them in such proportion as his wife thought fit, his intent being to oblige them to be dutiful to her. Out of the interest of this money, he would have them maintained according to their quality. And he appointed the principal money to be paid to them when the youngest of them should attain twenty-one years or sooner and in such proportion as his wife pleased to give it them.

He also gave his son Humfry £1500 to be paid when he attained the age of twenty-one years. And to Rachel and Ann, he gave £1500 apiece in the very same manner.

He gave to the plaintiff £200 a year until he attained the age of thirty, and, as soon as he attained that age, he gave to him and his heirs all his lands whatsoever. He gave to him and his heirs all the estate he lately bought at Keyston in trust that, until it be sold, the profits be applied for making good the interest of £3550, part of the said £4500, and, as soon as his son came of age, if he paid £3250 to his wife and younger children to be by her divided amongst them as was therein directed, then his said son and his heirs should have all that estate, but, if, within six months after he came of age, he did not pay that sum, then the estate should be sold and all the moneys arising thereby applied in part of the £4500 and to make good the residue thereof and all other bequests thereby given and his debts.

He gave his wife all his personal estate whatsoever until the plaintiff attained the age of thirty in trust to raise so much as should pay all his debts and legacies, and, if there should be any overplus, he gave the same to his wife.

The testator died soon after, and, having named no executor in the will, she took administration *cum testamento annexo.*

When the plaintiff came of age, he came to an agreement with his mother in consideration of having possession of £500 a year, part of his father's estate, and settling it on him and his heirs to charge the rest of his estate with the portions and with the raising of [ *blank* ] for making good the debts and other legacies and to release to his mother all demands he had against her as administratrix of her husband.

Accordingly, by lease and release dated 19 and 20 August 1706 between him and his mother and the younger children and others, several lands were conveyed to the plaintiff and his heirs, and other lands were limited to trustees for 500 years, remainder to the plaintiff for life, with divers remainders over. The trusts of the term were in the first place out of the rents to raise £270 a year for the maintenance of Humfry, Rachel, and Ann until their portions became payable, then, by sale or mortgage, to raise £9000 for the portions of Humfry, Rachel, and Ann in lieu of the legacies and portions given them by their father's will to be paid at twenty-one or marriage, *viz.* £4500 part thereof to be paid them in such proportions as their mother should appoint and, for want of appointment amongst them, equally, the remaining £4500 to be equally divided between them. And, if either died before his or her portion became payable, such portion to go to such person as would have been entitled to the same if the settlement had not been made, and upon further trust to raise £640 for the testator's debts and other legacies remaining unpaid.

By the same deed, the plaintiff releases to his mother all demands etc. he had against her as administratrix or otherwise.

Rachel died between the age of fourteen and fifteen, having made her will and thereby given several legacies, and she made her mother executrix and residuary legatee.

Judith, the mother, having proved her daughter's will, makes her own will. And she, thereby, directs that the £4500 left to her direction by the will of her husband should be paid to Humfry and Ann within one week after her death. And she made her son Humfry and the defendant Walcot executors.

The plaintiff, after the death of his mother, brought his bill to set aside the release he gave to his mother and to set aside the settlement he had made.

The defendants, the executors of the mother, pleaded the release, and the plea was allowed.

Upon the hearing the cause, the questions were:

First, how much of the £9000 given by the testator's will to his younger children ought to be raised and in what manner;

Second, whether the sum of £1500, as Rachel's share of the £4500, which was to be divided between them in such proportion as their mother should appoint, ought to sink into the real estate for the benefit of the plaintiff, Rachel dying before any division had been made by the mother.

Lord Keeper [Lord Harcourt] was of the opinion that the devise of that £4500 was a joint devise and, by the death of Rachel, survived to Humphry and Ann to be divided between them in such proportions as Judith should appoint, and, she having appointed the same to be equally divided between them, the said appointment is good, and Humfry and Ann are well entitled to that money in moieties between them with interest at £6 percent from the time it became payable according to the intention of the will of the father and the deed of trust as also the £1500 apiece devised to Humfry and Ann with interest at £5 percent from the time they became respectively payable.

As to the £1500 devised to Rachel, His Lordship [Lord Harcourt] was of the opinion the same was a legacy vested upon the death of the father and that he had a power to make a will and that the same ought to be raised with such interest as aforesaid of the fund left by her father decreed to be paid the executor before such time as the child, if she had lived, would have attained twenty-one was sufficient to have raised the whole £9000 and maintenance and interest and other legacies and funeral charges, His Lordship [Lord Harcourt] declaring that the portion of any younger child dying before such portions became payable was not intended by the deed of the 20th of August 1706 to be raised in any other manner than according to the said will. But, if the said fund should not be sufficient to answer the purposes aforesaid, then an abatement was to be made in respect to that legacy in proportion with the other legacies payable out of such fund for which purpose it was necessary an enquiry should be made into the value of the said fund, for, although the plaintiff, by his agreement with his mother, brother, and sisters, had so far directed the fund that his mother could not be called to an account for the same, yet the plaintiff's own estate ought not to be liable to make good more than such fund was before the agreement.

And to the end the value of the fund might appear, it was referred to the Master to take an account of the personal estate of the plaintiff's father and what the same after his debts and funerals paid amounted to.

Precedents in Chancery 316, 24 E.R. 149,
Gilbert Rep. 74, 25 E.R. 51

In this case, no dispute was made but that an infant male of fourteen years and a female of twelve years might make a will of the personal estate. And it was said to be so agreed by My Lord Keeper Wright in a Case of Sharp *versus* Sharp, wherein they followed the rule of the civil law of Justinian as, at those ages, they might consent to marriage.

British Library MS. Hargrave 81, f. 105

*Eodem die* [10 August].

Though a party in contempt is not to be heard in court either by petition or motion [as] a punishment for his disobedience and affront to the court, yet this is not an absolute and universal rule.

Here, the contempt complained of against the petitioner is his not paying Mrs. Hyde an annuity of £50 *per annum*. When the Master has made his report, it is a doubt whether she must have an annuity or not and therefore this is not a contempt within the meaning of this rule. And, therefore, he is to be heard notwithstanding the contempt.

And he was relieved upon his petition.

[Other copies of this report: British Library MS. Hargrave 82, f. 102, British Library MS. Hargrave 77, f. 26, pl. 1, British Library MS. Hargrave 303, f. 49v, pl. 1.]

## 305

## Whitcome v. Hoskins

(Ch. 1711)

*The Statute of Distribution and the custom of a city include posthumous children.*

*If one child of a citizen dies in the lifetime of his ancestor, his customary part survives to the other children.*

British Library MS. Hargrave 80, f. 63, pl. 2

[It was] agreed that a posthumous child shall come in with the rest upon the Statute of Distribution[1] and for his customary part. If one child dies, his customary part survives to the other children and does not fall. Under the Statute of Distribution, if a child be advanced by his father in part and the certainty of that part does not appear in writing, he shall be totally excluded from any customary part, but not if it does.

[Other copies of this report: Lincoln's Inn MS. Misc. 383, p. 118, pl. 2, Lincoln's Inn MS. Misc. 106, p. 67, pl. 1.]

## 306

## Anonymous

(Ch. 1711)

*Property held by a bankrupt as a trustee cannot be seized by the bankrupt's assignee for the benefit of his creditors.*

British Library MS. Hargrave 80, f. 63v, pl. 1

A tally for £500 was assigned to J.S. by J.N., to whom J.S. gave a note to be accountable for it to him. J.S. assigns it to A.B. as a security for £400, which £400 (I think) was paid over to J.N. Then, J.S. becomes a bankrupt, and A.B. paid the remaining £100 to the assignees. And they were decreed to pay it to J.N., the tally not being the proper goods of the bankrupt, but only deposited in his hands in trust to borrow money upon it for J.N. The assignees had not distributed the £100 among the creditors.

[Other copies of this report: Lincoln's Inn MS. Misc. 383, p. 119, pl. 1, Lincoln's Inn MS. Misc. 106, p. 67, pl. 1.]

---

[1] Stat. 22 & 23 Car. II, c. 10, s. 3 (*SR*, V, 720).

## 307

## Anonymous

(Ch. 1711)

*A client can have his solicitor's bill taxed by the court, but the solicitor cannot unless the client prevailed in the litigation, in which case the solicitor will be paid out of the proceeds of the recovery.*

British Library MS. Hargrave 80, f. 63v, pl. 2

A party may move to have his solicitor's bill taxed by a master upon undertaking to pay it. But a solicitor cannot have his own bill taxed unless there be a duty decreed to the party by the solicitor's care, in which case, the court will lay their hands upon it until the solicitor is paid out of it. By the Lord Keeper [Lord Harcourt] and the Master of the Rolls [Trevor].

[Other copies of this report: Lincoln's Inn MS. Misc. 383, p. 119, pl. 2, Lincoln's Inn MS. Misc. 106, p. 68, pl. 1.]

## 308

## Anonymous

(Ch. 1711)

*The question in this case was whether all executors must be sued jointly as co-defendants.*

British Library MS. Hargrave 80, f. 63v, pl. 3

A bill was brought against two executors and one only was brought to the hearing. And it was excepted for want of parties because the other executor might have paid the demands and have had a release or might have paid away all the assets in his hands and as much as the value of those in this executor's hands. And the exception was allowed.

But query whether there be not a difference where both executors were made defendants, as in this case, and another lately, where one of them was not so much as made a defendant.

And an exception was taken to that by *Vernon*, to which *Sir Peter King* replied that, at common law, one may sue one executor without the other, though, in [an action of] account brought by them, they must both join. The reason of that difference seems to be because a stranger may be ignorant who are executors, but an executor cannot but know his [fellow] executors.

And the exception was overruled by the Lord Keeper [Harcourt].

[Other copies of this report: Lincoln's Inn MS. Misc. 383, p. 119, pl. 3, Lincoln's Inn MS. Misc. 106, p. 68, pl. 2.]

## 309

## The Pennsylvania Company's Case

(Ch. 1711)

*Several subscribers of a company or creditors can sue a defendant or behalf of themselves and others similarly situated.*

British Library MS. Hargrave 80, f. 64

[In the] case of the Society of Traders to Pennsylvania, twenty out of 400 subscribers to this trade brought a bill against the representatives of the Deputy Treasurer, into whose hands they had paid their money. And an exception was taken for want to proper parties. It was urged that they ought to have sued in their corporate capacity; but it was replied that they were no corporation; secondly, that then all the subscribers ought to have been parties for, otherwise, the defendants might be liable to an infinite number of suits. It was replied that, if that exception prevailed, there would be a failure of justice, that it would be impossible to carry on a cause where so many must be concerned without continual abatements, and that one abatement either before or after hearing, would stop everything, that, upon this ground, this exception was overruled in the cases of Dr. Chamberlain and the Land Bank,[1] Hutchinson and the City of London, about Lamb's Conduit, and, in the Exchequer, between Eyre in Derbyshire and the inhabitants of the Hundred of Peake about an enclosure.

*Vernon* added that nothing was more usual than, where several creditors were to have a satisfaction out of a trust, for three or four of them to bring a bill in behalf of themselves and their other creditors and the decree may provide for the rest in case they come in and that one legatee may sue the executor without bringing the other legatees before the court, in which case, the executor may show what debts he has paid, what other legacies are owing, and shall retain a proportionable part to satisfy the other legatees, that they only desired their shares of gain and loss by the trade in proportion to their subscriptions or their subscription money again with interest in case it had not been paid over to the stock of the society, which was decreed accordingly.

[Other copies of this report: Lincoln's Inn MS. Misc. 383, p. 120, Lincoln's Inn MS. Misc. 106, p. 69.]

[1] Perhaps *Anonymous v. Briscoe* (Ch. 1706), see above, Case No. 49.

## 310

## Anonymous

(Ch. 1711)

*A suit for relief against a bond given by one who later becomes bankrupt does not affect the assignees in bankruptcy.*

British Library MS. Hargrave 80, f. 64v, pl. 1

The defendants became bankrupts after they had answered. And, though that did not appear, yet the parties being satisfied that the fact was so, the plaintiff chose to amend his bill and to make the assignees parties.

*Vernon* insisting that a decree against the bankrupt would not affect the assignees, the bill was brought for relief against the bond given by the bankrupts.

[Other copies of this report: Lincoln's Inn MS. Misc. 383, p. 121, pl. 1, Lincoln's Inn MS. Misc. 106, p. 70, pl. 1.]

## 311

## Sir Owen Buckingham's Case

(Ch. 1711)

*Where a trust beneficiary uses the trust estate to secure his debts, the creditors stand on equal equities and a third mortgagee cannot defeat the second by paying off the first encumbrance.*

British Library MS. Hargrave 80, f. 64v, pl. 2

Preference and tacking of debts in equity.

An estate was conveyed to trustees to the intent that the *cestui que trust* might take up money upon it. He first borrowed a large sum of J.S. and declared that the estate should stand a security for it. Then Sir Owen Buckingham [1650–1713] got a judgment against him for £1000, and then J.S. lent him a further sum on the same security.

Lord Keeper [Lord Harcourt]: None of those debts have anything more than an equitable security and, for that reason, though it should be admitted that J.S. had no notice of the judgment when he advanced his last sum, yet he cannot unite his two sums, but Sir Owen Buckingham's judgment must be satisfied before the last. If J.S. had a legal title as well as equity on his side, it would be otherwise.

Two cases were cited in point.

[Other copies of this report: Lincoln's Inn MS. Misc. 383, p. 121, pl. 2.]

## 312

## Sheers v. Sheers

(Ch. 1711)

*Where a younger son becomes an heir apparent, he will not take under a prior gift to younger children.*

*Where a deed has been lost, it will be presumed that there was a proper tenant to the praecipe.*

*A court of equity has jurisdiction to establish a lost deed.*

British Library MS. Hargrave 80, f. 64v, pl. 3

In this case, My Lord Keeper [LORD HARCOURT] cited the case of Chaddick and Sir Thomas Doleman,[1] which was this. Sir Thomas's father, having a power to charge his estate with £4000 for younger children, appointed £3000 of it to be for Sir Thomas, who was at that time his second son. I think some of the counsel said that the reason of that appointment was Sir Thomas's having married a lady with a great fortune. After this, Sir Thomas's older brother died, and then his father. And then the rest of the children brought their bill for the whole £4000 in regard the second son was become the eldest and so out of the meaning of the settlement. And Lord Cowper decreed the £4000 to them.

But my Lord Keeper [LORD HARCOURT] and *Vernon* said that that was going a great way. However, in the principal case, he decreed that the defendant, who was a second son at the time of the settlement and grew into an eldest in the life of his father, should be excluded from taking under a use limited to younger children and that it being the intent of the settlement to exclude only him that was to have the inheritance and to so provide for all the rest that an older daughter should come in for a share.

In the case before, it was admitted that, twenty years after a recovery, it would be presumed even at law that there was a proper tenant to the *praecipe* though the deed by which he was made so was lost.

But yet the Lord Keeper [LORD HARCOURT] seemed to allow that the loss of that deed was ground enough for coming into Chancery.

[Other copies of this report: Lincoln's Inn MS. Misc. 383, p. 121, pl. 3, Lincoln's Inn MS. Misc. 106, p. 70, pl. 2.]

---

[1] *Chadwick v. Doleman* (1706), 2 Vernon 528, 23 E.R. 941, 1 Eq. Cas. Abr. 344, 21 E.R. 1091.

## 313

## Anonymous v. Willmot

(Ch. 1711)

*A custom to have a mill in a manor must be established at common law before it can be enforced in a court of equity.*

British Library MS. Hargrave 80, f. 65

A bill was brought by a lady of a manor against Willmot to destroy a mill erected by him within the manor and for an injunction to hinder the tenants from grinding at that mill upon a suggestion that she had a mill there and had repaired it time out of mind and that the tenants had time out of mind etc. done suit of mill. [There was a] demurrer because, of her own showing, her title was founded on a custom, which is triable only at law.

*Sir Peter King*: We are entitled to a discovery here whether there is such a custom or not.

*How*: Whether a custom or not is triable at law and by a jury and not here, you ought to establish your title at law first and then you may be proper here.

The demurrer was allowed.

[Other copies of this report: Lincoln's Inn MS. Misc. 383, p. 122, pl. 1, Lincoln's Inn MS. Misc. 106, p. 71.]

## 314

## Ford v. Hale

(Ch. 1711)

*A defendant's plea must respond to the substance of the plaintiff's bill of complaint.*

British Library MS. Hargrave 80, f. 65v, pl. 1

A bill [was exhibited] to be relieved against a release. [There was a] plea of that release in bar without answering to the facts on which the plaintiff founded his equity, such as no account stated forcing him to make it by seizing his effects etc. And the plea was overruled.

[Other copies of this report: Lincoln's Inn MS. Misc. 383, p. 122, pl. 2, Lincoln's Inn MS. Misc. 106, p. 72, pl. 1.]

## 315

## Cock v. Wilkinson

(Ch. 1711)

*A demurrer on the ground that the bill prays a discovery of a penalty should go only to the prayer for discovery but not to the prayer for relief.*

British Library MS. Hargrave 80, f. 65v, pl. 2

*How*: We have demurred to that part of the bill that seeks a discovery of our pulling down of the plaintiff's wall etc. because the discovery might subject us to a penalty by indictment for a forcible entry and the plaintiff has his remedy at law and likewise to that part of the bill that seeks a discovery of what part of the timber we have felled upon the land we hold by lease from the plaintiff because he has not waived the penalty.

*Vernon*: Your demurrer goes farther; it goes to all relief as well as discovery, and there are several other things in the bill. If a matter be triable at law, yet a party may come hither for a discovery to save the trouble of examining witnesses.

The demurrer was overruled.

[Other copies of this report: Lincoln's Inn MS. Misc. 383, p. 122, pl. 3, Lincoln's Inn MS. Misc. 106, p. 72, pl. 2.]

## 316

## Anonymous v. Box

(Ch. 1711)

*Discovery of a title is only allowed where there is an impediment to obtaining the information otherwise.*

British Library MS. Hargrave 80, f. 65v, pl. 3

*Williams*: In all cases where a plaintiff sets forth a title, he is entitled to a discovery.

[It was] replied that they ought to have set forth an impediment and that, as they did not, the law was open.

And the demurrer was allowed.

[It was] said by *Williams* that a plea may, but a demurrer cannot, be supported by an answer.

[Other copies of this report: Lincoln's Inn MS. Misc. 383, p. 123, pl. 1, Lincoln's Inn MS. Misc. 106, p. 73, pl. 1.]

## 317

## Mince v. Peters's Lottery

(Ch. 1711)

*A court of equity will force a lottery promoter to pay the holder of the winning ticket, though the lottery was illegal, because the parties, though both are offenders of the same law, are not equal offenders.*

British Library MS. Hargrave 80, f. 66, pl. 1

The plaintiff drew the £1000 ticket in a lottery set up by Peters after the Act[1] that prohibits them and declares them to be common nuisances and subjects the projector to the penalty of £500 and the adventurers of £20 apiece. [It was] objected that she should have no relief in equity, being an equal offender with Peters, no more than, in the case of two gamesters, one could have a remedy against the other, or two pirates.

But the Lord Keeper [Lord Harcourt] thought their offenses were not equal and that the Act ought not to shelter Peters from making satisfaction. But, as the lot was made of two houses valued at £800 and of a silver cistern valued at £200, he decreed that the houses should be taken to be of that value, though they were really worth but £600, because the adventurers might have resorted to them and seen whether they were of that value or not. But as to the cistern, that having been never bought by Peters, he decreed that Peters should pay the £200.

[Other copies of this report: Lincoln's Inn MS. Misc. 383, p. 123, pl. 2, Lincoln's Inn MS. Misc. 106, p. 73, pl. 2.]

## 318

## Anonymous v. Wigmore

(Ch. 1711)

*Where a defendant appears and disclaims, he is entitled to receive court costs.*

British Library MS. Hargrave 80, f. 66, pl. 2

The plaintiff made a great number of persons to be defendants to his bill, which was chiefly for a discovery of deeds. They all disclaimed any title and denied that they knew anything of the deeds. But, however, the plaintiff brought on the cause to a hearing upon the bill and answer, and the only thing contended for by him then was that his bill might be dismissed with only 40s. costs apiece.

---

[1] Stat. 10 Will. III, c. 23 (*SR*, VII, 532–533); Stat. 9 Ann., c. 6, s. 57 (*SR*, IX, 383); Stat. 10 Ann., c. 112 (*SR*, IX, 669–670).

*Vernon*: You have made a vast number of persons defendants merely for vexation. If you had dismissed your bill before the hearing, we should have had our costs to have been taxed by a master by the Statute[1] and merely to avoid that to put us to a further expense, you have set this cause down for a hearing. He insisted that this was an abuse of the rule of court.

And though every defendant answered separately and appeared by a different counsel, Lord Keeper [HARCOURT] decreed them their costs to be taxed by a master.

It was said that each of the defendants had offered the plaintiff to take 40s. costs if he would dismiss his bill before hearing and that he refused it.

[Other copies of this report: Lincoln's Inn MS. Misc. 383, p. 123, pl. 3, Lincoln's Inn MS. Misc. 106, p. 74.]

## 319

## Anonymous

(Ch. 1711)

*Where a debtor is made the executor of his creditor's will, the debt is not thereby discharged.*

British Library MS. Hargrave 80, f. 66v, pl. 1

If a creditor makes his debtor executor in trust, this is no discharge of the debt in equity.

[Other copies of this report: Lincoln's Inn MS. Misc. 383, p. 124, pl. 1.]

## 320

## Anonymous

(Ch. 1711)

*Where a lease for years is bequeathed with a direction that it be renewed, the life tenant must pay one-third of the cost of the renewal and the remainderman two-thirds.*

British Library MS. Hargrave 80, f. 66v, pl. 2

A lease for years under the Church of Winton[2] was devised to J.S. for life, remainder to J.N. And the testator directed that the term should be regularly renewed.

And the court decreed that it should and that the tenant for life should pay one-third and he in remainder two-thirds of the fine. And the new lease being

[1] Stat. 8 Eliz. I, c. 2 (*SR*, IV, 486–487).

[2] *I.e.* Winchester.

to be taken in the name of a third person, it was directed that there should be a memorandum of the trust endorsed to prevent anybody's purchasing it without notice.

[Other copies of this report: Lincoln's Inn MS. Misc. 383, p. 124, pl. 2.]

## 321

## Witter v. Lutwidge

(Ch. 1711)

*When a testator in Ireland bequeaths money in 'sterling', it will be paid with English money.*

Lincoln's Inn MS. Misc. 10, p. 131

6 November 1711.

Henry Palmer, sometime a merchant in England, but, afterwards, residing at Dublin, made his will there. And, by his will, he gave several legacies to be paid in sterling money, and, among others, he gives to the plaintiff, then of Chester, the sum of £50 sterling to be paid within twelve months after his death.

The executor insisted that the testator's effects lay in Ireland and that this legacy ought to be paid according to the rate of money in Ireland and not in lawful money of England.

[It was] decreed that £50 sterling is £50 of lawful money of England and that the same should be paid accordingly with interest and costs.

In this case I [*Melmoth*] cited Blount's *Dictionary*, which says sterling was the ancient epithet for money current in this realm and took its name from this, that there was a certain coin stamped first in England by the Easterlings or merchants of East Germany by the command of King John; that the word 'sterling' is now much disused and, instead of £5 sterling, we say £5 of current or lawful English money.

By the Statute 17 Edw. III, which is mentioned in 3 Ins.[1] but not printed in the statute book, it is accorded to make money of good sterling in England of the weight and alloy of the ancient sterling, which shall be current in England etc. And, by the seventeenth of the same king, an English penny, which is called the sterling round shall weigh twenty-two grains of wheat well dried.

[1] Stat. 17 Edw. III (*SR*, I, 299); E. Coke, *Third Institute* (1644), p. 92.

## 322

## Mason v. Day

(Ch. 1711)

*Where a lease is surrendered and then renewed, the renewed lease is a new and different estate in land.*

Lincoln's Inn MS. Misc. 10, p. 99, pl. 1

13 November 1711.

A married woman has a lease to her and her heirs during the lives of A., B., and C. She dies, and this lease descends to the daughter as heir at law to her mother. She being an infant, her guardians enter, and two of the lives fall during her infancy. And, thereupon, the guardians surrender this lease and take a new one to the infant and her heirs during her own life and the lives of two others. And then she dies.

The question was between the uncles of the part of the father and the aunts of the part of the mother to whom this lease should descend.

It was insisted on for the latter that it belonged to them, for that it was the old estate.

But, to this, it was said on the other side that this was a new purchase, and, therefore, it ought to descend to the heirs on the part of the father.

And of that opinion was the Master of Rolls [TREVOR], who decreed accordingly.

And the Lord Keeper [LORD HARCOURT] coming into court in the interim, he declared he was of the same opinion.

Lincoln's Inn MS. Misc. 11, p. 227, pl. 1

A bishop's lease for three lives descended to Mary Mason from her mother. She being an infant and two lives having dropped, her guardian renewed the lease, having surrendered the old one, and took a new lease in the name of A.B. and his heirs in trust for Mary Mason. Mary died in her infancy and without issue. And the question was whether her aunts by the mother's side or her uncles by the father's side were entitled to this lease as heirs to Mary.

[It was] resolved by the Master of the Rolls [TREVOR] that, by the renewal, Mary became a new purchaser and that the lease was descended to her heir on the father's side. And Lord Keeper [LORD HARCOURT], after the decree, coming in and the Master of the Rolls [TREVOR] stating the case to him, he concurred in the same opinion.

Godbolt and Freeman, 3 Lev.[1] [was] cited.

[1] *Godbold v. Freestone* (1694), 3 Levinz 406, 83 E.R. 753.

[Other reports of this case: Precedents in Chancery 319, 24 E.R. 150, Gilbert Rep. 77 25 E.R. 54, 2 Eq. Cas. Abr. 494, 22 E.R. 419.]

## 323

## Price v. Solly

(Ch. 1711)

*Where a default decree is obtained by surprise, the defendant can move to have it set aside before court costs are taxed.*

Dickens 21, 21 E.R. 174

22 November 1711. Lord Harcourt.

A decree [was] obtained by surprise. On an application by a motion to discharge it, it was ordered that the defendant should be at liberty to show cause against the decree before the costs of his default were paid and that the whole costs should be reserved until the time of showing cause.

## 324

## Lord Ossulston v. Grey

(Ch. 1711)

*Where a person orders by his will that his debts be paid, this does not revive debts that are barred by the Statute of Limitations.*

*A court of equity cannot direct a trust to be executed contrary to the intention of the settlor.*

Lincoln's Inn MS. Misc. 10, p. 100

December 1711.

Ralph, lord Grey, by his will, devised all his lands in Northumberland, Durham, Sussex, etc. to the lord Somers and others upon trust that, by sale or mortgage, they should pay several debts and, among others, a mortgage upon an estate in Uppark in Sussex. And, subject to this trust, he entails these lands upon the defendant, Mr. Nevil, and the heirs of his body with remainders over.

It appeared that Lord Grey had no lands in Sussex but Uppark and, as to that, he was only tenant for life and, consequently had no power to dispose of it. And, upon his death, it came to the plaintiff's lady. And now the plaintiff came to have an execution of the trust and to have Uppark disencumbered out of the trust estate.

Lord Keeper [Lord Harcourt]: I am of the opinion in regard that Uppark could not go to Mr. Nevil, as the testator intended by his will, the trust that was created for discharging that and other estates of the encumbrances ought not to be executed as to Uppark in favor of one for whom it is plain the testator, by his will, has not shown the least regard.

It is manifest his intention was that Uppark should be disencumbered in favor and for the ease of Mr. Nevil, to whom he devised that and other lands. But, since his intention could not take place in one case, it is not reasonable it should in the other.

N.B. In this case, it was agreed that, if a man who owes a debt which is barred by the Statute of Limitations[1] does afterwards by his will create a trust for the payment of all his debts, this brings it out of the Statute again and puts it upon the same foot with the other debts. And this it was said was the Duke of Richmond's Case. But otherwise it is if a man makes a will and appoints executors and says as is usual 'I will that all my debts shall be paid.'

British Library MS. Hargrave 80, f. 66v, pl. 3

Statute of limitations discharging debts.

*Vernon*: That Statute[2] discharges the action only, not the debt. And, therefore, if a man creates a trust for payment of his debts, equity will let in those debts which the Statute barred the recovery of at law. But it was never pretended that, where a man devises his personal estate to his executor and wills that his debts be paid, that this shall revive such a debt, which Lord Keeper [HARCOURT] agreed to.

*Vernon* cited the Case of Sir Robert Carr and Cox,[3] where there was a general trust created by Sir Robert for the payment of his debts and the question was whether a debt to Cox, which Sir Robert had always litigated and denied to be due, should be let in, and, after much debate, [it was] decreed that it should.

In the principal case, Lord Grey had devised all his lands in Sussex etc. to trustees to be sold for discharging several encumbrances therein specified, one of which was a mortgage upon Uppark in Sussex and the residue in trust for Mr. Grey. The testator had no estate in Sussex but Uppark. He had agreed only to purchase lands of £1000 value there. But the conveyance was not made before his death. And Uppark, being in settlement, was not in his power to devise, but came upon his death to My Lady Ossulston. And My Lord sought by his bill to have the trust estate applied to discharge the mortgage upon Uppark. The chief argument for the plaintiff was that the will had expressly directed that encumbrance should be discharged out of the trust estate and that there could be nothing objected to it but loose and uncertain inferences drawn from his intention

[1] Stat. 21 Jac. I, c. 16, s. 3 (*SR*, IV, 1222).

[2] Stat. 21 Jac. I, c. 16, s. 3 (*SR*, IV, 1222).

[3] *Holles v. Carr* (1676), 3 Swanston 638, 36 E.R. 1004, 73 Selden Soc. 282, 334, 378, Reports *tempore* Finch 261, 23 E.R. 143, 2 Modern 86, 86 E.R. 956, 2 Freeman 3, 22 E.R. 1017.

and that the devise of all his lands in Sussex might operate upon those he had agreed to purchase.

But by Lord Keeper [Lord Harcourt], the plaintiff comes here for an execution of a trust, and I cannot direct a trust to be executed contrary to the intention of the party who created it. It is apparent that he intended to devise Uppark to Mr. Grey and that the encumbrance upon it and all the other encumbrances mentioned in the will should be discharged for the benefit of Mr. Grey only [so] that the residue of the estate might come clear to him. Though Lady Ossulston was his heir, yet there was not the least expression of kindness for her throughout the will. And, since the devise to Mr. Gray of Uppark cannot take effect, I cannot direct that the provision made for disencumbering it should.

Mr. Isles, one of the trustees in the will, had a mortgaged term in him of part of the lands devised to him and the other trustees and their heirs and had not intermeddled in the trust for fear of injuring his own term.

And Lord Keeper [Lord Harcourt] directed that he should assign his term in trust for himself and then release the inheritance to the other trustees.

*Mead* insisted upon his renouncing the trust in court without anything more.

But Lord Keeper [Lord Harcourt] said that would not be sufficient.

[Other copies of this report: Lincoln's Inn MS. Misc. 383, p. 124, pl. 3.]

## 325

## Anonymous

(Ch. 1711)

*A court of equity can order an account in order to enforce a restitution ordered by the Mayor of London's Court.*

British Library MS. Hargrave 80, f. 67v, pl. 1

The defendant attached goods in his own hands in London and procured them to be appraised. The plaintiff sued out a *scire facias ad disprobandum debitum*, which is to disprove or otherwise avoid the debt. The debt was thereupon disproved in the Mayor's Court, and the plaintiff had restitution awarded of the value according to the agreement, which was all that he could have there by the custom, the goods being sold, upon which the plaintiff brought a bill in Chancery.

And the Master of the Rolls [Trevor] decreed that the defendant should account for the value the goods were sold for beyond the appraisement and interest from the filing of the bill.

[Other copies of this report: Lincoln's Inn MS. Misc. 383, p. 125, Lincoln's Inn MS. Misc. 106, p. 75, pl. 1.]

## 326

## Anonymous v. Garton

(Ch. 1711)

*An arbitral award that is grossly excessive will be set aside by the court.*

British Library MS. Hargrave 80, f. 67v, pl. 2

The plaintiff, a freeholder of Oxfordshire, had been drawn to advance money for a place at court, but, afterwards, finding himself imposed upon, he brought a bill for his money, which was repaid to him, and to be relieved against an award which he had been drawn into by art. The thing submitted was an assault and battery by him and his wife upon a washerwoman of very ill reputation. And the umpire, to whose umpirage he was prevailed upon to submit by being told that he had said that, if the matters in dispute were referred to him, he would draw a stroke through the demands on each side and that the plaintiff should only give a dish of meat and that should end the dispute, awarded the plaintiff to pay £60.

*Vernon* cited the case of the butcher of Croydon,[1] who got an award for £100 for defamation, which for the unreasonableness, was set aside.

And the award in the principal case was set aside.

[Other copies of this report: Lincoln's Inn MS. Misc. 383, p. 126, pl. 1, Lincoln's Inn MS. Misc. 106, p. 75, pl. 2.]

## 327

## Carter v. Carter

(Ch. 1711)

*A court of equity can order a master in chancery to execute a provision in a will for making a purchase directed by the testator where the executors have failed to act.*

British Library MS. Hargrave 80, f. 68

The testator devised, *inter alia*, that his executors should purchase the tithes of Sudbury and settle them upon the parson and his successors. The tithes were worth £40 *per annum*. And the executors bid £800, but the proprietors demanded £1100 for them. And the devisees of the surplus after the charity brought their bill for a distribution of the surplus.

Lord Keeper [HARCOURT] directed that the master should examine into the clear yearly value of the tithes and how much they were worth to be sold and appoint a person to treat with the proprietor with power to give a year's purchase

---

[1] *Cooper v. Anonymous* (c. 1671), 3 Chancery Reports 76, 21 E.R. 733, 1 Eq. Cas. Abr. 50, 21 E.R. 866.

more than the value and that, in the meantime, the £800 that had been offered should be brought before the master and put out upon government security, the interest to be applied for the benefit of the parson until the purchase, but no interest to be paid for the four years from the death of the testator to the time of the decree in regard the executors had been always ready to purchase the tithes if they could have had them.

[Other copies of this report: Lincoln's Inn MS. Misc. 383, p. 126, pl. 2, Lincoln's Inn MS. Misc. 106, p. 76.]

## 328

## Allen v. Bolton

(Ch. 1711)

*A bill of discovery for a deed or writing that was alleged to be lost must be supported by an affidavit of the loss of it, whether relief is prayed or not.*

British Library MS. Hargrave 80, f. 68v, pl. 1

A bill [was exhibited] for a discovery of deeds, particularly of a lease for years, and an account etc. [There was] a demurrer for that the plaintiff did not annex an affidavit to his bill that he had none of the deeds in his custody nor the counterpart of the lease.

*How* insisted that he ought to give that satisfaction to the court to entitle him to a discovery.

But the Master of the Rolls [Trevor] asked *Vernon* and Serjeant *Hooper* their opinions, who both said that the old difference was that, where a man sought relief by his bill and to have something decreed as well as a discovery, he ought to annex an affidavit to his bill, but, where a bill was barely for discovery, that it was not necessary, but that this difference had been overruled sometimes of late.

His Honor [Trevor] overruled the demurrer.

[Other copies of this report: Lincoln's Inn MS. Misc. 383, p. 126, pl. 3, Lincoln's Inn MS. Misc. 106, p. 77, pl. 1.]

Lincoln's Inn MS. Misc. 10, p. 70

The plaintiff, as lord of a manor, suggesting that he had lost a counterpart of a lease which was made by his ancestor, prefers his bill for a discovery of that and likewise of what leases the plaintiff has of any part of the manor.

The defendant demurs because the plaintiff had not made oath of the counterpart. And he also pleads that some persons, affirming they had a title, made a lease to him, and this he pleads in bar of any further discovery in regard the plaintiff had not offered by his bill to confirm this lease.

Mr. *Vernon*: There is no need of making an affidavit when it is only for a discovery. If, indeed, you come for relief, as when you suggest the loss of a bond and pray a discovery of it and that you may be paid your money, you must make the usual oath, but not when you come barely for a discovery. And this he insisted strongly was the printed rule.

As to the plea, it is merely frivolous. The defendant says a person, affirming he had a title, made him a lease, but he does not say who that person was nor that he was seised or was in possession. And yet he insists that we must confirm this lease when, for aught we know, the person that made it had no title.

Lord Keeper [Lord Harcourt]: The plea is certainly too loose and must be overruled.

But as to the demurrer, I ever took it that, in all cases, when you come here for a discovery of a deed or writing supposed to be lost, you must make an affidavit of the loss of it, whether you pray relief or no. The reason is because the court will not permit you to bring a vexations bill to harass another person when perhaps you have the deed all the while in your own custody which you are pretending to seek after.

If you have such a printed rule as you speak of, the cause shall stand over, if you desire it, and let me see the rule. I am sure the reason of the thing is otherwise.

But Mr. *Vernon* not insisting any further upon it, the demurrer was allowed.

## 329

## Pierhouse v. Moore

(Ch. 1711)

*The doctrine of priority of suit applies to the equity courts of Chancery and Exchequer.*

British Library MS. Hargrave 80, f. 68v, pl. 2

The plaintiff purchased the equity of redemption of an estate pending a suit in the Exchequer about the redemption where there had been a decree for an account which was carrying on before the Deputy Remembrancer [John Morgan] there and brought his bill in Chancery for a redemption. [There was a] plea of this suit pending in the Exchequer.

*Vernon*: Priority of suit gives the preferment to either court. The plaintiff might have brought his bill in the Exchequer and gone hand in hand there with the plaintiff to see that there was no collusion in taking the account, but not here, for, should there be two accounts taken in two different courts at the same time, they might fall out to be stated differently.

The plea was allowed by the Master of the Rolls [Trevor].

[Other copies of this report: Lincoln's Inn MS. Misc. 383, p. 127, pl. 1, Lincoln's Inn MS. Misc. 106, p. 77, pl. 2.]

## 330

## Earl Rivers v. Bretland

(Ch. 1711)

*Where a trustee enters into the trust land and does not keep any accounts, he will be charged according to the annual value of the land.*

*Where a decree has been signed and enrolled, it can be revived upon a scire facias. But, if it has not been enrolled, a bill of revivor is necessary to revive it.*

British Library MS. Hargrave 80, f. 69, pl. 1

Lord Keeper [LORD HARCOURT]: If a trustee will enter and so far neglect his trust as to take what he can get and neither to give nor keep any regular account, he must be charged according to the annual value as well as a mortgagee.

In this case, there was a proviso in the deed of trust that Serjeant [Reginald] Bretland [d. 1703], the trustee and the father of defendant, should not be charged with more than he actually received, but yet he having kept no regular accounts, the Lord Keeper [LORD HARCOURT] declared that the Master had done well to charge the defendant with the annual value, allowing him for insolvencies of tenants and agents and for taxes, repairs, etc.

An exception to a master's report for not allowing more than the deposit for the costs of arguing the exception was overruled.

If a decree be signed and enrolled, a *scire facias* is proper to revive it. But, if it be not enrolled, a bill is necessary to revive it, though the party may plead to the *scire facias*. But, if he does not within the regular time, the proceedings will be revived upon a motion and, if a discovery of assets be necessary, the party may be examined to that upon interrogatories.

[Other copies of this report: Lincoln's Inn MS. Misc. 383, p. 127, pl. 2, Lincoln's Inn MS. Misc. 106, p. 78.]

## 331

## Compton v. Piggott

(Ch. 1711)

*Where a person has gotten an injunction to prevent a creditor from enforcing a judgment, a court of equity can order the sale of the land in the hands of a descendant of the judgment debtor in order to satisfy the judgment, including the principal, judgment interest, and court costs.*

British Library MS. Hargrave 80, f. 69, pl. 2

The defendant was the representative of a judgment creditor of the plaintiff's grandfather. A *scire facias* was sued out in the time of the plaintiff's father in order to extend a moiety of the lands descended. The father brought a bill and hung the judgment creditors up by an injunction all his time and devised the lands liable to the judgment to trustees for twenty-one years to raise daughters' portions. The trustees entered and received the profits. And the plaintiff, by his next friend, revived the suit.

The Master of the Rolls [TREVOR] decreed that the plaintiff, the infant, should pay the principal and interest due on the judgment in respect of the length of time that the defendant had been kept out of the receipt of the profits by an injunction, which, if he had received, his judgment might possibly have been satisfied.

But this decree for the infant to pay the judgment, who had received no part of the profits, being irregular, he appealed to Lord Keeper [LORD HARCOURT], who decreed a sale of the whole estate for the satisfaction of the principal and interest due upon the judgment and costs, which together amounted to near £6000. The judgment was but for £3000 and the principal due on the judgment £2000. But he decreed no account of the profits received under cover of the injunction.

[Other copies of this report: Lincoln's Inn MS. Misc. 383, p. 128, pl. 1, Lincoln's Inn MS. Misc. 106, p. 79, pl. 1.]

## 332

## Hoar v. Acton

(Ch. 1711)

*Where money is lent upon a chattel interest, a pawn, or a pledge, and, afterwards, more money is lent upon a bond, the latter loan is presumed to be upon the credit of that security and it will be tacked on to the amount due upon the redemption of a mortgage.*

Lincoln's Inn MS. Misc. 11, p. 9

December 1711. Richard Hoar v. Acton and Grant.

Grant, possessed of ten shares of the ship *Duke and Duchess of Bristol*, borrows £2000 of the defendant Acton, and he assigns over those shares to him upon trust to sell them and pay himself the £2000 and interest and what money he should advance in insuring those shares and to pay the overplus to Grant.

Afterwards, Acton lends Grant £1300 more upon bond, and then he becomes indebted to the plaintiff in £5000. And, reciting Acton's mortgage for £2000, he assigns over the equity of redemption of the shares to the plaintiff for securing his £5000 and interest.

And now, the plaintiff brings his bill to redeem Acton upon the payment of what was due for his £2000 and interest. But he insists that Acton never paid the whole £2000.

The defendant Acton insists that the plaintiff ought not to redeem but upon the payment of the £1300 and interest due on the bond as well as the £2000 on the mortgage, it being agreed that the mortgaged premises should stand charged with the money due on the bond.

But no such agreement could be produced, nor was there any proof that Grant had ever made any such agreement.

However the court [Lord Harcourt] was of opinion that, if the plaintiff will redeem, it must be upon the payment of the bond as well as the mortgage, for, the mortgage being of a chattel estate, it was in the nature of a pawn or pledge and differed from the case upon a mortgage of lands, for, there, a bond cannot be tacked to a mortgage without an agreement in writing, the Statute of Frauds etc.[1] standing in the way. But, where a man lends money upon a chattel interest, which is in the nature of a pawn or pledge, and, afterwards, lends money upon bond, he shall be presumed to do it upon the credit of that security.

It was insisted that the Master might enquire whether the £2000 were really paid.

But the court [Lord Harcourt] would not permit that inquiry, it being recited in the plaintiff's mortgage that the £2000 were due and he took his mortgage subject to that encumbrance. But, as to the £1300, the Master was directed to examine when and how it was paid.

See the case of Hallifax and Kirkland, Canc. Rep. 8vo, fo. 360.[2]

## 332a

## Lord Rockingham v. Penrice

(Ch. 1711)

*Where a lessor dies on the day that the rent is payable, the rent not having been paid, the rent is to be paid to the successor lessor, not the personal representative of the deceased lessor.*

1 Swanston 357, 36 E.R. 417

A tenant for life with leasing power dying on Michaelmas day before sunset, the rent due on that day from tenants under leases conformable to the power was declared payable, not to the executor of the lessor, but to the jointress taking a life estate in remainder on the ground that the lessor, dying before sunset, had no

---

[1] Stat. 29 Car. II, c. 3 (*SR*, V, 839–842).

[2] *Halliley v. Kirtland* (Ch. 1685), 2 Chancery Reports 360, 21 E.R. 687, Chancery Repts. *tempore* Jac. II, 178.

remedy before his death to compel payment, and the rent, therefore, passed to the jointress with the reversion.

The report in Peere Williams[1] states that, one of the lessees having paid his rent to the tenant for life on the morning of Michaelmas day, the court declared the payment good as to the lessee but directed the executor of the tenant for life to account for it to the jointress. And the reporter subjoins a question, why, if the payment was good at law, as it was according to Clun's Case,[2] it must not be so in equity?

On reference to the Register book, it appears that the payment was made, not on the morning of Michaelmas day, but on the 21st of September, the lessee, on the occasion of surrendering the old and taking a new lease, then paying the rent which would have become due on the 29th. The decree declared that 'Sir James Oxenden [the tenant for life], dying on Michaelmas day before sunset and before the tenants of the jointure estate were by law obliged to pay the half-year's rent, the said rent belonged to Lady Oxenden, the jointress, and not to the executor of Sir James Oxenden,' and directed an inquiry what had been received by Sir James Oxenden or his representative for the half-year's rent due at Michaelmas 1708 and what was still due from the respective tenants of the jointure estate, and, as to the tenant who had paid the rent before it became due, declared that Sir James Oxenden living until Michaelmas day, it was a good payment as to the tenant, but that the executor of Sir James Oxenden must make the same good to the jointress.

[Reg. Lib. 1711 A, f. 341.]

[Other reports of this case: 1 Peere Williams 177, 24 E.R. 345, *sub nom. Lord Rockingham v. Oxenden* (1705–1711), 2 Salkeld 578, 91 E.R. 487, Precedents in Chancery 239, 24 E.R. 116.]

## 333

## Barkham v. Darwin

(Ch. 1712)

*Where an executor gives a legacy to a devisee of the first testator, the second legacy is a payment of the first legacy, and the legatee cannot have both.*

[1] *Lord Rockingham v. Penrice* (1705–1711), 1 Peere Williams 177, 24 E.R. 345.

[2] *Clun v. Archer* (1613), 10 Coke Rep. 127, 77 E.R. 1117, Croke Jac. 309, 79 E.R. 265, 4 Leonard 247, 74 E.R. 850.

Lincoln's Inn MS. Misc. 10, p. 48

George Lassells, having a son John and a daughter Elizabeth, by his will, gave his daughter £500, which he charged upon eighty acres of meadow lands, out of the rents whereof he desires his executors to pay her £30 a year until the £500 should be paid her. Then he gives to his son the said eighty acres and to the heirs of his body. But, if he died before twenty-one, then he gave the same to his wife for life, with remainders over. And other lands he gives in like manner. Then he declared that, if his son died without issue or before twenty-one, then his wife should pay £500 more to his daughter, and, if she died before payment, then the next heir should pay this £500. And he made his wife and Robert, his brother, executors, and died.

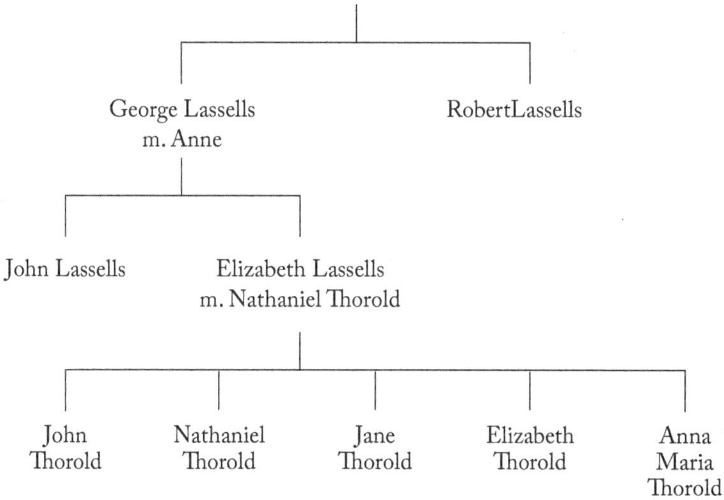


After the testator's death, Elizabeth brought a bill against her brother and the executors for the first £500. And, upon the hearing of that cause, it was decreed that the meadow land should stand charged with £30 a year until the £500 were paid and the surplus of the profits to go towards sinking the £500.

After this decree, Elizabeth was put into possession of this land by the executors, and then she married Nathaniel Thorold, by whom she had issue two sons, the defendants, John and Nathaniel, and three daughters, *viz.* the plaintiff Jane, Elizabeth, and Anna Maria.

Nathaniel Thorold made his will and gave to his son after his wife's death a leasehold house and another to his son Nathaniel, and he also gave him £400 and £300 apiece to his three daughters, and the residue he gave to his wife, whom he made executrix.

John, the son of the testator George, died without issue, whereby the other £500 became payable to the plaintiff's mother, Elizabeth, who died in 1704, having never received it. And before her death, she made her will and gave her two sons the same houses their father had given them and, also she gives to the plaintiff Jane and her heirs all her meadow land in Thurnholm, being the land charged with the first £500, and also the reversion of all her lands in Elston, which were the lands charged with the other £500, after the death of Ann, her mother. But no mention is made in the will of either of the two £500. She also gives to her son Nathaniel £400 and to the plaintiff Jane £78 and a moiety of her household goods. And she made her sister Ann Darwin, one of the defendants, executrix.

After her death, Anne, the widow of George Lassells, died, and the remainderman sold the lands in Elston and also the meadow land to the defendant, Robert Darwin, who kept back £1000 of the purchase money to satisfy the two £500s to the plaintiffs or to such of Mrs. Thorold's children as should appear entitled to them.

And, now, to have a satisfaction of those two sums, of the £300 given the plaintiff Jane by her father's will, and the £78 given her by her mother's will, is the bill brought.

Upon hearing this cause, the court was of the opinion that the devise of the lands to the plaintiff Jane by her mother's will was a devise of the moneys charged thereon and that the plaintiffs were entitled to both the £500s. But, then, the court declared also that that devise and the moiety of the goods and the £78 legacy was a satisfaction of the £300 legacy which the plaintiff Jane was entitled to by her father's will. And so, in like manner, the court was of the opinion that the £400 given Nathaniel by his mother's will should be looked on as a satisfaction of his £400 legacy given him by his father's will. And an account was directed to be taken as to the rents of the meadow land, and what the plaintiff's mother or the plaintiffs had received thereout above the £30 a year was to be applied towards satisfaction of the £500 charged upon those lands.

2 Eq. Cas. Abr. 352, 22 E.R. 299

A father gives legacies to his children and makes his wife executrix. She, not having paid the legacies, gives them legacies likewise, one of which was the same sum and the other a greater.

[It was] decreed they shall not have both, and the latter is a satisfaction of the former. And, where there was a devise of the lands with which one of the first legacies was chargeable, it was decreed that this was a devise of the money which is payable out of the lands.

[Related cases: Thorold v. Thorold (Ch. 1718), Chancery Reports *tempore* Geo. I, 472.]

## 334

## Anonymous

(Ch. 1712)

*A commission of bankruptcy that is sued out without giving public notice is fraudulent and will be set aside.*

*A court of equity will protect the purchase of a bona fide purchaser for value from an assignee under a fraudulent bankruptcy.*

British Library MS. Hargrave 80, f. 69v

Lord Keeper [Lord Harcourt]: If a commission of bankrupt be sued out fraudulently and a fair purchaser that had no notice of the fraud buy any of the bankrupt's effects of the assignee and the commission is afterwards superseded, though the purchaser can make no defense at law against an action brought by an assignee of a new commission, yet he may apply himself to this court and be protected in his purchase.

*How*: Two commissions were sued out against the same person. Upon the first, there was no notice given in the *Gazette* to the creditors to meet and choose an assignee.

Lord Keeper [Lord Harcourt]: That is a proof that it was intended to defeat all or some part of the creditors. [I will] supersede it without costs to those that sued it out.

[Other copies of this report: Lincoln's Inn MS. Misc. 383, p. 128, pl. 2, Lincoln's Inn MS. Misc. 106, p. 79, pl. 2.]

## 335

## Anonymous

(Ch. 1712)

*An action for a debt brought by a mortgagee includes a foreclosure of the mortgage.*

British Library MS. Hargrave 80, f. 70, pl. 1

Serjeant *Hooper*: If a mortgagee brings an action for his money, it opens a foreclosure.

[Other copies of this report: Lincoln's Inn MS. Misc. 383, p. 130, pl. 1.]

## 336

## Moor v. Moor

(Ch. 1712)

*Where both parties examine witnesses in a suit for discovery, neither party will be liable for the court costs of the other.*

British Library MS. Hargrave 80, f. 70, pl. 2

The bill was for discovery of several deeds etc. The defendant answered, and the plaintiff might have set down the cause upon the bill and answer and had what he sought by his bill decreed. But he replied and put some things in issue that were not material. And both parties examined [witnesses].

Lord Keeper [Lord Harcourt] declared that, if the plaintiff had examined alone, he should have paid costs. But the defendant having gone into the same examination, there should be no costs of either side.

[Other copies of this report: Lincoln's Inn MS. Misc. 383, p. 130, pl. 2, Lincoln's Inn MS. Misc. 106, p. 80, pl. 1.]

## 337

## Lord Anglesey v. Duke of Buckinghamshire

(Ch. 1712–1713)

*A peer does not have a privilege as such when he is a party to litigation that concerns only his wife.*

*A father, by his will, can direct the guardianship of his children to be given after his death to persons other than their mother.*

*A writ of sequestration lies against a party who is in contempt of court.*

*Where more than one person is made the guardian of an infant, the Court of Chancery can give the custody to one of them.*

British Library MS. Hargrave 80, f. 70, pl. 3

The late lord Anglesey [1674–1702] devised the custody of his daughter [Catherine] to three trustees with a particular direction that her mother should have nothing to do with her. The mother married the duke of Buckinghamshire [1647–1721]. And they, by *habeas corpus*, got the child. The duke insisting upon his privilege, it was resolved by the House of Lords that he had no privilege in this case because [of] no interest, not so much as a bare trustee, and it is a standing order of the House that no trustee has a privilege. It was objected that the duke was liable to a writ of ravishment of ward and, by that means, might be affected in point of interest. But they replied that that was not the case now before them and that it would be time enough to insist upon a privilege when that action was brought, besides it is against a rule of law that [no] man should take advantage of this own wrong.

[Other copies of this report: Lincoln's Inn MS. Misc. 383, p. 130, pl. 3, Lincoln's Inn MS. Misc. 106, p. 80, pl. 2.]

British Library MS. Hargrave 80, f. 74v

Lord Anglesey, the young lady's father and first husband to the duchess [of Buckinghamshire], devised the guardianship of her to My Lord Haversham until eighteen or marriage and, in the case of Lord Haversham's death, to the plaintiffs, Annesley, Coole, and Selby, provided that, if they or any of them should permit the young lady to cohabit or converse with her mother, that then the guardianship of the persons so permitting should cease. And he devised £3000 and £1200 *per annum* maintenance until that should be payable to the young lady upon the like condition to be void if she conversed with her mother. After the lord Anglesey's death, the duke of Buckinghamshire married his widow and, after lord Haversham's death, got the young lady into their possession. And the defendants Coole and Selby refusing to join with the plaintiff in recovering the possession of the ward, this bill was brought in the nature of a writ of ravishment of ward to recover the possession of her person and to restore her from a forfeiture.

To the first part, the defendants demurred because the interest of the ward was joint of the plaintiffs' own showing. And it was strongly argued that legal authorities not clothed with an interest nor in their creation made joint and several could not be executed but by the whole number and that was the present case, that, if there were two joint tenants of an advowson and they did not agree to join in, the law would throw it on the bishop after six months, and that, in this case, the guardians appointed jointly by the father not concurring, the guardianship devolved on the person appointed by the law where the father makes no appointment, and that person is the mother, that they had alleged in their bill that Coole was in Ireland and Selby they had prevailed upon not to act, and that allegation, if true, did not prove a forfeiture of their guardianship, that the will was a continuance of the cruelty to the duchess, which the legislature had before taken notice of, that there are a great many cases where equity relieves against, none where it assists such unnatural conditions, and that, if the plaintiff had any right and remedy at law, he had no occasion for coming here.

On the other side, the Solicitor General [*Raymond*] insisted upon the custody of infants being properly within the jurisdiction of this court and that the will was the proper measure to direct the guardianship, that they were without a remedy at law by reason the other two defendants would not join with the plaintiff, that, if a stranger had got the ward into his possession and two refused to join in returning her, it would be hard to say that this court should not assist the third in doing it, and that the rule of justice was the same in both cases.

*How*: The main part of the bill is to restore the young lady from a forfeiture and, for that purpose, she is properly made a plaintiff. In the other part, which is a necessary means to that end, the plaintiff prays in particular relief in case it should be the opinion of the court that the other two have forfeited their right of guardianship if otherwise a general relief, that the guardians were mere trustees and, in the case of a trust term, if two refuse to act, the third is proper in coming into this court to desire the direction of it, that nothing was more plain in case of infants than that this court has a proper, if not a more proper, jurisdiction than any court of law, that formerly, in cases of guardianship, they had proceeded by a summary way by petition but that His Lordship had been more cautious and that, since they had proceeded by bill, and that the memory of My Lord Anglesey's unkindness ought to be buried with him.

Lord Keeper [LORD HARCOURT]: The law of England would have given the guardianship to the duchess if My Lord Anglesey had not given it from her. But it is his will not mine. My direction must be guided by the rules of law. The condition annexed to the fortune is a strange one, but that is foreign to the present purpose. The Act[1] has indeed given the guardians a remedy at law and so has a guardian in socage. And the same reason would exclude the jurisdiction of this court in both cases. And, certainly, this court has not a more proper jurisdiction in any case than that of infants nor a more useful one for the public. The devise of the guardianship here is to three. It does not appear whether the other two will accept it or not. And the demurrer stands in the way of bringing the matter before the court. [He] overruled it.

[Other copies of this report: Lincoln's Inn MS. Misc. 383, p. 137, Lincoln's Inn MS. Misc. 106, p. 87.]

British Library MS. Hargrave 80, f. 132v

At the hearing of this cause, the duke and duchess [of Buckinghamshire] made default. And it appearing by the will of lord Anglesey, which was proved in the cause, that part of the young lady's fortune and maintenance was forfeitable if she lived with her mother, which forfeiture, the defendant, the lord Anglesey, waived in case she continued with her no longer and not otherwise, and the duke and duchess heaving used several delays in this cause and the young lady being so near twelve that she would attain that age before the decree could be made absolute and it being suggested by lord Anglesey that there was reason to think she might be married to her disadvantage in the meantime if she would be permitted to stay with the duke and duchess until the decree should be made absolute, a separate order was made for the duke and duchess to produce her in court the next seal [day]. This order was grounded on the proofs of the will etc. taken in the cause, which was said were a better foundation for such an order than barely a pe-

[1] Stat. 12 Car. II, c. 24, s. 8 (*SR*, V, 260).

tition supported by affidavits, which was the old way of proceeding in this [way] of guardianship, in this case, the party having an opportunity to cross-examine, which, in that of affidavits, they have not.

The order being not complied with, that of sequestration was ordered against the duke and a messenger for the young lady, upon which the duke and duchess sent her into court, where My Lord Keeper [Lord Harcourt] delivered her over into the hands of Mr. Annesly, one of the guardians, and not into a master's, which was done in the case of [ *blank* ] but ordered him not to permit her to marry nor a treaty for that purpose to be entered into without the leave of the court.

Besides the portion and maintenance subject to a forfeiture, she had £12,000 settled on her by a marriage settlement if she attained it or married and £100 *per annum* maintenance until then and the remainder in fee of the estate after some maintenances in tail.

[Other copies of this report: Lincoln's Inn MS. Misc. 383, p. 235, pl. 1, Lincoln's Inn MS. Misc. 106, p. 199.]

British Library MS. Hargrave 80, f. 134v, pl. 2

Upon the day for the duke and duchess to show cause against the last decree, *Sir Thomas Powys* then cited the Case of Auditor Curle, 11 Rept.,[1] where two made but one officer. And he resembled this case to that and inferred from thence that Mr. Annesly alone ought not to have the guardianship, the other two declining it, but that, in that case, it should devolve on the mother.

*Sir Joseph Jekyll* said that a guardian, by statute, is in the nature of a guardian in socage though appointed in a different manner except in some few instances which are stated in the case of Wheat and Castlehaven, in Lord Vaughan's time. Yet the condition was void being repugnant to the law of nature and the positive law of God, which requires an obedience to the mother as well as the father.

Lord Keeper [Lord Harcourt]: The father may dispose of the guardianship of his child to one or more, and, here, it is expressly devised to three. And they are undoubtedly entitled to it. They living separately, all of them cannot have the keeping of the young lady. Yet that is not inconsistent with their guardianship. If they do not agree, the court may appoint the custody to one. I think Mr. Annesly the most proper person to be entrusted with her, he having brought the bill and in respect to his relationship to her etc. but not so as to exclude the others from access or taking care of her education or from liberty to apply upon any occasion to the court. The £400 *per annum* is given to the guardians; nobody else can demand it, especially not one who possessed himself of the young lady in breach of her father's will. And, therefore, the duke is not entitled to the arrears of it while the young lady was with him, but, however, he must have an allowance for what he has actually expended or contracted for her necessaries that have

[1] *Auditor Curle's Case* (1610), 11 Coke Rep. 2, 77 E.R. 1147.

actually come to her use, provided it does not exceed the £400 *per annum*. I am of the opinion that, in respect of the nature of the condition and the young lady's tender years, she has not hither incurred any forfeiture by being with her mother.

Serjeant Selby and Mr. Coole by answer submitted to act as the court should direct and did not waive the guardianship.

[Other copies of this report: Lincoln's Inn MS. Misc. 383, p. 238, pl. 2, Lincoln's Inn MS. Misc. 106, p. 203.]

## 338

## Anonymous

(Ch. 1712)

*In this case, an injunctive order was made upon the parties' agreement even though no bill of complaint had been filed.*

British Library MS. Hargrave 80, f. 70v, pl. 1

Lord Keeper [Lord Harcourt] made an order upon a motion to stay the plaintiff's proceedings at law in an action of covenant and in ejectment upon the defendant's offering to pay the principal due on the mortgage with costs at law and in equity, though it was admitted that no injunction could be without a bill.

[Other copies of this report: Lincoln's Inn MS. Misc. 383, p. 130, pl. 4, Lincoln's Inn MS. Misc. 106, p. 81, pl. 1.]

## 339

## Ball v. Coggs

(Ch. 1712)

*Where two partners become bankrupts, the joint creditors must first resort to the joint estate for satisfaction and, if that proves deficient, then they may resort to the residue of the separate estates, if there be any, after the separate creditors are satisfied, who are in the first place to be satisfied out of the separate estates, and vice versa.*

British Library MS. Hargrave 80, f. 70v, pl. 2

[It was] held by Lord Keeper [Lord Harcourt], *Vernon*, *Cowper*, and *Sir Joseph Jekyll*, who was not of counsel in the cause, that, where two partners became bankrupts, the joint creditors must resort to the joint estate for satisfaction and, if that proves deficient, they may resort to the residue of the separate estates, if there be any after the separate creditors are satisfied, who are in the first place to be satisfied out of the separate estates, and *vice versa*, if the separate estates be not sufficient to satisfy the separate debts, they too may resort to the joint estate, if there be any, after the joint creditors are satisfied.

*Cowper* said that it had been often ruled so upon petitions and that the reason was that the joint creditors gave credit chiefly to the joint estates and, therefore, were entitled to a preference of satisfaction as to that estate and the separate creditors, who trusted to the separate estates, were for the same reason entitled to a preference of satisfaction.

*Sir Joseph Jekyll* cited the Case of the Land Bank[1] as adjudged in point.

*Vernon* said that this was so in case of a losing trade or where joint partners had wasted the joint stock equally but that, where one partner had wasted it, the joint creditors shall come in upon his separate estate *pro tanto.*

[Other copies of this report: Lincoln's Inn MS. Misc. 383, p. 130, pl. 5, Lincoln's Inn MS. Misc. 106, p. 81, pl. 2.]

[Affirmed on appeal: Ball v. Lord Lanesborough (1713), 5 Brown P.C. 480, 2 E.R. 809.]

## 340

## Greenhill v. Greenhill

(Ch. 1712)

*A testator can devise an equitable interest in land, such as an unexecuted contract to purchase land.*

British Library MS. Hargrave 80, f. 71

The testator articled in the name of one Young with a husband and wife. The articles bore date in April 1706, and there was a covenant in them that the land should be conveyed the Michaelmas following. In June, the testator made his will and devised his freehold estate to [ *blank* ] and that the surplus of his personal estate should be invested in land and settled to the same uses.

Upon a rehearing, *Sir Joseph Jekyll* insisted that, if a man articles for the purchase of lands, after the time is come for the performance of the articles, the vendor is a trustee for him and he is entitled to the profits and may devise this equitable interest. But yet, before that time, he has neither *jus ad rem* nor *in re* nor can devise it, that it was no answer to say that the land is bound by the articles. A judgment is a lien upon land. But, if the conusee devise it before an *elegit* is sued out, the devisee shall [not] enjoy it.

*How*: The will is intermediate between the articles and the time the conveyance was to be made. And the testator had then no right in law or equity. If the husband had died, the testator could have had no remedy against the wife for performance of the articles. If this devise be held good, the devisee will run away

[1] Perhaps *Anonymous v. Briscoe* (Ch. 1706), see above, Case No. 49.

with an estate worth £20,000 and the heir at law will have only the relics of an annuity of £100 *per annum* or £1500 in money.

*Vernon*, for the devisee: The will gives us all his freehold lands and directs the surplus of his personal estate to be invested in land for our benefit. Had not this money been tied down by the articles, we should have had the benefit of it by the will. But they are looking for a construction that would let this estate fall between the devise of his real and personal estate.

Lord Keeper [Lord Harcourt]: The testator had such a right by his articles as would have descended to his heir and the devisee might have compelled the executors to apply the personal estate for the performance of the articles. He decreed the devise to be good.

*Vernon* said in his argument that, if a man is entitled to the equity of a copyhold estate and the legal estate is in another, he may devise his interest without a surrender, for it is not in his power to surrender. And, in the principal case, the conveyance was made pursuant to the articles after the will and in the life of the testator.

Query whether the alteration of his estate from an equitable to be a legal one was not a revocation of his will and whether that and the articles shall be looked upon as one conveyance. But that point was not stirred by the counsel

I conceive it no revocation.

[Other copies of this report: Lincoln's Inn MS. Misc. 383, p. 131.]

[Other reports of this case: 2 Vernon 679, 23 E.R. 1041, Precedents in Chancery 320, 24 E.R. 151, Gilbert Rep. 77, 25 E.R. 54, 1 Eq. Cas. Abr. 174, 21 E.R. 968.]

## 341

## Taylor v. Langston

(Ch. 1712)

*Where a debtor refuses to pay the interest that is due, such interest can be turned into principal debt, thus creating compound interest.*

British Library MS. Hargrave 80, f. 71v

A mortgagee had occasion for her money. And the plaintiff, with the privity of the mortgagor and some intimation by his letter of request, advanced it to the mortgagee and took an assignment of the mortgage. He paid off the eleven years' interest that was due with the principal. And, in regard the mortgagor did not join in the assignment, the only question was whether that interest should be turned into principal and carry interest.

Lord Keeper [Lord Harcourt], upon a rehearing, declared it should and, further, that, where there was a great arrear of interest and the mortgagee pressed for the money and the mortgagor refused either to pay it or join in an assignment and the mortgagee could prevail with a stranger to pay the money and take an assignment, that the interest in such case should be turned into principal but that it would be otherwise if either a mortgagee made an assignment to another in trust for himself to swell the principal and swallow up the estate or if a stranger by fraud and with that view should procure an assignment to be made to him without the consent of the mortgagor.

[Other copies of this report: Lincoln's Inn MS. Misc. 383, p. 132, Lincoln's Inn MS. Misc. 106, p. 82.]

## 342

## Martin v. Duckett

(Ch. 1712)

*After a marriage contract has been made, a subsequent conveyance of the future wife's property in trust to her separate use is a fraudulent conveyance and will be set aside.*

British Library MS. Hargrave 80, f. 72

After the two plaintiffs [Martin *et ux.*] were contracted [to be married], the defendant, Duckett, an attorney, prepared a conveyance of the wife's estate to himself and two more in trust for her separate use during coverture with powers of leasing etc. to the trustees. The intended husband was no party, nor was there any proof of moment that he had notice of this conveyance before the marriage.

*Vernon* insisted that conveyances made by a woman pending a treaty of marriage in fraud of the husband are always set aside, and that this case was stronger than the common cases because there was a contract before the conveyance, that it was usual to make the intended husband a party to such conveyance that it might appear to be done with his privity and consent.

Lord Keeper [Lord Harcourt] agreed and decreed a re-conveyance from the trustees, I think, to the wife that the legal estate might stand as it did before this conveyance. The only difficulty that stuck with him was the wife's coming as a plaintiff before the court and not being present in court.

*Vernon* said it would have been more regular to have made her a defendant.

And My Lord [Lord Harcourt] directed notice to be given to her and the other trustees before the execution of the re-conveyance with liberty to apply to the court if she was aggrieved. The defendant Duckett, who appeared to have used some management in this cause to carve out work for himself, was ordered to pay all costs.

[Other copies of this report: Lincoln's Inn MS. Misc. 383, p. 133, Lincoln's Inn MS. Misc. 106, p. 83.]

## 343

## Higgins v. Higgins

(Ch. 1712)

*Specific performance of a marriage settlement contract will be ordered by a court of equity.*

*In this case, the court found a contract to have been made between the father of the husband and the married couple.*

British Library MS. Hargrave 80, f. 72v

The bill was for specific performance of marriage articles upon a treaty of marriage between the plaintiffs. The father of the young man treated with an aunt of the young lady about a settlement. And a draught was prepared by an attorney of the father's side and, afterwards, one or two more by attorneys of the other side, but the last were rejected by the father, and the draught made by his own attorney [was] amended by him and, in some places, some amendments were made by the aunt's directions. The father wrote to a third person that he would stand by that draught, but there was no evidence that the aunt agreed to it or that the proposal was closed with by her. But there was positive evidence of the minister that married them that the father directed him to go to the young people and prevail with them to marry without the aunt's knowledge and, at the same time, to assure them he would make good the agreement according to his draught. Upon this, they married. But the father never made a settlement pursuant to the articles but, instead of it, after some time, turned the young couple out of doors. And they were forced to take a lease of him of part of the land comprised in the articles for a place to live in. About nine years after the marriage, the draught and the letter fell into the plaintiffs' hands upon the death of the person to whom it was written, upon which, they brought this bill.

Lord Keeper [Lord Harcourt] decreed a specific performance. He laid great weight upon the evidence of the clergyman and seemed to say that, if the matter had rested upon the letter and nothing had been done after that, he could have done nothing upon it because [it was] not closed with by the aunt.

[Other copies of this report: Lincoln's Inn MS. Misc. 383, p. 134, pl. 1, Lincoln's Inn MS. Misc. 106, p. 84.]

## 344

## Shearman v. Fielder

(Ch. 1712)

*The appearance of the title to a copyhold on the court rolls is evidence of notice of title to the parties to a mortgage of the copyhold.*

*Where the tenant in tail of a freehold estate conveys to the use of a younger son and does not suffer a recovery, a court of equity will not supply it.*

Lincoln's Inn MS. Misc. 10, p. 102

4 February 1711[/12].

A man, apprehending he had a title to a copyhold estate, first, mortgages this estate and, then, sells it to the plaintiff, who pays off the mortgage.

The defendant, at the time of the mortgage, was entitled to this estate under a settlement made by his great-grandfather, and both solicited the lending of the money and was assisting to the plaintiff in treating for and making the bargain for the said purchase. And, afterwards, pretending that he was then ignorant of his title under the settlement, he set up a pretense to this estate.

And now, the plaintiff brings his bill to be quieted in his purchase.

The defendant's ignorance of his title was much insisted on. And it was said that it was by this accident that he discovered it. He was about to sell another copyhold estate, and, the purchaser consulting with the steward, he, upon searching the rolls, found out this settlement.

The Lord Keeper [LORD HARCOURT] said he would not presume a man to be ignorant of his title, but rather presume the contrary, and here the defendant persuaded the mortgagee to lend his money and the plaintiff to purchase. He decreed the defendant to join in suffering a recovery to the use of the plaintiff and his heirs.

British Library MS. Hargrave 80, f. 73

One of the plaintiffs was a mortgagee of part of a copyhold estate, and another plaintiff claimed another part of it under a voluntary surrender to his use for his portion or provision, he being a younger child of the person that made the surrender. The defendant's title to the estate was under an old entail that did not appear to have been barred. But, having been concerned in procuring the mortgage money to be lent to the mortgagee and likewise being one of the trustees by whose hands the surrender was made for the benefit of the other plaintiffs, the bill was to compel him to suffer a recovery to make good the conveyance to the plaintiffs.

*Vernon*, for the defendant, cited the case of Lower v. Webb,[1] where a tenant in tail mortgaged his estate and covenanted to suffer a recovery, which the court decreed him to do, but he refusing died in prison and the mortgagee was defeated and could have no relief. Upon his appeal, he said that the farthest the court ever had gone was in the case of Row v. Port, where the older brother employed the

[1] *Weale v. Lower* (1672–1689), Pollexfen 54, 86 E.R. 509, 2 Freeman 107, 22 E.R. 1089, 79 Selden Soc. 591, *Lord Nottingham's Prolegomena*, p. 340, 1 Eq. Cas. Abr. 266, 21 E.R. 1035.

younger to draw his marriage settlement where the younger knowing the estate to be entailed made the estate by lease and release and gave no notice to the lady of the entail and, after his brother's death, set up a title under pretense of this entail but was decreed to suffer a recovery and make good the lady's title.

*How* said that the reason of that and other like cases was the fraud of the party, the suppression of the truth by one that could and ought to have discovered it in order to draw in another.

*Vernon* said that that case was very different from this for that was in a case of a freehold where the parties could not have notice of the entail but that this estate was copyhold and that it was their duty to have searched the court rolls where they would have found the entail.

And both insisted that, though the defendant was privy to the mortgage, yet, he being ignorant of his own title, there was no reason that this court should take away the law from him.

Lord Keeper [Lord Harcourt] [said] that the appearance of the title on the court rolls was evidence of notice to the defendant as much as to the plaintiff.

*Vernon* replied, to both equally and, if both were presumed to have notice, then the mortgagee came in with his eyes open, but, if that should not be construed to amount to notice, then the defendant having denied notice by his answer and there being no proof that he had any, it could not be intended that he had any more than the mortgagee had.

Lord Keeper [Lord Harcourt]: It appears that the defendant was not only privy and consenting but intended for the advancing the money upon the mortgage. As to the soliciting, he had denied in his answer and, as to that, I think his answer was falsified. It is to be supposed that he had the copies in his custody. And I am not to imagine that he was ignorant of his title but rather that he was cognizant. Let him suffer a recovery to make good the title of the mortgagee. But to the other plaintiff, who was a volunteer, he gave no relief.

*Sir Thomas Powys* would have resembled this case to that where the court supplies a surrender to the use of a will in favor of younger children.

Lord Keeper [Lord Harcourt]: In case of a will, the testator may want an opportunity to surrender. It is rather like the case of a deed. Where the tenant in tail of a freehold estate conveys to the use of a younger son and does not suffer a recovery, this court will not supply it. I cannot take the law from the defendant. My Lord [Harcourt] said that he knew several manors in Staffordshire where the common recoveries have been frequently used to bar entails yet surrenders and enjoyments under them have been allowed to be good bars by all the judges that have gone that circuit.

[Other copies of this report: Lincoln's Inn MS. Misc. 383, p. 1134, pl. 2, Lincoln's Inn MS. Misc. 106, p. 85.]

345

## Lord Waring's Case

(Ch. 1712)

*Commissioners for charitable uses do not have the power or authority to award court costs.*

British Library MS. Hargrave 80, f. 74, pl. 1

In this case, Duke[1] was cited to prove that commissioners for charitable uses might decree costs and that the court might increase those costs if they saw reason.

But Lord Keeper [LORD HARCOURT] and *Vernon* held clearly that the commissioners had no jurisdiction to authorize them to give costs, but that the court, if they thought fit, might give the same costs that the commissioners had given before with or without an increase.

[Other copies of this report: Lincoln's Inn MS. Misc. 383, p. 136, pl. 1.]

346

## Young v. Cottle

(Ch. 1712)

*In this case, the court overruled a plea of res judicata because the point in issue had not been argued in the prior lawsuit.*

*An annuity charged upon a fund ceases when the fund ceases.*

*In this case, the plaintiffs were not estopped to have an account even though they had accepted payments for many years.*

British Library MS. Hargrave 80, f. 74, pl. 2

*Vernon* said that no rule is more settled than that you cannot come by an original bill to vary or add to a former decree. That practice would make suits endless. The only way is by bill of revivor or of review.

But Lord Keeper [LORD HARCOURT] overruled it and made a decree upon the construction of a deed that was fully disclosed in a former cause between the parties and relief might have been had in that cause upon the point in issue in this but it did not appear that that point was stirred then.

[Other copies of this report: Lincoln's Inn MS. Misc. 383, p. 136, pl. 2.]

---

1 G. Duke, *The Law of Charitable Uses* (1676); perhaps *Warreyn v. Eltham Inhabitants* (Ch. 1634), Chancery Repts. *tempore* Coventry 230.

British Library MS. Hargrave 80, f. 110, pl. 2

The three plaintiffs and the defendant were the only children of Mark Cottle, the haberdasher. Mark Cottle, the Register of the Prerogative Office, had a grant of it for lives and, by deed, appointed Wellham to officiate as deputy with a salary of £250 *per annum* and appointed several annuities to be paid out of it and the surplus to Alice, his widow, for the two first years after his decease and, from thence, to be divided between Alice and Mark Cottle, the haberdasher, share and share alike, provided there be first paid £100 *per annum* out of Mark Cottle's share to John, his son, the defendant, and, if Mark Cottle survived Alice, then he appointed the whole to Mark save what is beforementioned to be paid thereout for the benefit of John and his children and, if Mark die before A., his share to his children and so shall the moiety of Alice after her decease. This deed was dated in 1681. Soon after which, Mark, the Register, died. Mark, the heir, died in 1697, and Alice in 1698. The payments were made all along pursuant to this deed and £100 paid to the defendant after his father's death as well as before until the bringing the bill. Before this bill some years, there had been another brought to establish the deed of 1681 against a precedent one set up (I think by John) which appointed the whole profits for his use and a decree for the now plaintiffs for this deed.[1] After that, a second suit was commenced for the profits of this office, in which an account was decreed according to this deed. And upon litigating that account before a master, the point now in question was started, *viz.* whether the £100 *per annum* appointed for John Cottle did not cease upon his father's death, upon which their bill was brought as against John to have three-fourths of the £100 *per annum* received by him since that time refunded and as against him and Wellham to have the surplus distributed clear of the deduction for the future.

Upon the first hearing of this case, Lord Keeper [Lord Harcourt] was of opinion that the £100 *per annum* ceased upon the death of Mark, the heir. And it coming now to be reheard, My Lord called Chief Justice Trevor to his assistance.

*Cooper*, for the plaintiffs, insisted the £100 *per annum* was intended as an immediate provision for John during his father's lifetime, first out of his father's share and then out of the whole and, it being expressly reserved in both those cases and afterwards not mentioned when the whole was to be distributed among the children, as the reason ceased for continuing it, so the silence about it then was a strong argument it was to cease. To this, he added Mark, the Register, left John £200 *per annum* by his will and directed by this deed that he should have the first vacant place and that, upon the death of Mark, the heir, there was a new estate arose and that the defendants intended to annex this new charge to that new estate.

[1] *Young v. Cottle* (1707), 1 Peere Williams 101, 24 E.R. 312.

*How* said the father's share was the fund out of which the £100 *per annum* was to arise and that, that sinking by the father's death, the £100 *per annum* must fall with it.

*Hooper* observed that there was a clause in the latter end of the deed relating to the sale of the office and disposition of the money by which the defendant was to come in equally only with the plaintiffs, which he urged as an evidence that Mark, the Register, intended him but an equal share of the profits with the rest.

*Powys*, for the defendant, observed a difference in the wording of the deed. Alice's part is called a moiety; Mark his share and proportion, which is limited over to his children so that they are to have no more than he had, which is the surplus of the moiety after £100 *per annum* deducted.

*Vernon*: All the annuities granted by the deed are payable during the lives of the annuitants, which is an evidence that this was intended to be so too, nor will the death of the father determine it, for the proviso is not that he shall pay it, but that the trustees shall.

*Sayer*: Had the £100 *per annum* been appointed generally to be paid out of the trust estate, it must have been construed an estate for life. And there is no difference between that case and this but that, here, it is to arise out of a particular part of the trust estate.

Chief Justice [TREVOR], after taking time to consider, delivered his opinion that the £100 *per annum* ceased upon the death of Mark, the haberdasher, because it was charged upon his share, which determined by his death. And he said that the words 'share' and 'moiety' were synonymous and that the direction that Mark's share should be divided after his death among his children should be understood equally and that, if £100 was first to be paid out to John, it would be unequal besides that the absurdity that one-fourth of that must issue out of Mark's share.

Lord Keeper [LORD HARCOURT] added that the appointment of Alice and Mark, share and share alike, no estate being limited, was an appointment to them during their lives and that the subsequent proviso relating to the £100 *per annum* was not independent but restrictive of that clause and fell with it.

They both agreed that the plaintiffs' acceptance of their proportions from time to time and allowing the deduction of the £100 *per annum* would not bar them of having their shares of the £100 *per annum* from the death of Mark, the heir, refunded, they having placed an entire confidence in Wellham as to the distribution and its not applying that they were then apprised of their title not that they had seen the deed of 1681 until 1706 and they having pointed out this error in the accounts by their bill now.

And Lord Keeper [LORD HARCOURT] accordingly affirmed his first decree for refunding three-fourths of the £100 *per annum* from the death of Mark, the heir, and for the distributing the profits clear of that deduction for the future.

No notice was taken of what *Vernon* had objected that it was extraordinary to add to a former decree by an original bill and that this deed had been fully disclosed and put in issue in a former cause between the same parties.

[Other copies of this report: Lincoln's Inn MS. Misc. 383, p. 197.]

## 347

## Lord Craven v. Lady Craven

(Ch. 1712–1713)

*If a person sues for a discovery of title deeds, he must offer to confirm any relevant jointures.*

*A tenant in tail cannot confirm a jointure.*

*Where a person offers to confirm a jointure and then dies, his heir is bound by that agreement, and, if the heir be an infant, the court of equity will require him to confirm upon his coming of age.*

*A court of equity can order maintenance to be paid for unprovided for infants out of a decedent's estate during the pendency of its administration.*

*A counterpart of an indenture is good evidence against the party who produced it.*

British Library MS. Hargrave 80, f. 75v

A bill [was exhibited] by old Lord Craven for discovery of deeds etc. with an offer to confirm the defendant's jointure, to which the defendant answered. Then Lord Craven died, and the suit was revived by the young Lord with the same offer. [There was a] demurrer by reason the plaintiff is an infant and cannot confirm.

Lord Keeper [Lord Harcourt]: The offer of his ancestor will bind him and all claiming under his ancestor, and the court, upon that offer, may decree the defendant to hold and enjoy and the infant to confirm when at age. [He] overruled the demurrer.

A tenant in tail cannot confirm, and a plea to the old Lord Craven's bill was allowed because he was then only tenant in tail, upon which he suffered a recovery and amended his bill.

[Other copies of this report: Lincoln's Inn MS. Misc. 383, p. 139, pl. 1, Lincoln's Inn MS. Misc. 106, p. 90.]

British Library MS. Hargrave 80, f. 96, pl. 1

Lord Craven died without a will and without making any provision for younger children.

Lord Keeper [Lord Harcourt] directed an ample maintenance for the young lord, who was an infant, as well as the other children to the intent that they might be maintained with him out of his allowance until the quantum of the debts and personal estate could be settled. And an act of Parliament [was] got for their provisions.

[Other copies of this report: Lincoln's Inn MS. Misc. 383, p. 172, pl. 2, Lincoln's Inn MS. Misc. 106, p. 126, pl. 1.]

British Library MS. Hargrave 77, f. 26, pl. 4

*Eodem die* [15 October].

It was said by the Attorney General [*Northey*], of counsel for the defendant, the Lady Craven, and not denied by the counsel for the plaintiff or the court that, at law, a counterpart of an indenture was good evidence against the party himself who produced it.

[Other copies of this report: British Library MS. Hargrave 82, f. 103, pl. 3, British Library MS. Hargrave 303, f. 50, pl. 2.]

## 348

## Napier v. Weeden

(Ch. 1712)

*A defendant cannot demur or plead to a bill for an account that the plaintiff-executor has not properly proved the will.*

British Library MS. Hargrave 80, f. 76

Napier, executrix of Sir J. Napier v. Weeden.

[There was a] plea to a bill of revivor against the defendant, who was Sir John Napier's steward, for an account. [There was a] plea that the plaintiff was not entitled to revive not having proved her husband's will in any court where it ought to have been proved.

*Powys*: Where you demur to a bill, the bill is admitted to be true, and, where a plea is set down, the fact of the plea is admitted.

*Williams*: There is no rule more sure than that an executrix cannot sue until after probate.

*Vernon*: I never knew such a negative plea to come in but it was overruled. He takes upon him to swear a negative. It is wrong in form too, for he does not directly aver it, but it is not having proved. The bill alleges the will to be duly proved, and it will be incumbent upon us to show it at the hearing.

*How*: It is pleaded in bar, and that too is wrong.

The Lord Keeper [Lord Harcourt] overruled it.

[Other copies of this report: Lincoln's Inn MS. Misc. 383, p. 139, pl. 2, Lincoln's Inn MS. Misc. 106, p. 91.]

## 349

### Anonymous

(Ch. 1712)

*The question in this case was whether the widower of a copyholder of inheritance who died without an heir can levy a fine and defeat the escheat of the lord of the manor.*

British Library MS. Hargrave 80, f. 76v, pl. 1

A woman, tenant of a copyhold inheritance held of a manor, married and died without an heir. The husband continued in possession and levied a fine. And to a bill by the lord of the manor, whose title was upon the escheat, he pleaded a fine with proclamations and non-claim for five years.

*Sir Thomas Powys*: The possession of the husband was lawful and like the case of a termor that holds over. He is no trespasser. And as there is no pretense of a feoffment, he cannot come and call himself a disseisor; besides, the fine is pleaded Trinity 1704 and that may be though it was brought in long after, nor is it shown when the proclamation was, nor can it, therefore, be known from what time it is a bar.

Lord Keeper [Lord Harcourt]: Let it stand for an answer with liberty to except.

[ *blank* ] said in this case a mortgagor is a tenant at will to a mortgagee.

[Other copies of this report: Lincoln's Inn MS. Misc. 383, p. 139, pl. 3.]

## 350

### James v. Martin

(Ch. 1712)

*The Court of Chancery can give a mother the sole custody of her children and order the father to support them in order to prevent them from being raised as Roman Catholics.*

*If child support is charged on land and the land is sold or mortgaged, the charge does not bind the purchaser or mortgagee.*

British Library MS. Hargrave 80, f. 76v, pl. 2

Roger [Martin], the son of Sir Roger, both Papists, married a Protestant and had issue by her, two sons, whom he threatened and attempted to send to St. Omers to be bred Papists, to prevent which Mrs. Martin, their mother, concealed them and applied to Lord Chancellor Cowper by a petition for a competent allowance for their maintenance and education in the Protestant religion, the father and the grandfather refusing to maintain them. My Lord gave the guardianship of them to their mother. And it appearing that an estate of near £200 *per annum*, there being £1200 *per annum* in the family, had been settled by the grandfather upon the father, there was no order made upon the grandfather, but the father was ordered to pay her a moiety of that estate by quarterly payments.

Mr. Martin going beyond the seas to avoid this order, My Lord, upon the second petition, ordered the tenants in possession to pay her a moiety of the profits. Then there were two mortgages set up to cover the estate. The plaintiff, being the second mortgagee and in time too, subsequent to the first, brought his bill against the first mortgagee, Mr. Martin, his wife, and children to discover encumbrances and to redeem the first mortgage and set aside the orders for maintenance of the children out of the mortgaged estate. There were several circumstances of fraud, especially in the first mortgage, which was dated upon the order for attendance of the first petition and the order made upon that petition no money lent at that time but a pretended stated account and this mortgage made for securing the balance of it, which was £250, the mortgagee immediately put into possession, and a great part of the profits paid over by him to the mortgagor and the mortgagee, himself a person that had formerly paid down the consideration money for the purchase of the same estate to Sir Roger Martin taken a conveyance and then received his money again and, after that, swore the estate to be really his own to cover it from double taxes. Upon these circumstances, My Lord directed both mortgagor and mortgagee to be examined upon interrogatories touching the reality of their mortgage and the maintenance to be continued in the meantime.

But though it was urged that the orders of the court were a lien upon the estate and that whoever took a mortgage or purchased after must take the land *cum onere*, Lord Keeper [Lord Harcourt] was of a different opinion. He thought that part of the Act[1] as defective as the rest and a Papist might, notwithstanding the orders for maintenance, sell and mortgage the next day and defeat them. And, when he was pressed to enjoin the father not to sell or mortgage, he would not do it.

*Vernon* insisted that what had been paid by the first mortgagee of the profits of the premises to the mortgagor was a wrong payment. And, if his mortgage was a real one, it must be looked upon as satisfied so far with regard to the wife and children as well as in the case of a second mortgagee where the first gets into possession whatever he paid to the mortgagor abates his mortgage *pro tanto*.

But there too the Lord Keeper [Lord Harcourt] differed from him.

[Other copies of this report: Lincoln's Inn MS. Misc. 383, p. 140, Lincoln's Inn MS. Misc. 106, p. 92.]

[1] Stat. 11 Will. III, c. 4, s. 7 (*SR*, VII, 587).

## 351

## Colesworth v. Brangwin

(Ch. 1712)

*Where there are two co-executors and one of them is also a legatee and a relation of the testator, the residuum of the personal estate will be equally divided between them.*

British Library MS. Hargrave 80, f. 77v

There were two executors. One, who was a relation of the testator, had a legacy of £200 given him by the will; the other, who was a stranger, had nothing and now, contending that the legacy excluding his co-executor from any part of the residuum, which amounted to above £100, the whole ought to devolve upon him.

*Vernon, contra*: The surplus is always distributed equally between the residuary legatees or the next of kin though some of them have particular legacies.

Lord Keeper [LORD HARCOURT]: There is a great deal of difference between the cases where there are two executors and where but one. In the last case, the implication that the testator did not intend the whole for his executor when he gave him part is much stronger than the first, where the law would not have thrown the whole upon one executor if he had given him nothing but equally upon both and the giving a legacy to one might be to prevent that equality. And I do not remember any case where the court has gone so far as to throw the whole surplus upon one executor because the other had a legacy. The only question in this case is whether, there being but two executors, the one a stranger and the other a legatee, the whole surplus ought not to be distributed. But as the dispute is now between two executors only, it must be equally divided.

[Other copies of this report: Lincoln's Inn MS. Misc. 383, p. 141, pl. 1.]

[Other reports of this case: Precedents in Chancery 323, 24 E.R. 153, Gilbert Rep. 79, 25 E.R. 56, 2 Eq. Cas. Abr. 438, 22 E.R. 373.]

## 352

## Brown v. Brown

(Ch. 1712)

*The creditor of a husband can enforce the husband's right to receive his wife's legacy without making any provision for her out of the legacy.*

British Library MS. Hargrave 80, f. 78, pl. 1

Brown stole Selby's daughter, who was entitled to a legacy of £1000 charged upon her brother's estate. More than half of it was paid by the brother to the husband, who, afterwards, became indebted to the plaintiff Brown to the value of the residue. And he assigned his interest in it to the plaintiff as a security for his debt and then went away from his wife and left her without any provision. It was strongly urged that a creditor of the husband could not be in a better condition than the husband himself and that, if the husband had brought his bill for the residue of his legacy, equity would have laid hold of it for the benefit of the wife, who was otherwise unprovided for, and that the plaintiff had only an equitable interest. And, if he must have equity, he must do equity.

*Per contra, How* insisted that, if a husband, after marriage, assigned the term of the wife for her separate maintenance, even that assignment would not stand in the way of creditors, not of an assignee of a commissioner of bankrupt, much less should creditors be defeated where there was no assignment made to her separate use.

And Lord Keeper [LORD HARCOURT] was of opinion that the creditors would be in a better condition than the husband himself. And [he] decreed the residue of the legacy to the plaintiff.

[Other copies of this report: Lincoln's Inn MS. Misc. 383, p. 141, pl. 2, Lincoln's Inn MS. Misc. 106, p. 94, pl. 1.]

## 353

## Note

(Ch. 1712)

*An advancement must be in writing signed by the parent, and it must be for a certainty.*

British Library MS. Hargrave 80, f. 78, pl. 2

Custom of London.

[It was] agreed that the certainty of a child advanced by a father ought to appear by a writing signed by the father.

[Other copies of this report: Lincoln's Inn MS. Misc. 383, p. 142, pl. 1.]

## 354

## Smith v. Orm

(Ch. 1712)

*In this case, the legacy in issue was an express gift and it was not adeemed when the legatee paid off a previous debt to the testator in the testator's lifetime.*

British Library MS. Hargrave 80, f. 78, pl. 3

J.S devised £500 to his uncle, *viz.* 'that bond and judgment he gave me for about £400 that he owed me and £100 in money'. The uncle pays his nephew the £400, except £18, for which there was a new bond given after his will and before his death. And the single question was whether he should have £400 or £100. Several cases were cited out of Swinburne[1] upon the head of ademption of a legacy, as, if a man devises a house or ship or corn in a barn and, after that, repairs or in a great measure rebuilds the house or ship or spends the corn in the barn and brings in another crop, that, nevertheless, shall pass.

On the other side, it was said that, if a man devises his black horse in such a stable and sells that horse and buys in another, that shall not pass by the will. But the case nearer the point was that, if a man devises to his younger children £2000 apiece, *viz.* '£2000 due to me on a mortgage from J.S. to A.D. to B. etc.' and, after, calls in those mortgages and invests them in lands, those children shall go unprovided for.

*Vernon* said that the difference of this principal case, where the money was devised to the defendant, was where the testator called it in by suit or otherwise in his own life and where the devisee paid it involuntarily. In the first case, it did amount to an ademption of a legacy; in the second not. And there was another difference taken between a devise of the debt itself and the bond etc. and a devise of a certain sum of money with a '*viz.*' by way of explanation how to be paid.

Upon arguing this case the second time, the Attorney General [*Northey*] insisted that there was no foundation in law for Swinburne's distinction where the legatee paid in the money voluntarily and where by a suit, but that there was a difference where the money was owing from a legatee, as here, or where from a third person, as in Pawlet's Case, Raymond 335,[2] and that, in the first case, it could only operate by way of release.

*Cowper*: The civil law is the proper rule for construction of legacies. That divides ademptions of legacies into express and secret; every alienation, from which it may be presumed that the testator has changed his mind, is a secret ademption. If a man devises a watch and then pawns it, in regard the testator retains the ownership in some measure, this is no evidence that he changed his mind and, therefore, the executor shall be obliged to redeem it for the legatee. [It is] otherwise if the testator sells or gives away the watch. But in the principal case, the calling in the money was as much an evidence of the testator's having changed his mind as if he had got it in by a suit; there was no proof that the testator called it in, that it was the intent of the testator that his uncle should not be harassed for this debt by his executors, but that, by the devise of the £100 in money, it was plain he intended no more than £100 should be charged on his personal estate.

---

[1] H. Swinburne, *Brief Treatise of Testaments and Last Wills.*

[2] *Pawlet's Case* (1680), T. Raymond 335, 83 E.R. 174.

Serjeant *Hooper*, senior: The difference in Swinburne is this, if I give £100 in such a chest or £100 which J.S. owes me and there is no money in the chest or J.S. owes me none, that devise is void, but, if I give £100 to be paid out of the money in such a chest etc. and there happens to be none there, the devise is good, for, in that case, the devise is complete and the rest directs only the manner of payment and that, in this case, the kind declaration of the testator of his affection and kind intentions towards his uncle a little before his death, which were now proved in the cause, is an evidence that he intended the legacy should not be taken away.

*Vernon* admitted this that, in the case of Raymond, if the debt out of which the legacy was to have been paid had stood out and proved a desperate debt, that the legatee could not have resorted to the personal estate for satisfaction. And, here, if the money had not been paid in and desperate in the hands of the uncle, yet he must have contended himself with the delivery up of the bond and judgment as a satisfaction for the £400 etc., but that it was otherwise where the debts came to the hands of the testator that, if the nephew had taken a new security from his uncle for the £400 by mortgage after the will, the uncle would have had the benefit of that. And, therefore, [there is] no color to say it should operate by way of release.

Lord Keeper [Lord Harcourt]: The will proves his affection to his uncle at the time of making it, and these declarations of his are evidences that that affection continued to his death. It is an express gift of £500 and, therefore, stronger than that in Swinburne of the bequest of a bond. The subsequent words here are only directory as to the manner of payment. The justice of the uncle in paying in the greatest part of the £400 cannot be presumed to have lessened his nephew's affection for him. Let the defendant pay him the £500, the bond for £18 to be delivered up in part of payment, and the plaintiff to have his costs out of the assets.

[Other copies of this report: Lincoln's Inn MS. Misc. 383, p. 142, pl. 2.]

Lincoln's Inn MS. Misc. 506, p. 8

February 1711[/12], Lord Harcourt.

The plaintiff was indebted to the testator Smith by bond in the sum of £370 and gave a warrant of attorney to confess judgment. Smith makes his will, in which was this clause: 'I give and bequeath unto my only uncle [ *blank* ] Orme £500, *viz.* the bond and judgment which he gave me for about £400 he owes to me and £100 in money.' The plaintiff and testator, before his death, stated accounts, and the plaintiff paid him all that was due but £80. And the bond and warrant of attorney were delivered up, and the testator gave a warrant of attorney to enter up satisfaction, and the plaintiff gave the testator a new bond for £80.

And it was decreed he should be paid the whole £500, the bond of £80 being taken for part.

[Other reports of this case: Gilbert Rep. 82, 25 E.R. 58, 2 Vernon 681, 23 E.R. 1042, 1 Eq. Cas. Abr. 302, 21 E.R. 1061.]

## 355

## Dormer v. Bishop of Salisbury

(Ch. 1712)

*A married woman may make a gift of a lease out of her separate estate to her husband without it being considered to be a resulting trust.*

*A bequest of 'all the goods brought into a house' means goods brought for the convenience of the house, including plate and pictures, but not jewels, books, or money.*

*If a woman who has a separate maintenance lives with her husband and permits him to receive the profits of her separate estate, equity will not require the husband to account for them.*

*An agent or trustee of a party is not an interested party and can give evidence.*

*Parol directions to a steward for payments are admissible in evidence.*

Lincoln's Inn MS. Misc. 10, p. 103

Hilary vacation 1711[/12]. Judge Dormer[1] v. The bishop of Sarum and Mackney and *e contra*.

Upon the marriage of the bishop[2] with his late wife,[3] all her estate was settled on trustees for her separate use and to be at her disposal. She makes her will and the plaintiff executor. And she, thereby, gives to the bishop her watch and all her goods which she had brought into his house except such as were mentioned in a schedule annexed to her will. But there was no schedule.

The defendant Mackney, who was the bishop's steward, received the rents of the separate estate and paid the same from time to time to the order of the bishop's wife.

And now, the plaintiff, as her executor, exhibits his bill to have an account of the rents and profits of the separate estate come to the hands of the defendants.

And the bishop's cross-bill was to have the watch and other things given him by his wife's will and to be paid several sums of money which he had paid for his wife's debts and to have an allowance for her maintenance pursuant to an agreement she had made with him after her marriage.

Upon the hearing of these causes, several questions did arise.

The first was touching a lease of some houses which had been bought during the marriage. These houses belonged to some relations of the bishop's wife, and, being to be sold, she persuaded him to buy them. Accordingly, he does so,

[1] S. Handley, 'Dormer, Robert (bap. 1650, d. 1726)', *Oxford Dictionary of National Biography*, vol. 16, pp. 577–578.

[2] M. Greig, 'Burnet, Gilbert (1643–1715)', *Oxford Dictionary of National Biography*, vol. 8, pp. 908–923.

[3] F. Harris, 'Burnet [nee Blake, other married name Berkeley], Elizabeth (1661–1709)', *Oxford Dictionary of National Biography*, vol. 8, pp. 904–905.

and the lease was assigned to him, and he gives a bond got the purchase money, which was £250. Afterwards, she pays off this bond out of her own estate. And, by a verbal agreement between her and the bishop that she should receive the rents of these houses until she was reimbursed what she had so paid in case she lived so long, and, accordingly, during her life, she received the rents, which did not satisfy what she had paid.

And it was now insisted that this purchase was a trust for the wife and that the purchase money being paid by her, there was a resulting trust, and the rather because she was permitted to receive the rents during her life.

Lord Keeper [LORD HARCOURT]: At the time of the purchase, there is no doubt but the estate was the bishop's. He paid the consideration money or gave a bond for it, which was the same thing. Now, shall anything *ex post facto* alter the nature of this purchase? Surely no. Besides, when shall it be said that this trust resulted? As to what is insisted on, that she received the rents, that is answered by what the bishop says in his answer (and you have no other evidence) that she received them under an agreement to reimburse herself what she had paid in discharge of the bond.

The second question [was] what passed by the bequest of the watch etc. to the bishop.

Lord Keeper [LORD HARCOURT]: There was no schedule; so the exception is void, and it stands as if there had been no exception.

It has been said at the bar that the word '*bona*' in the civil law is a very comprehensive word and includes all the personal estate. [There is] no doubt but it does so, and, had it been a devise of all my goods generally, it would have passed everything. But here, it is restrained to all the goods which she brought into the bishop's house, so that I am of the opinion that, by 'goods brought into the house' must be understood such things as had been brought in for the accommodation or furniture of the house, in which I include plate but not jewels, rings, or ready money, nor the study of books and that nothing passes but what had been actually brought in at the time of the will.

The next question was upon the account. The plaintiff demanded from the bishop and Mackney an account of the rents of the separate estate which had been received by them during the marriage.

And, on the other hand, the bishop demanded an allowance for his wife's maintenance and for an extraordinary expense he was at upon the account of her going to the Spa and for debts which he had paid for her during the marriage and had said in his answer that there was discourse between her and him about her agreeing to allow him £100 a year for her maintenance by reason of the extraordinary expense he was at upon her account.

But this agreement being waived by the bishop in court, Lord Keeper [LORD HARCOURT] declared that, if a woman, upon her marriage, reserves her estate for her separate use and, notwithstanding, permits her husband out of kindness to him to receive the rents and profits of it, the husband, after the death of the wife, shall not account for this to her executors.

So, on the other hand, if the husband, notwithstanding his wife has such a separate provision made for her, will out of an indulgence to his wife pay any debts which she has contracted and not call upon her to pay them out of her own estate, he shall not after her death charge what he has so paid as a debt upon her executors, so that he would not decree any account from the bishop of what came to his hands during the marriage nor direct any satisfaction to be made him of any extraordinary expense he had been put to on her account or of any debts he had paid for his wife except what he had paid since her death.

Mackney [is] to account and to have all just allowances and, particularly, of what he had paid the bishop towards satisfaction of the £100 a year for the maintenance of his wife and of all the moneys he had paid the bishop by his wife's order or with her privity.

British Library MS. Hargrave 80, f. 79v

Mrs. Berkeley, before her marriage with the bishop of Salisbury [Gilbert Burnet (1643–1715)] and with his consent, assigned over all her real and personal estate to the value of £1000 *per annum* to trustees for her separate use with a power to dispose of it by will etc. during the coverture. A lease of four houses in Exeter Street that lay intermixed with Mrs. Dormer's estate and were formerly Mrs. Burnet's and her father's [was] purchased in the name of the bishop, the consideration [was] mentioned in the deed to be paid by him, and a bond [was] given by him for it. But, as the bishop disclosed in his answer, that bond was afterward discharged by Mrs. Burnet out of her separate estate. And it was agreed between them that she should receive the rents of the houses during her life to repay her as far as they would go and that, afterwards, the bishop should enjoy them. It was urged strongly that this was a resulting trust to Mrs. Burnet, the consideration being paid by her and that she received the rents and profits was an evidence of it and that the purchase being made out of her separate estate ought to follow the nature of that and go to her executor, Mr. Dormer, and not to the bishop.

On the other side, it was insisted and agreed to by Lord Keeper [Lord Harcourt] that here was no resulting trust at the time of the purchase, the consideration being paid or, which is equivalent, secured by a bond from the bishop nor was there anything *ex post facto* to make the trust result. The only evidence of Mrs. Burnet's discharging that bond was the bishop's answer. But then they must take the whole answer together, and, by that, it appears that it was intended to be for the bishop's benefit after her death. The receipt of rents would have been a strong evidence against the bishop had not that matter been set in a true light by his answer, upon which the Lord Keeper [Lord Harcourt] dismissed the bill as to those houses and decreed the bishop to hold and enjoy them.

Serjeant *Pratt* resembled this case to that of a purchase by a father in the name of a child, in which case no trust shall result because of the consideration of nature between them.

The next point was what should pass by these words in Mrs. Burnet's will, 'I give to the bishop of Salisbury my gold watch and all the goods I brought into his house' in the schedule annexed.

It was said by *Sir Peter King*, and I think agreed to by the Lord Keeper, that 'goods' is the most extensive word that can be made use of in a will and that, though in a grant, a term would not pass by that word, yet, in a will, which is to be interpreted according to the rules of the civil law, that and all other personal estate whatever would pass unless there were any others coupled with it to restrain it.

Serjeant *Hooper* said that, in Strode's Case, where there was a devise to the wife of his best bed and one of a sort of all his goods, that the bequest of the goods being introduced by that of the bed, the court restrained it to that of household goods.

But *Vernon* said that that devise was of one of a sort 'of all my goods in my house'.

Lord Keeper [Lord Harcourt]: The devise of the watch would be unnecessary if she intended to give goods of that kind by the general words of 'all the goods'.

*Sir Peter King*: That, [the watch,] was particularly devised as an instance of what kind of goods she intended. There was no schedule annexed or the least proof that there ever had been any.

Lord Keeper [Lord Harcourt]: The exception is void, and the devise is good in common cases. By a devise of 'all my goods', those that are acquired after making the will pass. But here, the subsequent words 'I brought into his house' restrains the devise to those she brought thither before the making of the will. The same words are explanatory of the nature of the goods she intended to give the bishop. And I cannot take them to be meant but of goods brought for the convenience of the house, in which plate and pictures will be included, but not jewels, books, or money.

Serjeant *Hooper* owned that pictures were always taken to be household goods, except in the Case of Sir Robert Geare,[1] where those that were not hung up were not reckoned so because he traded in pictures.

The next point was about money received by the bishop out of her separate estate and other sums expended by him for her separate use.

And as to that, the Lord Keeper [Lord Harcourt] declared that, if a woman that has a separate maintenance lives with her husband and permits him to receive the profits of her separate estate, equity will never oblige the husband to

[1] *Gayre v. Gayre* (1706), 2 Vernon 538, 23 E.R. 949, 1 Eq. Cas. Abr. 200, 21 E.R. 989.

account for them. On the other hand, if a husband supplies his wife with things for her separate use and does not call upon her to apply her separate estate to that purpose, equity will never allow him to make her executors debtors to him on that account, but that, if he paid debts of hers, he might, perhaps, have another consideration.

Serjeant *Pratt* said that, though a woman has a separate maintenance, the husband is chargeable with her debts if the creditors do not know of her having a separate maintenance, but not if they do.

And *Vernon* said that a woman that has a separate maintenance is considered in equity as a *feme sole*.

In this, the defendant Mackney, who was an agent for Mrs. Burnet and received a great part of her separate estate, was examined by the bishop *de bene esse*. And the plaintiff opposed the reading of his evidence because he was liable to be decreed against as to costs.

*Vernon*: A co-plaintiff cannot be read; but was it ever pretended that a trustee who is made a defendant may not be examined and read, and yet he is liable to be decreed to account and to costs too. In cases of a breach of trust, an apprentice or cashier may be read to prove payment of money, and yet that is in some measure to discharge himself.

The Lord Keeper [Lord Harcourt]: Read him.

In this case, Mrs. Burnet had a power of disposing of any part of her separate estate by a writing under her hand. And the plaintiff's counsel contended that Mackney ought not to be allowed for any payments made to the bishop for which he could not produce a writing signed by her.

Lord Keeper [Lord Harcourt] [held] *contra* that is to be intended of an alienation of any part of her separate estate. Parol directions to her steward for payment of the profits are sufficient.

[Other copies of this report: Lincoln's Inn MS. Misc. 383, p. 144, Lincoln's Inn MS. Misc. 106, p. 94, pl. 2.]

2 Eq. Cas. Abr. 322, 22 E.R. 274

A wife, having authority to make a will, devised to her husband her gold watch and all the goods which she brought into his house.

And it was decreed that such goods only passed as were then brought in, and not any brought in after, but that books, jewels, pictures, and money did not pass.

## 356

## Wood v. Webb

(Ch. 1712)

*Persons who have a bare fee determinable upon a life do not have the right to cut timber.*

British Library MS. Hargrave 80, f. 81

Sir Henry Wood, having devised his estate to J.S. for life, remainder etc. if the duke of Southampton died without issue by his daughter, and his daughter being dead without issue and no estate limited to the duke, who survived, the land during the life[time] of the duke descended to the heirs of Sir Henry Wood, who immediately began to fell the timber upon it.

But they having only a bare fee determinable upon a life, the court [LORD HARCOURT] stopped their felling any more by an injunction and directed the money arising by sale of what had been sold to be brought into court for the benefit of those that would be entitled to the timber.

[Other copies of this report: Lincoln's Inn MS. Misc. 383, p. 147, pl. 1, Lincoln's Inn MS. Misc. 106, p. 98.]

[Related cases: Wood v. Duke of Southampton (1685–1692), Shower P.C. 83, 1 E.R. 58, 1 Vernon 338, 23 E.R. 506, 2 Freeman 186, 22 E.R. 1151, Duke of Southampton v. Cranmer (1685–1692), Chancery Repts. *tempore* Jac. II, 122; Wood v. Webb (1695), Shower P.C. 87, 1 E.R. 60; Kirk v. Webb (1698), Precedents in Chancery 84, 24 E.R. 41, 2 Freeman 229, 22 E.R. 1177, 2 Eq. Cas. Abr. 743, 744, 22 E.R. 631.]

## 357

## Atkins v. Collingwood

(Ch. 1712)

*Where a person contracts to grant remainders, he cannot make himself a tenant in tail so as to be able to defeat his own grant.*

British Library MS. Hargrave 80, f. 81v

By marriage articles, the intended husband agreed to settle his estate to the use of himself and his intended wife and the heirs male of his body by her.

My Lord [Keeper LORD HARCOURT] decreed the conveyance to be made to the use of the husband and wife for their lives, remainder to trustees to preserve a contingent remainder, though the court seemed to think that limitation almost an *abundans cautela* since the 10th of William III, c. 16,[1] remainder to the first and every and every other son of that marriage in tail male.

The estate of the wife's father was agreed by articles to be settled to the use of the father and the heirs male of his body, remainder to the wife and the heirs of her body, remainder to father's right heirs, and a conveyance was executed by which the father was made tenant in tail, who immediately suffered a recovery and mortgaged his estate with other lands for £500 and then resettled to the former uses and conveyed the residue of the lands included in the mortgage to

[1] Stat. 10 Will. III, c. 22 (*SR*, VII, 532).

A. for life, with remainder etc. with a remainder to the wife. By the marriage articles, the father covenanted to give the wife £1500 beside the settlement and died without any issue but the wife. In the marriage articles, there was a power reserved to the father and likewise to the wife for charging the estate with £1000 and that being used as an argument to prove that it was not the intention of the parties that neither the father nor the wife should be tenants in tail for, then, that power would be needless.

*Lutwyche* cited the case of King v. Melling, in Levinz and Ventris,[1] which was that land was devised to A. and the issue of his body which he should have by a second wife with power to make a jointure and it was adjudged that A. was tenant in tail and that provision was added to save the trouble of suffering a common recovery.

Lord Keeper [LORD HARCOURT]: That estate was executed; this [is] executory. He directed all the persons claiming under the father, except the mortgagee, and the mortgagee upon payment of the principal and interest, to join in a conveyance to the use of the wife for life, remainder to trustees etc., remainder to the first and every other son of the body of the wife and the heirs of the body of such first and other son, remainder to the daughters of the wife as tenants in common and the heirs of their bodies with cross-remainders in case of the death of either without issue, remainder etc., these limitations being most agreeable to the intent of the marriage articles, for it is absurd to suppose that it could be the intent of the parties that the father should be tenant in tail and thereby enabled to defeat those very remainders he covenanted to limit.

The next point [was] out of what fund the £1500 should be satisfied.

The Lord Keeper [LORD HARCOURT] directed the personal estate should be first applied, then assets by descent, and if both [be] insufficient, the lands comprised in the voluntary settlement to be sold to make it up. This last was directed upon the head of fraud though there was a remainder in that voluntary conveyance to the wife.

*Vernon* and Serjeant *Hooper* insisted that, where a person that is indebted to others by specialties conveys his estate over voluntarily and dies, that this conveyance is fraudulent against those creditors.

Of this opinion, the Lord Keeper [LORD HARCOURT] seemed to be, though [it was] objected that the lands were not liable to those debts in the hands of the father nor could be in any hands but the heirs and, there, only assets by descent and that, if the father had devised those lands before the Statute of Fraudulent Devises,[2] even that would have defeated the creditors.

---

[1] *King v. Melling* (1672), 2 Levinz 58, 83 E.R. 448, 1 Ventris 214, 225, 86 E.R. 144, 151, also Pollexfen 101, 86 E.R. 526, 3 Keble 42, 52, 95, 84 E.R. 584, 589, 614, 3 Salkeld 296, 91 E.R. 835, 1 Eq. Cas. Abr. 181, 21 E.R. 973.

[2] Stat. 3 Will. & Mar., c. 14 (*SR*, VI, 320–321).

*Hooper* and *Vernon* said the reason of that was because the law would not admit any presumption of fraud in the case of a will but that voluntary conveyances by one in debt were always looked upon as fraudulent even before that Statute and, therefore, not taken notice of in the Statute.

*Vernon* cited the Case of Templeman and where a voluntary conveyance by one who had several creditors by specialty was ruled after his death to be fraudulent against them and said that that conveyance was both of leasehold and freehold estate.

The Lord Keeper [LORD HARCOURT] cited the case of Mrs. Willis, who claimed lands by a conveyance from Lord Culpeper two years before his death and yet that was made liable to his debts.

*Vernon* said that there had been several cases where voluntary remainders in a marriage settlement to those who were not privy to the considerations had been adjudged fraudulent in such a case.

The Lord Keeper [LORD HARCOURT] said that those cases had been both ways and that he would give his opinion on that case when it came before him. And the reason sometimes why they had been decreed not fraudulent [was] because the law would not presume fraud in a remainder limited after an estate tail which it was in the power of the tenant in tail to defeat. But he seemed to incline to Vernon's opinion.

And *Vernon* seemed to agree, that, if the wife had agreed to the limitation of the remainder to her in the voluntary conveyance, that then she could not be relieved against it upon the head of fraud.

As to the mortgage, it seemed agreed that a *haeres factus*, as a volunteer or a devisee, shall have the benefit of the personal estate to exonerate the real as well as a *haeres natus*. But the assets by descent shall not be applied for that purpose in favor either of a volunteer or devisee.

But in this case, part of the lands mortgaged being included in the marriage articles and part in the fee in the voluntary conveyances and the wife who was injured by this mortgage being likewise heir at law, My Lord [Keeper LORD HARCOURT] directed at first an estimate to be made of the lands included in the marriage articles and of those of the voluntary conveyance. And it being reasonable that the assets descended should be a satisfaction to the wife so far as they would go for the injury done her by her father, My Lord [Keeper LORD HARCOURT] directed that they should be applied to satisfy such a proportion of the mortgage as the lands in the articles bore to those of the voluntary conveyance and no further. Some difficulties arising about the estimate, the consideration of this point was reserved.

[Other copies of this report: Lincoln's Inn MS. Misc. 383, p. 147, pl. 2, Lincoln's Inn MS. Misc. 106, p. 99.]

## 358

## Westcome v. Briscoe

(Ch. 1712)

*A witness is estopped to testify to his own bad faith.*

*Brokers who have negotiable bills put into their hands have an unlimited power of disposing of them in the manner they please.*

British Library MS. Hargrave 80, f. 83, pl. 2

Westcome gave a note payable to J.S. or order at a future day for value received. J.S. endorsed it to C., who sent it to a broker to get it discounted. The broker carried it to Briscoe to discount, who refused. Upon that, the broker returned the note. Soon after, Briscoe brought notes for £300 to the same broker to discount, who then told him he had discounted them and paid him £160 of the money and no more. And Briscoe pressing for the rest of his money, the broker sent for Westcome's note again to discount it and delivered it over again to Briscoe without receiving any money upon it. Briscoe put it in suit. And Westcome and J.S. brought their bill to stay proceedings at law and to have the note delivered to them upon a surmise that it was fraudulently obtained by Briscoe, who knew that it was put into the broker's hands upon trust to raise money upon it and yet accepted in satisfaction of his own debt without advancing 1d. upon it. They would have read the broker's evidence to prove the contrivance and notice of Briscoe of the trust.

But Lord Keeper [LORD HARCOURT] would not allow it because it was to avoid his own act and prove himself a knave. He said that, if A. sells lands and takes the consideration money and then B. comes in against the vendee and surmises that A. was barely a trustee for him and that the vendee had notice, A., for the same reason, shall never be admitted to prove that notice. And, if A. covenanted that he was the true and lawful owner etc., it seems he cannot be a witness on the other hand to affirm his own act. The bill was dismissed because no trade could be carried on if brokers who have negotiable bills put into their hands should not have an unlimited power of disposing of them in the manner they please.

[Other copies of this report: Lincoln's Inn MS. Misc. 383, p. 150, pl. 2, Lincoln's Inn MS. Misc. 106, p. 103.]

## 359

## Anonymous v. Smart

(Ch. 1712)

*In this case, a life insurance claim was ordered to be paid, the insured not having done anything to forfeit it.*

*A witness who has an interest in the outcome of a case is not competent to testify.*

*A voluntary company created without the leave of the crown is illegal and indictable.*

Lincoln's Inn MS. Misc. 11, p. 7 [bis], pl. 1

8 July 11 Anne. A.B., a bond creditor of John Smart, plaintiff; Sarah Smart, executrix of John Smart, defendant.

John Smart subscribes and becomes a member of the Office of Assurance for Widows and Orphans on the behalf of M., his wife and children, and he makes his wife nominee. And he pays several claims for several years and dies.

Smart dies insolvent, and a bond creditor brings a bill in equity against Sarah, his widow and executrix, for a discovery of assets and to have the money received by this policy subjected to this debt.

The defendant, by her answer, insisted that her husband 4 February 1705[/06] subscribed to a policy of insurance for £500 on behalf of her and for Sarah, Mary, Charles, George, John, and Ann, her children, and the survivors upon the stock of the Assurance for Widows and Orphans subject to the agreement mentioned in the articles of settlement and paid £40 for claims. But, afterwards, refusing to go on with his payments or to comply with the articles, the defendant's mother, to secure the benefit of the policy to the defendant and her children, did for eighteen months before the death of Smart pay all the sums he ought to have paid. And, since his death, she admits she has in her own right and not as executrix to her husband received £71, which she hopes is not liable to her husband's debts.

On hearing the cause before the Lord Keeper, His Lordship [Lord Harcourt] directed that the Master should examine what was paid by John Smart for purchasing the policy and what payments were by him afterwards made upon the same. And so far, His Lordship declared the policy ought to be looked upon and taken to be the personal estate of the said John Smart and the defendant, his executrix, was to stand charged accordingly.

British Library MS. Hargrave 80, f. 83v

In the 12th article, every subscriber having paid his subscription money pursuant to the articles, his nominee is entitled to £500 upon his death. By the 16th article, if a subscriber refuses or omits to pay £5 towards the succeeding claim within seven days after notice, his policy is to be void and his former payment forfeited. In this case, the subscriber, whose nominee the plaintiff was, paid his subscriptions regularly until the 4th of March. Upon the 17th, there was another claim made and another upon the 25th. The plaintiff's subscriber died on the 4th of April following, and his wife, who was his nominee and who was represented by the plaintiff, lay sick in his house for ten days before her husband's death and died soon after him.

The payments on the second and last claims were paid in upon the day the subscriber died, but after his death, and were accepted by the office, who knew nothing then of his death and whose practice it is to receive the several £5s though not paid in due time, sometimes not within a twelvemonth after, provided the person that pays be in health.

It was insisted for the plaintiffs that this forfeiture like all others that are neither negligent nor willful is relievable in equity though they had proof, which in case of a forfeiture ought to be very clear and full, of notice and that the defendant had no regular proof of that. The words of the 16th article were urged to show that it was intended to be a forfeiture.

On the other side, Serjeant *Jekyll* insisted that it appeared from the 12th article, upon which the subscriber's title was built, that payments of the several £5s were to be in the nature of a condition precedent, the words being 'having paid' and that there was great reason for making it so for, if the society was to pay out the several claims before they received the subscription money, they might be driven to as many suits to get it in as there were subscribers and that this being in the nature of a condition precedent and not having been performed, nothing ever vested. And, therefore, [it] could not be forfeited and that neither infancy nor disability would excuse the non-performance of a condition precedent to prove notice.

He offered to read the deposition of a visitor, *alias* messenger, of the society, who was a subscriber. He said that, formerly, witnesses were rejected if they were ever so minutely concerned in interest but that it had been otherwise of late and that there had been several cases in Ventris and where freemen of a corporation or parishioners had been admitted to give evidence though some small advantages might accrue to them by it.

His evidence was read. And upon his examination before the hearing, he deposed that he gave notice on or about the 7th etc. But, in his deposition after the hearing by the Master of the Rolls, where this case had been heard and decreed for the defendants, he swore positively to the 17th day.

Lord Keeper [Lord Harcourt]: The plaintiff is well entitled to the £500 unless his subscriber has done any act to forfeit it. If he had no notice, he was guilty of no neglect. The only proof of notice is by an incompetent witness because a subscriber and, though he is concerned in interest no farther than £5, yet that is as much as any other member is. The reexamining of him to a point that he had been examined to before and deposing imperfectly is entirely wrong and introductive of perjury. He decreed the defendant the £500 (deducting some sums according to the articles) and interest from the time it ought to have been paid and costs. But he said it would be a great difference between this case of involuntary omission and the cases of a long and willful one or of a refusal. He said that this voluntary society, being erected without the leave of the crown, was illegal and indictable.

[Other copies of this report: Lincoln's Inn MS. Misc. 383, p. 151.]

## 360

## Greenwood v. Atkins

(Ch. 1712)

*Where it is uncertain whether a portion will ever arise, a court cannot give interest or maintenance upon it beforehand.*

British Library MS. Hargrave 80, f. 84v

The plaintiff's wife had a portion of £1000 charged upon the defendants', her brothers', estate [ . . . ][1] and had no fortune. The £1000 was charged upon the estate by her grandmother and made payable to her at twenty in case she lived so long and no provision for her maintenance [was made] in the meantime. By the plaintiff's marriage articles, £200 of the portion was recited to be sunk by the plaintiff's having maintained his sister for some years and the remaining £800 was agreed to be vested in trustees to the use of the husband and wife and the survivor of them, to the use of their children etc. And it was agreed by the parties that the husband should have a power of revocation as to £200, part of the £800, and of applying it to his own use. But, instead of that power, there was a clause inserted in the articles by which there were three or four trustees inserted of each side and a power reserved by the husband of revoking the whole £800 with the consent of any two of the trustees. And the husband brought his bill for the whole.

But Lord Keeper [Lord Harcourt] confined him to £200 and subjected that to the costs of this suit. The rest he directed to be settled to the use in the articles without a power of revocation and gave the wife liberty to apply to the court for further direction in case of necessity.

Mr. *How* insisted that the £200 ought not to have been deducted for maintenance and that, in case of a provision for a child where there was a portion given payable at a future day and no maintenance nor interest given in the meantime, equity would give interest.

But *Vernon* positively denied it unless there were any words in the will or settlement that would induce the court to do it.

[1] to the plaintiff himself was chose master: British Library MS. Hargrave 80, f. 84v, Lincoln's Inn MS. Misc. 106, f. 104.

And the Lord Keeper HARCOURT said that, where there was a certain portion given payable at a future day, equity would anticipate it and sink part by mortgage etc. for a present maintenance. But in this case, it was ever uncertain whether the portion ever would arise, and so [there is] no ground ever for making an allowance out of it beforehand.

[Other copies of this report: Lincoln's Inn MS. Misc. 383, p. 153, pl. 1, Lincoln's Inn MS. Misc. 106, p. 104.]

## 361

## Gibson v. Bayly

(Ch. 1712)

*Where a lawsuit is on the trial docket, a party's clerk in court can be served with a notice of trial.*

British Library MS. Hargrave 80, f. 85, pl. 1

The defendants were served regularly with a subpoena to hear judgment and appeared three years ago and, upon a suggestion of theirs that the suit was carried on without the plaintiff's direction, the cause stood over for that matter to be inquired into. And [it] was now brought on again. And the defendant's clerk in court [was] served with a subpoena to hear judgment.

Lord Keeper [LORD HARCOURT] asked *Vernon*, who was not in the cause, whether this was regular. And he said it was, the cause never having been struck out of the paper, upon which the cause was heard.

[Other copies of this report: Lincoln's Inn MS. Misc. 383, p. 153, pl. 2, Lincoln's Inn MS. Misc. 106, p. 105.]

## 362

## Lewis v. Whitehall

(Ch. 1712)

*A common law conveyance of an equitable right is not a voluntary conveyance.*

British Library MS. Hargrave 80, f. 85, pl. 2

J.S. married a young woman without the consent of friends, who had a £500 portion, the securities of which were taken in the names of trustees. The husband called on the trustees for the money, but they refused paying it unless he would agree to settle part of it upon the wife and, accordingly, £200 was paid to the husband and the other £300 [was] vested in trustees to the use of the husband during coverture and then to the use of the survivor. After[wards], the husband became a bankrupt and, after the bankruptcy, assigned his interest in the £300 for the separate use of the wife during coverture. The assignees brought their bill for the whole £300.

*How* insisted the assignees were in the nature of purchasers for a valuable consideration, they coming upon consideration of the debts due from the bankrupt, and that all voluntary conveyances made by a husband for the provision for his wife, children, etc. were by the Statute[1] void against purchasers.

*Vernon* cited Brown's Case,[2] fo. 141, as adjudged in point.

But Lord Keeper [Lord Harcourt] said it was hard to call that £300 settled for the benefit of the wife in case she survived fraudulent, which equity would have obliged him to do had he brought his bill against her trustees for the £500. And he decreed that she should have the benefit of that settlement but not of the other subsequent to the bankruptcy. He said that in Brown's Case, the creditors had got the legal interest (but that was not so) and, here, he could not give the assignees any assistance against the wife.

[Other copies of this report: Lincoln's Inn MS. Misc. 383, p. 154, pl. 1, Lincoln's Inn MS. Misc. 106, p. 106.]

## 363

## Bennett v. Bishop of Saint David's

(Ch. 1712)

*Where a person watches and is silent, he cannot later complain of action taken that he could and should have prevented.*

*Where an executor admits having assets of the decedent, the defense of laches will not later bar a creditor of the estate.*

*Paraphernalia extends only to the ornaments of the person.*

*Paraphernalia cannot be retained by a widow against her husband's creditors except necessary apparel.*

British Library MS. Hargrave 80, f. 85v

The bill demanded an account against Lady Plymouth, wife to the bishop, as executrix of her own wrong[3] to her first husband, who died about thirty years ago. And about 1687, the same party brought a bill for the same demand, and Lady Plymouth put in her answer to it, and no further proceedings were had. In that suit, the plaintiff was a creditor of the earl of Plymouth [1657–1680] and had a letter of attorney from him to receive the earl's pension out of the Exchequer and,

[1] Stat. 13 Eliz. I, c. 5, (*SR*, IV, 537–538).

[2] *Brown v. Brown* (Ch. 1712), see above, Case No. 352.

[3] *I.e. de son tort.*

afterwards, an authority under the hand and seal of the earl to apply the same to the satisfaction of his own debt. My Lady had a grant from the king of £1250 to put her in mourning upon the earl's death. But her agent that received it out of the Exchequer received it out of the arrears of the earl's pension whereby it became assets in her hands. And six or seven years after, several bond creditors sued her and recovered their principal, interest, and costs against her out of this money. In 1693, another bond creditor for £1000 principal money, besides interest, applied to her and she compounded the debt and the obligee either released the debt or acknowledged satisfaction upon a judgment on the bond.

It was insisted by *Sir Joseph Jekyll* that the plaintiff's demand was a specific lien on the £1250. He said that, if a person intended to sell his estate and directed a particular sum to be paid to J.S. out of the purchase money when it should be received, that this appointment is a specific lien upon the purchase money and it had been adjudged so in the case of Lord Kildare and Kent.[1] He admitted that, if the earl had only given a letter of attorney, that, being but a bare authority, had been no lien but that the authority after to his own use was in the nature of an assignment.

It was insisted on the other side that it was no lien, which Lord Keeper [LORD HARCOURT] seemed to agree to, and, that if it was, the Lady Plymouth had admitted that she had notice of the plaintiff's demand not long after her husband's death, yet she had not admitted nor was there any proof that she knew of the plaintiff's authority to receive and apply the same to his own use etc. And, if the plaintiff would stand by and see her who was ignorant of his title apply these assets to any debts by specialty, he could not afterwards call her to an account for a misapplication of them, to which My Lord agreed.

It was insisted by *Vernon* against the Lady's being decreed to an account that, though she had not pleaded the Statute of Limitations[2] in bar, yet, in this case and in cases to which the Statute of Limitations does not extend, if a man that is under no disability acquiesces until a defendant is, either by a loss of witnesses or otherwise, disabled from making so good a defense as he might have done at first, he cannot afterward be relieved here. An equity of redemption is a title purely relievable in this court, and yet, if a mortgagor lies still for a great number of years, he cannot afterwards come to redeem though the Statute of Limitations is no bar to his title.

In merchants' accounts, if a merchant make no objection to an account that is sent him within two or three posts after he receives it, he cannot afterwards contest it. And if an account between a master and his bailiff lies of sometime before a master and be not objected against, it is a bar to the master. The case of

[1] *Earl of Kildare v. Kent* (1702), 2 Freeman 253, 22 E.R. 1192, *sub nom. Shepherd v. Kent*, Precedents in Chancery 190, 24 E.R. 92, 2 Vernon 435, 23 E.R. 879, 1 Eq. Cas. Abr. 142, 21 E.R. 944, Colles 253, 1 E.R. 273, Lincoln's Inn MS. Misc. 10, p. 24.

[2] Stat. 21 Jac. I, c. 16 (*SR*, IV, 1222–1223).

Wescome v. Jones[1] was cited, where a bill was dismissed that sought an account against an executor after twenty-four years.

Lord Keeper [LORD HARCOURT]: You would not have me dismiss the bill where the defendant admits assets. Let her account, but let it be taken according to her answer without any liberty to the plaintiff to purchase or examine her upon interrogatories. The payment she made to the bond creditors for principal or interest due at the time she received £1250 and within a year after and for costs for, possibly, she was not satisfied of the reality of the debts before she contested them must be allowed her but not what she paid for interest that grew due upon those bonds after the year was expired, she having the assets to pay them and the surplus applied in a course of administration.

It was insisted by *Vernon* that the principal due on the several bonds amounted to more than the £1250 and that she had compounded the last bond for £300. The plaintiff ought not to have any benefit of that composition, for the obligee being induced to make it upon a supposition that she had no assets beyond that sum and, if it after appeared that she had, he might bring his bill and be relieved against his own release.

But nevertheless, [it was] decreed *ut supra*.

A coach and horses had been seized by the innkeeper of the earl for what the earl owed him for keeping them and which My Lady bought of the innkeeper. MY LORD [HARCOURT] would not look upon them as assets in her hands because she cannot be an executrix of her own wrong for what she bought, though under an ill title.

My Lord Keeper [LORD HARCOURT] said in this case that paraphernalia extend properly only to the ornaments of the person and that no paraphernalia could be retained by the wife against the husband's creditors except necessary apparel.

[Other copies of this report: Lincoln's Inn MS. Misc. 383, p. 154, pl. 2, Lincoln's Inn MS. Misc. 106, p. 107.]

## 364

## Cley v. Higgins

(Ch. 1712)

*An heir or legatee has an equitable interest in a bond given for repayment of assets of the decedent's estate. Such a person has an interest that has priority over a later creditor.*

---

[1] *Westcombe v. Jones* (Ch. 1711), see above, Case No. 275.

British Library MS. Hargrave 80, f. 87

The wife of Higgins was administratrix of her former husband. And she loaned out his assets upon bond, which she took in her own name and then married the defendant soon after, which she concealed, and, in a little time afterwards, she prevailed with the obligors to give a new bond for the same sum to her husband who, being in the Counter [Prison] for debt, assigned or pretended to assign it to a creditor only as a satisfaction for his debt and the residue in consideration of an equivalent advancement in money. And, a little after, being indebted to the crown, this bond was extended *inter alia*. The plaintiff, who was the only child unprovided for of her father, brought this bill for a distribution.

And Lord Keeper [LORD HARCOURT] decreed this bond to be distributed *inter alia* though taken in the name of Higgins, it appearing to be the assets of the plaintiff's father and the assignment, if real, could not stand in the way because no legal interest passed by it and the plaintiff's title in equity is prior to the assignee's, nor could the extent because, being assets of the plaintiff's father, it was not extendable for Higgins's debt any further than for the third that would belong to Higgins's wife upon a distribution and to him in her right.

Lord Keeper [LORD HARCOURT] said he did not know any case that went so far as to put a creditor that came in under a commission of bankrupts and, by that, is entitled to a satisfaction out of the debtor's lands upon an equal foot with a purchaser, that it was reasonable that a purchaser who contracts for the land itself should have liberty to protect his purchase against encumbrances that he had no notice of by getting in old terms etc., but that a creditor comes in upon a different foot. He does not contract particularly for the land but sweeps all he can get. And it seems that, if such a creditor should be allowed to cover himself against a precedent mortgage by getting in an old term etc., it would make an absurd transposition of debts and give one that was perhaps but a creditor by a simple contract a priority of satisfaction before a mortgagee out of the very mortgaged lands.

[Other copies of this report: Lincoln's Inn MS. Misc. 383, p. 157, Lincoln's Inn MS. Misc. 106, p. 110.]

## 365

## Stafford's Case

(Ch. 1712)

*In this case, various creditors had notice of the rights of prior creditors.*

British Library MS. Hargrave 80, f. 87v

The Plaintiff's father was tenant for life, remainder to the plaintiff in [ *blank* ]. The defendants were assignees of a mortgage created by the father. The first mortgagee had notice that the father was only tenant for life. But he having assigned over to a second and the second to a third, the father having joined in an assignment to a third, who advanced part of the money to a second mortgagee, and £50 new money to the father and it not appearing that the second or third mortgagee had notice, the plaintiff on the hearing submitted to redeem them on the common terms. But the mortgagees' having been in possession when the account of profits was taken, they contended that they ought not to be charged with more than £190 *per annum*, of which, by the last deed, it was agreed that the estate should be let to one Hall, especially both mortgagor and mortgagees' being parties to that deed though it was said the estate was worth £400 *per annum*. Upon reading the deed, the plaintiff discovered a clause in it by which £50 *per annum* was to be laid aside for insuring the life of the plaintiff's father and mother by which a sum was to be employed for supporting the suits which the deed took notice had been about this estate. Sometime before, the son had brought his action upon a supposition that the father had committed a forfeiture and, by another clause, almost a moiety of the second mortgagee's money was to be postponed to the third's. Upon these evidences of notice, the plaintiff petitioned for a rehearing, at which the defendant's counsel insisted that the plaintiff was tied down by his submission and that, if anything appeared after in taking the account which would affect the defendant with notice and which the plaintiff was not entitled to have a discovery of that he could have no benefit of it.

*Vernon* said almost the same thing, but said that, if that notice arose from anything which it would have been necessary for the defendant to have proved at the hearing, the plaintiff might take advantage of it, that, in this case, notwithstanding the plea of purchase without notice, that it was necessary to have proved the mortgage deed at the hearing and that it appeared from the last deed they had notice when that deed was made, that, in most cases, a *lis pendens* would affect a purchaser, but, here, the very deed took notice of suits and it was incumbent on the mortgagee to inquire what those suits were.

Lord Keeper [Lord Harcourt] was of opinion that these circumstances were a demonstration of notice, and he relieved the plaintiff against the £50 that was advanced though [it was] objected that £50 was satisfied by perception of profits in the life of the father. But the Lord Keeper [Lord Harcourt] refused to let those profits be applied to sink anything but the old debt. But, as between the second and third mortgagee, he reserved the consideration which should lose it.

[Other copies of this report: Lincoln's Inn MS. Misc. 383, p. 158.]

## 366

## Stevenson v. Hawkins

(Ch. 1712)

*A release that was induced by fraud will be set aside.*
*A limitation expectant upon a contingent estate tail is void.*

British Library MS. Hargrave 80, f. 88

The daughters of Sir Thomas Brograve was entitled to the sum of £5000, which was secured by a limitation in a lease subsequent to some estates for lives, which were spent. But the lease being set on foot and this estate being to be settled in jointure notwithstanding the invalidity of the daughters' title to the £5000 for want of a lease for a year, those for the lady insisted for the daughters' releasing their interest previous to the making the jointures, which they were prevailed on by Sir Thomas Brograve to do. The release took notice that there was no lease for a year and, therefore, their title [was] ill and that, in consideration of a competent sum of money, they did release etc. There were four or five hearsay witnesses that £400 was paid to the daughters for their release, but no other. Gill, a trustee in the lease and release (among whose papers the lease for a year was afterwards found after his death), was privy to this release. And there was a bill afterwards brought by Sir Thomas Brograve against the daughters for preserving the testimony of witnesses and discovering whether there was ever a lease for a year or not, to which the daughters, at Sir Thomas Brograve's expense, put in their answers, by which they said they believed there never was a lease for a year and founded their belief on Gill's information. Several witnesses were examined. But Gill, who knew the most of this affair, was not. One daughter died, and the survivor, who was thereby entitled to the whole, was married to the plaintiff.

The great question in this case was whether the release had extinguished the daughters' title to the £5000.

*Sir Joseph Jekyll*, for the defendants, agreed that a release shall not operate to extinguish any right but what was under the contemplation of the parties at the time of the release, but he insisted that the daughters' interest being doubtful at that time and that it being their intentions to extinguish that doubtful interest, it was accordingly extinguished by the release.

*Ward*: It is usual in purchases and assignments of mortgages to take in the title of everybody that there is the least color to think can have any, and, if one that joins in such a conveyance though for an inconsiderable consideration, should after discover that he had a good title and upon that discovery should be let in to defeat his own conveyance, no purchaser could ever be secure.

*Vernon*, for the plaintiffs, admitted that a person who was ignorant of his title when he joined in a conveyance to a purchaser could not be relieved against him and that, in this case, they did not seek to impeach the jointure that was made after their release but that, against Sir Thomas Brograve and all that claimed by voluntary conveyances under him, they were proper for relief.

*How* insisted that, where any person is drawn into a conveyance, either by a suppression of the truth or a suggestion of falsehood, equity will relieve him, that, in this case, there were strong presumptions that the lease for a year was designedly concealed and that, Sir Thomas Brograve and Gill being both dead, there was no possibility of having a discovery of that and that the recital in the release was a full evidence of a *suggestio falsi*.

Lord Keeper [Lord Harcourt]: There is no proof of any treaty between Sir Thomas Brograve and the daughters previous to the release to settle the value of their interest nor of any consideration paid. A competent sum of money generally means 5s. unless it be in cases where there is a reason for concealing the true consideration, as in assignments of church leases from one tenant to another. But, in this case, there is none. I am, therefore, of opinion that the release was a voluntary deed and it is evidently grounded on a false suggestion of there being no lease for a year, which it is plain there was. And, at a distance of time, it would have been presumed that there once was a lease for a year as well as a livery or attornment would have been presumed. There are several presumption that the truth was designedly concealed. But that not being fully proved, I do not found my decree upon that. The bill that was brought by Sir Thomas Brograve after the release to clinch everything is an evidence that he was conscious that there was something before that was not right. You ask nothing against the jointures, but, as against the rest, the release must be set aside.

[Other copies of this report: Lincoln's Inn MS. Misc. 383, p. 159, Lincoln's Inn MS. Misc. 106, p. 111.]

British Library MS. Hargrave 80, f. 90, pl. 1

In the case of Stevenson and Hawkins, goods were devised to J.S. for life, remainder to her first and every other son in tail, remainder over; J.S. never had a son and died; [it was] decreed that the limitations expectant upon this contingent estate tail were void and that, upon the death of J.S., the executors of the first testator and not the executor of J.S. were entitled to them.

[Other copies of this report: Lincoln's Inn MS. Misc. 383, p. 162, pl. 4.]

## 367

## Anonymous

(Ch. 1712)

*Where a purchaser of land takes a collateral security for the good title, this is evidence that he had notice that the title was imperfect; moreover, the true owner of the land has the benefit of such security.*

British Library MS. Hargrave 80, f. 89, pl. 2

J.S. devised his lands to A.B. etc. But before the witnesses subscribed, he went downstairs. And they subscribing when he was not present, the will was void. The devisees showed the will to the disinherited heir. And it appearing that there were three subscribing witnesses and it being concealed from the heir, though known to the devisees, that the subscription was not in the presence of the testator, they prevailed with him to release in consideration of £100 sterling, the estate being worth more than £3000, and conveyed over to the purchaser. The bill suggested that the purchaser took a collateral security and though he denied notice by his plea, yet not having denied that he had such a security, which, if he had admitted, would have either been a presumption of notice or, at least, the injured heir would have had the benefit of it, his plea was overruled.

*How* said that a disinherited heir had a right to contest his ancestor's will and that, if he failed, yet the court would not make him pay costs.

[Other copies of this report: Lincoln's Inn MS. Misc. 383, p. 161, pl. 2.]

## 368

## Anonymous

(Ch. 1712)

*A stated account can be re-opened to have an account for later payments.*

British Library MS. Hargrave 80, f. 89v, pl. 1

[To] a plea to a bill by an agent against the colonel's executors for an account after an account stated, [it was] objected that they had suggested in the bill that the agent had been forced to pay the officers several sums since the accounts with the colonel, which ought to have been allowed him in them, but were not, and that this plea stood in the way of their discovering these and other errors which they had suggested in the stated account.

*Hooper*: If an account that is solemnly stated is to be opened by such a bare suggestion, no account can ever be closed.

Lord Keeper [Lord Harcourt] overruled it.

[Other copies of this report: Lincoln's Inn MS. Misc. 383, p. 162, pl. 1.]

## 369

## Anonymous

(Ch. 1712)

*A bill for discovery and relief can be answered to the discovery and demurred to the relief.*

British Library MS. Hargrave 80, f. 89v, pl. 2

Where a bill is proper for a discovery only and seeks relief too, you may answer to the part that demands a discovery and demur to the relief.

*Vernon*: A demurrer must be maintained upon what appears in the bill only and cannot be supported by anything in the answer.

[It was] overruled for not pleading whether the mortgage was in fee, for life, or years.

[Other copies of this report: Lincoln's Inn MS. Misc. 383, p. 162, pl. 2.]

## 370

## Anonymous

(Ch. 1712)

*Upon a plea in abatement based upon the plaintiff's incompetency, being excommunicated, the defendant must prove the excommunication by a certificate under seal.*

*Where a party who is not competent to sue cures the incompetency, a new service of process is necessary.*

British Library MS. Hargrave 80, f. 89v, pl. 3

This plea is an abatement only, and the certificate of the excommunication must be pleaded under seal.

Query whether it must not be annexed to the plea; in this case, it was.

After the reversal of the excommunication, the plaintiff must re-summon the defendant.

[Other copies of this report: Lincoln's Inn MS. Misc. 383, p. 162, pl. 3.]

## 371

## Note

(Ch. 1712)

*Depositions cannot be objected to for irregularity after the hearing or after the Master's report.*

British Library MS. Hargrave 80, f. 90, pl. 2

A motion to suppress depositions for irregularity must be before hearing, and, if the depositions be taken upon a point directed to be examined to after hearing, before the Master's report.

[Other copies of this report: Lincoln's Inn MS. Misc. 383, p. 163, pl. 1.]

## 372

## Holles v. Duchess of Newcastle

(Ch. 1712–1713)

*A plaintiff who sues for a discovery of deeds relating to settled lands must both to be able to confirm the jointure and offer to confirm it.*

*An executor de son tort cannot be sued unless the proper executor or administrator of the estate is an party to the suit.*

*A defendant who refuses to answer because he may be a witness ought not simply to claim an interest, but he must disclaim.*

*In this case, the defendant was required to make discovery of a deed or the contents of it.*

*A writ of sequestration lies against a party who refuses to obey an order to answer interrogatories.*

*Ownership of property cannot be determined upon affidavits.*

*Sequestrators can be ordered to break locks in order to make an inventory of goods.*

*Where a sequestrator acts beyond his powers to sequester, he may be held in contempt of court.*

*In this case, a sequestration against the defendant was discharged when she agreed to be examined under oath and disclose various documents.*

British Library MS. Hargrave 80, f. 90, pl. 3

The first plea was in bar of discovery of deeds relating to the lands settled in jointure on the duchess, she being a purchaser and the plaintiff not having offered to confirm her jointure. The benefit of this plea was saved to the hearing, at which time, *Trevor* said the court might give proper direction about the deeds both for the security of the jointress and of the reversioner.

Lord Keeper [Lord Harcourt] said that the plaintiff that came for such a discovery ought both to be able to confirm the jointure and to offer to confirm it, which he supported by Lord Craven's Case, a demurrer to his bill having been allowed because [he was] but a tenant in tail and another for want of that offer; the case of the infant Lord Craven upon a bill of revivor, *ante* fo. 139,[1] seems to come nearer this case here, being a confirmation in the will under which he claims.

Query whether that extensiveness of this plea was taken notice of.

The second plea was in bar of a discovery of the title deeds of the Newcastle Estate, Duke Henry having, by his will, devised it to his wife for life subject to the payment of his debts, remainder to the defendant and her heirs, provided that such issue of her body on whom she settled it, which he willed should be only one for preserving his estate entire, should take the surname of Cavendish and that he by a subsequent conveyance by lease and release in consideration of a natural love and affection and for other good causes and considerations settled it to the use of himself for life, remainder to the countess of Clare, now duchess of Newcastle, and her heirs, he or she upon whom the inheritance of the premisses should descend taking upon him or her the surname of Cavendish in honor of the name of the most illustrious prince, William, duke of Newcastle, then deceased.

This limitation was opened by *Mead* to be upon an express trust for payment of Duke Henry's debts and no other, that, after the earl of Thanet and his wife, one of Duke Henry's co-heirs, brought their bill to set aside this will and deeds, and that the late duke of Newcastle and duchess brought a cross-bill to preserve the testimony of their witnesses to them, that the original case was heard and the bill dismissed, and that for the discovery of the deeds leading the uses of the fine, by which the duchess conveyed to the duke, would, if his will should take effect, tend to a breach of trust in carrying this estate into the family of the Pelhams and name of Holles. The plea was overruled.

They all waived giving their opinions whether those conveyances created any trust or condition, that being more proper to determine at the hearing, but said that, if the plea was allowed, that matter could not be brought in judgment before the court nor the plaintiff have an opportunity of controverting it unless the deeds were produced. The first demurrer as to that part of the bill by which the plaintiff demanded a discovery and account of the personal estate was for want of proper parties, the will not being proved nor any administration *pendente lite* before that court, and was allowed, Seymour's Case[2] being cited in point.

*Trevor* said that what Vernon had objected, that an executor *de son tort* might be sued at [common] law was true but that, in this court, he could not without bringing the rightful executor or administrator before the court and that the reason of it was to prevent circuity of actions.

---

[1] *Lord Craven v. Lady Craven* (Ch. 1712), see above, Case No. 347.

[2] *Seymour v. Seymour* (Ch. 1711), see above, Case No. 257.

The second demurrer was to that part of the bill by which the plaintiff demanded an account of several transactions relating to the making and keeping the will etc., which lay in the duchess's knowledge, to which the duchess demurred because the controversy touching the validity of the will was between the plaintiff and the Lady Harriet Holles and she might be examined as a witness to those facts, either at law or in equity and, by the rules of the court, what a witness could depose ought not to be known before publication.

*Trevor* said, and the Lord Keeper [Lord Harcourt], agreed that a defendant that will cover himself from answering because he may be a witness ought not barely to claim any interest but ought to disclaim, without which he might claim at any time, and that, in this case, the duchess had been so far from doing that that she had made a title to herself to the Newcastle estate by her second plea and not shown how it ever was taken from her, that the reason why a party concerned in interest was obliged to answer was because what he disclosed in his answer would be evidence against him and not for him, whereas, if he was examined as a witness, he must then be taken to be indifferent and whatever he deposed, either for or against himself, believed.

Note: They were unanimous in these resolutions. Observe that, on the second plea, the will of Duke Henry and everything built on it was quite out of the case, the will being revoked by a subsequent conveyance and that the decree pleaded was barely a submission of the plaintiff's bill that sought to impeach both will and deed which was regular though the deed alone were good and though no trust were created by it. The uses of the deed and will are different; so both could not stand. And, it does not appear that the cross-cause was brought to a hearing as it stands on the deed. The taking the name of Cavendish was said to be the consideration of the deed. The consideration expressed is natural affection and the deed [was] good on that alone.

Query whether there be any room for averring another consideration, that of his name, not to support a deed but to defeat a subsequent conveyance, a condition that would not be the precedent because limited to the countess of Clare and her heirs and no obligation on her to take the name of Cavendish though she had lost it before that time by marriage, which is an evidence that the duke was not very much concerned for his name, not subsequent because no proper words to create a condition or any clause of reentry, nor was it a trust if the deed was, as it was opened, upon an express trust for payment of debts and no other. The late duke, by taking in the encumbrances, seems to have answered that trust.

[Other copies of this report: Lincoln's Inn MS. Misc. 383, p. 163, pl. 2, Lincoln's Inn MS. Misc. 106, p. 114, pl. 2.]

British Library MS. Hargrave 80, f. 128v, pl. 2

Lord Pelham v. Duchess of Newcastle.

The Master reported the answer insufficient for not setting forth the deed that declares the uses of the fines and recoveries that were levied and suffered by the duke and duchess of the Newcastle estate.

And, upon the general exception to the report, *Sir Thomas Powys*, for the duchess, insisted, as the defendant did by her answer, on the very same matter in bar of the discovery of this deed that had been before pleaded and overruled with this further, that the intention for the preserving the estate in the name of Cavendish was continued to the making the deed and a clause in the deed that provided for it was set forth in the answer, that what was prayed by the bill, to have the deed set forth *in haec verba*, was worse than delivering it over to the plaintiff for that would discover it to all the world, that the duchess had an estate for life limited to her by that deed, and that the duke having agreed in consideration of her joining in that settlement that her estate for life should be protected from the encumbrances which amounted to £8000 and affected that estate, she was a purchaser of the benefit of those inheritances, and that those encumbrances being recited in the deed, the discovery might endanger her estate for life, that the plaintiff was not entitled to that discovery, being an infant and not capable of confirming her estate for life and not having proved the will nor having established their title at law. On the last head, he cited the case of the Duke of Hamilton and Mr. Fleetwood,[1] that Hamilton claiming under the remainder in fee and the estate tail being spent to all but one person, who was under an incapacity, the duke brought an [action of] ejectment and, after he had proceeded so far as to get a special verdict, that he brought his bill for discovery of deeds and writings and to stay waste, that, upon exceptions to a report of the insufficiency of Fleetwood's answer, the court would not oblige Fleetwood to answer because the duke had not affirmed his title at law. He cited likewise Woodcomb's Case,[2] which was a man left two daughters by a first wife, the second wife *enceinte* with a son who lived a year and the uncle, as heir to him, brought an [action of] ejectment but was nonsuited by terms being set up by the daughters, he then brought his bill for a discovery of deeds etc. and, particularly, of the leases of the estate to enable him to prove a possession in the infant and, upon exceptions to a report of the insufficiency of the answer for not setting them forth, the report was overruled, and, at the hearing, Lord Cowper would not compel the defendant to discover and declared that this court would not in all cases to help a person to deeds that he has a right to at law, that it would not help a first purchaser against a second without notice nor, where there is a very hard bargain made between two, this court will not help the person that would take an advantage of it to enable him to

[1] *Duke of Hamilton v. Fleetwood* (1714), see below, Case No. 583.

[2] *Whitcombe v. Whitcombe* (1709), see above, Case No. 144.

do so at law, and that the present case was much stronger, they coming here for a discovery before the hearing.

Note Whitecomb's Case was said to have been a case of great compassion and to have been compounded at last, and Lord Keeper [Lord Harcourt] seemed to think that decree [was] wrong.

*Hooper* insisted that the duchess was a purchaser and that the purchaser was obliged without confirmation and that, in the case of Sir Caplestone Bunfield,[1] a jointress subsequent to a marriage was not, nor in the case of Rook v. Rook,[2] where the deed comprised both the jointure and other lands.

*Chesshyre* [said] that a right to discovery is not substantive but dependent on a right at law, which the plaintiffs ought to establish first, and that they had room enough to try the validity of the will without discovery of the deed.

*Williams* put the case that, where coneys are tithable by custom and a bill is brought to discover the quantities and value, if the defendant denies the custom, he will not be obliged to set forth the quantities etc.

Lord Keeper [Lord Harcourt]: That is a matter of account; in this case, you say there are encumbrances. How shall the plaintiff be able to try his right?

*Chesshyre*: The court may direct an issue *damnificavit vel non.*

*Pratt*: We are purchasers though not of our estate for life, which is part of an old estate, yet of the encumbrances Lord Pelham has no right. We have denied the will and his title, and it must be taken now on our answer. And Your Lordship will not on a feigned suggestion oblige us to make any discovery. Our plea was overruled because the matter was not then fully discovered to the court. It is now, having disclosed in our answer the clause in the deed that relates to that matter. If the words that direct the taking the name of Cavendish be not formal enough to make either a condition or a limitation, there is the greater reason that they should inure as a trust, that continuing an estate in a name and family had been regarded in all ages, that was the reason of making the Statute.

*Peere Williams* [argued] that, if a plea was overruled for any mistake, the plaintiff might insist on the same matter by way of answer.

*Sir Joseph Jekyll* said, *inter alia*, that it could not be a trust, there being no obligation on the duchess to take the name, and, therefore, no trustee made by the deed nor *cestui que trust.*

Attorney General [*Northey*] [argued] that the duchess's fears of the encumbrances were groundless, she admitting by her answer that they were all assigned in trust for the duke before the deed of settlement and that there was a proviso in that deed that they should be assigned to protect the several limitations of that deed with agreement.

[1] Perhaps *Bampfield v. Popham* (Ch. 1704), see above, Case No. 20.

[2] *Rook v. Rook* (1702), Precedents in Chancery 202, 24 E.R. 99, 2 Vernon 461, 23 E.R. 895, 1 Freeman 519, 89 E.R. 389, 1 Eq. Cas. Abr. 210, 21 E.R. 996.

*How* said it was as effectual in equity as if they had been actually answered pursuant to the proviso.

*Vernon*: Two dilatories are never to be allowed by the printed rules of the court and, therefore, a man cannot plead twice or demur twice nor, where a plea in bar is overruled, can he insist upon the same thing by way of answer if it be overruled for informality only and not for the matter, which it was here. It is true they have thrown in here some additional circumstances. But, if that contrivance would avail, they might do so *in infinitum*, that what was said by the court before on their plea, *viz.* if there were such a trust etc., the discovery would not hurt them. And, if there were not, the concealing the deed were a manifest injury to the plaintiff and that, without a discovery of the deed, it could not be brought before the court in judgment, whether there was or not, was unanswerable, and that the plaintiff did not claim paramount to the duchess, that her son sought only a discovery of her own act, that he never heard it said that a purchaser was not compellable to disclose his own title nor that advantage might not be taken of any clause in the purchase deed.

*Cooper* [argued] that it was not possible for the plaintiff to go to law without a discovery of the deed, not even upon the issue *devisavit vel non*, for, if it was not in the duke, he could not devise it, and that was the only deed that brought the estate into him.

*How* [argued] that the apprehension of danger of any stranger's taking advantage of the discovery that was prayed was exploded in Lord Craven's Case[1] and, if there was any real danger of letting in any encumbrances of other persons by it, it ought to be particularly insisted on by answer, that there was no occasion here for confirming the duchess's estate for life, she not being a purchaser of it and it being created by the same deed under which the plaintiff claims and the duke having confirmed it by his will, which is much more effectual than a bare offer to confirm.

Lord Keeper [Lord Harcourt]: The duchess is said to be a purchaser and, therefore, not compellable to discover. She is no purchaser of any limitation in the deed. Those limitations are rather the consideration of her purchase of the benefit of the encumbrances. There is no reason of her being a purchaser of them for her not discovering the uses of the deed, which is another thing. The bill does not seek a discovery of the encumbrances but of a deed in which they are recited only. The fears of these are imaginary. Let her set it forth *in hoc loco*.

He, afterwards, proposed to both sides and they consented that, instead of that, she should deliver a copy of it and refer to it in her answer as a true copy.

Note that nothing was insisted on by way of answer in bar out of a discovery but what had been before pleaded and overruled or were allegations taken out of the deed itself. If they had been pleaded, the plea could not have been proved

[1] *Lord Craven v. Lady Craven* (Ch. 1712), see above, Case No. 347.

without producing the deed, which when produced, the plaintiff might take advantage on. It seemed, therefore, vain to allege that in bar of a discovery that could not be proved without giving the discovery they alleged against the duchess, a purchaser, of the reversion by encumbrances.

[Other copies of this report: Lincoln's Inn MS. Misc. 383, p. 227, pl. 4, Lincoln's Inn MS. Misc. 106, p. 189, pl. 3.]

British Library MS. Hargrave 80, f. 133v

The duchess pleaded in bar of a discovery of the deed that leads the uses of the fines and recoveries that have been levied and suffered of the Newcastle Estate; [it was] overruled, and, after that, two answers [were] reported and, upon exceptions, adjudged insufficient.

Lord Keeper [Lord Harcourt], by an order made on arguing the last exceptions, directed the duchess to answer three particulars relating to that deed and by a subsequent order directed a sequestration to issue without further motion if an answer did not come in in a fortnight's time agreeable to that order. That fortnight was by the easiness of the plaintiff enlarged to five weeks. And then a further answer was put in signed by three counsels. And after that, a petition was put in signed by the same three counsels and two more to rehear the last exceptions. That petition, upon an attendance, was dismissed as inconsistent with the answer put in before. Then, Lord Pelham moved for a [writ of] sequestration.

But *Sir Thomas Powys* declaring the duchess's intention to appeal from the order on exceptions, Lord Keeper [Lord Harcourt] would not grant it barely on reading the answer without having it first referred to a master lest he should be thought to break through the rules of the court purely to screen himself from an appeal.

The Master reported this answer not to be agreeable to that order on exception in any one particular. And, upon that report and the former order for the sequestration and for the common rule for defendant's answering interrogatories *in vinculis* after a third answer reported insufficient, a sequestration was again moved for and granted by the Master of the Rolls [Trevor], the Lord Keeper being absent by illness. And though the defendant pressed very much for a few days to file exceptions to the report or that the execution of the sequestration might be suspended for four days and, in which time, the Parliament was to meet or leave given to put in a farther answer in that time, the Master refused them and declared that the process of the court ought not to be stopped by their intentions to appeal. He said that, formerly, the court judged themselves of the sufficiency of answers upon opening the exceptions at the bar without filing them or referring them to a master, which practice was introduced purely in ease of the court. And, in this case, he had the orders and the last answer and report read and declared his opinion that the report was right. He said that all the orders and rules of the court, whether printed or not, were subject to My Lord Keeper's discretion and that he might vary them or adhere to them as he thought proper that only excepted which relates to the subpoena to hear judgment, in which the time could not be abridged by the Lord [Keeper] without the consent of parties.

[Other copies of this report: Lincoln's Inn MS. Misc. 383, p. 236.]

British Library MS. Hargrave 80, f. 145v

Lord Pelham v. Duchess of Newcastle *et al.*, Lady Henrietta Holles.

The sequestrators having entered into Powis House, to which Lady Henrietta Holles made title as heir, and sequestered all the goods etc. there belonging to the duchess, they were forcibly turned out of possession. And, upon an affidavit of it, Grandman, the duchess's solicitor, who directed it, was committed, and an injunction [was] awarded to restore the sequestrators to the possession.

But before they were actually restored, the Lady Henrietta moved the court that it might be referred to a Master to inquire what goods that were sequestered belonged to her and what to the duchess and that money in Sir Francis Child's hands, which had likewise been sequestered, might be discharged upon a suggestion that, though Sir Francis had given notes payable to the duchess or order, it was really the money of the Lady Henrietta.

But both parts of the motion were denied as irregular, the first being too early, before the sequestrators were restored, and, for the last, it was not proper for the court to determine the ownership of the money upon an affidavit.

It was then moved that Lady Henrietta might come in and be examined as to the money *pro interesse*. But that was denied too because the sequestrators had not made any return, and, until they have, it cannot appear to the court what is sequestered. After their return, anyone who claims a title to the thing sequestered may move to have the same examined *pro interesse*.

[Other copies of this report: 3 Swanston 311, 36 E.R. 867, Lincoln's Inn MS. Misc. 383, p. 260, pl. 1, Lincoln's Inn MS. Misc. 106, p. 226.]

British Library MS. Hargrave 80, f. 147, pl. 2

Lady Henrietta Holles moving that she might be admitted by guardian to be examined *pro interesse suo* touching the money in Sir Francis Child's hands and other things sequestered upon process against the duchess, she was directed to put her suggestions into an order and to specify what she claimed title to and how and that Sir Francis Child should give the plaintiff a copy of the account on which the balance in his hands that was sequestered arose to the end that the plaintiff might the better know how to form proper interrogatories.

Serjeant *Hooper*, for the young lady, said that, if a sheriff executed an execution upon goods that did not belong to the defendant, the party aggrieved might have his action, but, in a case of a sequestration, all the recompense a person could have whose goods were wrongfully sequestered was barely a restitution on proof of his right.

Lord Chancellor [LORD HARCOURT], as against the duchess, allowed the sequestrators to open boxes and rooms that were locked if the keys were denied them to schedule the goods in them, but to remove nothing from Powis House without the special order of the court.

[Other copies of this report: Lincoln's Inn MS. Misc. 383, p. 262, pl. 2, Lincoln's Inn MS. Misc. 106, p. 230, pl. 1, 3 Swanston 311, 36 E.R. 868.]

British Library MS. Hargrave 80, f. 151v, pl. 2

Lord Pelham v. Lord Harley.

Mr. Aislaby, one of the commissioners of sequestration, he likewise an attorney and agent for Lord Pelham, made use of the sequestration and injunction upon it in many instances to compel the tenants of the duchess's jointure and the Cavendish Estate and of the other estates of the late duke of Newcastle to attorn and pay their rents to Lord Pelham's use and, in several places, did the same thing by threats or remitting them the land tax or allowing for repairs where neither were allowed by their leases and giving them notes to indemnify them and receipts in full.

Lord Chancellor [LORD HARCOURT], upon the petition of Lord and Lady Harley complaining *inter alia* of this exceeding abuse of power in Mr. Aislaby, declared that the sequestration ought not be laid on any estate but the duchess's and that, though the duchess had possessed herself of the rest, her possession must be taken to be in right of and the possession of her infant daughter, that Mr. Aislaby's gaining possession for the plaintiff by the methods before mentioned was a great abuse of the process of the court, for which reason, he directed that he should show cause the last Thursday in term why he should not stand committed and pay Lord Harley his costs, that the sequestration should be discharged as to all the lands except the duchess's jointure and the Cavendish Estate, in which the tenants should attorn to the sequestrators and, in the others, re-attorn to Lord Harley, that the profits received by the sequestration or for Lord Pelham's use should be brought before a master and those that arose from the other estates be paid over to Lord Harley subject to the order of the court. The possession of Newcastle House, which was never sequestered, he directed to be delivered to Lord Harley and the goods to be removed unless Lord Pelham agreed to their being delivered over to Lord Harley on his giving security. And by the consent of both sides to save expense, he directed the sequestrators to be discharged out of the three great houses of Welbesk, Nottingham Castle, and the Roseaver and one person to be placed in each by the appointment of the master to take care of the goods sequestered. The evidence room in Welbesk was by consent to be locked up without inspection and a key delivered to each party.

Serjeant *Pratt* and *Sir Peter King*, for Lord Harley, cited the Case of Ridlesden, in the King's Bench, who, upon an erroneous judgment in [an action of] ejectment, took out a [writ of] *habere facias possessionem* and extended it as to part and for the rest only showed it to the tenants and, by that means, obliged them to attorn; the judgment being set aside, the court awarded a restitution of what he had got under the *habere facias possessionem*. He restored those lands where the writ had been executed only pretending that the tenants attorned voluntarily in the rest. But the court compelled him to make an entire restitution and committed him for his contempt.

And Serjeant *Pratt* said that, in all cases, where the process of the court was misused to obtain another and than that for which it issued, though that end were otherwise in itself lawful, it was a contempt of the court and the courts of the law always put things again *in statu quo*. And he instanced in the case where a man makes use of the process of the court at Westminster to bring a man within the process of an inferior court or jurisdiction that he may serve him with process of that inferior court.

[Other copies of this report: 3 Swanston 311, 36 E.R. 868, Lincoln's Inn MS. Misc. 383, p. 268, pl. 2, Lincoln's Inn MS. Misc. 106, p. 235.]

British Library MS. Hargrave 80, f. 170

Lord Pelham v. Duchess of Newcastle.

After a sequestration had issued against the defendant by order of the House of Lords for not complying with the order of the court, by which she was directed to set forth the deed of January 1693 *in haec verba* or deliver an attested copy of it and refer to that in her answer, the sequestrators were forcibly turned out of possession of Powis House and the day before they were to be restored to the possession of it, the duchess left the two deeds of January 1693 in a cupboard in her closet, of which she made an entry in her pocket book, sometime after[wards] she applied by petition for leave to search the house to enable her to put in her answer, which was granted, but to be in the presence of the Master and the plaintiff. The solicitor, Dummer, who with Auditor Harley, were the only persons privy to the duchess's having left the deeds there, was seen in the house and in that closet after he was told by the duchess where the deeds were left and before the public search in the presence of the Master. At that search, no deeds could be found nor were they afterwards. The duchess disclosed this matter by a further answer and set forth three abstracts of them, which she insisted was all she could do. She, after[wards], submitted to be examined upon oath, which she was. And she denied her being privy to their being removed or knowing what was become of them. Dummer too and several others were examined in open court, but no light could be got from them.

The court, upon the examination, was of opinion that they were taken away by somebody with a design to serve the duchess. But, however, afterwards, upon the duchess's producing the abstracts and submitting to be bound by them and bringing before a Master a settlement made by her of the Cavendish estate to different uses after the order for sequestration, she having done all now in her power to obey the order for setting forth the deed, though, when it was pronounced and for a long time, she had had the deeds in her custody, the court discharged the sequestration upon her paying costs and making a promissory affidavit to produce and discover the deeds if ever she should discover anything of them.

Lord Chancellor [Lord Harcourt] seemed to say that he could not have discharged the sequestration if the counsel for Lord Pelham had not closed with the duchess's offer to be examined upon oath and so put the matter into a different method of inquiry.

[Other copies of this report: 3 Swanston 311, 36 E.R. 869, Lincoln's Inn MS. Misc. 383, p. 291, pl. 2, Lincoln's Inn MS. Misc. 107, p. 13, pl. 2.]

[Other reports of this case: *sub nom.* Lord Pelham v. Duchess of Newcastle, 3 Swanston 311, 36 E.R. 865, 3 Brown P.C. 460, 1 E.R. 1433, 2 Eq. Cas. Abr. 377, 22 E.R. 321.]

## 373

## Bell v. Hyde

(Ch. 1712)

*Where a husband and wife are sued in regard to the wife's separate estate and the husband cannot be served with process, process of contempt can be served on the wife alone.*

*A married woman that has a separate equitable estate is considered in equity as a feme sole and may sue her husband and may be sued by him.*

Lincoln's Inn MS. Misc. 10, p. 107

14 March 1711[/12]. Pen v. Hide.

The wife had a separate estate, out of which she had made a security to the plaintiff, who brought his bill to have a satisfaction. The husband was beyond the sea and could not be served with a subpoena. But the wife was served, and an attachment issued out against her for want of an appearance.

And now, she moved by her counsel to stay all process of contempt in regard her husband had never been served, according to the Case of Dubois and Hole.[1]

Mr. *Vernon*, on the other side: In the Case of Dubois and Hole, the husband was never served. Here, we have a subpoena against the husband and wife, which was left at his house. The [writ of] attachment is against them both. We cannot find the husband, and we take the wife. Surely, we are very regular.

Lord Keeper [Lord Harcourt]: Mr. *Vernon* lays it down as a general rule that, whenever the husband and wife are both in contempt and you cannot find

[1] *Dubois v. Hole* (1708), 2 Vernon 613, 23 E.R. 1002, 1 Eq. Cas. Abr. 65, 21 E.R. 879.

the husband, you may take up the wife and she shall not be discharged until she has answered. I agree with it. But here, the husband was never regularly served. And I would be glad you would show me any precedent, where the husband was never served, that you could carry on process against the wife.

The Master of the Rolls [Trevor] said that, where a married woman has a separate estate, she is considered in this court as a *feme sole*, and, if a subpoena is served on her and she does not appear, the process shall run upon her though her husband was never served, for he only comes in for conformity. But then, it ought to appear that she has a separate estate.

Whereupon, it was ordered that the wife should put in her answer, and time was given her for that purpose.

British Library MS. Hargrave 80, f. 91v

The bill was against Hide and his wife, and it sought to charge the wife in regard of her separate estate. At the time of serving the process, the husband was in Holland and the process of contempt carried on against the wife only; query whether regularly.

*Vernon*: If there be an attachment against a husband and wife and the husband absconds, the wife may be taken up and cannot be discharged without applying to the court for leave to put in her separate answer, which it is incumbent on her to do. The only difference between this case and that of Dubois and Hole's is that, there, the husband was in the West Indies and the wife appeared, which, in this case, she had not, and the process there after appearance against the wife alone was adjudged regular.

*Cooper*, on the other side, laid great stress on the wife's not having appeared, which would have been a kind of submission to the process. He urged the great inconvenience that would ensue if the married woman by a bare suggestion in a bill after having a separate estate should be liable to be prosecuted without her husband and perhaps imprisoned.

Lord Keeper [Lord Harcourt] was of opinion that the process against the wife in this case was irregular. But he asked the Master of the Rolls [Trevor], who was of a different opinion because a married woman that has a separate estate is considered in this court as a *feme sole* and may sue her husband or may be sued by him. And note the truth of the suggestion of her having a separate estate cannot be tried unless she answers.

*Vernon*: In this case, there are two kinds of appearance, one to the bill, the other to the process of contempt. And a person may appear to the process of contempt to clear his contempt without his appearing to the bill.

Lord Keeper [Lord Harcourt] adjudged according to the Master of the Rolls' opinion that the process was regular.

*Vernon*: The costs of an insufficient examination after hearing cannot be taxed of course without applying to the court for them as the costs of an insufficient answer may.

[Other copies of this report: Lincoln's Inn MS. Misc. 383, p. 163.]

[Other reports of this case: Precedents in Chancery 328, 24 E.R. 155, Gilbert Rep. 83, 25 E.R. 58, 1 Eq. Cas. Abr. 65, 21 E.R. 879.]

## 374

## Anonymous

(Ch. 1712)

*A sheriff cannot take a bail bond upon an attachment for not paying court costs, but, in such case, a messenger is to go to bring in the party.*

Precedents in Chancery 331, 24 E.R. 156

Easter term 1712.

The plaintiff's bill being dismissed with costs and costs taxed to £160, a subpoena was awarded against him to pay those costs and, for not obeying it, a [writ of] attachment, upon which attachment, the sheriff of Leicester, to whom it was directed, took bail, and returned a *cepi corpus*.

And now, upon this return, a motion was made for a messenger to bring in the plaintiff. And it was urged to be the course of the court that a messenger should go in all cases where the sheriff takes bail, where the party is not bailable, as in this case he is not, and the rather for that, in this case, the bail bond was taken of a Member of Parliament, against whom, the Parliament being now sitting, they could have no remedy.

And one Hawkins's Case was cited, where, in a like case, a messenger was sent to bring in the party.

And so it was ordered in this case.

## 375

## Woodroft v. Soys

(Ch. 1712)

*Where a mortgagee holds the land after his debt has been satisfied out of the profits of the land and the mortgagor is forced to sue to redeem, the mortgagor will be receive his court costs instead of paying them.*

British Library MS. Hargrave 80, f. 92v, pl. 1

*Vernon* said in this case that, if a jointress joins with her husband in mortgaging the jointure lands, it is a good consideration for limiting the equity of redemption to her for life, but, if it be limited further to the heirs of her body, it had been adjudged that this consideration could not extend to them, that they are volunteers.

In the same case, Lord Keeper [Lord Harcourt] said that, if a mortgagee contrives to hold the land after he is satisfied by perception of profits, it is against conscience and the mortgagor that comes to redeem will be entitled to his costs instead of paying costs.

[Other copies of this report: Lincoln's Inn MS. Misc. 383, p. 167, pl. 1, Lincoln's Inn MS. Misc. 106, p. 119.]

## 376

## Marklove v. Allen

(Ch. 1712)

*A contract to make a will will be specifically enforced by a court of equity.*
*A husband has the right to use his wife's portion.*

British Library MS. Hargrave 80, f. 92v, pl. 2

Upon a treaty of marriage, the intended husband became bound in the penal sum of £1000; the condition of the bond recited that he was to have a considerable portion with the woman in land and money and that the bond should be void if he left £500 in money or land. The woman was entitled to an estate of inheritance of £12 *per annum* and her personal estate added to that did not amount to the value of £500. The marriage ensued, and the husband died. The wife's estate of inheritance continued unaltered by any conveyance.

Upon a bill to be relieved against this bond, the chief question was whether the wife's £12 *per annum* should be looked upon as part of the £500. [It was] objected that it ought not because it was her own estate and not her husband's, that there was no particular agreement for conveying it to the husband, nor could the husband have enforced such a conveyance by the aid of a court of equity, and, if he could, yet, not having called for it in his lifetime, he had waived and dispensed with that right.

Lord Keeper [Lord Harcourt]: If the husband had devised £500 to her or given it by any deed without calling for a conveyance from her, I should look upon it as a waiver of his right. But as the case stands singly on the agreement as disclosed by the bond and unperformed of either part, I must take it according to the nature of such agreement. The word 'portion' always signifies what the husband is to have to his own use. And the settlement to be made in this case by him is more than equal to the land and money brought by the woman. And it is, therefore, to be presumed that he was to have both. He engaged to leave her £500 in land or money. Let this £12 *per annum* be taken as part of that £500.

[Other copies of this report: Lincoln's Inn MS. Misc. 383, p. 167, pl. 2, Lincoln's Inn MS. Misc. 106, p. 120.]

## 377

## Lelliot v. Hockley

(Ch. 1712)

*Where a married woman does not have a particular power given to her for making a will, a will made by her cannot be proved in the ecclesiastical court.*

*However, a married woman can make a valid appointment of her separate equitable estate.*

British Library MS. Hargrave 80, f. 93

It was agreed by articles before marriage that the husband should have £500 of the intended wife's fortune to his own use and no more and that all the rest of her personal estate should be for her own use, separate from her husband, and that she should receive and dispose of it from time to time in such manner as she should think fit. She made a will and devised it away. The spiritual court would not allow it to be proved as a will. And the question here was whether it was a good appointment or not.

*Vernon*: Where a woman has not a particular power given her of making a will, a will made by her cannot be proved in the spiritual court. In this case, it is not limited that she shall dispose of it by deed or will, but her power is the greater for her not being confined to any particular manner of executing it. A married woman is considered in equity, as to her separate estate, as a *feme sole* and has the same power over it by way of appointment, though not by way of conveyance, and, though this is not a will, it is a good appointment.

And it was decreed accordingly.

[Other copies of this report: Lincoln's Inn MS. Misc. 383, p. 168, Lincoln's Inn MS. Misc. 106, p. 121, pl. 1.]

## 378

## Anonymous

(Ch. 1712)

*Co-executors must sue as co-plaintiffs, but, if a co-executor refuses to be joined as a co-plaintiff, he must be joined as a co-defendant.*

British Library MS. Hargrave 80, f. 93v, pl. 1

An executor cannot bring a bill without making his co-executor a party. And, if he refuses to let his name be used as a co-plaintiff, he must be sued as a defendant.

[Other copies of this report: Lincoln's Inn MS. Misc. 383, p. 169, pl. 1, Lincoln's Inn MS. Misc. 106, p. 121, pl. 2.]

## 379

## Anonymous

(Ch. 1712)

*A writ of sequestration lies against the assets of a municipal corporation.*

British Library MS. Hargrave 80, f. 93v, pl. 2

Upon a sequestration against the Corporation of Hereford, *Cowper* said, and it was not denied, that a sequestration would reach even the insignia of a corporation and that the sword carried before the Lord Mayor of London had been taken upon a sequestration.

[Other copies of this report: Lincoln's Inn MS. Misc. 383, p. 169, pl. 2, Lincoln's Inn MS. Misc. 106, p. 122, pl. 1.]

## 380

## Lord Widdrington v. Anonymous

(Ch. 1712)

*A court of equity will grant a bill to redeem a mortgage after a great length of time where the plaintiffs and their privies have been under a disability, such as marriage or infancy.*

British Library MS. Hargrave 80, f. 93v, pl. 3

The plaintiff's ancestors, in 1658, granted a rent charge of 200 marks *per annum* to those under whom the defendant claimed, redeemable upon payment of £2000. In 1659, by a subsequent agreement, the time for redemption was enlarged until 1661, from which time until this, the persons entitled to the lands charged had been continually either infants or married women. And this bill now was for a redemption. The chief argument against it was the great length of time, which it was admitted would foreclose a mortgagor as well as a decree. And it was insisted that this length of time would run upon married women, though not upon infants.

*Vernon* said that a married woman may release or be foreclosed by a decree without having a day to show cause, which an infant cannot.

Lord Keeper [Lord Harcourt]: But length of time will not run upon a married woman in this case no more than a fine and non-claim. He decreed a redemption upon payment of the principal money with costs and the arrears of the annuities until the principal is paid, but no account of the profits of the one side nor interest of the other.

[Other copies of this report: Lincoln's Inn MS. Misc. 383, p. 169, pl. 3, Lincoln's Inn MS. Misc. 106, p. 122, pl. 2.]

# 381

## Leith v. Leicester

(Ch. 1712)

*Where a person has a power of appointment, if a first appointment fails, a second appointment can be made.*

Lincoln's Inn MS. Misc. 10, p. 108

16 May 1712. Leigh v. Leicester.

A settlement was made with a power for tenants for life, by deed or will, to grant an annuity of £50 a year during the life of such grantee. A tenant for life, being indebted to A.B. in £300, in pursuance of this power, grants an annuity of £50 a year to A.B. during his life towards securing the repayment of this debt. The grantee dies, and, then, the tenant for life grants another annuity of £50 a year to the plaintiff without any consideration.

The question was if, by the first grant, the power was so fully executed that the tenant for life could not make the second grant.

Lord Keeper [Lord Harcourt]: I am of opinion that the grant to A.B. was not so full an execution of the power but that, after his death, the tenant for life might make a second grant, for the first was only a counter-security to indemnify the grantee against bonds that he was bound in for the tenant for life. But then, the second grant being voluntary, the plaintiff must stand in the room of the tenant for life. And, therefore, it appearing that the grantor, at the time of the second grant, was a debtor to the defendant, the infant's estate, out of which this annuity is payable, if the plaintiff comes to have the assistance of this court, he must answer out of this annuity what moneys the grantor owned this estate, And, therefore, there must be an account taken of what moneys the grantor has received out of the defendant's estate, which must be made good to him out of the annuity so far as it will extend.

British Library MS. Hargrave 80, f. 94, pl. 1

A woman, to whom an estate is limited for her life in a settlement, had a power given her by the same deed to appoint a rent charge of £50 *per annum* out of the estate settled to any person for his life either by deed or will. She made this appointment to one for life, who died in her lifetime, upon which she made a second appointment.

Lord Keeper [Lord Harcourt] decreed that the second was good, the power not being fully executed by the first.

[Other copies of this report: Lincoln's Inn MS. Misc. 383, p. 169, pl. 4, Lincoln's Inn MS. Misc. 106, p. 123, pl. 1.]

## 382

## Nisbett v. Nisbett

(Ch. 1712)

*Where a trustee becomes bankrupt, the beneficiaries of the trust have priority over the bankrupt's other creditors.*

Lincoln's Inn MS. Misc. 11, p. 164

19 May 1712.

Thomas Nisbett, being an executor in trust, possesses the assets of his testator and becomes a bankrupt.

And, upon a bill exhibited against the assignees under the commission awarded against the bankrupt for an account by the testator's children, an account was decreed and that the plaintiffs should be let in as creditors for what should be found due prior to the other creditors of the bankrupt.

## 383

## Mansfield v. Dugard

(Ch. 1712–1714)

*A devise with a condition subsequent lapses if and when the condition becomes impossible.*

British Library MS. Hargrave 80, f. 94, pl. 2

The testator devised certain lands to his wife until his son should attain the age of twenty-one years if she should live so long and, when his son should attain that age, then he devised to him and his heirs. The son died before twenty-one. And the single question was whether the heir of the son was entitled to the land immediately upon his decease, for it was agreed, by that limitation, a certain interest vested in the son immediately, which would descend to his heir, or whether the wife should enjoy it until the son would have attained that age had he lived so long.

It was insisted for the wife that it could not be the testator's intention that the heir of the son should be in a better condition or come to the estate sooner than the son himself could.

On the other side, the Bishop of Bath's Case, 6 Co., and Boraston's Case, 3 Co. 19,[1] were cited, and, though, in the last, the court resolved that the devisee's interest would continue until the son would have attained his age of twenty-one

[1] *Bellamy v. Fish* (1605), 6 Coke Rep. 34, 77 E.R. 303, Croke Jac. 71, 79 E.R. 61; *Hynde v. Ambrye* (1587), 3 Coke Rep. 16, 76 E.R. 664, 1 Eq. Cas. Abr. 190, 194, 21 E.R. 980, 984.

years, yet the reason of that was because the devise there was for payment of debts and the court supposed that the testator computed in what number of years the profits of his estate would do that and carved out a proportional term.

*Vernon* urged that this was a provision for the wife, which was favored by equity equally with a provision for debts, which was agreed, if the wife was otherwise unprovided for, which she was not in this case.

Lord Keeper [LORD HARCOURT] decreed that the wife's interest determined on the death of the son.

*Vernon* cited the case of Lawrence v. Lawrence,[1] where the testator devised part of his lands to his wife for life, another part during widowhood, and gave several terms to her, and then devised the rest over; though it was looked upon that this will was intended to be a complete settlement of the husband's estate, yet, upon a bill of review, dower was decreed to the wife.

Lord Keeper [LORD HARCOURT]: A mortgage made after publication of the will is a revocation only *pro tanto*.

[Other copies of this report: Lincoln's Inn MS. Misc. 383, p. 170, Lincoln's Inn MS. Misc. 106, p. 123, pl. 2.]

Lincoln's Inn MS. Misc. 384, p. 17, pl. 1

5 February [1714].

[There was] a devise to the wife 'until her son should attain his age of twenty-one' and then to him in fee. He dies at thirteen. The question was whether the wife shall hold until such time as the son might have attained twenty-one had he lived. Boraston's Case, 3 Co. 13.

*Curia*: That case was to perform the will and for the payment of debts. I think, in this case, she shall not hold after her son's death.

[Other reports of this case: Gilbert Rep. 36, 25 E.R. 26, 1 Eq. Cas. Abr. 195, 21 E.R. 984.]

## 384

## Nichols v. Hooper

(Ch. 1712)

*In general, a person is said to die without issue whenever the issue fail.*

*In this case, the legacies arose upon the death of the testator's son or never.*

---

[1] *Lawrence v. Lawrence* (1699), 2 Vernon 365, 23 E.R. 829, 2 Freeman 234, 22 E.R. 1180, 3 Brown P.C. 483, 1 E.R. 1448, 1 Eq. Cas. Abr. 218, 21 E.R. 1002, 2 Eq. Cas. Abr. 386, 388, 22 E.R. 330, 331, *sub nom. Lawrence v. Dodwell*, 1 Lord Raymond 438, 91 E.R. 1190, 3 Lord Raymond 151, 92 E.R. 615, 1 Lutwyche 734, 125 E.R. 384.

Lincoln's Inn MS. Misc. 10, p. 110, pl. 1

18 May 1712.

A.B., by will, gives the residue of his estate to his wife Mary for life and, after her death, to her son Thomas and his heirs, provided that, if his son shall die without issue, then he gives £200 apiece to his two nieces, the plaintiffs, to be paid within six months after the death of the survivor of his said wife and son. And, in case it be not then paid, then he gives his said estate to his said nieces to raise the legacies out of the rents thereof. The son died after his mother, leaving issue a son, who died three months after his father.

[It was] decreed the legacy did not vest. Dying without issue in this case must be understood of the son's leaving no issue at the time of his death.

British Library MS. Hargrave 80, f. 94v

Lands were devised by the testator to his wife for life, remainder to his oldest son and his heirs, provided that, if he shall depart this life without issue of his body, then he gave to J.S. and J.N. £200 equally to be divided between them and paid to them out of the said lands by the person that shall inherit the same within six months 'after the death of the survivor of my said son and wife and, for default of payment, then I give the said lands to them to raise the said £200'. The son survived and died leaving issue, a daughter, who died three months after him. The bill was brought for this legacy. And the only question was whether it ever arose or not.

*Page*, for the plaintiff: If, instead of the legacy, the lands had been limited over, the remainder had been unquestionably good. The great question is the testator's having confined it to be raised within six months after the death of the survivor, but that is obviated by the death of the daughter within three months, by whose death, he is properly dead without issue, and, if he had meant a dying without issue living at the time of his death, it would have been so expressed.

*Vernon*, for the defendant: The devisees have an absolute fee, and there are no words after to vary it. [There was] no limitation of the estate over. The legacy was to rise upon a contingency. And it was plainly the intent of the testator that the contingency should appear at the death of the son from the time he has limited for payment of it.

Lord Keeper [LORD HARCOURT]: To many purposes, a man is said to die without issue whenever the issue fail. But such a construction cannot be in this case. It is evident from the time that is limited for the payment of them that the legacies ought to arise upon the death of the son or never. If the direction had been for payment within six months after the death of the son without issue, it would have been otherwise. If you think yourselves aggrieved, the land being limited to you in case of non-payment, you may go to the law. He seemed to say that their right was more properly triable at law for that reason than in equity.

*Page* insisted that, wherever land is limited as a security for money and the person to whom it is limited would by his entry make himself accountable, he may resort to equity if he will for his money and cannot be compelled to subject himself to an account.

[Other copies of this report: Lincoln's Inn MS. Misc. 383, p. 171.]

[Other reports of this case: 2 Vernon 686, 23 E.R. 1045, 1 Peere Williams 198, 24 E.R. 353, 1 Eq. Cas. Abr. 202, 21 E.R. 990, 2 Eq. Cas. Abr. 559, 22 E.R. 471.]

## 385

## Regina v. Corporation of Liverpool

(Ch. 1712–1713)

*It is improper to seal a writ after the return of it, and also it is improper to amend a writ after it has been sealed without leave of court.*

*An appeal upon a bill of exceptions lies to proceedings in the common law side of the Court of Chancery.*

British Library MS. Hargrave 80, f. 95

A *scire facias* was taken out against the Corporation of Liverpool to reverse the charter directed, according to custom, to the Sheriff of London and then a *testatum scire facias* to the sheriff of the proper county. The first was not sealed until after the return of it. And the second was sealed before it was quite engrossed and opened again and twenty lines that had been left blank filled up and some erasures and alterations made and the wax put on again but not sealed a second time but sent down to the sheriff. This appearing to be the fact upon a motion to quash both the writs, there was little said to defend the last.

But for the first, the Attorney General [*Northey*] said that it was taken out for form only, for it was notorious that Liverpool was not within Middlesex and that a *nihil* must be returned and that it had been the common practice to seal such writs after the return and that there were several instances of like practice in the other courts in cases of the like nature and particularly in the Queen's Bench, where, formerly, they always took out the *scire facias* against the principal and that against the bail together until that practice was broken by Holt and that the rule he made looked forward only but did not impeach anything that had been done pursuant to anything that had been the practice of the court before.

Lord Keeper [Lord Harcourt] sent the clerk to the Fleet [Prison], who had been concerned in sealing and filling up the blank writ and quashed both. He said that, perhaps, he might not have quashed the first if there had not been so much iniquity in the second but should have contented himself in making an order to prevent so absurd a practice for the future, which, however, he would make but that, as the case stood, they should both go for company.

When this was moved before, *Sir Peter King* said that, though in cases of private property, where a man was entitled to a fair, warren, etc., and another person set up one to his prejudice, he was entitled to a *scire facias* as of right, that yet, in cases of corporations, there was not one instance in all the law books that a freeman was entitled to a *scire facias* against a charter as a writ of right and that, according to that doctrine, as there were 40,000 freeman in London, they might have as many *scire facias*es.

[Other copies of this report: Lincoln's Inn MS. Misc. 383, p. 172, pl. 1, Lincoln's Inn MS. Misc. 106, p. 124.]

British Library MS. Hargrave 80, f. 133

The former *scire facias*es being quashed by order of the court, new ones were brought, to which the pendency of the former *scire facias* was pleaded in abatement. It was said they were not effectually quashed at the *teste*s of them.

This plea, upon motion, was overruled by Lord Keeper [Lord Harcourt], upon which *Sir Joseph Jekyll, Sir Peter King*, and Mr. *Lechmere* tendered a bill of exceptions.

But being unprecedented, Lord Keeper [Lord Harcourt] [said] that he may neither lessen the power of the court by admitting it if it did not lie nor injure the corporation by rejecting it if it did. He referred it to all the judges in Michaelmas term last [1712] whether it lay in this case or not. The beginning of this term [Hilary term 1712/13], a letter from the Chief Justice of the King's Bench to His Lordship was by his order read in court and entered in the Register's book importing that he, the said Chief Justice, and the rest of the judges had considered the question referred to them and that none of them, from their own experience or reading, could find any precedent for a bill of exceptions upon a proceeding in the Petty Bag in Chancery, nor could the counsel give them any instance of it but the words of the Statute of Westminster II, c. 31,[1] are *extensive*, and that for promoting justice, they have always had a very liberal construction and that the case in question was in equal mischief with those expressly provided for by the Act, for which reason, they were unanimously of opinion that a bill of exceptions did lie upon proceedings in the Petty Bag.

Upon this, Lord Keeper [Lord Harcourt] declared he would seal the bill provided the matters contained in it were true.

[Other copies of this report: Lincoln's Inn MS. Misc. 383, p. 235, pl. 2, Lincoln's Inn MS. Misc. 106, p. 200.]

[1] Stat. 13 Edw. I, Westminster II, c. 31 (*SR*, I, 86–87).

Georgetown Univ. Law Sch. MS B88–10, p. 988

Upon a writ of *scire facias* in Chancery, upon a question whether a bill of exceptions lies upon proceedings in the Petty Bag Office in Chancery, all the judges of England, at the desire of My Lord Keeper Harcourt, heard counsel the 8th of December 1712 on both sides in Serjeants' Inn hall in Fleet Street. And, upon a meeting of all the judges at Lord Chief Justice Parker's chamber the 22nd January following, they were all unanimously of the opinion that a bill of exceptions did lie upon proceedings in the Petty Bag, which is a law court, as well as in the Queen's Bench, Common Pleas, Exchequer, or other law court whatsoever, though there was no precedent of any such bill of exceptions in the Petty Bag ever heard of, the mischief endeavored to be remedied by the Statute of Westminster II, ca. 31, which gives the bill of exceptions, being as great there as in any other law court and, therefore, ought to be as well within that Statute as any other law court whatsoever. And they desired His Lordship to signify that, their opinion, to the Lord Keeper.

## 386

## Tonge v. Stote

(Ch. 1712)

*In this case, the court enforced a portion for a daughter even though it was to be paid out of her own inheritance.*

*A court of equity will not enforce a married woman's portion unless her husband will make a reasonable settlement to her separate use.*

British Library MS. Hargrave 80, f. 96, pl. 2

Serjeant [Richard] Stote [d. 1682],[1] having issue a son and three daughters, by deed, created a term to his wife and trustees for raising such portions for his daughters as they should think fit. These were afterwards adjusted to £1800 for the oldest and £1500 apiece to the other two. And upon the death of the father, the inheritance came to the son, who encumbered it. The trustees were likewise executors to the serjeant, having a power to appoint the portions out of the personal as well as the real estate. They appointed a mortgage due to the first for £1200 to the oldest daughter in part of her portion. The son died, and the lands descended to the daughters. The £1200 and the £700, which was the personal estate of the serjeant, were applied to exonerate the debts of the son on the land by the joint consent of all the sisters. The oldest sister married the plaintiff, who brought this bill for the portion appointed to his wife and to have a partition.

[1] Stoke *MS.*

*Vernon* insisted that, the sisters being equally entitled to the lands out of which the portions were to be raised, their several portions so far as they were equal were to be sunk in the land. He cited the cases of Worthington v. Taylor and Fletcher v. Worthington, where two coheirs had a term in trustees for raising portions and, then the land descended upon them and they wanting to raise money procured the term to be assigned for that purpose reserving the equity of redemption to them and their heirs, though there was no expression of sinking the portions, yet the terms having been once directed to attend the inheritance, Dr. Fletcher, who married one of the coheirs, could not prevail to have it set up again to entitle himself to the portion but, having issue by her, he was let in by Lord Cowper as tenant by the curtesy notwithstanding the term. He said that the case of Henrys v. Thomas was decreed upon this reason: the young lady was but seventeen, at which age, she had power over her personal, though not over her real, estate and had accordingly disposed of it by a nuncupative will, and the court would take her to be in of what was then her better right, but that, had she been twenty-one years, the court would have looked upon her to have been in her other right, that to the inheritance, which, in that case, would have been the better.

*How*, for the plaintiff, insisted that his wife's £1200 having been applied to exonerate the real estate, she stood in the place of those creditors and that she had an election at least whether she would have her portion and that, having by her marriage submitted her will to her husband's, that election was now in the breast of the husband, who had made it to have the portion by bringing this bill.

Lord Keeper [Lord Harcourt] decreed a portion but that the plaintiff's wife's portion charged on the estate being £300 more than either of the other sisters, the part to be allowed to her should be worth £300 more than either of the other two parts and that her part should stand charged with £1800. But the consideration how it should be raised for the husband was reserved until after he had made proposals before the Master for making a settlement on his wife and the Master's report, no settlement having then been made.

The wife, in this case, was a defendant and the husband alone plaintiff.

[Other copies of this report: Lincoln's Inn MS. Misc. 383, p. 173, Lincoln's Inn MS. Misc. 106, p. 126, pl. 2.]

## 387

## Goodman v. Peach

(Ch. 1712)

*Where a testator is indebted to his legatee, the legacy is not a satisfaction of the debt.*

British Library MS. Hargrave 80, f. 97, pl. 1

The father, jointly with another as executors of J.S., was indebted to one of his daughters in the sum of £50, and then he devised to his three daughters £400 apiece.

Lord Keeper [Lord Harcourt] decreed that this was no satisfaction of the debt and chiefly because it seemed to be the father's intentions to be equally kind to all his daughters and, if the legacy should be looked upon as a satisfaction of the £50, that will make the gift to this daughter £50 less than any of the others.

[Other copies of this report: Lincoln's Inn MS. Misc. 383, p. 174, pl. 1, Lincoln's Inn MS. Misc. 106, p. 128.]

## 388

## Hennekenius v. Jacobsen

(Ch. 1712–1713)

*A business partnership can exist even though one of the partners made no financial contribution.*

*The debt of a decedent to a deceased creditor will be distributed according to the law of the place where the debt is located.*

*The question in this case was whether a bill of review lies for new matter discovered after the final decree that should have been discovered earlier.*

British Library MS. Hargrave 80, f. 97, pl. 2

A merchant, who was a single man, made an entry in his books of £10,000 as a stock in trade for himself and his eldest nephew, and the account of this copartnership was carried on regularly for three or four years. Invoices etc. [were] made in both their names, but no part of the profits of the trade [was] brought to the separate account of the nephew, and the trade itself [was] not carried on for some years before the death of the uncle, who, in his lifetime, had set on foot a treaty of marriage for his nephew, which took effect, and had made proposals for a settlement, but there was not evidence enough of them to ground a decree upon for an execution. After the death of the uncle and nephew, the representatives of the nephew, his widow and children, brought their bill for their share of this stock in trade.

*Inter alia*, it was insisted for the defendant that, as there was no part of the £10,000 advanced by the nephew nor any of the product of it brought to his account in the books nor subject to his control, that his name was made use of in trust for his uncle or, at most, to give the nephew credit in the world and bring him by degrees into the trade.

*Vernon*, on the other side, insisted that this case was the same as to that of a child to whom the father gives credit in his books for a sum of money, in which case, unless there be an express declaration of trust, equity will presume that it was intended for the advancement of the child.

Lord Keeper [Lord Harcourt] decreed that the representatives of the nephew were entitled to the benefit of this co-partnership, but would not make the uncle a debtor so far as to give interest for the money due on account from the end of the partnership to the death of the uncle. The nephew died in Hamburg, and his widow was a woman of that place. But yet this debt lying here and not having been disposed of by him, My Lord [Lord Harcourt] decreed it should be divided according to the Statute of Distribution[1] and not according to the laws of Hamburg.

[Other copies of this report: Lincoln's Inn MS. Misc. 383, p. 174, pl. 2, Lincoln's Inn MS. Misc. 106, p. 129.]

British Library MS. Hargrave 80, f. 146v, pl. 1

Jacobsen v. Hennekenius.

The plaintiff brought a bill of review to reverse the former decree partly for new matter and partly for errors appearing in it. The new matter was a letter from the defendant's uncle declaring that he intended to let his nephew into the partnership upon certain conditions only, therein mentioned, which were not afterwards performed and the defendant annexed an affidavit that he never saw or knew of this letter until after the decree, since which he found it in a trunk of papers which had been sent over to him from Hamburg before the former bill but it was not opened until after the decree. One error alleged was that the enrollment was not according to the decretal order. To this, the defendant demurred.

*Vernon*, for the defendant: Though a bill of review may be brought for new matter, yet it is not necessary to answer it without first having the judgment of the court, whether it be sufficient to open the enrollment or not, and the plaintiff must make an affidavit that it first came to his knowledge after the decree, but, here, the letter appears to have been in his custody after the first bill and, if he was ignorant, it was through his own neglect. Besides, it is in itself frivolous. It is dated a year before he wrote his nephew [as a] partner in his books and cannot control an act done after. If the enrollment does not pursue the decretal order, which is the warrant of it, it is to be set aside by a reference for irregularity, but it is no ground for a bill of review.

The Chancellor [Lord Harcourt]: If the plaintiff suffers in this case, it is by his gross neglect, and, were the letter ever so material, I had rather he should suffer than make so ill a precedent as the opening of this decree would be. He dismissed the bill.

---

1 Stat. 22 & 23 Car. II, c. 10 (*SR*, V, 719–720); Stat. 1 Jac. II, c. 17, ss. 5–8 (*SR*, VI, 19–20).

Note: This order [was] reversed by the Lords.[1]

[Other copies of this report: Lincoln's Inn MS. Misc. 383, p. 261, pl. 2, Lincoln's Inn MS. Misc. 106, p. 228.]

[Other reports of this case: 5 Brown P.C. 482, 2 E.R. 811.]

## 389

## Anonymous

(Ch. 1712)

*A profit a prendre cannot be barred by the Statute of Limitations or by a conveyance of the servient estate.*

British Library MS. Hargrave 80, f. 97v, pl. 1

A bill [was exhibited] for an account. [There was a] plea of payment of a certain sum and of a release given thereupon. The bill suggested a surprise into the agreement and that that was no account stated. The plea denied the surprise.

Lord Keeper [Lord Harcourt] allowed the plea though there was no account stated, there not appearing to have been any fraud or misrepresentation.

[It was] said by the Lord Keeper [Lord Harcourt] and *Sir Joseph Jekyll* that a profit to dig coal is a profit *a prendre* and, therefore, not barred by the Statute of Limitations[2] or fine of the lands and non-claim.

[Other copies of this report: Lincoln's Inn MS. Misc. 383, p. 175, pl. 1.]

## 390

## Anonymous

(Ch. 1712)

*The discounting of a bill is not within the Statute of Usury.*

British Library MS. Hargrave 80, f. 97v, pl. 2

[It was] said by *Sir Joseph Jekyll* that discounting bills though at £20 percent is not within the Statute of Usury[3] because of the hazard.

[Other copies of this report: Lincoln's Inn MS. Misc. 383, p. 175, pl. 2.]

[1] *Jacobsen v. Hennekenius* (1714), 5 Brown P.C. 482, 2 E.R. 811.

[2] Stat. 21 Jac. I, c. 16 (*SR*, IV, 1222–1223).

[3] Stat. 21 Jac. I, c. 17 (*SR*, IV, 1223–1224).

## 391

### Anonymous

(Ch. 1712)

*The question in this case was the method of enforcing an arbitral award that has been made an order of the court.*

British Library MS. Hargrave 80, f. 97v, pl. 3

In this case, there was a submission to arbitration by rule of assizes afterwards made a rule of the Common Bench. And a verdict found for £30 and security of what should be awarded. The referees awarded £53 to the defendant for the debt and costs. And this award was pleaded by him in bar of an account and allowed, notwithstanding it so far exceeded the sum given by the verdict as a security.

*Hooper* said that their way to get the £53 was by attachment upon the rule of court, not by judgment upon the verdict.

[Other copies of this report: Lincoln's Inn MS. Misc. 383, p. 176, pl. 1.]

## 392

### Darth v. Buggins

(Ch. 1712)

*Where there is a contract to buy a parcel of land of a particular acreage, if the conveyance is for a smaller acreage, the price will be abated proportionally.*

British Library MS. Hargrave 80, f. 98, pl. 1

This case was cited thus by *Vernon*. The plaintiff articled for purchase of lands with the defendant and there was no mention made in the articles of the number of acres, but a particular of them at the same time was delivered signed by Buggins and, they falling short of the particular, Darth was allowed to retain a proportional part of his purchase money.

[Other copies of this report: Lincoln's Inn MS. Misc. 383, p. 176, pl. 2, Lincoln's Inn MS. Misc. 106, p. 130.]

## 393

### Henning v. Ferrers

(Ch. 1712)

*Where a life tenant makes a lease without informing the lessee that he has only a life estate and the remainderman observes the lessee making large improvements on the land and fails to inform the lessee that his lease is valid only for the life of the lessor, the re-*

*mainderman will be estopped to eject the lessee if the lessor dies before the expiration of the lease as contracted for.*

*Where a person is estopped to eject a hold-over lessee, the ejector having acted inequitably, he may be allowed to regain possession upon payment of the lessee's expenditures on improvements.*

British Library MS. Hargrave 80, f. 98, pl. 2

The plaintiffs were Dutchmen and took a lease of the defendant's father of a mill for the term of thirty-one years under the rent of £100 and a £95 fine. At the same time, they took an assignment of a term in these mills, of which there were twelve years to come from the former tenant. The rent reserved by his lease was £105 and no fine for this assignment. They paid £600 to the former tenant. There was a small piece of land included in the second, which was not in the first but, however, was enjoyed by the first tenant without any addition of rent. After the first lease and before the second, the father, for a valuable consideration, limited the estate to himself for life, remainder to the defendant for life, remainder to the first and every other son of the defendant in tail, remainder etc. The plaintiffs were ignorant of his being only tenant for life and, taking their term for thirty-one years to be good, not only rebuilt a corn mill (which there was a consideration in the first and second lease for doing) and expended £600 in that but laid out £1800 more in building an oil mill and a thimble mill then. The defendant did not live upon the place, nor was he privy to the making of the lease. But, however, he had notice of those great improvements soon after they were begun and yet did not inform the plaintiffs that his father was only tenant for life. And, after the death of his father and the expiration of the twelve years, he brought an [action of] ejectment, whereupon, the plaintiffs brought their bill to stop proceedings at law and to be quieted in the enjoyment of the mills during the residue of the thirty-one years.

The plaintiffs' counsel cited several cases where equity had relieved against frauds in suppressing the trust, that of Clare, who was a mortgagee and engrossed a second mortgage without discovering his own and was, therefore, postponed to the second mortgagee, that of Taylor, who stood by while his neighbor rebuilt his house and came every day among the workmen and, a few inches of the new house being placed upon his ground, he would afterwards have pulled it down, which, by law, he might, but this court stopped him because he did not inform his neighbor that he encroached upon his ground nor hinder him while he was building, and that of St. John, where, at a meeting at a funeral, there was a discourse about selling an estate and one of the company had a mortgage upon this estate and yet did not discover it and the purchaser was relieved against him, the defendant having for several years after his father's death but during the term of twelve years accepted the rent of £106, this was urged to amount to a confirmation of the last lease, that being the rent reserved upon that and only £105 upon the first.

The counsel for the defendant urged his right upon the death of the father as tenant for life and that no acceptance could make the lease for thirty-one years good, that the cases cited differed widely from this, that, in those cases, there was a fraudulent concealment in the commencement and an immediate right in the person that concealed, that, here, it was not pretended the defendant was privy to the making the lease, and that the plaintiffs had a possibility of enjoying the mills for the whole term, for the father might have lived so long (but note the improvements were most of them made after the father's death or some of them however), that, in all events, they were secure of enjoying them for twelve years and they urged the inconvenience of obliging every remainderman that knew of a lessee under the tenant for life his making any improvement to give notice to him not to proceed in them upon pain of having the lease established against his remainder and the remainder so far defeated.

Master of the Rolls [Trevor]: The plaintiffs are foreigners. And it is plain that they bought in the term of twelve years in order to have a longer lease. I agree that the second lease is void at law and that no acceptance can make it good there, but it may here. I agree too that this case differs from all the cases that have been put to or resolved upon this head. Here is no concealment nor fraud at the commencement. But it is the business of equity to abate the rigor and to supply the defects of the law. It does not appear that the plaintiffs had notice of the father's being only tenant for life. He had notice of the defendant's lease when it was made. The evidence is that the defendant's hearing a rumor about it, afterwards, he came over to his father to inquire about it, who told him that he had made such a lease, to which the defendant said it was not in his power. The father replied that it would be good however during his life. There is no manner of proof of his sending or going upon this to the plaintiffs. Though he was informed of the great improvements they were making, he took care indeed, as appears by a letter from him, to put them in mind of repairing his corn mill (for which there was a covenant in the lease for twelve years), but, at the same time, he took no care to hinder their building the oil and thimble mills, though he was then resolved to make use of his title at the end of twelve years. Here it is that the plaintiffs' equity arises.

The question is whether he was obliged to give notice to the plaintiffs. And I am of the opinion that, in conscience and equity, he was. And there are cases even at law to support this opinion. The Book of Cases 27 of Hen. VIII is thus:[1] a married woman gave goods to a third person in the presence of her husband, who said nothing; this was adjudged to be a good gift, for this case, Serjeant Maynard told me, was founded upon the 30th of Numbers.[2] So to permit waste is by a construction of law *facere vastum*. There is another rule to that *qui non vetat cum*

[1] *Holygrave v. Knightsbridge* (1535), YB Mich. 27 Hen. VIII, f. 24, pl. 3, 93 Selden Soc. 7, 94 Selden Soc. 256.

[2] Numbers, chap. 30, verses 6–7.

*potest et debet jubet.*[1] Upon these grounds, he decreed the plaintiffs to hold and enjoy during the residue of the thirty-one years if the defendant should so long live. There was no room for making the lease good against his sons, they not having been guilty of any undue suppression of the truth.

[Other copies of this report: Lincoln's Inn MS. Misc. 383, p. 176, pl. 3, Lincoln's Inn MS. Misc. 106, p. 131.]

British Library MS. Hargrave 80, f. 113v, pl. 2

Upon rehearing this cause, Lord Keeper [LORD HARCOURT] so far varied the former decree as to give the defendant an election to pay the plaintiffs what they had expended in building, improving, and repairing more than they would have been obliged to have done had they been barely assigns of the term and that, upon repayment of that with costs and likewise upon the repayment of the £95 fine out of the father's assets, that the plaintiffs should deliver up the lease and the possession to the defendant but, in default of it, the former decree to stand.

The defendant elected to pay etc. St. Johns' Case[2] was again cited.

But *Vernon* said that was a round decree.

And Lord Keeper [LORD HARCOURT] seemed to disapprove of it and asked if it stood unrepealed, and it was said that it does.

[Other copies of this report: Lincoln's Inn MS. Misc. 383, p. 202, pl. 2, Lincoln's Inn MS. Misc. 106, p. 146, pl. 1.]

## 394

## Bottomley v. Lord Fairfax

(Ch. 1712)

*Land held in trust is not subject to dower.*

*Dower does not attach to land that has been leased until the lease expires.*

British Library MS. Hargrave 80, f. 99v, pl. 1

*Vernon*: Where the inheritance is conveyed to trustees antecedent to marriage, equity has never gone so far as to give dower of the trust. But, where a term is vested in trustees only for a particular purpose by a conveyance before marriage, there equity will let in dower after the purpose is answered. At law, a term is no bar of dower, but there will be a *cesset executio* until the end of the term.

[Other copies of this report: Lincoln's Inn MS. Misc. 383, p. 179.]

---

1 *Qui potest et debet vetare jubet*; [he] who can and ought to forbid [but does not] directs. *Black's Law Dictionary* (rev. 4th ed. 1968), p. 1414.

2 *Pyot v. St. John* (1613), Croke Jac. 329, 79 E.R. 281.

[Other reports of this case: Precedents in Chancery 336, 24 E.R. 158, 1 Peere Williams 334, 24 E.R. 413, 2 Vernon 750, 23 E.R. 1090, 1 Eq. Cas. Abr. 144, 217, 21 E.R. 945, 1001.]

## 395

## Gage v. Gage

(Ch. 1712)

*A peer must give his evidence under his oath and not upon his honor even though the parties agree otherwise.*

*A court of equity will grant relief against a conveyance that was made through fraud.*

British Library MS. Hargrave 80, f. 99v, pl. 2

In this case, the commissioners had taken the depositions of [Lord] Fauconberg *super honorem*, and he was examined in that manner by both parties.

And at the hearing, *Vernon*, for the defendant, objected that the depositions could not be read no more than a private person's evidence without oath and that, though both sides had taken his depositions *super honorem*, yet either was at liberty to object to their being read. He said it had been resolved so more than once in this court and affirmed upon appeal in the House of Lords.

Lord Keeper [Lord Harcourt] would not let them be read.

It seemed to be agreed that, if the parties agree beforehand to take a nobleman's depositions without oath and apply to the court for that purpose, it may be done as well as an answer of a common person may be taken without oath upon such application and consent.

In the case *supra*, the defendant, being a younger brother of the plaintiff, had conveyed to him the reversion of his estate after his own life for less than half the value and afterwards married and the conveyances were taken away by a sister to them both and concealed and she could not be found to have her answer though an attachment was issued against her. The bill was brought against the defendant to procure the deeds to be redelivered or to execute a new conveyance. The defendant insisted that he was no way privy to the tort, that the consideration of the conveyance was but a trifle, that there was no evidence that even that was paid, and that, at the time of the conveyance, it was agreed that, in case he should marry, that his brother should re-convey at the same rate, but that it was likewise agreed that this agreement should not be inserted in the deeds.

This last point Lord Keeper [Lord Harcourt] looked upon as hardly to be conceived that it should be so nor was the defendant proper to pray a conveyance having no bill. As to the fraud, there were several suspicious circumstances. But what My Lord chiefly relied upon as an evidence of his being concerned in the fraud was that he alone could possibly gain by suppressing the deeds. He, therefore, decreed him to be examined upon interrogatories for the finding both the deeds and the sister that took them and that he should produce the deeds in three months or execute a new conveyance to the use of himself for life, remainder to the plaintiff and his heirs.

The plaintiff's counsel did not deny that his estate for life in the first conveyance was without impeachment of waste. But it not being fully made out, the Lord Keeper [LORD HARCOURT] would not let him have that privilege in the new conveyance that he might the more readily produce the old. For the same reason, he said he would give the plaintiff leave to examine him upon interrogatories *in infinitum* for the discovery of the old deeds. No new conveyances could be so beneficial as the old, for, if, in the meantime, this defendant should have conveyed to a purchaser without notice, the plaintiff would hardly find relief against such purchaser.

Lord Keeper [LORD HARCOURT] decreed likewise that the plaintiff should hold and enjoy against the defendant and all claiming under him, but he said that, if the defendant had any equity with regard to the agreement he insisted on the consideration, he might get the deeds produced and bring his bill and that this decree would not hurt him.

[Other copies of this report: Lincoln's Inn MS. Misc. 383, p. 180, Lincoln's Inn MS. Misc. 106, p. 134.]

## 396

## Clement v. Russell

(Ch. 1712)

*The question in this case was whether the conveyance in issue created a resulting trust or cross-remainders.*

British Library MS. Hargrave 80, f. 100v

Lands were conveyed by deed to trustees in fee in trust to pay the profits to A. during his life and then in trust to convey them to the use of B., the wife of A., for her life, remainder to the first and every other son of A. in tail, remainder to the daughters of A. and the heirs of their bodies, and, if R., who was the son of A., and E., the daughter of A., die without issue of their or either of their bodies respectively living at the time of their respective deceases, then, after such deceases of R. and E. without issue etc. as before in trust to convey to C. and D. and their heirs. A. left two daughters, Eleanor and Alice, and now A. and B. being dead and R., who was the only son, and Alice being dead without issue and Eleanor being likewise dead and having left issue, the question was whether the remainder over were good for a moiety or not.

It was urged that, by the limitation to the daughters of A. and the heirs of their bodies, his two daughters were joint tenants for life with several inheritances and that the subsequent words ought to be taken *reddendo singula singulis* and then E. and A. being both dead and Alice without issue, her moiety remained over. The case of Cook v. Gerrard in Sanders, Ventris, and Levinz was cited.[1]

It was agreed by the other side that, by the limitation, the two daughters could be but tenants for life with several inheritances. But great stress was laid upon the subsequent words that they amounted to a condition precedent and that, unless Eleanor had died without issue living at the time of her decease, the trustees could not be compelled to convey it to the remaindermen in fee. It was urged that it was not the intent of him that made the conveyance that his estate should go over to remote relations, which those remaindermen were, while there was any issue descended from his own body in being. This trust was executory and, therefore, to be guided by the intent as much as a will, that it was admitted by the other side that, in case of a will, subsequent words would have made cross-remainders in the two daughters and that, at most, it could be but a resulting trust in case these words should not be construed to create cross-remainders.

Lord Keeper [Lord Harcourt] decreed against the remaindermen. But whether the issue of Eleanor took the moiety of Alice as heir at law and under a resulting trust or under a cross-remainder was not determined.

It seems Robert and Eleanor were the only children of A. that were born at the time of the conveyance, but that was not much insisted on or proved.

[Other copies of this report: Lincoln's Inn MS. Misc. 383, p. 181, Lincoln's Inn MS. Misc. 106, p. 137.]

## 397

## Radcliffe v. Roper

(Ch. 1712)

*The question in this case was whether a Roman Catholic over the age of eighteen and a half is capable of receiving a devise of land.*

British Library MS. Hargrave 80, f. 101v

Radcliffe and Hewitt and Roper and Radcliffe.

John Radcliffe, a Papist, conveyed his estate by lease and release dated 17 and 18 January 1708 to Constable, Snow, and Hickman, and their heirs in trust to sell the whole or in parcels to the best purchasers and with the money arising from the sale, first, to pay off a mortgage which stood a charge upon part of the

[1] *Cook v. Gerrard* (1668), 1 Williams Saunders 170, 85 E.R. 171, 1 Levinz 212, 83 E.R. 374, also 2 Keble 206, 224, 84 E.R. 129, 140.

estate, then, to pay his debts mentioned in a schedule and to dispose of the surplus as his deed or will should direct, and, for want of such appointment, in trust for himself and his heirs. By will dated 5th March following and taking notice of this deed of trust, he charged the surplus with some legacies and then devised the rest of his real and personal estate to Radcliffe, Hewet, Constable, and Hickman, their heirs, executors, and administrators. Radcliffe and Constable were Papists and more than 18 [years] and 6 months [old] at Michaelmas 1700. The other two were Protestants. By a codicil afterwards, he gave all his remainder, whether in lands or personal estate, to Radcliffe and Constable, and he died.

*Sir Joseph Jekyll*, for the Protestant heir: The first question is whether the devise to the Papists be void and, second, whether the devise in the codicil will amount to a revocation of the will. To the first, he said that, by the words of the second branch of the fourth section of the Statute of the 11th of Will.,[1] Papists are disabled to purchase lands and profits out of lands and that, if a trust were created to raise money out of the profits of an estate, money raised by the sale of the land was always counted such a profit and that, if the second branch of the section should be confined to purchasing in the strictest sense, that the third branch would reach this case, by which all estates etc. to be made etc. for the benefit or relief of any such person or persons shall be void etc.

Lord Keeper [Lord Harcourt]: The word 'such' couples this to the precedent branch, and, that affecting purchasers only in the strict sense, this can extend no further.

*Jekyll*: Then the third clause is totally void and impertinent for the second is effectual to that purpose and, if, notwithstanding both these clauses, a Papist that was at full age Michaelmas 1700 is still capable of taking by devise, such a construction will make this Act more severe and penal to infant Papists than to old inveterate ones.

Lord Keeper [Lord Harcourt]: The first clause is more strict than the others because it was the principal intent of the Act to prevent the education of infants in the religion and perhaps it would be too severe to lay the same incapacities on one that is grown old in his error and thereby wedded to it before the Act was made. He said that, upon a trial at the bar, it was ruled that none but those under eighteen and a half at May 1700 were within the first branch.

*Lechmere*: The last is a substantial branch independent of the former; the three make but one entire section, and the last is as distinct from the second and the second from the first. The last, as well as the second preceding, mentions the time from whence it is to take effect and, though it be the same time, yet would it have been needless to have named it had the word 'such' entirely confined this branch to the second, but that word relates to persons only, *viz.* Papist above eighteen and seventeen and does not include the fact too, *viz.* purchasing, that

[1] Stat. 11 Will. III, c. 4, s. 4 (*SR*, VII, 587).

the word 'such' does not include purchasers seems plain from the word 'relief', for an estate that a man purchases cannot with any propriety be said to be conveyed in trust for his relief, that word implying a voluntary gift though it may be for his benefit. The next point upon the validity of this devise was whether this was to be esteemed in this case a real or personal estate, for, if it was personal, it was said to be clearly out of the Act, it being the intent of the Act to procure the way for their turning their real estates into money.

*Chesshyre* said that, the surplus not having been yet sold, the heir or devisee, whichever was entitled to it, might bring his bill and thereby prevent the sale of it and that, therefore, it was to be deemed a real estate.

*Vernon*: Where lands are conveyed to trustees to be sold for payment of particular debts, if the deed is silent as to the surplus, it will go to the heir and not to the executor, equity presuming it to be the intent of the parties that it should. But, in this case, their intent is more evident, for here, for want of an appointment, the surplus is expressly limited to him and his heirs.

The questions as to the codicil were whether it was a revocation of the will and how far. And it was said that, if the devise of the codicil were void, yet would it be a good revocation according to the first, Rolls 614,[1] and it being insisted that there being no words of inheritance in the devise and codicil, nothing passed but an estate for life and that, therefore, it was a revocation *pro tanto* only. It was replied that the words in the codicil were 'all the remainder of my estate', which would carry his estate in the lands as well as in the land itself without words of inheritance.

This case was argued a second time before the two chief justices [PARKER and TREVOR] and POWELL at their chambers. The questions referred to them were, first, whether a Papist be disabled to create a trust for selling his estate and to demise a surplus arising by sale to a Papist, the second whether a Papist be disabled to take by such a devise, and the third whether a Papists above eighteen etc. be disabled to take lands by devise.

The same questions were again solemnly debated in court in Michaelmas term 1712 before the Lord Keeper, the two chief justices, the Master of the Rolls, and Powell.

*Sir Thomas Powys*, for the Popish devisees, upon the first and second questions, insisted that ancient seats and estates of Papists being the common receptacles and shelter for their priests and that religion descending in a manner hereditary with their estates, it was the intent of the Act to encourage their disposing of their real estates and turning them into personal and to prevent their turning personal into real, that nobody could say that a Papist could not in his lifetime sell his estate and give the money to whom he pleased, and that there was no difference in reason between his doing so himself and appointing another to

[1] *Anonymous* (1572), 1 Rolle, Abr., *Devise*, p. 614, pl. O, 1.

do it for him, that the money arising by sale was personal estate and had no earmark. He agreed that the devisee of a surplus might have a decree for the lands discharging the onus, but that the court would not interpose and say the land shall not be sold. And the devisee, by his bill, prays it may, that, if he were silent and the will, by construing it a real estate, would be void and by taking it for a personal good, the court would put the construction upon it that would made the will good, that, if a Papist devised lands to be sold to raise portions for younger children or to pay creditors who are Papist, should they be defeated of their portions or debts. To the third question, he said that the first part of the Act creates a disability, but it is *sub modo* only and does not totally strip them for, if they omit their opportunity of complying, they incur but a kind of sequestration of profits until they do and that provides expressly against devisees and settlements as well as descents, that, by a second, a total disability was inflicted but related only to purchasers in the strictest sense, that it was true that that word, as opposed to descent, took in all other acquisitions but that, in common parlance, it does not, and, even in courts, it was used as opposed to volunteers, and that Coke had a tract of words that *arbitramentum, testatum, et parliamentum* were to be construed in a favorable sense and that the words in the latter part of the clause were only explanatory.

The Attorney [General, *Northey*] and the Solicitor General [*Raymond*] spoke both to the same effect.

Serjeant *Pratt*, of the same side, to the first and second, the reason why equity does not decree a sale where the devisee of the surplus will take the estate and discharge the encumbrances is because the court will not order a vain thing but the primary equity of the devisee is to the surplus of the money and that, in this case, the court could not in conscience decree a conveyance of the lands to the devisees. If they would have it, they being disabled to take them, and, therefore, as to the land, they had neither *jus in re* nor *ad rem*, and that the only consideration was whether they could take the money, that, if it were the case of an alien, he, being disabled to take, could not ask nor the court decree the land to him, but the money they might. To the third question, he said that, by the first part of the Act, Papists are disabled to take only upon this, failing to comply with the terms by the second absolutely and immediately and that therefore the two clauses would be repugnant unless the word 'purchaser' in the second be restrained to purchasers for a valuable consideration.

*Sir Joseph Jekyll*, for the Protestant heir of the testator: It has been said that this Act encourages Papists to sell. I see no distinction made between real and personal estates. It is called too a penal act, but, improperly. A man cannot lose what he never had. It has been said too that he had no real estate to devise. He had the trust of the deed [which] was to him and his heirs, not executors. He would have been interested had it been sold. This court has often looked upon money to be real estate so far as to decree dower and tenancy by the curtesy of it. If the party had been silent, the trust of the surplus would have resulted to his heirs because it arose from land. In the case of Sir John Packinton and Sir Cyril Wiche,[1] the House of Lords decreed the trust of a surplus of a term to result to the heir because it was taken out of the inheritance.

If it is not land, the next question is whether it is a profit out of land. If money is directed to be raised by rents and profits, though the profits are coupled with the rents, which are permanent, a sale is often decreed.

To the objection that he might have sold it himself and given the money away as he pleased, he said there was no provision in the Act to meet with that case, but there was with this. The case of younger children and creditors was not now before the court. But, if it was, as they have no lien upon the land but by the voluntary act of the parties, the Act would extend to it.

*Lechmere*, of the same side: To the third question, it was admitted by Mr. Attorney General that, if the third was a substantive clause, it would include the case of a devise. It is the same thing if it be explanatory, for then, the judgment of the court about the meaning of the word 'purchaser' must be directed by this clause, and it is explained here *ex vi termini*. A devise is an estate made by the act of the party. If no Papist is to be looked upon as a purchaser within the Act but one that is so for a valuable consideration, the provision is vain. The whole Act will be defeated by letting in voluntary conveyances. It is only changing the method of conveying, and the Act is eluded. And such a construction evacuates all the last clause whether it be explanatory or substantive.

To the repugnancy objected by Pratt, that the provision by the first clause was a special one, that, by the second, general and, therefore, not to be extended by any rule of construction to what was particularly provided for before, for *expressum facit cessare tacitum* and that they being applicable to different cases could not be repugnant, he urged the third clause to be an independent one from its appointing a time for its commencement as well as the other two, which would have been needless had there been but one provision intended by that and the former clauses, that the word 'such' related to the persons only, and that there was but one sort of persons described by the Act, *viz.* Papists and that expression was used to avoid repetition, and, that there was a plain gradation in the Act, the first related to persons under eighteen [years and] six months only and to all kinds of acquisition, second, to persons above that age and strictly purchasers, and, third, to all cases of voluntary conveyances and everything but descents, that declaring them to be void puts an incapacity to convey estates vesting at law without the act of the party that is to take.

To the objection that they chose the money and the court would not decree them the land, it was strange if there should be one rule in equity for a Papist and

---

[1] *Packington v. Wyche* (1707–1712), Eq. Cases Exch. 619, order of 9 December 1707: Public Record Office, E.126/18, f. 681; order of 30 May 1709: Public Record Office, E.126/19, f. 153, 3 Brown P.C. 44, 1 E.R. 1166, 2 Eq. Cas. Abr. 507, 744, 22 E.R. 429, 632, Lords' Journal, vol. 19, p. 448, Lincoln's Inn MS. Misc. 503, p. 281.

another for a Protestant, one for a Papist that desires the money and another for a Protestant that desires the land, that it was to be looked upon as a real estate in equity, it would have been assets by descent and subject to an execution within the Statute of Frauds.[1] And it is equally real in the hands of an assignee or devisee. This would have been the case of a Papist before the Act and had the Act made that personal estate in favor of the Papist which was real before the Act, that the case of an alien was different, his incapacity was by the common law and he could not have come hither before the Act for conveyances, which Papists might, that the case of children and creditors was different from a legacy, being considered in equity as money, nor could they or creditors pray a decree for the lands but only for a sale.

*Peere Williams*, of the same side, insisted that there was greater reason to guard against a devise than anything else, that being the time the priests insinuated themselves most, and that it was a strange construction of the Act to say that a Papist shall take an estate that he pays nothing for and not one that he does pay for, that an alien could take but for the crown not himself.

Serjeant *Chesshyre*, for the two Protestant devisees: It was the design of the Act to put difficulty upon Papists. Therefore, saying such a thing will be a difficulty upon them is saying nothing. The case of younger children and creditors would be a pretty harsh construction, but that differs from the present case of the surplus, that the second clause was first in the intent of the legislature being to take effect first and, indeed, immediately, that Coke's observation upon the Statute of Mortmain,[2] about the clergy, was applicable to the present Papists, *viz.* that they were hard to be bound, that, therefore, such constructions should be put on the word 'purchaser' as would render it most effectual. Thus they had a great many shifts to evade it, the one by making a will and giving a bond not to revoke it and changing the possession immediately. That, as the surplus being real estate, construction must be made of it as it stood at the testator's death, not according to the election of the party, that, even at law, land and the profits of land were the same thing.

*Vernon*, of the same side, that the surplus was real and not personal, if it had been undisposed by the testator, it would have gone to his heirs notwithstanding. If he had given them the residue of all his personal estate only, it would not have carried this surplus of the testator to the devisees. And, if not disposed of by them, it will go to their heirs, not executors. The rents and profits are for their benefit. If the devise be good and are applicable to ease them, that, if, by such persons, purchasers only had been meant in the strict sense, it would have been easy to have expressed it and better than leaving it to the construction of an ambiguous word.

---

[1] Stat. 29 Car. II, c. 3 (*SR*, V, 839–842).

[2] Stat. 7 Edw. I (*SR*, I, 51).

*Atcherly*, of the same side, insisted on the word 'relief' as not applicable to purchasers for a valuable consideration.

*How*, of the same side, [argued] that it was a real estate even in the opinion of the testator and was disposed of and trusted as such by the deed, will, and codicil. There was but little said to the point of revocation, whether it was a total one which shuts out the Protestant devisees during the life of the Papist devisees, in which case, it was said that the two Papists not being capable to take by the will, the two Protestants would have the whole during their lives, as, if a legacy be given to two *conjunctim divisim* and one dies before the testator, by the *Institute* of Justinian,[1] the survivor shall have the whole upon the revocation. A case was cited first Lect. 172; devise of land to A. and all the remainder to B., the fee passed, and [he] inferred from thence that this was a total revocation.

The court took time to consider before they delivered their opinions. Between the seals after Hilary 1712, the court delivered their opinions in this case *seriatim*.

Powell, to this effect, *viz*. the two first questions run into one and are only whether a Papist can take the surplus by devise. I think he may because it is merely personal and neither within the letter nor the mischief of the Act. It is personal at law and, therefore, not otherwise in equity. He cited the 19 Hen. VI, 34, etc., and Cro. El. 750, Miller and Eathrow,[2] in [an action of] debt for money raised by sale of land, the defendant may wage his law because it is merely personal, but, if rent be reserved on a lease, there the contract is rent. Lands devised to be sold are assets to an executor. Two witnesses would have been enough to this will since the Statute of Frauds. This case is not within the words of the Act. The surplus is not lands or tenements, nor is it a profit out of land. It arises indeed out of a contract for the land, but it is not properly the profit of the land. Rents, services, vestures, *terrae, pasturae*, estovers, etc. are properly the profits of lands. Raulins etc., the 4 Co.;[3] a lease was made for years for a fine of £20 to be paid at several days and at £20 rent with a proviso to reenter accepting a re-demise suspends the rent because it issues out of the land, but not the fine, because it is collateral to the land and issues out of the contract for the land, not out of the land. The word 'relief' is pretty general, but it depends on what went before and must be understood for continuing interests. It is true that some disabling statutes have been extended by an equitable construction, as those that restrain bishops etc. from making leases,[4] a grant of a rent charge, or a recovery of an annuity by default against a person and his successors though these are no charges on the possessions but on the persons only in respect of the possessions, they have

[1] Justinian, *Institutes*, 2. 20. 8.

[2] *Miller v. Eastcrowe* (1600), Croke Eliz. 750, 78 E.R. 982.

[3] *Rawlyns v. Somerford* (1587), 4 Coke Rep. 52, 76 E.R. 1007, also 4 Leonard 116, 74 E.R. 767, Gouldsborough 89, 93, 75 E.R. 1015, 1018, Jenkins 254, 145 E.R. 180.

[4] Stat. 1 Eliz. I, c. 19, s. 4 (*SR*, IV, 381–382).

been held to be within those acts though not within the letter of them. And had this Act been to disable Papists from disinheriting their Protestant heirs, I would have gone so far in the construction of it here. But that was not the mischief intended to be remedied by this Act. The mischief this Act was made to prevent was the growth of popery.

The landed interest is an invitation and shelter for priests. Therefore, the Act designed to get the lands out of popish hands to hinder their purchasing more. He cited Sir George Curson's Case, 6 Co. 75,[1] that a feoffment for the advancement of younger children or payment of debts was not within the Statute of Marlbridge, *de hiis qui primogenitos etc.*[2] There can be no collusion in a man's doing what he is obliged to do by the laws of God and nature. And this he applied to the Statute in 11 Will. III, c. 2.[3] The disposition of the surplus he said was a *casus omissus* and that creating a trust to sell answers not the intent of the Act. He said that the statute made to hinder religious houses purchasing lands were equally for the public good with this. The services which were to be performed for those lands and were necessary for the defense of the realm being lost by the lands coming into religious hands, but that, however, the courts of Westminster Hall never thought fit to extend those statutes by equity beyond the letter, but left the defect of each act to be supplied by the Parliament by a subsequent act. Magna Charta, c. 36,[4] provides against their buying the lands held of other lords; they nevertheless bought lands held of themselves and long terms and the secular clergy and lay corporations were held not to be within it. Then the Statute *de Religiosis*[5] was made and that was avoided by feigned recoveries, they not being *ratione donationis*. Then [came the Statute of] Westminster II, c. 32.[6] Then they got conveyances by way of feoffments to others for their use, which was then the same as a trust now, yet equity could not prevent that evasion. Then, in the Marquess of Winchester's Case,[7] uses were held not to be comprised within the word 'hereditaments' though they are a sort of one, upon which the Statute 15 Ric. II, c. 5,[8] was made to remedy that defect. None of the cases that have been put to prove this surplus to be a real estate come up to the case in question. In all of them, the construing it a real estate falls in with supporting the will here. It would destroy it where lands are devised to be sold for payment of debts and the

[1] *Attorney General, ex rel. Leveson v. Curson* (1607), 6 Coke Rep. 75, 77 E.R. 369, also Croke Jac. 157, 79 E.R. 137.

[2] Stat. 52 Hen. III, c. 6 (*SR*, I, 20–21).

[3] Stat. 11 Will. III, c. 2 (*SR*, VII, 545–581).

[4] Stat. 25 Edw. I, Magna Carta, c. 36 (*SR*, I, 118).

[5] Stat. 7 Edw. I (*SR*, I, 51).

[6] Stat. 13 Edw. I, Westminster II, c. 32 (*SR*, I, 87).

[7] *Regina v. Marquess of Winchester* (1583), 3 Coke Rep. 1, 76 E.R. 621, 1 Leonard 270, 74 E.R. 246, Moore K.B. 95, 125, 323, 72 E.R. 464, 483, 606.

[8] Stat. 15 Ric. II, c. 5 (*SR*, II, 79–80).

surplus is given to J.S. This may draw the land after it if J.S. will take upon him the payment of the debts and prays to have the land. But if he does not pray it, the trustee may sell all and J.S. can have only the surplus and that is merely personal. If the surplus be given to the Dean and Chapter of St. Paul's and they bring their bill for a sale and have the surplus in money, they may have it. Here, the devisee is incapable to take the lands, and, there, the dean and chapter are incapable to take them effectually. The testator's calling it real or personal in his will or codicil will not alter the nature of it. I take it that it will pass as a personal estate and that it is such. To the third question, he said nothing as not material to the decision of the case in question of this personal estate.

Lord Chief Justice TREVOR sent his opinion in writing that the devise of the surplus was good because it was a personal estate and, therefore, not void in the words or intent of the Act.

The Master of the Rolls [TREVOR], *ad idem*, that it was properly personal and that the court ought to decree a sale.

Lord Chief Justice PARKER [held] that the surplus is real; the trust of it is reserved by the deed to the testator and his heirs and devised by him to the four and their heirs, nor is there anything else to answer the words 'land and real estate' in the will and codicil, that it was plainly an interest in land, that a release to the trustees would extinguish it, a grant of all right in the lands pass[es] it, and that it was a devised hereditament, that a use before the Statute of the 27th Hen. VIII[1] was a mere trust, that whosoever is seised of lands has a right to take the profits as a use. If a man, after several limitations, limits an estate to the use of himself and his heirs, it is an old use. A trust in equity is the same and results as an ancient trust, a devise, or conveyance to trustees to pay debts carries the whole legal estate, but part only of the trust, the rent, results.

Culpeper and Austin, 2 Canc. Cases; 2 Ventris 349, 359; and Sir John Packinton and Wyche,[2] these cases were ruled upon terms for years, the inheritance being in the heirs. And the reason of these cases is because the whole term passed, yet but part of the trust passed and the rest descended to the heir. And the case is the same where the whole estate passes and but part of the trust of it. 1 Ch. Canc. 346,[3] and other cases. The single question was whether the whole trust passed with the legal estate, and [there is] no question but that what was undisposed of resulted. The grantees here are bare trustees. And the only question is about the nature of the trust, whether descendible or not. He cited the case of Cote and

---

[1] Stat. 27 Hen. VIII, c. 10 (*SR*, III, 539–542).

[2] *Culpeper v. Aston* (1676–1682), 2 Chancery Cases 115, 221, 22 E.R. 873, 919, also 1 Eq. Cas. Abr. 272, 21 E.R. 1040, 73 Selden Soc. 443; *Anonymous* (1680), 2 Ventris 349, 86 E.R. 480; *Anonymous* (1683), 2 Ventris 359, 86 E.R. 485; *Packington v. Wyche* (1707–1712), *ut supra*.

[3] *Moore v. Bennett* (1678), 2 Chancery Cases 246, 22 E.R. 928, also 1 Eq. Cas. Abr. 331, 21 E.R. 1082.

Moor[1] and said it had been the constant opinion that the trust of the surplus is inheritable. A devise of such a trust is a disinheriting of the heir. A devise of all his personal estate would not pass it. The devise here does not alter it. It is given by the name of real estate. It was rightly said that the intent of the Act was to take the lands out of their hands and to prevent their conspiracies against the government. But such an inference as this will have the same influence as where the legal interest is coupled with it. If the devisees satisfy the creditors and legatees, the sale may be deferred as long as they please and the profits in the meantime and the management of the estate be under their direction. A term is within the Act, but this interest is not likely to be so short as a term, nor to cease sooner than the devisees would have it, for who should compel a sale if the legatees and creditors are once satisfied, not the trustees, who are chosen on those occasions out of their intimate friends, not the heir, he has no interest. Such a construction would open a way to buy, for, if it be not within the Act, it may be bought as well as given. The arguments drawn from hardships are of little force where hardships are intended. The disability to provide for younger children may be prevented by a father's selling in his lifetime and giving them their portions in money. The Act makes no difference between continuing and not continuing interests, nor between real and personal estates etc.

To the question whether a devise of lands be within the Act, he said, *inter alia*, that the Act did not refer to any particular sort of conveyance and, therefore, no reason to exclude a devise, that the word 'purchase' was a legal term signifying any acquisition but by act of law, Hob. 30,[2] purchasing and taking by purchase is all one, and that law term in law ought to be taken in a legal sense, that some statutes had distinguished between purchasers for valuable considerations and others, but yet not so as to confine the meaning of the word to them only, that there was no ground for that distinction here, nor was it material whether the acquisition was for money or no, if there be any difference, the acquiring an estate for nothing and keeping the money too is most mischievous and the prevention of the mischief ought to be the measure of construing an act, whether anything or nothing concerns only the grantor and grantee is all one to the public, that the last words if considered not as independent but barely explanatory put this out of all doubt, that they extend to purchasers in the largest sense, and that 'such' is such Papists, not such purchasing Papists. Upon the whole, he concluded that the surplus ought to be looked upon as a real estate and that the devisees were incapable of taking it since the Statute. He thought the codicil an entire revocation of the will and not *pro tanto* only. In his argument, he enumerated several means of evading the Act if it should not extend to voluntary conveyances.

[1] *Moore v. Coote* (H.L. 1692), 9 Modern 189, 88 E.R. 391, Lords' Journal, vol. 15, p. 151.

[2] *Counden v. Clerke* (1613), Hobart 29, 80 E.R. 180, also Moore K.B. 860, 72 E.R. 955, 1 Eq. Cas. Abr. 213, 22 E.R. 998.

Lord Keeper [Lord Harcourt]: The surplus ought to be considered as a personal estate. The disposition of it, therefore, is not restrained by this Act. Any Papist may sell his lands and give the money to a Papist. The first part of the Act creates a disability *sub modo* only. But that does not concern this point. The third clause is not an independent one. If it be considered without reference to the precedent, it is unintelligible. It is harsh in equity to say that a Papist cannot raise a portion for a child or any sum in gross for payment of debts etc. The true meaning is that the interest which the Act is to obviate should be a continuing interest of the surplus. Here is to be looked upon as a profit out of the land. The devisees would have been equally incapable of taking by a sale in Mr. Roper's life as now. I will rather be silent than show how the Act may be eluded. If any such case comes before me, I will endeavor to obviate it. In the case upon the Statute to hinder purchases by religious houses, if any defect appeared in an act, the judges did not supply it by construction, but, as it becomes us here, left that to the wisdom of the legislature. If this be deemed real estate, creditors by simple contact and legatees whose legacies do not affect land will be defeated. Am I to make a construction to avoid a will? If it can be taken two ways, it ought to be taken that way which will support the will. Suppose it was executed in the presence of two witnesses only, should I by a rigorous construction void it? I am of opinion that it ought to be looked upon as a personal estate and do decree the estate to be sold and the heir at law to join. By the will, the four are tenants in common. But the codicil is a total revocation of the will. Creditors that had a lien upon the estate are to be preferred before the rest, it being a trust estate, to come in equally and in average upon the head of extending disabling statutes by equity.

Powell seemed to take a difference between those which created a disability to give, as the Statute about church leases, which may be extended, and those which restrain taking, as the Statute of Mortmain, which never were.

But note the Statutes of Mortmain were against the religious; those of Elizabeth for them, and that it was their interest that the first should be extended by equity and that the second should. The Statute of Will. III is in favor of the established religion and, therefore, by parity of reason as well as because it is *pro bono publico* ought to be construed favorably though it be a disabling act.

[Other copies of this report: Lincoln's Inn MS. Misc. 383, p. 182.]

[Other reports of this case: 9 Modern 167, 181, 88 E.R. 380, 387, 10 Modern 89, 230, 88 E.R. 639, 706, 5 Brown P.C. 360, 2 E.R. 731, 2 Eq. Cas. Abr. 508, 620, 621, 622, 625, 771, 22 E.R. 430, 520, 521, 525, 655.]

## 398

## Jones v. Etheridge

(Ch. 1712)

*A legacy limited over to the person entitled under the will upon a condition that the legatee will not challenge the will is in the nature of a forfeiture and different from a limitation to a third person.*

*In this case, the court did not enforce the forfeiture except to have the expenses resulting from the interfering with the will reimbursed out of the conditional legacy.*

British Library MS. Hargrave 80, f. 107v

A testator devised lands to trustees to be sold for payment of his debts and legacies and gave the surplus to the plaintiff and a legacy of £500 to the defendant [Sir James Etheridge] and his heirs upon condition that he did not interrupt the trust and, if he did, he gave the £500 over to the plaintiff.

*How*, for the plaintiff, insisted that the limitation over distinguished this from the common cases where a legacy is given to an heir provided he does not contest the will. In this case, the defendant had entered a *caveat* at Doctors' Commons [and] procured an assignment of a mortgage of the premises that was standing out to be made to Thornhill on purpose to keep the plaintiff and her trustees out of possession and both forbade the tenants to pay the rents due and used indirect means to avoid accepting the mortgage money at the day in the assignment after a promise to receive it and after the plaintiff had procured it at no little expense.

*Vernon*, for the defendant, [argued] that the entering of a *caveat* was no forfeiture of the defendant's legacy, that the cases were frequent where such restraints were laid upon heirs by wills, but that notwithstanding that the heir had a right to inquire into the validity of his ancestor's will, and that it never yet was adjudged a forfeiture, that, whether the legacy in this case was to be forfeited or revoked or devised by a subsequent condition, the creation of the condition was to be strictly performed, and that, in this case, there was no proof of any interruption of the execution of the trust.

Lord Keeper [Lord Harcourt]: The legacy being limited over to the person entitled to the land under the will, it is in the nature of a forfeiture and different from a limitation to a third person. If the heir had gone no farther than entering a *caveat* or putting them upon proving the will, it had been too hard to make it amount to a forfeiture. But the procuring the assignment of the mortgage and stopping the rents and preventing the receiving the mortgage money are not justifiable. Let the plaintiff have as much of the legacy as will make her satisfaction for what she has lost by stopping the rent in the tenants' hands and for her expense in procuring the mortgage money at the day and in keeping it by her afterwards (and, I think, her costs).

[Other copies of this report: Lincoln's Inn MS. Misc. 383, p. 195, Lincoln's Inn MS. Misc. 106, p. 138.]

## 399

## Hopkins v. Newman

(Ch. 1712)

*The question in this case was whether a purchaser of land is deemed to have notice of heirship and copyhold court rolls.*

British Library MS. Hargrave 80, f. 108

*Vernon*: If a purchaser buys of a wrong person, supposing him to be the heir, which he is not, he cannot defend himself against the right heir by saying that he had no right notice that he was heir, for this is a matter that he ought to take notice of at his peril and is not like the case of a settlement that may be kept secret. He said too that anything that appears upon the court rolls is constructive notice to a purchaser of a copyhold estate because he may and should search them.

*Sir Thomas Powys* denied because the rolls are carried up and down by stewards and the search would be infinite. And a judgment, he said, a purchaser is not obliged to take notice of at his peril, though, if he would search, he might find it upon record.

*Vernon* said privately that, in the case of the Attorney General v. Stepney Manor, they were affected by notice appearing upon the rolls.

[Other copies of this report: Lincoln's Inn MS. Misc. 383, p. 196, pl. 1, Lincoln's Inn MS. Misc. 106, p. 140, pl. 1.]

## 400

## Freestone v. Rant

(Ch. 1712)

*An equity court will supply the want of a surrender of a copyhold estate in favor of a grandchild otherwise unprovided for.*

British Library MS. Hargrave 80, f. 108v, pl. 1

In this case, the Case of Kettle v. Townshend[1] was cited where the House of Lords refused to supply the want of a surrender of a copyhold estate in favor of a grandchild otherwise unprovided for.

[1] *Kettle v. Townsend*, 1 Salkeld 187, 91 E.R. 170, 1 Eq. Cas. Abr. 123, 21 E.R. 929.

But Lord Keeper [Lord Harcourt] said that that was a single instance and that, if ever a case of that nature came before him, his opinion would be otherwise.

[Other copies of this report: Lincoln's Inn MS. Misc. 383, p. 196, pl. 2, Lincoln's Inn MS. Misc. 106, p. 140, pl. 2.]

## 401

## Page v. Page

(Ch. 1712)

*A mortgage to a London freeman's daughter's husband for her portion is an advancement.*

*A London orphan can elect to bring her advancement into hotchpot and take her customary share.*

British Library MS. Hargrave 80, f. 108v, pl. 2

A freeman of London mortgaged his estate to his daughter's husband for £400 for her portion.

Lord Keeper [Lord Harcourt] declared that this was an advancement though, had he given his daughter part of the lands, it would not and that the certainty of it appearing excluded her from any share of the orphanage part unless she would bring the £400 into hotchpot, which he gave her the election to do and time to make her election until after the account of her father's personal estate was taken.

[Other copies of this report: Lincoln's Inn MS. Misc. 383, p. 196, pl. 3, Lincoln's Inn MS. Misc. 106, p. 141, pl. 1.]

## 402

## Rawlins v. Powell

(Ch. 1712)

*Where a close relative or a wife of the testator is given a legacy and also made the executor, he or she takes the legacy as well as the residuary estate.*

British Library MS. Hargrave 80, f. 108v, pl. 3

In this case, the Attorney General [*Northey*] mentioned it as a point settled by the Lord Keeper that a specific legacy would not exclude a wife or near relation who was made executor from taking as executor. And he said that, in the case

Littlebury and Buckley,[1] the executor, though a stranger and a specific legatee, went away with the whole against the brother upon proof of the testator's intention to give him the whole.

[Other copies of this report: Lincoln's Inn MS. Misc. 383, p. 196, pl. 4.]

## 403

## Anonymous

(Ch. 1712)

*A witness cannot be required to give evidence against himself of a crime, but he can be of his general reputation.*

British Library MS. Hargrave 80, f. 110, pl. 1

Lord Keeper [LORD HARCOURT] said, in the case of Woden and Woden, it was held by the Court of King's Bench *seriatim* that no question could be asked as to any particular crime affecting a witness but to his reputation in general.

[Other copies of this report: Lincoln's Inn MS. Misc. 383, p. 196, pl. 5.]

## 404

## Beard v. Higginson

(Ch. 1712)

*Where an executor is given a legacy, he is not entitled to receive any further compensation for his services except for a commission on the sale of the testator's goods for the benefit of the estate.*

Lincoln's Inn MS. Misc. 10, p. 137

30 April 1712, Beard, *et al.*, children of John Beard v. Higginson, administratrix of A. Higginson, her husband.

The plaintiff's father, being a merchant in the East Indies, remitted over to the defendant's husband divers considerable effects with directions to dispose thereof and invest the produce in stocks and other public securities. He makes his will and the defendant's husband executor, to whom the testator gave a legacy of £50.

The plaintiffs exhibit a bill to be paid their portions given them by their father's will. And, upon the hearing, an account was directed.

[1] *Littlebury v. Buckley* (1711), 1 Eq. Cas. Abr. 245, 21 E.R. 1021, 2 Vernon 677, 23 E.R. 1040, 3 Brown P.C. 43, 1 E.R. 1165, Lincoln's Inn MS. Misc. 10, p. 86.

The Master, in taking the account, allowed the defendant commission money for what moneys the defendant's husband had received and paid during the testator's lifetime. But the defendant insisting upon an allowance of commission money for goods which came to her husband's hands after he proved the will and which had been remitted to him by the testator in his lifetime and also for moneys which her husband had put out on government securities and for interest which he had received on those and other securities and the defendant likewise insisting on commission money for what she had received and paid since her husband's death, the Master reported that matter specially.

And, now, it came on upon the special matter of the Master's report for the judgment of the court.

The court said there was a difference where a man makes his factor or agent his executor and where he makes another person his executor. And, in the principal case, he allowed commission money for what goods the defendant's husband had sold after he had proved the will, which were consigned to him by the testator in his lifetime, but not for any other money which he had received and paid after he took upon him the executorship. And, as to the defendant herself, the court would not allow her any commission money, for she was in the case of an ordinary executor or administrator.

405

## Clifton v. Burt

(Ch. 1712)

*Where debts by specialty are paid out of a decedent's personal estate and there is not sufficient assets left for the payment of the debts by simple contract, the creditors by simple contract shall stand in the place of the bond creditors and, so far as they have been paid out of the personal assets, have a satisfaction out of the real assets, but such marshalling does not apply to legatees.*

*Where freehold and copyhold lands are both charged with a decedent's debts, the court will not supply the defect of a surrender of the copyhold lands unless the freehold is not sufficient.*

Lincoln's Inn MS. Misc. 10, p. 114

4 July 1712.

Mr. Bignal, having a freehold and copyhold estate and also a personal estate consisting of leases and other personal chattels, makes his will, and, thereby, gives his freehold estate to his son John in tail, remainder to the defendant Burt and his heirs. He gives his copyhold estate to trustees for the payment of his debts, and makes the plaintiff Clifton and one of the defendants executors.

The plaintiff Clifton is a legatee for £500, and the other plaintiffs are creditors of the testator by simple contract. And they bring their bill to have an account of the real and personal estate of the testator.

And, as to the plaintiffs, the creditors, it was prayed that, in regard the personal assets had been exhausted in the payment of the bond debts, they might now stand in the room of the bond creditors and have a satisfaction out of the freehold lands, which were assets at law for the payment of the bond debts, in case the personal estate was not sufficient to pay them.

Note the testator made no surrender to the use of his will; so it was likewise prayed that it might be supplied by the court.

As to the marshalling of the debts, the court was of the opinion that, where debts by specialty are paid out of the personal estate and there is not sufficient assets left for the payment of the debts by simple contract, the creditors by simple contract should stand in the room of the bond creditors and, so far as they have been paid out of the personal assets, have a satisfaction out of the real assets.

As to the supplying the defect of a surrender, Mr. *Vernon* said that, in the case of Kettle and Townesend, decreed by Lord Somers and affirmed in the House of Lords,[1] the want of a surrender was not aided in favor of a grandchild unprovided for, nor will the court supply that defect in favor of creditors where there is a sufficient fund to satisfy those debts another way.

Lord Keeper [Lord Harcourt]: It is true, where freehold and copyhold lands are both charged with debts, the court will not supply the defect of a surrender unless the freehold is not sufficient. But here, the copyhold only is charged.

As to the plaintiff Clifton, the legatee, it was insisted for him that this defect of a surrender might be supplied and that the creditors by simple contract might stand in the room of the bond creditors and take their satisfaction out of the real assets and that then he might stand in the room of the creditors by simple contract. And have a satisfaction of his legacy out of the copyhold lands.

Lord Keeper [Lord Harcourt] seemed to be of the opinion that he might marshal the assets in that manner.

But this was strongly opposed by Mr. *Vernon* as going a great way farther than ever the court had yet gone. He said, had the copyhold estate been legally charged with those debts and the debts had been paid with the personal assets which should have satisfied the legacies and there is not sufficient [assets] left to pay them, the court, in that case, would have allowed the legatees to have stood in the room of the creditors and to have had a satisfaction out of the copyhold estate. But, in regard the copyhold, for the want of a surrender, can no ways be charged but by the assistance of a court of equity, the court will never supply the want of a surrender in order to let in the legatees to stand in the room of the creditors. And this difference, he said, had been always allowed.

---

[1] *Kettle v. Townsend*, 1 Salkeld 187, 91 E.R. 170, 1 Eq. Cas. Abr. 123, 21 E.R. 929.

The court directed the Master should enquire what debts there were and what fund there was for the payment of them, and reserved the consideration of the whole matter until after the Master's report.

The testator's son, John, was dead, and his executor was a defendant before the court and set up a title to the leasehold estate, which he said was assigned upon the testator's marriage to trustees upon trust for the testator for life, then to his wife for life, then in trust for such person as should be heir of the body of the testator begotten on his wife, with remainders over.

Lord Keeper [Lord Harcourt]: This is a *descriptio personae*, and the leasehold belongs to the executor of John, the testator's son, who was the heir of the body of his father and mother, and the remainder over was void.

The executor, likewise, claimed £500, which, upon the testator's marriage, was agreed by him to be laid out in a purchase and settled to the use of himself for life, then to his wife for life, remainder to the heirs of their bodies, remainder to his own right heirs, and there was a proviso in the articles that, if the £500 should not be laid out in the life of the testator and his wife, then the same should be paid to such person or persons as should be entitled to the lands in case a purchase was made.

[It was] agreed on all sides that this £500 belonged to the son and, consequently, to the defendant, his executor.

Lincoln's Inn MS. Misc. 10, p. 145

Clifton *et al.*, creditors of John Bignold, plaintiffs; Joseph Burt *et al.*, defendants.

John Bignold, in consideration of marriage, settles freehold lands for the jointure of his wife of the yearly value of £25, and she, on her part, settles copyhold lands of £50 a year, both which settlements were to the use of John Bignold for life, then to his wife for her life, remainder to the heirs of their two bodies, remainder to his right heirs.

The wife died leaving issue only one son. John Bignold makes his will, and devises the reversion of the freehold lands expectant on failer of issue of his son to the plaintiff Burt and his heirs without any trust, and he devised the reversion of the copyhold lands expectant on failer of issue of his son to the said Burt in fee (but no surrender was made to the use of the will) upon trust to sell the same and, therewith, to pay his debts and legacies.

The testator owed at his death by bond £357 besides his simple contract debts, and his personal estate amounted to £491.

Note the defendants Folwell and May and the plaintiffs Clifton and Burt were the executors.

The reversion of the freehold lands not being assets in the hands of the plaintiff Burt, as devisee and he and the other executors being sued at law by the bond creditors, they paid off all the bonds and applied the rest of the personal assets towards satisfaction of the simple contract creditors in the life of John Bignold's son. And, afterwards, he died without issue.

The plaintiff Clifton having a legacy of £500 given him by the will to be paid three months after the death of the son without issue, he and seven of the simple contract creditors brought their bill, complaining that the administration of the assets was a mal-administration and praying that they might stand in the room of the bond creditors and be paid their debts and legacy respectively out of the freehold lands.

[It was] decreed the freehold lands should be sold and that the money arising by the sale together with the rents and profits from the death of John, the son, should be applied to pay the plaintiffs their debts and the £500 legacy what the personal estate should fall short of satisfying and that the simple contract creditors and legatees should stand in the room of the bond creditors so far as such creditors had been paid out of the personal assets and that they should have a satisfaction out of the real estate and that the copyhold estate should be liable to pay such part as the personal estate and freehold lands would not suffice to pay.

The defendants petitioned to rehear this cause for these reasons:

First, for that the reversion in fee was not assets to pay debts by specialty, it being a mere possibility, which might never happen or might have been barred by the tenant in tail, and for that the reversion was not made liable to the debts and legacies by the will;

Second, for that, when the personal estate was applied in the payment of the debts, the legacy was not payable, but was a remote possibility and might never have become payable, and, therefore, the administration of the personal estate being made before the estate tail determined, it was a right application of it by the executors.

[It was] ordered to be reheard.

[Later proceedings in this case: Clifton v. Burt (Ch. 1720), 1 Peere Williams 678, 24 E.R. 566, Precedents in Chancery 540, 24 E.R. 242, 2 Eq. Cas. Abr. 556, 22 E.R. 467.]

## 406

## Shaw v. Hull

(Ch. 1712)

*Parol evidence cannot be introduced against the words of a will to show the intent of the testator.*

Lincoln's Inn MS. Misc. 10, p. 118

5 July 1712.

Anne Shaw, being entitled to a portion of £2000 given her by her father's will and, thereby, charged upon his real estate, makes her will in this manner, *viz.* 'I desire my brother John Shaw to pay three hundred [without saying pounds, shillings, or pence] to my Aunt Hull and £50 to another' without saying anything more.

This was proved by John, who took administration *cum testamento annexo.* And he dies, having made his will and the defendant B. executor, who proved that will and took administration *de bonis non* of Anne.

One question was whether this bequest of 'three hundred' shall be taken to be £300.

[It was] decree it shall. It can be taken in no other sense, and the rather because it is directed to be paid with interest and, besides, the word 'pounds' is added to the other legacy.

Another question was between Mrs. Hull and her husband, to whom the legacy should be paid, for, at the time of the will, she was parted from her husband and had a separate maintenance settled on her by him, and, therefore, she insisted to have the legacy paid to her for her own separate use. And this was said was the intention of Anne Shaw, the testator, to prove which Mrs. Hull had examined several witnesses.

But the Lord Keeper [Lord Harcourt] would not suffer them to be read, for he said he must collect the meaning from the words of the will and not from any parol proof. And he decreed the legacy to the husband.

But Mr. *Vernon*, in his private opinion, seemed to think it ought to have been decreed to the wife, she living separate from her husband at the time of the will.

Another question was in respect of the residue of the £2000, to whom it belonged, whether to the executrix of John or should go in a course of administration, *viz.* between John and the daughter of another sister, who was dead, for the land out of which the £2000 was payable descending to John, it was said that it seemed to be the intention of Anne that her brother should have all the £2000 except what she had desired him to pay.

But notwithstanding, it was decreed that the residue of the £2000 should go in a course of administration.

British Library MS. Hargrave 80, f. 111

The defendant Hull lived separately from the [co-]defendant Hull, her husband, and had a small separate maintenance ill paid. Anne Shaw, her niece, who had lived with her during her separation and knew her necessities was entitled to £2000 charged upon a real estate. And, when she was at the point of death, having nobody to make her will, she wrote to her brother, in whom the legal interest of the estate charged with the £2000 vested on her death, the following words:

Brother, as binding in conscience, though not at law, my will is that you pay to my Aunt Hull 300; if not paid within a year after, interest to be paid to the daughter of my brother Thomas the full sum of £50. /s/ *Anne Shaw.*

Administration was taken to her with this will annexed. And, upon a bill to compel all parties to join in a sale of the estate, it was held clearly that this was a good gift of £300 though the word 'pound' was not inserted immediately after 300 but, being added after £50, it extended to both.

But Lord Keeper [Lord Harcourt] decreed it to the husband, there being no words to the will that excluded him and would not hear any parol proof of Mrs. Anne Shaw's intentions, though there was very full proof of that kind that she intended it for her aunt's separate use and to support her during her separation.

[Other copies of this report: Lincoln's Inn MS. Misc. 383, p. 199, pl. 1, Lincoln's Inn MS. Misc. 106, p. 141, pl. 2.]

## 407

## Frewin v. Goodseal

(Ch. 1712)

*In this case, where a settlement provided imperfectly for the daughters of the settlor, the court of equity gave the settlor an election to provide better for his daughters if the court would compel the trustees to assign the trust to different uses.*

British Library MS. Hargrave 80, f. 111v

Sir Edward Frewin, before his marriage and in consideration of it, conveyed his real estate to the use of himself for 99 years if he lived so long, remainder to trustees to preserve contingent remainders, remainders to the first and every other son of that marriage in tail male, remainder to trustees for a term of 500 years upon trust that, if there should be no issue male of the marriage living at the time of his decease or if all such issue male should die without issue male and before twenty-one, then to raise £6000 for the portion of any daughter of that marriage if but one, if two, then to raise £8000, if more than two, £10,000 etc., remainder to his own right heirs. Sir Edward had issue by that lady, a son and two daughters. The eldest was married and amply provided for; the second was unmarried and about twenty. The son [was] at age and a match [was] agreed upon for him and his estate was to be settled on his marriage. And the bill was brought by Sir Edward and his son against the trustees to preserve contingent remainders and the unmarried daughter to compel the trustees to join in a common recovery or to assign their trust. They, by answer, stated the fact and submitted to the direction of the court.

*Sir Thomas Powys*, for the plaintiffs, insisted that they were trustees to preserve the contingent remainders only, that the term of 500 years depended upon no contingencies, and that obstructing the person whose remainder they were to preserve from suffering a recovery was rather against than pursuant to their trust.

*How*, for the trustees, said that they were placed there as guardians of the whole settlement and that, though the legal estate of the term for 500 years depended upon no contingency, yet the trust did, for, until Sir Edward died, it could not be known whether he would die without issue male living at the time of his decease, in which case, the portion was to be raised.

Lord Keeper [Lord Harcourt] observed a defect in the settlement, there being no provision for daughters but in case of failure of issue male and, for that reason, he would not decree the trustees to join in barring the contingent limitations for their benefit, but that he would so far consider the convenience of the family that, if Sir Edward would secure a portion for the unmarried daughter in all events, he would ground a decree upon that.

He, therefore, referred it to a master to inquire into the value of the estate settled, the agreement relating to the marriage of Sir Edward's son, and the proposal that Sir Edward should make about settling a certain portion upon his unmarried daughter.

[Other copies of this report: Lincoln's Inn MS. Misc. 383, p. 199, pl. 2, Lincoln's Inn MS. Misc. 106, p. 142.]

## 408

## Attorney General v. Thompson

(Ch. 1712)

*Where a legacy is payable at a future date, the legatee will receive interest on it from the testator's death if the testator had a duty to support the legatee.*

Lincoln's Inn MS. Misc. 13, p. 38, pl. 3

8 July 1712.

The case was thus. Robert Thompson had issue by his first wife, one son named Carrier Thompson and two daughters, Elizabeth and Mary. Robert Thompson married a second wife named Mary Cust, whose fortune was £2000 secured by a mortgage. And Mr. Thompson made a settlement of a jointure. And, in the settlement, there was an agreement that the £2000 should be laid out in lands to be settled in this manner, *viz.*, as to one moiety, to the use of the said Robert Thompson for life, remainder to the first, second, and other sons of that marriage in tail, and, if there should be one daughter of that marriage and no issue male, then to the use of that one daughter and the heirs of her body, remainder to the said Robert Thompson and his heirs.

The second marriage took effect. [In] 1707, Robert Thompson made his will, and, apprehending that his wife was then pregnant, he devised that, if his wife was pregnant of a daughter, then he gave the whole £2000 so secured by the mortgage to that daughter. He gave to his eldest daughter Elizabeth £1500 to be paid at her age of twenty-one or marriage so as she married with the consent of his trustees. He gave the like legacy to his daughter Mary upon the same terms.

And, then, he directed that, if his wife was not then pregnant of a daughter, that his executors should pay out of the said £2000 to his said daughters Elizabeth and Mary £500 apiece as an addition to their said portions within twelve months after their ages or marriage with such consent as aforesaid. He gave all the rest and residue of his estate, real and personal, to his only son, Carrier Thompson, and his heirs forever, and he made him sole executor of his will.

The wife was not pregnant of a daughter at the time of the will. But, about one year and a half later, a daughter was born named Jane Thompson. Afterwards, the testator made a codicil and, thereby, gave to his daughter £300 and some specific legacies. He directed that, if any of his daughters should die under twenty-one or should marry without such consent, then the whole portion should fall and go to his said heir and residuary legatee. He directed that, if his personal estate should prove deficient to pay his debts and legacies, then such deficiency should be made good out of his real estate.

The personal estate proved deficient, and a great part of the legacies was to fall on the real estate.

Jane, the daughter, died an infant without issue.

At the hearing of this cause, it was argued that those two legacies of £500 each out of the £2000 were not a direct gift, but a direction that his executor should pay £500 to each within twelve months after twenty-one or marriage, that, since a deficiency was to fall on the real estate, it seemed reasonable that the heir and residuary legatee should have the interest as part of the surplus bequeathed to him to enable him to pay the legacies and save his lands, that these legacies were contingent and not vested, because Elizabeth and Mary might die before twenty-one or might marry without consent, in either of which cases, their legacies of £500 each were (according to the codicil) to fall to the heir and residuary legatee.

But the Lord Harcourt decreed that, in regard one moiety of the £2000 belonged to Jane, the same to be laid out in lands and settled on her and the heirs of her body, the same moiety, on her death without issue did by the will belong to Elizabeth and Mary to be paid within twelve-months after twenty-one or marriage with consent. And he decreed to them the interest in the meantime from the death of Jane, the £2000 being out upon a mortgage that paid interest.

Lincoln's Inn MS. Misc. 10, p. 119

9 July 1712.

A man, by his will, gives to his two children £1500 apiece to be paid at twenty-one or day of marriage. And then, he takes notice that he had £4000 out upon a mortgage, and, out of this money, he gives his children £500 apiece more to be paid at the same time. And he makes no provision for maintenance nor for the payment of any interest in the meantime.

And, among other questions in the cause, this was one, whether the children should be allowed any maintenance or interest until their portions became payable.

Mr. *Vernon* insisted strongly they should not. And he said it never had been done in any case when it was opposed, for, when a legacy is to be paid *in futuro* and no interest is given in the meantime, the interest shall sink into the estate for the benefit of the executor to pay the debts and perform the will.

But Mr. *How* took this difference. He allowed it to be as Mr. Vernon said, where the legacy is given by a stranger or a collateral ancestor, but, where it is given by a parent, who is bound to provide for his children and makes no provision for maintenance until the legacy becomes payable, the court will do it out of the interest of the portion.

But Mr. *Vernon* insisted strongly it had been never done in any case.

Lord Keeper [Lord Harcourt] seemed to incline to the contrary. However, he went no farther in this case than to order the children the interest of the £500 apiece towards their maintenance, it appearing that the sum of money last mentioned was out at interest.

British Library MS. Hargrave 80, f. 112v, pl. 1

In this case, *How* said that, where a legacy is given payable at a future day and no interest or maintenance in the meantime, if the legacy moves from a parent of the legatee or one who is bound to provide for and maintain the legatee, the court will decree the legatee interest in the meantime but not if the legacy is given by a stranger, to which Lord Keeper [Lord Harcourt] seemed to agree and, in the principal case, gave the legatee interest though *Vernon* insisted that there was no difference between those cases and that, in both of them, the interest ought to fall into the testator's estate.

[Other copies of this report: Lincoln's Inn MS. Misc. 383, p. 200.]

[Other reports of this case: Precedents in Chancery 337, 24 E.R. 158, 1 Eq. Cas. Abr. 301, 21 E.R. 1061.]

## 409

## Anonymous

(Ch. 1712)

*Process for contempt of court can be issued only for matter appearing in the affidavit, and, if that is insufficient, it cannot be aided by other evidence of contempt.*

British Library MS. Hargrave 80, f. 112v, pl. 2

The plaintiff carried on the process of contempt against the defendant and grounded it upon an affidavit that the defendant had been duly served with a subpoena. Upon examining into the regularity of the process, it appeared that the defendant never had been served with a subpoena but the plaintiff's solicitor went to the defendant's house and, not seeing the defendant, told a relation of hers that he had a subpoena against the defendant and the defendant afterwards, in the hearing of the plaintiff's solicitor, ordered an appearance for her[self]. And it was insisted that the order for an appearance saved the regularity of the subsequent process though, in strictness, she never had been served with a subpoena.

But *Vernon*, for the defendant, said that the process of contempt is grounded upon the affidavit and can only be supported by the matter alleged in the affidavit and not by any other fact.

Lord Keeper [Lord Harcourt] held the process of contempt irregular in this case.

[Other copies of this report: Lincoln's Inn MS. Misc. 383, p. 201, pl. 1.]

## 410

## Anonymous

(Ch. 1712)

*A deposition can be amended to add the deponent's name, age, and place of abode and to the correct the style of the lawsuit.*

British Library MS. Hargrave 80, f. 112v, pl. 3

The court, upon motion, allowed a deposition to be amended by adding the name, age, and place of abode of a witness, for which purpose those of the commissioners that could be got near, I think, [were] to attend the Six Clerk.

I think too that there had been but this single witness examined in another case. The clerk that made out that commission mistook the title of the cause writing it '*inter J.S. et ux. et al., querentes et J.D. et ux. et al., defendentes*' whereas J.S. alone was plaintiff, and the words '*et ux. et al.*' after J.S. should have been omitted. This too was ordered to be amended, there being no room to doubt but that the depositions were taken in the right cause though *Sir Joseph Jekyll* objected that the depositions ought to be suppressed for no witness that had been examined at this commission could be indicted of perjury though they swore ever so extravagantly, there being no such cause in court as that in title of the depositions. And, if the title was amended, they might plead to an indictment that they were not examined in a cause in which J.S. alone was plaintiff.

Lord Keeper [Lord Harcourt] said he remembered a case where one that was the only witness to a bond was afterwards executor to the obligee and being obliged to put the bond in suit and incapable of being a witness for himself, he was forced to bring one to prove his own hand though he himself was then present in court.

*Vernon* said that, where both parties had barely equitable titles, he that had the prior equity held the prior right.

[Other copies of this report: Lincoln's Inn MS. Misc. 383, p. 201, pl. 2.]

## 411

## Key's Case

(Ch. 1712)

*Public taxes, such as the land tax, are not included in the word 'reprises'.*

British Library MS. Hargrave 80, f. 113

The testator [Sir Arthur Key] subjected his real estate to the payment of debts and legacies and made no disposition of the surplus of his personal estate by his will.

Lord Keeper [LORD HARCOURT] held clearly and decreed that the personal estate must in the first place be applied and the real only come in aid. He said some cases had gone further and applied the personal first though devised to an executor in the same clause where he is made executor.

Upon which last point, *Vernon* mentioned the case of Coxetor v. Cutler and Wilkinson's Case.[1]

In this case, there was a covenant that a jointure should be £400 *per annum* beyond reprises.

*Jekyll* and *How* insisted that all kinds of deductions were reprises, such as parish rates, tithes, and, particularly, the land tax, and that the common expression in conveyances that lands are worth or to pay beyond all reprises, the land tax only excepted, was an evidence that the land tax is looked upon to be included in the word 'reprises' because, otherwise, the exception would be idle.

*Powys* and [ . . . ]: Reprises are only what a tenant may account out of his rent, such as a rent charge paid by him with which the premises were charged or a rent due to a superior lord, such as quit rents etc., but not taxes or parish rates.

*Vernon*: The only way to ascertain what land is worth beyond reprises is to enquire what it is worth to be let. And if a jointress enters and makes secure anything of it by ill management, she shall not have the aid of the covenant to make

[1] *Cutler v. Coxeter* (1693), 2 Vernon 302, 23 E.R. 794, Lincoln's Inn MS. Misc. 10, p. 198; *Wilkinson v. Wilkinson* (1681), 1 Vernon 23, 23 E.R. 277, 1 Eq. Cas. Abr. 413, 21 E.R. 1142.

what she received up [to] £400 but shall be looked upon to have received what a tenant would have paid for the land.

Lord Keeper [Lord Harcourt] directed the Master to enquire into the value of the jointure lands beyond reprises, but said that public taxes were not to be included in that word.

[Other copies of this report: Lincoln's Inn MS. Misc. 383, p. 201, pl. 3, Lincoln's Inn MS. Misc. 106, p. 144.]

## 412

## Bishop of Litchfield v. Walmsley

(Ch. 1712)

*A bill of discovery lies in a court of equity for the discovery of grants of an office.*

British Library MS. Hargrave 80, f. 113v, pl. 1

In this case, *Sir Joseph Jekyll* said that, in the Case of Flower v. Bease, that no grant of the office could be produced prior to the restraining statutes and that two grants subsequent to it were admitted at a trial at the bar to the evidence of the custom of granting that office before the Statute and that, in this case, they had not only several subsequent grants for as many lives as that to the defendant but one antecedent to the Statute, which Lord Keeper [Lord Harcourt] seemed to think good evidence but admitted the bill to be proper for a discovery of several old grants and in defendant's custody and retained it with liberty to the plaintiff to proceed at law in an action for the profits of the office and the tenant was to admit that he had received £5 from it.

[Other copies of this report: Lincoln's Inn MS. Misc. 383, p. 202, pl. 1, Lincoln's Inn MS. Misc. 106, p. 145.]

## 413

## Bradwell v. Catchpole

(Ch. 1712)

*A trustee is liable in full to the trust where a co-trustee received trust funds and absconded with them.*

*A question in this case was whether the assignee of a mortgage has notice of a partial re-payment of the debt where the mortgagor does not join in the assignment.*

British Library MS. Hargrave 80, f. 113v, pl. 3

In this case, the defendant was a co-executor with James Maykew in trust and co-devisee with him of certain lands in trust by sale to raise money to discharge a mortgage etc. And the lands mortgaged descended to the plaintiff as heir. The mortgage term was assigned after to Maykew. Catchpole joined with Maykew in a conveyance of the lands devised to them to sell and in a receipt for the purchase money, but he never received 1d. for it. Maykew had enough in his hands to discharge the mortgage but, however, assigned it over for the principal sum without notice of the trust for clearing it. And that assignee assigned to another with notice. Maykew had appeared to the bill but never answered nor could be found to be served with process, which was carried on against him to a commission of rebellion. And it was said he was broke. He not being served to hear judgment, there could be no decree against him, but the process of contempt having been carried on to the end of the line (less would not have done), the other defendants could not object for want of parties, for, otherwise, there might be a failure of justice.

And now upon hearing the cause, Lord Keeper [Lord Harcourt] decreed the defendant Catchpole to make satisfaction for the breach of trust in his co-trustee in running away with the purchase money though [it was] objected that he joined in the sale merely for conformity and never intermeddled farther.

*Sir Joseph Jekyll* cited a late case at the Rolls, where one who was trustee for a woman and her children did with the woman's consent assign his trust to another who was guilty of a breach of trust and the first trustee [was] decreed to make satisfaction because trustees cannot divest themselves of their trust at their pleasure, and another before Lord Somers, where one trustee received the whole trust money and both were charged.

Another part of the bill was against the assignee of the mortgage to have the plaintiff's inheritance discharged of it, Maykew having had sufficient [assets] in his hands to pay it off while the mortgage was in him and the mortgagor not having joined in an assignment from Maykew to J.S. nor from J.S. to the defendant. And it was insisted, and agreed to by *Vernon* of the other side, that, if any person will take an assignment of a mortgage in which the mortgagor does not join, he must at his peril inquire what is due upon it, and, if all or part of the principal has been before paid off by the mortgagor or discharged by perception of profits, the assignee, though he comes in without notice, cannot set it up again against the mortgagor; and that for that reason, where the mortgagor does not join in the assignment, it is the constant course to take a covenant from the mortgagee who assigns that the mortgage is in force and unsatisfied etc., and that, in this case, where Maykew having money enough in his hands to satisfy the mortgage and which, by the trust, was to be applied to that purpose, it ought to be considered as applied against the mortgagee.

But *Vernon* insisted that an assignee was not obliged to take notice of such a collateral satisfaction.

And there having been some length of time and several assignments, Lord Keeper [LORD HARCOURT] would not look upon the mortgage as satisfied, though it was objected that, though the first under Maykew came in without notice, yet his assignee came in with notice.

But *Vernon* replied that, if you would affect a purchaser at a third or fourth hand with notice, you must affect everyone under whom he claims and it is not sufficient to prove notice in him only or in the second or third, for, if it were, a purchaser without notice might be brought under an impossibility of selling by giving notice to those who intended to purchase of him.

[Other copies of this report: 3 Swanston 90, 36 E.R. 781, Lincoln's Inn MS. Misc. 383, p. 203, Lincoln's Inn MS. Misc. 106, p. 146, pl. 2.]

## 414

## Chapman v. Chapman

(Ch. 1712)

*Where an executor does not pay money that is due and which he has in his hands, he is liable to pay interest on it.*

*The payment of maintenance of children is favored in equity.*

*Where a maintenance is due and payable and not paid, interest is due on it.*

British Library MS. Hargrave 80, f. 114v

The executors of the plaintiff's testator, in trust for the plaintiff, put out part of the trust money on a mortgage. And, afterwards, one of the executors, without the privity of the co-executors, called in this money. The defendant was the representative of this executor and pretended that his testator, in his lifetime and the defendant since his death, had been always ready to pay this money over to the plaintiff, an infant, and that, therefore, he ought not to be charged with interest for it. It was twelve years since it had been called in.

And Lord Keeper [LORD HARCOURT] decreed the defendant to pay £5 percent, being the interest upon the mortgage, for both principal and interest that was then paid in from that time.

Another point in this case was this, by the plaintiff's father's marriage settlement, some lands were conveyed to her father for life, remainder to trustees for 99 years, with remainder over, and another part over to her mother for life, remainder to the first son in tail etc., remainder to trustees for 500 years, remainder over; the trust of the first term was to raise a portion of £500 for the plaintiff at twenty-one or marriage and £30 *per annum* for maintenance in the meantime of the second to raise a £1000 additional portion and £20 *per annum* maintenance.

The mother died without issue male in the lifetime of the father. And the question was whether the £20 *per annum* maintenance should commence from her death or not until the death of the father.

It was objected that this was barely an additional maintenance and that, therefore, it could not commence before that which was to be increased.

On the other hand, it was urged that the estate after the 500 years term was not limited to the father but to a stranger and that, therefore, the sinking the maintenance could be no advantage to him.

Lord Keeper [Lord Harcourt]: Maintenances are always favored here if there be any ground to decree them by construction of law. The £20 *per annum* commences with the 500 years term. And why should I take away the law from the plaintiff? He decreed that it should commence accordingly. And there being a great arrear of maintenance and the defendant having received the profits of an ample estate out of which [it] was to arise, he decreed interest to the plaintiff for the several sums in arrear from six months after they respectively became payable.

[Other copies of this report: Lincoln's Inn MS. Misc. 383, p. 204, Lincoln's Inn MS. Misc. 106, p. 149.]

## 415

## Cox v. Miller

(Ch. 1712)

*The question in this case was whether a devise of a lease is revoked when the testator afterwards conveys the same to the use of his will.*

British Library MS. Hargrave 80, f. 115

The defendant's testator, to whom the plaintiff was heir, purchased two long terms in the manor of D. and then devised these terms expressly to the defendant. And being afterwards about to purchase the inheritance, he assigned these terms to the use of himself for life, remainder to the use of such person or persons as he had or should by his will appoint and then took a conveyance of the inheritance to himself. After that, he had purchased the manor of S. and of that, likewise, he took a conveyance of the inheritance to himself. And there being an old term standing out that was conveyed to the defendant in trust for him after that, he made a codicil and thereby devised the manor of D. to the defendant and his first heirs and the manor of S. to a third person under whom the defendant purchased. But this codicil being subscribed by five witnesses in the room under that in which the testator was, it was agreed that the inheritance of these manors could not pass by it, the farthest that the courts had ever gone on that head being where the witnesses have subscribed in another room where the door was open and where the testator might possibly see them whether he actually did or not. The question was how far the defendant's title to the terms would hold to those in the manor of D.

*Vernon* said that the assignment subsequent to the will was so far from revoking it that it declaring the trust of these terms for the benefit of such person to whom he had or should devise them amounted to a confirmation of the will and that, if that were otherwise, yet the codicil would be a good appointment of the trust of those terms, the testator's intent being evident. The term in the manor of S., he owned, was a term attendant upon the inheritance. But he said that, in several cases, a person who had the inheritance and the trust of a term attendant upon it might sever them and that frequently a court of equity would do it with or without his consent.[1] In the Case of Baden and Lord Pembroke,[2] a term attendant of the inheritance was in favor of creditors and subjected their debts and that, in this case, the devise of the manor would carry the term, though it could not the inheritance.

Lord Keeper [LORD HARCOURT]: Suppose he had died intestate.

*Vernon*: The heir would have had the benefit of this term against the administrator; so would a devisee of the inheritance against an executor. But had he expressly devised this term by his codicil, it would undoubtedly have passed to the devisee. And his intent here that the devisee should have it is unquestionable, though there is a necessary formality wanting to carry the inheritance.

*Et adjornatur.*

[Other copies of this report: Lincoln's Inn MS. Misc. 383, p. 205, Lincoln's Inn MS. Misc. 106, p. 150.]

## 416

## Beake v. Brown

(Ch. 1712)

*A devise of lands to a person for the payment of the testator's debts makes the devisee a trustee for that purpose, and he must pay all of the debts proportionably not favoring bond creditors or himself by retainer.*

*A decedent's creditors must be paid before his legatees. One must be just before being generous.*

[1] would do it without or against his consent: Lincoln's Inn MS. Misc. 106, f. 152.

[2] *Baden v. Earl of Pembroke* (1688), 2 Vernon 52, 23 E.R. 644.

British Library MS. Hargrave 80, f. 116

A man, before the Statute of Fraudulent Devises,[1] devised lands to his second son and his heirs subject to the payment of such debts as his personal estate should not be sufficient to satisfy and of a legacy of £500 and made his wife and second son his executors. The debts amounted to more than the personal estate and the value of the land. And the questions were, first, in what order the creditors should have a satisfaction against the land and paid by whom; secondly, whether the legatee for £500 should come in equally with the creditors.

Upon the first, it was insisted that the second son, being a creditor and executor, might retain out of what the land should be sold for towards his own satisfaction as he might out of personal assets against creditors in equal degree and that, if lands were devised to executors to be sold for payment of debts and legacies, the money arising by sale would be assets even at law and be administered as personal assets, which last was admitted.

But the counsel of the other side took a difference between a devise of lands to executors to be sold for payment etc. and to anybody else. In the first case, it is an implied intention of the testator that the money should be applied in a course of administration, but there is no such implication in the second case and that, here, the devise not being to the executors but to one of them, it could not be looked upon as a devise to him as executor and that he being, therefore, barely a trustee of those lands for payment of debts and all debts being equal in equity, they all ought to come in equally for satisfaction whether they are due by bond or simple contract, nor can the son give himself a preference by retaining.

Lord Keeper [Lord Harcourt] decreed accordingly upon that distinction.

Upon the second question, it was urged for the legatee that the lands being not otherwise liable to the payment of debts and legacies, that as they were subjected to it by the will of the testator, he having subjected them to both, both ought to be equally satisfied. The Case upon Sir John Churchill's will [was] cited as adjudged in point.

But to this, it was said that there were precedents both ways.

Lord Keeper [Lord Harcourt]: I will construe the testator's meaning to have been what it ought to be and that, when he made a provision for payment of his debts and legacies, he intended to be just before he was charitable and to pay his debts in the first place. And he decreed that all the creditors should be satisfied before the legatee.

[Other copies of this report: Lincoln's Inn MS. Misc. 383, p. 206, Lincoln's Inn MS. Misc. 106, p. 152.]

---

[1] Stat. 3 Will. & Mar., c. 14 (*SR*, VI, 320–321).

## 417

## Rogers v. Hodkins

(Ch. 1712)

*A defendant who claims to be a bona fide purchaser for value must allege in his pleading what the consideration was and the date of the purchase.*

British Library MS. Hargrave 80, f. 116v, pl. 1

*Vernon*: Where a person pleads himself to be a purchaser for a valuable consideration without notice, it is necessary for him to set forth what the consideration was [so] that it may appear to the court to be valuable and also the time of the purchase [so] that the plaintiff may, if he can, assert him [to be] with notice.

Lord Keeper [Lord Harcourt]: Let the plea stand for an answer with liberty to except.

[Other copies of this report: Lincoln's Inn MS. Misc. 383, p. 207, pl. 1, Lincoln's Inn MS. Misc. 106, p. 154, pl. 1.]

## 418

## Long v. Earl

(Ch. 1712)

*A party cannot avoid a discovery of documents by giving them to his lawyer.*

British Library MS. Hargrave 80, f. 116v, pl. 2

A plea [was] given in bar of a discovery of deeds, that he knew nothing but as counsel, and [he] disclaims.

*Vernon*: He ought to have said that he had divested himself of the deeds for, otherwise, the plaintiff, by a defendant's paying over the deeds into his counsel's hands, would be remediless.

[It was] overruled.

[Other copies of this report: Lincoln's Inn MS. Misc. 383, p. 207, pl. 2, Lincoln's Inn MS. Misc. 106, p. 154, pl. 2.]

## 419

## Kemble v. Stroud

(Ch. 1712)

*Where a defendant is successfully sued for money payable out of an estate and the defendant then dies, the plaintiff's court costs and interest are payable out of the defendant's estate.*

British Library MS. Hargrave 80, f. 116v, pl. 3

The defendant's testator purchased an estate which was subject to the payment of £500 to the plaintiff and with notice of the trust. The plaintiff brought his bill to have this sum raised for him with interest out of the estate. And he had a decree by which costs were reserved. The defendant's testator died leaving the defendant executor and devisee. And the matter coming on afterwards upon the Master's report and reservations of costs, the plaintiff had an order for his costs from the beginning out of the estate. It was admitted, where a demand is merely personal and the person on whom the demand is dies pending the suit, the costs die with him. But it is otherwise in that case and in the case of a mortgagee where the demand is upon the estate. Upon motion for costs reserved by a decree, it was ruled that they were grantable upon a motion and likewise interest reserved by a decree.

Lord Keeper [Lord Harcourt] said, in our court as well as at law, costs will follow a recovery although the defendant had a probable cause of defense but that the court was sometimes induced by the circumstances of some special cases to remit them.

[Other copies of this report: Lincoln's Inn MS. Misc. 383, p. 207, pl. 3, Lincoln's Inn MS. Misc. 106, p. 155, pl. 1.]

## 420

## Pace v. Mosely

(Ch. 1712)

*A conveyance that is void at law for inconsistency can be enforced in a court of equity.*

British Library MS. Hargrave 80, f. 117, pl. 1

[There was a] conveyance by feoffment to a husband and wife and their heirs *habendum* to them and their heirs to the use of the husband for life with several remainders over. [It was] objected that this limitation in the *habendum* was repugnant to the preceding limitations by which a fee passed and therefore void.

But [it was] ruled by Lord Keeper [Lord Harcourt] to be a good limitation of the trust of the lands as to the remainder though void at law. And he decreed accordingly.

[Other copies of this report: Lincoln's Inn MS. Misc. 383, p. 207, pl. 4, Lincoln's Inn MS. Misc. 106, p. 155, pl. 2.]

## 421

## Herne v. Merick

(Ch. 1712)

*Where a testator's debts have exhausted his personal estate, a pecuniary legacy is payable out of his real estate.*

British Library MS. Hargrave 80, f. 117, pl. 2

The father of the plaintiff and defendant devised to the plaintiff a legacy of £500 and an annuity of £25 to be issuing out of his real estate, which he had devised to the defendant, who was his heir, likewise in tail, and made him executor and residuary legatee and left personal estate suggested to be sufficient to pay his bond and simple contract debts and no more. And the defendant having applied it to that purpose, the single question was whether the plaintiff, as to her legacy of £500, should stand in the place of the bond creditors to have a satisfaction out of the real assets, the personal being exhausted by them.

The Master of the Rolls [Trevor] made a decree upon the defendant personally to pay the £500.

But that decree, upon the rehearing now by Lord Keeper [Lord Harcourt], it was agreed to be wrong, though the plaintiff should be entitled to the £500 out of the real estate.

It was urged by *Vernon*, for the plaintiff, that the devise to the defendant was within the Statute of Fraudulent Devises,[1] that it was as much the intent of the testator that the plaintiff should have her legacy as the defendant out of the real estate, and that he intended the defendant should take it subject to the debts and legacies, that, if a third person had been made executor and the bond creditors had come against the devisee, he could not have protected himself against them and, if he afterwards brought his bill against the executor and legatees to be reimbursed, he could have no relief in equity.

To which last point, Lord Keeper [Lord Harcourt] said he thought so too.

On the other hand, it was insisted by *How*, and agreed by the Lord Keeper [Lord Harcourt], that the devise to the defendant was not fraudulent, there being no creditors to be defeated.

He said that, if several legacies were given and the personal estate was insufficient to satisfy them all, they must abate in proportion, but that, if any of the legacies were specific ones, the court never decreed them to abate, that, if the estate here devised to the defendant had been a term for years which, if it had not been devised, would have been assets and liable to the payment of the legacy and the court would not have decreed it to abate.

---

[1] Stat. 3 Will. & Mar., c. 14 (*SR*, VI, 320–321).

Lord Keeper [Lord Harcourt]: Though that case was very like the case in question and, though there was a difference between the present case of a devisee and the case of an heir and that, if the lands had descended as they would have been assets and liable to the payment of debts by specialty, a legatee might have stood in the place of a specialty creditor and had satisfaction out of them. But, however, he directed an inquiry of the quantum of the personal estate and of the debts and into the nature of them and how they had been satisfied and the value of the real assets. And he reserved the consideration of the main point until after the report.

[Other copies of this report: Lincoln's Inn MS. Misc. 383, p. 208, Lincoln's Inn MS. Misc. 106, p. 156.]

[Other reports of this case: 2 Salkeld 416, 91 E.R. 362, 1 Peere Williams 201, 24 E.R. 355, 1 Eq. Cas. Abr. 143, 21 E.R. 944.]

## 422

## Dawson v. Rason

(Ch. 1712)

*Where an assignee of a bankrupt who is the beneficiary of a trust sues in regard to the trust, the trustees and the other beneficiaries should be made parties to the suit.*

British Library MS. Hargrave 80, f. 118, pl. 1

The defendant, upon marrying his daughter to J.S., covenanted with him to pay £400 to A. and B. to be invested in land to be settled for the use of J.S. for life, remainder to his daughter for life, with remainder to the issue of the marriage, and the interest until purchase was made payable to the same uses. The money continued after the marriage in the defendant's hands, and J.S. mortgaged his estate for life in it to the defendant and became a bankrupt. The plaintiff was assignee and brought his bill for the interest due and to be due during the life of J.S., suggesting the act of bankruptcy to have been precedent to the mortgage and consequently to overreach it, and, I think, he prayed an execution of the trust.

[It was] objected by *Vernon* and *How* that the principal being payable to the trustees to be invested in lands, they ought to have brought them before the court, that, otherwise, the defendant could not be discharged of his covenant, which he was to be upon payment of his money, and that there were greater reasons for them to have brought the wife of J.S. before the court for that, she being a *cestui qui trust* in remainder, if the court should direct the money to be laid out and it should be accidentally lost, she, being no party to the suit, might notwithstanding the decree resort again to the party for her money and the decree would not protect him.

This first objection the Master of the Rolls [Trevor] thought might be got over though it would have been more regular to have made the trustees parties. But the second he allowed to be a good one and, however, directed an issue to try whether [he was] bankrupt or not before the mortgage, the defendant not opposing it. And [he] reserved the consideration of everything else until after the trial and directed the wife and the trustees to be brought before the court.

[Other copies of this report: Lincoln's Inn MS. Misc. 383, f. 209, pl. 1, Lincoln's Inn MS. Misc. 106, p. 158.]

423

## Anonymous v. White

(Ch. 1712)

*A court of equity will not grant specific performance of a contract where the purpose of the contract has been defeated by third persons.*

*Where specific performance of a contract cannot be granted, a court of equity can give common law damages for the breach of contract.*

British Library MS. Hargrave 80, f. 118, pl. 2

The bill was for a specific performance of an agreement by which the defendant was to take a lease of a wayleave over the plaintiff's close at the yearly rent of £10 for the use of a colliery, which the defendant intended to take and was likewise to employ the plaintiff's son in the colliery during the term and allow him £20 *per annum* during the first seven years and £30 the second. At the close of the articles, the defendant obliged himself to the performance under a penalty. After the execution of them, some other colliers took a lease of other lands which, as well as the plaintiff's, lay between the colliery and the river and so rendered the plaintiff's wayleave useless to the defendant. And the defendant could not obtain a lease of the colliery and the lease that he was to take being for the use of the colliery though there was no fraud proved in the plaintiff from hindering the defendant from taking the other wayleaves or the colliery.

Yet My Lord [Lord Harcourt] would not decree a specific performance but directed only a [writ of] *quantum damnificatus* by the defendant's not taking the lease. And that part that related to the employing the son, he totally rejected, there being no colliery to employ him in.

[Other copies of this report: Lincoln's Inn MS. Misc. 383, p. 209, pl. 2, Lincoln's Inn MS. Misc. 106, p. 159.]

## 424

### Anonymous

(Ch. 1712)

*A guardian of an infant does not have the power to make capital improvements on his ward's lands and will not be reimbursed for them.*

British Library MS. Hargrave 80, f. 118v, pl. 1

Upon a bill brought by an infant against his guardian for an account, My Lord [LORD HARCOURT] refused to allow the guardian for lasting improvements upon his account and said he had no power to make them.

[Other copies of this report: Lincoln's Inn MS. Misc. 383, p. 210, pl. 1, Lincoln's Inn MS. Misc. 106, p. 160, pl. 1.]

## 425

### Anonymous

(Ch. 1712)

*A lease to begin in the future can be sold in order to raise a portion payable out of it.*

British Library MS. Hargrave 80, f. 118v, pl. 2

The plaintiff was entitled to a £400 fortune payable at twenty-one or marriage for the raising of which a term had been carved out by a settlement expectant upon an estate for life which was yet in being. The term was directed to be sold for raising it, notwithstanding the mesne estate for life, but no interest [was] given but from the filing the bill though it had been payable sometime before.

[Other copies of this report: Lincoln's Inn MS. Misc. 383, p. 210, pl. 2, Lincoln's Inn MS. Misc. 106, p. 160, pl. 2.]

## 426

### Anonymous

(Ch. 1712)

*An oral trust will be enforced if the trustee admits to its existence.*

British Library MS. Hargrave 80, f. 118v, pl. 3

[It was] said by *Sir T. Powys* that the Statute of Frauds[1] does not extinguish a trust though not created by a writing signed by the party but that, if the trustee would have the honesty to own such a trust, he would be decreed to perform it.

[Other copies of this report: Lincoln's Inn MS. Misc. 383, p. 210, pl. 3, Lincoln's Inn MS. Misc. 106, p. 160, pl. 3.]

## 427

## Dinly v. Dinly

(Ch. 1712)

*The questions in this case was whether a certain condition in a devise had occurred or not so as to defeat the plaintiff's title and whether a mortgage should be redeemed.*

British Library MS. Hargrave 80, f. 118v, pl. 4

Mark Dinly devised the manor of Peopletown in Worcestershire to the heir male of his own body, the remainder to Sir Edward Dinly for life, remainder to his first and every other son in tail male, remainder to the defendant for life, remainder to his first and every son in tail male, and for default of such issue, remainder to the plaintiff for life etc., provided that Sir Edward Dinely should have the custody and education of the defendant until he attained his age of twenty-one to the intent he might be bred up in the Christian religion according to the Church of England and that, if the defendant's father refused to let the defendant be bred up by Sir Edward according to the will or if he refused to be so bred up after he came to twelve years old, that then the limitations to him and the heirs male of his body and their heirs should cease and be void.

The bill was brought against the defendant Dinely and mortgagee precedent to the will to redeem the mortgage or to have that and all impediments removed in order to try his title at law and to be relieved generally. There was full proof of the defendant's being an Anabaptist. And one witness swore positively that Sir Edward, after the testator's death, requested the defendant's father to let the defendant be bred up by the deponent, who was a clergyman, and that he positively refused. On the other hand, it was proved that this witness had declared it was over a bottle in a cellar, that the defendant was but five years old when his father died, and that, after his father's death, his mother tendered him to Sir Edward, who refused to take him. And, after her death, he was bred up by one Harwood, an Anabaptist, until twenty-one, that Sir Edward knew of it and told Harwood that he could demand him if he would, but he was well satisfied with his being there, and that Sir Edward married him to his granddaughter and gave him pos-

[1] Stat. 29 Car. II, c. 3 (*SR*, V, 839–842).

session of part of the estate upon his marriage, and that the defendant was heir at law to the testator.

It was urged by *Vernon* that the limitation to the plaintiff was not to take place but in default of issue male of the defendant and, therefore, the proviso should defeat the limitation to the defendant and his issue yet the plaintiff's title would not arise until failure of the issue male of the defendant.

*Lechmere* insisted that, the breach of the proviso being to be incurred by the act of the third person, it ought to be taken strictly, that the proviso was that if the father refused to let him be bred up by Sir Edward and that the deposition showed a request by Sir Edward to let him be bred up by the deponent Hodge not by himself and so different.

Lord Keeper [Lord Harcourt] decreed the plaintiff to proceed by [a feigned action of] ejectment and to insist on his title only under the will or as heir at law, the mortgage not to be set up. The farther consideration [was] reserved until after the trial. Lord Keeper [Harcourt] thought he might have gone farther and decreed for the plaintiff.

[Other copies of this report: Lincoln's Inn MS. Misc. 383, p. 210, pl. 4, Lincoln's Inn MS. Misc. 106, p. 160, pl. 4.]

## 428

## Wingold v. Plume

(Ch. 1712)

*An annuity is more properly chargeable on realty than personalty, and, therefore, taxes can be deducted from it.*

British Library MS. Hargrave 80, f. 119v, pl. 1

The plaintiff's testator subjected his real and personal estate to the payment of an annuity to the plaintiff for life and made the defendant his executor, who was likewise his heir. The annuity was £12 *per annum*, personal estate £10,000, leasehold and freehold lands £500 *per annum*. And the single question was whether taxes could be deducted for this annuity.

*How*, for the plaintiff: If the annuity was charged singly upon the lands, whether freehold or leasehold, taxes must have been deducted out if it. But the personal estate being likewise subject to the payment of it and that being the proper fund for it to arise from, for, if the personal estate and real assets were in two hands, the heir would have aid of the personal to discharge the real, it is otherwise.

Lord Keeper [Lord Harcourt]: It would if they were in different hands, but, here, they are in one. And the annuity being permanent and the personal assets transitory, I take the real estate to be the proper fund for the annuity to be charged upon. And he decreed taxes to be deducted.

[Other copies of this report: Lincoln's Inn MS. Misc. 383, p. 211, pl. 1, Lincoln's Inn MS. Misc. 106, p. 162.]

429

## Payne v. Bareford

(Ch. 1712)

*A bond creditor who is also the executor of the debtor's will can retain assets to satisfy the bond to himself.*

*In this case, the trustees of an estate breached their trust by failing to properly secure the trust assets for the benefit of the beneficiary.*

British Library MS. Hargrave 80, f. 119v, pl. 2

The bill was brought by bond and simple contract creditors of J.S. against the defendant Bareford, his executor, who was likewise trustee in his marriage settlement, the other trustee, and the eldest son of J.S., an infant, for a discovery of assets and satisfaction of debts.

It was insisted on for the defendant that J.S., in consideration of marriage, conveyed all his real estate and, among other things, some tithes, to the use of himself for life, remainder to his intended wife for life, remainder to preserve etc., remainder to the first and every other son of the marriage in tail male, remainder to his own right heirs, that it was provided by the deed that it should be lawful for J.S. to sell the tithes with the approbation of the trustees and, in case of such sale, he covenanted with the trustees to convey other lands to the same use, that the tithes were afterwards sold by J.S. with the trustees' consent for £2000, and that the trustees took a bond from him upon the sale for their indemnity and for his performing the covenant, that he died without performing it and left but £800 assets, which the executor insisted to retain towards satisfaction of this bond.

Lord Keeper [Lord Harcourt] thought he might and dismissed the plaintiff's bill but without costs, they being creditors, and without prejudice to their bringing another bill upon a further discovery of assets. But My Lord [Lord Harcourt] being of opinion the trustees, consenting to a sale and trusting J.S. with the money for twelve years (which he lived after) upon his single bond without seeing it paid into court or invested in land or other lands settled pursuant to the covenant, had notoriously broken their trust. Though, by the proviso, they were not otherwise to join in the sale but by consenting, nor was the money to be paid to them, he directed a bill to be brought against them in the infant's name by a Six Clerk as his *prochein ami* for satisfaction of his breach of trust.

[Other copies of this report: Lincoln's Inn MS. Misc. 383, p. 211, pl. 2, Lincoln's Inn MS. Misc. 106, p. 163.]

## 430

## Robert v. Millechamp

(Ch. 1712)

*Where the style of the case in a commission to take depositions is mistaken, the commission can be amended at the cost of the negligent party.*

Dickens 22, 21 E.R. 174

16 July 1712. Lord Cowper.

The plaintiff sued out a commission. The defendant's commissioners joined and signed the plaintiff's interrogatories, and witnesses were examined on the part of the plaintiff, and the defendant's commissioners signed the depositions, after which it was discovered that the title of the cause in the commission was mistaken.

Upon an application to suppress the depositions, Lord Chancellor [Lord Harcourt] ordered the Six Clerk to amend the commission in respect of the title of the cause, but the plaintiff to pay the costs of the motion and to be at the expense of sealing a new commission for the examination of the defendant's witnesses and the Master to settle a time and place for the execution of the commission.

## 431

## Marquess of Dorchester v. Davies

(Ch. 1712)

*In this bill to foreclose a mortgage, the interest contracted for was ordered to be paid.*

British Library MS. Hargrave 80, f. 120

Upon a bill to foreclose, the single question was upon a covenant in the mortgage that it should be lawful for the mortgagor in case he paid £5 percent within three months after it should become due to retain the other one percent reserved by the mortgage towards clearing all taxes that might be imposed upon the mortgage money and the surplus for his own benefit to the year 1696. The interest had been paid, though not regularly, but sometimes two years interest together, and the mortgagee had, nevertheless, to that time accepted the £5 percent and given acquittances in full. From 1696 to 1703, the interest ran in arrears. Then the mortgagee entered and, between that time and the decree, was satisfied all the arrear of interest and the greatest part of the principal by perception of profits.

*Sir Joseph Jekyll*, for the mortgagee, said that there had been a difference taken formerly between reserving interest at £5 percent and then covenanting that £6 should be paid if the interest was in arrear from a time prefixed and reserving £6 and covenanting to take £5 if paid by such a time but that, in the case of Tony v. Coxe, in Lord Keeper Wright's time, six was decreed though five was there first reserved and the covenant was to pay six in case of not paying five.

*Mead* cited the case of Pollexfin and Mitchell, at the Rolls lately, where £5 was reserved upon the mortgage and £6 agreed to be paid by another deed in case of failure to pay £5 at the time limited and, upon that failure, £6 [was] decreed.

Lord Keeper [Lord Harcourt], in the principal case, directed £6 to be paid from 1696 to the time the mortgagee was repaid all the arrear of interest by perception of profits and no longer.

[Other copies of this report: Lincoln's Inn MS. Misc. 383, p. 212, Lincoln's Inn MS. Misc. 106, p. 164, pl. 1.]

432

## Matthews v. Cartwright

(Ch. 1712)

*A trustee cannot lease the trust property to himself.*

*A trustee who has committed fraud against the beneficiaries of the trust will be ordered to make an account to them.*

British Library MS. Hargrave 80, f. 120v, pl. 1

The plaintiff's father, having a considerable real and personal estate, part of which was a wharf in London, left the care of that and his children to the defendant, Cartwright, and distributed everything equally among his children born or to be born. The plaintiff was a posthumous son and entitled to a share. The defendant, three years after the plaintiff came of age but before he was out of his apprenticeship, invited him to his house at Christmas and, when he had him there, took him into his closet and showed him that his brother had signed his accounts and, by that means, prevailed with him to sign them. They were drawn up and stated accordingly, but all signed together. But there appeared a great deal of fraud on the part of the defendant in several instances and particularly in driving away the custom of the wharf and then granting a lease of it at a very low rent to another person in trust for himself, which practice of a trustee leasing to himself and accounting for the rent only My Lord [Harcourt] declared was not to be endured. The bill was to open these accounts and, though the plaintiff's father had been dead thirty years and the accounts signed, yet, in regard to the means of having them signed and several instances of fraud in them on the defendant's part, My

Lord [LORD HARCOURT] decreed the defendant to account from the death of the plaintiff's father.

[Other copies of this report: Lincoln's Inn MS. Misc. 383, p. 213, pl. 1, Lincoln's Inn MS. Misc. 106, p. 164, pl. 2.]

## 433

## Smith v. Baker

(Ch. 1712)

*The administrator of an administrator can be ordered to distribute property of the first intestate.*

British Library MS. Hargrave 80, f. 120v, pl. 2

The Master of the Rolls [TREVOR] decreed the defendant, who was administratrix of an administratrix, to distribute a leasehold estate of the first intestate, who had been dead twenty-six years, though a distribution had been made many years before, this leasehold estate being omitted out of the inventory.

In this case, there was full proof of the plaintiff's having sold his right to another, of part of the money being paid and an assignment executed, and an agreement to pay the rest of the consideration money out of what should be recovered. But notwithstanding this champerty, [it was] decreed *ut supra*.

[Other copies of this report: Lincoln's Inn MS. Misc. 383, p. 213, pl. 2, Lincoln's Inn MS. Misc. 106, p. 166.]

## 434

## Johns v. Gale

(Ch. 1712)

*A trust for the poor of several Baptist congregations is a superstitious use and will not be enforced.*

*A devise to an improper charitable use does not lapse, but it will be re-directed by the crown to a proper charitable purpose.*

British Library MS. Hargrave 80, f. 121

Pierce Johns, having two sons, whom he apprehended to be dead, conveyed his real estate, *inter alia*, subject to an annuity of £50 *per annum* to his wife for life to the use of himself for life, remainder to his two sons successively in tail, remainder to trustees for a term for one hundred years, remainder to the plaintiff, who was no relation to him, in fee, the trust of the term was declared to be that, out of the rents and profits, £15 *per annum* should be paid to five traveling ministers of the General Assembly of Anabaptists, £5 *per annum* to the minister and congregation of Anabaptists in Dunning's Alley, London, the like sum to four other meetings, and all the residue to the minsters and poor of the congregation within certain districts particularly described, provided that, if the General Assembly be dissolved and that there be no such traveling ministers or if one or more of those congregations change their faith in the opinion of the trustees, the sum limited to them should accrue to the rest and, if all change their faith or are dissolved or the trust premises or any part of them be transferred or applied to any other use, that then the term of one hundred years should cease and the lands enure to the only use of the plaintiff and his heirs. The questions were whether those charities were to be supported by equity and, if not, whether the plaintiff had any title during the term.

The Lord Keeper had referred it to Sir James Montagu, then Attorney General, to enquire whether any and what charity could be collected from the deed and ascertained so as to be established, who certified he could not gather any. It was then sent to a master to enquire what congregations were in being that were within the description of the deed and to certify them and the constitution of them. A report was accordingly made and, among other things, it was certified that they all continued in the same places and in the same condition they were in at the times of this settlement. It now came on again upon the master's report.

And Serjeant *Hooper*, for the plaintiff, insisted that it was an encouragement to faction and schism and, therefore, not to be established, that the limitation of the term to these uses was void by 23 Hen. VIII.[1]

But Lord Keeper [Lord Harcourt] said that Statute extended only to superstitious uses, that, in My Lord Jeffreys' time, money was given to good dissenting ministers such as Mr. [Richard] Baxter should nominate and the court would not establish it,[2] and that there was a like case in Lord North's time and the money applied to the Chelsea Hospital, that the trust was incapable of being reduced to any certainty and therefore void, and that, by the proviso, the term was to cease [if] the profits were misapplied by the trustees to pay law charges and tavern reckonings.

*Vernon*: Where the term is raised out of the inheritance for a particular use, if either the end for which it is created is accomplished or if it is impossible to be performed, it always attends the inheritance. The £15 *per annum* limited to five traveling ministers of the [General] Assembly of Anabaptists is incapable of being applied, no such assembly being lawful, nor can those sums be applied that are given to the several ministers and assemblies, the ministers not being incorporated and it not being practicable to keep up a succession among them or to

1 Stat. 23 Hen. VIII, c. 10 (*SR*, III, 378).

2 *Attorney General v. Baxter* (1684), 1 Vernon 248, 23 E.R. 446, 1 Eq. Cas. Abr. 96, 21 E.R. 907, Lincoln's Inn MS. Misc. 498, p. 9, pl. 2.

know how long to apply those sums and that, therefore, the term in the trusts of it not being possible to be performed ought to attend the inheritance.

The Attorney General [*Northey*], for the defendants, took a difference between the cases cited by Serjeant Hooper, which were before the Toleration[1] and those since, those meetings not being contrary to law now, though they were so then, and that the Brief Act[2] has given a farther countenance to them by directing the briefs to be read by the ministers of the separate congregations. It seems hard to imagine that the law should direct the collecting of money for charity from those people and prohibit the giving anything to them, that, before those acts, if a charity was misgiven, that the Court of Chancery always applied it to a proper use.

*Vernon* said that the rule was to apply it to a charity *ejusdem generis*, as for the purpose, what was given to a dissenting minister to a minister of the Church of England, and what was given to the poor to the poor of a hospital, but that the donor here had prevented the application by directing the term to cease, but that it has been the practice of the Court of Exchequer for these last twenty years to decree what is given to superstitious uses to be forfeited to the Crown. And he instanced the Case of Savoy by a bequest to Jesuits.[3]

The Attorney General [*Northey*] and the rest of the counsel of that side agreed that the appointment of £15 *per annum* to the five traveling ministers etc. was void but insisted that that sum fell into the residue.

*Sir Peter King*: The bequests in the instances cited by Serjeant Hooper were applied to other charitable uses and not for the benefit of the heir, nor ought to be here for the *haeres factus* though they were for superstitious uses, which, since the Toleration, they are not, that this trust is in effect but to ease the parishes of their poor and that surely is not superstitious, that a devise to a church or the poor of the town is good, and the congregations and ministers of churches are no more permanent than those of the Baptists.

*Hooper*: We have no bill to establish this charity. Our only business is to defend ourselves against the plaintiff. If the appointment had been to the minister, a congregation of a parish church, it would have been interpreted [to the] poor. We do not contend for the ministers of these separate congregations, but for the poor. And the trustees know how to apply it, which is a sufficient certainty, at least for our defense against the plaintiff.

*How* insisted the limitation to the plaintiff was voluntary and expectant on the determination of the term for 100 years and that, while any trust of that term remained to be performed, the plaintiff had no color of right to the lands, that the donor had an absolute power of disposing of this land as he pleased, and that the

[1] Stat. 1 Will. & Mar., c. 18 (*SR*, VI, 74–76).

[2] Stat. 4 & 5 Ann., c. 25 (*SR*, VIII, 513–515).

[3] *Attorney General v. Burdett* (Ex. 1705), Equity Cases Exch. 521, Orders of 28 February and 25 October 1705: Public Record Office, E.126/18, ff. 474, 539v.

trustees sought no assistance from the court. He cited a case where £4 *per annum* was devised to trustees by the will of one Russell for the benefit of the poor of the Low Dutch Church and, though the poor are fluctuating, it was applied to the poor that frequent that church, and a bill was brought by the Attorney General to establish it, and there has been an enjoyment and acquiescence ever since, that this appointment was as certain as that, and that this court will not interpose to take it from them. He cited another case in Moore 784, 785, 786,[1] where Lord Chancellor Ellesmere, assisted by two chief justices and the Master of the Rolls, decreed land given to superstitious uses to the heir of St. John against the plaintiff in case the trust for the charity should be adjudged void. But query whether in that case there was any limitation over, as there is here.

Lord Keeper [LORD HARCOURT]: Can you show me any case where the heir in cases of superstitious uses has prevailed against the Crown? I take it that the Crown, in these cases, always directs the application. He thought there would be a great difference between the Dutch, French, or Lutheran churches and the English dissenting congregations. An appointment to the first, he seemed to say, he should make no difficulty of establishing. But for the last that there was a great deal of difference between conniving at them and making good such an appointment for their benefit, which in time might set them on a level with the Church and the next step would be to jostle that out its place and that, therefore, he would not make the first precedent, but that was not the question now, that he could not see that the plaintiff could possibly prevail against the Crown. And, therefore, he would have dismissed the bill but without costs.

Serjeant *Hooper* insisted upon retaining it that they may try their title in an [action of] ejectment, which he [the Lord Keeper] gave them liberty to do.

[Other copies of this report: Lincoln's Inn MS. Misc. 383, p. 213, pl. 3, Lincoln's Inn MS. Misc. 106, p. 167.]

## 435

## Regina v. Hill

(Ch. 1712)

*Where an ecclesiastical court has jurisdiction, it can excommunicate a party for non-payment of court costs.*

*A writ de excommunicato capiendo will not be quashed for the lack of a proper addition to the party's name.*

---

[1] *Croft v. Evett* (Ch. 1605), Moore K.B. 784, 72 E.R. 904, also 117 Selden Soc. 342.

Lincoln's Inn MS. Misc. 10, p. 138

I [*Melmoth*] moved for a [writ of] *supersedeas* to a writ of *excommunicato capiendo* taken out upon a [writ of] *significavit* from the bishop that [Richard] Hill was excommunicated for his contempt in not paying costs.

The exceptions I [*Melmoth*] took were:

First, for that it was said in the *significavit* that a suit was brought in the spiritual court, *quae fuit ad primam instantiam causa defamationis sive opprobrii* and it is not said what the defamation was, which ought to be, that the court might judge whether it was a defamation of a spiritual nature and of which the ecclesiastical court has cognizance.

And upon this exception, without showing any other, the Master of the Rolls [Trevor] granted a [writ of] *supersedeas nisi.*

Second, a second exception I [*Melmoth*] intended to have taken was because it was said that *placit*[*um*] *Ricardi Hill in facie ecclesiae parochialis de D. 16 die mensis Septembris placit. palam et publice pro ex*[*communicato*] *denunciatus et declaratus fuit* and it is not said by whom he was so pronounced excommunicated and it might be by one not authorized to declare him excommunicated. *Vide* for this Trollop's Case, 8 Co.[1]

Third, a third exception I [*Melmoth*] would have taken was for that the *significavit* prays that Richard Hill may be taken and imprisoned *secundum leges et statuta regni Angliae* whereas since the Union, there is no such kingdom as England, for, by the Act of Union,[2] the two kingdoms of England and Scotland are united into one kingdom by the name of Great Britain.

But the first exception being allowed, I [*Melmoth*] had no mind to mention the two last.

Note I [*Melmoth*] moved in this matter once before and took the first exception and another, which, as the writ was then, was *secundum leges et Statuta Magnae Britannicae*, and I excepted to that for there was no such laws, for the law upon which the writ of *excommunicato capiendo* was grounded was the Statute of Queen Elizabeth,[3] which was not made part of the laws of Great Britain by the Act of Union, and then the Master of the Rolls [Trevor] allowed this exception, but he did not think there was any great matter in the first. And, upon that, they amended the writ and made it '*Regni Angliae*', which was as bad, for it ought to have been *secundum leges et statuta ejusdem partis Magnae Britannicae vocatae Angliae.*

[1] *Richeson v. Trollop* (1608), 8 Coke Rep. 68, 77 E.R. 577, also Croke Jac. 213, 79 E.R. 185.

[2] Stat. 6 Ann., c. 11 (*SR*, VIII, 566–577).

[3] Stat. 5 Eliz. I, c. 23 (*SR*, IV, 451–453).

British Library MS. Hargrave 80, f. 122v, pl. 1

Upon a motion for a [writ of] *supersedeas* to a writ *de excommunicato capiendo*, it was alleged the excommunication was for costs and, therefore, wrong, that not being one of the causes mentioned in the Statute of Elizabeth.

But that was overruled by Lord Keeper [Lord Harcourt], who held clearly that the spiritual court, having jurisdiction of the principal cause, might excommunicate for non-payment of costs, especially since they have no other remedy to compel the payment of them.

The second objection to the writ was the want of a right addition to the name of the party pursuant to the Statute.[1]

But it, likewise, was overruled, that addition being necessary only in respect of the penalties inflicted by the Act upon the party's not surrendering himself upon proclamation made. Without such addition, the party cannot incur those penalties, but may be liable to a writ *de excommunicato capiendo* however.

[Other copies of this report: Lincoln's Inn MS. Misc. 383, p. 216, Lincoln's Inn MS. Misc. 106, p. 172, pl. 1.]

[Related cases: 12 Modern 517, 88 E.R. 1489, 1 Salkeld 294, 91 E.R. 260.]

436

## Lee v. Curzon

(Ch. 1712)

*A court of equity can supply the lack of a surrender of a copyhold to the use of a will in favor of a widow.*

British Library MS. Hargrave 80, f. 122v, pl. 2

The father of an idiot, being possessed of a copyhold estate of inheritance and of a personal estate, devised £300 to his son, who was an idiot and his heir, and devised all the rest of his land and personal estate to his wife. He made no surrender to the use of his will.

And it was insisted by *Vernon* that equity, in this case, would not supply the want of it. He admitted that it would in favor of a wife or child otherwise unprovided for and where the copyhold lands were expressly devised to them, but that, here, it did appear that the wife had other provision. On the contrary, the bequest of all but his personal estate to her was an evidence *prima facie* that she had a provision from thence, nor was the copyhold here devised by express words nor did it appear but that the testator had other lands with which the general words of

[1] Stat. 1 Hen. V, c. 5 (*SR*, II, 171).

all the rest of his estates might be satisfied. He cited the case of Parker v. Jenny,[1] where equity would not supply the want of a surrender in favor of a younger child against an heir otherwise unprovided for.

The Master of the Rolls [Trevor] declared that it appeared to him from the preamble of the will, *viz.* 'as for such estate wherewith' etc., that the testator intended to make a clear disposition of his whole estate, both real and personal, and that it not appearing that the wife had any other competent provision, the copyhold passed to her for life but that, if it had appeared that she had been otherwise provided for, it would not. The wife had boarded out the idiot and, by his board, clothes, and physic besides the interest of £300, which she had applied to that purpose, the principal was reduced to £187.

But the Master declared he would presume the testator had calculated what would be necessary for the support of the idiot when he left him £300 and that the wife ought not to have broken in upon the principal without the direction of the court. And, therefore, he decreed the wife's representatives to make good the principal sum again though it was alleged that the wife at the time when she broke in upon it was the only person entitled to it in case she survived her son and, therefore, could not be brought to have lessened it unnecessarily. In this case, the plaintiff, who was administrator to the idiot, had been drawn into a release by a misapprehension of his title. And it was, therefore, set aside in this case.

*How* cited the case of Fothergill v. Fothergill,[2] where a defective execution of a power to make a jointure was supplied by the Master of the Rolls, upon the consideration of precedents, though made after marriage and, therefore, voluntary.

[Other copies of this report: Lincoln's Inn MS. Misc. 383, p. 217, Lincoln's Inn MS. Misc. 106, p. 172, pl. 2.]

## 437

## Eloyson v. Hutchison

(Ch. 1712)

*In this case, although the marriage had already occurred, an oral marriage settlement contract was ordered to be specifically performed because the negotiations had begun before the marriage took place and the defendant was acting in bad faith.*

[1] *Baker v. Jennings* (1699), 2 Freeman 234, 22 E.R. 1180, 2 Eq. Cas. Abr. 230, 22 E.R. 195.

[2] *Fothergill v. Fothergill* (1702), 2 Freeman 256, 22 E.R. 1194, 1 Eq. Cas. Abr. 222, 21 E.R. 1004.

British Library MS. Hargrave 80, f. 124

The plaintiff's son was a clerk to one Mowbrey, and the defendant sent his daughter for some time to be at Mowbrey's house. The daughter was very handsome, and the plaintiff's son falling in love with her, she was sent back to her father. He said upon her coming back Mowbrey was afraid of one of his rich clerks. However, the courtship proceeded with the privity of the defendant, who declared (as he owned by answer) that he would give his daughter £500 provided they married with the plaintiff's consent and so as she would settle £100 *per annum* on her son. The young couple married without the privity of the plaintiff. And there was no positive proof of the defendant's being privy to the marriage, but his son was present at it, and he received them soon after. And being pressed to give his daughter a fortune, he was prevailed upon to write to the plaintiff, and, in his letter, he offered to give £500 with his daughter if she would settle £100 *per annum* on her son. The person that carried it deposed that she was angry at first and declared the whole letter was a cheat and that she was sure the defendant would do nothing but, however, to try him, bid the deponent tell him she would comply with his proposal. When the defendant heard that she would, he fled off and would do nothing. The young couple were afterwards maintained by the plaintiff, who allowed them £100 *per annum*. And now, being eight years since these transactions, she brought her bill against the defendant for a specific performance of his proposal, offering to settle £100 *per annum* on her part.

*Vernon*, for the defendant, insisted that there is a difference between a proposal made before and one [made] after marriage, that, after is but a *nudum pactum* and there is no precedent for carrying such a one into an execution. A settlement made after marriage, though expressly in consideration of it, is voluntary and that the first case of this nature was that of Moore and Dr. Hart,[1] and the next that of Wangford and Fatherly,[2] both which cases were adjudged to be out of the Statute of Frauds[3] by reason of a letter which was sent in each of them with a proposal, but that the ground of those resolutions was to obviate frauds. There having in the first case been a treaty depending for a considerable time and, at last, Dr. Hart sent word by a letter that he would give £1500, whereupon the marriage proceeded, and the Doctor was decreed to made good his proposal, though no acceptance was proved on the other side, that the second case was the same; only, there, the defendant would have retracted his proposal after the young couple had proceeded upon it so far as to engage their affections, but, there likewise, he was decreed to perform it. Both those cases went up to

[1] *Moore v. Hart* (1683), 1 Vernon 110, 201, 23 E.R. 352, 412, 2 Chancery Reports 284, 21 E.R. 680, 1 Eq. Cas. Abr. 22, 21 E.R. 844.

[2] *Wankford v. Fotherley* (1694), 2 Vernon 322, 23 E.R. 807, 2 Freeman 201, 22 E.R. 1159, 1 Eq. Cas. Abr. 22, 21 E.R. 844.

[3] Stat. 29 Car. II, c. 3 (*SR*, V, 839–842).

the House of Peers and were affirmed. And he cited the case of Coleman and Uprott,[1] where there being a treaty between the plaintiff and defendant about the purchase, which was pretty dear, and the main inducement to the plaintiff was a seat in a church, which his wife had a mind to, the defendant wrote a letter to the plaintiff in which he told he should have it if he would advance £50 more than he had offered; the plaintiff sent an answer that he would the next day, though a neighbor stepped in and bid more for it, the plaintiff, following his letter, immediately brought his bill; the defendant was decreed to perform his offer by his letter, but that, in the principal case, there had been a long acquiescence, nor was the obligation here mutual, there having been no compliance with the proposal on the part of the plaintiff but only a message to try the defendant, nor could the plaintiff on a bill brought by the defendant be decreed £100 *per annum*.

*Mead*, on the same side, cited the case of Ackworth and Sir Peter Mew; Ackworth was executor of Andrews, a lessee under the bishop of Winchester, and he treated with Sir Peter as agent for the bishop about renewing; letters were proved from Sir Peter proposing the terms of a fine, but, there being no evidence of acceptance of the other hand, the court would not decree performance.

Lord Keeper [Lord Harcourt]: I am fully satisfied that the marriage was had with the privity and contrivances of the father. The answer that denies it is fully falsified. His letter owns he was privy to the courtship. His sending his daughter to Mowbrey was purely to ensnare one of the clerks. His not acquainting the mother with the courtship, but, on the contrary, giving the young man opportunities are a strong proof of his contriving the marriage and his son's being at it and his receiving the young couple at his house soon after and then sending the proposal shows he did not dislike it. The admission in his answer of his offer before the marriage to give his daughter £500 takes it out of the Statute of Frauds, though it were but a verbal one. And that is a ground for a decree, but that, afterwards, was qualified with respect to the plaintiff's estate. Though the letter was subsequent to the marriage, yet I will consider it jointly with the transactions before and the rather because of the contrivance of the defendant in those cases and the irregularity of the value of the settlement to be made by the mother and that, by him, the mother closed immediately with his proposal. Let him pay the £500 within a month after the plaintiff shall execute a settlement of £100 *per annum* and, if he does it within that time, without interest or costs, but, in default of his paying it in time, to be paid with interest from the filing of the bill with costs. On the other hand, though the mother's offer by the bill and the terms demanded of her by the defendant's letter were in general to settle £100 *per annum* upon her son, yet, Lord Keeper [Lord Harcourt] declared he would take that according to the common way of settling estates upon marriage and, therefore, decreed her to convey lands to that value to the two senior Six Clerks

[1] *Coleman v. Upcot* (1707), see above, Case No. 64.

and their heirs in trust for herself and her heirs until the defendant should pay the £500 and then in trust to the husband and wife for their lives, remainder to preserve contingent remainders, remainder to the first and every other son of that marriage in tail male, remainder to the right heirs of the husband with power to the husband to charge the land with £500, the wife's fortune, for younger children but so as not to affect the jointure and in default of payment of £500 by the defendant in trust to reconvey to the plaintiff and her heirs.

*Sir Joseph Jekyll*, of counsel with the plaintiff, chose to have the conveyance thus, by way of trust rather than by limitation of uses. He said that a limitation to the use of a husband and his heirs until marriage and then to the use of a husband for life etc. had been held not a fee upon a fee, but he doubted whether it would not be a fee upon a fee if the limitation in this case were for the use of the mother and her heirs until the defendant should pay the £500 and then to the use of the husband and wife for life etc.

*Quaere diversitatem.* There were some other circumstances in this case that were mentioned to show they intended the world should think his daughter worth £500, such as his giving a bond for £500 to her and taking a defeasance of it privately and showing his will in which he gave her that sum.

[Other copies of this report: Lincoln's Inn MS. Misc. 383, p. 219, Lincoln's Inn MS. Misc. 106, p. 176.]

## 438

## Bellasis v. Churchill

(Ch. 1712)

*A captain of marines or his personal representative can compel an account of money due to the company from the colonel and his agent.*

British Library MS. Hargrave 80, f. 125v

The plaintiff's wife was the widow and executrix of a captain of marines, who died in the service in Spain. And the bill was brought against the Colonel [Churchill] and [his] agent for an account of the money due to the company before the captain's death.

It was urged for the defendants that, as to all but the captain's personal pay, neither the plaintiff nor defendant were entitled to it but that both one and the other in whose hands it was were but trustees for the soldiers or their representatives and, in case no soldiers or representatives of them appeared, that then the public was entitled to the money issued for them, that, by the words of the Acts for punishing mutiny and desertion,[1] the agents were liable to account to the

[1] Stat. 9 Ann., c. 9, s. 3 (*SR*, IX, 389–390).

soldiers for their respective pay as well as the captain for his and that, though, in the case of the land army, the captain might be entrusted with the pay of their companies where the soldiers had necessarily their subsistence of 6d. per day paid them weekly and where, therefore, there could be no great arrear due to them, that it was otherwise in case of marines, who were supported while they were aboard by the public and, by that means, had frequently great arrears due to them and though, by the laws of the Admiralty, an account lay for seamen against the captain of the ship, no account would lie here for the marines against their captain, but they might have one against the agent, who ought, therefore, to keep the money for his indemnity.

But Lord Keeper [Lord Harcourt] declared that the captain was the proper person to receive the pay and distribute it to them, that the captain in this having been dead five years and no demand being made by any of the company for the pay that accrued before his death, he would presume that he had satisfied them and that his executrix was, therefore, entitled to a satisfaction of the agent and Colonel, that, in this case, neither captain nor agent ought to gain anything from the pay of the private men, but that, if anything was to be gained, it was more reasonable that the captain, who lost his life in the service, should have it than the agent, who sat at home and preyed upon the regiment. And, therefore, he declared an account against the defendants but with liberty to deduct what they had paid to private men or afterwards should pay with the privity and consent of the plaintiff and approbation of the Master, and that the plaintiff should indemnify the defendants against the demands of the private men, the defendants' giving the plaintiff notice when any such demand is made.

The case of Constable and Leshingson was cited as adjudged in point.

[Other copies of this report: Lincoln's Inn MS. Misc. 383, p. 222, Lincoln's Inn MS. Misc. 106, p. 180.]

[Other reports of this case: 2 Vernon 682, 23 E.R. 1043, 1 Eq. Cas. Abr. 6, 21 E.R. 832.]

## 439

## Earl of Warrington v. Worrall

(Ch. 1712)

*A court of equity can order a partition of a reversion in expectancy.*

British Library MS. Hargrave 80, f. 126

The defendant was tenant for two lives and had a term for thirty-one years expectant upon the death of the survivor of those lands and was also entitled to an undivided third of the residuum and inheritance, and the plaintiff was entitled to the other two-thirds of it. And he brought his bill for a partition that he might know the land out of which the rent payable to him issues or might be able to prevent waste or bring his action for it.

And a partition was decreed though the plaintiff had only a reversionary interest but to be made in such manner by means of stakes etc., not fences as not to prejudice the defendant's possession and at the equal costs of both parties though the plaintiff sought it and the defendant did not and the plaintiff had two-thirds of the residuum, partitions of portions being generally looked upon for the benefit of both.

[Other copies of this report: Lincoln's Inn MS. Misc. 383, p. 223, Lincoln's Inn MS. Misc. 106, p. 182.]

## 440

## Morgan v. Morgan

(Ch. 1712)

*Where a testator's personal estate is expressly devised, it is not subject to raise portions, but it is to liable to pay debts in ease of the real estate.*

British Library MS. Hargrave 80, f. 126v

The father of the plaintiff and defendant, having issue, the defendant, the elder, the plaintiff, and two more younger children, charged his estate, real and personal, with raising £200 *per annum* to his wife for life and £1500 for his three younger children for their portions and directed that his wife should receive the profits of his estate until his son came to twenty-one and raising her own £200 *per annum* and paying debts and encumbrances and at twenty-one should let the son into possession. And he made his wife executrix and gave her all his personal estate. She, after his death, married the defendant Manwaring. They received the rents and profits many years, but paid no part of the portions. And, then, the wife died, and Manwaring became insolvent.

And the bill was brought against him, the heir at law, and the other two children to have their portions raised out of the estate.

The personal estate being expressly devised to the wife, My Lord [Lord Harcourt] decreed the personal estate not to be subject to raise the portions, but that it was to pay debts in ease of his real estate, notwithstanding the devise of it. And for the profits of the real estate, he decreed that, so far as the surplus of them beyond £200 *per annum* to the wife, the maintenance, and the charges which the personal estate did not satisfy which were received by the wife or her second husband during the eldest son's minority amounted to, so far the estate ought to be taken and to have borne its burden and the portions to have been satisfied as against the eldest son, notwithstanding the misapplication by the wife or her second husband, she being during that time the person entrusted by the testator to receive them, but that no profits received by her or her second husband after the son came to age, at which time her trust was to cease, and not applied to the payment of the portions should be looked on as applied or the estate discharged by them. But he gave the son leave to prosecute the accounts against Manwaring in the name of the young children, but [he] must indemnify them.

[Other copies of this report: Lincoln's Inn MS. Misc. 383, p. 224, pl. 1, Lincoln's Inn MS. Misc. 106, p. 183.]

441

## Head v. Barret

(Ch. 1712)

*In this case, the estates given to children by a marriage settlement in issue never vested.*

Lincoln's Inn MS. Misc. 10, p. 136

19 November 1712. Sir Francis Head, administrator of Catherine Head and one of the executors of the Lady Sarah Barret, John Lynch, administrator of Sarah, his late wife, and one other of the executors of the said Lady Barret, Richard Head, another executor of the said Lady Head, and several others, plaintiffs; Thomas Barret, William Boys, and Anne, his wife, defendants.

Sir Paul Barret, upon his marriage with the Lady Sarah, his wife, settles a lease which he held for three lives of the Dean and Chapter of Canterbury upon trustees and their heirs upon trust to permit him to receive the profits during his life, then to permit his wife to receive the profits during her life, and, after her decease, to dispose of the profits from the decease of the survivor of them until the eldest heir male of their bodies from time to time should attain the age of twenty-one years for his maintenance and, after he should attain that age, upon trust to convey to him and his heirs during the lives of the *cestui que vie*s. And, if the said Dame Sarah Head should happen to die without any heir male of her body by Sir Paul or if such heir male should die before twenty-one without issue and if there should be then living any issue female by the said Sir Paul Barret on his wife begotten, then the trustees were to raise £2000 for such daughter as should live to eighteen.

Sir Paul Barret died leaving issue by his wife, one son and one daughter. The son attained the age of twenty-one and died. The daughter, who survived the son, attained the age of eighteen and died intestate. And, then, the Lady Barret, the mother, died.

In this cause, amongst other things, it was decreed that the daughter was never entitled to the £2000 portion and that the trust estate was never vested in the son in regard that the daughter and son died in the lifetime of their mother. And the bill was dismissed as to the demand of the £2000.

## 442

## Hudson v. Hudson

(Ch. c. 1712)

*A contract for a wife's separate maintenance will be specifically enforced in a case of spousal abuse.*

Lincoln's Inn MS. Misc. 10, p. 137

The plaintiff, the defendant's wife, being used very ill by him, as appeared by the proofs in the cause, he came to an agreement under his hand with his wife to make her a separate maintenance. And refusing afterwards to perform that agreement, she brought a bill to have an execution of it.

It was insisted for the defendant that this was in the nature of a bill for alimony, that to decree this agreement was to decree a separation, which all courts would endeavor to prevent, and that the defendant was willing to live with his wife and had invited her home.

But, notwithstanding, the court decreed the agreement to be performed, it appearing very fully upon the proofs that the defendant had used his wife very ill.

Note Serjeant *Hooper*, in arguing for the defendant said he believed no precedents of this nature could be produced, upon which My Lord Keeper [LORD HARCOURT] told him he might cite one tomorrow if he pleased, meaning the decree he was going to make.

## 443

## Dew v. Craven

(Ch. 1712)

*A bill of discovery can be brought by a tenant against his lessor to discover the lessor's title to the leased premises.*

British Library MS. Hargrave 80, f. 127, pl. 1

Sir Anthony Craven, being barely tenant for life of a manor by a family settlement, took upon him to grant several leases for lives. The tenants, upon hearing of his title, brought a bill for discovery of it, to which he demurred. And the demurrer was clearly overruled.

[Other copies of this report: Lincoln's Inn MS. Misc. 383, p. 224, pl. 2, Lincoln's Inn MS. Misc. 106, p. 184, pl. 1.]

## 444

## Churchill v. Fitch

(Ch. 1712)

*The question in this case was whether the unexecuted contract for a lease of land was within the Statute of Frauds.*

British Library MS. Hargrave 80, f. 127, pl. 2

Churchill agreed with Fitch for the purchase of a leasehold estate. And after an assignment [was] engrossed but not executed and the purchase money prepared, an advantageous under-lease dropping after the day, from which the purchase was to take place, Fitch would have flown off. And to a bill for a specific execution, he pleaded the Statute of Frauds[1] and that there was no agreement in writing.

But the plea was overruled, he having sent a letter to the plaintiff with an assignment in which he took notice of it and said he would come and execute it and he said by his plea that the plaintiff drew him to write that letter on purpose to bring this case out of the Statute.

*Vernon* cited the case of Sir Thomas Mears and Lord Stourton, where there were two pieces of paper and but one of them signed by Sir Thomas, but the court decreed the last to be a continuation of the first, and that of Butcher v. Butcher, where the possession being changed pursuant to a parol agreement, it was decreed to be out of the Statute.[2]

[Other copies of this report: Lincoln's Inn MS. Misc. 383, p. 225, pl. 1, Lincoln's Inn MS. Misc. 106, p. 184, pl. 2.]

## 445

## Slack v. Coward

(Ch. 1712)

*Where a father buys land in the name of his son and later destroys the conveyance and takes a conveyance in his own name and then mortgages it, this is not an advancement to the son, but it is a resulting trust, and the son and heir is a trustee for the father and is liable to redeem the land or be foreclosed.*

[1] Stat. 29 Car. II, c. 3 (*SR*, V, 839–842).

[2] *Meers v. Lord Stourton* (Ch. 1711), see above, Case No. 303; *Butcher v. Stapely* (1686), 1 Vernon 363, 23 E.R. 524, 1 Eq. Cas. Abr. 21, 21 E.R. 843.

British Library MS. Hargrave 80, f. 127, pl. 3

The defendant's father purchased lands of the plaintiff in the name of the defendant, then an infant, and entered and enjoyed them himself. But, afterwards, wanting money, he could get none upon them, the conveyance not being in his own name. He then applied again to the plaintiff and got a second conveyance to himself in his own name dated before the first and burned the first. And about a year afterwards, he mortgaged these lands to the plaintiff, who now brought his bill against the son that he might redeem or make a further assurance.

Serjeant *Hooper*, for the defendant, urged that the first conveyance to the son, though the money [was] paid by the father, ought to be looked upon as a provision made by the father for him. And, it being the case of a father and child, no trust would result to the father.

*How* [argued] that the plaintiff could have no relief, that his equity being founded on a fraud, that he was privy to burning the first deed and executed a second with an antedate, that such acts were evidences that both he and the father looked upon the first conveyance to have been intended a provision for the son.

*Vernon*, for the plaintiff, insisted on the Case of Sir Charles Sidney, who purchased a house in the name of a lady (I think his second wife) intending it should be a provision for her and, though, at law, the conveyance could not be adjudged fraudulent, the legal estate never having been in Sir Charles, yet, upon a rehearing, the house was decreed to be liable to Sir Charles's debts, that this case resembles that, and that the father's taking of the profits and his mortgaging the lands to the plaintiff overthrew that construction, that the conveyance to the son should be deemed a provision for him so far at least as to let in the plaintiff's mortgage, that they did not found their equity upon the deeds being destroyed nor desired to take any advantage of it, and that was only a foolish, unadvised act of the defendant's father without any design of fraud nor was the plaintiff privy to it.

Lord Keeper [Lord Harcourt]: The rule that all purchases made by fathers in the son's name are to be looked upon as advancements of the son is too general. There does not appear to have been any fraud in this case. The plaintiff had no view of lending when he executed the second deed. The first was burned after that was executed and without the plaintiff's direction, and the money [was] lent a year after that. I look upon this case to be the same as if the first deed were in being and, if it were, the son would be a trustee for the father's mortgage. Let the defendant redeem within six months or make farther assurance.

[Other copies of this report: Lincoln's Inn MS. Misc. 383, p. 225, pl. 2, Lincoln's Inn MS. Misc. 106, p. 185.]

## 446

## Kent v. Curzon

(Ch. 1712)

*A supplemental bill lies in equity to compute interest that has accrued pendente lite.*

British Library MS. Hargrave 80, f. 127v

In this case, there had been a former bill to foreclose, and, after issue joined, an account [was] stated between the parties by a deed, and then [there was] a decree by which interest was to be computed from the beginning for the principal money only, and not from the foot of the stated account, for what was due upon that account not being in issue in that cause though witnesses were examined for it then. And now, a supplemental bill was brought in aid of that decree after it was enrolled to have the account taken from the foot of that stated account.

*Vernon*, for the defendant: No rule is more certain or more constantly allowed on pleas or demurrers than that you cannot bring an original or supplemental bill to add or to vary a former decree. If a new matter arises after a bill and before publication and before the hearing, a supplemental bill will lie, but not after a decree, and if a man would have a second decree in the same cause, he may bring another after that and so *in infinitum*.

But Lord Keeper [Lord Harcourt] overruled the objection and decreed the account to be taken from the foot of the stated account.

*Vernon* allowed in this case that a bill in aid was proper after a decree. And, in a motion afterwards in another cause, he said that those bills were a more ancient method of proceeding than examining the party to interrogatories after the decree, and that, now, they are at liberty to proceed either way. But, however, his client's bill was there dismissed upon motion with costs, the bill being only a verbal recital of the former bill, answer, and decree between the same parties and the charge or discharge brought in by the other side and seeking a discovery of something relating to the account and the court's being in opinion that this method of proceeding was vexatious when he had a much easier way of obtaining what he sought by moving only and that the other side might be examined on those matters upon interrogatories.

*Vernon* insisted here that, if a bill were improper, they ought to have pleaded to it. If the recitals verbatim were the objections, they might refer it for impertinence, but that neither was a ground to dismiss it upon a motion.

[Other copies of this report: Lincoln's Inn MS. Misc. 383, p. 226, Lincoln's Inn MS. Misc. 106, p. 187.]

## 447

## Rice v. Pine

(Ch. 1712)

*Money given to a person to prosecute a lawsuit is an unlawful consideration for an assignment, being maintenance and champerty.*

British Library MS. Hargrave 80, f. 128, pl. 1

The bill was to be let in to have the benefit of a debt due to Ann Andrews, which the plaintiff entitled himself unto under an assignment from her, he having maintained her and supplied her with money to prosecute the suit she was engaged in, for prosecuting this suit for the recovery of this debt were alleged in the bill as consideration of the assignment.

To this bill, the defendant demurred. And his demurrer was allowed because [it was] plain maintenance and champerty.

[Other copies of this report: Lincoln's Inn MS. Misc. 383, p. 227, pl. 1, Lincoln's Inn MS. Misc. 106, p. 188.]

## 448

## Anonymous

(Ch. 1712)

*A parol demurrer is allowed in equity for an infant heir of an obligor.*

British Library MS. Hargrave 80, f. 128, pl. 2

*Vernon*: If the heir of an obligor be under age, the parol will demur in equity as well as at law.

[Other copies of this report: Lincoln's Inn MS. Misc. 383, p. 227, pl. 2, Lincoln's Inn MS. Misc. 106, p. 189, pl. 1.]

## 449

## Anonymous

(Ch. 1712)

*A defendant who pleads by confession and avoidance has the burden of proof as to the defense.*

British Library MS. Hargrave 80, f. 128v, pl. 1

*Vernon*: If the defendant confesses to anything in his answer and then avoids it, he must prove his avoidance for, otherwise, his confession will bind him.

[Other copies of this report: Lincoln's Inn MS. Misc. 383, p. 227, pl. 3, Lincoln's Inn MS. Misc. 106, p. 189, pl. 2.]

## 450

## Elborough v. Glenworth

(Ch. 1712)

*An inter vivos gift by a London freeman is not a fraud on the custom of the City.*

*The London custom of widow's chamber applies even though the freeman lives outside the City.*

*The value of a London widow's chamber is one-fourth of the value of the deceased freeman's personal property.*

British Library MS. Hargrave 80, f. 130

The husband of the plaintiff and uncle of the defendant was a freeman of London and, having no child, about three or four months before his death and being then in an ill state of health with the approbation of the plaintiff, made his will, by which he gave considerable legacies to the plaintiff and the residuum unto the defendant. Soon after making his will, he gave £1500 sterling to the defendant to advance him in the way of his trade and directed £300 Bank stock, which he had in the hands of Mr. Kech, a scrivener, to be sold, intending the £300 for the defendant. And £200, part of it, was paid by Mr. Kech in his uncle's lifetime to him but, the transfer books being shut up, the rest was not disposed of until after his death. And, a little before his death, being told that what he had given his wife was not equal to what she would be entitled to by the custom, he made a codicil and by it gave her farther the sum of £1000. She now brought her bill and, waiving her right under the will and codicil, insisted upon her customary part. And the chief question was whether £1500 and £300 ought to be looked upon as given in fraud of the custom. Upon that head, the case of Turner v. Jenny[1] was cited, which was thus. A freeman of London having but one child, a daughter, and grandchildren by a son, who was dead, made an assignment of a leasehold estate in trust for himself during his life, then, in trust for his grandchildren, and this assignment, though for a provision for his grandchildren by his son, who could not come in with his daughter on the foot of the custom, was set aside as made in fraud of the custom.

But the court distinguished that case from this, there being a trust in that for the freeman during his life, but, here, the money as to all but £100 was paid over to the defendant in his uncle's life and it was proved from his letters that he had the giving of this sum to his nephew to advance him in his trade in his thoughts

[1] *Turner v. Jennings* (1708), 2 Vernon 612, 685, 23 E.R. 1000, 1044, 1 Eq. Cas. Abr. 152, 21 E.R. 952.

for almost a year before his death and it would have been hard to have construed an act of so great generosity and kindness a fraud.

It was urged by *Vernon*, as the defendant ought to be looked upon as a debtor to his uncle for the money thus advanced or, if it should be taken as a gift, that, it being subsequent to the will, that it ought to go in satisfaction of what was given by that, the cases being many where £1000 has been given to one by will and, afterwards, the testator has given £1000 in his lifetime to the same person and that has been adjudged a satisfaction of the £1000 given by the will.

But the court had no regard to either of those cases. It seems hard to make a trust result in the first case to the uncle, the nephew being his nearest relation, and this [was] plainly intended for his advancement. And the last case differs entirely from this, the sum given by will being uncertain, the residuum, and that, as it fell out, much more valuable than the money given in his lifetime.

He then said that the nephew ought not to be in a better case than a child would have been, that, if it had been the case of a child, the money given in his father's lifetime would have excluded him unless the certainty of it appeared or if it did unless he brought [it] into hotchpot.

Lord Keeper [Lord Harcourt], pronouncing his decree, seemed to think the defendant in a better case than a child would have been.

But query whether a child, in this case, would have been excluded, it not being the customary part, but the dead man's part, that the defendant claiming under the will the £100 that was not paid in the uncle's lifetime.

Lord Keeper [Lord Harcourt] would not decree to the defendant the £100, that he considered it as promised to be paid him only by the uncle and not excluded.

The plaintiff demanded her chamber. And it being suggested that her husband was a lodger only in town and had no house furnished anywhere but in the court, *Sir Peter King*, who was the plaintiff's counsel, was asked by My Lord [Lord Harcourt], as Recorder, whether the custom extended to a chamber in the country, and he was not positive whether it did or not.

But the court seemed to be of opinion that, in reason, the custom ought to extend to that as well as to any other personal estate out of London.

The next query was as to the value of the chamber. And to that *Sir Peter King* said, as counsel, that several disorders and inconveniences having arisen from widows' crowding everything they could into the best chamber while their husbands were dying, the City had of late agreed to reduce that to a certainty to prevent those disorders and that it was now the constant practice in the Court of Orphans to estimate the widow's chamber at a fourth part of what the personal estate amounted to, provided that a fourth part did not exceed £100, which they did not allow the widow's chamber to do in any case.

This rule My Lord [Lord Harcourt] held reasonable to check those fraudulent contrivances of the women and to defeat them where they had heaped things together beyond that value, but, if the chamber happened not to be worth a fourth part, he thought it ought not to be made up to them.

[Other copies of this report: Lincoln's Inn MS. Misc. 383, p. 230, Lincoln's Inn MS. Misc. 106, p. 194.]

## 451

## Kitson v. Kitson

(Ch. 1712)

*A widow of a citizen can take both a devise and her customary share unless the devise is inconsistent with the custom of the city and, then, she must elect one or the other.*

British Library MS. Hargrave 80, f. 131

A freeman of London devised part of his real and all his personal estate to his wife for her life with a power to dispose of £500 of it. She brought her bill to have the devise established as to the freehold and moiety of the personal estate and to have the other moiety absolutely under the custom, there being no child. The case of Lawrence *contra* Lawrence[1] was cited, where lands were devised to the wife, part freehold, part copyhold, part leasehold, and yet [it was] ruled this devise was no bar of her dower, there being no expression in the will that it should and the implication not being necessary, and the case of Sir J. Hern's will,[2] where the lady was compelled to abide by the will or the custom, but not to resort to both, and that of Nowis v. Mordant,[3] where a man intended to provide for his children by his will, gave an estate to one, which, afterwards, appeared to be entailed and made a provision for the other two out of his fee simple lands, the two would have taken advantage of the entail to defeat the third and, as to the fee simple lands, would have had the benefit of the will, but were obliged to abide entirely by the will or renounce it quite.

In the principal case, Lord Keeper [Lord Harcourt] declared that the will, as to the personal estate, all which it gave the widow [for] her life only was inconsistent with the custom, which gave her a moiety forever, and, as to that, he decreed her to elect which she would abide by. And she elected her customary part. But the devise of the freehold, he thought was not inconsistent, and, therefore, he established that.

---

[1] *Lawrence v. Lawrence* (1699), 2 Vernon 365, 23 E.R. 829, 2 Freeman 234, 22 E.R. 1180, 3 Brown P.C. 483, 1 E.R. 1448, 1 Eq. Cas. Abr. 218, 21 E.R. 1002, 2 Eq. Cas. Abr. 386, 388, 22 E.R. 330, 331, *sub nom. Lawrence v. Dodwell*, 1 Lord Raymond 438, 91 E.R. 1190, 3 Lord Raymond 151, 92 E.R. 615, 1 Lutwyche 734, 125 E.R. 384.

[2] *Herne v. Herne* (1706), 2 Vernon 555, 23 E.R. 959, 1 Eq. Cas. Abr. 203, 21 E.R. 991.

[3] *Noyes v. Mordaunt* (1706), 2 Vernon 581, 23 E.R. 978, Gilbert Rep. 2, 25 E.R. 2, Precedents in Chancery 265, 24 E.R. 128, 1 Eq. Cas. Abr. 273, 21 E.R. 1041.

[Other copies of this report: Lincoln's Inn MS. Misc. 383, p. 232.]

[Other reports of this case: Precedents in Chancery 351, 24 E.R. 164, Gilbert Rep. 28, 25 E.R. 20, 2 Eq. Cas. Abr. 275, 22 E.R. 232.]

## 452

## Button v. Powell

(Ch. 1712)

*In this case, the bonds in issue were not set aside, the plaintiff having unclean hands.*

Lincoln's Inn MS. Misc. 10, p. 169, pl. 2

24 November 1712. Sir John Button, baronet v. Rachel and Mary Powell.

The plaintiff, being upwards of eighty years of age, was prevailed on by the defendants to give each of them a bond for the payment of £500, which bonds were executed at The Angel Inn at Marlborough.

And, now, he brought his bill to be relieved against these bonds, suggesting that he was superannuated and, by reason of his great age and infirmities, impaired very much in his understanding and not capable to transact and manage his own affairs and that he had been prevailed on by the said defendants to meet them at Marlborough and other places and had been inveigled by the defendants after they had given him strong liquors to execute these bonds.

The defendants, by their answer, did insist that the bonds were freely and voluntarily given and did pretend some merit by reason of services formerly done the plaintiff by their father.

It appeared by the proofs that Sir John was a very weak man and, both before and after the time he gave the bonds, had done many foolish, mad, and extravagant actions which plainly showed him to be a man not right in his understanding. And there was some proof of some obscene words which fell from him when he was in the defendants' company at Marlborough. It was also proved that, the next day after he executed the bonds, he said he would do the same thing again if it was to be done.

Upon the hearing, the Master of the Rolls [Trevor] declared that, as this case was circumstanced, the bonds could not be set aside because they were voluntarily entered into without any practice or circumvention on the part of the defendants and, on the part of the plaintiff, it appeared that he had filthy and unclean thoughts and lustful intentions and all his transactions showed that he was libidinously and lecherously given and the plaintiff's iniquity in this case does take away his equity. And such courses and temptations are of very ill example and not fit to be countenanced, but the plaintiff ought to pay for the public scandal he has given. And he decreed that, upon paying principal, interest, and costs in this court and at law, the defendants acknowledge satisfaction on the judgments they had obtained upon the bonds.

The plaintiff died soon after the decree, and his executors revived. And, upon a rehearing before Lord Harcourt, the decree was affirmed.

## 453

## King v. Withers

(Ch. 1712)

*Where a legacy is given at age twenty-one or marriage with a condition, the condition does not apply if the legacy vests upon becoming twenty-one.*

*Where a husband sues for his wife's legacy, a court of equity will not give relief unless he makes a reasonable settlement to his wife's separate equitable use.*

Lincoln's Inn MS. Misc. 10, p. 139

6 December 1712.

The plaintiff's wife's father, by his will, gives her £2500 to be paid her at her age of twenty-one or day of marriage. And, then, he adds a clause that, if she should marry or enter into a treaty of marriage in the lifetime of his wife without her consent first had in writing under her hand, then £500 part of the portion should be applied towards the payment of the debts. And he subjects his real estate to the payment both of his debts and this portion.

The plaintiff's wife attained her age of twenty-one and then married without the consent of her mother. And, now, she and her husband bring their bill for the portion. And if the £500 was forfeited was the question.

It was insisted on for the plaintiffs that the portion was vested at twenty-one and that the daughter might then have demanded it, and, had she received it and, afterward, married without consent, the court would never have ordered the £500 to be paid back again, that the condition could only extend to a marriage before twenty-one, for, when she was twenty-one, she was capable to judge for herself and the testator could never intend to extend the proviso further. And, besides, here was no bequest over, and, therefore, [it was] only a condition *in terrorem*.

On the other side, it was said that, had the wife received her portion at twenty-one and married afterwards without consent, the court might have fetched back the £500, that this was a reasonable condition being to keep children within the bounds of their duty, that here was a devise over, for the £500 is devised for the payment of debts, which is as much a devise over as if it had been actually devised to the son, whose estate is now to be exonerated by it. And, as this portion is charged upon the real estate and must be raised out of that fund (for it is agreed the personal estate is not sufficient to pay the debts), it must be considered as money issuing out of land, and a charge upon land is of the same nature as land itself. And, had this condition been annexed to a devise of land, it would have been a forfeiture of the land to have married without the consent of the mother, according to Fry and Porter's Case.[1]

Lord Keeper [Lord Harcourt]: I do not think this is to be considered as a devise of land, nor do I think, as this case is, there is any devise over, for it is not pretended that the land is not sufficient to pay the debts. And, therefore, I am of the opinion that the plaintiffs are entitled to the whole portion, for I must consider it as if there was no devise over.

Let the Master certify what provision the plaintiff is able to make for his wife, and, then, I will give directions how the money shall be paid. Costs [are to be paid] out of the estate.

British Library MS. Hargrave 80, f. 131v

The testator bequeathed £2500 to his daughter at twenty-one or marriage which should first happen provided that, if she should marry during her mother's life and without her consent in writing attested by two credible witnesses, that then £500, part thereof, should go to be disposed of for payment of his debts and the performance of his will. He directed the £2500 to be raised out of his real estate, which he subjected to the payment for his debts and legacies, and he appointed the mother guardian of his daughter during her minority. The daughter married King after twenty-one without the knowledge or consent of the mother, who was afterward reconciled and declared her approbation of the marriage in the answer to the bill of King, the plaintiff, and for the £2500.

And in court at the hearing, *Sir Thomas Powys* and the Attorney General [*Northey*], for the plaintiff, said that conditions to restrain marriage being annexed to legacies are held by Swinburn[2] to be generally unlawful and good only with certain limitations such as not to marry a particular person or without the consent of a certain person, and that it was very unusual to restrain marriage without consent after twenty-one, that, in this case, the legacy vested at twenty-one and the condition ought to be applied to the case of marriage only under twenty-one and her entitling herself to the legacy by that, and that there was no devise over, the disposition for payment of his debts and the performance of his will being no more than the law would have said, nor was there any deficiency in the fund provided for that purpose.

---

[1] *Fry v. Porter* (1670), 2 Chancery Reports 26, 21 E.R. 606, 1 Chancery Cases 138, 22 E.R. 731, 1 Modern 300, 86 E.R. 898, 1 Eq. Cas. Abr. 111, 282, 333, 21 E.R. 918, 1047, 1083, *sub nom. Williams, ex dem. Porter v. Fry*, 1 Modern 86, 86 E.R. 752, 1 Freeman 31, 89 E.R. 26, 2 Levinz 21, 83 E.R. 434, 1 Ventris 199, 86 E.R. 135, T. Raymond 236, 83 E.R. 122, 2 Keble 756, 787, 814, 867, 84 E.R. 478, 498, 515, 548, 3 Keble 19, 84 E.R. 570.

[2] H. Swinburne, *Brief Treatise of Testaments and Last Wills.*

*Vernon*, for the heir at law: If the proviso had been general, it might have borne that construction. But, here, time is expressed, *viz.* during her mother's life. I agree that the legacy vested at twenty-one, but the proviso may direct it, and there is a sufficient devise over and such as equity will favor, it being in effect to exonerate the whole estate.

*How*: If such a condition were annexed to lands and broken, the party might recover at law, and equity would give no relief. This issues out of lands and is to be considered as such.

Lord Keeper [Lord Harcourt]: I cannot fall in with the common opinion that conditions of this kind are only *in terrorem*. The legacy here is not considered as land but as a sum in gross. And there being no deficiency in the fund, there is no devise over. The testator in the considering his creditors only as they are amply provided for, the legacy was to vest in all events at twenty-one or marriage. And it is reasonable to confine the condition to a marriage under twenty-one. She could not have entitled herself to it by a marriage under that age without having performed the condition, but she claims now by being twenty-one and the clause that places her under the guardian's part of her mother falls in with this construction. Let the legacy be brought in before the Master, and let him certify what settlement the husband is able and proposes to make on his wife, and let the plaintiff have the costs out of the estate.

[Other copies of this report: Lincoln's Inn MS. Misc. 383, p. 233.]

[Other reports of this case: Precedents in Chancery 19, 24 E.R. 163, 1 Eq. Cas. Abr. 112, 21 E.R. 920, note also Cases *tempore* Talbot 117, 25 E.R. 693, Gilbert Rep. 26, 25 E.R. 19, 3 Peere Williams 414, 24 E.R. 1125, Precedents in Chancery 348, 24 E.R. 163, 2 Eq. Cas. Abr. 656, 22 E.R. 551.]

## 454

## Talman v. Plukenett

(Ch. 1712)

*A question in this case was whether, after a final decree and then the infant comes of age, he can re-open the case and plead a different defense or whether he is limited to filing a new lawsuit.*

*A testator can devise a conditional estate.*

British Library MS. Hargrave 80, f. 132

In this case, there was a decree at the Rolls *nisi* against an infant. And, after he came to age, an ill defense appearing to have been made for him, he obtained an order from the Master of the Rolls [Trevor] for leave to put in a new answer, by which he put several other matters in issue and examined to them. But the plaintiff did not join with him in that examination.

Upon an appeal before Lord Keeper [Lord Harcourt], *Vernon* and *How* insisted that the practice was wholly irregular and would make suits where infants or married women are concerned endless, that, if an infant came of age or a wife was unmarried after an answer put in and before publication, they might, if they apprehended an improvident defense had been made for them, apply for leave to put in a new answer but not after publication, when the strength of a cause was known, much less after a decree, and, though the court indulges infants with six months after they come to age to show cause against the decree, they are tied down to show cause out of the record and upon the face of the pleadings and decree.

And, if any fraud or contrivance has been used in putting an ill answer for an infant, *Vernon* said that he may come by an original bill on that matter to be relieved against the decree and that there were several precedents of that but none of putting in a new answer after the decree.

*Sawyer*, for the defendant, said there were precedents to support this cause.

But the new matter put in issue by the second answer being not sufficient to vary the former decree, Lord Keeper [Lord Harcourt] did not determine that point, but he seemed to incline to Vernon's opinion.

The single question upon the merits was this. A man devised his real estate to trustees to pay debts and to pay the surplus profits and convey the estate to his son when he should attain his age of twenty-three and, if he died before twenty-three, he devised over; the son, after twenty-one and before twenty-three, made his will and thereby devised his estate and lived until he was past twenty-three.

Lord Keeper [Lord Harcourt] held clearly that the devise was good.

[Other copies of this report: Lincoln's Inn MS. Misc. 383, p. 234, Lincoln's Inn MS. Misc. 106, p. 197.]

British Library MS. Hargrave 83, p. 33, pl. 2

Upon a petition *ex parte*, an order was made by Sir John Trevor, Master of the Rolls, that the infant might be at liberty to take his former answer off the file and put in a new answer. This was done, and the infant so much bettered his case by the new answer that a decree was made for him.

Against this decree, there was an appeal, and, in the petition of appeal, this order was *inter alia* complained of. But Lord Harcourt reversed the decree upon the merits, and this matter did not come in question before him.

[Note Talman v. Pluckenett (1719), Lincoln's Inn MS. Misc. 11, p. 113, pl. 1.]

## 455

## Attorney General, ex rel. Watford School v. Shelly

(Ch. 1712)

*In a suit to enforce a charge on land, the plaintiff need not sue all of the terre tenants, but any of the terre tenants who are not sued can voluntarily intervene.*

1 Salkeld 163, 91 E.R. 151

Sir R. Combe devised an annuity out of his land for the maintenance of Watford School. And, now, upon a bill in Chancery brought by the Attorney General on the behalf of the charity, it was objected that all the terre tenants of the lands charged ought to be brought before the court.

*Sed curia contra*, for every part of the land is liable and the charity ought not to be put to this difficulty, but the terre tenants may, if they seek a contribution, undertake to make them parties to the information or help themselves by such course as they think fit.

## 456

## Norman v. Fagg

(Ch. 1713)

*Where the consideration for a land sales contract fails, the contract is cancelled.*

Lincoln's Inn MS. Misc. 10, p. 142

28 January 1712[/13].

The defendant was possessed of a lease for years determinable upon the death of one Chapman. In November, the plaintiff and the defendant enter into articles that the defendant should assign this lease to the plaintiff in consideration of £120. The plaintiff pays £5 in part [payment] upon the sealing of the articles and covenants to pay the remainder upon the 28th of December following, at which time, the assignment was to be made.

Chapman dies at the beginning of December, and the plaintiff exhibits his bill to have the articles delivered up.

Mr. *Vernon*, for the plaintiff, insisted that he ought not to pay his money in regard, by the act of God, it was not in the power of the defendant to make good his part of the articles, the lease being determined. And, therefore, the articles ought to be delivered up.

He cited a case touching lands in Port Royal in Jamaica, which, after a man had articled to sell, were swallowed up by an earthquake, and, a bill being brought, the articles were decreed to be delivered up, and that decree was afterwards affirmed in the House of Lords.[1]

Serjeant *Hooper*, for the defendant: By the articles, the plaintiff had an equitable right to this lease and ought to be considered as though the purchase had been actually completed, and, since he agreed to purchase a contingent interest, he ought to be the loser if the contingency has happened, especially since the defendant has been in no fault. And, therefore, he insisted that the bill should stand dismissed. If the plaintiff can defend himself at law, let him go there if he pleases.

Mr. Baron Price: It would be against conscience to let the defendant loose to go to law. The plaintiff has been guilty of no neglect. He was not obliged to pay his money before the 25th. Now, before that time, the *cestui que vie* dies. What has the defendant to convey? He has no estate either in law or equity. The articles are mutual, and it would be against conscience that one should pay his money and that the other should not perform his part of the bargain.

He decreed the articles to be delivered up and releases given on both sides.

## 457

## Markant v. Twisden

(Ch. 1713)

*In this case, the words of the will in issue did not pass the testator's real estate.*

Lincoln's Inn MS. Misc. 10, p. 144

Markham v. Twisden; 4 February 1712[/13].

A.B., after several money legacies, gives all the rest of his estate, chattels real and personal to his wife, and he makes her executrix.

The question was if the reversion of the wife's jointure and other lands, of which the testator was seised in fee, passed by this general devise.

Mr. *Vernon*: 'All my estate' being coupled with 'chattels', nothing more could be meant by it than all his chattels, real and personal. It is true, had he given away any lands before, it might have been of another consideration. But here is nothing but money legacies given away before.

Attorney General [*Northey*]: The word 'estate' is very comprehensive. A devise of all my estate, both real and personal, will not only pass land but carries an estate in fee in that land. And this was the Case of the Duke of Bolton and Lord Bridgwater.[2]

---

1 *Cass v. Rudell* (1692), 2 Vernon 280, 23 E.R. 781, 1 Eq. Cas. Abr. 25, 21 E.R. 847.

2 *Countess of Bridgewater v. Duke of Bolton* (1704), 6 Modern 106, 87 E.R. 866, Holt K.B. 281, 90 E.R. 1054, 1 Salkeld 236, 91 E.R. 209, 1 Eq. Cas. Abr. 177, 21 E.R. 970, 2 Eq. Cas. Abr. 299, 22 E.R. 252.

Lord Keeper [Lord Harcourt]: I am of the opinion no freehold land passes by this devise. There is no disposition of any lands before in the will, and, therefore, I think, by the word 'estate', nothing more could be intended than all the rest of his personal estate, or, as the words following explain it, all the rest of his chattels, real and personal.

British Library MS. Hargrave 80, f. 134, pl. 2

The testator gave several pecuniary legacies but made no devise of his real estate. Then followed these words, 'all the rest of my estate chattels real and personal, I give and devise to my wife, whom I make executrix' etc. It was urged from the word 'devise', which is properly applicable to a real estate, that his estate of inheritance should pass to his wife, especially the testator's being a lawyer, that, otherwise, the word 'estate' must be rejected, for the subsequent words are sufficient to carry all the personal estate and that no word ought to be rejected unnecessarily.

On the other hand, it was said the word 'rest' was plainly relative to what went before and that he had before taken notice only of his personal estate and that the subsequent words 'chattels real and personal' were only explanatory of the word 'estate'.

Lord Keeper [Lord Harcourt] took time to consider of it and, then, decreed that the lands of inheritance did not pass, though they had passed by the word 'estate', he did not seem to doubt but the whole inheritance would have passed without words of inheritance. The Case of Murray and Wise, 5 Ann.,[1] was cited where a testator gave £30 to his heir and then, without mentioning lands before, gave all the rest of his estate real and personal to his wife and [it was] decreed that the inheritance passed to her.

[Other copies of this report: Lincoln's Inn MS. Misc. 383, p. 237, pl. 2, Lincoln's Inn MS. Misc. 106, p. 201, pl. 2.]

[Other reports of this case: Gilbert Rep. 30, 25 E.R. 22, 1 Eq. Cas. Abr. 212, 21 E.R. 997.]

## 458

## Lanyon v. Williams

(Ch. 1713–1714)

*In this case, a debtor refused to bar an entail in favor of his creditor and died in prison for his contempt of court for such refusal, and, thereupon, the remainderman's estate in the land became vested, and the court of equity upheld the remainderman's title.*

[1] *Murray v. Wise* (1706), 2 Vernon 564, 23 E.R. 968, Precedents in Chancery 264, 24 E.R. 127, 1 Eq. Cas. Abr. 177, 21 E.R. 970.

Lincoln's Inn MS. Coxe 89, vol. 3, pt. 2, p. 15

5 February 1712[/13].

The defendant's father, in 1668, made a mortgage to the plaintiff's father of the lands in question for 1000 years. And the mortgage was by a decree in 1681 foreclosed, and [he was] decreed to suffer a common recovery to bar the entail. But the mortgagor died in prison in contempt for not performing the decree. The mortgagee having sometime after lost his mortgage deed, the heir of the mortgagor brought an [action of] ejectment for the recovery of the possession and obtained a verdict at law, upon which the plaintiffs, who claimed under the mortgage, brought their bill to be quieted in their possession.

The defendant insisted that William Williams, father of the mortgagor and grandfather of the defendant, upon marriage, by deed dated 31 May 1635, settled these lands to the use of himself and the heirs male and female of his intended wife and, for default of such issue, to the heirs of the body of the grandfather, that Thomas Williams, the defendant's father, was the eldest son of the marriage and the defendant [was] the eldest son of said Thomas and entitled under the settlement in 1635, his father having suffered no recovery to dock the entail, and that the mortgagee was a witness to the deed of 1635.

Upon reading the proceedings in the former cause, the indenture of 1635, and endorsement of livery thereon, it was decreed by the Master of the Rolls [TREVOR] that the defendant should try his title under the settlement of 1635 by [an action of] ejectment and was to admit the mortgage deed and, after the trial, to resort back again to the court. An [action of] ejectment was brought, and the defendant obtained a verdict.

Upon the hearing on the equity reserved, the defendant's counsel prayed that the bill might be dismissed with costs.

The plaintiff insisted that the lands for which the verdict was obtained were more than those comprised in the deed of 1635 and, the defendant's father, not performing the decree by not suffering a recovery, had occasioned this suit and, therefore, he hoped the defendant should not have costs.

Upon reading the *postea* and several deeds, the defendant was upon oath to produce before the Master all deeds relating to the lands in question and the Master to see what lands were comprised in the deed of settlement and, as to those, the plaintiff's bill was to be dismissed. And, as to costs, the court gave none except as to the last trial at law and the defendant to be examined on interrogatories and the plaintiff also as to the loss of the said mortgage deed if the defendant thought fit and the plaintiffs not to bring any writ of error but to release errors and to deliver possession of the lands comprised in the deed of settlement in 1635 as the court should direct on hearing the Master's report.

The defendant appealed from this decree to the Lord Chancellor [LORD HARCOURT] as to the producing his deeds before the Master and thereby subjecting his title to a new examination which tended to impeach his verdict at law upon a mere suggestion that part of the lands were purchased subsequent to the deed of 1635, which was never mentioned until the hearing on the equity reserved. Besides, the defendant, being by the decretal order to admit all the lands in the plaintiffs' possession to be contained in the deed of mortgage, could recover only what he made title to under the deed in 1635 and also appeared.

As to the matter of costs and on a hearing before Lord Chancellor [Lord Harcourt] 5 February 12 Anne [1714], the plaintiffs' bill was absolutely dismissed. And, so far as the bill sought to impeach the deed of entail or to establish the mortgage, the Master [was] to tax the defendant his costs. And, as to the costs at law, the defendant should be at liberty to proceed at law for them and to take back his deposit.

## 459

## Milkins v. Bythesea

(Ch. 1713)

*A resulting trust can be proved by parol evidence.*
*The ecclesiastical courts have no jurisdiction over trusts.*

Lincoln's Inn MS. Misc. 10, p. 147

10 February 1712[/13].

The defendant [Bithersey] and another were made executors and residuary legatees in a will. And the bill was to have an account of the testator's personal estate, it being insisted that the executors were only trustees for the plaintiff's wife, who was the testator's sister.

The bill was likewise to have a conveyance of some lands called Barhams, which were purchased in the testator's name, but there was no deed of trust.

It was fully proved that the testator declared that the executors were only trustees for his sister and so intended by him and that one of the executors renounced and declared that they were only trustees and that the other said when the inventory was taken that the personal estate did not belong to him.

And the question was upon the Statute of Frauds and Perjuries,[1] which says a clause in a will shall be revoked but by a writing.

And it was insisted for the defendant that, if the executors should be decreed to be trustees for the plaintiffs, it would be to alter the will upon parol proof, for, by the will, they are executors and residuary legatees in their own right.

Indeed, in the Case of Mr. Thinne of Egham,[2] he was decreed to be an executor in trust upon parol proof, but there was fraud. In that case, Mr. Thinne's

---

[1] Stat. 29 Car. II, c. 3 (*SR*, V, 839–842).

[2] *Thynn v. Thynn* (Ch. 1685), 1 Vernon 296, 23 E.R. 479, 1 Eq. Cas. Abr. 380, 21 E.R. 1116, Chancery Repts. *tempore* Jac. II, 47.

father, being about to make his will and his wife executrix, his son desired him to make him executor, which he said would be a credit to him and that it should be all one, for he would be a trustee for his mother and would account to her. After this, he sets up for himself and denied the trust. But, it being fully proved, the court decreed the trust as being a manifest fraud. But it was said this was the only case of this kind which had ever been in the court.

Lord Keeper [Lord Harcourt]: As to the land, it is fully proved that the wife paid the consideration money and received the profits of that estate, and, therefore, here was a resulting trust for the plaintiff's wife.

As to the executorship, the proofs are very strong that the executors were only trustees, and, therefore, surely, the Statute cannot stand in the way. The defendant must account for the personal estate.

British Library MS. Hargrave 80, f. 137v, pl. 1

In this case, *Sir Thomas Powys* insisted that a resulting trust ought to arise from something appearing on the face of the deed itself not by matter *dehors* supported by parol proof, as if, in consideration of £500 paid by C., A. conveys lands to B. and his heirs to the use of B. and his heirs, there, the consideration appearing within the deed, a trust will result to C., but, if the foundation of the resulting trust was left to be proved by parol, the Statute of Frauds would easily be eluded.

But Lord Keeper [Lord Harcourt] overruled the objection and admitted of parol evidence of the payment of the consideration money and perception of profits of the plaintiff and of the admission of the person under whom the defendant claimed that he was but a trustee to be a sufficient evidence of a resulting trust to the plaintiff.

The Case of Mr. Thyne of Eggham's will was cited by the counsel thus. Mr. Thyne intended to make his wife executrix, but his son desired him to let him have the credit of being his executor and promised to account to the wife, upon which Mr. Thyne named his son executor in the will and, though there was nothing in writing to build a trust on for the wife, the son was nevertheless decreed to be barely a trustee for her. But it was said that this decree was founded upon the son's fraud in this etc.

Lord Keeper [Lord Harcourt] said the ecclesiastical courts have no authority to judge matters of trust.

[Other copies of this report: Lincoln's Inn MS. Misc. 383, p. 243, Lincoln's Inn MS. Misc. 106, p. 208.]

## 460

## Coates v. Watford

(Ch. 1713)

*A contract to educate a child is an obligation to educate according to the child's social quality and condition.*

British Library MS. Hargrave 81, f. 60

15 February.

The plaintiff, upon his marriage with defendant's testator, who was a widow and had two infant daughters, covenants to maintain, educate, and bring up the said children at his own expense until they should attain the full age and be married and that their mother may dispose of £400 of her own fortune, who, afterwards, by her will, devises the £400 to the defendant in trust for her two daughters and, if they should both die before their full age and marriage, then she gives £300 of it to the defendant and the other £100 to the plaintiff, her husband. And she dies. The plaintiff brings his bill to know how the defendant has disposed of the money that it might be secured for the benefit of the children and to answer the contingent legacy to him.

*Curia* [LORD HARCOURT]: The bill is proper because of the contingent interest which the plaintiff has in the money and, as to the words in the covenant to maintain, educate, and bring up, they must be construed according to the quality and condition of the parties. And their fortune being but £200 apiece when grown up, their education should be adapted to and proper for their circumstance. And as probably they must be obliged to go to service, the father-in-law, by those words in his covenant, should only be obliged besides their maintenance to have them taught to read and sew, but not to write.

[Other copies of this report: British Library MS. Hargrave 82, f. 58; British Library MS. Hargrave 77, f. 16v, pl. 1, British Library MS. Hargrave 303, f. 30v, pl. 2.]

## 461

## Wareing v. Wareing

(Ch. 1713)

*In this case, maintenance for children was ordered by the court.*

British Library MS. Hargrave 77, f. 13v, pl. 2

No interest [being] provided, let the child have part of the principal. [It was] heard before the Master of the Rolls [and] reheard before the Lord Chancellor. The trustee allowed the principal.

*Vernon*: [There is] no interest but from the time the duty arises, payable only in respect of the defendant's not complying and, where an estate is charged, to arise as soon as may be convenient. It is but to have it ready to answer when payable. And the parties [are] to have six month's time to do it. And interest only from the time the computation of as late is not the method, for, if this case had been heard and no portion had been given, this court had given one.

*How*: The agreement of the parties is to be the measure of the judgment of the court, and it cannot enlarge nor abridge the agreement of the parties by the settlement. No maintenance or interest is thought to be provided for. And, therefore, they must take the portion upon the terms they are given by.

*Curia*: This is a strong case for maintenance. No pretense of interest is another circumstance. The testator gives them an apartment in the house for three years. He did not intend they should starve there.

[Other copies of this report: British Library MS. Hargrave 303, f. 23v.]

## 462

## Palmer v. Allicock

(Ch. 1713)

*The question in this case was whether a voluntary conveyance should be set aside.*

British Library MS. Hargrave 77, f. 13v, pl. 3

The father dies intestate and leaves a child. Though no administration was taken by the child, which, afterwards, dies, the plaintiff went as representative of the child, not of the father.

*Sir Joseph Jekyll*: T.B. heard in this court and, afterwards, went to trial. [It was] decreed that a voluntary covenant made by one at the time indebted is a fraudulent conveyance and, as against creditors, was void. Here, the conveyance to the lady, then another's wife, was a voluntary [one]. The now lord is a purchaser for a valuable consideration under his father's marriage articles and is a creditor in respect of the breach of the articles, by which the estate is to be settled on the issue of the marriage and was to be £950 and was deficient £150 *per annum*, for which he ought to have satisfaction, and, against that satisfaction, a voluntary conveyance shall not stand.

[ . . . ] the above [cases] and several others in this court and, though there be not any articles, express words of covenant, as covenants, articles, agreements, or promises, yet where there are several cases in Roll's reports.

[Other copies of this report: British Library MS. Hargrave 303, f. 24.]

## 463
## Fisher v. Hawley
## Attorney General v. Hawley
(Ch. 1713)

*A court of equity will order a copyhold to be sold in favor of a charity, but not a legatee.*

*In this case, the assets of a decedent's estate were marshalled so as to provide for creditors, legatees, and charities so far as possible.*

Lincoln's Inn MS. Misc. 384, p. 1, pl. 1

3 March 1712/13.

*Jekyll*, for the plaintiff: A charity will charge a copyhold estate and also an entailed [one]. A want of a surrender will be supplied for a charity as debts, but not in favor of a legatee.

*Vernon*: A court of equity ought not to take away from an heir to give to a remoter relation. 1 Salk. 187, Kettle v. Townsend,[1] a surrender of a copyhold was not supplied for a grandchild. There is no precedent that assets have been marshalled and a surrender supplied in favor of a legatee only.

Lord Keeper [LORD HARCOURT]: The copyhold estate must be sold to satisfy the charity only and not the other legacies. That being no surrender, the freehold lands devised for the payment of debts and legacies must be equally subject to the charity and the other legacies, for I do not know that a charity is to have a preference to the other legacies where the fund is equally subject, but all must abate in proportion. If there be a deficiency, the rest of the charity must be charged on the entailed estate. *Vide* recovery made good.

British Library MS. Hargrave 80, f. 139

A man, seised of a freehold estate of £33 *per annum* entitled to a copyhold of an inheritance of £26 *per annum* and also to a reversion in tail expectant upon an estate for life of lands of £80 under a marriage settlement and being possessed of some personal estate, made his will and, thereby, devised £40 *per annum* to several charities forever, two annuities of £10 *per annum* each to two poor relations, and £1100 to eleven other poor relations, and charged all his estates in possession or in reversion with the payment of these charities and legacies. The personal and freehold estate out of settlement not being sufficient to satisfy the legacies and charities, the legatees sought by their bill to have their bequests so marshalled that the charities might be satisfied out of the copyhold and entailed estates and the freehold and personal, by that means, left entire for their satisfaction. And

[1] *Kettle v. Townsend*, 1 Salkeld 187, 91 E.R. 170, also 1 Eq. Cas. Abr. 123, 21 E.R. 929.

the Attorney General's bill was for satisfaction of the charities generally out of the whole estate.

It was insisted for the legatees that, where a man has a power to dispose of an estate by any regular conveyance, be it by fine or recovery etc., and makes an appointment of that estate to a charitable use, equity, since the Statute of Elizabeth,[1] will make good that appointment and supply the want of a recovery etc. or other defects in the conveyance that, in this case, the testator might have barred the estate tail by a fine and subjected the copyhold to be disposed of by his will by surrender and that, therefore, he having expressly subjected all his lands in possession or reversion, which words could be satisfied only by the entailed lands, to the charities, equity would make them liable to the charities, *quod fuit concessum* by Lord Keeper [Lord Harcourt].

And by *Sir Thomas Powys*, for the defendant, it was urged for the legatees that the real estate unsettled and the personal estate not being sufficient to satisfy both the charities and the legacies and the entail and copyhold land being chargeable with the charities and not with the legacies and the intention of the testator being manifest that all his lands should be charged and both legacies and charities satisfied, equity would marshal them in such manner that the intent of the testator should be fully performed, which could not be in this case otherwise than by laying the charities upon the entailed and copyhold estates and the legacies upon the rest, that, if the testator had particularly charged them in that manner, there could have been no doubt of their having been well charged, that, though he had done it in general terms, yet his intent being evident, equity ought to distribute the charge in such a manner as would be more agreeable to his intent.

On the other side, it was said that, though where a mortgagee or a judgment creditor, who have a lien upon the real estate, sweep away the personal assets, equity will let creditors by simple contract and, I think, legatees stand in their places, yet there was not the same reason for doing it in this case where both stood singly on the foot of the will, that the defendants were purchasers of the entailed lands, they claiming as issue in tail and under a marriage settlement, and that, if the legatees could not affect those lands at law, equity would never interpose in their favor against purchasers.

Lord Keeper [Lord Harcourt] decreed that the copyhold lands should in the first place be applied to the charities, that what remained unsatisfied an estimate should be put upon, and that the charities and legacies charged equally on the freehold estate unsettled and the personal estate, and, if they were deficient, they should abate in proportion, and what the charities suffered by that abatement should be made good to them out of the entailed estate. A mortgage, which was of the copyhold estate and the fine paid for admittance upon the descent,

[1] Stat. 43 Eliz. I, c. 4 (*SR*, IV, 968–970).

he directed to be satisfied out of the copyhold estate, that the personal [estate] should not be diminished by their being turned upon it.

*Vernon* [said] that, in the case of Peacock v. Spooner,[1] a term was limited in consideration of marriage to the husband for life, remainder to the heirs of the body of the husband and wife, remainder to the heirs of the body of the wife; in this case, the last remainder was supported and the issue of the wife looked upon as purchasers. But even in these cases, this has been overruled by the Lord Keeper and the remainder decreed to be void.

[Other copies of this report: Lincoln's Inn MS. Misc. 383, p. 246, Lincoln's Inn MS. Misc. 106, p. 213.]

## 464

## Earl of Warrington v. Booth

(Ch. 1713)

*The question in this case was whether a marriage brokage bond should be enforced.*

Lincoln's Inn MS. Misc. 384, p. 1, pl. 2

16 March 1713.

A bill [was brought] to be relieved against a brokage bond of £1000. The defendant pleaded the Statute of Limitations[2] and answered that he had paid the whole sum to J. for procuring the match.

*Jekyll*, for the plaintiff: We are proper here, for an action on the case will not lie. B. enters into a bond to J., and the plaintiff gives B. a counterbond. It is not like an action of debt or trover.

*Howe*: If A. be bound to B. and employ C. to pay B., who does not, and, thereupon, B. sues A., who does not discover the fraud until after the time limited by the Statute, it does not extend to it.

*Curia*: If the plaintiff has since discovered that the defendant did not really pay any money for him, he may be relieved notwithstanding the Statute. Save the benefit of the plea.

[Affirmed on appeal: 4 Brown P.C. 163, 2 E.R. 111, Chancery Cases *tempore* Harcourt, p. 431.]

[1] *Peacock v. Spooner* (1688–1690), 2 Vernon 43, 195, 23 E.R. 638, 727, 2 Freeman 114, 22 E.R. 1094, Chancery Repts. *tempore* Jac. II, 429.

[2] Stat. 21 Jac. I, c. 16 (*SR*, IV, 1222–1223).

## 465

## Newman v. Warner

(Ch. 1713)

*A lost will can be established in a court of equity, and a legacy can be ordered to be paid without any probate of the will.*

British Library MS. Hargrave 80, f. 134, pl. 1

A will relating to the personal estate was destroyed by the defendant's contrivance, who was one of the next of kin and obtained administration and made a distribution. This bill was brought several years after by the plaintiff, who was an infant when the will was destroyed, for a legacy, which was decreed, though no proof was ever made of the will in the spiritual court.

[Other copies of this report: Lincoln's Inn MS. Misc. 383, p. 237, pl. 1, Lincoln's Inn MS. Misc. 106, p. 201, pl. 1.]

## 466

## Davis v. Peers

(Ch. 1713)

*A bill of review lies for errors in an account that are apparent on the record.*

British Library MS. Hargrave 80, f. 134v, pl. 1

A bill was brought in the name of infants against executors in trust for an account. They annexed an account for a schedule to their answers, and that was decreed to be taken as a stated account without reference to a Master.

But Lord Keeper [Lord Harcourt], upon a bill of review brought several years after, partly for the irregularity of the former decree and partly for errors apparent in the account, reversed the former decree and opened the account. Now upon a rehearing, he affirmed his own decree.

*Vernon* said that, in cases by consent, accounts had been afterwards taken, though they had been referred to and stated by a master. Query.

*How* cited the Case of Danvers and Hickeringall, where an executor had a specific legacy and two were equally entitled to the surplus; upon a distribution, one of them made up and stated accounts with the executor. And he being the proper party with whom it ought to be stated, the court, upon a bill brought by the other, would not lay the account entirely open but only gave him leave to surcharge or falsify.

[Other copies of this report: Lincoln's Inn MS. Misc. 383, p. 238, pl. 1, Lincoln's Inn MS. Misc. 106, p. 202.]

## 467

## Hele v. Bond

(Ch. 1713)

*Where a power of appointment is not renewed in a deed revoking uses, it is gone and cannot be used to declare uses in a later deed.*

British Library MS. Hargrave 80, f. 135

A tenant for life, remainder to A. for life, remainder to B. in tail, remainder to the right heirs of the tenant for life, with power to him at any time or times during his life, by deed etc., to revoke the use limited to B. and appoint new uses and to revoke those new uses and appoint others and so *toties quoties*, the tenant for life by deed reciting his whole power *in haec verba* revoked the uses to A. and appointed other uses not reserving expressly by that deed a new power of revocation and then, by a subsequent deed, revoked the uses of the second deed and limited others. The tenant for life being dead and A. [being] dead without issue, the question was whether anyone could take under the limitations in the last deed.

*Sir Thomas Powys* insisted that a power of revocation once executed is at an end unless renewed. And for that propose, he cited Digs's Case, 1 Reports 173 B; 1 Ventris 198; 2 Rolle's *Abridgement*, 262; Beckwith's Case, Lane 118, 119; 1 Siderfin 243, 244, 2 Keble 269, 270; Jones and Countess of Manchester.[1]

*Hooper*: If a tenant for life with a power to lease assigns his estate, the power is determined.

*Sir Peter King*: *Infinitum in jure reprobatur*; there is no express limitation to the power here. And, therefore, it must have a reasonable construction. Before Digges's Case, it was doubted whether a man could revoke by parcels, and before Beckwith's [Case] whether he could reserve a new power in the deed by which he revoked the old and limited new uses. The express reservation of a power here to revoke *toties quoties* was made to obviate those doubts. But here, as well as in Beckwith's Case, if the power were intended to be continued, it should have been expressly reserved in the second deed, that, if the power were well executed in the third deed, yet those limitations coming in the place of the use limited to A. in tail could have no longer continuance than that in whose place they stood

[1] *Digges v. Palmer* (1598–1600), 1 Coke Rep. 157, 76 E.R. 352, also Moore K.B. 603, 72 E.R. 787, 2 Anderson 205, 123 E.R. 622; *Jones v. Countess of Manchester* (1672), 1 Ventris 197, 86 E.R. 133; *Becket's Case* (Ex. 1610–1612), 2 Rolle, Abr., *Powers*, p. 262, pl. B, 2, Lane 91, 118, 145 E.R. 325, 347, also Exch. Repts. 1604–1648, p. 83; *Ward v. Lenthall* (1667), 1 Siderfin 343, 82 E.R. 1146, 2 Keble 269, 84 E.R. 167.

might have had and, therefore, ceased upon A.'s dying without issue. For which, he cited the case of Gilmore and Harris, 3d Levinz 213.[1]

*How*: The power to revoke the new uses is void unless inserted in that deed, for, otherwise, a purchaser under that deed might be defeated.

Attorney General [*Northey*] etc.: The reservation here is no more than if he had said his last deed or his last will should direct the uses. The power is and may be ambulatory during life at least, that, in Beckwith's Case, a power of revocation in the second deed was held good though there was no authority expressly given by the first to reserve that power in the second, that, here, it is expressly reserved in the first according to the precedent settled by the Lord Keeper and Rolle to obviate the doubt made in Beckwith's Case. Digges's Case is for us. It is true that a man cannot revoke the new uses without a new power to revoke, but that we have by Beckwith's Case that power must arise out of the first agreement. Here, it arises out of the first deed itself. And the recital in the second deed is a sufficient contrivance of it if it were necessary. If a man, having a power to revoke a use limited to A. in tail, revokes it and limits it to B. in tail, nobody ever thought that B.'s estate would determine on the failure of issue by A.

Lord Keeper [Lord Harcourt]: Is anything more expressed in the first deed than would have been implied without it?

Solicitor General [*Raymond*]: We are in a case of uses. And, where no inconvenience will follow, no rule of law be broken by it, they are always directed according to the intention of the parties. There is no mischief in having a use ambulatory during life nor any greater inconvenience where the second power of reservation is reserved in the first deed than where it is in the second, nor can a purchaser be defeated, for, as against him, the power would be fraudulent by the Statute of Elizabeth.[2] And a conveyance to him inconsistent with the power would destroy it. This seems to be so as to purchasers immediately from the person that has the power of revocation.

(But query as to a purchaser under him to whom the uses are limited by the second deed were not the power there recited.)

Lord Keeper [Lord Harcourt], after taking time to consider, referred it to the Court of Queen's Bench whether the uses of the second deed were well revoked by the third by virtue of the power reserved in the first or the recital of that power in the second. This method of referring he chose as less expensive and more expeditious than either a trial at law or leaving it to the parties to state a case. The case he said was new, no authority in point, nor no power so fully expressed.

---

[1] *Gilmore v. Harris* (1685), 3 Levinz 213, 83 E.R. 656, also Skinner 324, 90 E.R. 144, Carthew 292, 90 E.R. 773.

[2] Stat. 13 Eliz. I, c. 5 (*SR*, IV, 537–538).

This was in the House of Lords. It was decreed that the power not being renewed in the first deed, if a revocation, it was gone, and, therefore, the uses declared in the second deed of revocation were without authority and void.

[Other copies of this report: Lincoln's Inn MS. Misc. 383, p. 239.]

## 468

## Aswin v. Charlotte

(Ch. 1713)

*A power to require a surrender of a copyhold expires upon the death of the holder of the power and is not an asset of the holder's estate.*

British Library MS. Hargrave 80, f. 136

Richard Charlotte had issue, the defendant, his eldest son, Richard, his second son, and the plaintiff's wife. A copyhold estate was granted to the father and the two sons likewise. Then, the father agreed with the defendant that he should postpone himself to his younger brother and suffer his younger brother, though named after him in the copy, to take before him. And the father likewise settled a leasehold estate upon his eldest son, in consideration of which, he agreed to surrender all his interest in the copyhold estate upon his request to such uses as his father should direct. The younger son died; then the father died intestate and without making any request. And the defendant took out administration to him.

And the bill was brought by the plaintiff, as administrator to his wife, for a distribution of the personal estate of the father and *inter alia* of the copyhold estate. The power the father had for calling in the son to surrender was used as an evidence of the son's being a trustee for the father.

And *Vernon* said that, if a man purchased a copyhold estate from a copyholder and took security from him to surrender upon request, the copyholder was a trustee for the purchaser, that this was the same case here, there being a bond given here to surrender on request, as there was, and the father having purchased this by settling the leasehold estate, that the trust of this copyhold estate being in the father went upon his death to his administrator and is distributable, that though the copyhold of inheritance were never adjudged assets, those *pur auter vie* had frequently been decreed to be testamentary estates and to the executor or administrator and to be distributory.

He admitted that, upon a distribution, the plaintiff must bring the portion given his wife by her father in his lifetime into hotchpot but that, on the other side, the defendant, the heir at law, must likewise bring into hotchpot whatever personal estate he had received from his father in his lifetime, that the only difference between an heir at law [and] a younger child as to bringing into hotchpot was with regard to a real estate settled by the father upon either in his lifetime.

A younger child is obliged to bring even that into hotchpot, but an heir is not. And this point he said was settled so on consideration of the Statute[1] in the case of Phinny v. Phinny by My Lord Cowper.[2]

On the other hand, it was insisted that the power which the father had of calling upon the son to surrender was ambulatory during his life, that he might have called upon him to surrender if he had thought fit, but he not having done it, that power dropped with him, and that there was no reason for a court of equity to set it up again after his death against an heir at law for no purpose in the world but for to make the estate distributable, that, in the case of Pickering v. Pickering, in the King's Bench,[3] an estate *pur auter vie* was ruled not to be distributable, that a copyhold *pur auter vie* is not.

Note there seems to be a difference between a freehold estate *pur auter vie* and a copyhold; in the last, the lives inserted in the copy regularly take successively, either in their own right or in trust for others and are not barely a limitation of the trust, but, in the case of a freehold *pur auter vie*, there is not so much as a bare legal interest in the person for whose life etc., but his life is singly a limitation of the continuance of the estate and such a freehold is not distributable. Query whether a trust, which seems to be all the interest that a man can have in a copyhold for another's life, may not be distributed.

And *How* denied that an heir who comes for a distribution would be obliged to bring anything, even personal estate received in his father's lifetime, into distribution, the Act plainly intending to favor the heir and making no distinction between real and personal estate received by him.

The Master of the Rolls [TREVOR] laid great weight on the father's not having called on his son to surrender, the power being reserved singly to the father, and he would not give the plaintiff any relief.

[Other copies of this report: Lincoln's Inn MS. Misc. 383, p. 241, Lincoln's Inn MS. Misc. 106, p. 204.]

## 469

## Atkyns v. Barns

(Ch. 1713)

*An heir cannot retain, but an executor may.*

---

[1] Stat. 22 & 23 Car. II, c. 10 (*SR*, V, 719–720).

[2] *Phiney v. Phiney* (1709), 2 Vernon 638, 23 E.R. 1018, 1 Eq. Cas. Abr. 249, 21 E.R. 1025.

[3] *Oldham v. Pickering* (1696–1698), 2 Salkeld 464, 91 E.R. 400, Carthew 376, 90 E.R. 819, 1 Lord Raymond 96, 91 E.R. 960, 3 Salkeld 137, 91 E.R. 738, Comberbach 388, 475, 90 E.R. 545, 600, Holt K.B. 503, 90 E.R. 1176, 1177, 12 Modern 103, 88 E.R. 1195.

*Where the words of a will are doubtful and uncertain, parol evidence is admissible to explain what could not be explained by the will itself.*

Lincoln's Inn MS. Misc. 10, p. 141, pl. 2

Hilary term 1712[/13].

[It was] decreed by the Master of the Rolls [TREVOR] that an heir shall not retain for his own debt, as an executor may.

British Library MS. Hargrave 80, f. 137

By articles made on the marriage of the plaintiff, the wife's father covenanted to pay her £1500. And, in the conclusion of the articles, each party bound himself to the other in the penalty of £2000 for performance of covenants. The father dying without paying leaving a real estate sufficient to answer that sum to descend to her, she being his heir, and the bill brought by her and her husband against a bond creditor of her father for an injunction to stay his prosecuting them at law and for liberty to retain the lands descended towards satisfaction of the £1500, for the plaintiff, it was said that the reason why an executor might retain was because, when the assets came to the hands of a creditor, it was deemed as payment and because he cannot sue himself, that the same reasons held in the case of an heir *ubi eadem ratio etc.* that in the case of Willcocks and Willcocks,[1] there were articles to settle lands to the value of £2000 and the party dying before he made a settlement and leaving £100 *per annum* to descend to the same person on whom the settlement was to be made, Lord Cowper decreed that it should be taken as a satisfaction of the £2000 and retained against bond creditors.

And it being objected by the Master of the Rolls [TREVOR] that the bond in the principal case was only for performance of covenants and the defendants for a certain sum and, therefore, to be preferred by the constant practice of the court, Serjeant *Hooper* replied that it would be so if the covenant sounded in damages, but that, here, the covenant was for a sum certain.

But, however, the Master [of the Rolls TREVOR] seemed to be of opinion that an heir could not retain, though an executor might. And he would have dismissed the bill, but the plaintiffs desired to attend him with precedents, which he agreed to.

Upon this head, *Vernon* cited the case of Litton Stroude and Litton,[2] where Lord Cowper admitted parol evidence to explain the words in Mr. Litton's will 'all my estate out of settlements', which were sufficiently uncertain and, if it were reasonable to admit it in any case, it was in that. He said that, upon an appeal to the House of Lords, he was very much censured for admitting it.

---

[1] *Wilcocks v. Wilcocks* (1706), 2 Vernon 558, 23 E.R. 961, 1 Eq. Cas. Abr. 26, 21 E.R. 847.

[2] *Litten v. Lady Falkland* (Ch. 1708), see above, Case No. 107.

The Master of Rolls [Trevor] said that he was in that case of Lord Cowper's opinion and so was the Chief Justice and that he was still of the same and that, where the words of a will are doubtful and uncertain, he should always admit parol evidence to explain what could not be explained by the will itself.

[Other copies of this report: Lincoln's Inn MS. Misc. 383, p. 242, Lincoln's Inn MS. Misc. 106, p. 207.]

470

## Hyde v. Viveane

(Ch. 1713)

*A power of appointment cannot be exercised otherwise than by its own terms.*

British Library MS. Hargrave 80, f. 137v, pl. 2

The defendant's wife's father gave £4500 by his will to his three daughters to be divided among them in such proportions as their mother should think proper to engage them to be dutiful to her. One daughter died in the mother's lifetime. And the mother gave by her will the £4500 to be equally divided between the plaintiff's wife, who was one of the daughters, and the defendant's wife, the other, and paid to them within a week after her decease subject to this condition, *viz.* that, if the defendant should marry without the consent of J.S., she did thereby revoke and make void all her legacies, dispositions, and orders given to her and then devised them over to J.S. By the same will, some jewels were a given to the defendant, who, after her mother's death, married the defendant, Viveane, the clerk in court, in good business and without asking the consent of J.S. She had near £2000 more subject to no condition, part by her father, part by her mother's will.

*Sir Joseph Jekyll* [said] that conditions to restrain marriage were void by the civil law, that this being in case of a pecuniary legacy, though this court has a jurisdiction as well as the ecclesiastical [court], yet they would guide themselves by the same rules to avoid the inconveniences which would arise from different determinations in different courts.

But this Lord Keeper [Lord Harcourt] seemed to overrule and, I think, said that such a condition though annexed to a personal thing had been held good in this court.

He then insisted that the devise over being to the person whose consent was to be had, it was not so necessary so much as to ask it. He cited the case of Garritt v. Pretty, by Lord Somers adjudged in point, and that of Warburton v.

Warburton,[1] where there was a disposition among children in such a portion as Dr. Warburton, who was one of them, should appoint, the defendant carved out almost all for himself and left but a trifle for the rest, but his appointment was set aside, it being contrary to natural justice for the same party to be judge and party.

But, however, Lord Keeper [Lord Harcourt] seemed to think it necessary to ask consent though the devise over be to the same person, but, in case he should refuse his consent to a reasonable match, he said equity would control him. But he thought the mother who had a power only of distributing and, therefore, could not give the whole from either had exceeded the power in her will. He seemed to think too that she had no power of annexing any condition to the appointment she was to make.

[Other copies of this report: Lincoln's Inn MS. Misc. 383, p. 244, Lincoln's Inn MS. Misc. 106, p. 209.]

[Related cases: Hyde v. Hyde (Ch. 1711–1713), see above, Case No. 304.]

## 471

## Man v. Wyne

(Ch. 1713)

*Masters of hospitals are subject to the oversight of the commissioners for charitable uses. An election made without reasonable notice given to the electors is void.*

British Library MS. Hargrave 80, f. 138v, pl. 1

The minister, two churchwardens, and four parishioners had the power of electing the master, brethren, and sisters of a hospital and to remove them for special causes, as drunkenness etc., and to take their accounts. And an exception was taken to the decree of commissioners for charitable uses that their power did not extend to hospitals which have special visitors, governors, and overseers and, therefore, not to this.

Lord Keeper [Lord Harcourt]: The visitors etc. intended by the Act[2] are such as have a general visitorial power equal to what the commissioners have in other places but that the master etc. have not here. He overruled the exception.

By their construction, notice was to be given of the election of a master, who was to be chosen by the minister, two wardens, and four parishioners to be elected by the rest of the parish. In this case, no notice had been given. The four parishioners were not chosen by the rest but called out of them by the minister

[1] *Garret v. Pritty* (1693), 2 Vernon 293, 23 E.R. 790; *Warburton v. Warburton* (1701), 2 Vernon 420, 23 E.R. 869, 4 Brown P.C. 1, 2 E.R. 1, 1 Eq. Cas. Abr. 265, 345, 21 E.R. 1034, 1091.

[2] Stat. 43 Eliz. I, c. 4 (*SR*, IV, 968–970).

*ceteris tacentibus* and the master before his election articled with the minister to serve him as his curate, *inter alia*, and gave him a general bond of resignation.

The commissioners declared this election void though he had acted as master for seven years and decreed him to account for the profits.

Lord Keeper [Lord Harcourt] was of the same opinion and seemed to think either the want of notice or of a due choice of the four or the bond sufficient to annul his election in this case.

*Sir Thomas Powys* said that the commissioners not having power to give costs, he had known the party to whom they had given [judgment] except to that part of the decree in order to have them given by this court.

[Other copies of this report: Lincoln's Inn MS. Misc. 383, p. 245, pl. 1, Lincoln's Inn MS. Misc. 106, p. 211.]

## 472

## Hickman v. Chappell

(Ch. 1713)

*A lease for lives that is devised cannot be renewed in order to extend the length of the devise.*

British Library MS. Hargrave 80, f. 138v, pl. 2

One, seised of an estate for three lives, by a bishop's lease, devised an annuity of £40 out of it to A. for her life and to be disposed of by her at her death, another of £10 *per annum* to her and her heirs etc., and devised the estate to a third person, who, one of the lives dropping, took a new lease for the two old lives and a new one.

It was insisted on by the Attorney General [*Northey*] that the testator intended the annuity should continue as long as his interest in the estate out of which they were to issue and that the annuitants had an interest under their testator as well as the devisee of the land in the right of renewing and that, therefore, upon their paying their proportion of the fine from time to time, their annuities ought to be continued as long as the renewed estates lasted.

But Lord Keeper [Lord Harcourt] decreed that they should enjoy their annuities during the two old lives only.

[Other copies of this report: Lincoln's Inn MS. Misc. 383, p. 245, pl. 2, Lincoln's Inn MS. Misc. 106, p. 212.]

## 473

## Loeffes v. Lewen

(Ch. 1713)

*In this case, the bond in issue was deemed voluntary and fraudulent against creditors.*

Precedents in Chancery 370, 24 E.R. 167

In this case, the question was whether the plaintiffs, who were creditors of one Eyton, should have the benefit of a bond for payment of £1500 entered into by one Bayly to Eyton or if the said bond should be looked upon to be voluntary and fraudulent as against the creditors of Bayly, who were defendants, and they [were] to be accordingly first satisfied out of Bayly's assets, they being creditors only by simple contract. And, as to that, the case appeared to be thus.

One Mason, a vintner and freeman of London, made his will about twenty-four years since and, thereby, he devised one third part of his personal estate to Letitia, his wife, and the other two thirds to his children. And he died, leaving only two daughters, Letitia and another, who, afterwards, died intestate and unmarried. Letitia, the widow, afterwards, intermarried with Bayly, who was a vintner likewise. And the widow, as well before marriage as she and her husband after marriage, continued to employ the whole stock left by Mason in the carrying on of their trade, without making any distribution or division to the children.

Some time after, upon a treaty of marriage to be had between Letitia, the daughter, and Eyton (the other daughter being then dead), a computation was made of what fortune would be coming to Letitia, the daughter. And, the same appearing to be short of what Eyton expected, Bayly agreed to make up her fortune the sum of £4000. But there was no writing or memorandum of it under hand, but Bayly did afterwards pay all but £1500 of the fortune agreed on.

About four years after the marriage, Bayly makes his will, and, at the same time, prepares a bond to Eyton of £3000, conditioned for the payment of £1500 to him at such a time. And then sends for Eyton and his wife, and shows them the bond and will, whereby he had likewise given them a legacy, but he never delivers the bond to Eyton or his wife, but kept it in his own custody. And Bayly, some time after, dying suddenly, this bond was delivered over to one Owen, who was a defendant, to be kept by him, as an indifferent person, until it should appear how things were like to go.

Bayly dying considerably indebted, his executors renounced. And administration with the will annexed was granted to the defendant Lewen, as principal creditor for about £2000 by simple contract. And Bayly was likewise indebted to several others by simple contract.

Afterwards, Eyton becomes a bankrupt, and this bond of £1500 was assigned by the commissioners to the plaintiffs, who were his creditors.

So this bill was brought to have the bond delivered to the plaintiffs and to have an account of Bayly's personal estate and satisfaction thereout for the said £1000.

Several proofs were read on the plaintiff's part to prove the due execution of the bond, and that seemed to be out of all doubt. Eyton and his wife likewise, being examined as witnesses by order of the court, did both by their answer and depositions swear the agreement by Bayly to be to pay or secure £4000 for the wife's portion.

On the other side, it was proved that, if this £1500 should be taken out of Bayly's assets, there would not be enough to pay above 4s. 6d. in the pound to his creditors. So, the only question was who should have the preference.

But another question was made, Whether the dead daughter's portion should survive wholly to the other daughter or be distributed between her and her mother, according to the Statute.[1] And, as to this, a difference was taken and agreed by the court that, as to the orphanage part, which belonged to the daughters by the custom of London, the survivor should have the whole, even after a division and partition made between them, but, as to the testator's part devised to them, that was under the direction of the Statute as a legacy, and must be distributed between the mother and surviving daughter accordingly.

And, as to the other point, the court was of opinion that this bond was to be looked upon as voluntary against the creditors of Bayly.

But My Lord [Harcourt] said that the agreement to pay or secure £4000 in consideration of the marriage, though it were only by parol and, by consequence, not binding within the Statute of Frauds and Perjuries,[2] yet it was binding in conscience. And, therefore, so far as Bayly afterwards executed that contract by payment of part of the money agreed upon, it was an effectual performance, and not to be set aside in a court of equity. And he never would call that fraudulent which was just. But, as to the £1500 bond, you cannot tack that to the parol agreement so as to make it any evidence in writing of that agreement or as a performance of it for that appears to have been given four years after and without any application of Eyton or his wife. Besides, if it had been intended to be in execution of the former agreement, it is natural to conclude it would have been immediately delivered over to the obligee or his wife, which here it was not. But Bayly, the obligor, always kept it by him. It was made at the same time with his will, shown to them at the same time with his will, and, after his death, found with his will, and, therefore, he could take it not otherwise than in the nature of a legacy and voluntary. And, therefore, he decreed an account to be taken of Bayly's personal estate and that to be applied in the first place towards payment of his own creditors, and, if any surplus remained, the plaintiffs were to come in for a satisfaction of their bond, in the next place, before the legatees of Bayly.

---

1 Stat. 1 Jac. II, c. 17, s. 7 (*SR*, VI, 19).

2 Stat. 29 Car. II, c. 3 (*SR*, V, 839–842).

And costs on all sides were to come out of Bayly's personal estate, he being the occasion of this suit.

But the plaintiffs thought there would be no surplus at all, and, therefore, desired a farther day to consider whether they would not choose to have their bill dismissed, rather than enter into the account.

And My Lord Chancellor [LORD HARCOURT] gave them time accordingly to consider of it.

[Other copies of this report: Gilbert Rep. 32, 25 E.R. 23.]

[Other reports of this case: 2 Eq. Cas. Abr. 257, 22 E.R. 217.]

## 474

## Wallis v. Pudman

(Ch. 1713)

*The discounting of a bill of exchange is not within the Statute of Usury.*

British Library MS. Hargrave 80, f. 139

*Sir Joseph Jekyll* [said] in the case of Wallis v. Pudman that discounting bills though at £20 percent is not within the Statute of Usury[1] because of the hazard.

[Other copies of this report: Lincoln's Inn MS. Misc. 383, p. 247, pl. 1, Lincoln's Inn MS. Misc. 106, p. 215, pl. 1.]

## 475

## Anonymous

(Ch. 1713)

*Where a submission to arbitration is made a rule of court, the award should be enforced by contempt of court proceedings.*

British Library MS. Hargrave 80, f. 140, pl. 1

A verdict for £30 was to be a security of what should become due on an arbitration, and a rule of assizes was made, and, afterwards, [it was] made a rule of court for submission to an award; £55 was awarded, and this matter was pleaded in bar of an account allowed.

Serjeant *Hooper*: Our way to come at it is by a [writ of] attachment upon the rule of court not by judgment upon the verdict.

[1] Stat. 13 Ann., c. 15 (*SR*, IX, 928).

[Other copies of this report: Lincoln's Inn MS. Misc. 383, p. 247, pl. 2, Lincoln's Inn MS. Misc. 106, p. 215, pl. 2.]

## 476

## Anonymous

(Ch. 1713)

*A profit a prendre, being a property right, is not within the Statute of Limitations, nor can it be defeated by a conveyance by a fine or by non-user.*

British Library MS. Hargrave 80, f. 140, pl. 2

[It was said] by My Lord Keeper [Lord Harcourt] and *Sir Joseph Jekyll*, a right to dig for coal etc. is a profit *a prendre* and, therefore, not barred by the Statute of Limitations[1] nor by a fine or non-claim.

[Other copies of this report: Lincoln's Inn MS. Misc. 383, p. 247, pl. 3, Lincoln's Inn MS. Misc. 106, p. 215, pl. 3.]

## 477

## Conquest v. Froud

(Ch. 1713)

*A plea of payment and release is a good defense to a bill for an account though the account was not stated.*

British Library MS. Hargrave 80, f. 140, pl. 3

[Upon a] bill for an account [and] a plea of payment of a sum and a release, the bill suggested a surprise in the agreement and that there was no account stated. The plea denied the surprise.

Lord Keeper [Lord Harcourt]: Here is no fraud nor misrepresentation; I allow the plea though the account was not stated.

[Other copies of this report: Lincoln's Inn MS. Misc. 383, p. 247, pl. 4, Lincoln's Inn MS. Misc. 106, p. 216, pl. 1.]

[1] Stat. 21 Jac. I, c. 16, s. 3 (*SR*, IV, 1222).

## 478

## Roberts v. Isham

(Ch. 1713)

*The question in this case was whether, where an estate is limited in trust by way of a mortgage, the equity of redemption can be barred by a fine or recovery.*

British Library MS. Hargrave 80, f. 140, pl. 4

Sir Richard conveyed lands to himself for life, remainder to his wife for life, remainder to trustees for 1000 years for raising portions if any son should come to twenty-one years, remainder to the first and every other son in tail male, remainder to all the daughters and the heirs of their bodies until £4000 should be raised out of the rents and profits, remainder to such uses as Sir Richard should appoint, remainder to his right heirs. No sons living to twenty-one, the widow and one daughter join in a bargain and sale to make a tenant to the *praecipe* and suffer a recovery, which was pleaded in bar to a bill brought by the plaintiff as heir to Sir Richard against the daughter to redeem.

*Sir Thomas Powys*, for the plea: The limitation to the daughters is a legal limitation determinable on their dying without issue on receiving £4000 out of the rents and profits. The recovery being suffered before either limitation determined, the estate tail is barred and the reversion [and], consequently, the account of profits to which the plaintiff is entitled only in respect of his reversion. 2 Lev. 28 and 1 Mor. 111, Benson v. Hodson and Lord Hales;[1] a gift in tail determinable of non-payment of £1000 at a day, remainder in tail to another, remainder over; the first in tail suffers a recovery before the day of payment; he gains a fee; so it is if a limitation be to one and the heirs of this body while such a tree shall stand. If a term for portions should be raised after an estate tail, as, formerly, they have been, and the son should suffer a recovery, equity could not aid the children by this means unprovided for. If a trust be limited in tail, remainder over, a recovery though not a legal is yet an equitable bar, from whence he concluded that equity ought not to interpose here in favor of the reversion which was barred at law and with the account of profits, the right to which would have passed by a grant of the reversion had it not been barred.

The Solicitor General [*Raymond*]: A recovery will bar a condition to re-enter though not a rent. He relied on the case of Page v. Heyward, Trinity 4 Queen;[2]

[1] *Benson v. Hodson* (1674), 2 Levinz 28, 83 E.R. 438, 1 Modern 108, 86 E.R. 768, also T. Raymond 236, 83 E.R. 123, 1 Freeman 362, 89 E.R. 269, 3 Keble 274, 287, 292, 84 E.R. 717, 724, 727.

[2] *Page v. Hayward* (1704), 2 Salkeld 570, 91 E.R. 481, 3 Salkeld 96, 135, 91 E.R. 714, 736, 11 Modern 61, 88 E.R. 886, Holt K.B. 618, 90 E.R. 1242, 2 Eq. Cas. Abr. 362, 22 E.R. 308.

'all my lands I give to my niece upon condition only and provided she marry with and have issue by one whose name is Sherkserle' etc.; *vide* the case. The equity of redemption here is incident to the reversion and barred with it.

*Chesshyre*: It is an estate tail at law and must have all incidents and, consequently, to be barred by a recovery; the death of the tenant in tail without issue after a recovery is no determination of the estate derived under it nor, consequently, is the happening of any limitation annexed to the estate tail. In Page's Case, the court took it to be no more than a limitation to her and the heirs of her body to be begotten by a Serle. If the recovery here should not be a bar, there might possibly be a perpetuity established in the pernancy of the profits; the daughter could not have compelled the remainderman to redeem. Therefore, it is reasonable that it should be able to make the estate permanent in order to a sale to raise their portion. And an equity of redemption ought to be mutual if any.

*Williams*: If the remainder in fee had been limited to a stranger, the redemption would have been to him. It is, therefore, incident to the reversion.

*Vernon*, for the plaintiff: The plea is informal and not good in substance. To the last, he said that the equity of redemption is not subsequent but concomitant with the estate tail that equity makes no difference whether the estate pledged be an estate tail or a fee, whatever it be, it is to be reconveyed on payment of the money. In the Case of Lloyd v. Whithrong, there were the same limitations and no recovery and [it was] decreed to be redeemable. In that of Sheldon v. Justice Dormer,[1] a portion being to be raised out of rents and profits, a sale was decreed. [He said] that there is a difference where a charge lies upon an estate and where it comes subsequent to it. In the case of White v. Gearish, Cro. El.,[2] the reversion was barred by a recovery, not the rent. In this case, the reversion is barred but not the right of redemption. If an estate be limited in trust by way of mortgage, the equity of redemption cannot be barred by a fine or recovery. Equities of redemption are creatures of this court, and this court will consider the intention of the parties, which plainly, in this case, was only to secure the £4000 for the daughter.

Lord Keeper [Lord Harcourt] overruled the plea but saved the benefit of it until the hearing.

[Other copies of this report: Lincoln's Inn MS. Misc. 383, p. 248, Lincoln's Inn MS. Misc. 106, p. 216, pl. 2.]

---

[1] *Sheldon v. Dormer* (1693), 2 Vernon 310, 23 E.R. 802.

[2] *Whyte v. Gerish* (1599–1600), Croke Eliz. 727, 769, 78 E.R. 961, 1000, also Moore K.B. 575, 72 E.R. 769, Owen 126, 74 E.R. 949.

## 479

## Walker v. Tilly

(Ch. 1713)

*A solicitor can sue a client for his fees without first delivering a bill of fees.*

British Library MS. Hargrave 80, f. 141, pl. 1

Walker and Sir James Tilly.

A demurrer to relief by a bill brought by a solicitor for his fees and a plea of the Statute of 3 Jac. I[1] and that there was no bill of fees first delivered were both overruled.

[Other copies of this report: Lincoln's Inn MS. Misc. 383, p. 250, pl. 1, Lincoln's Inn MS. Misc. 106, p. 218.]

## 480

## Child v. Frederick

(Ch. 1713)

*The question in this case was whether the Statute of Limitations is tolled where a suit for the accounts in issue are in litigation in another suit.*

British Library MS. Hargrave 80, f. 141, pl. 3

There had been dealings between the defendant and Sir Stephen Evance[2] for a great many £1000s before 1695, he depositing cash and tallies with Sir Stephen and Sir Stephen buying stock etc. for him. The bill was brought by the plaintiff [Sir Caesar Child] under a commission of bankrupts against Sir Stephen and against the defendant for an account from the years 1690 to 1695.

The plea admitted the dealings but alleged that the defendant was a gentleman and kept no book and that, in 1691, accounts were stated and adjusted between then by comparison of notes, which were entered on two sheets of paper, that, afterwards, Hale, Sir Stephen's partner, pretending theirs was lost, borrowed the defendant's sheet and never returned it, upon which the defendant brought a bill against Sir Stephen for an account, who put in three insufficient answers and then stood out to a sergeant at arms and never put in another, that Sir Stephen snatched a note of £4000 out of his hands and destroyed [it], that,

[1] Stat. 3 Jac. I, c. 7 (*SR*, IV, 1083–1084).

[2] H. Lancaster, 'Evance, Sir Stephen (1654/5–1712)', *Oxford Dictionary of National Biography*, vol. 18, p. 660.

since 1695, there had been no dealings between them nor no promise to account, wherefore, he insisted on the Statute of Limitations.[1]

*Vernon*: We have lost several witnesses and our vouchers, the paper, and note, and the benefit of a discovery from Sir Stephen not by our default but by the length of time and the act of Sir Stephen. In the case of the Countess of Plymouth,[2] her steward pleaded in bar to a bill brought by her for an account that she had taken all his books and papers of account from him, and she never could proceed until she had made oath that she had returned them all.

*Sir Joseph Jekyll*: There was a bill brought by Sir Stephen about the time of the defendant's bill against him, and that was never dismissed, which takes this case clearly out of the Statute, like filing an original. The note, if there was ever any such, will stand a charge upon us etc.

Lord Keeper [Lord Harcourt] overruled the plea but saved the benefit of it at the hearing.

[Other copies of this report: Lincoln's Inn MS. Misc. 383, p. 250, pl. 3.]

[Other reports of this case: 1 Peere Williams 266, 24 E.R. 383, 2 Eq. Cas. Abr. 180, 22 E.R. 154.]

## 481

## Trafford v. Ashton

(Ch. 1713)

*A plaintiff cannot allege his own bad faith.*

*A monopoly is not illegal unless it is used for extortion.*

*A monopoly is not per se illegal.*

British Library MS. Hargrave 80, f. 142

The plaintiffs and defendants were lessees of the several wharves between the Bridge and the Tower [of London] and entered into articles for the using them all jointly in partnership and dividing the profits *pro rata* for twenty-one years. If any lease was renewed during the term, it was agreed it should be in trust for the partnership. The defendant's lease in three of the wharves expiring at the year's end of four years, he took a new one for fourteen years in his own name. The first twelve years, he acted in concert, but being then removed from being manager for several mismanagements by an order from the directors made pursuant to the articles, he, afterwards, continued in the possession of the three wharves included in the lease to him.

[1] Stat. 21 Jac. I, c. 16 (*SR*, IV, 1222–1223).

[2] *Countess of Plymouth v. Bladon* (1687), 2 Vernon 32, 23 E.R. 630, 1 Eq. Cas. Abr. 11, 21 E.R. 836.

The plaintiffs' bill was for an account of the profits of those wharves, *inter alia*. He submitted and answered to account for the first twelve years and brought a cross-bill for an account of the other wharves to the time of the hearing.

It was urged for him by the Attorney General [*Northey*] etc. that the articles were illegal tending to a monopoly and to the raising of the price of wharfage, that, where people had acted in partnership, either without any articles or with void ones or even in an illegal combination, there was a sort of justice that, while they so acted, they should account to one another, but that the defendant having quitted a partnership illegal in the beginning ought not to compelled by a court of equity to account for any time after his quitting it and that the bill was in a manner to establish this unlawful agreement.

But it was answered and ruled by Lord Chancellor [Lord Harcourt] that Mr. Ashton, who was a party to the articles had submitted to them for twelve years and now brought a bill under them for an account for that time, ought not to be heard to say they were unlawful.

Lord Chancellor [Lord Harcourt] thought them not illegal unless made so by an actual abuse of them after by extorting immoderate prices for wharfage and that, even that abuse would not make them void, though it would expose the parties to an information. And he decreed an account to this time and to be carried on the remaining three years of the term.

[Other copies of this report: Lincoln's Inn MS. Misc. 383, p. 253, pl. 1, Lincoln's Inn MS. Misc. 106, p. 219, pl. 2.]

## 482

## Palmer v. Shribb

(Ch. 1713)

*The word 'desire' can have a testamentary effect.*

*A devise to an uncertain legatee is void.*

Lincoln's Inn MS. Misc. 384, p. 3, pl. 1

13 April 1713.

A husband makes his wife residuary legatee. And, in his will are those words 'I desire my wife to give her estate among her and my relations equally.'

Lord Chancellor [Lord Harcourt]: 'I desire and request' will go a great way in a will if it be plain and certain. But here, they are general and uncertain and are, therefore, to be considered as a recommendation only.

*Howe*: We submit it to Your Lordship whether the clause in the will does not amount to a declaration of trust. If it had been a real estate, the wife had been a trustee upon the construction of a court of equity upon the word 'relations'. [This] is according to the rule in the Statute of Distributions.[1]

*Curia* [LORD HARCOURT]: The court does not go from the Statute without a particular reason.

British Library MS. Hargrave 80, f. 141v, pl. 1

A man devised a sum of money to his wife and, in his will, desired her, after her decease, to give it among his and her relations.

*Vernon* and *Curia*: A desire in a will is equivalent to a devise, but the words 'among his and her relations' are too general and void for the uncertainty.

[Other copies of this report: Lincoln's Inn MS. Misc. 383, p. 251, pl. 1, Lincoln's Inn MS. Misc. 106, p. 219, pl. 1.]

2 Eq. Cas. Abr. 291, 22 E.R. 244

Easter 12 Ann. [1713].

J.S. devises the residue of his estate to his wife and desires her to give all her estate at her death to his and her relations. *Quaere* if this does amount to a devise on a trust in the wife for all the estate which the husband gave her by his will.

HARCOURT, Chancellor, thought these words too general to amount to a devise over of his estate after the death of the wife, nor can it be taken as a trust, because the words extend to all the estate which she shall be possessed of at the time of her death, which the husband has not any power over, and, therefore, it must be taken over as a recommendation, and not as a devise or trust. But, if the testator had desired his wife by his will to give at her death all the estate which he had devised to her to his and her relations, there, the estate devised to her ought to go after her death to his and her relations according to the Statute of Distributions. The bill was dismissed.

## 483

## Anonymous

(Ch. 1713)

*Where a legacy to a charity is impractical or extremely inconvenient, a court can re-direct it so as to be as near as can be to the donor's intent.*

British Library MS. Hargrave 77, f. 25, pl. 2

23 April 1713.

Dr. Hans, by his will, devised £1000 for building a more convenient lodging for the queen's scholars at Westminster [School]. And the executor, on petition,

[1] Stat. 22 & 23 Car. II, c. 10 (*SR*, V, 719–720).

prayed the direction of the court touching the application of his money, being a case of charity, and suggested that the Dean and Chapter of Westminster, who were the governors of the school, had refused to find out new ground for erecting such new building.

On the other hand, it was said that they had no new ground for that purpose and that an additional building was unnecessary and rebuilding on the old foundation would cost above £4000.

*Curia* [Lord Harcourt]: The intent of the testator is to be observed especially in cases of charity, yet, where the intent is impractical or extremely inconvenient, this court is to come as near the intent as conveniently it can. And, here, the primary intent of the testator was to render those lodgings more commodious and not to have a new set of buildings. And this may best be answered by repairing and altering the old rooms thereof. He ordered the executor to pay the £1000 to the Chapter's clerk upon his giving security and the same to be paid out by order of the Dean and Chapter with the advice of Sir Christopher Wren[1] in repairing and making the scholars' rooms more commodious.

## 484

## Barnardiston v. Bennet

(Ch. 1713)

*An infant legatee should be given only the interest from his legacy.*

Lincoln's Inn MS. Misc. 384, p. 2, pl. 1

25 April 1713.

[It was] said by *Vernon*, in the infancy of a legatee, the executor or guardian ought not to allow him more than the interest of his legacy.

## 485

## Prideaux v. Harvey

(Ch. 1713)

*In equity, the plaintiff, having the burden of proof, cannot prevail against the defendant's oath unless he has two witnesses or one witness and strong circumstantial evidence.*

*Marriage brokage bonds are illegal and unenforceable.*

[1] K. Downes, 'Wren, Sir Christopher (1632–1723)', *Oxford Dictionary of National Biography*, vol. 60, pp. 406–419.

British Library MS. Hargrave 80, f. 141v, pl. 2

The defendant was physician to the plaintiff and his father, Sir Edward Prideaux's, family for several years. He was instrumental in the plaintiff's marriage and, pending the treaty, got two promissory notes, each for £100 from Sir Edward, one payable on his son's, the other on his own second intermarriage. And, at the same time, he gave Sir Edward a receipt in full for £200 for twelve years attendance. He, likewise, got pending the treaty two bonds from the plaintiff, one for payment of £300, the other of £200. And about a month after the marriage, he prevailed with plaintiff, on cancelling the bonds, to give him a new one for £500 and a warrant of attorney to confess judgment upon it. The money due on the notes was paid by Sir Edward, all but £30. This bill was brought to be relieved against the bonds.

Lord Chancellor [Lord Harcourt]: The defendant, in his answer, says the bonds were voluntarily entered into by the plaintiff as a gratuity for acts of friendship which the defendant had shown him. He denies, too, that the two notes were given on consideration of marriage brokage, but he insists they were for physic. But, in the last, he is falsified. And Sir Edward who swears that, before he gave the notes, the defendant said he could and would hinder the marriage unless he was gratified. If it stood singly on Sir Edward's oath against the defendant, equity would decide it without putting it to a farther trial. But Sir Edward is not concerned in interest, which the defendant is, nor is it probable that the defendant would have accepted of such notes, which might happen never to become payable, as a satisfaction for a just debt and, though the defendant swears in answer only that they were payable at a future day, that does not contradict what Sir Edward swears, that they were payable on these contingencies they were given to pending the treaty. And Sir Edward swears the receipt given by the Doctor at the same time was to color the consideration of the notes, his answer being falsified as to the notes and they appearing to be given on consideration of the marriage, it is an inducement to suppose the bonds were given on the same account. There is no positive proof of the consideration of the bonds. But it arises from circumstances they were entered into pending the treaty to the person who proposed it to one who it is plain thought he had influence in it by the young gentleman to be married, who had no estate in possession but a precarious annuity of £80 *per annum* and that ill paid. It is not probable that, under these circumstances, he should voluntarily and out of an act of friendship bind himself to pay £500, not after his father's death but a day certain. The sum is too great and not proportioned to any services pretended to have been done. For these reasons, I take them to be entered into in consideration of brokage of marriage. I suspect the changing the bonds after marriage to have been because he might think one entered into after marriage better. However, that the warrant of attorney stands on the same foot as the former and they being *ex turpi causa*, they ought to be set aside though, were they given voluntarily and without any such consideration, this court would never interpose. Let the plaintiff have a perpetual injunction and all the bonds and warrant of attorney be delivered up and satisfaction be acknowledged on the record of the judgment if there be any. The plaintiff comes to relieved against his own act. If the defendant performs this decree in a month, he shall be excused his costs.

Now, LORD COWPER said on the rule of equity not to decide where there is a single oath against the defendant that it seemed needless to send it to law where the defendant's oath would not be evidence, and on what the plaintiff's witnesses swore he would certainly have a verdict.

And note that the Dr. Harrison brought a *quantum meruit* for his attendance, and, upon the trial of the issue at the Guildhall, LORD TREVOR directed the jury to find for the defendant.

[Other copies of this report: Lincoln's Inn MS. Misc. 383, p. 252, pl. 2.]

Lincoln's Inn MS. Misc. 384, p. 2, pl. 2

29 April.

Brokage bonds will be set aside and a perpetual injunction awarded.

## 486

## Greenhill v. Waldoe

(Ch. 1713)

*Interest is not due on portions before they are payable.*

*In this case, under the terms of the settlement in issue, an uncle was liable to pay reasonable and necessary maintenance for his nieces.*

Lincoln's Inn. MS. Misc. 11, p. 97, pl. 2

8 May 1713.

By the marriage settlement of Mr. Edward Waldo, a remainder was limited, the trusts whereof were declared to be that, in case the said Edward Waldo should leave no issue male by his wife and should have issue female at his death, then the trustees should with all convenient speed after his death by and out of the rents of the premises or by mortgage, demise, or sale raise and pay £3000 for the portions of such daughters to be equally divided between them and to be paid at their respective ages of eighteen or marriage or within six months after, so as they married with consent etc., provided, if any of the daughters died before the portions became payable, then the share of such daughter to go to the survivor and, if all died under eighteen and unmarried, the portions were not to be raised.

Edward Waldo, having afterwards two daughters and one son, makes his will and gives his daughters £500 apiece if they lived to the age of eighteen or married. But, if either of them died before, then the survivor was only to have

£3000 provided by the settlement. And he gives the lands charged with the portions to the defendant, his brother, and his heirs. And, soon afterwards, he died.

The eldest daughter was sixteen at her father's death. And, after she had attained the age of eighteen, she married the plaintiff. And they now bring their bill to have her portion paid with interest from the death of the father.

It was insisted on for the plaintiffs that they ought to have interest until the portion became payable as well as after or, at least, an allowance for maintenance in the meantime.

On the other side, it was insisted that there being no interest or maintenance provided for by the settlement, this court could not decree any to be paid, for the court is not to consider what was reasonable to have been done when the settlement was made but what is done.

And the case of Wareing and Wareing, before the present Keeper,[1] was cited, where portions were charged on lands to be paid at twenty-one or marriage and no maintenance [was] provided in the meantime and the children spent £300 in their maintenance, which was paid by the trustee, and he was decreed to be allowed it out of the principal, but the children could get no allowance for maintenance.

Lord Keeper [Lord Harcourt]: There is no pretense for interest. The question is if any maintenance ought to be allowed. And I think this is a strong case for maintenance.

Accordingly, it was decreed that the portion should be paid with interest at £5 percent from the time it became due and an allowance to be made for maintenance in the meantime and the Master to settle the allowance.

British Library MS. Hargrave 80, f. 142v

The defendant's brother, in consideration of marriage and of £3000 portion, conveyed this estate to himself for life with limitations for a jointure and to the issue male in tail and then to trustees for 200 years in case there should be no son to raise £3000 with all convenient speed by sale, lease, or mortgage for one or more daughters to be paid them at eighteen or marriage or within six months after, if one died before eighteen or marriage her share, to accrue to the survivors, if all died before, the £3000 [was] not to be raised; if raised, to be paid over to the remainderman, remainder to his own right heirs. His wife died leaving no son but two daughters; then he died. And by his will, he devised the whole estate above £500 *per annum* to his brother, the defendant, and gave his two daughters only £500 apiece as an increase of the portion if they attained eighteen or marriage and to be paid as the portion was by the deed and, if either died before eighteen or marriage by which the other would have the £3000 and the settlement, this legacy to cease. He left them too the use of a chamber in his house for themselves

[1] *Wareing v. Wareing* (Ch. 1713), see above, Case No. 461.

and one for a servant and the furniture, but made no provision by deed or will for their maintenance until eighteen or marriage. The eldest was sixteen at his death and, after eighteen, married the plaintiff. And the younger was now past eighteen within a short time after their father's death. No care being taken of them by the defendant, they were forced to leave the house and get credit for their board.

The plaintiff's bill was for the portion and legacy. And the single question was whether they were entitled to interest or maintenance until eighteen.

*Sir Thomas Powys*, for the plaintiff, cited the Case of the Lady Torrett and her daughter and that of Gough and Warth, in both which he said a portion in a family settlement being made payable at a future day and no maintenance provided, the court gave interest in the meantime.

*Peere Williams*: Though it was our father's pleasure to disinherit us, it can never be presumed to have been his intention that we should want bread. At least, the defendant who takes so plentiful an estate by the bounty of our father ought not to say that it was. But, if we are not entitled to interest or maintenance until eighteen, we might have wanted it. The portions are not payable until eighteen or marriage and, if both had died unmarried and under eighteen, not at all had we been but two instead of sixteen at our father's death with this contingent prospect only of a portion and without maintenance or interest in the meantime, the defendant might have been sure of having the portions fall into the estate, we must have been starved. The court will never make so harsh a construction if it can be avoided. The direction that the portions should be raised with all convenient speed implies the father's intention to make an immediate provision for their maintenance though the portions themselves were not to be paid until eighteen etc., for, had the trustees raised them immediately upon the father's death, what should have been done with the interest? The defendant would have no title to it. The principal is only directed to go over to him in case the portions being raised and our dying before eighteen.

*Vernon*, for the defendant: It is made a question of the other side whether it is possible for a man to provide a portion for a child without providing a maintenance or that will not carry interest before it is payable. They complain of the hardships of the case. It had been much harder if the father had given them no portion at all. And, if he had not, what could the court have done for them? But the question is not what would have been proper for the father to have done, but what is done if the remainderman would give security for the payment of the portions at the time appointed. They are directed not to be raised at all. Had they died under eighteen and unmarried, nothing had vested in them. The convenient speed in which the trustees were to raise them must be construed such as would have been sufficient to enable them to have the money ready against it should [they] become payable. If there had been any undesigned omission in the settlement, he had time enough after to have supplied it. He had the settlement in his thoughts when he made his will and, even then, did not think fit to give them any maintenance. In the Case of Waring and Waring, [it was] decreed by Lord Cowper [and] the Master of the Rolls where portions were charged on land payable at twenty-one or marriage and no maintenance [was] provided in the meantime, the trustees laid down £300 for maintenance and was allowed it by the court out of the principal.

Lord Chancellor [LORD HARCOURT]: I shall not give any interest for the time before the portions were payable. But it is a strong case for maintenance. It is directed to be raised with all convenient speed. He has given them room in the house. He knew nobody could maintain them there but his brother. They had nothing. It implies that none should maintain them. If the court can lay hold of anything to help them to maintenance, it ought, but yet not such a maintenance as would be proportional to their portion but as much as is reasonable and necessary. Let the defendant pay the plaintiff £30 *per annum* for the maintenance until the portions become payable. Let the portion with interest at £5 percent from the time it was payable and the £500 with interest at £6 percent be brought before the Master until he makes proposals for a settlement of his wife and the defendant pay the plaintiff his costs.

[Other copies of this report: Lincoln's Inn MS. Misc. 383, p. 253, pl. 2.]

[Other reports of this case: Precedents in Chancery 367, 24 E.R. 166, Gilbert Rep. 31, 25 E.R. 22, 2 Eq. Cas. Abr. 146, 640, 22 E.R. 125, 537.]

## 487

## Lilly v. Long

(Ch. 1713)

*Interest does not arise before a sum certain is payable.*

Lincoln's Inn MS. Misc. 384, p. 2, pl. 4

8 May.

A portion is given by a will, which happens to be payable ten years before the trust out of which it was to be paid did commence. The query was whether it should carry interest before it could possibly be raised.

*Curia*: There is no case where interest has been given before the term did arise, especially where no bill was brought before. Where a bill has been brought by a child which had no other provision, the court would give interest if possible. Here, the plaintiff must have interest only from the commencement of the term.

## 488
## Aldrich v. Stratford

(Ch. 1713)

*The question in this case was whether the Vice-Chancellor's Court of the University of Oxford has jurisdiction over matters in equity.*

Lincoln's Inn MS. Misc. 384, p. 3, pl. 2

21 May.

Upon a motion, the University of Oxford claimed jurisdiction. The bill was for discovery of what goods of the testator came to the defendant's hands.

*Powys*: The University have had a court time out of mind and have power to hear causes, both of common law and equity. They judge chiefly by the civil law. Lord Cook, 4 Inst.,[1] takes notice that the City of London has a court of equity by prescription, though it cannot be granted by a charter; it extends to all causes personal. Cognizance of pleas is in the nature of a *supersedeas*.

Lord Chancellor [Lord Harcourt]: Has the jurisdiction of the University been allowed upon a claim as well as upon a plea?

*Powys*: Some of the precedents go upon a plea and some upon a claim. Cognisance of pleas in equity cannot be granted by a patent, but it may be by prescription or statute. Hardress 506.[2] [There is] no precedent where it has been disallowed in a personal cause.

Lord Chancellor [Lord Harcourt]: Have they a jurisdiction which may exclude this court, they must proceed according to the charter or custom. If they have a court of equity by prescription, the crown may grant cognisance. Yelvert. 11. The demand of cognisance has usually been upon a plea, but it may be otherwise. It is admitted this court has jurisdiction unless the University claim cognisance. I think it proper to look into the clause of the patent. There being no one on the other side, I will put it off until another day.

3 June.

Lord Chancellor [Lord Harcourt]: I have had time to look into the precedents and am of the opinion that the claim of the University is to be allowed. There is a precedent where the jurisdiction was allowed even upon the plea of a party. Therefore, I dismiss the bill without costs.

---

[1] E. Coke, *Fourth Institute* (1644), p. 227.

[2] *Castle v. Lichfield* (1669), Hardres 505, 145 E.R. 570, also Lincoln's Inn MS. Misc. 500, f. 25, pl. 2.

British Library MS. Hargrave 80, f. 143v, pl. 2

Mr. Aldrich, as a student, having preferred a bill against Dr. [William] Stratford [d. 1729] a canon of Christ Church, for a discovery of some matters relating to his estate, Dr. Aldrich's estate. Mr. Aldrich was, thereupon, cited to appear in the Vice-Chancellor's Court at Oxford for presenting a member of the University for a matter determinable there, contrary to the privileges of the University, upon pain of expulsion. Upon this citation, he moved the court in Hilary term last and obtained an injunction both to Dr. Stratford and the Vice-Chancellor to stay proceedings against him where the first seal before this term the Chancellor and Vice-Chancellor etc. appeared in court and demanded conusance in form, and, nobody appearing for Mr. Aldrich, a day was given. And, in the meantime, several precedents were laid before My Lord Chancellor [Lord Harcourt] by the University.

At the day appointed, the plaintiff's counsel not being prepared, Lord Chancellor [Lord Harcourt] said that though Mr. Aldrich should give up his cause, yet His Lordship must do justice to the jurisdiction of the Court of Chancery, that he should be very glad the counsel of the University could satisfy him that he ought to determine in their favor, but that several difficulties occurred to him which he would state to them. And he gave them a further time to answer. He laid it down as a principle agreed on all hands that the crown cannot grant conusance of causes in equity and, that being admitted, the question is whether, by the general words in their charter of conusance of all pleas, personal debts, contracts, accounts, injuries, etc., conusance of pleas in equity, which is not expressly mentioned and which the crown could not grant by express words, shall be understood to be granted. The words that the justices of the Common Pleas *aut alii judices quicunque* shall not intermeddle must be understood *secundum subjectam materiam* in the cases in which conusance is granted. As for Lord Hale's opinion in the case of Castle v. Smithfield in Hardres,[1] this matter was no otherwise to his purpose than barely whether those general words of *alii judices* would extend to the Exchequer, which he thought they would. If conusance of pleas in equity is not granted by the charter, it is not given by the Statute,[2] which confirms only and does not enlarge the grant. And if it be not granted by the charter nor consequently by the Statute, the University, whose right stands purely on the charter and the Statute, have no right to conusance of causes in equity. Their power of ending by the civil law is granted to them by the charter in express terms, and the crown can grant no such power. Yet the charter that was void in that part before is made good by the Statute.

To the precedents that had been laid before him, he said that some were upon suspicions only and these were certainly wrong because it could not appear

[1] *Castle v. Lichfield* (1669), *ut supra*.

[2] Stat. 13 Eliz. I, c. 29 (*SR*, IV, 585–586).

whether the thing in dispute were matter of freehold or not. In cases of freehold, the University has no pretense of conusance. He took a difference to be between a claim of conusance and a plea of it. In the last case, the facts of the plea are always supposed to be true when the plea is argued and the allowance of it, therefore, no conclusive determination in favor of the party that pleads it, who must afterwards prove the facts alleged in the plea. He said that there was no such case as that of Pratt v. Taylor in the Chancery Reports,[1] but that there was one like it in which a claim of conusance by the University was disallowed and a plea of it afterwards allowed. The University produced the order by which the plea was allowed but not that for disallowing their claims. In the case of Sir Thomas Draper and Dr. Crowder, 2 Ventris,[2] the bill being brought for a special performance, a plea of conusance in the University was overruled. He said that, in the time of Lord Ellesmere, one of the greatest of his predecessors, this point arising, Lord Ellesmere, though most of the precedents produced by the University must have been fresh in his memory, would not determine it but referred it to the Master of the Rolls and the two judges of the Oxford Circuit, and, they not being able to decide it, he then referred it to the twelve judges, that the University had produced the two orders of reference and, afterwards, a third order made as upon a motion of course in which their claim was allowed without the least notice taken of the solemn proceedings before or of the opinion of the judges, that he was wonderfully surprised when he saw this order and sent thereupon to search the proper office for it, that he found the two orders of reference and several things done the same day, that the third order bore date but no footsteps of that, but he verily believed there never was any such order wherein the resolution of the judges did appear.

Mr. *Lutwyche* saying that Mr. Aldrich would consent to dismiss this bill and content himself with Dr. Stratford's affidavit about matters of which he sought a discovery by his bill provided the University would consent to drop their proceedings against him, Lord Chancellor [LORD HARCOURT] said I will not suppose that the University can entertain so wild a design as punishing Mr. Aldrich for suing here. My Lord North declared this to be such a case as their conusance did not extend to. Lord Nottingham denied their conusance. Lord Ellesmere and the Master of the Rolls and the two judges doubted of it. And shall Mr. Aldrich suffer for not being wiser than all these great men?

*Lutwyche*: Where an inferior court has conusance, the courts of Westminster Hall may proceed until they come into court and demand it regularly.

Attorney General [*Northey*]: The rule in the books is that, where there are words in the charter exclusive of the courts above, conusance may be either

[1] *Prat v. Taylor* (1674), 1 Chancery Cases 237, 22 E.R. 778, 1 Eq. Cas. Abr. 14, 21 E.R. 838.

[2] *Draper v. Crowther* (1684), 2 Ventris 362, 86 E.R. 487, also 1 Eq. Cas. Abr. 136, 21 E.R. 940.

pleaded or demanded. He said too that, by the opinion of the twelve judges, the Court of Chancery was within the word 'justices' in the Statute of Car. II, of bills of exceptions.[1]

But My Lord [HARCOURT] said that was a remedial act.

This matter was spoken to on another day by the counsel for the University, nobody appearing on the behalf of Mr. Aldrich. I was told they then grounded their right on prescription, which it was allowed might be a foundation for conusance of pleas in equity.

Lord Chancellor [LORD HARCOURT] at another day allowed their conusance, but I do not hear that he gave any reasons for his allowing it.

[Other copies of this report: Lincoln's Inn MS. Misc. 383, p. 256, Lincoln's Inn MS. Misc. 106, p. 221.]

## 489

## Stroud v. Twiford

(Ch. 1713)

*A lawyer can charge his client for work done as a barrister or for work done as a solicitor, but not for both.*

British Library MS. Hargrave 80, f. 143v, pl. 1

The plaintiff's testator, a barrister having an account between him and the defendant, his client, charged him with several items for drawing briefs and doing other things as a solicitor and for fees for moving etc. as a counsel.

Lord Chancellor [LORD HARCOURT] directed a master in taking the account to put the plaintiff to his election and to allow him what was due to his testator as solicitor or as counsel, but not both.

[Other copies of this report: Lincoln's Inn MS. Misc. 383, p. 255, Lincoln's Inn MS. Misc. 106, p. 220.]

## 490

## Wilkes v. Wilkes

(Ch. 1713)

*In this case, various inter vivos gifts were held to be part satisfaction of a settlement.*

[1] Stat. 16 & 17 Car. II, c. 8 (*SR*, V, 556–557).

British Library MS. Hargrave 80, f. 144v

A father entered into a bond conditioned to invest £800 in land to be settled to the use of the mother for life, remainder to the heirs of his own body. And he died, having first conveyed a small parcel of land to his eldest son in consideration of £60 and left him a legacy of £100 by his will charged on land, and a copyhold estate descended on him. The question was whether these not be equivalent to the £800 intended so to be settled should be taken by the son as a satisfaction *pro tanto*. It was urged that all the precedents on the head of satisfaction are, where the same given is equal to or exceeds the debt, that, though the words of the bond extended to lands generally, that freehold lands could only be intended, copyhold not being so regularly capable of being entailed nor are they so beneficial a freehold estate, being subjected to several services and the tenant of them without a particular custom, having no power to fell timber. On the other hand, the Case of Willcock and Lane was cited where lands descended were decreed to be a satisfaction of an agreement to settle.

Lord Chancellor [LORD HARCOURT] decreed the copyhold to be taken as a satisfaction *pro tanto* and the freehold conveyed in consideration of £60 unless that money was really paid by the son, but the £100 legacy, though charged in land, yet, being of a different nature from land which was agreed to be settled, he would not decree to be applied in part of satisfaction.

The case of Lawrence and Lawrence[1] was cited, where part of the estate was devised to the wife without saying in satisfaction of dower and the rest to others, and [it was] decreed by Lord Somers to be a satisfaction for her dower out of the rest because the whole will could not otherwise be complied with and he that will take advantage of one part of the will must comply with the rest. That decree was reversed by Wright.

*Jekyll*: I heard the Master of the Rolls deny the authority of that reversal.

Lord Chancellor [LORD HARCOURT]: It stands however.

[Other copies of this report: Lincoln's Inn MS. Misc. 383, p. 258.]

Lincoln's Inn MS. Misc. 384, p. 4, pl. 2

6 June 1713.

A bill [was brought] to have a specific performance of an agreement contained in a bond. The condition was to settle an estate of £100 a year on A. for life, remainder to B. for life, remainder to the heirs of the body of A.

*Vernon*, for the plaintiff: The plaintiff's late father enters into this bond on the plaintiff's marriage. The chief question is whether there has been an equitable

---

1 *Lawrence v. Lawrence* (1699), 2 Vernon 365, 23 E.R. 829, 2 Freeman 234, 22 E.R. 1180, 3 Brown P.C. 483, 1 E.R. 1448, 1 Eq. Cas. Abr. 218, 21 E.R. 1002, 2 Eq. Cas. Abr. 386, 388, 22 E.R. 330, 331, *sub nom. Lawrence v. Dodwell*, 1 Lord Raymond 438, 91 E.R. 1190, 3 Lord Raymond 151, 92 E.R. 615, 1 Lutwyche 734, 125 E.R. 384.

satisfaction of the condition of this bond. I admit, where a man is indebted to another and, by will, gives him a greater sum, it will be deemed a satisfaction, but not where he gives a lesser sum. Here, the father, after entering into this bond, purchases a copyhold estate of £60 a year, which he suffers to descend on the plaintiff. This cannot be a satisfaction, being of a lesser value. There was another estate conveyed to the son, but that cannot be a satisfaction, neither because the son paid £60 for it, neither can the bequest out of the personal estate be a satisfaction for a real settlement. Hooper v. Pollexton; Sim v. Sim.[1] We hope the Master shall see a settlement made according to the condition of the bond.

*Jekyll*, for the defendant, the executor: We hope to have an allowance of what the plaintiff has received out of the estate of his father and that it shall go in satisfaction of the bond. If the plaintiff will take advantage of one part of the will, he must have it by a construction of the whole will. Here, if the condition of the bond is to be performed, it will defeat part of the will. Lawrence's Case. The conveyance in fee, being a better estate than the plaintiff would (Vernon's Case) have by the condition of the bond, ought to be a satisfaction *pro tanto*.

*Mead*: We are in the common case. Where lands are conveyed or suffered to descend, they ought to be a satisfaction according to the value.

Lord Chancellor [Lord Harcourt]: The money paid by the father for the purchase of the copyhold estate must go in part of satisfaction. As to the conveyance of the real estate to the son, if it was voluntary, I shall take it to be a satisfaction *pro tanto*, not if the son paid £60. Therefore, let the Master look into it. The condition of the bond so far as it is not satisfaction must be carried into execution. The plaintiff must have a satisfaction of the marriage agreement with interest at £5 percent from the defendant, the executor, who has admitted assets. And then, the bond must be delivered up to the defendant.

2 Eq. Cas. Abr. 35, 22 E.R. 30

Trinity 12 Ann. [1713].

A marriage agreement was contained in a condition of a bond, *viz*. 'that the husband should purchase lands of £800 value to be settled upon himself for life, remainder to his wife for life, remainder to the heirs male of the husband begotten on the body of the wife, remainder to the husband's right heirs'.

The eldest son of the marriage brings his bill against his father's executors to have the benefit of this agreement.

The defendants insisted that the father in his lifetime purchased a copyhold estate which descended to plaintiff and, likewise, by his will devised £100 legacy to be raised out of land to the plaintiff and that this copyhold and legacy shall be

---

[1] *Hooper v. Pollexten and Davy* (Ch. 1710), see above, Case No. 182; *Pym v. Pym* (Ch. 1705), see above, Case No. 39.

taken as a satisfaction of the marriage agreement, especially in this case where the husband and wife were tenants in tail and might bar the issue.

HARCOURT, Chancellor, decreed the plaintiff a satisfaction of the agreement in the bond, and £4 percent interest of the £800 from his father's death, that the copyhold estate descended to him must be taken as a satisfaction *pro tanto* of the agreement according to the value of the land and the purchase money. But the £100 legacy, being devised out of land, is not to be taken in part of the satisfaction. As to a conveyance of six acres said to be made by the father to the plaintiff in his lifetime, [a Master is] to inquire whether it was a voluntary conveyance and then to go *pro tanto* in satisfaction of the agreement, but, if the purchase money was paid to the father, then [it is] to be no part of the satisfaction.

[Other copies of this report: 2 Eq. Cas. Abr. 218, 22 E.R. 185.]

## 491

## Anonymous

(Ch. 1713)

*A power when executed relates back to the time of its creation.*

British Library MS. Hargrave 80, f. 145, pl. 1

A Papist, by a marriage settlement made several years before the Statute 11 Will., c. 4,[1] reserved a power to himself of charging the estate settled with an annuity, this power to be executed after the Statute for the benefit of a Papist.

[It was] said by *How* and admitted by the Lord Chancellor [LORD HARCOURT] without [ *blank* ] that a power when executed has relation to the time of its creation and that the annuitant here was in paramount [to] the Statute and, by that means, would avoid it. *Sed quaere.*

[Other copies of this report: Lincoln's Inn MS. Misc. 383, p. 259, pl. 1.]

## 492

## Lord Kilmurry v. Geery

(Ch. 1713)

*In a suit to redeem a mortgage, the plaintiff will be ordered to pay all of the accrued interest plus the principal and court costs or be dismissed.*

[1] Stat. 11 Will. III, c. 4 (*SR*, VII, 586–587).

Lincoln's Inn MS. Misc. 384, p. 2, pl. 3

12 May. Lord Kilmorry v. Gery.

The plaintiff's father had a power by a settlement to charge the estate with £3000. And he mortgaged it to the defendant for that sum. Query whether the plaintiff can redeem without paying the interest.

Lord Chancellor [Lord Harcourt]: Is not the interest a consequence of the charge?

*Vernon*: If a tenant for life has a power of charging, he cannot exceed that power so as to bind the remainderman. Here, the interest ought to go out of the personal estate.

*Curia* [Lord Harcourt]: This is not a bare power to charge, but to raise a term, which is the same with a mortgage. The interest is a consequence upon the payment of the principal, interest, and costs. The defendant must re-convey.

British Library MS. Hargrave 80, f. 145, pl. 2

Lord Kilmory by *prochein ami* v. Dery.

By a settlement by the plaintiff's father upon marriage, the estate was limited to himself for life, remainder to the first son etc. in tail, with remainders over, and a power was reserved to the tenant for life to raise a term by deed or will for securing any sum not exceeding £3000. The plaintiff's father did thereupon borrow £3000 of the defendant and created a term for securing the repayment of it with interest in pursuance of this power. At the death of the plaintiff's father, there was above £500 due for interest. The bill was for a redemption upon payment of the £3000 and the interest that had accrued since the father's death and, there being great quantities of timber on the estate, to have that felled and applied to pay the mortgage.

*Vernon* and *How*, for the plaintiff, insisted on the power being expressly confined to a sum not exceeding £3000 on the defendant's coming in under and consequently with notice of that power and on his neglect in suffering interest to run so far in arrear, which a tenant for life of an equity of redemption is in common cases where there is no such restriction obliged to keep down and, if he suffers anything here, it is owing to himself, and on the great inconvenience if, by construction, the power should be confined to principal money only, in which cases, should a tenant for life live a great many years after executing this power, the interest might swell the debt to the value of the estate and so defeat the whole settlement.

But [it was] replied by the Lord Chancellor [Lord Harcourt] that there is no time fixed by the deed for the plaintiff's father's raising the money. He might do it at any time during his life by deed or by his will at his death. The interest is a necessary consequence of the charge. And though, as between a tenant for life and the reversion[er], the tenant for life is obliged to keep the interest down, yet, with respect to the encumbrance, his title to his debt cannot suffer by a tenant for life's not doing it. He, therefore, decreed a redemption to the plaintiff upon payment of the principal, all the interest due before and since his father's death, and costs within a year after the report, and, on a failure, his bill to be dismissed. And, on the prayer of the plaintiff and consent of the defendant, he directed a commission to issue, the plaintiff being an infant, to see what timber there was on the estate fit to be felled, upon the return of which, proper directions are to be given.

[Other copies of this report: Lincoln's Inn MS. Misc. 383, p. 259, pl. 2, Lincoln's Inn MS. Misc. 106, p. 224.]

2 Salkeld 538, 91 E.R. 456

Easter 12 Anne.

It was held that, if a man has power to charge land with any sum not exceeding the sum of £3000, he may charge it with £3000 and the interest besides, for the intention is to charge the premises with £3000 principal money, and that, of course, carries interest, and none would lend such sum on such security if the law were otherwise.

[Other reports of this case: Lincoln's Inn MS. Misc. 384, p. 2, pl. 3, 1 Eq. Cas. Abr. 341, 21 E.R. 1089, 2 Eq. Cas. Abr. 665, 22 E.R. 559.]

## 493

## Lelliot v. Devenish

(Ch. 1713)

*The true owner of a bearer instrument does not have any claim in equity against a bona fide purchaser for value.*

British Library MS. Hargrave 80, f. 146, pl. 1

The bill was brought for four bearer lottery tickets which had been left in the hands of Bennett by the plaintiff after three payments had been made upon them and were delivered by Bennett to the defendant for a valuable consideration and without notice of the plaintiff's right to them and for an account of what had been received upon them after they came to him. The defendant had made the fourth payment upon them after they came to him.

The Attorney General [*Northey*], for the plaintiff, insisted that the plaintiff's right was not barred by the delivery to the defendant, that [an action of] trover would lie for them at law, and that it was ruled by Chief Justice Hale, where J.S. picked tickets payable to bearer out of the pocket of A. and sold them, trover was maintainable for them by A. against the vendee. And he said privately that the trover would undoubtedly lie here against the defendant.

But Lord Chancellor [LORD HARCOURT] would not relieve the plaintiff. It would be a great hindrance to the common way of dealing if a fair purchaser of a note or ticket to bearer should be afterwards defeated. But he dismissed the bill without costs, the plaintiff's being a real sufferer, Bennett having afterwards become a bankrupt.

The Attorney [General *Northey*] desired it might be without prejudice to their action.

But, by *Vernon*, a bare dismission hinders no action.

[Other copies of this report: Lincoln's Inn MS. Misc. 383, p. 260, pl. 2, Lincoln's Inn MS. Misc. 106, p. 227.]

## 494

## Anonymous

(Ch. 1713)

*Where a London orphan dies intestate, underage, and unmarried, his orphanage share lapses, but his legacies go to his personal representative.*

British Library MS. Hargrave 80, f. 146, pl. 2

[As to the] custom of London as to orphans, [it was said] by *Vernon* it has been often settled that, if an orphan dies intestate, underage, and unmarried, his orphanage part shall survive to the other orphans and not to be distributed according to the Statute of Distribution,[1] but what he is entitled to as a legatee shall be distributable.

[Other copies of this report: Lincoln's Inn MS. Misc. 383, p. 261, pl. 1.]

## 495

## Garlick v. Jennins

(Ch. 1713)

*The privilege against self-incrimination applies to bankruptcy; however, this privilege can be voluntarily waived.*

British Library MS. Hargrave 80, f. 146v, pl. 2

The bill was *inter alia* to discover what acts of bankruptcy the defendant had been guilty of, to which he demurred.

---

[1] Stat. 22 & 23 Car. II, c. 10 (*SR*, V, 719–720).

And *How* insisted that, the Statute of Bankruptcy[1] being penal, a man is not obliged to discover anything that will expose him to them.

Lord Chancellor [LORD HARCOURT] seemed to be of the same opinion, but he overruled the demurrer, the defendant having confessed by his answer that he had executed a composition deed for paying 10s. per pound to his creditors, which is an act of bankruptcy.

[Other copies of this report: Lincoln's Inn MS. Misc. 383, p. 261, pl. 3, Lincoln's Inn MS. Misc. 106, p. 229, pl. 1.]

## 496

## Upcott v. Coleman

(Ch. 1713)

*In this case, the payment of interest that was contracted for was enforced by the court.*

Lincoln's Inn MS. Misc. 384, p. 7, pl. 1

23 June 1713.

The query was whether a mortgage should carry 5 or 6 percent. There was an endorsement on the mortgage [that], provided the mortgagor paid interest within three months after the end of every year, it should be at 5, otherwise at 6 percent.

*Jekyll*, for the plaintiff: The mortgagee is dead. The administrator *durante minore aetate* gave a receipt to the defendant, the mortgagor, for part of the interest at 5 percent. He cannot give a release or extinguish any right thing.

*Vernon*: Where a lesser sum is to be paid in lieu of a greater, the condition must be punctually performed, which it is not in this case. Whatever is endorsed on a deed at the time of the execution is of the same force as if contained in it.

*Hooper*, for the defendant: We took up money at 6 percent to pay the interest. But there was none to receive it.

Lord Chancellor [LORD HARCOURT]: The Master must take the account of the interest according to the endorsement.

British Library MS. Hargrave 80, f. 147, pl. 1

It was admitted by *Vernon* and Lord Chancellor [LORD HARCOURT] that, where there is a provision in a mortgage to accept £5 percent instead of £6 [percent] if paid within three months after the end of the year and the mortgagor fails in paying within three months, that shall not entirely destroy the proviso, but, if, afterwards, the mortgagor pay the subsequent interest within the respective three months, he shall have the benefit of it in such payment. But, in the first

[1] Stat. 1 Jac. I, c. 15 (*SR*, IV, 1031–1034).

case, interest was decreed after the rate of £6 percent *ab initio*, no payment having been made in due time.

[Other copies of this report: Lincoln's Inn MS. Misc. 383, p. 262, pl. 1, Lincoln's Inn MS. Misc. 106, p. 229, pl. 2.]

## 497

## Abbott v. Hart

(Ch. 1713)

*Where there is a lease for years made by a tenant for life and the lessor dies before the term expires, the lessee has no remedy in equity against the lessor's estate.*

British Library MS. Hargrave 80, f. 147, pl. 3

The plaintiff's mother, being barely tenant for life, demised lands to the plaintiff for twenty-one years rendering £90 *per annum* with a clause of reentry for her and her heirs and assigns. There was a covenant in the deed on the plaintiff's part to permit her, her heirs, and assigns to sue any persons in the plaintiff's name that should hawk or hunt there during the term, and, on the defendant's mother's part, that the plaintiff should hold and enjoy against her and her heirs and all claiming under her. She died in the middle of the term, making the defendant executor, who brought an [action of] ejectment as next in remainder. And, thereupon, the plaintiff brought his bill to be quieted in the possession during the remainder of his term or to have satisfaction out of the assets, which the defendant admitted the lands being worth £30 or £40 and more than the reserved rents.

It was insisted upon for the plaintiff that his rent made him a purchaser for a valuable consideration, that it was plain from the lease that he contracted for an absolute term of twenty-one years, that the clause of reentry for herself and her heirs and the tenant about suing plainly showed that she dealt with the plaintiff as one that had the inheritance, and that, though the lease could not be established, her assets ought to make good her contract, at least in equity, upon the mention of Nokes' Case,[1] where a special covenant restrained the general covenant, which the law would have implied.

*Pauncefoot* cited the case of Johnson v. Proctor in Yelverton,[2] where one joint tenant for years assigned over his part and died and the other took upon him to grant the whole without taking notice of the severance of the jointure and covenanted that he had done no act etc., and notwithstanding this special covenant, it was ruled that the general implied that one was not restrained by it.

[1] *Nokes v. James* (1599), 4 Coke Rep. 80, 76 E.R. 1056, Croke Eliz. 674, 78 E.R. 912.

[2] *Johnson v. Procter* (1610), Yelverton 175, 80 E.R. 116.

But it not appearing here that the plaintiff had paid any fine or was bound by covenant to lay out anything in improvement or had done so, the Master of the Rolls [TREVOR] did not think this case proper in equity and dismissed his bill.

[Other copies of this report: Lincoln's Inn MS. Misc. 383, p. 262, pl. 3, Lincoln's Inn MS. Misc. 106, p. 230, pl. 2.]

## 498

## Tooker v. Wilson

(Ch. 1713)

*Upon the default of a debtor, a creditor cannot sell Exchequer annuities that were mortgaged without a bill in equity to foreclose unless there is a specific covenant in the mortgage that he can. It is otherwise where shares of stock have been mortgaged.*

Lincoln's Inn MS. Misc. 384, p. 6, pl. 1

A bill [was brought] to have an account of Exchequer annuities which were mortgaged to the defendant and which the defendant had sold without foreclosing the mortgage.

*Conyers*, for the plaintiff: The annuities cost £6400 and were mortgaged to the defendant for £500. In the Case of East India stock, a mortgage was sold, yet a redemption [was] decreed.

Solicitor General [*Raymond*], for the defendant: If, in the City, upon every mortgage of this nature recourse must be to a court of equity, it will lessen the credit of stocks. It is the common custom there, if stocks are not redeemed according to the agreement, the mortgagee may sell.

*Vernon*: The plaintiff has not brought this bill against the purchaser. Therefore, it is improper. We gave notice to the plaintiff that he would sell the annuity, and he desired us to respite it until a further day, which he did. And we sold the annuity for the full value. Woodcroft v. Staines.

Lord Chancellor [LORD HARCOURT]: The usurer will have an admirable trade if this be allowed. I take the Exchequer annuity to be of the same nature with land and not like the other stocks. It is a certain security. The defendant, the mortgagee, has done what he ought not without foreclosing the mortgage. And, therefore, he must assign the annuity of like value to the plaintiff upon his paying principal and interest. I will not give the mortgagee his costs hitherto.

N.B. This decree was reversed in the House of Lords upon an appeal.

British Library MS. Hargrave 80, f. 147v

The plaintiff, as administrator to Mr. Thyne, brought his bill against the defendant, a goldsmith, for the redemption of four Exchequer annuities, each of £100 *per annum* for ninety-nine years, which were purchased by the intestate for £6400 and assigned in 1703 to the defendant for £5000; the assignment was defeasanced that, on payment of the £5000 with [ *blank* ] at six months end, the defendant should reconvey, and there was a covenant in the assignment from the intestate to pay the £5000 and interest. In 1712, the defendant sent notice to the plaintiff that he intended to sell the annuities and desired him to be present at the sale to see that they were fairly sold. The plaintiff, in answer, desired him to respite the sale for a few days, which the defendant did and then sold them at eleven years and a half's purchase and, they at that rate not amounting to the debt by £170, he brought an action of covenant for that against the plaintiff, who first pleaded *plene administravit* and then brought a writ of error and, afterwards, this bill.

The defendant insisted on the matters above by answer and that it was the practice among merchants that, where these fluctuating securities were mortgaged, if they were not redeemed by the day specified, the mortgagee had liberty to sell, that the sale here was made *bona fide* and at the common price of those annuities at that time, which three brokers[1] swore to be the then market price. It was insisted that the nature of government securities and stock being more variable and uncertain than land made a difference between a mortgage of one and the other and that, though the redemption of land could not be lost but by the act of the party or decree of this court, it was not usual to bring a bill to foreclose the redemption of the other and that the common practice of the Exchange having been to sell on failure of payment at the day without foreclosing by a bill, it would be dangerous to break into it however erroneous it might be at first and would very much lessen the value of those securities and hinder the making pledges of them if, afterwards, they could not be sold without coming to a court of equity, that the plaintiff was improper in this case to pray a redemption without bringing the vendee before the court, a redemption following the thing redeemable, especially in this where the vendee must come in with notice of the defeasance, nor could the plaintiff demand any satisfaction on account of any fraud or breach of trust in the defendant in setting to sale, the sale having been made *bona fide* at the market price and [there was] no proof on the other side to impeach it.

*How* cited a case where an agent of a regiment pledged army debentures to J.S.; from time to time, J.S. sold them and, afterwards, the agent brought his bill for an account and to redeem, but he said that the sale was ruled to be good, both at the Rolls and here.

But the Lord Chancellor [Lord Harcourt] took a difference between stock, whose value depends chiefly upon imagination, and Exchequer annuities, which are a certain permanent interest. And he decreed a redemption, and the defendant on payment to reconvey the same annuities or others on the same fund.

---

[1] brothers *MS.*

It was said that, in mortgages of annuities, stock, etc., it was usual to insert a covenant that the mortgagee, on failure of payment at the day, should have liberty to sell, which was not done here.

I think the defendant, for his ill defense, had no costs to the time of the decree.

[Other copies of this report: Lincoln's Inn MS. Misc. 383, p. 263.]

[Other reports of this case: 1 Peere Williams 261, 24 E.R. 379, 5 Brown P.C. 193, 2 E.R. 622, 2 Eq. Cas. Abr. 597, 608, 634, 22 E.R. 502, 511, 532.]

499

## Napier v. Aisham

(Ch. 1713)

*Upon a sale of land, money retained out of the purchase price to pay off encumbrances can be first used to compensate for a deficiency in the value contracted for.*

Lincoln's Inn MS. Misc. 384, p. 4, pl. 1

6 June.

The defendant, upon the purchase of the plaintiff's estate for £9700, was to retain £2400 out of the purchase money to discharge encumbrances. The bill charges that the defendant did not pay off the encumbrances in due time, but suffered them to run at interest.

*Vernon*, for the plaintiff [Napper]: We hope to have an account of the interest. The defendant was but a trustee for us. He insists that the land did not hold out in the number of acres, but it did in value, which is sufficient.

Solicitor General [*Raymond*], for the defendant: There are other debts which will exhaust the £2400. And, there being a covenant that the land is free from encumbrances, we must retain to save ourselves harmless. £1000 is retained to answer the deficiency in value.

Lord Chancellor [Lord Harcourt]: If there be a deficiency in value, the defendant must have a satisfaction out of the money in his hands. The rest must be applied to pay off the encumbrances. I reserve the consideration of interest until after the Master's report.

Note *Vernon* said, if a bill be dismissed against some defendants, they may be examined as witnesses, but not as parties.

## 500

## Beak v. Wilson

(Ch. 1713)

*A court of equity will enjoin a common law action by a creditor against his debtor who has been discharged in bankruptcy.*

British Library MS. Hargrave 81, f. 57, pl. 1

8 June 1713.

If a bankrupt be discharged by a certificate and a creditor afterwards sues him at law and he brings his bill to be relieved, it is now of course to grant an injunction on producing the certificate. And so it was done here on motion.

[Other copies of this report: British Library MS. Hargrave 82, f. 54, British Library MS. Hargrave 77, f. 15v, pl. 1, British Library MS. Hargrave 303, f. 28v, pl. 1.]

## 501

## Atherton v. Rook

(Ch. 1713)

*The terms of a contract reduced to writing cannot be varied by parol evidence.*

Lincoln's Inn MS. Misc. 384, p. 5, pl. 1

12 June.

A bill [was brought] to have a settlement rectified. The limitation was to the defendant Rook for life, remainder to his wife for life, remainder to the heirs of his body. Rook covenants in the settlement that the estate shall go according to the uses. But, afterwards, he levies a fine and suffers a recovery. The bill prays that Rook may be made but a bare tenant for life.

*Vernon*, for the defendant: Whatever parol discourse there were before or after the settlement, it cannot be varied after it is reduced into writing. The covenant that the estate should remain to the uses in the settlement will not hinder him from suffering the recovery, which, by law, he had a power to do.

N.B. It had been.

Lord Chancellor [Lord Harcourt] dismissed the bill with costs.

## 502

## Anonymous

(Ch. 1713)

*The words of a will 'worldly goods and live cattle' carries the live and dead stock that is proper to be kept in barns or granaries.*

Lincoln's Inn MS. Misc. 384, p. 5, pl. 2

2 July.

Lord Chancellor [Lord Harcourt]: Upon the words of a will 'I give all my worldly goods and live cattle to' A., it carries the live and dead stock that is proper to be kept in barns or granaries.

## 503

## Attorney General, ex rel. v. Brampston

(Ch. 1713)

*Funeral expenses are to be paid out of a decedent's estate.*

*Where it is impractical for co-executors to act, they can be discharged.*

British Library MS. Hargrave 77, f. 15v, pl. 3

9 July.

The Lady Johanna Thornhill devised several money legacies to charities and also the residue and surplus of her personal estate. She gives several specific legacies to several persons and money legacies to her executor and others. She orders her body to be buried in the parish church of Wye and a monument to be set up there for her, her executors to have the distribution of some of those churches and, after them, the minister of Wye and four ministers of the nearest parishes. And she makes the defendant Dr. Brampston and the relators, Sir George Wheeler and Dr. Wells, executors. Dr. Brampston, being the only executor in town at the lady's death, possesses himself of the estate and proves the will. Mr. Thornhill, the testatrix's nephew, desired Dr. Brampston order for the church of Wye to be put into mourning. And, the Doctor afterwards refusing to pay for it, Mr. Thornhill is sued, and a verdict [is found] against him for £18 damages besides costs. And he being a defendant here insists to have satisfaction.

*Curia*: As to the damages recovered, they shall be looked upon as part of the funerals, being done at the executor's desire. But it was Thornhill's own fault to suffer himself to be sued for the money. Therefore, he is not to have any allowance for the costs. The executors being too remote from the place where the charity is, [are] to be discharged. Dr. Brampston [being] in London, Dr. Wells in Worcester, and Sir George Wheeler at Durham, it is impracticable for them to distribute. Therefore, he orders the minister of Wye and the four next parishes [to do it].

[Other copies of this report: British Library MS. Hargrave 303, f. 29.]

## 504

## Lane v. Hubert

(Ch. 1713)

*Where testamentary trustees are required to convey an estate tail to a bankrupt, they must convey a fee simple in the land to the assignees of the commissioners of bankrupts.*

Lincoln's Inn MS. Misc. 384, p. 7, pl. 2

A., by his will, directs his trustees to convey an estate tail to B., who becomes bankrupt.

Lord Chancellor [Lord Harcourt]: It is as strong as if he had devised the land to such uses. It vests a fee simple in the assignees of the commissioner of bankrupts. The trustees must convey a fee at the costs of the assignees.

## 505

## Iveson v. Greathead

(Ch. 1713)

*Gambling debts are void and unenforceable.*

Lincoln's Inn MS. Misc. 384, p. 7, pl. 3

16 July 1713.

*Jekyll*, for the plaintiff: A bill [was brought] to be relieved against a bond of £60 given for money lost by gaming. The bond bore date since the Statute of Gaming, 9 Ann.[1] The plaintiff had given the defendant notes which were dated before the Statute, but the defendant, not thinking himself secure, made the plaintiff give him this bond. And the covenant of it being the delivering up of the former notes, the plaintiff could not in the action brought against him by the defendant upon the bond give in evidence that the money was won at play. It is time this Statute should be put in execution.

Lord Chancellor [Lord Harcourt]: I will construe the Act as liberally as I can. I am sure I am within the words of the Statute. Let there be a perpetual injunction. The defendant must deliver up the bond to the plaintiff. If he give the

[1] Stat. 9 Ann., c. 19 (*SR*, IX, 476–477).

plaintiff a general release within a month, he shall be excused costs. Upon his default, he shall pay costs to the plaintiff.

## 506

## Nortwick v. Faning

(Ch. 1713)

*A parish vestry can be ordered to pay the debts of the parish.*

British Library MS. Hargrave 81, f. 58

10 August.

The plaintiff had been a churchwarden of the parish of [ *blank* ] in London and had expended considerable sums in carrying on and defending several suits for the said parish at the desire and request of the vestry, of which the parish had repaid part, and, by an order of the vestry when he went out of his office, auditors were appointed to examine and state his accounts, which they did and so settled them. And they were allowed by the vestry. Afterwards, in the time of new churchwardens, several sums were paid to them for fines to be excused from parish offices, which they refusing to pay to the plaintiff Nortwick towards satisfaction of his said demand without an order of the vestry, and neglecting to call any for that purpose, the plaintiff brings his bill against the present churchwardens setting forth this case and praying that the said money received by the defendants for fines might be applied towards his satisfaction and that the defendants may be ordered to call a vestry and that, on this extraordinary occasion, the defendants might be directed to raise an extraordinary rate on the parishioners to pay the plaintiff the remainder of the money due to him.

Lord Chancellor [Lord Cowper]: It is my opinion the plaintiff ought to be paid what is justly due to him. But I will not meddle with the money in the churchwardens' hands by fines etc., for that is for the ordinary uses and occasions of the parish. The plaintiff ought to have applied to the vestry for satisfaction before he brought this bill. If an application of this kind be encouraged, I shall bring all vestry business into this court, which I will not do. Therefore, let the churchwardens call a vestry that the parish may be satisfied and see what justly remains due to the plaintiff. And for so much as shall appear due, let the vestry make an extraordinary rate on the parish to reimburse him.

[Other copies of this report: British Library MS. Hargrave 82, f. 55, pl. 2, British Library MS. Hargrave 77, f. 16, pl. 1, British Library MS. Hargrave 303, f. 30.]

## 507

# Anonymous

(Ch. 1713)

*A court of equity will cure defective devises in favor of creditors but not in favor of legatees.*

British Library MS. Hargrave 81, f. 59

*Eodem die* [10th August].

Where a tenant in tail by will devises his entailed lands to charitable uses or for payment of debts, equity, in favor of those and because the party had it in his power to make a perfect conveyance of his estate for those purposes and defeat the remainders and that, in conscience, every man ought to be just and pay his debts where it is in his power generally speaking, will supply this defect against the heir at law and execute the intention of the party. And it is daily experience so to do and decree according to the intent of the parties so far as may be done and is just. But equity will not supply the defect against an heir at law to defeat him in favor of legatees, who are mere volunteers and whose demands arise from a mere generosity of the party.

[Other copies of this report: British Library MS. Hargrave 82, f. 57, British Library MS. Hargrave 77, f. 16, pl. 2, British Library MS. Hargrave 303, f. 30v, pl. 1.]

## 508

# Taylor v. Lee

(Ch. 1713)

*A question in this case was whether a court of equity will rectify a defect in a deed of settlement for the benefit of a child of the settlor.*

*A devise to a specific person who is described as the testator's wife is valid even though they were not married.*

*In settlements, where the intention of the parties is clearly evident and does not take effect through the unskillfulness of the conveyancer, a court of equity will supply the defect. However, in this case, the intent of the grantor was not clearly contrary to the words of the conveyance.*

British Library MS. Hargrave 77, f. 16v, pl. 2

31 October.

The plaintiff's father, being seised in fee of divers lands in Kent and also of the rectory of Tentor, on the plaintiff's marriage, settles the lands in Kent to the use of himself for life, remainder to the plaintiff for life, remainder to the intended wife for her jointure, then to the issue of the marriage in tail male. And as to the rectory of Tentor, he limits that to himself for life, remainder to the heirs male of his body, remainder to the heirs of his body generally, remainder to his right heirs. The intended marriage took effect. And, afterwards, the plaintiff's father married or cohabited with the defendant and levied a fine of the rectory and then, by will, devises it to the defendant and dies.

The plaintiff exhibits his bill setting forth this whole matter and taking notice that, in the settlement, there were no trustees to support the contingent uses, which must be by mistake, it not being possible to suppose that, in a settlement of marriage, it could be the intention of the parties that the person who makes that settlement should have it in his power to destroy it and defeat the purchasers of their purchase at his will and pleasure. And he prayed, therefore, to have this defect in the settlement rectified by a decree and that the defendant should account for the rents and profits.

[Other copies of this report: British Library MS. Hargrave 82, f. 59, British Library MS. Hargrave 81, f. 61, British Library MS. Hargrave 303, f. 31.]

British Library MS. Hargrave 80, f. 154

The plaintiff's father, in consideration of his son's marriage and of a considerable portion, conveyed an estate more than adequate to the portion to the son for life, then to the wife for her jointure, remainder to the first and every other son of the marriage in tail etc. And, by the same deed, he limited another estate to himself for life, remainder to trustees for five hundred years to raise £100 to be disposed of by him, remainder to the heirs male of the body of the son and of his intended wife, remainder to the heirs of the body of the son etc. In the same deed, there was a proviso for the son to make a jointure to any second wife and to lease the lands limited to him in present possession and, after his father's death, those limited to his father for life. The father afterwards died in the son's life[time] and, by his will, devised the last mentioned estate partly to a woman with whom he had long lived as a wife by the name of his 'beloved wife Phyllis' and partly to his son by her and his heirs. The bill was brought chiefly to impeach the will upon the insufficiency of the devise in regard the plaintiff's father, as he alleged, had never been married to the person he called his wife in his will.

But for that, the court seemed clearly of opinion that, they having lived together and being reputed for man and wife, the devise would be good whether they proved the marriage or not.

The second thing sought by the bill if the first failed was to have a supposed defect in the conveyance supplied.

It was urged for the plaintiff by *Sir Joseph Jekyll, Chesshyre, Vernon*, and *How* that equity always carries articles into execution according to the intent of the parties and that, in conveyances executed where the intent of the parties appeared and did not fully take effect through the unskillfulness of the drawer, equity, in favor of purchasers, would supply the defect as if, in a settlement for valuable consideration, lands were limited to a man for 99 years if he should so long live, remainders to the heirs of his body or, if the father were made tenant for life, remainder to his first son etc. in tail and no limitation to trustees to preserve contingent remainders and the father, before the birth of a son, should levy a fine, equity, in each case, would interpose, in the first, take care that the limitations should be made effectual, in the last, preserve the estate for the first son. So, if livery or enrollment were omitted, equity would supply them in favor of a purchaser. The case of Finch v. Lord Winchelsea[1] was cited where an omission in a conveyance executed was supplied, and that of Cholmonly v. Cholmonly.[2] In the present case, it was said that there was a plain omission in not limiting the second estate to the plaintiff for life. The powers of making a jointure and, especially, that of leasing was urged as evidence of the parties' intention that the plaintiff should take the estate for life, it being absurd to give him a power to make leases of which he was to reap no benefit. And the plaintiff being a purchaser, it was insisted that, if the bill had been brought against the father in his lifetime, he would have been compelled to join in making the settlement agreeable to the parties' intention and that the defendants, being voluntary devisees, stood in his place, that, if they would not be compelled to make a conveyance to the plaintiff for life, yet, at least, they ought to make good the limitation to the heirs of his and his wife's body and that to the heirs of his body, who were equally purchasers of those limitations, and which it could not have been presumed to have been the intention of the parties to have left so precarious [an estate] as to be defeated by the death of the plaintiff's father before the plaintiff.

Lord Chancellor [Lord Harcourt]: A difference has been always observed between articles that are executory and settlements executed. But in settlements where the intention of the parties is evident and does not take effect through the unskillfulness of the conveyancer, this court ought to supply the defect. But then, the intention ought to be extremely plain. In the case of a limitation for 99 years and then to the heirs of his body, I would rectify it because of an apparent mistake. He seemed to say the same of supplying livery, enrollment, etc. But the intention of the parties is not so plain here. If there was as certain a provision intended for the issue out of the second estate as out of the first, why was the expression varied? There being a sufficient provision made before, it might be the parties' intention that this should be contingent. The mistake may be as well in inserting the power as in omitting a limitation. And were there unquestionably a mistake, here is no evidence of the intention of the parties but what arises from the deed itself. And nothing can be collected from thence certain enough whereby to rectify it. He gave no relief to the plaintiff on that head but affirmed the decree of the Master of the Rolls [Trevor] in that respect.

---

[1] *Finch v. Earl of Winchelsea* (Ch. 1713), see below, Case No. 509.

[2] *Chomley v. Chomley* (1688), 2 Vernon 47, 82, 23 E.R. 642, 663, 1 Eq. Cas. Abr. 66, 160, 161, 21 E.R. 880, 958, Chancery Repts. *tempore* Jac. II, 440.

In the Case of Finch v. Lord Winchelsea, My Lord [Lord Harcourt] relied on letters to prove the parties' intent, and, in that of Cholmonley v. Chomonley, [it] was said to be about parcel or not parcel and there was written evidence to guide the court. In this, it was said that the wife and child, for so they were to be presumed, were not to be considered as volunteers.

[Other copies of this report: Lincoln's Inn MS. Misc. 383, p. 271, pl. 2, Lincoln's Inn MS. Misc. 106, p. 239.]

## 509

## Finch v. Earl of Winchelsea

(Ch. 1713)

*A partially executed oral contract will be specifically enforced in equity.*

British Library MS. Hargrave 80, f. 149

Lord Chancellor [Lord Harcourt]: I think the plaintiffs are entitled to the relief they seek by their bill. The case is thus. The Dowager Lady Winchelsea, widow of Earl Charles's grandfather, was a jointress of part of the estate, remainder to Charles, late earl of Winchelsea, in tail, with remainders to his uncles successively for life and their first sons etc. in tail, remainder to the heirs of Lord Nottingham etc. of the rest of the estate. Charles, earl of Winchelsea, was tenant for life, remainder to his first son etc. by his then lady in tail, remainder to himself in tail with the like remainders over, *prout* the jointure estate and with a power to revoke his own estate tail and all the subsequent remainders. His estate being thus settled and he in great straits for money, nobody would advance any upon the last estate, in regard of the contingency of issue by his lady nor should he bar the remainders of the jointure estate or let in any charge upon them without the consent of the jointress. Under those circumstances, he comes to an agreement with the jointress, who has acted in the case as a common trustee for the issue male of her husband, to join with him in a recovery in order to let in £6000 on the remainders. And, in consideration of it, he, on his part, agrees not barely to depart with his power of revocation, but to secure both estates to the remaindermen and their first etc. sons in tail. It has been objected that this agreement stands singly on parol evidence. If that were so, though I have the greatest honor for the witnesses that have been examined and for their credit, I could not ground my decree upon it. But here are letters to the jointress from Lord Weymouth, who acted between them, and from Charles, earl of Winchelsea, himself acknowledging the agreement, which has been fully executed on her part and imperfectly on the other. The lady appears to have been hurried on in this affair. The transactions which Mr. Johnson was solely entrusted with, he only provided a release of the power of revocation and got that executed. And, at the same time, he left

Earl Charles tenant in tail, and he, afterwards, suffered a recovery and barred the remainders over, which, by the agreement, were intended to have been preserved. It was plainly a defective execution of the agreement on the part of Earl Charles, and such defective executions in case of purchasers are daily relieved here. In this case, the remaindermen are purchasers by the £6000 being let in upon them by the consent of the jointress.

Let the Master prepare a conveyance according to the agreement and the heirs of Earl Charles and all proper parties join in it, but the creditors of Earl Charles who have a legal lien upon this estate after he became seised in fee of it under the recovery and who shall not be satisfied by this personal estate, their demands are not to be impeached, but let a part of the estate be conveyed to trustees to be sold for their satisfaction.

The case of Lester v. Foxcraft was cited, where a parol agreement about a building lease was partly executed and the tenant, in confidence of it, laid out great sums of money, the landlord was compelled to perform it by the Lords, not here.[1]

[Other copies of this report: Lincoln's Inn MS. Misc. 383, p. 264, Lincoln's Inn MS. Misc. 106, p. 232.]

[Other reports of this case: 1 Peere Williams 277, 24 E.R. 387, 2 Eq. Cas. Abr. 257, 460, 683, 22 E.R. 218, 392, 574.]

## 510

## Attorney General v. Kemies
## Kemies v. Potter

(Ch. 1713)

*An executor can enforce an accounting between his decedent and an agent for money due to the decedent.*

British Library MS. Hargrave 80, f. 149v

The defendant Kemys was executrix of her husband, who died a major and captain of a company in Mr. Hill's regiment of foot [soldiers]. The question was about his and his company's pay at two periods, one for some years before his death, and that account was between him and Potter, the agent.

And My Lord [Lord Harcourt], in that, directed what was due to him or his company to be paid out of what the agent had received for the company. In the other, where the Attorney General was plaintiff and which concerned the pay for some time immediately before his death, My Lord [Lord Harcourt] directed the executrix only what was due to the testator for his personal pay

[1] *Lester v. Foxcroft* (1700), Colles 108, 1 E.R. 205.

and that of the servants allowed him and for what he had actually disbursed for his company for their subsistence or otherwise. He distinguished his case from that of Lillingston, which was affirmed in the House of Lords, and Bellasis v. Churchill,[1] in which he retained his opinion, in neither of which the Attorney General was a party and the contest was only between the officer's representative, who died in the service, and either the colonel or agent, and, if anything was to be gained, it was more reasonable that it should be got by the captain's representative than by the colonel and much more by the agent.

[Other copies of this report: Lincoln's Inn MS. Misc. 383, p. 265, Lincoln's Inn MS. Misc. 106, p. 233.]

## 511

## Anonymous

(Ch. 1713)

*Where a sum certain has been ordered to be paid, it must be paid before the defendant can bring a bill of review.*

British Library MS. Hargrave 80, f. 150, pl. 1

If a bill of review be brought before what is decreed upon an account be ascertained by a report, there is no necessity to pay anything to the other party. If after the sum is ascertained, [it] must be paid before the bill of review can be brought.

[Other copies of this report: Lincoln's Inn MS. Misc. 383, p. 266, pl. 1, Lincoln's Inn MS. Misc. 106, p. 234, pl. 1.]

## 512

## Anonymous

(Ch. 1713)

*Process for contempt of court can be issued only for matter appearing in the affidavit, and, if that is insufficient, it cannot be aided by other evidence of contempt.*

British Library MS. Hargrave 80, f. 150, pl. 2

Attachments are taken out at the party's peril. They must be grounded on an affidavit, and you cannot go out of your affidavit to support them; the contempt must appear on the face of the affidavit, both by *Vernon* and the Court.

[Other copies of this report: Lincoln's Inn MS. Misc. 383, p. 266, pl. 2.]

---

[1] *Bellasis v. Churchill* (Ch. 1712), see above, Case No. 438.

## 513

## Anonymous

(Ch. 1713)

*Where commissioners in bankruptcy make an assignment of the bankrupt's estate and then the creditors choose a different assignee, the first assignee will be ordered to assign the estate to trustees for the benefit of all of the assignees.*

British Library MS. Hargrave 80, f. 150, pl. 3

The commissioners, immediately after declaring the party a bankrupt, made an assignment to prevent the assignment's being overreached by a [writ of] extent bearing *teste* before it.

[It was said] by the Attorney General, another day, it was ruled with great solemnity on a special verdict in the Case of Nowell, a bankrupt,[1] that an extent binds from the *teste* not only from the inquisition.

Afterwards, the creditors met and chose the assignee of the commissioners and one more assignee. And the Statute[2] directing the commissioners to assign over to the assignees chosen by the creditors, there was an application to the court by petition for the direction of it what to do. They durst not vacate the first assignment and take a new one from the commissioners lest they should let in an extent tested between the two assignments and the first assignee, they apprehending, could assign to himself and another.

Lord Chancellor [LORD HARCOURT] directed that he should assign real estate to trustees to the use of himself and the other chosen assignee by the creditors. The personal [estate] he directed to continue as it was, but the first assignee not to transact anything about it without the concurrence of the second. It was proposed that he should assign an undivided moiety but apprehended it might create some difficulty if it were necessary to bring any actions.

[Other copies of this report: Lincoln's Inn MS. Misc. 383, p. 266, pl. 3.]

## 514

## Anonymous

(Ch. 1713)

*Where a judgment debtor dies, the judgment creditor can sue out a new writ of execution against the lands and goods of the decedent.*

---

[1] *Regina v. Arnold* (Ex. 1710), Dodd 356, 5 Price 631, 146 E.R. 716, Harvard Law Sch. MS. 537, pt. 2, p. 147.

[2] Stat. 6 Ann., c. 22, s. 5 (*SR*, VIII, 601).

British Library MS. Hargrave 80, f. 150, pl. 4

[As to the] death of a party in execution, the Statute 21 Jac. I, c. 24,[1] is a declaratory law and was made to quiet the disputes arising from the different resolution in 5 Co., Blanfield's Case, and Hobart, Foster and Jackson.[2]

[Other copies of this report: Lincoln's Inn MS. Misc. 383, p. 266, pl. 4.]

## 515

## Fawkner v. Fancourt

(Ch. 1713)

*A contract to indemnify for a marriage settlement is void and unenforceable.*

Lincoln's Inn MS. Misc. 10, p. 151

27 October 1713.

Mr. Fancourt, the plaintiff's [Susan Fawkner's] husband's father, upon his son's marriage with the plaintiff, covenants with the plaintiff's father that the lands which he had settled for the plaintiff's jointure were of the yearly value of £250 beyond all charges and reprises. But, before he entered into this covenant, he gets his son into articles wherein, taking notice of this covenant which he was about to enter into, the son covenants that, if his father should at any time be required to make good his covenant as to the jointure, then he would settle lands for that purpose and indemnify his father.

The father dies leaving little or no assets, and then the son dies, leaving one child only by the plaintiff, *viz.* a son, who died an infant, upon whose death, the reversion of the jointure lands descended upon the defendants, who were sisters and heirs at law to the plaintiff's husband.

The jointure falling much short of the £250 a year, she brings her bill to have it made up out of the assets of her husband, which were descended to the defendants, by virtue of the covenant which he had made with his father.

Lord Chancellor [Lord Harcourt]: It was a fraud both in the father and the son, and, though the son might have been relieved against the father upon his articles, yet as to the plaintiff, they are both answerable, and she ought to have a satisfaction out of both their estates, for, though the son has not covenanted with his wife's trustees, yet he having covenanted with the father, who had been guilty of the fraud, the plaintiff ought to stand in his room and have the benefit of that covenant. And he decreed her to be recompensed out of both their estates.

---

[1] Stat 21 Jac. I, c. 24 (*SR*, IV, 1233).

[2] *Blumfield v. Usewick* (1596), 5 Coke Rep. 86, 77 E.R. 185, also Moore K.B. 459, 72 E.R. 693, Croke Eliz. 478, 555, 573, 78 E.R. 730, 800, 817; *Foster v. Jackson* (1609), Hobart 52, 80 E.R. 201, also 2 Brownlow & Goldesborough 311, 123 E.R. 960.

It was insisted that her paraphernalia ought to go towards her satisfaction, but the court denied it upon the circumstances of this case.

## 516

## Humphreys v. Houblon

(Ch. 1713)

*A final judgment of the Court of Admiralty is res judicata in the Court of Chancery.*

*Depositions taken in the Court of Admiralty to prove a crime are not admissible in a court of equity.*

*A judgment in the Court of Admiralty that wages were forfeited because of mutiny is a good defense to a suit in equity for the wages.*

British Library MS. Hargrave 80, f. 153v

The bill was brought by seamen for their wages. The defendants disclosed in their answers that the plaintiffs had proceeded against them in the Admiralty for the same wages and that the sentence was against the plaintiffs there. And they insisted too on the plaintiffs' having forfeited their wages by mutiny. It was agreed that the depositions taken in the Admiralty Court could not be read here as evidence of the mutiny, but both they and the sentence there might be used to show that the same matter had been under consideration and determined there.

And upon reading them, it appearing that the libel there had been for the same matter and the plaintiff [was] barred there, Lord Chancellor [Lord Harcourt] dismissed their bill. The same plea had been good in bar. And a defendant might have the same advantage of it by insisting upon it by way of answer or disclosing it in the answer, which is the same thing, there being no particular form of insisting upon a thing in bar in answer, which *How* said he knew of. Where there are two concurrent jurisdictions, if the decision of the first should not be a good plea in bar in the second, it would be the utmost confusion. It is so if a bill be brought for a legacy after a libel for it in the spiritual court and a sentence against the plaintiff there.

[Other copies of this report: Lincoln's Inn MS. Misc. 383, p. 271, pl. 1, Lincoln's Inn MS. Misc. 106, p. 238.]

Lincoln's Inn MS. Misc. 384, p. 8, pl. 2

30 October. Humfreys v. Mouslin.

A bill [was exhibited] for seamen's wages. The defendant, by an account, insisted that the wages were forfeited by mutiny and that there was a sentence against the plaintiff in the Admiralty.

*Howe*: If there be a sentence against one upon a conditional legacy in the spiritual court, he cannot be relieved here.

*Vernon*, for the plaintiff: The depositions in the Admiralty are no evidence here, and the sentence should be pleaded.

Lord Chancellor [Lord Harcourt]: It is the same by way of answer. I dismiss the bill.

## 517

## Attorney General, ex rel. v. Eales

(Ch. 1713)

*The question in this case was whether a charitable devise for the poor of a dissenting congregation should be settled for that congregation or for the poor of the entire parish.*

Lincoln's Inn MS. Misc. 10, p. 157

8 November 1713. Attorney General, at the relation of the Deacons and [ . . . ] of a congregation of people commonly called Anabaptists frequently meeting at the house of A.B. in the parish of C. against Eales.

J.S., by will, devised part of his real estate to the poor of a congregation of people commonly called Anabaptists frequently meeting at the house of A.B. in the parish of C. And the bill is now brought to establish this devise against the defendant, the heir at law of the testator, who insisted that this was a void devise.

It was said for the relators that here was no legal estate given by the will and, therefore, they were very proper to come for the assistance of this court to direct the application of the estate.

In the Case of Johns and Strode before Lord Cowper,[1] there was a settlement made and a term limited to trustees upon trust to apply the rents for the poor of a congregation of Anabaptists, and the heir brought his bill to set aside the deed of trust, but the court would not take away the legal estate from the trustees and dismissed the bill and left the heir to go to law if he thought fit. But ours is a different case, for here is no legal estate devised. And, therefore, the Case of Johns and Strode is no precedent to govern this case.

Lord Chancellor [Lord Harcourt]: The mischief will be the same in both cases. If such trusts are allowed to be good where a legal estate is given or settled, it will be very easy to fix the legal estate in trustees. For my own part, I am not satisfied in establishing charities of this kind, for it may be a means to draw people from the Church [of England] by establishing charities for the support of the poor of separate congregations. It is one thing to tolerate the Dissenters[2] and another thing to establish a perpetual fund for their support.

I will consider of it. In the meantime, let me be attended with precedents. I shall make no scruple to settle the estate for charity. But the question is whether

[1] *Johns v. Gale* (Ch. 1712), see above, Case No. 434.

[2] Stat. 1 Will. & Mar., c. 18 (*SR*, VI, 74–76).

I shall do it for the poor of the whole parish or for that particular part which are of this congregation.

518

## Beaw v. Maddocks

(Ch. 1713)

*In this case, the defendant's plea of outlawry did not contain the required allegations.*

Lincoln's Inn MS. Misc. 10, p. 158

25 November 1713.

A plea of outlawry was overruled because the defendant had not averred that the person outlawed and the plaintiff were one and the same and because he had not averred that the outlawry was in force and unreversed, but it only said it was not reversed as he knew, had heard, or believed.

519

## Pinckney v. Young

(Ch. 1713)

*A bill of review lies for new matter discovered after a final decree, as well as for error on the face of the record, but an original bill is barred by the former decree.*

*Such an allegation of newly discovered matter must be supported by an affidavit, and the bill of review must be allowed by the court.*

Lincoln's Inn MS. Misc. 10, p. 159

The plaintiffs, Pinckney and A.B., had married the two daughters of John Young, who, by his will, had given part of his estate to trustees to be sold for the payment of his debts and for raising portions for his daughters. And the rest of his estate, he had given to the defendant Young, a remote relation.

After the testator's death, the defendant brought a bill against the daughters and the trustees for proving the will. And witnesses were examined the cause was heard and the will was established and the trusts were decreed to be executed.

After this decree, the plaintiff Pinckney, who married one of the daughters, discovered that a settlement was made by John Young upon his marriage, by which settlement, part of the lands was come to the daughters.

And they now bring a bill to have a discovery of this settlement, which it was charged was secreted by the defendant.

The defendant Young pleaded the will and the decree in bar of so much of the bill as tended to impeach the will or invalidate the decree. And he answered that he had never seen the settlement set forth in the bill.

And it was said by Mr. *Vernon* and so ruled that no decree of the court ought to be set aside by an original bill and that this bill was in effect to overthrow the decree and, therefore, if the plaintiffs had discovered any new matter which had arisen since the decree, they must bring a bill of review, though even that could not be done without leave of the court and making an affidavit of the discovery of such new matter.

And of that opinion was the court.

Then, it was objected for the plaintiffs that though the plea might be a good plea in bar to the relief, yet the defendant ought to answer as to the discovery prayed by the bill.

But, to this, it was answered that the plaintiff was not entitled to any discovery which tended to overthrow the decree upon an original bill, but he must have it upon a bill of review.

And of that opinion was the court, and [the court] allowed the plea.

British Library MS. Hargrave 80, f. 161, pl. 2

Pinkley v. Young.

The defendant's testator, by his will, devised the estate in question to the defendant charged with portions to his daughters, the now plaintiffs. And, upon a bill brought by the defendant against them as heirs, the will was established and the portions decreed to be raised and were accordingly, or part of them at least, raised and paid. Sometime after this decree, the plaintiffs got information, as they suggested by their bill, of a deed by which their father was only tenant in tail and, he not having suffered a recovery, his will as to this estate was void. This deed they sought a discovery of and relief by their bill, to which the defendant pleaded the will and former decree in bar of a discovery and of relief.

*Vernon*, for the defendant: A bill of review lies as well for new matter discovered after publication in the former cause of which no advantage could be taken there, as for error in the record. But, even the[re], the court is so tender that they must first apply to it for leave to bring such a bill and make an affidavit of their having discovered the new matter since publication. And, if they want a discovery of anything they have been informed of after the decree, for that too, a bill of review is proper and the defendant will be obliged to answer to the new matter in it. But that discovery is not to be had upon an original bill, nor has the court ever suffered a decree to be broken through or varied by an original bill.

Lord Chancellor [Lord Harcourt] agreed to Mr. Vernon's distinction and allowed the plea, the plaintiffs' being an original bill.

[Other copies of this report: Lincoln's Inn MS. Misc. 383, p. 283, pl. 2.]

## 520

## Waller v. Moore

(Ch. 1713)

*A court of equity will not grant relief against a discontinuance of a title to land.*

British Library MS. Hargrave 80, f. 150v, pl. 1

*Vernon* cited the case of Stapleton v. Straid in Lord North's time,[1] where the court would not oblige one who claims under a discontinuance to discover so much as a tenant to the *praecipe*. In the principal case, the defendant pleaded himself a purchaser under one who was tenant in tail by a feoffment in 1653 and did not deny notice, yet the court would not compel him to discover the deed in tail to enable him the plaintiff, whose title accrued to him as heir in tail within a few years, to bring an [action of] formedon etc.

Lord Chancellor [LORD HARCOURT] seemed to think this court never relieved against a discontinuance.

[Other copies of this report: Lincoln's Inn MS. Misc. 383, p. 266, pl. 5, Lincoln's Inn MS. Misc. 106, p. 234.]

## 521

## Carr v. Lord Burlington

(Ch. 1713)

*In this case, it was not the intent of the testator to take away the priority of the judgment creditors, but, as against the trust estate for the payment of debts, the judgment creditors came in upon an equal foot with the other creditors.*

*Interest is not due where it results from the delay of the creditor.*

British Library MS. Hargrave 80, f. 150v, pl. 2

The late Lord Burlington conveyed an estate in Ireland to trustees for payment of all such debts as he should owe at his death in equal proportion and without preferring one to another. He, afterwards, became indebted to several persons by judgments, bonds, and simple contracts. The first questions was between the judgment creditors and the others, whether they, having resorted to the personal estate for a satisfaction and using the preference there which the law gives them, having entirely exhausted that, should come in for a satisfaction for the residue of their debts, which the personal estate had not been sufficient to make good out

[1] *Stapleton v. Sherrard* (1683–1687), 1 Vernon 212, 305, 314, 432, 465, 23 E.R. 421, 485, 491, 567, 590, 2 Chancery Reports 257, 21 E.R. 672, 1 Eq. Cas. Abr. 76, 161, 21 E.R. 890, 958, Chancery Repts. *tempore* Jac. II, 61.

of the trust estate, *pari passu* with the other creditors or should bring the personal estate into hotchpot, it being subsequent to the deed of trust and acknowledged in England and the trust estate lying in Ireland, for their bringing the personal into a hotchpot or being postponed until the other creditors had received as much in proportion to their several debts out of the trust as they had out of the personal estate. It was alleged that it was plainly the intention of My Lord Burlington that all his creditors should have an equal satisfaction and that all debts were equal in equity and that My Lord might unquestionably have provided by express words that such of his creditors as made use of their priority at law against his personal estate should be postponed *pro tanto quoad* the trust estate and that his intention to make them all equal was [as] plain as it could have been had he made the express provision.

*Vernon*, who was for the other creditors, said that the resolutions where there was no such express provision had been both ways.

For the judgment creditors, it was said that, as against the personal estate, they had made use only of the preference which the law gave them and equity would not take it away, that it did not appear to be My Lord's intention to take away their priority anywhere but as against the trust estate and there they [were] contented to come in upon an equal foot with the rest.

Lord Chancellor [Lord Harcourt] directed that they should for the residue of their debt unsatisfied by the personal estate.

The next question relating to the judgment creditors was how long interest should be carried on upon their judgments. If any of them were not for a penalty, it was agreed they would not, and, if they were, as most or all were, the question was whether the interest should be carried on to this time or only to the death of Lord Burlington. The judgment creditors laid by for several years after Lord Burlington's death before they laid hold of his personal estate and contended to apply it in the first place to the interest accrued since My Lord's death, by which almost all the principal would have charged a charge upon the trust estate.

But My Lord [Lord Harcourt] was of opinion that they ought not to take that advantage of their own delay but that the personal estate ought to be applied towards what was due to them at My Lord's death and they came in upon the trust estate for the residue only of what was then due.

The question between the bond and simple contract creditors was whether interest should be carried on upon the bonds subsequent to the death of Lord Burlington.

And as to that, it was said and agreed to by Lord Chancellor [Lord Harcourt] that the principal interest due on the bonds at his death added to it and the simple contract debts became then equally a charge upon the trust estate and, being a charge on lands, would both equally carry interest from them.

But it being agreed that the trust estate would not pay what was due at his death, no interest was directed to be carried on after that time.

[Other copies of this report: Lincoln's Inn MS. Misc. 383, p. 267.]

[Other reports of this case: 1 Peere Williams 228, 24 E.R. 364, 2 Eq. Cas. Abr. 529, 22 E.R. 446.]

## 522

## Anonymous

(Ch. 1713)

*Fixtures erected by a tenant are removable by him.*

British Library MS. Hargrave 80, f. 151v, pl. 1

Lord Chancellor [Lord Harcourt] refused to grant an injunction to stay a tenant from carrying away iron gates and rails put up by himself. And he thought it not such a waste, if any, as the Court of Chancery would interpose in.

[Other copies of this report: Lincoln's Inn MS. Misc. 383, p. 268, pl. 1.]

## 523

## Whiting v. Ustick

(Ch. 1713)

*The heir or executor of a defendant may revive a suit.*

British Library MS. Hargrave 80, f. 152v, pl. 1

It was agreed in this case that the heir or executor of a defendant may revive; query whether in a bill for an account only. And [it was] ruled that the plaintiff, as devisee, might have brought a bill in the nature of a bill of revivor against the defendant to revive a suit at law in which the now defendant was plaintiff against his testator. The proceedings in that cause and three several verdicts by which a release in question was affirmed and another intermediate verdict obtained by the now plaintiff at which trial he had set up a demise of the trustee of the releasor to avoid trying the validity of the release were pleaded in bar of this bill, which sought to impeach that release and the plea being allowed, though the defendant failed in proving that the release was produced at the first trial.

Yet proving the residue, My Lord [Lord Harcourt] was of opinion that he had proved the material part of his plea and dismissed the bill with costs.

[Other copies of this report: Lincoln's Inn MS. Misc. 383, p. 269, Lincoln's Inn MS. Misc. 106, p. 237, pl. 1.]

## 524

## Child v. Sherman

(Ch. 1713)

*A purchaser of land has the right to redeem a mortgage on the land.*

British Library MS. Hargrave 80, f. 152v, pl. 2

Sir Richard Child purchased a country seat upon which the defendant had a mortgage and was in possession. And the defendant covenanted that, upon payment of the mortgage money on or before the end of twelve months, he would reassign to Sir Richard, his heirs, or assigns. Sir Richard sold the seat in the middle of the year to the plaintiff [Sir Caesar Child], who sent to the defendant to meet him at Mr. Gibson's, a scrivener, and there tendered him the money, which the defendant refused to accept because the year was not expired. At the end of the year, the plaintiff made him a second tender in specie and Exchequer bills and offered to have them immediately turned into money, if he had any objection to them. The defendant declared he had none, but refused to accept them, being unwilling to leave the house until he had provided himself with another to his mind. Upon this, the plaintiff brought this bill to redeem and the defendant brought a cross-bill to foreclose, but, after the tender and before the cross-bill, the plaintiff had made a forcible entry and detained the possession, whereupon, the defendant brought an [action of] ejectment.

Lord Chancellor [Lord Harcourt] decreed the plaintiff a redemption on payment of the principal and interest to the time of the second tender and from thence of the interest that he had received of the Exchequer notes that had been tendered for the time they continued in his hands, to which he was to be examined on interrogatories. And, in regard of the forcible entry made by the plaintiff about four months after the tender, he directed the accounts of profits to be carried on against the defendant only to the time of the tender. He gave the plaintiff his costs here in both causes and at law.

[Other copies of this report: Lincoln's Inn MS. Misc. 383, p. 270, pl. 1, Lincoln's Inn MS. Misc. 106, p. 237, pl. 2.]

## 525

## Churchill v. Hobson

(Ch. 1713)

*Under the circumstances of this case where one co-executor became a bankrupt, it was held to be too harsh to charge the solvent co-executor with the loss.*

British Library MS. Hargrave 80, f. 153

Churchill v. Lady Hobson and her infant children and Goodwin, executor.

Sir Charles Hobson distributed his personal estate by his will among his wife and children and made the plaintiff and the defendant Goodwin executors in trust for them. Goodwin was cashier to Sir Charles several years before his death and to his Lady afterwards. And when the personal estate of Sir Charles was got in after his death, the plaintiff joined with Goodwin in the receipts that were given. But Goodwin received all the money. Other parts of the personal estate were received by the plaintiff and paid over to Goodwin, who afterwards became a bankrupt, having at the time of his bankruptcy £15,000 or more of his testator's estate in his hands. The bill was brought by Churchill to be discharged of his executorship and indemnified against the loss occasioned by Goodwin's bankruptcy.

*Vernon* for the children took a difference between the case of co-trustees for the sale of lands and that of co-executors. In the first, there is a necessity of their joining both; without it, a title cannot be made out. And he thought it a little hard there to charge one trustee who only joined for conformity for what was received by the other. *Sed quaere.* In the case of Bradwell and Cachpole, in Chancery,[1] where such a co-trustee was charged, but that, in the case of co-executors, it was otherwise, for there was no necessity for their joining; one alone could give a sufficient discharge and, without joining, one would not be answerable for the other by law, from whence he inferred too that the words of this will, that one should not be answerable for the receipt of the other, had no effect, they being no more than what the law implied. He cited the case of Williams and Allen, decreed by Lord Keeper Wright and affirmed by Lord Cowper; in that case, two co-executors sold their testator's goods by public auction; one received all the money and (I think) gave receipts alone and after[wards] broke; the other was charged with the whole; and the Case of Murrell v. Cox and Pratt,[2] where two executors joined in a sale of bank stock and divided the money; then one broke and the other was charged with the companion's share, but all the counsels for the defendant allowed the case to be extremely hard.

Lord Chancellor [Lord Harcourt]: It is too hard to punish the plaintiff for depositing the trust money in the hands where it is probable Sir Charles himself would have lodged it and which he always trusted with his cash, besides the loss will not fall on creditors, but legatees.

[Other copies of this report: Lincoln's Inn MS. Misc. 383, p. 270, pl. 2.]

---

1 *Bradwell v. Catchpole* (Ch. 1712), see above, Case No. 413.

2 *Murrell v. Cox* (1707), see above, Case No. 62.

British Library MS. Hargrave 81, f. 81

The defendant Goodwin and one Churchill were executors of Sir Charles Hobson's will, and they both joined in giving receipts for money part of the testator's estate but Goodwin only received the money and he sometime after having failed, the residuary legatees bring their bill against Churchill for an account of the testator's estate and to charge him with what thereof Goodwin had received.

*Sir Joseph Jekyll*: There is a clause in the will that one executor shall not be charged with the receipts or defaults of the other. Churchill ought not to be charged because of joining in the receipt for the satisfaction of debtors since it appears that he did not receive any part of the money. In the Case of Fellows and Owen,[1] My Lord Somers declared that it was against natural justice that one executor or trustee should be charged with the receipt of the other. And in the case of Pitt and Murrell,[2] heard at the Rolls and afterwards affirmed here, where two joined in the sale of East India Stock, [it was] decreed that both should not be answerable, but that person only who received the money.

Of the other side, a distinction was made between executors and trustees, for, if trustees join in a conveyance and one only receive the money, this shall not charge the rest, because of the necessity of joining. But, in the case of two executors, there is no such necessity, for a discharge from or sale by one executor is good without the rest. Therefore, if more joined, they ought to be charged. And so it was adjudged in the Case of Wilkins and Allen, in the Lord Keeper Wright's time; goods were sold at public auction in the name of Wilkins, and the other executor received all the money and then proved insolvent; Wilkins was decreed to answer the money to the residuary legatees.

*Curia* [Lord Harcourt]: This is not a case of creditors, and it is too hard to charge Churchill by reason of joining in the receipt only for the satisfaction of such as were indebted to the testator's estate. It is against natural justice. Goodwin was a person entrusted in the testator's lifetime as his cashier and no part of the money ever came to Churchill's hands or was applied to his use. [It was] decreed that he should not be charged.

[Other copies of this report: British Library MS. Hargrave 82, f. 78, British Library MS. Hargrave 77, f. 21v, pl. 1, British Library MS. Hargrave 303, f. 41.]

1 Salkeld 318, 91 E.R. 280

Michaelmas 12 Anne.

Sir Charles Hobson made Churchill and Goodwin his executors, men of good credit. Goodwin, being a banker, received all the money, but Churchill

---

[1] *Fellows v. Owen* (1705), 2 Freeman 283, 286, 22 E.R. 1212, 1215, 1 Peere Williams 81, 24 E.R. 302, 2 Vernon 504, 515, 23 E.R. 922, 929.

[2] *Murrell v. Cox* (1707), *ut supra*.

joined with him in the receipts, taking his note to show that he received not the money.

*Et per* HARCOURT, Lord Chancellor: If two trustees join in a receipt and one receives the money, he only that receives shall be liable. If there be two executors and they join in a receipt and one only receives the money, as to creditors, who are to have the utmost benefit of the law, each is liable for the whole, though one executor alone might give a discharge and the joining of the other was unnecessary. But, as to legatees and those claiming distribution, who have no remedy but in equity, the receipt of one executor shall not charge the other, for the joining in the receipt is only matter of form; the substantial part is the actual receiving, and this only is regarded in conscience.

[Other reports of this case: 1 Peere Williams 241, 24 E.R. 370, 1 Eq. Cas. Abr. 247, 21 E.R. 1023.]

## 526

## Gale v. Croft

(Ch. 1713)

*Where the testator's personal estate is not expressly exempted from the payment of his debts, it is first so liable even where the testator devised lands to be sold for the payment of his debts.*

*In this case, the intent of the testator was found to be that his personal assets should be used to discharge a mortgage and that the encumbered land should not go to the devisee cum onere.*

Lincoln's Inn MS. Misc. 10, p. 149

4 November 1713. Gale v. Crofts, Boxil, Sedgwick, *et al.*

Crofts, by will, gives a farm and other lands, which he had mortgaged to one Andrew, to the defendants Boxil and Sedgwick upon trust to sell the same and, out of the moneys arising thereby, to pay all his own proper debts except his funeral charges. And, after the payment of his debts, he gives £200 out of the moneys for which those lands shall be sold and the residue to such person as shall be his heir at law. And he makes Boxil and Sedgwick his executors, but he made no disposition of the surplus of his personal estate.

There were two questions:

First, if the devisees of the mortgaged land must take it *cum onere* and the mortgage be paid out of the moneys arising by the sale of the other lands;

Second, if the personal estate, as this case is, shall be applied to exonerate the real [estate], and, if so, yet whether the mortgage ought to be paid out of the personal assets.

*Sir Joseph Jekyll*: As to the first point, if a man gives an estate in mortgage by a will, it is the constant course of this court to decree that he must take it *cum onere*. And there could have been no question in this case as to that matter had not the testator made a provision for the payment of his debts. However, that will not alter the case.

*Sir Peter King, contra*: It is plain the testator's intent was that all his debts whatsoever should be paid out of the fund provided for that purpose.

As to the second question, which was between the heir and the executors, it was insisted on for the heir that here are no words to exempt the personal estate from the payment of the debts, and, therefore, the testator, having directed part of his real estate to be sold for the payment of his debts, shall be looked upon to have done it out of caution to supply any deficiency there might be of his personal estate.

And so it was decreed in the Case of Christ's Hospital and Garraway and in Took and Sir Robert Atkins in 1697,[1] there being no negative words to exempt the personal [estate]. And upon the same reason, it was decreed in Sir William Bassett's Case,[2] where the residue of the personal estate was given to the executors and the real [estate] charged with the debts. But, there being no words of exemption, the personal estate was decreed to be applied in exoneration of the real.

Lord Chancellor [Lord Harcourt]: The testator having directed all his debts to be paid out of the fund he provided for that purpose, it is plain he intended the mortgage should be paid as well as the rest of his debts and the devisee have the lands discharged of the mortgage. And this is the more evident because he has excepted his funerals out of his debts, for, though that could not be called a debt, yet, by the excepting of that, it showed his intention to be that everything that he apprehended could have the appearance of a debt should be paid out of the trust lands except his funeral expenses.

As to the personal estate, he decreed an account of it and that it should come in aid of the real.

British Library MS. Hargrave 80, f. 155, pl. 2

A testator devised a real estate to his executors to sell and that, out of the money arising by sale, they should pay all his proper debts except for funerals and pay the surplus to such person as should be his heir. Another real estate, which was mortgaged almost to the value, he gave to J.S. in fee, and he made two executors but no express devise of the personal estate to them. Two questions arose upon this will: first, whether the personal estate or the money arising by the sale of the real [estate] should be first applied to pay debts; second, whether either should be applied to exonerate the estate devised to J.S. of the mortgage.

---

[1] *City of London v. Garway* (Ch. 1705–1706), see above, Case No. 42; *Tooke v. Atkins* (1687), 1 Vernon 451, 23 E.R. 579.

[2] *Symmes v. Symonds* (1703), 4 Brown P.C. 328, 2 E.R. 222.

For the executors, the deposition of Goddart, the drawer of the will, was offered to be read to show that the testator, at the time of making his will, made a computation of his debts, the money his estate would sell for, and his personal estate, that he reckoned the surplus of what would be left of his real estate after payment of the debts would make his heir equal, as he intended he should be, to his executors for whom he designed his personal estate, and that he gave him instructions to devise the personal estate to them, which he omitted, apprehending it to be implied in naming them executors.

*Sir Joseph Jekyll* cited the Case of Lady Gainsborough,[1] where the personal estate was devised to the executor and a real estate subject to the payment of debts and the evidence of Milburne, the drawer, was admitted to prove he had instructions to exempt the personal estate from payment of debts and the personal [estate was] thereupon decreed to the executors and the real subject to the debts.

*How* cited the case of Roberts v. Smith, in Lord Cowper's time, where the drawer's evidence of his instructions was admitted to rebut an equity.

It was added by *Sir Peter King* that a real estate devised to executors to be sold is assets at law. The Duke of Beaufort's Case[2] was cited likewise, where the evidence of Mr. Price carried the personal estate to the duchess.

Mr. *Cowper*, of the other side, made a distinction between evidence that supports the legal construction of a will and that which overthrows it and said the reasons why parol evidence was admitted in the Case of Littlebury v. Buckley[3] was because it was to prove the testator's intention to be agreeable to law, *viz.* that the executors should take, but the evidence offered in the present case was to show that the testator intended that they should take as devisees not as executors. He said an express devise to them would not have exempted the personal estate from being liable without negative words. In the Case of Christ's Hospital v. Mr. Jarroway,[4] there was an express devise of the personal estate to her, who was both widow and executrix, and yet it was made subject to debts in exoneration of the real, which was likewise liable, and the court said that, there, it would be liable unless discharged by express words.

*How*, in that case, said there was no evidence in that case of the testator's intent to exempt his personal estate and, there being two funds liable and neither exempt, the only question was which should be applied.

---

1 *Countess of Gainsborough v. Earl of Gainsborough* (1691), 2 Vernon 252, 23 E.R. 764, 2 Freeman 188, 22 E.R. 1152, 1 Eq. Cas. Abr. 230, 21 E.R. 1010.

2 *Duke of Beaufort v. Lord Dundonald* (1716), 2 Vernon 739, 23 E.R. 1083, 1 Eq. Cas. Abr. 201, 21 E.R. 989.

3 *Littlebury v. Buckley* (1711), 2 Vernon 677, 23 E.R. 1040, 3 Brown P.C. 43, 1 E.R. 1165, 1 Eq. Cas. Abr. 245, 21 E.R. 1021, Lincoln's Inn MS. Misc. 10, p. 86.

4 *City of London v. Garway* (Ch. 1705–1706), *ut supra.*

*Sawyer* cited the Case of Sir Robert Atkyns v. Tooke,[1] where Lord Somers said that, where a real estate is made subject to debts and [there are] no words that the personal estate shall not be liable, the real [estate] only comes in aid.

Lord Chancellor [LORD HARCOURT]: I am to judge of the intention of the testator as it arises from the will. It is dangerous to collect it from foreign evidence. Those cases have gone full far enough already. I shall not go a hair's breadth farther. In this cause, the personal estate is not exempted; the debts must be paid out of the surplus of the personal estate beyond the funeral expenses in the first place and the residue arising by sale of the real.

On the second head, it was contended that the lands were given in the same plight that they were in in the testator's custody and that *transit terra cum onere*. On the other hand, it was insisted that a *haeres factus* ought to have his estate exonerated as well as a *haeres natus*.

A great stress was laid both by the counsel and Lord Chancellor [LORD HARCOURT] upon the extensiveness of the words 'all my proper debts' and the exception of funerals as speaking the intention to extend the provision he was making to all debts whatsoever, funeral only excepted.

And My Lord [LORD HARCOURT] was of opinion that the mortgage on the estate devised was within those words, and he decreed that the estate should be exonerated in favor of the devisee.

[Other copies of this report: Lincoln's Inn MS. Misc. 383, p. 270, pl. 2, Lincoln's Inn MS. Misc. 106, p. 243.]

Dickens 23, 21 E.R. 175

4 November 1713.

The testator bequeathed his personal estate to his executor, and he devised his real estate to be sold for the payment of his debts, the surplus of which he gave for his heir at law. The heir at law insisted that the personal estate ought to be first applied towards the payment of the debts in ease of the real estate.

The Lord Chancellor [LORD HARCOURT] would not permit parol evidence to be read of the testator's intention, that the devise of the personal estate should be exempt from debts. And he decreed the executor to account for the personal estate.

[Other reports of this case: 2 Eq. Cas. Abr. 415, 494, 22 E.R. 352, 419.]

[1] *Tooke v. Atkins* (1687), 1 Vernon 451, 23 E.R. 579.

## 527

## Rush v. Hayward

(Ch. 1713)

*A remainder over that is more durable than the estate granted is nevertheless valid.*

British Library MS. Hargrave 80, f. 165v, pl. 2

A lease for three lives was vested in trustees in trust to convey the use of it so as T. Gape and the heirs of his body might receive the rents and profits and, for want of such issue, remainder to his trustees and their heirs.

*How* contended that the remainder over was void, the limitation in tail being greater and more durable in the eye of the law than the term for lives.

But it was ruled clearly by Lord Chancellor [LORD HARCOURT] to be good and this point [was] said to have been so settled by him in the Case of Sir Randolph Massenacs upon great deliberation.

*How* said that a distinction was taken in that case, where the first freehold continues and where the lease is renewed, all the lives in the original lease being dead. But in the principal case, one of the first lives was still in being.

[Other copies of this report: Lincoln's Inn MS. Misc. 383, p. 275, pl. 2, Lincoln's Inn MS. Misc. 106, p. 246, pl. 1.]

## 528

## Sherman v. Whitter

(Ch. 1713)

*A bill of discovery lies in equity to discover whether a bill of exchange has been accepted or not.*

British Library MS. Hargrave 80, f. 157, pl. 1

The plaintiff suggested that he had a foreign bill of exchange drawn upon the defendant and payable to the plaintiff, which he tendered and the defendant accepted, and that it was accidentally lost. And he brought his bill for a discovery and relief. The defendant demurred for not annexing an affidavit of the truth of the case.

*How*: It is a matter properly cognizable at law. This court has no jurisdiction but upon a supposition that the note is lost. And the plaintiff to entitle himself to sue here ought to have satisfied the court that the note is lost by an affidavit.

*Vernon*: The demurrer is too large. It goes as well to a discovery as the relief. It is proper if a man comes into equity for a thing recoverable at law, but, if we had the bill in our hands, we are certainly proper to have a discovery whether he accepted it or not.

Lord Chancellor [Lord Harcourt] overruled the demurrer.

[Other copies of this report: Lincoln's Inn MS. Misc. 383, p. 277, pl. 1, Lincoln's Inn MS. Misc. 106, p. 246, pl. 2.]

## 529

## Ridout v. Ridout

(Ch. 1713–1714)

*In this case, the intent of the testator was to convey only a life estate.*

*Where lands are given to an heir, he paying a sum of money, this is a limitation and not a condition.*

Lincoln's Inn MS. Misc. 10, p. 160

The plaintiff's father, by his will, devises lands to the plaintiff, his eldest son. And he gives to the defendant, who was his youngest son, his farm at A. and all his lands at B. And, then, he gives £500 to his daughter to be raised as soon as may be out of the estate and premises aforesaid and, if possible, within three years.

The question was if the devise to the youngest son was for life only or in fee.

*Curia* [was] clear of the opinion that this was only an estate for life. The charge is upon the estate and not upon the person of the devisee. There are no words to make it a condition, as in Collier's Case;[1] it is not said 'paying' etc.

Note, where lands are given to the heir at law, paying a sum of money, this is a limitation and not a condition.

Lincoln's Inn MS. Misc. 384, p. 16, pl. 1

*Vernon*: The question was whether the defendant has an estate for life or in fee by a devise. The words are 'I give the lands to A. and £500 to B. to be paid out of the profits.'

*Hooper*, for the defendant: The profits will not satisfy the legacy in many years. We hope we have a fee. If a man devise his lands to A., paying such a sum, it carries a fee. Here is no devise over, and the estate [is worth] but £40 *per annum*; so the tenant for life can take nothing. 5 Coke, Collyer's [Case].

*Curia*: The intent of the testator does not appear to carry a fee. And I can construe this but an estate for life.

[1] *Collier v. Walker* (1595), 6 Coke Rep. 16, 77 E.R. 276, also Croke Eliz. 379, 78 E.R. 625.

## 530

## Anonymous

(Ch. 1713)

*Where interrogatory answers are insufficient and a second examination is ordered, court costs are taxable.*

British Library MS. Hargrave 81, f. 101

The defendant was decreed to be examined upon interrogatories. And his first examination was reported insufficient, but his second was full. And he would have the plaintiff take 40s. costs only, as for an insufficient answer.

Lord Chancellor [LORD HARCOURT] asked Mr. Browning, the Master, how the practice was in that point, who declared that, formerly, 40s. only had been given, but, of late, costs had been taxed.

And His Lordship ordered it accordingly.

[Other copies of this report: British Library MS. Hargrave 82, f. 98.]

[Other reports of this case: British Library MS. Hargrave 77, f. 25, pl. 1, British Library MS. Hargrave 303, f. 48, pl. 1.]

## 531

## Loft v. Jones

(Ch. 1713)

*Where a legacy is charged on the testator's real estate but not exclusively, if the real estate is insufficient, the personal estate is liable for the deficiency.*

British Library MS. Hargrave 81, f. 102

If a legacy be charged on the real estate and there is no exclusion by express words of the personal or any collateral verbal proof, as in Lady Gainsborough's Case,[1] an account must be taken of the personal estate, and, if the real be insufficient, it must be satisfied out of the personal.

[Other copies of this report: British Library MS. Hargrave 82, f. 99, British Library MS. Hargrave 77, f. 25v, pl. 2, British Library MS. Hargrave 303, f. 49, pl. 1.]

[1] *Countess of Gainsborough v. Earl of Gainsborough* (1692), 2 Vernon 252, 23 E.R. 764, 2 Freeman 188, 22 E.R. 1152, 1 Eq. Cas. Abr. 230, 21 E.R. 1010.

## 532

### Crump v. Shale

(Ch. 1713)

*In this case, the court of equity ordered the maintenance of an infant daughter to be paid out of the decedent's estate presently.*

British Library MS. Hargrave 80, f. 157v

By a marriage settlement, the wife was made tenant in tail of the greatest part of the estate and the rest was limited to the husband for life, remainder to trustees in fee in trust by sale thereof and out of all of the rents and profits until sale to raise portions for the younger children, if any, to be paid at twenty-one. The wife was prevailed upon to join with her husband in selling the part settled on her, and, by that means, she and her eldest son were wholly destitute of any provision. There was no younger child, only a daughter about seven years old, and the son was eleven. The defendant, who was the surviving trustee, scrupled allowing the daughter any maintenance, none being allowed by the settlement and the whole rents etc. directed to be applied to raise portions.

Upon a bill against him by the two children for maintenance, *Vernon*, for the plaintiffs, admitted that they could not strictly ask any for the son but that cases had been frequent, where there was a large estate settled on the eldest and no provision for the other children, the court had made a liberal allowance to the parent or person that was to maintain the eldest that the younger children might find their account in it. Here, the whole estate was but £28 *per annum*.

And the defendant declining the trust, Lord Chancellor [Lord Harcourt] directed that he should assign and the whole rents be paid to the new trustees for the maintenance of the daughter.

[Other copies of this report: Lincoln's Inn MS. Misc. 383, p. 278, pl. 1, Lincoln's Inn MS. Misc. 106, p. 249.]

## 533

### Bullock v. Bullock

(Ch. 1713)

*The drafter of a will cannot testify as to the testator's intention, but it must be found from the words of the will itself.*

*In this case, the court held that nothing in the will or codicil in issue gave the younger sons more than estates for life.*

*Copyhold lands do not pass by a devise of all of the testator's lands where they have not been surrendered to the use of his will.*

British Library MS. Hargrave 80, f. 160

The father of the plaintiff and the defendant, having three sons, made his will. It began 'as to my worldly estate' etc.; then he gave £100 to his eldest son provided he would execute a lawful general release to the second younger within three months after the testator's decease such as his trustees should advise. He made his three sons his executors and devised all his lands, goods, and chattels, real and personal, and money etc. to the three sons equally to be divided among them, share and share alike. By a codicil, he directed that, if either of his sons should die or marry without consent under age, his portion should go over to the other. And he devised a particular estate to trustees to be sold for certain purposes and the surplus to be equally divided among his three sons or reinvested in lands and they divided between them.

Upon a bill for a partition, the question was whether the two younger sons took an estate for life only in the lands devised to them or the inheritance. The person that drew the will was examined to prove the intention of the testator that the inheritance should pass.

But Lord Chancellor [Lord Harcourt] would not suffer his deposition to be read.

It was said for the younger children that the introduction to the will showed the intention of the testator to pass his whole estate, that the release he directed his heir to give could have no operation but upon the lands, that the lands were blended in the same devise with the goods, which spoke the intention of the testator to make as complete a disposition of the one as of the other, that the word 'portions' in the codicil ought to be understood of the shares both of the lands and goods given to his sons, and the directing them to go over upon the death of either under age showed his intention that each of them should take more than an estate for life, and that, in the clause where part of the estate was directed to be sold and the surplus reinvested and settled, there were no words of inheritance and yet it was not doubted but that the inheritance was to be sold and the inheritance of the new purchased lands settled which was an evidence of the opinion of the testator and of him that drew the will that the inheritance would pass without any words of inheritance.

On the other side, *Vernon* insisted that an heir ought not to be disinherited but by express words or a necessary implication, that the introductory words were the common formal words in all wills, that nothing certain could be collected from the release, that, from the mixing lands and goods in one devise, they had rather reason to insist that none but leasehold lands should pass if the testator had had any, that the inference from the word 'portion' would be strong were there not other things with which that word could be satisfied and that more properly the personal estate.

Lord Chancellor [Lord Harcourt] was clearly of opinion that, if the question had stood singly upon the clause of the devise of all his lands, goods, etc., nothing would pass but an estate for life. But, on the other clauses, he doubted and seemed to think that the testator intended to pass the inheritance.

But he took time to consider. And, at another day, he declared that he saw nothing in the will or codicil that gave the younger sons more than estates for life.

Another question was whether copyhold lands should pass by the devise of all his lands, they not having been surrendered to the use of his will.

And [it was] ruled that they should not, they not being particularly named or described and there being other lands to satisfy the words of the will.

[Other copies of this report: Lincoln's Inn MS. Misc. 383, p. 281, Lincoln's Inn MS. Misc. 106, p. 250.]

2 Eq. Cas. Abr. 231, 22 E.R. 196

Michaelmas 12 Ann. [1713].

B., having several freehold and copyhold lands, devises all his lands, goods, and chattels to his three sons, equally to be divided between them. And he also devises £100 to his eldest, provided he gives a lawful, good, and general release to his two younger brothers. And, by his codicil, he appoints that, if one of his younger sons should die or marry in his minority without the consent of his executors, then his portion to go to the other younger son.

Lord Chancellor [Lord Harcourt] was of the opinion that the copyhold lands do not pass by the devise for want of a surrender to the use of the will, though in the case of younger children, because there are freehold lands to satisfy the words of the will.

2 Eq. Cas. Abr. 311, 22 E.R. 264

Michaelmas 12 Ann. [1713].

B., having several freehold and copyhold lands, devises all his lands, goods, and chattels, to his three sons, equally to be divided between them. And he devises over and above this £100 to his eldest, provided he gives a lawful and general release to his two younger brothers. And, by his codicil, he appoints that, if one of his younger sons should die or marry in his minority without the consent of his executors, then his portion [is] to go to the other younger son.

*Per* Harcourt, Chancellor: There being no words of limitation of estate in the devise to the two younger sons, they can take only an estate for life in the lands. And, as to the general release directed by the will to be given to the younger sons, that is satisfied by releasing his right to the personal estate without affecting the real estate; so the devise over to the younger son in case of the death of one under age etc. may be satisfied by the personal [estate]. And the word 'portion' properly signifies nothing.

## 534

## Opery v. Oly

(Ch. 1713)

*Oral promises in reference to a written agreement are unenforceable under the Statute of Frauds.*

British Library MS. Hargrave 80, f. 161, pl. 1

The plaintiff married the defendant's daughter and, by his bill, suggested that there was a mistake in the marriage articles and that £500, part of the portion, which the defendant, by the articles, was left at liberty either to give or not at his pleasure; he had both before and after the articles agreed to give absolutely. And he prayed a discovery of this agreement and of some discourses and circumstances relating to it and relief.

The defendant pleaded the Statute of Frauds[1] in bar of the discovery sought by the bill of any agreement or discourse concerning it not reduced into writing and in bar of relief upon any such agreement.

*Cowper*: If a parol agreement be admitted by an answer, the court may ground a decree upon it that, therefore, the plaintiff ought to have a discovery of it.

*Vernon* and *How*, for the defendant, [said] that, if a defendant would admit of a parol agreement by his answer, he could not afterwards defend himself against it, but that, since the Statute of Frauds, he was not obliged to admit it.

*Vernon* added that, before the Statute, when an agreement was reduced into writing, all previous parol treaties were gone and that this was much stronger since.

Lord Chancellor [Lord Harcourt]: I cannot compel the defendant to answer to a parol agreement though the court will decree upon it if it be voluntarily admitted. He allowed the plea.

[Other copies of this report: Lincoln's Inn MS. Misc. 383, p. 283, pl. 1, Lincoln's Inn MS. Misc. 107, p. 1.]

## 535

## Darrell v. Darrell

(Ch. 1713)

*A legacy given to a Roman Catholic lapses.*

*A sum of money charged on an estate can be raised by felling timber growing upon it.*

1 Stat. 29 Car. II, c. 3 (*SR*, V, 839–842).

British Library MS. Hargrave 80, f. 161v

The plaintiff demanded *inter alia* a legacy given to her sister by her brother's will to which she made title under an assignment from her sister by virtue of a letter of attorney. And she made her case by her bill that her sister had retired into a nunnery, was in her year of probation at the death of the testator, and was since become a professed nun. At the hearing, it was urged that, by her going beyond the sea to be bred up in a Popish seminary, she was disabled to take and that disability arising before the death of the testator, the legacy never could arise. And, though it was objected that the disability did not attach until a conviction and that she never had been convicted, it was answered that the confession of the plaintiff by the bill was equal to a conviction.

And of that opinion was Lord Chancellor [LORD HARCOURT]. And he dismissed the bill.

As to that demand, it was objected to them by *How* that the nun should have been a party, for that an assignee of a chose in action would not bring a bill without having the assignor before the court and that the Attorney General ought likewise to have been made a party. The statutes of 1 and 3 of James I and 3 of Charles II[1] were mentioned in the argument.

In this case, there was a sum of money charged upon an estate, of which the defendant was tenant for life but not without impeachment of waste, remainder to another in tail etc. to be raised by lease or mortgage.

And the court directed such timber as was fit to be cut leaving sufficient for repairs to be felled and the money applied for that purpose and a commission to issue to see what timber was fit and could be spared.

[Other copies of this report: Lincoln's Inn MS. Misc. 383, p. 284, pl. 1, Lincoln's Inn MS. Misc. 107, p. 2.]

## 536

## Terry v. Thomas

(Ch. 1713)

*A debtor is required to repay the loan even though the security for the repayment is destroyed and lost.*

British Library MS. Hargrave 80, f. 162

The plaintiff had a bill of sale by way of mortgage from the defendant's testator for some shares in a ship and a covenant for the repayment of what the plaintiff should pay for insurance if he thought fit to insure her, but no covenant or bond

[1] Stat. 1 Jac. I, c. 4 (*SR*, IV, 1020–1022); Stat. 3 Jac. I, cc. 4, 5 (*SR*, IV, 1071–1082); Stat. 3 Car. I, c. 3 (*SR*, V, 25–26).

for payment of the money lent on the mortgage. The ship was afterwards insured by the plaintiff for one voyage. But the next, she went without being insured, the plaintiff thinking the terms of insurance too high. And she was lost. The plaintiff brought his bill against the executor of the mortgagor for satisfaction of his money out of the assets.

It was objected that a mortgage might be so framed as to exempt the person of the mortgagor and leave the thing mortgaged the only security for the money, that the Welsh mortgages were commonly a conveyance of land to hold until repayment of the money and without any covenant to repay and that, if the land were deficient, the mortgagee must bear the loss, that it was in the plaintiff's power to have made this security good by insurance and his fault that he did not, and that his taking a covenant for the repayment of the insurance money and none to repay the principal money was an evidence that the person of the mortgagor was not a debtor for that, but, however, if the law implied a contract, he might go to law and need not come into equity.

*Vernon*, for the plaintiff: There is no doubt but that, if the plaintiff had lent his money without any security, it would have been a debt. It is the same thing where he takes a defective one. In the common mortgage of copyholds by surrenders, it is on condition to be void on payment and without a covenant to pay; it is, however, a debt, though but by a simple contract. In this case, the plaintiff did insure as far as it was reasonable and for that he is a creditor by specialty and, for the mortgage money, by simple contract.

Lord Chancellor [Lord Harcourt]: The bill of sale is but a security and so far as that proves deficient, the plaintiff is a creditor, though but by simple contract. He having no covenant for the payment, he must have his debt and costs out of the assets.

[Other copies of this report: Lincoln's Inn MS. Misc. 383, p. 284, pl. 2, Lincoln's Inn MS. Misc. 107, p. 3.]

[Other reports of this case: *sub nom.* Thomas v. Terry (1714), Gilbert Rep. 110, 25 E.R. 77, 1 Eq. Cas. Abr. 139, 21 E.R. 942.]

## 537

## *Ex parte* Ashton

(Ch. 1713–1714)

*Marriages by idiots are good in law, but they ought not to be made.*

*A suit cannot be maintained in the name of a married woman against her consent, but it may be in the case of an infant who is presumed not capable of judging for himself.*

*A writ de homine replegiando does not lie against a husband for his taking his wife.*

British Library MS. Hargrave 80, f. 163

A writ *de homine replegiando* having been ordered *nisi* against R., who took away the daughter of Mrs. Ashton, the daughter had £500 of her own and was the only child of her mother, who was said to be worth £20,000, it was showed for cause that she was married voluntarily to R. and that she was twenty-eight years old. And several affidavits were read of her consent, one sworn by herself.

On the other side, they read several affidavits to prove her an idiot.

And Master of the Rolls [Trevor] said that the marriages of idiots were good in law though they ought not to be made and that, she being married, the writ should not issue. But without being pressed to it on the other side, he ordered the husband, parson, and several others to stand committed.

He did the same sometime since in my Case of Sir Edward Hand's daughter; she was an infant but not under the care of a guardian assigned by the court but of one appointed by her father but, upon submission, the party there [was] afterwards enlarged.

*Vernon* laid it down as a rule that, though both an infant and a married woman may sue by their *prochein ami*s, yet a suit cannot be carried on in the name of a married woman against her consent, as it may in that of an infant who is not presumed capable of judging for himself.

To which, the Master of the Rolls [Trevor] agreed. And, upon his motion, he referred it to a master to enquire whether the suit had been carried on with or without her consent.

Against an order for making their election, it was urged that the bill was only for a discovery and sought no relief.

*Vernon*: Then, your bill must be dismissed with costs. You have had the discovery you sought by our answer and may make use of that at law after your bill is dismissed.

To which the Master of Rolls [Trevor] agreed.

[Other copies of this report: Lincoln's Inn MS. Misc. 383, p. 285.]

Dickens 23, 21 E.R. 175

21 November 1713, 28 November 1713, 20 January 1713–14. Lord Cowper.

A woman of weak mind, supposed to be an infant, being seduced from her friends in order to marry, a writ *de homine replegiando* was granted on the first of the above days [21 November 1713]. On her being afterwards married, although no ward, on the second of those days [28 November 1713], the husband and the clergyman were committed to the Fleet [Prison]. It being afterwards discovered she was neither an idiot nor under age, they, on the last of the above days [20 January 1714], were discharged.

British Library MS. Hargrave 77, f. 27, pl. 2

One Acton's daughter, an only child and an idiot but of full age, was, unknown to her mother, carried away by her maid, Jane Mines, and one Raynor in the evening and, that night, was married to Raynor. And being concealed from her mother, she put out an advertisement offering considerable rewards and, afterwards, petitioned for a writ *de homine replegiando*, which was granted but, afterwards, discharged because it could not be against a man for his wife, but the maid, husband, parson, and one more who had been concerned in contriving this matter were ordered to stand committed, two of which were taken, but the rest kept out of the way.

And now, a motion was made in behalf of them all to have the order discharged, which was done accordingly.

*Curia*: Though this court be a guardian of idiots, lunatics, and infants, yet there must be some cause depending or that was depending in the court to authorize the taking cognizance of what relates to them or their estates and bring any person into a contempt or make him liable to the censure of this court. So it was in the case of Dr. Han's daughter, who was about thirteen and married in the like manner. But their being no such thing in this case, the court has no manner of cognizance of this marriage or the transactions relating to it. There can, therefore, be no contempt for the court to punish.

[Other copies of this report: British Library MS. Hargrave 82, f. 107, pl. 2, British Library MS. Hargrave 303, f. 51, pl. 2.]

## 538

## Richards v. Gore

(Ch. 1713)

*In this case, under the terms of the will in issue, the executors were only trustees and the estate was distributable, and the court ordered a certain lease to be sold to pay off a creditor.*

British Library MS. Hargrave 80, f. 164

Gilbert Raylegh, being possessed of a leasehold estate for years of the College of Winchester upon and in consideration of his son Sir Charles Rawlegh's marriage, conveyed it subject to some annuities to trustees in trust for Sir Charles and the heirs male of his body and his intended wife. Sir Charles left issue Carew Raleigh, his only son, and three daughters. His real estate was inconsiderable. And his personal estate he devised to his wife and Mr. Hobly, his executors, to be distributed equally among his daughters. And he gave his son 5s. in full of all demands. The use of his household goods he gave to his wife for life and £10 apiece to her and Mr. Hobly for their mourning. But he took no notice of this leasehold estate, which was of the value of £700 *per annum*, in his will. Upon his death, Carew Raleigh entered and came to an agreement in writing with Mr. Coles, with whom Sir Charles' executrix intermarried, in which Mr. Coles was to accept of 500 guineas in full satisfaction of his wife's right to this leasehold estate. Carew Raleigh likewise took in the right of two of his sisters and renewed the lease in the name of the same trustees once or twice and, at length, renewed it again in the name of other trustees, and the trust of one-fourth and two-thirds was declared to be for the benefit of his other sister as her distributive share. She, afterwards, joined with these new trustees in a mortgage of this new lease to the plaintiff for £1242 and died. In the mortgage, there was a covenant from him to renew it from time to time and assign the new leases as a security to the plaintiff. After his death, his administrator and the trustees renewed the lease without the plaintiff.

And the bill was to have this new lease sold for the satisfaction of the plaintiff's debt. Cole and his wife insisted on their apprehending themselves to be entitled to no more than a third at the time of their agreement with Carew Raleigh and that, therefore, the agreement ought to be confined to what the parties had in view and to bind them only as to that third and that they were in truth entitled to the whole, she being the surviving executrix.

But that the Master of the Rolls [Trevor] overruled, that, there being no fraud, the will and settlement being in Cole's hands and the words of the agreement being general, the agreement fully executed on both sides, an acquiescence for several years, and enjoyment of the estate by Carew Raleigh under it, and, after all, a conveyance for a valuable consideration from him to the plaintiff. He relied much upon the opinion of Sir Thomas Twisdon that, where a lease for years is entailed, which, by law, it cannot, yet, if there has been an enjoyment under it, it ought not to be broken through. He was of opinion that the lease did vest in the executors but, from the frame of the will and the £10 legacies, that they were executors in trust and that it was distributable.

Mr. Wilcocks, who married the third sister, and his wife insisted upon having the two-thirds of the children divided into thirds and not fourths upon a supposition that Carew was excluded upon his father's giving him 5s. in full of all demands.

But there being no evidence of any want of affection in the father to him and he having no provision but this lease and the will not naming the lease, the Master of the Rolls [Trevor] was of opinion that it was rather an evidence of his father's thinking he would be entitled to the whole under the settlement than of his intention to exclude him from any part of it. He decreed the lease to be sold and reserved the consideration of the distribution of the surplus after payment of part between Wilcocks and the administrator of Carew Raleigh.

[Other copies of this report: Lincoln's Inn MS. Misc. 383, p. 286, Lincoln's Inn MS. Misc. 107, p. 4.]

539

## Upton v. Pepper

(Ch. 1713)

*A contract to arbitrate can be made an order of court provided that the order is entered before the end of the term next after the award.*

British Library MS. Hargrave 80, f. 165

In this case, it seemed agreed that a submission [to arbitration] may be made an order of court after the award made, but, then, it must be before the end of the term then next ensuing the award, for, otherwise, the party to be bound by it should be precluded from any opportunity of complaining to the court against it, the Statute of 9 & 10 Will. III, c. 15,[1] confining him to complain before the end of the term next ensuing the arbitration made and published to the parties.

And it was said by *Vernon* that he can complain of nothing but corruption and undue practice in the arbitrators.

*Sed quaere de hoc.*

[Other copies of this report: Lincoln's Inn MS. Misc. 383, p. 287, pl. 1, Lincoln's Inn MS. Misc. 107, p. 6.]

540

## Soudswell v. Soley

(Ch. 1713)

*A settlement made after the marriage may be fraudulent as against creditors.*

British Library MS. Hargrave 80, f. 165v, pl. 1

In this case, a settlement of a lease for years after marriage as an additional provision for the wife and children, though there was no proof of its being made on a parol agreement before marriage and though this, with what was settled before marriage, amounted to a little more than £100 *per annum* and the portion was £2000, [was] adjudged fraudulent against creditors. The settlement did not recite the agreement.

[Other copies of this report: Lincoln's Inn MS. Misc. 383, p. 287, pl. 2, Lincoln's Inn MS. Misc. 107, p. 7, pl. 1.]

[1] Stat. 9 Will. III, c. 15 (*SR*, VII, 369–370).

## 541

## Anonymous

(Ch. 1713)

*A suit to foreclose a mortgage need not be brought against all of the persons who have a right of redemption because a decree of foreclosure does not bind persons who were not parties to the suit.*

British Library MS. Hargrave 80, f. 165v, pl. 2

*Vernon*: A mortgagee may bring a bill to foreclose without making all that have a right to redeem parties. It is his own loss if he does not, for it will still lie open to a redemption by those that are not parties to his bill though he foreclosed those that are. Those, therefore, who are not cannot object to him that he has not brought the rest before the court.

[Other copies of this report: Lincoln's Inn MS. Misc. 383, p. 287, pl. 3, Lincoln's Inn MS. Misc. 107, p. 7, pl. 2.]

## 542

## Burton v. Lloyd

(Ch. 1713)

*Where a court of equity supplies the defect of a surrender to the use of a will in favor of younger children, no difference is taken between those that have and those that have not any other provision, except where the heir would be totally disinherited by it.*

British Library MS. Hargrave 80, f. 165v, pl. 3

By Lord Chancellor [Lord Harcourt] and *Vernon*: In the cases where equity can supply the defect of a surrender to the use of a will in favor of younger children, no difference has ever been taken between those that have and those that have not any other provision. Whether the copyhold devised be the sole portion or an augmentation of a portion, whether it be an immediate or future provision, it is all one. The father is the only judge of a quantum of the child's portion, and this court never enters into a consideration of that. The only distinction that has been made in those cases is where the heir would be totally disinherited by it. And, there, equity will not supply the want of a surrender.

In the principal case, the copyhold devised was a remainder in tail expectant upon an estate tail to the eldest son and was an additional portion.

[Other copies of this report: Lincoln's Inn MS. Misc. 383, p. 288, pl. 1, Lincoln's Inn MS. Misc. 107, p. 7, pl. 3.]

[Affirmed on appeal: 2 Brown P.C. 281, 1 E.R. 945.]

## 543

## Lake v. Mason

(Ch. 1713)

*Where a mortgagee pays off a prior mortgage, such payment is not a part of the mortgagor's debt to him, the second mortgagor.*

British Library MS. Hargrave 80, f. 166

The plaintiff's father lent money to Mason upon a mortgage and, afterwards, took an assignment of a prior mortgage, of which he had notice when he lent his money. Mason did not join in the assignment. And there being two years interest due at the time of the assignment, the question was whether it should be deemed principal in the hands of [Sir Bibye] Lake, who paid it off. The necessity Lake was under of taking the assignment to protect his mortgage was urged as a reason for making it principal though Mason did not join.

And the case of Lord Conway and Shrimpton[1] was cited by *Sir Joseph Jekyll*, where the interest due at the time of the assignment was made principal by the House of Lords, though the mortgagor did not join.

Lord Chancellor [LORD HARCOURT]: There was an arrear of sixteen years here but two, and the prior mortgage you had notice of. He directed that it should not be looked upon as principal in the account.

The Duke of Bucks and Sir Robert Clayton's Case was maintained by *Vernon*, where a scrivener had inserted a covenant in a mortgage that it should stand as security likewise for such other sums as should be afterwards advanced. And he said it was with great difficulty that the court was brought to allow it to be good.

[Other copies of this report: Lincoln's Inn MS. Misc. 383, p. 288, pl. 2, Lincoln's Inn MS. Misc. 107, p. 8.]

[On appeal: 2 Brown P.C. 495, 1 E.R. 1088.]

[Related cases: Mason v. Lake (Ch. 1709), see above, Case No. 142.]

[1] *Conway v. Shrimpton* (1710–1711), 5 Brown P.C. 187, 2 E.R. 617, 2 Eq. Cas. Abr. 596, 738, 22 E.R. 510, 627, and see above, Case No. 172.

## 544

## Shish v. Bewis

(Ch. 1713)

*A minority share owner of a ship is liable for his proportion of the expense of repairs to the ship unless he gets an order from the Court of Admiralty for the majority owners to buy out his share or give him security for the loss of the ship.*

British Library MS. Hargrave 80, f. 166v

The plaintiff was a shipwright. And the defendant [was] a party owner of one sixteenth of the ship called *The Prince of Orange*. The plaintiff brought his bill against the party owners for satisfaction for work done by him in repairing the ship for a voyage to Guinea, in which the ship was lost, and at the request of the major part of the partners. Bewis insisted that he had all along disapproved of the voyage and the repairing of the ship and ought not to contribute.

*Vernon*, for the plaintiff, agreed that none of the party owners were liable to make the plaintiff satisfaction but *pro rata*. But he insisted that the act of the major part of the party owners would bind the rest and that Bewis, if he had intended not to have been bound, ought to have protested against the voyage in the Court of Admiralty, where the rest of the party owners would have been obliged either to have paid for his share or given security to Bewis for his and then must have navigated the ship at their own peril and that, he not having protested, his barely disagreeing to the voyage and repairs would not excuse him from contributing his proportion.

The Master of the Rolls [Trevor] decreed Bewis to make the plaintiff satisfaction for his share.

[Other copies of this report: Lincoln's Inn MS. Misc. 383, p. 288, pl. 3, Lincoln's Inn MS. Misc. 107, p. 9, pl. 1.]

## 545

## Meaburne v. Mascal

(Ch. 1713)

*A bill to perpetuate testimony lies in the Court of Chancery in regard to witnesses who live outside of the jurisdiction of a palatinate court for the use of proceedings in the palatinate court.*

British Library MS. Hargrave 80, f. 167v, pl. 2

The plaintiff brought his bill for an injunction to stay proceedings in the Court of Durham upon a bill brought there by the defendant against the plaintiff to examine witnesses to a will in order to perpetuate their testimony upon a suggestion that some witnesses necessary to be produced by the defendant there lived out of the jurisdiction of that court and that part of the lands too lie out of the county palatine. To this, the defendant pleaded that Durham is a county palatine, there is a court of chancery there, which has exercised jurisdiction in causes of this nature time out of mind, and that he had brought his bill there before the commencement of the suit, to which the plaintiff had appealed.

*Vernon*, for the defendant: All courts of equity are by prescription, and priority of suit gives a jurisdiction where there is no prior suit in the court of a county palatine. Surmises that part of the lands lie out of the jurisdiction of the court below or that the witnesses are not within the process of that court are often thrown into bills brought here to avoid a plea in bar to the jurisdiction of this court and with success. But a bill to stay proceedings in Durham upon a bill brought there before the commencement of this suit, to which the defendant there has appeared. and where the lands, parties, and witnesses are all within the jurisdiction of that court is unprecedented.

*Jekyll*, for the plaintiff: It was solemnly ruled in Ratford's Case, in Dyer, and in the Baron of Kinderton's Case that the jurisdiction of counties palatine does not extend to counties in which, by means of the witnesses living out of their jurisdiction or the like, they cannot do justice, those courts being supposed to have been excepted out of the grant from the crown, upon which the jurisdiction of all counties palatine is founded, and that, in this court, his clients' witnesses not being examinable by the process of that court, whatever those of the other side might, that court could not do complete justice.

*How*: It is charged by our bill and admitted by the defendant's answer that part of the lands lie out of the county palatine, that part is attractive of the jurisdiction and gives this court a jurisdiction as to the whole. If we had brought this bill after examination, there, it had been too late. But we come before the examination.

*Vernon*: There is no pretense for an injunction to stay proceedings in the court below unless there had been a priority of suit here. In the Mayor's Court in London or any spiritual court, where there is a priority of suit, this court never enjoins. But, if, in a cause depending there, any witnesses are not answerable by the process of that court, you may bring a *certiorari* bill and remove the proceedings hither. But even in that cause, after examination, that court remits the whole for the final determination of the court below; upon a bill here, the plaintiff is entitled to an answer and to examine such witnesses as could not be reached by the process below.

And *Sir Joseph Jekyll* alleging that no *certiorari* bill would lie to a county palatine, Lord Chancellor [Lord Harcourt] asked Mr. *Vernon* where he ever knew a bill brought here to examine witnesses that lived out of the jurisdiction of a county palatine and the proceedings after examination sent thither.

And he [*Vernon*] said that there was a bill of that nature within two or three years and the proceeding sent down to the county palatine of Durham. But he did not name the cause.

Lord Chancellor [Lord Harcourt] allowed the plea.

*Sir Joseph Jekyll* said in this cause that it had been held that a bill would lie here for lands in Ireland upon this ground, that proceedings in a court of equity follow the conscience of the plaintiff not the thing itself.

[Other copies of this report: Lincoln's Inn MS. Misc. 383, p. 289, pl. 2, Lincoln's Inn MS. Misc. 107, p. 9, pl. 2.]

## 546

## Langston v. Langston

(Ch. 1713–1714)

*The settlement of a woman's fortune from her family is not a composition in lieu of her customary widow's share of a London freeman's estate.*

*A London freeman's widow is entitled to retain her paraphernalia.*

British Library MS. Hargrave 80, f. 169

Lieutenant General Langston, before his marriage with the plaintiff Agnes, [settled] that £2200, which was the plaintiff's portion, should be vested in trustees in trust to pay the interest thereof to the husband during his life, then to the wife during her life, afterwards to the issue of the marriage, and, for default of issue, the money to be paid to the survivor etc. The lieutenant, afterwards, makes his will and, therein, gives all his estate, plate, jewels, and equipage, and £1000 in money and an annuity of £400 a year for life to his wife.

The plaintiff had discovered that her husband was a freeman [of London] and brings her bill to have her customary share and also the £1000 and the specific legacies but waives the annuity.

It was urged by the defendant's counsel that the settlement of the £2200 before marriage was in the City language compounding for her customary part and that she was thereby barred from demanding the same. But the counsel for the defendant, who was the residuary legatee, determined to give that point up.

And it was decreed that she should have her customary part. It was said by the Lord Chancellor [Lord Harcourt] that the settlement of her own fortune was not to be taken as a composition. But as to the legacies claimed by her under the will, Lord Chancellor [Lord Harcourt] decreed she should take no benefit whatsoever by the will and that she should deliver up all the jewels etc. except her paraphernalia, which he allowed her to retain, though it was insisted that the freemen of London were supposed to be tradesmen and, therefore, their wives not entitled to any paraphernalia.

[Other copies of this report: Lincoln's Inn MS. Misc. 383, p. 290, Lincoln's Inn MS. Misc. 107, p. 12.]

Lincoln's Inn MS. Misc. 384, p. 21, pl. 1

28 February [1714].

The plaintiff's husband, being a freeman of London, before the marriage, settled the plaintiff's own fortune on her. And, by his will, he gives her some legacies and a real estate. She brings her bill to have her customary share of his personal estate.

*Vernon*, for the defendant: If the husband had settled on the plaintiff out of his own estate, it had been a composition with her, and she had been barred of her customary share.

*Curia*: In this case, the plaintiff has only her own money settled, and, therefore, it is not the same as if the settlement had been out of her husband's estate. The plaintiff must have her customary share and her widow's chamber and paraphernalia if there be a surplus. But she shall take nothing by the will.

## 547

## Thomas v. Davis

(Ch. 1713)

*An executor, though without notice of a bond made by his decedent, is liable for that bond debt if he pays the decedent's simple contract debts and has no assets of the estate remaining.*

British Library MS. Hargrave 80, f. 171, pl. 1

*Vernon* cited a cause of Mr. Allen, a relation of [Henry] Pollexfen [d. 1691], in which it was determined by the Court of Chancery assisted by the judges upon great deliberation, which Pollexfen was Attorney General [1689], that a bond debt which had been concealed for twenty years after an executor had paid the assets away in discharging debts of an inferior nature should notwithstanding be paid by the executor.

And, in the principal cause, Lord Chancellor [Lord Harcourt] decreed that a bond should be satisfied of which the executor had no notice until after administration of the assets in payment of simple contract debts.

I think *Vernon* said that, in the Case of Lord Oxford, the question was whether an executor, pending a bill against him for an account, might pay a debt of an equal nature and [it was] resolved that he might.

[Other copies of this report: Lincoln's Inn MS. Misc. 383, p. 292, pl. 1, Lincoln's Inn MS. Misc. 107, p. 14.]

## 548
## Hilton v. Earl of Scarborough

(Ch. 1713–1714)

*A bill of peace does not lie to enjoin and bind the general public.*

British Library MS. Hargrave 80, f. 171, pl. 2

The plaintiff, as owner of an ancient ferry which was navigated by a rope, brought his bill against many owners of boats that carried coals up and down the river to be quieted in the enjoyment of his wherry and rope upon a suggestions that they frequently cut it to get a passage for their boats.

*Chesshyre* and *Vernon* insisted upon this bill being in the nature of a bill of peace that actions, if they were to be brought upon every cutting of the rope, would be infinite, that it was therefore proper for a court of equity to interpose and direct proper issues to try the right upon which an injunction might be grounded to quiet the possession, especially against force.

Lord Chancellor [Lord Harcourt]: A ferry is a highway. Did you ever know that where the right of a highway was in controversy and one side only brought a bill, a court of equity would interpose? If there are cross-bills, it may. And in a late case of commoners, where those that claimed a right are certain, it does. But here, all the queen's subjects in general are concerned and a decree could not possibly bind those that are not parties to it.

He dismissed the bill with costs.

[Other copies of this report: Lincoln's Inn MS. Misc. 383, p. 292, pl. 2, Lincoln's Inn MS. Misc. 107, p. 15.]

2 Eq. Cas. Abr. 171, 22 E.R. 147

Easter 13 Ann. [1714].

A bill to be quieted in the possession of an ancient ferry used with a rope over the River Ware was brought against twenty defendants, who had cut the rope, to avoid the multiplicity of actions.

*Per* Parker, Chancellor: The plaintiff may have [an action of] trespass for cutting the rope. A ferry is in the nature of a highway, and a bill does not lie to be quieted in possession of an highway. A bill lies to be quieted in the possession of a common, but that is of a different nature. This is a navigable river, and the rope to the ferry is an obstruction to the navigation. If the plaintiff has any such right, there is a proper remedy for him at law. The bill was dismissed with costs.

## 549

## Hill v. Alleyne

(Ch. 1713)

*The executor of the estate of a deceased person who was under a disability must pay a rent in arrear that was due from the decedent out of the income of the estate but cannot sell the estate for that purpose.*

*A committee of a person under a disability cannot compromise that person's rights without an order of the court.*

British Library MS. Hargrave 80, f. 171v

In this case, a rent issuing out of an estate for the life of a lunatic who was dead had run in arrear almost to the value of the inheritance.

*Vernon* desired that, in default of payment within six months, the estate might be sold.

Lord Chancellor [Lord Harcourt]: Did you ever know a sale decreed in such a case?

*Vernon*: I cannot say I have.

Lord Chancellor [Lord Harcourt]: I cannot go further than the [Statute] 32 Hen. VIII[1] enables me. Let the executors of the lunatic hold the estate until they are satisfied the arrears.

They both agreed that, if a trust had been created for raising the annuity, there might undoubtedly have been a sale decreed.

In this case, Lord Chancellor [Lord Harcourt] declared that a committee of a lunatic ought not to presume to make an agreement for accepting a less annuity instead of a greater without the express directions of the court. And he set aside one of that kind that had been made some years before and in the lunatic's life; there were some circumstances of fraud in it of the other side.

[Other copies of this report: Lincoln's Inn MS. Misc. 383, p. 293, pl. 1, Lincoln's Inn MS. Misc. 107, p. 16, pl. 1.]

## 550

## Lord Coventry v. Lady Ann Coventry

(Ch. 1713)

*A conveyance pursuant to a marriage settlement should not be varied or set aside as contrary to the original intent of the parties except upon clear and convincing evidence.*

[1] Stat. 32 Hen. VIII, c. 37 (*SR*, III, 791).

British Library MS. Hargrave 80, f. 172

The bill sought to have a re-conveyance of some lands that passed by the general words of Lady Ann's marriage settlement, made before her marriage to her for life, upon a suggestion that they were not intended to be conveyed, that they were not mentioned in the particular of the lands agreed to be settled, and that the other lands without these being of the full value agreed to be settled for her jointure. To support the bill, several cases were cited of purchases when the particulars have been delivered and the treaty proceeded upon them and the general words of the conveyances been controlled by those particulars. Mr. Dash bought an estate by a particular as containing a certain number of acres at so much per acre, and, some years after the conveyance upon an admeasurement, the estate was found to fall short a good many acres, and the vendor was decreed to refund *pro rata*.

*Sir Joseph Jekyll*, of the other side, took a difference between contracts for sales where there is no room for bounty but each side has a *quid pro quo* and marriage treaties which proceed upon honor, especially among people of great distinction and where what they give is to their own family and posterities and that, therefore, a marriage treaty ought not to be examined with the same strictness as sales.

*Vernon* added that, if there had been articles, which there was not, and their settlement being repugnant to them, yet, being precedent to the marriage, it must be looked upon to contain the last resolution of the parties and would control the articles, that treaties of this kind varied daily, and that there would be no security in deeds if they were to be broken into by a foreign and uncertain evidence of the intent of the parties.

Lord Chancellor [Lord Harcourt] approved of Sir Joseph Jekyll's distinction and declared that, if a settlement was to be impeached as repugnant to the intent of the parties, that intent ought to be undeniably evident, that, in this case, there was no certain evidence of the parties' intent. And, therefore, he dismissed the bill but without costs, the particular having given My Lord Coventry some color for bringing it.

[Other copies of this report: Lincoln's Inn MS. Misc. 383, p. 293, pl. 2.]

[Related cases: Lord Coventry v. Lady Coventry (Ch. 1714), see below, Case No. 608.]

## 551

## Andre v. Browne

(Ch. 1713–1714)

*An offer to pay a debt tolls the Statute of Limitations.*

*A deposition taken before a replication cannot be used in evidence if the replication is withdrawn afterwards.*

*Additional questions can be put to a deponent if he is examined by one of the official examiners of the court, but not by a commissioner in the country.*

*Where a defendant has filed a new answer after depositions have been taken, further depositions may nevertheless be taken.*

British Library MS. Hargrave 80, f. 173

The plaintiff, being possessed of a bill for £300 from Valentine Duncombe dated almost thirty years ago and payable to bearer and it not appearing that it ever had been satisfied and, on the contrary, the proof that it had not being pretty strong and a reasonable account being given of the long acquiescence occasioned by Valentine Duncombe's breaking and going beyond the seas, was decreed his principal with interest from the time of filing the bill and costs against the defendant, the executor of Sir Charles Duncombe, who was the executor of Valentine. The defendant had pleaded the Statute of Limitations,[1] but the plea was overruled. And the same defense was again overruled at the hearing. The defendant having caused an advertisement to be published in the *Gazette* that, if any person had any demand against the estate of Sir Charles Duncombe or Valentine, they might repair to Mr. Lewis's chambers in the Temple for their satisfaction, which, though general, the court thought sufficient to take this particular debt out of the Statute of Limitations.

In this case, after some witnesses had been examined, the defendant obtained leave to amend his answer, and, upon that, the replication was withdrawn and a new one filed and other witnesses [were] examined.

It was ruled by the court that the deposition taken before the replication was withdrawn fell with it and the plaintiff lost the benefit of [it] at the hearing. In this case, it was insisted on by *Vernon* and ruled by the court that you cannot add an interrogatory after an examination at a commission in the country without leave of the court, the commissioners being named by the parties and not sworn, yet, in the office, you may add as many as you please with an order for it, the officer there being sworn and, therefore, not to be suspected of any foul practice in disclosing what was sworn before by the parties.

[Other copies of this report: Lincoln's Inn MS. Misc. 383, p. 294, Lincoln's Inn MS. Misc. 107, p. 16, pl. 2.]

British Library MS. Hargrave 81, f. 114, pl. 3

7 May 1714.

The defendant answered. The plaintiff replied and examined witnesses in the office, and the defendant gets leave to put in another answer, and, then, the plaintiff withdrew his replication and filed a new set of interrogatories and exam-

[1] Stat. 21 Jac. I, c. 16 (*SR*, IV, 1222–1223).

ined to them and, at the hearing, the reading of the last deposition was objected to and they were prayed to be suppressed.

Mr. *Vernon* answered, and it was agreed to by the Court, that either party might not only add an interrogatory but also exhibit an additional set of interrogatories in the office without an order for it and that, where witnesses are to be examined only in the office, there, no subpoena to rejoin is served though there must be where the examination is to be upon a commission. He said also that, if a bill be to discover assets, where the plaintiff is a creditor by bond or note, after the dismission of assets, the plaintiff may proceed at law if he please, yet the bill may likewise pray payment of the debt and the plaintiff may proceed properly to a hearing and to have a decree for his debt and interest, and his having a remedy at law first shall not be objected to him at the hearing.

And where a debt, an action, or a right is not otherwise barred than by the Statute of Limitations, a very small matter will serve to revive that right etc.

[Other copies of this report: British Library MS. Hargrave 82, f. 128, British Library MS. Hargrave 77, f. 31v, pl. 3, British Library MS. Hargrave 303, f. 58, pl. 3.]

## 552

## Buetell v. Tilden

(Ch. 1713)

*In this case, the devise in issue was a pecuniary bequest secured by land and not a life estate.*

British Library MS. Hargrave 80, f. 173v

A man, having created a term for years determinable upon the life of J.S. and made it a security to J.S. for £400, by his will, devised the same £400 to J.S. and, afterwards, devised the land to his own heir at law. After the death of J.S., [it was] decreed that J.S. did not take an estate for life, the implication not being necessary, but the natural construction upon the whole will rather being that his heir should take immediately subject to that charge to J.S., which he plainly had then in view. And the security he had made seemed the reason of devising to the heir after the death of J.S.

[Other copies of this report: Lincoln's Inn MS. Misc. 383, p. 295, pl. 1, Lincoln's Inn MS. Misc. 107, p. 17.]

## 553

## Crispe v. Crispe

(Ch. 1713)

*The plowing of uncultivated land is waste.*

British Library MS. Hargrave 80, f. 174

Upon a motion for an injunction to stay the defendant, who was a tenant for years under the plaintiff, from committing waste upon lands in Oxfordshire by plowing and burning them, it was alleged for the plaintiff that, in the case of Sir Simon Stewart and Worsley, this had been adjudged to be waste in the Exchequer and the decree was affirmed in the House of Lords.[1]

But in that case, *Vernon*, who was for the plaintiff, [said] that the tenant had been allowed to take one crop from the land he had so plowed before the bill was brought.

Lord Chancellor [LORD HARCOURT], in this case, allowed the defendant to turn the land, which was plowed before the filing the bill, and sow it once only and enjoined him from breaking up any more or sowing that a second time.

[Other copies of this report: Lincoln's Inn MS. Misc. 383, p. 295, pl. 2, Lincoln's Inn MS. Misc. 107, p. 18, pl. 1.]

## 554

## Symondson v. Tweed

(Ch. 1713)

*A court of equity can decree specific performance of a parol contract if the contract be set forth in the bill and confessed by answer.*

Precedents in Chancery 374, 24 E.R. 169

In this case, the court declared, and the counsel agreed likewise, that, if a man brings a bill for a specific performance of a parol agreement, setting forth the substance of it in his bill, and the defendant, by his answer, confesses the agreement that the court may in such case decree an execution thereof, notwithstanding the Statute of Frauds and Perjuries,[2] because the defendant confessing the agreement, there can be no danger of perjury from contrariety of evidence, which was the only mischief that Statute intended to obviate.

---

[1] *Stewart v. Worsely* (Ex. 1711), Eq. Cases Exch. 673, *Worsley v. Stuart* (1712), 4 Brown P.C. 377, 2 E.R. 255, Lords' Journal, vol. 19, p. 393.

[2] Stat. 29 Car. II, c. 3 (*SR*, V, 839–842).

But, in the principal case, the defendant had not by his answer confessed the agreement charged in the bill, which was only by parol, to settle some lands and houses on the plaintiff in consideration of his marrying the defendant's daughter.

And, therefore, the bill was dismissed. And it was said, in all cases where the court had decreed a specific execution of a parol agreement, yet the same had been supported and made out by letters in writing and the particular terms stipulated therein as a foundation for their decree; otherwise, the court would never carry such an agreement into execution.

[Other copies of this report: Gilbert Rep. 35, 25 E.R. 25.]

[Other reports of this case: 1 Eq. Cas. Abr. 19, 21 E.R. 842.]

## 555

## *Ex parte* Alpe

(Ch. 1713)

*A court of equity will not order the conveyance of land of infants under the age of discretion.*

British Library MS. Hargrave 81, f. 103

10 August.

Mr. *Mead*, for the petitioner, prayed that the heir of the mortgagee might assign to the mortgagor on payment of principal, interest, and costs, the executor of the mortgagee consenting to it, that the Statute of [ *blank* ][1] had directed this summary way and, though the infant was but a year old, yet, in the eye of the law, an infant of twenty was equally incapable and under the same disability as one of a year only.

*Curia* [Lord Harcourt]: There are degrees of discretion[2] in an infant, and such a one may be guilty of murder, felony, etc. at one age though not at another. An infant who is to do such an act as you are desiring ought to be of such an age as to know what he is doing or at least to be capable of doing what you would have him. I will not order a child of a year old anymore than a child in the cradle to execute a deed, which he cannot do. But you may go before a master and let him see what is due for principal, interest, and costs. Let that be brought before the Master and the executors assign over as the mortgagor directs, and let the Master inquire who is guardian for the infant, for there is not any appointed by the will. And the mother, who is one of the executors, has an interest by the will and is not, therefore, a proper person in this case.

---

1 Stat. 7 Ann., c. 19 (*SR*, IX, 89).

2 direction *MS.*

Secondly, the Statute mentions that those conveyances by infants shall be by petition, and a bill here is a petition only. And why should not a bill be brought [is] answered because that was a tedious expensive way which would load a mortgagor's estate who was ready and willing to pay the money and that was the very thing the Act intended to remedy by this summary way. And the court, upon a bill without the Statute, could not have directed an infant to convey or, if it had, the conveyance had not been good. And now, since the Statute, the court cannot direct otherwise or in any other manner upon a bill than it may upon a petition without a bill. And, as the latter is the most easy and least expensive, it best answers the end of making the said Statute.

[Other copies of this report: British Library MS. Hargrave 82, f. 100, British Library MS. Hargrave 77, f. 25v, pl. 3, British Library MS. Hargrave 303, f. 49, pl. 2.]

## 556

## Anonymous

(Ch. 1713)

*A bond given in consideration for an out of court settlement that is for a greater sum than the settlement is unenforceable.*

British Library MS. Hargrave 77, f. 26, pl. 2

14 October.

It was said by the plaintiff's counsel and not denied by the defendant's or the court that, where a person compounds his debts and a creditor who signs that instrument of composition with the rest takes a bond from the debtor for a greater sum to sign, equity constantly relieves against such bond.

[Other copies of this report: British Library MS. Hargrave 82, f. 103, pl. 1, British Library MS. Hargrave 303, f. 49v, pl. 2.]

## 557

## King v. Mitchell

(Ch. 1713)

*A general report of a master in Chancery can be excepted to on the grounds of insufficient evidence to support it or ultra vires.*

British Library MS. Hargrave 77, f. 26, pl. 3

15 October.

Where a master reports generally or a sum in gross, the party aggrieved may take a general exception, as that he had not evidence or had not authority by the decree so to do. But where the report is founded on particulars or refers to items in the schedule of the report or expressed in a book with reference to [ *blank* ], a general exception is nought, for, there, the exception ought to be particular.

If several persons are appointed to manage an affair, as the care of a cargo of a ship or the disposing of it and they are to have a satisfaction for it, the owners afterwards on making up their accounts take a part of the produce and release the managers, all the surplus of the produce shall be intended to be given them for their trouble and shall be equally divided between them.

[Other copies of this report: British Library MS. Hargrave 82, f. 103, pl. 2, British Library MS. Hargrave 303, f. 50, pl. 1.]

## 558

## Wase v. Whitfield

(Ch. 1713)

*In this case, it was the intent of a testator according to his will that his personal estate should not be liable to exonerate his real estate for the payment of his debts.*

Lincoln's Inn MS. Misc. 11, p. 97, pl. 1

6 November 1713.

[It was] decreed that, by a devise of 'all my household goods', linen in trunks, as also pictures, passed.

British Library MS. Hargrave 80, f. 165v, pl. 1

A man devised his lands to be sold for payment of debts and gave his wife a legacy of £600 to be paid out of the money arising by the sale. The surplus he directed to be reinvested in lands and settled to the use of his wife for life, remainder to his senior brother in tail, with a like remainder to his second, remainder to his own right heirs. He gave several specific legacies to his wife and appointed her his executrix and residuary legatee. The second brother died without issue.

And upon a bill brought by the plaintiff, heir to the testator, against the defendant, executor to the wife, My Lord [Lord Harcourt] decreed the personal estate to the executor of the wife. And, if it should not be applied in exoneration of the real [estate], though there were no negative words to exempt it, it was given her by the name of the residue. He relied chiefly on the giving her a legacy out of the rent as an evidence of his not intending that she should bring in the personal estate in ease of the real [estate].

*Tamen quaere.*

[Other copies of this report: Lincoln's Inn MS. Misc. 383, p. 275, pl. 1, Lincoln's Inn MS. Misc. 106, p. 245.]

559

## Matthews v. Pufford

(Ch. 1713)

*Where a mortgagor afterwards enters into a bond to the mortgagee, the heir of the mortgagor must pay off the bond as well as the original debt when he comes to redeem.*

*He who will have equity, must do it.*

Lincoln's Inn MS. Misc. 11, p. 99

10 November 1713.

Edward Pufford, upon his marriage, settles lands to the use of himself for life, after to his wife for life, remainder to the heirs of his body begotten on his wife, remainder to himself in fee.

Edward Pufford borrows £300 of the plaintiff, and he and his wife levy a fine of the premises, which he declared to be to the use of the plaintiff and his heirs, subject to a proviso that, if Pufford paid the £300 with interest at a day therein mentioned, then the same should enure to the same uses as are limited in the settlement. After the mortgage becomes forfeited, Pufford borrows two sums more of £30 each of the plaintiff and gives him bonds for them payable with interest. And then Pufford dies.

The plaintiff brings his bill against the defendant, the son and heir of the mortgagor to foreclose him of the equity of redemption unless he paid not only the money due on the mortgage but likewise the £60 due on the bonds.

And the question was if the defendant should redeem without paying both.

Mr. *Vernon*, for the plaintiff, insisted that, the proviso not being performed, the entail under the fine could not take effect.

However, if the limitation of the uses of the fine had been subject to the mortgage to the very same uses as are limited in the settlement and they had been expressly limited over again, yet that would not have helped the defendant, for the second settlement was voluntary and, therefore, shall not stand in the way of a bond creditor.

And, for this, he cited the Case of Templeman and Bertie,[1] where a tenant in tail under a settlement levied a fine to the use of the mortgagee, and he settles the equity of redemption on himself in tail and then borrows money on bond of divers persons, and he dies; [it was] decreed the second settlement was voluntary and fraudulent against the bond creditors.

*Sir Joseph Jekyll*: The new uses were not fraudulent at the time of their creation, for what could be more just than when he had let in the mortgage to limit the estate to the old uses. The defendant comes in under the consideration of the first settlement.

---

[1] *Templeman v. Beke* (K.B. 1689 x 1710).

Master of the Rolls [TREVOR]: This is a new case. And I do not remember any such in the court before. The plaintiff is a creditor on bond for £60 really advanced as well as a creditor on mortgage. It is true the land is not particularly charged with the bond debt, but the obligor has bound his heirs, which at law is an express lien on the land.

I agree, if the money had been paid at the day, the uses would have arisen. But the money was not paid, and, therefore, at law, the plaintiff had an absolute estate and the mortgagor has nothing but an equity of redemption.

Now, the heir can never come at this equity of redemption but by the assistance of a court of equity. And, if he comes here to have the assistance of equity, he ought to do equity.

Upon the whole, I am of the opinion the estate is open and that the bonds are a lien upon the equity of redemption.

Note it was agreed on both sides that, if a man mortgages and, afterwards, borrows more money of the mortgagee on bond, the mortgagor himself may redeem without being obliged to pay off the bond. But, if the heir comes to redeem, he must pay the bonds of his ancestor, for the equity of redemption is assets, and this [is] for preventing circuity.

British Library MS. Hargrave 80, f. 157, pl. 2

A tenant in tail in remainder expectant upon an estate for life mortgaged in fee by a fine, provided that, if the money were paid at the day, that then the mortgagee should stand seised to several uses, which were the same as were limited in the first settlement. The mortgage became forfeited, and the mortgagor, after having entered into several bonds to the mortgagee, died. Upon a bill against the heir of the mortgagor to foreclose, the single question was whether these bonds should be tacked to the mortgage and affect the equity of redemption.

For the defendant, it was urged that his title to the equity of redemption being as heir in tail, the debts of his ancestors could not affect him, that a bond could not be tacked to a mortgage against the mortgagor himself, the only reason why it might against the heir of a mortgagor was in respect of his having assets by descent, which reason ceased in this case, the estate tail not being assets.

*Vernon*, for the plaintiff, insisted that the limitation of the equity of redemption in tail was voluntary and fraudulent against creditors.

And *Sir Joseph Jekyll* urged that the deed could not be fraudulent that was not so at the time of making it and that this was not, the bonds being given after.

*Vernon* insisted that it was nevertheless fraudulent against the plaintiffs and cited the case of Templeman v. Beeke, where an equity of redemption was referred to be tried by Chief Justice Holt and [it was] ruled to be fraudulent against debts contracted after.

*How*, on the same side, insisted that the defendant's father, having an estate tail in the equity of redemption, had consequently a power over it and that, his estate being only an equitable one, it was not necessary for him to levy a fine or suffer a recovery to bar it, but any other solemn act would be sufficient and that his entering into the bonds was equivalent to bind it.

Master of the Rolls [Trevor]: Complaints have been frequent here of married women being drawn in to let in a charge upon their estates and, upon a neglect in penning the proviso, several of them have been ruined and the mortgagees gained absolute estates upon the husband's failure to pay the money. The equity of redemption here is subject to the bonds though, by proper words, it might have been exempted from subsequent debts, but the estate is open. The mortgagee on failure had an absolute estate and the heir cannot have a redemption anywhere but in equity, and, if he will have equity, he must do it.

[Other copies of this report: Lincoln's Inn MS. Misc. 383, p. 277, pl. 2, Lincoln's Inn MS. Misc. 106, p. 247.]

## 560

## Tipping v. Piggott

(Ch. 1713)

*Trustees to preserve contingent remainders are not trustees to mere remote volunteers but only to remaindermen who are purchasers and their issue.*

British Library MS. Hargrave 80, f. 158

Sir Richard Piggott, in 1676, in consideration of an intended marriage which was afterward had between Thomas Piggott, his nephew and who was afterwards his heir, and Letitia and of £3000 portion paid to Sir Richard, conveyed a very considerable estate, part to trustees and their heirs to the use of Thomas Piggott for 99 years if he should so long live, remainder to the trustees to preserve contingent remainders, remainder to the first and every other son of the marriage in tail, remainder to the heirs of the body of Thomas, remainder to the right heirs of the body, remainder to the right heirs of Thomas, the other part was conveyed to trustees and their heirs to the use of Sir Richard for life, remainder to Thomas for 99 years if he should live so long, remainder to the trustees for his life to preserve contingent remainders, remainder to Letitia for her life, remainder to the first son etc. in like manner as the other part. After the death of Richard, Thomas, having no issue, prevailed with the defendant Meime, who was the surviving trustee, to join in levying a fine of the whole estate, the uses of which were declared in the same manner as the uses in the settlement of 1676 except only the last remainder, which, instead of being to the right heir of Thomas, was to Thomas and his heirs. Thomas, afterwards, died without issue and, by will, devised this estate to the defendant Piggott, a very remote, if any, relation. At the death of Thomas, Mrs. Spikely was his heir. But she dying, Sir Thomas Tipping became his heir, the relation being pretty remote, their great-grandfather being the common ancestor. And he brought this bill against Piggott for a reconveyance of the estate and, if he failed there, against Maime for a satisfaction for the injury done him by his breach of trust.

It was agreed on both sides that the remainder to the first son etc. and to the heirs of the body of Thomas and to the right heirs of Thomas were continent and that those that were limited for that part of the estate in which Letitia had no jointure were destroyed by the fine in the part that was limited to her for her life, she not having joined in the fine and being still alive. It was insisted that her particular estate or the present right of entry which she had preserved the contingent remainders and that there the plaintiff's title was good at law but, in regard he could not try it there, yet, there being an estate of freehold in being in Letitia, she was proper to litigate it in equity and, he having confirmed her jointure, he was likewise proper to pray that the deeds that concerned that part of the estate might be preserved.

But to this, it was replied by *Hooper* that, though the remainders were contingent, yet they were to arise out of the fee limited to the trustees and that fee being conveyed away by the surviving trustee before the contingency happened upon which they were to arise, those contingencies never should arise but were destroyed. For this, he cited the Case of Chudleigh as in point; Cro. 102.[1] And if it should be said that the fee resulted to Sir Richard until the contingency happened, that would not avail them, for then Thomas being heir to Sir Richard at the time of the fine, it was in him, and it seems that the estate of Letitia was turned to a right by the fine and, her husband joining in it, his act so far bars her, that she could not then have a present right of entry for that part of the estate where the contingent remainders were admitted to be destroyed.

It was urged by *Vernon*, for the plaintiff, that the trustees were singly interested here to preserve the contingent remainders and that no trustee had any power to defeat his trust without the concurrence of the party *que* trust, nor was there any defence in equity against a breach of trust where there was no purchaser in the case and yet, in this, the defendants were surely volunteers, that, where a trust was broken, the injured person might follow the trustee for satisfaction or rather, if a purchaser did not intervene, the thing itself.

*Cowper* added that the estate moving from Sir Richard in consideration of the marriage and of a portion received by him, the last remainder ought to be looked upon as a purchaser's as well as the issue of the marriage.

On the other side, it was insisted by *Sir Joseph Jekyll* and *Hooper* that the plaintiff was a volunteer as well as the defendant, the consideration of a marriage and of the portion extending only to the issue of that marriage, and that, both being volunteers, a court of equity had nothing to do to interpose between them,

[1] *Dillon v. Freine* (1589–1595), 1 Coke Rep. 113, 135, 76 E.R. 261, 305, 1 Anderson 309, 123 E.R. 489, Popham 70, 79 E.R. 1184; *Biggot v. Smith* (1628), Croke Car. 102, 79 E.R. 691.

that, though the several remainders were contingent, yet the trustees could not be understood to preserve those that were voluntary but only those to the issue of the marriage, and that Maime was not therefore guilty of any breach of trust, all the limitations of the issues of the marriage being preserved in the deed declaring the uses of the fine to the last remainder, which was voluntarily destroyed.

Lord Chancellor [Lord Harcourt]: There is no difference between the two estates. The remainder to the right heir of Thomas is destroyed in both by the fine. All the three remainders are contingent but fall under a different consideration. The issue of the marriage are purchasers of those limited to them; the others are merely voluntary and, being barred at law, equity ought not to interpose. He added that the plaintiff was a very remote relation and not heir at the death of Thomas. The opinion of conveyancers formerly, who did [not] scruple passing titles where contingent remainders had been destroyed by trustees joining in fines having been mentioned, he said that the experiment was dangerous; where the remaindermen were purchasers, that was possible; there might be a cause of that kind where this court would not relieve. But, if, in any case, a breach of trust ought to be punished, it ought in that where a trustee comes in to destroy the limitations of the issue of the marriage. And care ought to be taken that the issue may not suffer by it.

The bill was dismissed without costs.

[Other copies of this report: Lincoln's Inn MS. Misc. 383, p. 278, pl. 2.]

Lincoln's Inn MS. Misc. 384, p. 9, pl. 2

13 November.

A bill [was brought] to be relieved against a breach of trust. In the marriage settlement, the limitation was to A. for 99 years if he lived so long, remainder to trustees to preserve contingent remainders, remainder to the wife for a jointure, remainder to the first and other sons in tail, remainder to the plaintiff. A., having no issue, joins with the trustees in levying a fine and suffered a recovery.

*Hooper*, for the defendant: Where the issue of the marriage is defeated, they being purchasers, it is a breach of trust; not where it is a remote remainder[man] that is defeated, for he is merely a volunteer.

Lord Chancellor [Lord Harcourt]: The issue of the marriage are to be esteemed purchasers, and this court would punish a breach of trust in favor of them. But the subsequent remainders are merely voluntary. And, therefore, a court of equity ought not to interpose. It is [not] impossible that [there] may be a case of a remainderman, where it is for the support of a family, which this court will relieve. I dismiss the bill.

Lincoln's Inn MS. Misc. 11, p. 102

13 November 1713.

On the marriage of Thomas Piggott, nephew of Sir Richard Piggott, Sir Richard conveyed lands to Sir Edward Atkyns and Simon Mayne and their heirs to the use of himself for life, then to his wife for her life, then to Thomas Piggott for ninety-nine years if he lived so long, remainder as to part to Lettice, his intended wife, for her life, remainder as to the whole to the trustees to support contingent remainders, remainder to the first and other sons of Thomas and Lettice, remainder to trustees for ninety-nine [years] for raising portions for daughters of the marriage, remainder to the heirs of the body [of] Thomas, remainder to the right heirs of Thomas.

Thomas and his wife died without issue and his sister was his heiress at law. And she being since dead and Sir Richard and his lady being likewise dead, the plaintiff claims title to the lands under the settlement as heir at law of Thomas.

And, now, he brings his bill to have the settlement and the other title deeds relating to the premises delivered to him.

The defendants set forth by answer that, after the death of Sir Richard and his lady, Thomas Piggott having no issue, he and Simon Mayne, the surviving trustee, by feoffment and fine, in 1700, conveyed the premises to trustees to other uses, and the defendants claim under this last settlement.

Mr. *Vernon*, for the plaintiff, insisted much on the great breach of trust in Mr. Mayne in joining with Thomas Piggott to destroy the contingent remainders and that he ought to answer for this breach of trust.

Mr. *Cowper*: I believe, if there had been issue of Thomas born after the remainders were destroyed and such issue came to be relieved, there could be no question but such issue might follow the estate. Now, the limitations to the heirs of Thomas was as much a contingent remainder and intended to be preserved as the limitation to the first and other sons. And the plaintiff, claiming under this contingent remainder, ought to be relieved against the breach of trust in Mayne.

*Sir Joseph Jekyll*, for the defendants: The plaintiff is not the person injured. If anyone was, it was the sister of Thomas. But she is now dead. And, therefore, the plaintiff and defendants being both volunteers, the court ought to stand neuter.

We have the estate in law us. The limitation to the jointress would not support the contingent remainders. She could have no right of entry. The right of entry that must support a contingent remainder must be some person whose inheritance is endeavored to be defeated as a tenant in fee or in tail. I do believe, if it was in the case of the issue, the court would look upon it as a great breach of trust. But that is not our case.

Serjeant *Hooper*, on the same side: There is no doubt but the limitation to the heirs of Thomas was a contingent remainder. Now, how must this contingency arise? It must arise out of the estate that was limited to the trustees. And, if that estate is gone, the contingency is gone too.

I agree, if it was in the case of issue, the trustees would be answerable. But this is a notion but of late years. I think it was started within these ten years.

Lord Keeper [Lord Harcourt]: it is a very good notion. The remainder to the right heirs of Thomas and to the heirs of his body were contingent remainders as well as the limitation to the first and other sons. But there is a great difference between them; the two first were partly voluntary and do no come within the consideration of the settlement. Now, these being destroyed, I do not think this court ought to interpose in favor of the plaintiff, who is a mere volunteer.

I believe it has been formerly thought that trustees might safely join in destroying the contingent remainder in a settlement. For my part, I think it is a plain breach of trust, and, if it should ever come in question in favor of issue, the trustees would find they had made a dangerous experiment. But this is not the case now before me.

The bill must be dismissed, but without costs.

[Other reports of this case: Gilbert Rep. 34, 25 E.R. 25, 1 Eq. Cas. Abr. 385, 21 E.R. 1120.]

## 561

## Anonymous

(Ch. 1713)

*A court of equity will supply a defective surrender of a copyhold in favor of a child unless it will totally disinherit the heir at law.*

Lincoln's Inn MS. Misc. 384, p. 9, pl. 1

14 November.

Lord Chancellor [Lord Harcourt]: This court always supplies a defective surrender [of a copyhold] in favor of a child unless it tends to the total disherison of the heir at law.

## 562

## Broderick v. Broderick

(Ch. 1713)

*A conveyance can be set aside on the ground of fraud in the inducement.*

Lincoln's Inn MS. Misc. 384, p. 10, pl. 3

14 November.

*Vernon*: Where there is a *suppressio veri* or a *suggestio falsi*, this court will set aside deeds, as in Webb and Hill's Case, though perhaps not a will. *Vide* Bodvile and Roberts in Bath and Monts, 61.[1]

British Library MS. Hargrave 80, f. 159

The plaintiff was heir and the defendants [were] devisees of Broderick, who devised his real estate to be sold for payment of debts and the surplus to the defendants. The will was executed by the testator and attested by three witnesses, but they did not subscribe in his presence.[2] This defect was soon after disclosed to the devisee, who immediately proved the will in the Prerogative Court and produced it under probate to the heir and upon pretense that the estate was charged with debts almost to the value and that there would be a necessity of selling and that, though it was not necessary, the estate would sell the better if he would release. They obtained a release from him of 100 guineas, which recited the will, that it was duly executed. They, afterwards finding that the release was ineffectual, the will bring merely void, for 50 guineas more, got the plaintiff to join with them in a lease and release to one Day. The consideration mentioned in the deed was adequate to the value of the land, but the sale was fictitious. And Day [was] only a trustee for the defendants. The plaintiff, afterwards being informed of the defect in the will, brought his bill to be relieved against the conveyances as being obtained by concealing the truth and suggesting the will was duly executed though it really was not.

And upon that head, *Vernon* cited the case of Webb and Hill, where there were but two witnesses to a will and the devisee concealed it and got the heir to join in a conveyance and though there were several repeated acts, yet the heir, upon discovering it three or four years after, was relieved and the conveyances [were] set aside by the Master of the Rolls, and this decree [was] affirmed by Lord Cowper.

*How* cited the case of Dr. Dent and Sir William Buck,[3] the Doctor demanded tithes in kind of Sir William; he pretended a *modus* of £40 *per annum* and produced an exemplification of a [writ of] prohibition in Queen Elizabeth's time grounded on a suggestion of that *modus* but concealed the award of a [writ of] consultation in the end of it; the Doctor was prevailed upon to agree by this authority to accept £40 *per annum* in lieu of tithes and, upon a discovery

[1] *Roberts v. Wynn* (1664), 1 Chancery Reports 236, 21 E.R. 560; *Earl of Bath v. Earl of Mountague* (1693), 3 Chancery Cases 55, 103, 22 E.R. 963, 992.

[2] Stat. 29 Car. II, c. 3, s. 5 (*SR*, V, 840).

[3] *Dent v. Buck* (1701), Colles 182, 1 E.R. 240, 2 Eq. Cas. Abr. 244, 481, 22 E.R. 208, 408.

after[wards] of the imposition was not relieved in the Exchequer but was upon an appeal from thence to the House of Lords.

*Jekyll*, of the other side, said that, in the Case of Pen and Ford, there had been several accounts stated and an error in the first run through all of them and, though the error was fraudulent, yet, after so many repeated acts, Lord Cowper would not break through them and relieve the plaintiff, and Pen submitted.

Lord Chancellor [Lord Harcourt]: The release and subsequent conveyance were fraudulent, gained by misrepresenting the will as duly executed though the defendants all that time knew the contrary. He, therefore, decreed them to be set aside and a re-conveyance to be made to the plaintiff but 150 guineas to be discounted out of the profits. Barker, who had purchased part under the defendants having, though he denied express notice, admitted that he had heard some random discourse about the defect in the execution of the said will, his purchase was decreed to stand only as a security for his money. And the other defendants were to account for that they having received it but were to be allowed out of that and the profits for what debts they had paid which the personal estate did not amount to. But costs were reserved until after the accounts were taken of other debts and legacies that effect the real estate.

[Other copies of this report: Lincoln's Inn MS. Misc. 383, p. 280.]

[Other reports of this case: 1 Peere Williams 239, 24 E.R. 369, 2 Eq. Cas. Abr. 244, 480, 22 E.R. 207, 408.]

## 563

## Hooke v. Grove

(Ch. 1713)

*In this case, a legacy to a widow was not taken as the satisfaction for an unperformed marriage settlement in her favor.*

Lincoln's Inn MS. Misc. 384, p. 8, pl. 3

20 November 1713.

Upon the marriage of the plaintiff with Sir Hele Hook, who was an infant, there were articles entered into by his guardian for settling lands of £500 *per annum* on the plaintiff for her jointure. After the marriage, Sir Hele settles his lands on the plaintiff of £250 *per annum*, which prove defective in title. After[wards], he gives the plaintiff £4000 by a will.

The plaintiff brings her bill to have the marriage articles carried into execution. And the question was whether the legacy of £4000 was a satisfaction.

*Cowper*, for the defendant, the heir: If Sir Hele had covenanted to make a jointure and had died, leaving personal assets, they would be liable to the breach of the covenant. Here, the legacy ought to be a satisfaction.

Lord Chancellor [Lord Harcourt]: The plaintiff must have her marriage articles made good. I cannot construe the devise of £4000 to be any satisfaction. Marriage agreements are not like purchases, for, though a purchaser shall have no more than he contracts for, yet here is room for bounty. The second settlement, being defective in title, is no satisfaction. The £500 *per annum* must be settled on the plaintiff clear of all charges except taxes.

Lincoln's Inn MS. Misc. 10, p. 167

21 November 1713.

Sir Eli Hooke, upon his marriage with the plaintiff, entered into articles to settle £500 a year upon her for a jointure. He makes a settlement which falls short of that value. In pursuance of these articles, afterwards, he settles other lands upon her for her life, but no notice is taken of any defect of the yearly value of the first settlement or that this second settlement was made to supply any deficiency in the first settlement. Then, he comes by his will and devises other lands to the plaintiff, his wife, for her life, which lands, together with the lands in the second settlement, exceed the £500 a year. And he also gives her a considerable legacy by his will.

After Sir Eli's death, the lands in the first settlement are evicted from her by a prior title. And she now brings her bill to have her jointure made good. And if the settlement and will shall be looked upon to be a satisfaction of the articles was the question.

It was said by Mr. *Vernon*, in the Case of Wilcox and Wilcox,[1] a man upon the marriage of his son entered into articles to settle £100 a year. He neglected to make a settlement in his lifetime, but suffered lands of that value to descend upon his son, and this was decreed in this court to be a satisfaction of the articles.

It was also said by Mr. *Cooper* that, if an infant, upon his marriage, enters into articles to settle a jointure and receives his wife's portion, this shall bind him in this court and, when he comes of age, he shall be compelled to make the settlement, and, if he dies before he does so, it shall bind his heir or executor to make good these articles.

Note the lands in the first settlement were evicted after Sir Eli's death so that it was objected that he could not intend that the second settlement and what he gave by his will should go in satisfaction of the articles.

Lord Chancellor [Lord Harcourt]: The Lady [Hooke], being disappointed of the settlement, ought to have the benefit of the articles. Had the first settlement stood, she would have had the benefit of the second settlement. Is not the reason the same that she should have it now the first settlement is defeated? Sir Eli could never intend the second settlement and will to be any satisfaction of the

[1] *Wilcocks v. Wilcocks* (1706), 2 Vernon 558, 23 E.R. 961, 1 Eq. Cas. Abr. 26, 156, 21 E.R. 847, 955.

marriage articles, for he looked upon the first settlement to be a full performance of the articles. Let the Master set out lands of £500 a year for the plaintiff out of the lands whereof Sir Eli died seised in fee or tail in regard she was dowable of the latter as well as the former.

Note another question followed on this determination, *viz*. whether the second settlement was good, for that settlement was made in pursuance of a power, for, as to those lands, Sir Eli was tenant for life with a power to make a jointure so it be in bar of dower. Now, he executed this power. But it falls out that this is not a settlement in bar of dower, being made after the marriage, and the question was if this settlement should be made good in this court, being only a voluntary settlement.

It was said by Mr. *Vernon* that a defective execution of a power was never supplied in favor of a volunteer.

The court inclined at first to have made it good, but, at last, said he would do nothing in it, but leave them to the law.

May 14, this decree was affirmed in the House of Lords.[1]

[Other reports of this case: 2 Eq. Cas. Abr. 218, 389, 22 E.R. 186, 332.]

[Affirmed on appeal: 4 Brown P.C. 593, 2 E.R. 404.]

## 564

## Brandon v. Bowles

(Ch. 1713)

*The title deeds of a bankrupt that are in the hands of his creditors must be given to the assignees of the commissioners of bankrupts.*

Lincoln's Inn MS. Misc. 384, p. 10, pl. 2

25 November.

A bill [was brought] by the assignees of the commissioner of bankrupts to compel the defendant to deliver up deeds and writings which the bankrupt had deposited in his hands until such time as he should make the defendant a mortgage to secure a debt due to him.

*Vernon*, for the plaintiff: There is a great difference between deeds that are pledged until the debt is paid and this case where the estate, and not the writings, is to be the security.

Lord Chancellor [Lord Harcourt]: The defendant must deliver up the writings to the plaintiffs and come in under the commission with the other creditors and pay costs.

[1] *Grove v. Hooke* (1714), 4 Brown P.C. 593, 2 E.R. 404.

Lincoln's Inn MS. Misc. 10, p. 169, pl. 1

25 November 1713.

A. became indebted to the defendant in £240 for goods sold. Afterwards, A. promised to assign over a mortgage to the defendant for securing this debt. Accordingly, he delivers the mortgage writings to the defendant in order to have an assignment of the mortgage made to him. But, before such assignment was made, A. becomes a bankrupt.

And the assignees now bring their bill to have these deeds delivered up.

[They were] decreed to be delivered up, and the defendant [was ordered] to pay costs. And the court would hardly allow it to be spoken to.

[Other reports of this case: Precedents in Chancery 375, 24 E.R. 169, Gilbert Rep. 35, 25 E.R. 26, 2 Eq. Cas. Abr. 112, 22 E.R. 96.]

## 565

## Anonymous

(Ch. 1713)

*Where an oral agreement is reduced to writing, parol evidence cannot be used to contradict the written memorandum of the contract.*

British Library MS. Hargrave 77, f. 26, pl. 5

25 November.

Where a parol agreement is made and that is afterwards reduced into writing, the latter has totally destroyed the former and the party cannot go out of the writing. Where a parol agreement is charged and a bill founded upon it, the defendant may answer to it if he will, but the court will not compel him because [it is] against the Statute of Frauds and Perjuries[1] and the court is against countenancing or establishing such agreements and the party may plead the Statute to such a bill, as here it was done and allowed.

[Other copies of this report: British Library MS. Hargrave 82, f. 104, pl. 1, British Library MS. Hargrave 303, f. 50, pl. 3.]

## 566

## Richardson v. Swinborne

(Ch. 1713–1717)

*In this case, the decedent's personal estate was ordered to be used to pay off a mortgage.*

1 Stat. 29 Car. II, c. 3 (*SR*, V, 839–842).

Lincoln's Inn MS. Misc. 10, p. 202

Michaelmas 1713. At the Rolls.

The plaintiff was the son and heir of William Richardson, who surrendered his copyhold estate to trustees and their heirs on condition that, if Richardson should pay Jane Fowler £36 *per annum* for life and £600 to her daughters in six months after her death, that then the trustees should stand seised to the use of Richardson and his heirs.

Richardson died intestate, leaving the plaintiff his heir, but Anne Swinborne, the plaintiff's sister, took administration to her father and possessed his estate and also, as one of the executors of Robert Fairberd, the assignee of the mortgage, was in possession of the copyhold premises.

The bill was to compel the defendant Swinburne to exonerate the mortgage on the copyhold estate out of her father's personal estate and for a redemption, which was accordingly decreed.

This cause was reheard Hilary [term] following [1714] before LORD HARCOURT, and [there was] no variation in this respect. And, afterwards, it was heard on the Master's report before the present Lord Chancellor [LORD COWPER], and there was no variation.

And now [28 October 1717], it came on upon the equity reserved.

Mr. *Cowper*: This is a debt in equity, and we have a precedent in point where the personal estate was applied to exonerate the real estate of a debt which was only a debt in equity, *viz*. Popley v. Popley, Hilary 33 & 34 Car. II.[1] This was in the case of a devisee of lands. But there is no difference between the heir and the devisee, for, if the personal estate is to be applied to exonerate the real estate in the hands of the devisee, it is as strong at least that it ought to be so in the case of the heir where lands descend to him.

In this case, there are assets sufficient to satisfy all the debts and legacies. And, therefore, the surplus of the personal estate being given to the executrix and not to a stranger, it ought to be applied to exonerate this mortgage, which is a debt in equity.

Serjeant *Hooper*, for the defendants: This was no debt, either at law or in equity. No action could be maintained at law, nor could they come into this court to compel the payment of it.

Suppose a man creates a term in his marriage settlement for raising younger children's portions. Will anyone say that the heir, in this case, shall come in and say let the personal estate be applied to pay these portions? Surely, it never was done.

Mr. *Vernon*: The mortgagor has made his daughter, who was also his heir at law, and his wife executors. It is true the daughter is now dead. But shall a remote

[1] *Popley v. Popley* (1681), 2 Chancery Cases 84, 22 E.R. 858, 1 Vernon 36, 23 E.R. 290, also 1 Eq. Cas. Abr. 270, 21 E.R. 1038.

heir come now and pray that the personal estate shall be applied to exonerate the real estate? No, surely, for this right was extinguished during the lifetime of the daughter, she being entitled to the real estate as well as to the personal estate, and, therefore, it cannot now be revived.

Why, suppose a man makes a mortgage and dies and this land descends to his son and he dies. Shall his heir come and pray that the son's personal estate shall be applied to exonerate this mortgage? No. It was no debt of his, nor was the personal estate liable to the payment of it. And as often as this has been attempted, it has been denied.

Lord Chancellor [Lord Cowper]: Thomas Davis, in consideration of £300 to him in hand paid, makes a conveyance in fee to Thomas Reynolds with a covenant for quiet enjoyment and that the premises are free from encumbrances; then comes the proviso that, if the mortgagor, his heirs, and assigns shall pay £300 to Reynolds at Michaelmas 1702 or at any other Michaelmas day following with all rent and arrears of rent due for the same (which must be interest, for there are no lands that the word 'same' can refer to), then the mortgagor may enter. Interest is paid annually. The only question then is if this is a debt. I take it that it is a debt. It is a debt secured by a pledge or mortgage of land. And it is not a debt without a remedy.

It is true it is confined to a point of remedy, for the remedy is that, if the interest should not be paid, the mortgagee may bring his [action of] ejectment and recover the land and hold it until the mortgagor shall think fit to redeem.

The daughter and wife being joint executrices destroys that part of the argument of the suspension of the remedy mentioned by Mr. Vernon.

He decreed the personal estate should be applied to discharge this mortgage.

## 567

## Anonymous

(Ch. 1713)

*The filing of a lawsuit can constitute an entry or a claim.*

Lincoln's Inn MS. Misc. 384, p. 10, pl. 1

28 November.

*Vernon*: The Statute of Fines and Nonclaim[1] shall not incur on an infant *cestui que trust* on a default of the trustee, nor so as to prejudice a purchaser. A bill in this court amounts to an entry or claim.

[1] Stat. 4 Hen. VII, c. 24 (*SR*, II, 547–548).

## 568

## Ellis v. Anonymous

(Ch. c. 1713)

*In cases of accounts, after a hearing, a witness can be re-examined by the other party.*

British Library MS. Hargrave 81, f. 108

28 November.

The cause was heard, and an account decreed. And a witness, who was examined before the Master on the account and had finished his deposition and signed it, was now prayed to be examined on the other side.

It was said on the other side that this was irregular and that a witness once examined and publication passed could not be examined again, that, if this was allowed, great inconveniences would follow, for then, after examination, the party for whom such witness was examined would find by the witness how far he had gone in his deposition for or against him and, accordingly, might work him to enlarge or vary his testimony upon a second examination as might be most for his purpose. And, therefore, to procure a person to make an affidavit in a cause touching matters in that cause was looked upon to be an indirect practice and a trick to draw in a witness and pin him down by that affidavit to swear the same things in his deposition as a witness in the cause. And the practice was looked upon to be such a contempt in the case of Fairbank and Moor that the party was committed for the doing of it.

*Curia*: That case was upon procuring an affidavit before hearing in order to his being examined afterwards in chief as a witness and was of a dangerous consequence, and, therefore, the party was justly punished for it. But, in cases of account after a hearing, there was no such danger, and it had been often done. And, therefore, here he was ordered to be examined again before the Master and he to settle the interrogatories.

[Other copies of this report: British Library MS. Hargrave 82, f. 122, British Library MS. Hargrave 77, f. 30v, pl. 1, British Library MS. Hargrave 303, f. 56, pl. 2.]

## 569

## Hoblethwaite v. Bland

(Ch. 1713)

*A devise where the devisee is to make a payment is a conditional devise.*

British Library MS. Hargrave 77, f. 26, pl. 6

1 December. Rolls.

If lands are devised to J.S. paying and discharging etc., this, by the Master of the Rolls [Trevor], amounts to a condition according to Collier's Case, 6 Coke, fo. 16, and a devise in fee upon the condition.

[Other copies of this report: British Library MS. Hargrave 82, f. 104, pl. 2, British Library MS. Hargrave 303, f. 50v, pl. 1.]

## 570

## Bland v. Graham

(Ch. 1713)

*Where there is a condition in a lease that it will be void for non-payment of the rent, if the rent be not paid, the lessor can elect to terminate the lease or accept the late rent.*

Lincoln's Inn MS. Misc. 384, p. 10, pl. 4

7 December.

Lord Chancellor [Lord Harcourt]: If a lessee for years be rendering rent upon a condition to be void on non-payment, it is at the election of the lessor whether it shall be void or not.

*Jekyll*: The lessor may confirm it, but, without such confirmation, it will be void.

Solicitor General [*Raymond*]: It is absolutely void upon non-payment and cannot be confirmed. But, if it were an estate for life, it might be confirmed because it cannot be void without an entry.

## 571

## Lady Haversham v. Lord Haversham

(Ch. 1713)

*A court of equity will supply the defect of a surrender to the use of the will in cases of creditors or portions for younger children otherwise unprovided for, but not for a grandchild.*

Lincoln's Inn MS. Misc. 384, p. 11

11 December 1713.

Morrice Thompson, the father of the late Lord Haversham, settles a term in gross on himself for life, then to the late Lord Haversham for life, then to the first and other sons in tail male. And he has issue, John, who died an infant, and Arthur, who died without issue in his lifetime. The question was whether it belonged to the third son of Morrice Thompson under the settlement or to the administrator of Morrice Thompson.

It was decreed to Lord Haversham, the third son, because, the other sons dying in the life of the father, it was not vested as it would have been if the sons had been named by their proper names.

[This was] affirmed in the House of Lords. See Basse v. Grey, A, 11.[1]

T[hompson], possessed of a term in gross, covenants to settle it on himself for life, then to his first and other sons in tail.

Solicitor General [*Raymond*]: This term will go to the administrator of T[hompson]. The legal estate was in him. There being then no son, the limitation is void. Where a person was entitled to administration before the Statute of Distributions[2] and dies and administration is granted after the Statute, it is to be construed within the Statute. The administrator is only a trustee for those that are entitled to a distribution. Query whether a court of equity will supply the want of a surrender for a grandchild. Kettle v. Townsend, Salk. 187.[3]

*Vernon*: A term in gross cannot be limited further than to two persons in being and to one not in being. The copyhold estate being purchased after the articles cannot be bound by them. Where the heir at law is provided for and a grandchild is not, this court will aid the want of a surrender, but not otherwise.

*Jekyll*, for the defendant: If a man surrenders his copyhold estate to the use of one for life with a remainder over with a power to make a jointure, the power is void.

*Sir Peter King*: It is a new notion that the Statute of Distributions should extend to persons dying intestate before. If a man covenants to make A. an estate tail, who comes into equity to have a specific performance, he shall be but a tenant for life, remainder to his issue in tail, because the court regards the intent of the parties. As to the surrender of the copyhold, there is no real difference between a child and a grandchild unprovided for. The grandfather is bound to provide for his grandchild.

*Vernon*, for the plaintiff: As to the limitation of a term, there is no difference between a settlement executed and articles executory. Bath v. Coleman's Case.[4] If a man devise all his lands, tenements, and hereditaments, his copyhold estates will not pass.

Lord Chancellor [Lord Harcourt]: The intent of the parties is to be observed as far as possible. The terms for years might be carried to the first son if he attains his age of twenty-one, then to the heirs male of his body, but, if he died

---

[1] *Basse v. Gray* (1715), 2 Vernon 692, 23 E.R. 1049, Gilbert Rep. 97, 25 E.R. 67, 1 Eq. Cas. Abr. 363, 21 E.R. 1104.

[2] Stat. 22 & 23 Car. II, c. 10 (*SR*, V, 719–720).

[3] *Kettle v. Townsend* (1693 x 1700), 1 Salkeld 187, 91 E.R. 170, 1 Eq. Cas. Abr. 123, 21 E.R. 929.

[4] Perhaps *Baile v. Coleman* (Ch. 1708–1711), see above, Case No. 115.

before that age, then to the other sons, As to the copyhold, the plaintiff is entitled to if for life under the will; after her death, it goes to the defendant.

[It was] decreed the limitation was good to the third son, the others dying before the father.

British Library MS. Hargrave 81, f. 68

18 December.

[It was said] that this court did supply the defect of a surrender to the use of the will in case of creditors or for portions for younger children unprovided for, yet not for a grandson, that was too remote, yet, in the case of Kettle and Townsend, the Lord Somers did do it in the case of a grandson. But this was a single instance and, upon an appeal to the House of Lords, the decree was reversed.

[Other copies of this report: British Library MS. Hargrave 82, f. 65, British Library MS. Hargrave 77, f. 18v, pl. 3, British Library MS. Hargrave 303, f. 35v.]

572

## Davis v. Philips

(Ch. 1713)

*In this case, the surplus of the decedent's estate in issue was taken as an intestate estate.*

*A court can make a decree for one defendant against another.*

Lincoln's Inn MS. Misc. 384, p. 12

12 December.

Ann Harris, by will, gives the defendant Philips, her executor, for his pains, £20 in money and a silver tankard. Then, she devises all her goods not before disposed of to four nieces and leaves a surplus in money of £200.

The first query is whether the word 'goods' carries all the residue of the personal estate or only in contradistinction to money.

The second query is whether the surplus goes to the executor, who has a specific legacy, or is to be taken as an intestate estate.

The third query is whether, if the plaintiffs, who claim the residue under the word 'goods', be not entitled, the court can make a decree for one defendant against another.

*Hooper*, for the defendant executor: When an executor is made, it hard to make a man die intestate. The Case of Foster and Munt[1] was the first that broke

[1] *Foster v. Munt* (1689), 1 Vernon 473, 23 E.R. 598, 1 Eq. Cas. Abr. 243, 21 E.R. 1020, 2 Eq. Cas. Abr. 433, 443, 22 E.R. 368, 378, Dodd 78, Chancery Repts. *tempore* Jac. II, 368.

in upon the common law, and that was founded upon a fraud. The four nieces, the plaintiffs, are by a clause in the will not to have any more money, and the word 'goods' will not take away that exclusion. Therefore, they are not entitled to the surplus. If the plaintiffs are excluded and their bill dismissed, the court will not decree against one defendant for another.

Lord Chancellor [Lord Harcourt]: This case is stronger than Foster and Munt, except the fraud. The specific legacy excludes the defendant from taking as executor anything more than is given him. The plaintiffs are likewise excluded. The surplus must be taken as an intestate estate. It is common for the court to make a decree for one defendant against another. If there should be another suit, the surplus would be swallowed up. The legacy of £200 given to B. extinguished the debt of £74, which the testator owed him. The father of H., by will, gave S. an annuity of £20 and made H. executor; H., by will, gave the same S. £20; this is not a satisfaction of the annuity of £20.

## 573

## Bird v. Culler

(Ch. 1713)

*The question in this case was whether a judgment creditor can redeem a prior mortgage and re-open a decree of foreclosure.*

Lincoln's Inn MS. Misc. 384, p. 13, pl. 1

15 December 1713.

A bill [was brought] by a judgment creditor to be admitted to redeem a prior mortgage and to open a decree of foreclosure, not being a party to that suit. The defendant pleaded.

*Hooper*, for the defendant: Our mortgage being prior to the plaintiff's judgment, he could only extend the reversion. It is true a judgment creditor may redeem, but he ought to take matters as they were in the former cause which he had notice of.

*Vernon*, for the plaintiff: A judgment creditor has as much right to redeem as a subsequent mortgagee. Bennet v. Western's Case, in Lord Cowper's time. The defendant had notice that we were a judgment creditor and should have made us a party to his former bill if he would have concluded us.

Lord Chancellor [Lord Harcourt]: I overrule the plea. It must stand for an answer with liberty to except.

## 574

## Magan v. Stepkin

(Ch. c. 1713)

*A court of equity will not take jurisdiction over a purely common law dispute.*

Lincoln's Inn MS. Misc. 384, p. 13, pl. 2

A bill [was brought] to establish the plaintiff's pedigree.

[There was a] demurrer for that the plaintiff's title is merely at law.

*Curia*: I allow the demurrer.

## 575

## Anonymous

(Ch. 1713)

*An agent who has received money on behalf of his principal is not a proper party to a suit for an account of the money paid.*

British Library MS. Hargrave 77, f. 26v, pl. 1

16 December.

If an agent or servant employed in the receipt and payment of moneys is afterwards sued in equity for an account and satisfaction touching those moneys suggesting a misapplication in the payment of the money, it is a good plea for him to say he received the money not otherwise than as an agent or servant to the other and paid it by his order and has accounted with him. [This was said] by *Vernon* and not denied.

[Other copies of this report: British Library MS. Hargrave 82, f. 104, pl. 3.]

## 576

## Bayly v. Stone

(Ch. 1713)

*Where all of the commissioners to examine witnesses sign the deposition certificate, any deficiencies prior to the examination are cured.*

British Library MS. Hargrave 77, f. 26v, pl. 2

17 December.

If a party be to be examined before a master and a commission issues for the party's examination, the interrogatories ought to be signed by the master and enclosed in the commission. But if the interrogatories be sent apart from the commission and not signed by the master but engrossed from an authentic copy and the commissioners of both sides join in examining the parties upon those interrogatories and sign the *jurat* upon them and join in the return thereof, this is now regular or, at least, a dispensing with the irregularity.

*Curia* [LORD HARCOURT]: The master upon a reference touching this irregularity enquired of the ancientest practicers in the Six Clerk's Office, who answered that the commissioners on both sides joining in the execution was regular, and so he reported it. And the court overruled the exception.

[Other copies of this report: British Library MS. Hargrave 82, f. 105, pl. 1, British Library MS. Hargrave 303, f. 50v, pl. 2.]

## 577

## Stroud v. Garrard

(Ch. 1713)

*In this case, the court admitted parol evidence as to a will.*

British Library MS. Hargrave 77, f. 26v, pl. 3

*Memorandum* in the case of Litton Stroud *versus* Garrard, the court admitted parol evidence as to a will.

[Other copies of this report: British Library MS. Hargrave 82, f. 105, pl. 2, British Library MS. Hargrave 303, f. 50v, pl. 3.]

## 578

## Richardson's Case

(Ch. 1713)

*A certificate of excommunication must state that the offender remained excommunicate for forty days after the public announcement.*

British Library MS. Hargrave 77, f. 26v, pl. 5

19 December.

Upon a [writ of] *significavit*, an exception was taken that it is not said in the ordinary's certificate that he stood excommunicate forty days *post publicationem in facie ecclesiae* these last words being material, [it was] ordered *nisi*.

[Other copies of this report: British Library MS. Hargrave 82, f. 106, pl. 1, British Library MS. Hargrave 303, f. 50v, pl. 5.]

## 579

## *Ex parte* Waite

(Ch. 1713)

*A person who lends money to a bankrupt after the bankruptcy cannot participate in the liquidation and payment of the bankrupt's assets.*

*A creditor to a bankrupt can assign his security to a third person.*

British Library MS. Hargrave 77, f. 26v, pl. 6

Carnell was a creditor to Waite, and, after Waite had committed an act of bankruptcy and before the commission issued, Watts lent so much money to Waite as paid Carnell. Afterwards, the commission issuing, the commissioners refused to admit Watts as a creditor because his debt was contracted after the bankruptcy [was] committed. But Watts insisted that, having paid off Carnell, he ought to stand in his place and, as he might have come in as a creditor, so ought Watts now as representing him.

*Curia* [Lord Harcourt]: The commissioners have done well. The money was lent to the bankrupt after the act of bankruptcy was committed. The dealing was not between the creditor and Watts. If it had and Watts had an assignment from Carnell of his security if he had any, it had been another thing.

[Other copies of this report: British Library MS. Hargrave 82, f. 196, pl. 2, British Library MS. Hargrave 303, f. 50v, pl. 6.]

## 580

## Rose v. Giles

(Ch. c. 1713)

*One co-defendant can get a common injunction to stay a common law action against him by another co-defendant.*

British Library MS. Hargrave 81, f. 107, pl. 1

One defendant answered and, being sued or threatened to be sued at law by another of the defendants who had not answered nor was in contempt, moved for an injunction against the co-defendant, which was said to be irregular for one defendant to pray an injunction against another, as in this case.

But the Master of the Rolls [Trevor] said it had been often done and granted the injunction.

[Other copies of this report: British Library MS. Hargrave 82, f. 120, British Library MS. Hargrave 77, f. 30, pl. 1, British Library MS. Hargrave 303, f. 55v, pl. 1.]

## 581

## Wheeler v. Wayn

(Ch. c. 1713)

*A conditional devise will not be enforced where the condition is broken.*

British Library MS. Hargrave 81, f. 107, pl. 2

Woolcott devised to his daughter, the plaintiff Wheeler's wife, an annuity of £10 *per annum* and makes executors and directs that, if she married with their consent and approbation, they should pay her out of his copyhold lands £150 in money instead of the annuity. She, afterwards, marries the plaintiff Wheeler without their advice or consent, and they have no subsequent approbation. And now they bring their bill *inter alia* for arrears of the annuity and for the £150.

Serjeant *Hooper*, for the plaintiff, [said] that, there being no devise over of the £150, it was but a devise *in terrorem* and, therefore, the court might well decree them now the £150. And he cited the Case of Bertie and Lord Falkland, *ante*, fo. 38b.[1]

*Curia*: Neither that case nor any other of devises *in terrorem* is like this, for, here, the father, having in contemplation the provision he intended for his daughter, gives her £10 *per annum* in all events but, if she would marry with the advice of his executors, £150 instead of the said annuity so that here is not a cautionary provision which is to be totally lost and the party have nothing if the condition be not observed but an alternative given by the devise if she marries with consent etc. £150, if not, £10 *per annum*, so that having affected not to observe the condition but to take the annuity. I cannot give her the money. I do not sit here to make wills for other men and otherwise than they ever intended.

[Other copies of this report: British Library MS. Hargrave 82, f. 121, British Library MS. Hargrave 77, f. 30, pl. 3, British Library MS. Hargrave 303, f. 56, pl. 1.]

## 582

## Roffe v. Harding

(Ch. 1713)

*Furze is not underwood for the purpose of paying tithes.*

*Tithes are due for furze made into faggots and sold.*

[1] *Bertie v. Lord Falkland* (1697–1715), 3 Chancery Cases 129, 22 E.R. 1008, 2 Freeman 220, 22 E.R. 1171, 1 Salkeld 231, 91 E.R. 205, 2 Vernon 333, 23 E.R. 814, 12 Modern 182, 88 E.R. 1248, Holt K.B. 230, 90 E.R. 1026, 1 Eq. Cas. Abr. 110, 21 E.R. 917, Colles 10, 1 E.R. 155, Dickens 25, 21 E.R. 176, Chancery Cases *tempore* Geo. I, 143.

British Library MS. Hargrave 80, f. 155, pl. 1

Rolfe v. Harding.

Upon a bill for tithes of furze, it was objected that underwood there paid no tithes and that furze were of the nature of underwood.

But [it was] ruled clearly by Lord Chancellor [Lord Harcourt] that they were not to be esteemed underwood, but were tithable.

A difference was taken and seemed to be allowed between furze that are sold and such part of them that are used in fencing the premises or for fuel in the owner's house there and that the latter should pay no tithes.

It was said by the Attorney General [*Northey*] that, if a *non decimando* for wood [be] laid in a hundred or county, [it] is good, but not for a single parish.

[Other copies of this report: Lincoln's Inn MS. Misc. 383, p. 270, pl. 1, Lincoln's Inn MS. Misc. 106, p. 242.]

2 Eq. Cas. Abr. 732, 22 E.R. 619,
1 Rayner 125, 2 Gwillim 610, 1 Eagle & Younge 705

Michaelmas 12 Anne.

A bill [was exhibited] for a discovery of tithes of furze and payment thereof.

The defendant, by answer, insists that furze spent upon the premises is not tithable and also that underwood and furze generally are not tithable in that parish etc.

The plaintiff admits that no tithes are due for underwood or furze spent upon the premises, but he insists upon tithes of furze made into faggots and sold by the defendant. That underwood or furze spent for firing or fencing of the premises is not tithable, but underwood or furze sold is tithable, he cites Moor 909.[1]

In the proofs of the cause, there was some evidence or 1d. a year paid, called smoke money, in lieu of tithes or furze. But that was not insisted upon by the answer, but a general *non decimando* for underwood and furze.

Lord Chancellor Harcourt decreed the defendant to account for tithes of furze made into faggots and sold, but not furze burnt or used upon the premises, and the defendant to pay costs.

## 583

## Duke of Hamilton v. Fleetwood

(Ch. 1714)

*A suit in equity by a husband and wife to enforce the wife's rights does not abate upon the death of the husband.*

[1] *Austin v. Lucas* (1598), Moore K.B. 909, 72 E.R. 990, also Croke Eliz. 609, 78 E.R. 852, 1 Rolle, Abr., *Dismes*, pl. Z, 3, p. 644, 1 Eagle & Younge 142.

British Library MS. Hargrave 77, f. 27, pl. 1

20 January.

They [the duke and duchess of Hamilton] exhibited their bill touching lands which they claimed in the right of the duchess as her inheritance. In November 1712, the duke was killed, and no further proceedings were had. And, upon a certificate of it, it is moved that the bill should stand dismissed for want of prosecution. It was first doubted by the court whether here was not an abatement by the duke's death.

But is was said and ruled by the court, as that the suit was concerning the duchess's inheritance, the duke's death made no abatement, but her suit continued and, she not proceeding in one term after the duke's death, the bill was ordered to stand dismissed.

[Other copies of this report: British Library MS. Hargrave 82, f. 107, pl. 1, British Library MS. Hargrave 303, f. 51, pl. 1.]

[Other reports of this case: 2 Eq. Cas. Abr. 377, 22 E.R. 321.]

## 584

## Pike v. Heathcott

(Ch. 1714)

*A Quaker can put an answer without an oath or affirmation where otherwise it would be an intentional oppression of him by the plaintiff.*

British Library MS. Hargrave 77, f. 27, pl. 3

21 January.

The plaintiff and defendant were both Quakers, the plaintiff one that would take the affirmation and the defendant one who would not, as conceiving it an oath in effect. And for want of swearing an answer, he was committed. And, afterwards, on account of his health, he had an order for leave to go into the country, giving a security. The defendant now petitions to continue in the country unless the plaintiff would take his answer without an oath. And Mr. Attorney General [*Northey*], *Sir Joseph Jekyll*, the Serjeant *Hooper*, all as *amici curiae*, said there were many precedents both in Lord North's and Lord Somers's time where the court in case Quakers who, on a religious account, though it be a weakness or mistake in conscience or opinion not to take an oath, yet, if bringing the suit appeared to be to take advantage of that weakness or for oppression, the court had ordered the answer to be taken without oath.

And so the Lord Chancellor [Lord Harcourt] declared he would and ordered it accordingly.

[Other copies of this report: British Library MS. Hargrave 82, f. 108, British Library MS. Hargrave 303, f. 51v, pl. 1.]

## 585

## Dixon v. Dixon

(Ch. 1714)

*In this case, The legacy in issue was a present gift, though it was to be paid at a future day.*

Lincoln's Inn MS. Misc. 384, p. 15, pl. 3

26 January 1713[/14].

A bill [was brought] to have a legacy of £200 brought before the Master. It was given to the plaintiff to be paid her when she came to twenty-one.

Lord Chancellor [Lord Harcourt]: The legacy is a present gift, though it be to be paid at a future day. It must be brought before the Master with interest at 5 percent from the death of the testator to be preserved for the plaintiff's benefit when she attains twenty-one. And, if she die before, then [it is] to be paid to her representatives.

## 586

## Crossland v. Fillmer

(Ch. 1714)

*A trustee is liable to pay interest on rents and profits received on the behalf of a beneficiary of the trust.*

British Library MS. Hargrave 81, f. 119

29 January. The defendant Fillmer petitions against Thomson, executor of Thompson and co-defendant.

The testator had lent defendant Fillmer's father a considerable sum upon bond and, afterwards, Fillmer, advancing a sum of money to Mr. Bertie on a mortgage, takes the mortgage in the name of Thomson, the testator, and, before the money was repaid, he died. The testator Thomson borrows the deeds and then entered upon the mortgaged premises and got the tenants to attorn to him, his own debt not being paid.

On the hearing, it was decreed that Thompson was but a trustee for Fillmer as to the mortgage and that the defendant, his executor, should account for the rents and profits received by him or his testator. But no directions were given touching interest for the money received, and the decree was signed and enrolled.

And now a petition was preferred to His Honor [Trevor] signed by the defendant Fillmer. And Thomson, stating the case as above but not taking notice of the enrollment, therefore, prayed interest. And Thomson submitted the matter of the petition to His Honor.

The question was whether any interest could be directed after the decree was signed and enrolled or whether Thompson's submission had not waived the objection.

The Master declared that, by the submission and no notice being taken of the enrollment, Thompson had waived the objection, which otherwise had been clear, and interest could not have been directed, but, by reason of that waiver and that the monies were received by a trustee, who, as such, was accountable for them and ought to have paid them over but, contrary to the trust, had detained them. Therefore, he ought to pay interest. And he directed it to be paid yearly, three months after the end of each year, and after the same rate as he himself was to have for the money which he lent by the bond.

[Other copies of this report: British Library MS. Hargrave 82, f. 132, British Library MS. Hargrave 77, f. 33, pl. 1, British Library MS. Hargrave 303, f. 60, pl. 2.]

## 587

## Cope v. Futor

(Ch. 1714)

*A witness to a will can give evidence of the testator's intent where the words of the will are unclear.*

British Library MS. Hargrave 81, f. 120v

*Eodem die* [29 January].

A witness to the codicil of Lady Fowler's will and who drew both will and codicil was examined as a witness and allowed, though objected against, to prove the testator's intention as to a revocation and how far it was intended by her to extend, which was not very clear by the words of the codicil.

And Mr. *Mead* said that His Lordship had allowed the like in a cause before him the last term.

[Other copies of this report: British Library MS. Hargrave 82, f. 134, pl. 1, British Library MS. Hargrave 77, f. 33, pl. 2, British Library MS. Hargrave 303, f. 60v, pl. 1.]

## 588

## Lord Harcourt v. Harcourt

(Ch. 1714)

*The joining in levying a fine to confirm a jointure is not a forfeiture of a term in equity or of a power of leasing.*

Lincoln's Inn MS. Misc. 384, p. 17, pl. 2

29 January.

Lord Harcourt [1661–1727],[1] being entitled to a term of ninety-nine years after the death of his mother with a power of leasing, joins in levying a fine the better to confirm her jointure. The question was whether this was a forfeiture of the term in equity or of the power of leasing.

The Master of Rolls [TREVOR] was of the opinion that the fine being levied only for a special purpose, a court of equity would control and qualify the legal operation of it and, therefore, that, in this case, the fine only operated so as to corroborate the settlement and was neither a forfeiture of the term nor an extinguishment of Lord Harcourt's power of leasing.

## 589

## Bayly v. Heath

(Ch. 1714)

*Where an estate devised is substantially altered thereafter, the alteration will be taken as a revocation of the devise or an ademption.*

British Library MS. Hargrave 81, f. 121

*Eodem die* [29 January].

*Sir Joseph Jekyll*: If a mortgage in fee be and the mortgagee devises all his real estate, the mortgage does not pass by the word 'real' but as personal estate because a mortgage is always considered here as such.

J.S. having two daughters by different marriages took a mortgage for years of copyhold lands. And, afterwards, the mortgage was forfeited. He makes his will and devises this copyhold estate and a sum of £20,000 to his daughter by the first marriage and, afterwards, purchases the inheritance of the copyhold and assigns the mortgage in trust to attend the inheritance. And he dies without having made any surrender to the use of his will.

And for the daughter of the second marriage and co-heiress, it was said that, there being so great an inequality in the disposition of the testator's estate, equity would not supply the want of a surrender in favor of one co-heiress so amply provided for in prejudice to the other, who had so slender a provision.

*Curia*: Wherever it is for a provision for a child, equity will supply the want of a surrender. But here, the inheritance of the mortgaged premises being purchased after the will was made so altered the nature of the estate that he had at

[1] J. Campbell, *Lives of the Lords Chancellors of England* (1874 ed.), vol. 5, pp. 296–351; S. Handley, 'Harcourt, Simon, first Viscount Harcourt', *Oxford Dictionary of National Biography*, vol. 25, pp. 131–134.

the time of the making the will that it amounted to a revocation of the devise to the daughter. And, therefore, the estate must descend to both daughters as coheiresses, and the term being assigned to attend the inheritance must necessarily be for their equal benefit.

[Other copies of this report: British Library MS. Hargrave 82, f. 134, pl. 2, British Library MS. Hargrave 77, f. 33, pl. 3, British Library MS. Hargrave 303, f. 60v, pl. 2.]

## 590

## Paston v. Ellison

(Ch. 1714)

*In this case, a power of appointment to increase a child's legacy was properly exercised and was enforceable.*

Lincoln's Inn MS. Misc. 10, p. 163

1 February 12 Anne. Wolfstan Paston and Barbara *uxor*, daughter of Joseph and Elizabeth Ellisson, plaintiffs; Francis Ellisson, son and heir of Joseph.

Joseph Ellisson, by will dated the 21st January 1685, gave his house in The Close in Newcastle to Elizabeth, his wife, for life, remainder to the heirs male of his body, remainder to his heirs female, remainder to his own right heirs. And another house, he gave to his wife for life, remainder to his heirs male, remainder to his heirs female, remainder to the rights heirs of his wife. He gave the plaintiff, his daughter, out of his real and personal estate £300 or so much, more or less, as his wife should think fit. And he made his wife and Robert Ellisson executors.

The wife proved the will. And the personal estate was not sufficient to pay the testator's debts.

The plaintiff Wolfstan [Paston], after the testator's death, married the plaintiff Barbara, and, about a year after the marriage, she [Elizabeth Ellisson] executed a writing wherein, reciting the will and that her daughter had behaved herself dutifully and had married with her consent, it is witnessed that she, being minded, pursuant to the power and trust reposed, to ascertain the portion of her daughter and to increase it and advance her as far as the circumstances of the testator's estate would allow, did think fit, determine, and appoint that the same to be paid by her out of the estate of the testator was and should be £600 in the whole, that is to say £300 mentioned in the will, and £300 more which she thought fit her said daughter should have and should be raised and paid her out of the said estate thereunto liable by the will. Elizabeth, the mother, afterwards, died. And she made her will and her daughter executrix. And she gave her another house of her own and her personal estate.

And the testator's real estate being come to the defendant, his son, the plaintiffs prefer their bill to have the £600 raised and paid them.

The defendant insisted that, as to one of the houses, it was settled upon his father's marriage and he had no power to devise it by will. As to the other house, which is about £40 a year, his mother received the rents during her life and left the same at her death much out of repair, and he insists his mother had not the power to increase the plaintiff's portion to £600 or to charge the same on the defendant's said estate, which is all he had to live upon.

[It was] declared by the Master of the Rolls [TREVOR] that the plaintiff Barbara's portion of £300 might be made more or less by her mother, and, she having doubled the same and made it £600, the same ought to stand a charge upon the real and personal estate. And he ordered the Master to compute the interest at £5 percent from the mother's death and to tax the plaintiffs their costs and the defendant to pay the same in twelve months or, in default thereof, the house in The Close, which was not in the marriage settlement, to be sold to the best purchaser and the money arising thereby and the rents in the meantime until sold (for which the defendant was to account before the Master) was to be applied to pay the plaintiffs what the Master should report due to them and the surplus to be paid the defendant. But, if the defendant should think fit to enter into the account of the testator's personal estate, then the plaintiffs were to account for the same before the Master and the personal estate that should be remaining was to be applied in the first place towards the payment of the £600, interest, and costs.

Lincoln's Inn MS. Misc. 384, p. 15, pl. 4

3 February. Master of the Rolls.

*Vernon*: Where a tenant for life is subject to a charge or mortgage, it is in his election to pay off one-third of the principal or to keep down the interest.

591

## Minshall v. Hutchins

(Ch. 1714)

*In this case, the testator's intention was that his children by his first wife should not take under the will until there was a total failure of issue by the second wife.*

Lincoln's Inn MS. Misc. 384, p. 16, pl. 2

3 February 1713/14.

The plaintiffs are daughters of Sir G. Hutchins by his first wife. He, by will, gives the residue of his real and personal estate to the children of his second wife, equally to be divided between them, but, if there should be no such issue or the issue shall die before twenty-one or marriage, then to the children of his first wife. He has issue, the defendant and another child by his second wife, who dies before twenty-one or marriage. The question is whether the plaintiffs are entitled to the share of the child so dying or the defendant.

*Jekyll*, for the plaintiff: By the words 'equally divided between them' the children were tenants in common and the share of them so dying goes over to the plaintiffs. This is not a remainder, but an executory devise. This cannot be a cross-remainder, but an executory contingent devise. He left £25,000 personal estate.

*Vernon*: The rents and profits of the real [estate] must be taken as personal estate. Though there be a devise over, if the child die before twenty-one, the profits in the meantime will not go over. 'If such issue die' before twenty-one is the same as if any of the children die.

*Hooper*, for the defendant: It is plain that the surplus of the personal estate cannot go over to the plaintiffs; it is to the children of the first wife after the failure of issue of the second. The plaintiffs had £7500 apiece portions out of the personal estate, which is more in proportion than the defendant, the heir at law, will have by the surplus. The children dying before the legacies were due, they fall into the surplus.

*Hooper*: If the defendant had been the only child of the second wife, he had taken the whole; so he ought now he becomes the only child. The testator intended the surplus wholly for the benefit of the issue of the second wife, the children of the first [wife] being so well provided for. A necessary implication is as strong as an express limitation. There can be no cross-remainders between [ . . . ]. The word 'issue' is always taken collectively at law.

Lord Chancellor [LORD HARCOURT]: The intent of the testator was that the children of the first wife should not take until there was a total failure of issue of the second. I am not barely to collect the intent of the testator, for he has plainly declared it by the codicil. Therefore, the share of the child of the second wife, which died, does belong to the defendant. And, as to that demand, the bill must be dismissed.

## 592

## Ludlow v. Noyes

(Ch. 1714)

*A power of appointment is personal to the parties, and it is not an asset of a bankrupt's estate.*

Lincoln's Inn MS. Misc. 384, p. 14, pl. 3

22 February.

[The question was] whether a power in a bankrupt to raise a sum not exceeding £3000 shall after his death be transferred to the assignees. Lassells v. Cornwallis' Case.[1]

[1] *Lassells v. Lord Cornwallis* (1704), 2 Vernon 465, 23 E.R. 898, Precedents in Chancery 232, 24 E.R. 113, 2 Freeman 279, 22 E.R. 1210, 1 Eq. Cas. Abr. 242, 21 E.R. 1019,

*Jekyll*, for the defendant: This is out of the Statute of Bankrupts.[1] A power is personal and cannot be transferred, being upon a special purpose.

Lord Chancellor [Lord Harcourt]: The defendant is a purchaser. She has for a special purpose joined in a fine and given this power. I must take it in the strictest sense and not impeach her jointure, this being a hard case.

British Library MS. Hargrave 80, f. 141, pl. 2

Lord Cornwallis's Case cited was thus. Lord Cornwallis had a power to charge an estate with a certain sum either for debts or portions; he charged it with part of the sum for portions only; equity raised the rest for creditors.

[Other copies of this report: Lincoln's Inn MS. Misc. 383, p. 250, pl. 2.]

## 593

## Butler v. Allington

(Ch. 1714)

*A devise to pay debts out of rents and profits can be satisfied by selling off timber to pay the debts.*

Lincoln's Inn MS. Misc. 384, p. 14, pl. 1

22 February 1713[/14].

B[utler], by his will, devises premises to the plaintiff for life, with remainders to his first and other sons in tail. Then are these words 'I charge my real estate with payment of my debts, which my personal estate will not, out of the rents and profits, but not by sale.'

*Cowper*, for the plaintiff: Where debts are to be paid 'out of the rents and profits', it may be by mortgage. Sir G. Rook v. Banks;[2] a devise of the rents and profits carries the land.

*How*, for the defendant: That can be no color for a mortgage, which may amount to a sale if the mortgagor should be foreclosed. The timber ought to be felled towards the payment of the debts.

Lord Chancellor [Lord Harcourt]: Let the Master see what timber is proper to be felled. I reserve further directions until after the Master's report.

2 Eq. Cas. Abr. 250, 466, 467, 22 E.R. 212, 397.

[1] Stat. 1 Jac. I, c. 15 (*SR*, IV, 1031–1034).

[2] Note *Mills v. Banks* (Ch. 1723–1724), 3 Peere Williams 1, 24 E.R. 943, 2 Eq. Cas. Abr. 491, 22 E.R. 417, Misc. Chancery Cases (1714–1730), 163.

British Library MS. Hargrave 81, f. 69

22 [December].

One Butler, by his will, devises that his debts should be paid out of the rents and profits of his lands except his capital seat and park and that his house and garden, the Goods and Greens, shall be as heirlooms and kept in repair and the park well stocked with deer. And he devises, after his wife's jointure and debts paid, his estate to his cousin J.B. for life, with remainder to his first and other sons in tail male, remainder over. And he dies greatly indebted by a mortgage, specialties, and otherwise. J.B., the devisee for life, brings his bill to have the timber on the estate sold to discharge the debts and that, in regard he could not legally enter by virtue of the devise by reason of the mortgage, he might have a reasonable allowance out of the estate for the support of himself and for educating his son suitable to the estate he was to have.

Mr. *Vernon, pro querente*, [said] that, by the words 'rents and profits', this court has constantly understood a power to lease or mortgage the estate for performance of the trusts but not always a sale. It has not generally been carried so far, and this construction is founded upon this, that a devise or conveyance of the rents and profits is a devise or conveyance of the land itself out of which they issue, for what is the land but its profits. *Vide* Cooke upon Littleton.[1] And so it was adjudged in the case of Sir George Rooke and Sir Jacob Bancks. Sir Jacob by his marriage settlement directed his daughter's portions should be paid out of the rents and profits of certain lands. And, Sir George Rooke having married one of the daughters, upon application to this court, it was decreed that a mortgage should be made for the immediate raising the portion and that Sir George should not wait the slow method of raising it out of the annual rent. So in the Case of Lord Roseberry,[2] though [it was] otherwise decreed by my Lord Nottingham, yet, upon appeal to the Lords, it was decreed to be raised immediately by lease or mortgage.

Where lands are settled or limited upon trust for the payment of debts, the trusts shall be executed in a reasonable manner so as shall be most for the benefit of the parties interested in that trust that the creditors in all events may have a satisfaction for their debts. And so it is also in the cases of portions and maintenance. In the Case of Warburton,[3] a term was devised that, by and out of the rents and profits thereof, portions should be raised by the testator's sisters, and the sisters, by their bill for the performance of this trust, insisted to have the money raised out of the annual income as the rents and profits should come in that so they might keep a clog upon the estate, but the court decreed that so

[1] E. Coke, *First Institute* (1628).

[2] *Viscount Roseberry v. Taylor* (1702), 6 Brown P.C. 43, 2 E.R. 921, 2 Eq. Cas. Abr. 643, 22 E.R. 539.

[3] *Warburton v. Warburton* (1702), 4 Brown P.C. 1, 2 E.R. 1.

much of the term should be sold as the Master should find necessary for raising portions immediately. And, here, that the estate may be preserved, the plaintiff desires no sale but that the timber may be applied to discharge the debts on the estate.

And, as to that part of the bill that desires a maintenance, it is the constant practice of this court where there is a settlement but subject to the payment of debts or raising of portions that the party entitled to the estate thus subject should have a reasonable allowance out of it for his support and should not be exposed to starve while the trusts are executing and especially when the trusts are secured in all events as hereby the reason of the largeness of the estate.

And the court decreed the timber to be sold and applied to the payment of the debts but so as not to spoil and disfigure the seat and that the plaintiff should have the seat and park and £400 *per annum* paid him by the receiver for the maintenance and education of himself and son.

[Other copies of this report: British Library MS. Hargrave 82, f. 66, British Library MS. Hargrave 77, f. 19, pl. 18, British Library MS. Hargrave 303, f. 36.]

## 594

## Wood v. Crofts

(Ch. 1714)

*It is the mortgagor, and not the mortgagee, who is entitled to present to an advowson.*

Lincoln's Inn MS. Misc. 384, p. 14, pl. 2

23 February.

Lord Chancellor [Lord Harcourt]: A mortgagor is entitled to present to an advowson, and the mortgagee is but a bare trustee for him, at least until the mortgagor is foreclosed.

## 595

## Sayer v. Sayer

(Ch. 1714)

*An unexecuted contract cannot bar an entail.*

Lincoln's Inn MS. Misc. 384, p. 21, pl. 3

24 February.

Lord Chancellor [Lord Harcourt]: A court of equity has never gone so far as to bar the issue in tail in equity unless the ancestor had done some act which plainly showed his intent to bar the entail, as by making a feoffment of the entailed lands, but not by a bare covenant which he had not executed in his lifetime.

*Vernon*: A bargain and sale or other conveyance by a tenant in tail in equity has been ruled to be a bar to the issue in tail.

## 596

## Harris v. Cope

(Ch. 1714)

*Where a mortgagee of land held in trust purchases the equity of redemption and agrees to pay off the debt, he must satisfy the beneficiaries of the trust.*

Lincoln's Inn MS. Misc. 10, p. 163 [bis]

4 March 1713[/14].

Abraham Dashwood mortgages lands to A. and B. for £2400, of which sum, £2000 was trust money agreed by articles to be put out at interest for the benefit of Samuel Cope's wife. And the remaining £400 was the proper money of Samuel Cope.

Cope, afterward, purchases the mortgaged premises for £2700, and it is agreed between him and the mortgagor that no advantage shall be taken of the breach of the covenants in the mortgage, and Cope released those covenants, but [there was] no express covenant on Cope's part that he would pay the £2000 to his wife's trustees.

Cope being dead, the question was between the heir and the executor whether the personal assets should be applied to exonerate the encumbrances on the purchased estate, the £2000 belonging now to the wife by virtue of the articles. And it was much insisted on that this was different from the common case where a man mortgages his own estate and covenants to pay the money which is a personal lien upon the personal estate.

But Lord Chancellor [Lord Harcourt was] of the opinion that the deed between Cope and the mortgagor did amount to an agreement on Cope's part that he would discharge the £2000. And he decreed it should be paid out of his personal assets.

In this case was cited the case of Holt and Holt, in Lord Somers's time,[1] where a man purchased an estate and took the conveyance in his own name and an assignment of an encumbrance in the name of another. And, though it was declared that this assignment was in trust for the purchaser, his executors, and administrators and [there was] no declaration that it should attend the inheritance, yet [it was] decreed that it should attend the inheritance in favor of the heir and not go to the executor.

[1] *Holt v. Holt* (Ch. 1693 x 1700), 1 Peere Williams 374, 24 E.R. 431.

But note [it was] said by the Master of the Rolls [Trevor] that, in this case, the purchaser gave directions to one Sutton, an attorney, who drew the writings.

A like case was said to be in Lord Cowper's time.

## 597

## Watts v. Goddard

(Ch. 1714)

*A joint tenant of a mortgage can made an inter vivos gift of his share, but he cannot make a devise of it.*

Lincoln's Inn MS. Misc. 10, p. 164

15 March 1713[/14]. Watts *et ux.* v. Goddard and Collis *et al.*

Goddard mortgages lands to one Rampko, the plaintiff, Watts's wife's former husband, for £400 and takes the mortgage in his own and his wife's name. And the consideration money was said in the mortgage to be paid by them both. Rampko dies. And, before his death, he makes his will and gives £200 out of the mortgage to the defendant Collis, and, all the residue of his estate, he gives to his wife. And he makes the defendants A. and B. executors.

The mortgage being survived to the wife, she and her now husband bring their bill that the defendant Goddard may redeem or be foreclosed.

The question between the plaintiffs and the legatee was whether this money belonged to the wife or whether the defendant should have his legacy, which was given out of it by the will.

[Trevor] decreed the money to the wife and that, he having made his wife in the nature of a joint purchaser with him, he could not give away the money by the will though he might have done it by a deed in his lifetime.

## 598

## Cook v. Gerrard

(Ch. 1714)

*In this case, the devise survived because the intent of the testator was that, as to the principal devised by the will, the devise over should not take place until all of the children by the second marriage died.*

British Library MS. Hargrave 77, f. 27v

Sir G. H., by his will, devises to his daughter Sarah by the second marriage £5000. 'And the residue of any estate, both real and personal, I give to my children begotten or to be begotten on my dear wife equally to be divided amongst them and, if all my children by her die before their full age or marriage, I give all to my daughters by the first marriage.' And by a codicil, he devises copyhold lands to his wife for life, then to his son and his heirs 'and, if I have no son, to my daughters by my now wife, and, if I die without issue by her, then to my three daughters by the first marriage as tenants in common.' The wife dies. And, afterwards, Sir G. H. dies, leaving a son and daughter by the second marriage and three daughters by the first. Sarah, the daughter by the second marriage dies an infant and unmarried. The son is living and about thirteen. And now, the question is how the part of Sarah shall go, whether the whole shall survive to the brother or whether it shall go to the issue of the second marriage or whether distributed according to the Statute of Distributions.[1]

*Sir Joseph Jekyll*, for the children of the second marriage: It is objected here that only one of the children being dead, the contingency upon which the estate was limited over has not happened and, therefore, the children by the second marriage cannot take, that being the express terms of the limitation to them. In the Case of Willies, cited in the Case of Cocke and Gerrard,[2] three houses were devised to three sons, that is one to each, and, if they all died without issue, then to the wife; one of the sons died without issue, and, there, it was held the wife should not wait until all the sons died, but the devise should be taken distributively, not conjunctively, not as a limitation by way of a remainder, for, then, nothing could vest in the wife until the whole contingency happened, and, in case one died, the others could not take because not given to them. And yet something must be done with the estate. It was, therefore, construed an executory devise, and so the deceased son's part was adjudged to go immediately to the mother. So here.

Mr. *Vernon, ad idem*: The question is whether the part devised to Sarah be devised over, the words 'such issue' subsequent to the mention of the several children must be understood such issue as are to take by my will. And this seems plain by the will itself, for he who best understood his own mind declared them tenants in common and that they should not taken jointly. But, if the court should be of opinion that the words are to be take conjunctively and not distributively so that the limitation over cannot take place until the whole contingency happen, then the estate being personal must be distributed according to the Statute in which the plaintiff, though of the half blood, must have an equal share with those of the whole.

Mr. *How*: There is no dispute as to the profits incurred in Sarah's lifetime; that is first fallen and not subject to the will. The word 'any' in the clause 'if I shall not leave any such issue' etc. must go throughout the will and then the construction must necessarily be distributive. The usual limitation in settlements of lands

---

[1] Stat. 22 & 23 Car. II, c. 10 (*SR*, V, 719–720); Stat. 1 Jac. II, c. 17, s. 7 (*SR*, VI, 19).

[2] *Gilbert v. Witty* (1623), Croke Jac. 655, 79 E.R. 566, 2 Rolle Rep. 281, 81 E.R. 801; *Cook v. Gerrard* (1668), 1 Williams Saunders 170, 85 E.R. 171, 2 Keble 206, 224, 84 E.R. 129, 140, 1 Levinz 212, 83 E.R. 374.

is to daughters for want of issue male and, in default of such issue, remainder over. And yet, if there be two daughters and one of them die without issue, her part shall go over to the next remainder and not survive to the other sister. And cross-remainders are not to be taken by implication nor favored.

Serjeant *Hooper*: The case slightly touched by Sir Joseph Jekyll is expressly in point against the plaintiff as to real estate. There, the devise was to them three equally to be divided between them and, if they should all die without issue, remainder over, it was adjudged that nothing passed to the remainder until all were dead. In this case, nothing can be taken by such a contingent devise because the contingency has not happened.

Mr. Attorney General [*Northey*], for the defendant: The main point is as to the third part of the residue of Sir G. H.'s personal estate, who that shall go to on Sarah's death. In the case of Holmes and Meynell,[1] a devise to two daughters and their heirs, equally to be divided between them, and, in case they happen to die without issue, remainder over, one died without issue, and it was adjudged that her part should go to the other sister by way of cross-remainder and should not go to him in remainder over, the intention of the testator being apparently that it would not go over until both daughters were dead without issue. If the testator's intention here appeared to be that the estate of either should go over upon the death, the court would consider the words distributively in order to answer the intent. But should it be so construed here, it would plainly contradict the intention of the testator, for he designed that nothing should go over in part but the whole together and that only when there was not any child remaining of the second marriage. And the court constantly governs itself in the construction of wills according to the intent so as may best stand with or answer the meaning of the testator. And this constructive conjunctive is a necessary implication which is as strong as an express direction. Notwithstanding the objection in Holmes and Meynel's Case, there would be an inconvenience in allowing cross-remainders among three and that it should only be between two, for my part, I cannot see any such inconvenience. And in Dyer, fol. 303, cross-remainders were allowed among five persons; *vide etiam* Dyer 330.[2] Executory devises are let in and allowed by the construction upon the words in the Statute of Wills,[3] *viz.* that a man may devise at his will and pleasure, and, therefore, executory devises are allowed which settle and carry estates quite contrary to the rules of law.

Mr. *Lutwyche*: The provision by the testator here is in two cases, if there be no child or if such child or children die before age or marriage. The word 'such'

---

[1] *Holmes v. Meynel* (1680–1681), T. Jones 172, 84 E.R. 1202, T. Raymond 452, 83 E.R. 236, Skinner 17, 90 E.R. 9, 2 Shower K.B. 136, 89 E.R. 842, *sub nom. Maynell v. Read* (1677), Pollexfen 425, 86 E.R. 599, Dodd 35.

[2] *Anonymous* (1571), 3 Dyer 303, 73 E.R. 682; *Glover v. Berry (Clache's Case)* (1573), 3 Dyer 330, 73 E.R. 747, also 110 Selden Soc. 288, Benloe 212, 123 E.R. 149.

[3] Stat. 32 Hen. VIII, c. 1 (*SR*, III, 744–746).

in this case, being a relative word, must be as extensive as the words in the first clause to which it relates, that is if all such children shall die etc., and according to this construction in the [Court of] King's Bench, 2 Ann. [1703 x 1704], where the words did not plainly and expressly create an estate in common, the court construed it a joint tenancy. The words in the special verdict were 'in a devise to several to be equally divided between them during their lives and, if they should all die without issue, remainder over'. The court judged this a joint devise and the survivors to be tenants in tail of the whole. 13 Hen. VII[1] was the first case of a devise by implication, and, there, it was because the construction was absolutely necessary as a devise to the heir at law, after the death of the wife, she must have it for her life by a necessary implication because the testator's intent is plain that the heir should not have it during her life, and, it not being expressly devised, nobody else can.

Mr. *Mead*: If the words here were to be construed distributively and not conjunctively, it would be very much to the prejudice of the parties, for, then, the son, when of disposing age, this being a chattel, might devise it away, though he should not live until the age of twenty-one.

*Curia*: As to the profits of Sarah's estate, to her death, they must go in distribution as an intestate's estate. But, as to the principal devised by the will, that must survive to the brother, the defendant, for, by the will, the intent is plain that the devise over should not take place until all the children by the second marriage died.

[Other copies of this report: British Library MS. Hargrave 82, f. 109, British Library MS. Hargrave 303, f. 51v, pl. 2.]

## 599

## Symes v. Symes

(Ch. 1714)

*Where the profits of a person's estate are wrongfully received, the wrongdoer must account for them only from the date of the filing of the suit or the entry; however, in the case of an estate of a person under a disability, the account is taken of all the profits received.*

British Library MS. Hargrave 80, f. 175v, pl. 1

The distinction taken by the court in this case seemed to be that, if a man receives the profits of another's estate wrongfully for ever so many years and the party injured be under no impediment, he is entitled to an account only from the filing of his bill or making an entry or bringing an account. But otherwise it is if he be under any impediment, as infancy or non-sane memory, or, if his title deeds be

[1] YB Hil. 13 Hen. VII, f. 17, pl. 22 (1498).

in the hands of the adverse party or he be beyond the seas etc. and, particularly, in the case of infants, whoever receives the profits of their lands is accountable.

[Other copies of this report: Lincoln's Inn MS. Misc. 383, p. 296, pl. 2, Lincoln's Inn MS. Misc. 107, p. 19.]

## 600

## Elderfield v. Moxton

(Ch. c. 1714)

*A court, in the case of a doubtful devise, will not construe the will so as to exclude a child who is not otherwise provided for.*

British Library MS. Hargrave 81, f. 72

One Ray, by his will, devises as follows, *viz*. 'Item to my niece Elderfield [the plaintiff] I give £600 with condition that, during the life of her husband, the said money shall remain in the hands of my executors as they with the advice of my trustees shall judge convenient for the benefit of my said niece and her daughter Margaret'. And [he] appoints executors and trustees and dies, and, after[wards], the husband of the devisee Elderfield dies. And now she brings this bill to have the whole £600 and exclude her daughter.

Mr. *Vernon, pro querente*: The devise is first to the plaintiff entirely and then by reason of the circumstance of her husband, who soon after died insolvent, and that she might have the money effectually secured to her, it is ordered that, during his life, he should lie in the hands of the executors, but, he being now dead, the reason of that provision ceases. The condition was but temporary, and, the time being now expired, she is well entitled to the whole and to the interest or improvement.

*Curia* [Lord Cowper]: The words are doubtful whether the principal or only the interest or improvements was intended to be divided between the mother and daughter. The daughter here is wholly destitute of any other provision, and the mother cannot have the whole by clear and express words in the devise, but by implication and construction only. And I cannot construe but that, out of that money, there might be a provision intended for the daughter since there is no other made for her and that money is directed to be kept and improved for her as well as the mother's benefit. And, where two parties claim and both by construction, I shall favor most that party which without a favorable construction would be without any provision at all. And he decreed the money between them but that the mother should have the interest of the daughter's part to breed her up.

[Other copies of this report: British Library MS. Hargrave 82, f. 69, British Library MS. Hargrave 303, f. 37, British Library MS. Hargrave 77, f. 19v, pl. 1.]

## 601

## Hamond v. Tench

(Ch. 1714)

*In this case, the sum of money promised by the decedent and not paid was only an unenforceable gift.*

British Library MS. Hargrave 77, f. 20

Hamond *et al.* v. Fisher Tench, heir and executor of Nathaniel Tench, deceased.

Nathaniel Tench had two daughters, A. and E. On the marriage of A. with Ambrose Ashe, he agrees to give him £2500 of his own money and £500, which was a legacy given her by her grandmother by marriage articles. He covenants with Ambrose that, in case he gave in marriage with E. or any other more than £3000, he would give A., if living, or leave to the issue of Ambrose and A. as much as would make the portions equal. And, by this covenant, he binds his heirs etc. He, afterwards, on a treaty for the marriage of E. to Francis, insisted on the like covenant which Ambrose had, which was refused. Then J. solicits Ambrose to release that covenant, and he refuses. [He] threatens, if there was any trick in law, he would evade that covenant, and he accordingly advises with counsel [and] is told he must change [?] hands. The match being by this delayed for some time, the defendant Fisher, who had also a £500 legacy by the grandfather and lay in his father's hands and having no other immediate estate of his own, by a deed poll, reciting the treaty and that Francis insisted on £3500, for natural love and affection, assigns to E. the £500 legacy. And, two days after, Nathaniel Tench, by articles, covenants to give £3000 in marriage with E. The marriage is had, and the £3500 paid by Nathaniel Tench.

A. dies, leaving six children. Nathaniel Tench dies. He makes the defendant executor and residuary legatee. And one of the children being married to the plaintiff Hamond, he and [ . . . ], the child, bring a bill against the defendant, as executor, to have satisfaction for that covenant.

He, by answer, insists it was not broken, that the £500 was his own free gift without any promise or security of recompense or payment.

Witnesses [were] examined on both sides.

*Curia*: This was only a parol covenant and a matter of personal conscience, both in the defendant and Nathaniel Tench, his father. The father might have more kindness for one than another daughter and might have an opportunity of marrying the younger daughter better than the elder. And these sort of covenants unreasonably fettered and perplexed parents. And, therefore, [they] were not to be taken strictly, and [they] might endeavor to avoid such a covenant. [They] are of opinion he had effectually done here, but would not be the adviser of such a method, that there were cases that, according to regular equity, he could not relieve against. He could not construe that such a fraud that was proper for relief in this court. But he left [it] to the defendant's conscience, and he dismissed the bill.

## 602

## Cross v. Cross

(Ch. 1714)

*A court of equity has the jurisdiction to construe a will and order an account to be taken of the estate.*

British Library MS. Hargrave 77, f. 41, pl. 1

27 April 1714. Lord Chancellor.

A bill [was brought] by executors to have judgment of the court on a will and the testator's schedules or codicils, being eight in number and all with date refers to the will and short notes of intended alterations. One of the schedules or codicils beings in the form of a will and says 'I hereby revoke all former wills' this being without a date *non constat* whether made before or after the will that is proved. And, by order of the ecclesiastical court, the schedules are proved together with the will. In the schedules, many particulars are absolutely unintelligible, in others inconsistent with the will. By the [will], annuities are given to several infants and the residue to charitable uses. The will and schedules [were] proved in the ecclesiastical court. The charity entitled to the residuum [was] no party to the bill, only the executors, all but the widow [were] executors in trust; so indifferent. *Quoad* the schedules, the widow has a benefit by the schedules. What therein relates to her [is] intelligible. But, if the schedules be established, then the charities would be defeated and the annuities be prejudiced.

The doubt here was whether they should by an appeal to the [Court of] Delegates from the probate. If the executors appeal and not prevail, the costs must be borne by the appellants.

*Curia* [Lord Harcourt]: I decree an account of the estate. The Master is to state all parties' demands, and, if [there is] anything difficult in the will or the schedules, to state the same specially.

## 603

## Bolt v. Damer

(Ch. 1714)

*The question in this case was whether, in a suit to redeem a mortgage, the beneficiary of a trust residing outside the jurisdiction of the court must be served with process.*

British Library MS. Hargrave 77, f. 41, pl. 2

3 May 1714. At the Rolls, Mr. Justice Powys.

The plaintiffs brought their bill to redeem, as trustees of the estate, under the will of Baker, the mortgagor.

The defendant, by answer, says that the complainant borrowed money at interest of one Jos[eph] Damer of Dublin in Ireland and that a mortgage was thereupon made to the defendant and one Edward Damer, deceased.

And the plaintiff prayed [leave] to amend and that service of George Damer's trustee's clerk in court might be good service as to the *cestui que trust*, Joseph Damer. And the answer of the said defendant, George, was read to the effect above. Yet, as to the service of the subpoena, the motion [was] denied.

[It was] said that the plaintiffs ought to produce an affidavit that he was in Ireland, that they had done what they could to find him but could not, and should have served him with a subpoena in Ireland, and, if he refused to appear, as he might choose whether he would or not, then the plaintiff might apply, else the plaintiff would proceed here by way of contempt to conclude him without hearing him.

It was answered this could not be any prejudice to him, for the bill was to redeem. He could have but what principal and interest the Master should find due to him and his costs. And the trustee and his clerk in court being both served, it could not be supposed that they would not give notice of it to the *cestui que trust* and pray a commission to take his answer. It was needless to serve him in Ireland, because no affidavit of service could be made there which would be read here, because there is no master extraordinary of this court there and then it could not be made to appear to this court that he was served. And so, after all, the plaintiff would be in the same difficulties as now. Ireland was in the same consideration as to this or any of His Majesty's foreign plantations or factories. And, if the *cestui que trust* had been in the East or West Indies to send the plaintiffs to serve a subpoena there as to the affidavit, it was needless because the fact appeared by the defendant's own answer, which was more than an affidavit.

## 604

## Anonymous

(Ch. 1714)

*Where legatees receive their legacies out of an insolvent estate, the legatees must refund what they received with interest.*

Lincoln's Inn MS. Misc. 10, p. 165, pl. 1

31 May 1714. At the Rolls.

The plaintiffs, being executors and residuary legatees of one A.B., paid the defendants legacies given them by the said A.B.'s will. Afterwards, it appeared that A.B. left no personal estate, she having taken upon her to give away the estate of her husband, which she had no power to dispose of.

And, now, the executors bring their bill against the legatee to refund.

And they were accordingly decreed to refund with interest but without costs. And His Honor [Trevor] declared the precedents of the court had been so and that it was natural equity that the defendants should refund.

## 605

## Jenner v. Harper

(Ch. 1714)

*A devise to charitable uses must be made according to the requirements of the Statute of Frauds.*

British Library MS. Hargrave 80, f. 175v, pl. 2

Trinity term 1714.

A tenant in tail, by a nuncupative codicil, made in the year 1651 charged his lands with a rent of £20 *per annum* forever for a school. Upon exceptions to a decree of commissioners for charitable uses, the question was whether this was a good appointment. The objection that it was made by a tenant in tail was scarcely insisted upon, that point having been fully settled in other cases.

But it was urged by Mr. *Vernon* and Mr. *Williams* that lands were not devisable at common law unless by special custom, that the Statute of Hen. VIII,[1] which gave a power to devise, did it by will in writing and that, before the Statute of Frauds,[2] unless a will was reduced into writing by the testator himself or some other by his directions in his lifetime, it was void as to lands, that the condition men are usually in when they make their wills, their being liable to impositions when they are *in extremis*, was the reason of the laws guarding their inheritance in case of wills, that this being the case of a rent out of land was rather stronger than that of land itself, a rent not being capable of being granted by the party by any act in his lifetime without a deed, and that charities as well as other things are to be bound by the rules of this court, that the civil law did not allow charities to abate in proportion with other legacies where there happened to be deficiency of assets, but that, in this court, they always abate in proportion.

*Vernon* cited a case in Lord Cowper's time between Johnson and [ *blank* ] College in Cambridge,[3] where a charity was given since the Statute of Frauds by a will attested by two witnesses, and [it was] resolved by Lord Cowper upon great deliberation that, though it was in the case of a charity, yet, since the testator intended to make an appointment by a will and it was a void will, it was, therefore, a void appointment, and a like case of Dr. Shermeers upon a charity to the poor of the parish of St. Clement's determined upon the like reason by Wright and

[1] Stat. 32 Hen. VIII, c. 1 (*SR*, III, 744–746).

[2] Stat. 29 Car. II, c. 3 (*SR*, V, 839–842).

[3] *Attorney General v. Baines* (Ch. 1707), see above, Case No. 74.

alleged that a will being in writing was necessary before the Statute of Frauds as the subscription of three witnesses, which is only a further circumstance since, and that, if the want of a third witness made it a void appointment since the Statute of Frauds, there was the same reason that the want of its being in writing should make it void before.

In answer to this, it was urged by *Sir Joseph Jekyll* that the case of a will by a tenant in tail, its being a good appointment, was much stronger than the case at bar, that, there, though the estate was generally under the control of the tenant in tail, yet, at the time, he might not have it in his power to suffer a recovery, and that the case of Johnson [and] (query Keys) College was resolved by Lord Cowper upon the Statute of Frauds being subsequent to the Statute of Elizabeth[1] and *leges posteriores priores contrarias abrogant*[2] and by the Lord Chancellor enrollment required by the Statute of Hen. VIII and fine or recovery [by a] tenant in tail are dispensed with by Statute 43 Eliz., that Act being subsequent to the Statute Hen. VIII and *donis*,[3] why should not the writing be dispensed with here for the same reason.

*Williams*: In those cases, the [Statute of] 43 Eliz. only restores the common law. But if it abrogates the Statute Hen. VIII, of Wills, as being subsequent, and restores the common law, even there, the will is void.

Lord Chancellor [Lord Harcourt] took time to consider. And afterwards without any further debate, he declared his opinion that the exceptions ought to be allowed. He said it might be a precedent of very ill consequences if, for the sake of charity, he should get out of the Statute in a case of the greatest danger.

[Other copies of this report: Lincoln's Inn MS. Misc. 383, p. 296, pl. 3.]

Lincoln's Inn MS. Misc. 384, p. 18, pl. 3

4 June.

The question was whether a charity given by a nuncupative will in 1651, before the Statute of Frauds, will charge land.

*Vernon*, for the plaintiff [Gonner]: A nuncupative will is not sufficient to charge lands. I admit a tenant in tail may charge the entail and the remainder by a charity without a sufficient recovery. The Statute of Wills requires it to be in writing where lands are charged. Johnson's Case, in Lord Cowper's time; where there was a will in writing since the Statute of Frauds signed by two witnesses, yet it could not charge a charity on lands. You cannot aver a charity by parol.

*Jekyll*, for the defendant: It is not necessary a will should be put in writing by the testator himself, but it may be by his direction. The Statute of 43 Eliz., of

1 Stat. 43 Eliz. I, c. 4, s. 1 (*SR*, IV, 968–969).

2 Later laws abrogate contrary prior ones. *Black's Law Dictionary* (rev. 4th ed. 1968), p. 1045.

3 Stat. 13 Edw. I, Westminster II, c. 1 (*SR*, I, 71).

charitable uses, does dispense with the Statute of Wills. If a man directs or appoints a charity, though not in a legal way, yet it is good. Here has been an execution of part of the charity, for lands have been purchased and a school built and the salary of the schoolmaster paid for some time out of the personal estate. We are not at this distance of time to prove that the nuncupative will was put into writing by direction of the testator.

Lord Chancellor [LORD HARCOURT]: Suppose this stood barely upon a nuncupative codicil; the Statute of Enrollments,[1] though required by an Act of Parliament, is dispensed with; so, upon the Statute *de Donis*, a fine is dispensed with. Why not so in this case?

*Vernon*: Though, in the civil or canon law, charities are preferred to legacies, yet, in this court, they are equal. There might indeed have been an appointment to a charity by parol, as in Dr. Shalmer's Case, but not in this way, by a will. This did bind the personal estate, which was applied until there was a failure of assets.

*Peere Williams*: There is a case in the books where a man sends for a scrivener and directs him to give an estate to A. upon a condition. He writes the will, but, before the writing of the condition, the testator died. Therefore, it was a void devise. If it be a void will, it is a void appointment.

Lord Chancellor [LORD HARCOURT]: Is there no instance of an appointment of lands to charitable uses by parol since the Statute of Frauds? ([It was] answered, no.) If the plaintiff will not consent to pay the arrears for four years directed by the decree of the charity commissioners, I will make him go back further if I can. I will consider of it. If either side can show me precedents, let them attend me.

25 June.

I have considered of it and find I cannot charge land by a nuncupative will. Therefore, I allow the exceptions to the decree, which must stand reversed.

1 Salkeld 163, 91 E.R. 152

Trinity 1714.

A., tenant in tail, made a nuncupative will and gave a rent of £20 *per annum* out of the estate tail for the erecting of a free school. And he ordered that his executors should purchase other lands for the maintenance of the said school. This will was made before the Statute of Frauds, but the testator died after.

And, now, it was held by HARCOURT, Lord Chancellor, that, at common law, lands were not devisable, that the [Stat.] 31 Hen. VIII, empowers the owner to devise, but as much requires that his will of lands shall be in writing, as the Statute of Frauds requires his will of lands should have three witnesses. And, therefore, if such will want but one witness, it is void to all intents and purposes.

[1] Stat. 27 Hen. VIII, c. 16 (*SR*, III, 549).

And the Statute of the 43 of Eliz. which favored appointments to charities is now repealed *pro tanto* by the Statute of Frauds.

[Other reports of this case: Lincoln's Inn MS. Misc. 384, p. 18, pl. 3, 1 Peere Williams 247, 24 E.R. 374, Gilbert Rep. 44, 25 E.R. 31, Precedents in Chancery 389, 24 E.R. 175, 2 Eq. Cas. Abr. 191, 22 E.R. 163.]

## 606

## Loo v. Everand

(Ch. 1714)

*The presumption of payment of a note made many years before the demand for payment can be rebutted by evidence of non-payment.*

British Library MS. Hargrave 80, f. 177

Loo, a pauper v. Everand.

The plaintiff's father, in August 1665, deposited £500 in the defendant's grandfather's hands, a goldsmith, and took a note payable the first of November following with interest at £4 percent and left the town to avoid the plague. The goldsmith died before the first of November of the plague. And the next year, a great part of his estate, consisting in houses, was consumed by the Fire of London [in 1666]. The plaintiff's father lived until 1689 and then died intestate. Then his brother took administration and went abroad and died. Among his effects returned home, the plaintiff found the note in 1700 and took administration *de bonis non* to his father and demanded it of the heir and executor of the goldsmith, he having died before it was payable.

And after his death, one Dee, who took administration during his son's minority, having accounted in the Prerogative Court and this note not appearing in those accounts to have been paid and the son who afterwards proved the will and lived to answer the plaintiff by his answer not pretending to have paid it himself, the Master of the Rolls [Trevor] thought the presumption of satisfaction from the length of time quite off by these circumstances and decreed the plaintiff a satisfaction of the entire note with interest from the date at £4 percent.

Lord Chancellor [Lord Harcourt], upon an appeal to him, was of the same opinion until one of the goldsmith's books was produced by the defendant, in which there was an entry of £110 paid in part of this note. And, thereupon, he varied the decree *pro tanto* but confirmed it for £300 and interest.

[Other copies of this report: Lincoln's Inn MS. Misc. 383, p. 298, pl. 1, Lincoln's Inn MS. Misc. 107, p. 20.]

## 607

## Andrews v. Anonymous

(Ch. c. 1714)

*Undersheriffs and their bailiffs are not the agents of the parties to litigation.*

British Library MS. Hargrave 81, f. 111

Complaint was made to the court against Mervyn, undersheriff of Buckinghamshire, and some other of his bailiffs for having broken an injunction. The undersheriff had taken the plaintiff's goods in execution. And, while they were in execution and undisposed, the defendant at law, now plaintiff, exhibits his bill against the defendant, who was plaintiff at law, for want of an answer, [and] had the common injunction directed to the defendant, his counsel, attorney, and agents, which the plaintiff served on the undersheriff and his bailiffs. The undersheriff, notwithstanding, removes his goods from one part of the house to another, but did not carry away or sell any of them.

Mr. Baron Price, sitting this day for the Lord Chancellor, was of opinion that the undersheriff or his bailiffs were not persons within any of the descriptions in the injunction and, therefore, could not be guilty of a breach of it.

[Other copies of this report: British Library MS. Hargrave 82, f. 125, British Library MS. Hargrave 77, f. 31, pl. 1, British Library MS. Hargrave 303, f. 57.]

## 608

## Lord Coventry v. Lady Coventry

(Ch. 1714)

*A court will not construe general words in a deed narrowly unless it is clear that the party did not intend that anything more than is particularly expressed and described in the deed should pass by the general words.*

British Library MS. Hargrave 81, f. 145

5 April 1714.

The late Lord Coventry, on the treaty of the marriage of his eldest son with the duke of Beaufort's daughter, proposes a settlement. The duke requires £1500 *per annum* to be settled in particular lands. The Lord Coventry orders his steward to lay before the duke for that purpose an account of what estates he was seised in fee, either in possession, reversion, or remainder, and also of what he was only tenant for life, which was accordingly done. And, afterwards, the marriage being agreed on, a settlement was made whereby several manors, towns, and lands particularly mentioned were settled on the wife and the tenant's name expressed. And then followed several words of reversion and reversions, remainder and remainders, etc. as usual in conveyances by lease and release. The lands in question were not expressed, and the then lord was seised only in reversion of them at the time of making the settlement. The marriage was had; the Lord Coventry, the father, dies. Then, the son dies without issue male; so the title comes to the plaintiff. And, by these deaths, the estate in question, which was before but a reversion, fell into the possession of the defendant. The lady brings her [action of] ejectment, claiming under the general words in the settlement, and recovers the land. The Lord Coventry brings his bill to be relieved and to have a recompense made by the lady in regard she had without that full £1500 *per annum*, which was all that was agreed upon or intended to be settled.

And for the plaintiff, it was said that, where a purchase was made by a particular or wherever a conveyance was made and lands particularly expressed and described, there, the general words were to be looked upon but as words of course and form and were to be restrained to the particulars expressed and specified before. So it is in the case of releases or discharges; a receipt at the bottom of a bill of particulars, though it be said in full of all accounts, yet it shall be restrained to the former particulars. So, if a general release be given, the release, notwithstanding the general words, shall be restrained to the particular matter. And he cited the case of Taylor and Beversham, 2 Ven. 345,[1] a re-conveyance was decreed where, by the general words in the conveyance, copyhold lands would have been carried which were not in the particular by which the purchase was made. So, in the case of C. v. C., nephew and uncle join in a conveyance by lease and release and, by reason of the general words in the conveyance, the nephew brought [an action of] ejectment for land of the uncle which, at law, passed by the general words, upon which the uncle brought his bill to be relieved and to have a re-conveyance because none of his lands were intended to pass, and he was made a party only for form and to corroborate the nephew's settlement; the court went into the consideration of the agreement for the uncle's joining in the conveyance and what was intended really to be conveyed and the uncle, being only joined for conformity, had a decree according to the prayer of his bill the 26 of October 1709.

*Curia* [Lord Harcourt]: Whenever this court restrains the operation of law by general words, it must be very manifest and clear that the party did not intend that anything more than is particularly expressed and described in the deed should pass by the general words. And it is incumbent on the plaintiff to make this out, which His Lordship had not done, for the arguments made use of by his counsel of impossibility that it should be intended, because the Lord Coventry had not at the time of settlement any possession in those lands to settle and their argument of improbability that, if he were apprised of his title to this, he would settle it when he had before made a settlement to the full value required do not at all make out that these lands were not intended to pass; what was required was

[1] *Taylor v. Beversham* (1674–1680), 2 Ventris 345, 86 E.R. 477, also 2 Chancery Cases 194, 22 E.R. 908.

£1500 *per annum* or upwards. The settlement with the lands in question agree very well that the whole after deduction of outgoings being very little more than £1500 *per annum*. And this being in the case of a settlement between persons of great quality, it is very easy and natural to imagine that this estate, which, at that time, was remote, was thrown into the settlement *ex abundanti* [*cautela*] as what there might be a possibility but no probability of the lady's having any benefit of because of the several persons who must die before she could be entitled to it. And, therefore, it was cast in as a bounty.

And, as to the cases that have been cited, they do not come up to this, for there is a difference between a stranger purchaser for money and a purchaser by marriage settlement; the first shall take nothing but what he actually agrees for and for which he pays a valuable consideration, and no construction of bounty or gift can be intended between a vendor and vendee. But, in the other case, there is room justly for such imagination and construction because it is between parent and child and very near relations; it is on an occasion where people are usually liberal and bountiful, and, by such construction, nothing is lost to the family of the party, but it is made a gift to them. And, therefore, in such cases, the party shall have advantage of the general words in a settlement notwithstanding particular words and parcels in the grant.

[Other copies of this report: British Library MS. Hargrave 82, f. 158, British Library MS. Hargrave 77, f. 38v, pl. 2, British Library MS. Hargrave 303, f. 68v, pl. 2.]

Lincoln's Inn MS. Misc. 384, p. 18, pl. 1

15 April 1714.

A bill [was brought] to have leasehold lands excepted out of Lady Coventry's jointure, which passed at law by the general words. In consideration of £10,000, the countess's fortune, there was a covenant to settle £1500 *per annum*, which the estate is worth, without the leasehold estate, which the bill would have excepted.

Lord Chancellor [Lord Harcourt]: There is a great difference between a purchaser and a jointress, for a purchaser shall not have an acre more than he pays for, but, in a jointure, there is room for bounty. I dismiss the bill without costs.

[Related cases: Lord Coventry v. Lady Ann Coventry (Ch. 1713), see above, Case No. 550.]

## 609

## Kent v. Whetred

(Ch. 1714)

*A former partner will be ordered to account for fraud committed during and in the course of the former business.*

British Library MS. Hargrave 81, f. 150

16 April 1714.

The defendant being possessed of Byfleet Mills for the remainder of a term of years, which mills had been paper and corn mills, and by him altered into brass wire mills and having made some new works and out buildings to them, in January 1703, the plaintiff and defendant treat for the plaintiff's becoming joint partner with the defendant in the mills upon his paying half the purchase money paid by the defendant and half the charge of the alterations [of the] new works and buildings. The defendant gives the plaintiff a particular of the purchase and of the pretended several articles and sums of the several materials and things used therein and paid for carriage and workmen's wages. This particular is put into a schedule annexed to articles indented and executed between them. The plaintiff accordingly paid him one-half of the total amount, and the partnership goes on. The defendant, presently after, takes away the books and accounts from the clerks of the works and destroys them to prevent a discovery of the fraud in the particulars. After some years continuance, the plaintiff being informed the defendant had wronged him but not being able to make out in what particulars, he complains of the wrong to the defendant, who thereupon pays him £500, which he now would have to be in full of all the wrong. In the articles, there was a clause that, if the plaintiff thought fit within the year, the partnership should determine. In some time, the partnership was dissolved by consent. And, afterwards, the complainant, having discovered the particular wrongs in omissions, false charges, and over-charges in the said schedule, the half of which amounted to £1200, and being able to make a reasonable proof of them, exhibits his bill to be relieved and to have a discovery of the particulars from the defendant and satisfaction made him, and he sets out the payment of the £500 as in part towards satisfaction and offers to allow it.

And the cause being this day at hearing, by the defendant's counsel, it was said that he could not be relieved because he neglected the time in the articles, *viz.* the first year, secondly, for that it was his own negligence and default not to have inquired better into the particulars before he executed the articles and paid the money, thirdly, because the £500 was paid and accepted in full of all demands as to any wrong or over-charge, fourthly, for that, by this payment and dissolving the partnership and selling the interest in the mills, the plaintiff had fully acquiesced in what had been done and in such length of time his complaint ought not to be countenanced nor relieved.

Mr. *Vernon*, for the plaintiff: This is a case of most notorious fraud in the defendant, who has abused the confidence put in him by the plaintiff to that degree that in £4500, which is the total amount of the particulars in the schedule, there is above £2400 over-charged and, in one item only of £1300, there is above [ *blank* ] over-charged, that, by paying £500, he has given judgment against himself as to the fraud and, notwithstanding his answer, he has not made any proof of the £500 being paid or accepted in full or ever been agreed to be so and his destroying the books and accounts cannot be supposed to have been done but with an ill design to conceal the truth and is a plain indication of a premeditated fraud. And the length of time cannot in this case be a just objection, for the plaintiff has all along been in pursuit of and endeavoring to make out and discover the particulars of the fraud, and the practice of the defendant's suppressing the books has been the occasion of the length of time and delay. The particular or schedule annexed to the articles cannot be taken to be more binding than an account stated would be. And pointing out particulars in a stated account upon complaints, persons are usually relieved in equity. That is done here, we having set out the particulars we complain of and the particular of each over-charge and omission. And, in the case of Sale and Shoppins, in this court, the plaintiff was relieved though he had had the partnership account for four years together in his custody to peruse and inspect without making any objection to the account. And, in the case of the Earl of Warrington and Booth,[1] which has been up in the House of Lords and the decree here below affirmed there, which was a fraud committed by Booth in concealing from the earl part of the fortune which his lady really had and which His Lordship ought to have had but his uncle, Mr. Booth, vested to his own use, it was the opinion of all the judges and so resolved that, in the case of fraud, time should not affect and that the Statute of Limitations[2] should not in such case take place. And in the case of Mr. Death and Major Bugge,[3] where he had sold his estate in Kent to Mr. Death by a particular wherein he had charged the woodlands at a greater number of acres than in truth they were, although conveyances were executed and all the purchase money paid, yet all this being founded upon a confidence and supposition that the particulars were just, he, after he had discovered the falsity, brought his bill in this court and had a commission to measure and survey the woodlands and, upon the commissioner's certification that they contained less than given in for, the major was decreed to refund in proportion and to pay costs, which he hoped the defendant here would likewise be decreed to do.

*Curia* [Lord Harcourt]: The defendant having by answer admitted he repaid £500 in respect of what he had over-charged and it not appearing that the £500 was taken in full [satisfaction], he directed the Master to inspect the schedules and see what items were over-charged and, if the moiety thereof amounted to more than £500, then that the defendant should pay so much more as would make up a full moiety, but, if less, then the plaintiff to refund a moiety of what should be less. And, in regard to the length of time [since] the fraud committed,

---

[1] *Earl of Warrington v. Booth* (H.L. 1714), 4 Brown P.C. 163, 2 E.R. 111, Chancery Repts. *tempore* Harcourt, p. 431, see also above, Case No. 464.

[2] Stat. 21 Jac. I, c. 16, s. 3 (*SR*, IV, 1222).

[3] *Darth v. Buggins* (Ch. 1712), see above, Case No. 392.

he decreed the items in the schedule to be taken for granted unless the plaintiff satisfied them.

[Other copies of this report: British Library MS. Hargrave 82, f. 161, British Library MS. Hargrave 77, f. 39, British Library MS. Hargrave 303, f. 70.]

## 610

## Scholefield v. Pack

(Ch. 1714)

*Bond and judgment creditors cannot levy upon their debtor's copyhold lands.*

British Library MS. Hargrave 81, f. 155

19 April 1714.

Cannon, a grocer, was seised of a copyhold estate, part of the manor of Sovaffin, in the County of Suffolk. And, in the year 1680, he withdraws[1] to the house of the defendant's father, who assisted him in compounding his debts. And, during that time, he took a conditional surrender from him for £140 and interest. And, in 1687, he died without issue. Cannon was also indebted to Pack, the defendant's father, in a bond of £500. And owing J.S. £220 on a judgment, the same was compounded for £100 and assigned to Pack, the defendant's father, who died leaving issue, the defendant, his only son. Cannon, at the time of his decease, had three nieces, his co-heiresses, *viz.* Rose, the mother of the plaintiff, Ann Scholefield, and Ann Salter. The plaintiffs now brought their bill to redeem the premises and to have an account of the rents and profits received and have a surrender on paying what should appear due on the surrender only, for that the premises, being copyhold, were not liable to the bond or judgment [creditors].

The defendant, by his answer, set forth what of the rents etc. his father or he had received and set forth the judgment and bond.

The plaintiffs reply, but never serve the defendant to rejoin or examine one witness.

And, at the hearing, it was insisted by *Sir Joseph Jekyll*, for the defendant, that the cause came to a hearing upon the bill and answer, for the replication was nothing, there not being any order for publication nor anything done on the replication. And he admitted that neither judgments nor bonds could affect the copyhold estate. But he said that, the mortgage having been made above twenty years since, the plaintiffs ought not after so great a length of time be let into a redemption. And, therefore, being precarious in this redemption, they ought to have it on the defendant's terms only, *viz.* for paying the bond and judgment [creditors].

[1] *I.e.* absconds from his creditors.

Mr. *Vernon*, on the same side, [said] that the plaintiffs, coming into a court of equity for a favor, *viz.* to redeem after so great a length of time, ought to do equity themselves and stand in the place of the debtor to be just, as he should have been, by paying the defendant what his father had advanced and paid for Cannon upon the bond and judgment though, perhaps, in strictness, it could not be tacked to the estate; besides, Cannon failed, and, upon a commission of bankruptcy, it ought to have been sold to pay the creditors. And the defendant stands in the creditors' place and ought to be paid.

*Curia* [Lord Harcourt]: Here is no agreement between the parties to charge or subject the estate to the bond and judgment [creditors]. And, without a special agreement for that purpose, a copyhold estate cannot be liable to debts. And, though the copyhold might be sold by a commissioner of bankruptcy, yet, no commission of bankruptcy having issued in Cannon's lifetime, it is too late now for any such. And, as the creditors themselves could not have affected the copyhold estate, so neither the defendant, who stands in their place. To decree a redemption upon paying what, upon an account, the Master shall find remaining due for principal, interest, and costs over and above the receipt of rents and profits and what, without willful default in the defendant or his father, might have been received and to be examined upon interrogatories as to his own receipts only and, upon payment of what shall so appear due to the defendant, to surrender to the plaintiffs at their charge and deliver all deeds and writings and, in default of payment, the bill to be dismissed with costs.

[Other copies of this report: British Library MS. Hargrave 82, f. 166, British Library MS. Hargrave 77, f. 40, British Library MS. Hargrave 303, f. 71v.]

## 611

## Nicholson v. Masters

(Ch. 1714)

*The Court of Chancery can order a parish tax to pay for a steeple to the parish church.*

Lincoln's Inn MS. Misc. 384, p. 18, pl. 2

26 April 1714.

A bill [was brought] by the churchwardens of Woodford, who, by an order of the vestry, had laid out a sum of money in building a steeple to be reimbursed by a parish rate. There have been precedents of this nature, as St. Clement's Danes, St. Mary [ *blank* ], where an organ was erected by an order of the vestry. Bishop v. Eagle;[1] where the church warden was allowed the money he had expended by

[1] *Bishop v. Eagle* (1708–1711), 10 Modern 22, 88 E.R. 607, 11 Modern 186, 263, 88 E.R. 978, 1028.

a parish rate. The plaintiffs have been in the spiritual court, but were not allowed all their charges.

The *Curia* granted a parish rate to reimburse the plaintiffs.

[Other reports of this case: 2 Eq. Cas. Abr. 203, 2 E.R. 173.]

## 612

## Holder v. Buxton

(Ch. 1714)

*Where a defendant sets a date for a hearing, he must give notice thereof to all of the parties.*

British Library MS. Hargrave 81, f. 112, pl. 1

27 April 1714.

Where a cause is set down to be heard *ad requisitionem defendentis*, it is incumbent on the defendant to serve all parties and bring them on to a hearing, as the plaintiff should had it been set down at his request.

[Other copies of this report: British Library MS. Hargrave 82, f. 125, pl. 2, British Library MS. Hargrave 77, f. 31, pl. 2, British Library MS. Hargrave 303, f. 57v, pl. 1.]

## 613

## Lord Coningbsy v. Plane

(Ch. 1714)

*Where lands are heriotable, whoever has any legal estate or interest in any estate in the land and dies must pay a heriot.*

British Library MS. Hargrave 77, f. 32v, pl. 3

27 April 1714. At the Rolls before Mr. Justice Dormer.

Where lands are heriotable, the heriots shall be multiplied as the land is parceled out to various purchasers and each shall pay a heriot. But where lands are conveyed to a husband and wife or others and one or more die, no heriot is due because, as long as any of the joint tenants remain, the estate continues, for it was but one estate in them all. Whoever has any legal estate or interest in any estate or interest in possession of the land and dies shall pay a heriot.

[Other copies of this report: British Library MS. Hargrave 82, f. 132, British Library MS. Hargrave 81, f. 118, pl. 2, British Library MS. Hargrave 303, f. 60, pl. 1.]

## 614

## Bellows v. Reginson

(Ch. 1714)

*Where a Master in Chancery makes a report as to a party's contempt of court, the report must be based on the evidence of witnesses and not on mere affidavits.*

British Library MS. Hargrave 81, f. 112, pl. 2

29 April 1714.

The plaintiff was indebted to the defendant for goods sold and delivered. The defendant recovers by verdict at law and has judgment and execution executed before the now plaintiff brought his bill. But before any goods were sold or removed, the bill is filed and, for want of an answer, the plaintiff obtains the common injunction but no order to stay the goods. The bailiff of Westminster, who had taken the goods, sells them, and the plaintiff, upon this, takes out an attachment against the defendant as having broken the injunction by the goods being sold. The defendant, being examined upon interrogatories touching the contempt, denied it. The plaintiff moved that the Master might certify whether he was in contempt or not. Upon this, the plaintiff produces before the Master an affidavit of one of the bailiff's followers, who was in possession of the goods, that the defendant had given money to the appraisers and to him for their trouble in keeping possession and appraising and selling the goods. The Master, hereupon, reports the defendant in contempt. And exceptions being taken to the report, it was insisted that the Master had no power in that case to read an affidavit or to ground any certificates or reports on an affidavit but, where, on an examination, the contempt is denied, the prosecutor must prove the contempt by examination of witnesses on interrogatories.

And, therefore, the Lord Chancellor [Lord Harcourt] discharged the report.

[Other copies of this report: British Library MS. Hargrave 82, f. 126, British Library MS. Hargrave 77, f. 31, pl. 4, British Library MS. Hargrave 303, f. 57v, pl. 3.]

## 615

## Anonymous v. Hord

(Ch. 1714)

*A London citizen's widow is entitled to her common law dower rights, even though she has contracted to not receive her customary rights upon her husband's death.*

*The creditors of a decedent cannot levy upon his copyhold lands.*

*Where a testator devises property to be sold to pay his debts and the secured creditors are paid out of this fund, the unpaid, unsecured creditors are subrogated to the secured creditors' rights to go against the debtor's real property.*

*Where a testator devises property to be sold to pay his debts, the secured and the unsecured creditors will be all paid pro rata out of this fund.*

British Library MS. Hargrave 81, f. 158

3 May 1714. At the Rolls.

A citizen of London, at his marriage, being possessed of some copyhold estate besides his stock in trade and although seised in fee of some freeholds lands and being to have a portion of £2000 with his intended wife, covenants to make her a provision which shall be in full satisfaction and bar of all her demands by the custom of London or otherwise howsoever. And, afterwards, the marriage is had. And then he surrenders the copyhold to the use of his will. And, being afterwards considerably indebted by special and simple contracts, he makes his will, and takes notice of the surrender, and desires his copyhold and freehold estate to be sold for payment of his debts, and wills that the money arising from such sale should be deemed as part of his personal estate. And he dies without making any provision for his wife, according to his covenant.

The simple contract creditors bring their bill for satisfaction of their debts and to have the estate sold and that the assets might be so marshaled that, as to what the specialty creditors should take out of the personal estate, they may stand in their places and have the benefit of the securities in order to have a satisfaction for their simple contract debts out of the real estate.

One question in this case was whether the words 'in full satisfaction etc. or otherwise howsoever' exclude the widow of her right of dower in the freehold lands.

*Curia* [Trevor]: This exception is only as to particular customary interests. As widow of a freeman, she might claim notwithstanding her dower at common law. Therefore, she must have her dower, and the freehold must be sold or a value may be set on her dower, which may be paid her in money. The personal estate is the proper and immediate fund for the satisfaction of the simple contract creditors. And, if that estate will not discharge both and the specialty creditors insist on satisfaction out of that, then the simple contract creditors must stand in their place to have satisfaction out of the real. The copyhold is not by law liable to any debts; it is not assets. And so the specialty creditors cannot have any lien upon it. Therefore, as to that, there cannot be any preference to the specialty creditors in point of satisfaction out of the money arising out of the sale of that. And the devise being generally for payment of debts and all debts being alike in conscience, the specialty and simple contract creditors shall be paid alike and in proportion out of the money arising from the sale of the copyhold estate.

[Other copies of this report: British Library MS. Hargrave 82, f. 168, British Library MS. Hargrave 77, f. 41v, British Library MS. Hargrave 303, f. 73v.]

## 616

## Sayer v. Salisbury

(Ch. 1714)

*Where a wife has a separate living allowance and the husband and wife are sued jointly, the wife can put in a separate answer without her husband.*

British Library MS. Hargrave 81, f. 114, pl. 1

3 May 1714.

If there be a decree between a man and wife that she shall have a separate allowance and, afterwards, a suit is brought against the husband and wife, upon showing this decree without notice the wife shall be allowed on her motion to answer separately. And so it was ordered here.

[Other copies of this report: British Library MS. Hargrave 82, f. 127, pl. 1, British Library MS. Hargrave 77, f. 31v, pl. 1, British Library MS. Hargrave 303, f. 58, pl. 1.]

## 617

## Sherston v. Knowling

(Ch. 1714)

*Elderly and infirm witnesses can be examined de bene esse after the complaint has been filed but before the defendant has been served with process.*

British Library MS. Hargrave 81, f. 114, pl. 2

*Eodem die [3 May 1714].*

The plaintiff brings his bill in order to establish a prescription to a footway over the defendant's grounds and, before any subpoena [was] served on the defendant or that he had appeared or had any notice of the suit, the plaintiff, on a certificate of the bill being filed, may have a commission to examine aged and infirm witnesses *de bene esse.*

[Other copies of this report: British Library MS. Hargrave 82, f. 127, pl. 2, British Library MS. Hargrave 77, f. 31v, pl. 2, British Library MS. Hargrave 303, f. 58, pl. 2.]

## 618

## Cardonell v. Morgan

(Ch. 1714)

*A court of equity cannot order an issue to be tried out of its geographic jurisdiction, but it may send a commission to examine witnesses out of its jurisdiction.*

*A sheriff, upon executing a writ of elegit, can put the plaintiff into possession without any further proceedings.*

British Library MS. Hargrave 81, f. 116

25 May 1714.

The matter in question was touching the title to an estate in Ireland, part of the forfeited estates there, of which the plaintiff had a lease. And whether the defendant had any legal eviction or interruption, he being tenant of the premises and decreed to an account with the plaintiff for the rent, was the question.

And, upon an issue being directed touching the interruption, it was said to the court that there was not any precedent of directing an issue to be tried in another kingdom because there could be no *venire* ordered, though, perhaps, by consent of the parties, it might be done. But, if it be insisted that the trial should be here, the party who desires it should make an allowance for the witnesses to be brought from beyond the sea or else he may have a commission to examine witnesses there and the depositions may be made use of at the trial here.

It was said by *Sir Joseph Jekyll*, and not denied by the Court, that the sheriff, upon executing a [writ of] *elegit*, might deliver possession to the plaintiff and not put him to the trouble of a second suit by [an action of] ejectment and that this practice of ejectments in these cases had been introduced only for the sake of attorneys.

[Other copies of this report: British Library MS. Hargrave 82, f. 129, British Library MS. Hargrave 77, f. 32, pl. 1, British Library MS. Hargrave 303, f. 58v.]

619

## Clayton v. Anonymous

(Ch. 1714)

*A contract that was made by an infant's guardian that is favorable to the infant can be enforced after the infant comes of age.*

British Library MS. Hargrave 81, f. 161

1 June 1714. At Westminster, Lord Chancellor.

The plaintiff sued to compel the defendant to take a lease of lands purchased by the plaintiff pursuant to articles made with the defendant's guardian on his behalf. The defendant insisted on his infancy and that, had he executed the articles itself, it would not have bound him but at his own election, and they being executed and the agreement made by another for him could not make it more binding upon him than if the whole had been transacted by himself.

But, for the plaintiff, *Sir Joseph Jekyll* said that every act that was done or every contract was not void or even voidable by him during his minority or afterwards, for an infant may put himself out apprentice, may contract for schooling or necessaries, and all those shall bind him notwithstanding his infancy and, generally, what contracts infants make that are for their benefit shall stand and not be avoided by them. These articles and the lease agreed to be taken was for the benefit of the defendant, who, though then an infant, was about twenty years of age.

And, therefore, the court decreed for the plaintiff.

[Other copies of this report: British Library MS. Hargrave 82, f. 171, British Library MS. Hargrave 77, f. 42, British Library MS. Hargrave 303, f. 74v, pl. 1.]

## 620

## Shiply v. Shiply

(Ch. 1714)

*A purchaser of land can sue a doweress who has contracted with the seller to release her dower rights, and a court of equity can require her to release her dower and record a satisfaction of any relevant judgment at common law.*

Lincoln's Inn MS. Misc. 384, p. 19

8 June.

A bill [was brought] to be relieved against a judgment in [an action of] dower.[1] The defendant, upon a consideration, agreed to release her dower to her son, from whom the plaintiff purchased.

The defendant is decreed to acknowledge satisfaction upon record and to release all her right of dower and pay the costs of this suit, but not the costs at [common] law.

## 621

## White v. Thornborough

(Ch. 1714)

*Where a contract for a marriage settlement is to be specifically enforced in a court of equity, the court will order a strict settlement, but the court will not defeat a right of dower.*

British Library MS. Hargrave 80, f. 177v

Abraham married an orphan of the City of London and, after marriage, covenanted with the Chamberlain in consideration of her portion to levy a fine of lands whereof he was seised in fee to the use of himself for life, remainder to his

[1] *Shiply v. Shiply* (1714), 10 Modern 225, 88 E.R. 703.

wife for life, remainders to his heirs male of his body by her, remainder to his heirs of his body by her, remainder to his right heirs. He died without levying any fine, leaving a son, Isaac, and a daughter, the now plaintiff, by his wife, who survived him. Isaac, in his mother's lifetime, borrowed a sum of money of the defendant Thornburgh and covenanted to levy a fine of the same lands to the use of Thornburgh for 500 years by way of a mortgage, remainder to the use of Isaac and his heirs. The deed took notice of the former deed of covenant made by Abraham. Isaac died, leaving a widow, and made a disposition of the estate by his will. And the question was whether the right of the plaintiff, the daughter, under the covenant of her father or that of Thornburgh under Isaac's covenant should have the preference.

*Vernon*, for Thornburgh, [argued] that, upon the death of Abraham, all the limitations subsequent to the estate for life of the wife of Abraham vested in Isaac, who, if a fine had been levied pursuant to the articles, would have an estate in tail male, remainder in tail general, remainder in fee, all which he might have barred by a fine, that, a fine not being levied, the entire legal interest descended upon him in fee and the trust after his mother's estate agreeably to the limitations in the deed of covenant, and that he, having the remainder in tail etc. of the equitable interest, might bar it by any kind of conveyance without levying a fine, which in her case, was needless and would have been to no purpose, the whole legal interest being in him, that a fine or recovery was not necessary to bar an equitable entail, a decree of this court will do it as effectively, that even a bargain and sale or feoffment had been resolved by My Lord Nottingham to be sufficient bars, that, in the case of Alley and Alley, Lord Somers had decreed that a conveyance by feoffment was a good bar to an equitable estate tail to which a man was entitled under articles for conveying lands to him in tail, and that, in the case of Dorse and Collison, a bargain and sale had been decreed to be a good bar, and that, in Otway and Dove,[1] before Lord Cowper, a *cestui que trust* of a copyhold in tail had required his trustees to surrender to the use of his will and to bar the entail and, they refusing, he died before any surrender and devised the lands by his will and [it was] ruled to be a good devise. He admitted that, in this case of Lower and Weal,[2] where one that had a legal estate in him in tail had mortgaged it and covenanted to suffer a recovery and, afterwards, refused it and died without doing it, though decreed to do so, that this court could not supply the want of it because of the Statute *de Donis*,[3] but that, in the present case, there was only

[1] *Otway v. Hudson* (1706), 2 Vernon 583, 23 E.R. 981, 1 Eq. Cas. Abr. 122, 21 E.R. 928.

[2] *Weale v. Lower* (1672–1689), Pollexfen 54, 86 E.R. 509, 2 Freeman 107, 22 E.R. 1089, 79 Selden Soc. 591, Lord Nottingham's Prolegomena, p. 340, 1 Eq. Cas. Abr. 266, 21 E.R. 1035.

[3] Stat. 13 Edw. I, Westminster II, c. 1 (*SR*, I, 71).

an equitable entail in Isaac which was sufficiently barred by his covenant to levy a fine to Thornburgh.

*Vernon* admitted that those that claimed under the first covenant were not to be looked upon as volunteers, though the covenant was subsequent to the marriage, the marriage being with an orphan and the covenant with those that had the care of her and her fortune in their power.

*Hooper*, for the plaintiff, insisted that the covenant of Isaac could not operate further than a fine by him would have done had the estate been executed which were intended by the covenant, that, if this court had carried that agreement into execution, it would have directed the uses to be limited to Abraham for life, remainder to his wife for life, remainder to their first son etc. in tail general, remainder to their daughters in tail or remainder to Abraham in fee, in which case, a fine by the son would not have barred the daughters, that Thornburgh had no legal estate in him, no fine being levied by Isaac. And though he was a purchaser, he was so with notice of the plaintiff's title, who was likewise a purchaser.

Lord Chancellor [LORD HARCOURT] decreed the estate to be conveyed to the plaintiff in tail, remainder to the right heirs of Abraham.

Another question was made, whether the widow of Isaac was entitled to dower.

And [it was] ruled by Lord Chancellor [LORD HARCOURT] that she was, the other side not much opposing because the legal estate was in her husband and she was a purchaser for the highest consideration, marriage, and without notice for aught that appeared.

But *Vernon* said privately that he thought her not dowable, her husband being in the nature of a trustee, and the wives of trustees are not entitled to dower out of those estates.

[Other copies of this report: Lincoln's Inn MS. Misc. 383, p. 298, pl. 2.]

British Library MS. Hargrave 77, f. 30, pl. 2

J.S., seised in tail of freehold and copyhold, upon his marriage, covenants to settle the principal and levy a fine of the freehold and surrender the copyhold for the use of himself and [his] intended wife for life, then to the first and every other son in tail, remainder over. The marriage is had. They have issue, sons, and die. No settlement being made or fine levied of the freehold but the copyhold [was] surrendered. Afterwards, the son mortgages the freehold [and] covenants to levy a fine and surrender the copyhold to the use of the mortgagee. He surrenders the copyhold but levies no fine, and he dies. The issue in tail brings his bill to have the benefit of this intended settlement, no fine being levied.

The cause was heard before LORD HARCOURT, who decreed that, there being marriage articles executed, the settlement was in equity to be deemed executed although the fine was not levied and that the issue in tail upon the mortgage not having levied a fine, a fine had not barred or discontinued the entail. And so, as to the copyhold, there not being any recovery suffered, the cause being now [for] rehearing, His Lordship [LORD HARCOURT] declared the same opinion as to the freehold. But, as to the copyhold, both parties being only in equity and it not appearing there was any usage or custom in the manor to suffer recoveries, he would intend that all was done that was necessary to bar the entail. And so he decree the copyhold to the mortgagee.

[Other copies of this report: British Library MS. Hargrave 303, f. 55v, pl. 2.]

Lincoln's Inn MS. Misc. 11, p. 63

9 June 1714.

On the marriage of the plaintiff's father, there were articles entered into whereby the father agreed to settle lands to the use of himself for life, then to his wife for life, remainder to the heirs male of his body begotten on the wife, remainder to the heirs of his body, remainder to his right heirs. The father dies without making a settlement, leaving a son and a daughter. The son, during the life of his mother, mortgages these lands to the defendant and covenants to levy a fine. But he dies without issue before the fine was levied. And the plaintiff, his sister, brings her bill to have an execution of these articles.

It was insisted on for the plaintiff that, if a bill had been brought in the life of the father, the court would have decreed the lands to have been settled according to the usual methods of marriage settlements, *viz.* to the first and other sons etc. And for this was cited by Serjeant *Hooper* the case of Pin v. Pin, decreed by Lord Keeper Wright and, upon a rehearing, affirmed by Lord Cowper.[1] A man, on his marriage, enters into a bond to settle lands to the use of himself for life, then to his wife for life, then to the heirs male of his body, with remainders over. He makes a settlement according to these uses and, afterwards, suffers a recovery. Twenty years afterwards, the son brings his bill to set aside this recovery for that the settlement ought to have been made to the first and other sons in tail male and then it would not have been in his father's power to have barred the entail. And, for this reason, the recovery was decreed to be set aside.

On the other side, it was insisted that, if the lands had been settled according to the articles, the son might have barred the entail by a fine and, if they had been settled in a strict settlement, yet he might have suffered a recovery and have barred the entail in that case and, he being in the nature of a tenant in tail of a trust estate, a conveyance by lease and release was as effectual as a recovery would have been in case the settlement had been made. In the Case of Otway and Hudson, in Lord Cowper's time,[2] where a copyholder in tail of a trust estate had devised it by his will, it was decreed to the devisee.

---

1 *Pym v. Pym* (Ch. 1705), see above, Case No. 39.

2 *Otway v. Hudson* (1706), 2 Vernon 583, 23 E.R. 981, 1 Eq. Cas. Abr. 120, 21 E.R. 926.

LORD COWPER: This case differs from the cases of deeds executed by tenants in tail of a trust estate where they might have levied a fine or suffered a recovery, for, in the present case, the son could not suffer a recovery during the life of his mother.

This court ought to consider the estate when the mortgage was made to be under the same limitations as they would have directed it to have been then settled in case a bill had been brought for that purpose, that is to say, to the father for life, then to his wife for life, then to their first and other sons in tail male etc. Now, if the estate had been settled in such manner, the son would have had no power over it during his mother's life.

He decreed the estate to be conveyed to the plaintiff.

Lincoln's Inn MS. Misc. 384, p. 20, pl. 1

9 June.

A., tenant in tail male, remainder in general tail unto himself and the heirs of his body, has issue, a son, who levies a fine. The question was whether the heir general shall not be barred.

Kusack v. Kusack, in the House of Lords;[1] a covenant to make an estate to A. for life, then to his first and other sons in tail, then to the daughters in tail. It was decreed to be without prejudice to the wife's dower.

*Vernon*: Where a copyhold may be entailed, a surrender may bar it and the remainder also unless the custom be contrary. Sims v. Pim's Case;[2] P., on his marriage, entered into a bond to settle an estate upon himself and the heirs of his body, which he, accordingly, did. But, afterwards, he suffered a recovery. The son, in this court, set aside the recovery and had it settled on P. for life, remainder to his wife for life, remainder to his first and other sons in tail, remainder to his daughter in tail.

*Hooper*, for the defendant: If articles are entered into and after[wards] executed, the wife will not be entitled to dower.

*Curia*: If articles are to be carried into execution in this court, it will be by way of strict settlement. Here, the defendant is entitled to dower at law, and this court will not take it away from her.

[Other reports of this case: Gilbert Rep. 107, 25 E.R. 75, Precedents in Chancery 425, 24 E.R. 190, 2 Vernon 702, 23 E.R. 1056, 2 Eq. Cas. Abr. 231, 714, 22 E.R. 196, 601.]

---

1 *Cusack v. Cusack* (1714), 5 Brown P.C. 116, 2 E.R. 570.

2 *Pym v. Pym* (Ch. 1705), see above, Case No. 39.

## 622

## Luff v. Anonymous

(Ch. 1714)

*Cheese is fungible, and, therefore, a dairyman cannot sue a cheesemonger for cheese delivered to a cheese factor that the dairyman was not paid for.*

British Library MS. Hargrave 81, f. 162

11 June 1714. At the Rolls.

The plaintiff was a cheesemonger in London, and one Blower was a factor for many dairymen in Suffolk to sell their cheeses. And he sold great quantities of them, among others, to the plaintiff, some of them being one dairyman's and some another's. Blower receives for the plaintiff part of the money for the cheeses and after[wards] becomes greatly indebted to the dairymen and to several others. The defendant, one of the dairymen, inquiring into the disposal of his cheeses, finds that part of them was sold by Blower to the plaintiff and, thereupon, brings his action at law against the plaintiff for the cheeses as sold and delivered to him by the plaintiff being so by his factor and recovers at law. The plaintiff, upon this, brings his bill on this equity, that the cheese factor's being employed promiscuously by great numbers of dairymen and dealers in cheese and their several goods not having any particular marks by which the cheesemongers can distinguish one from the other so as to know whose they are nor informed by the factors and being liable to an action for the whole at the suit of the factor, if they should likewise be liable to distinct actions at the suit of every particular person to whom any of the cheeses belonged, it would not only introduce multiplicity of actions and suits, which this court abhors and is its office to prevent, but would be the ruin of both the cheesemongers and the dairymen and destroy the trade by rendering it too dangerous. And it was so decreed lately upon these reasons in the Case of the Dairymen of Cheshire.[1]

And a perpetual injunction was granted here against the defendant.

[Other copies of this report: British Library MS. Hargrave 82, f. 172, British Library MS. Hargrave 77, f. 42v, pl. 1, British Library MS. Hargrave 303, f. 74v, pl. 2.]

[1] *Ives v. Hankey* (1687), cited in *Tovey v. Young* (1702), Precedents in Chancery 193, 24 E.R. 93, 2 Vernon 437, 23 E.R. 880.

## 623

## Hunt v. Hunt

(Ch. 1714)

*Where a settlement is made void by the non-performance of a condition, a re-conveyance can be ordered.*

Precedents in Chancery 387, 24 E.R. 174

The defendant was son and heir apparent to the plaintiff, who had an estate of about £200 *per annum*. And the defendant being about to marry Elizabeth Wright, who was not above sixteen years of age, the plaintiff, by lease and release, the 14th and 15th of October 1708, settles and conveys his estate to trustees and their heirs, and, as to one part, to the use of himself for life, remainder, as to that part, after his death, and, as to the other part in possession, to the use of the defendant for his life, remainder to the intended wife for her life for her jointure, remainder to the first and other sons etc. in the usual form. And, in the release, was a proviso that, if the marriage did not take effect or, if it took effect, and Elizabeth should not when she came of age by fine or otherwise join in charging an estate she was then entitled to of about £250 *per annum* with the sum of £2000 to be paid to the plaintiff, then the said indentures of lease and release and settlement were to be absolutely void to all intents and purposes.

The marriage took effect. And, about half a year ago, the wife attained her age of twenty-one years, but, finding her own estate of more value than that settled upon her in jointure, she and her husband refused to join in charging it with the £2000, whereupon this bill was brought against them and the trustees to have a re-conveyance.

It was insisted for the defendants that here needed none, because, by the proviso, on the defendant's refusal, the estate limited to them was to cease and be void.

But the court thought that not sufficient without a re-conveyance, being in a case of a freehold.

Then, it was insisted for the plaintiff, and the bill was for that purpose likewise, that he might have an account and satisfaction of the mesne profits received by the defendants from the time of the settlement. And it was said that, by the proviso, the estate being to cease and be void on the defendant's refusal, the plaintiff ought to be restored to all benefits and advantages which he had parted with, as if no settlement had been made and, consequently, to the rents and profits received by the defendants.

But My Lord Chancellor [Lord Harcourt] decreed a re-conveyance and an account of the rents and profits only from the defendant's refusal after his wife came of age and no costs on either side, for it was said this was not a condition precedent, but subsequent to the vesting of the estate in the defendants.

[Other copies of this report: Gilbert Rep. 43, 25 E.R. 31.]

[Other reports of this case: 2 Eq. Cas. Abr. 209, 22 E.R. 177.]

## 624

## Andrews v. Cradock

(Ch. 1714)

*Where a married woman disowns a lawsuit brought in her name and for her benefit, the case will be dismissed.*

Lincoln's Inn MS. Misc. 10, p. 165, pl. 3

12 June 1714. Oliver Andrews and Elizabeth Cradock, wife of the defendant Francis Cradock, by the said Oliver, her father and next friend, and Richard Cradock, her infant son, plaintiffs, and John Cradock and Francis Cradock, defendants. Upon an appeal from a decree at the Rolls.

Richard Lucas made his will, and he gives £1000 to the plaintiff Elizabeth, and he makes her the residuary legatee, and he makes the defendant John Cradock the executor. Francis, son of John, married the plaintiff Elizabeth, and, two years after the marriage, John entered into articles with his son to leave him by his will or give him in his lifetime £1500.

The plaintiff Andrews, without the consent of the wife, brings a bill to have an execution of these articles and an account of the personal estate.

Upon hearing this cause, an account was decreed and the defendant John was to give security to make good the articles.

The defendants appeal from this decree for that the plaintiff Andrews had brought this bill without and against the consent of the defendant's wife, that they are all at rest, and it is of ill consequence to allow such bills to be brought.

*Sir Joseph Jekyll*: In the Case of Lord Warrington and Sir James Langham,[1] a bill was brought to have security for making good a covenant to leave a sum of money at his death. The bill was dismissed, and the decree was affirmed by the Lords.

If the defendant Francis's wife was consenting to this suit, what is now attempted could not be obtained. The wife is the residuary legatee, and the right she had is vested in the husband, who might have gone into the ecclesiastical court and had it paid to him. If he had come into this court, it would be hard to say he should have other terms put upon him than what would have been done in the ecclesiastical court.

[1] *Earl of Warrington v. Langham* (1698–1699), Precedents in Chancery 89, 24 E.R. 43, Colles 149, 1 E.R. 224, 1 Eq. Cas. Abr. 132, 21 E.R. 936.

Indeed, if the money was perfectly trust money and they could not have it without coming into this court, the court may put such terms upon the parties as are reasonable.

Mr. *Vernon*: This attempt is very new. I believe there never was any suit admitted to be brought in this court on the behalf of a married woman against her consent. This bill is barely to alter the law. It is to say that what the law gives the husband shall be taken from him in equity. The utmost length this court ever went was in the case of a trust where a man comes for the aid of the court is to put what terms upon him [as] are just. But did this court ever enjoin a husband from suing in the ecclesiastical court for a legacy given his wife or from releasing a debt due to his wife?

The wife, being examined, disavowed the suit in open court, and the decree was reversed, and the bill was dismissed.

British Library MS. Hargrave 80, f. 182

This bill was brought by Andrews, the defendant Craddock's wife's father, in her name as her next friend and in the name of their infant son and his own against the husband and his father, who was the only acting executor under the will of the wife's grandfather by her mother's side. By that will, £1000 was given to the wife and the residuum, which amounted to several £1000s more. She was likewise devisee of the real estate. And, after her grandfather's death, she, being under the care of the defendant Craddock, married a younger son of his, for whom there was little or no provision made by the father. But he was the person that her grandfather had in his lifetime expressed his desire that she should marry. And her own father, the plaintiff, gave her in marriage to him. And, after they had lived together well for three or four years, he brought this bill without, and even against, the consent of the wife for an account of the personal estate of the grandfather and for the rents and profits of the real estate that had been received by the husband that they might be settled for the benefit of the wife and the issue of the marriage. And he obtained a decree at the Rolls for an account. But how the money that should be coming upon the account should be disposed of, that decree did not provide. It was said to have been founded upon the defendant Craddock's breach of trust in marrying an infant under his care and for whom, as residency legatee, he was executor [and] was a trustee to his younger son.

But upon an appeal to Lord Chancellor [Lord Harcourt], *Sir Joseph Jekyll* and Mr. *Vernon* said, for the defendants, that it was true that a married woman was considered in equity as a *feme sole* and might sue her husband but that, as she might sue, she may dismiss her own bill, that anybody might bring a bill in the name of an infant, who are not thought capable of judging for themselves, even without his consent, but not of a married woman who, in equity, are not thought to be under that incapacity, if they might, it would indeed *ampliare jurisdictionem* but would be attended with many inconveniences, and that no instance could be given of a bill brought in the name of a wife against her will and, where they are brought with their consent, they always sue by a *prochein amy* or a guardian that, if their suit be groundless, there may be somebody liable to costs, but that, in the present case, if the wife was in earnest and consented to the suit, there could be nothing decreed for her, that, if the husband had brought his bill for the legacy and it were a *res integra*, it would be pretty hard to maintain that he should have other terms put upon him here than the ecclesiastical court, which, in that case, has an original and a proper jurisdiction, would put upon him though, in the case of trust money, which is only recoverable here, the court had often interposed as a parent and obliged the husband to make a reasonable settlement, but that this bill was not to have an execution of a trust but to change the law to take what the law gives the husband away from him in equity for asking for that the profit of the real estate which had been received by him he was entitled to by law and that he was decreed to an account even for those profits, that the right to the legacy of £1000 and the residuum vested in the husband by the intermarriage, and he had a power to demand, receive, or release them, that no bill ever was brought before to hinder a husband from disposing of a legacy given to his wife, no husband [was] ever enjoined from releasing such a legacy or suing for it in the spiritual court, no bill [was] ever brought by the wife to set aside a release but that the farthest that the court has ever gone is, where the husband prays the aid of the court to have the benefit of a trust, to grant that aid upon terms and as he would have equity to make him do it, that, though the decree for the defendants to account and the consideration of the disposal of what they have received is reserved, that that is yet a great grievance to be harassed with an account with those who have no right to the balance of it nor can give any legal discharge, that neither the plaintiff Andrews nor the infant had any color of right to anything and the right of the wife was vested in the defendant, her husband.

The wife was in court and was examined by Lord Chancellor [Harcourt], and she disowned the suit and desired no account might be taken, upon which the former decree was reversed and the bill was dismissed but without costs.

[Other reports of this case: Gilbert Rep. 36, 25 E.R. 26, Precedents in Chancery 376, 24 E.R. 170, 1 Eq. Cas. Abr. 65, 72, 21 E.R. 879, 884.]

## 625

## Parker v. Parker

(Ch. 1714)

*Where a power of appointment is coupled with an interest, a court of equity will cure a defective execution of it.*

Lincoln's Inn MS. Coxe 89, vol. 3, part 2, p. 12, pl. 3

15 June 1714; *coram* Lord Harcourt.

Hugh Parker, son and heir of Henry Parker, on his marriage to Anne Smith, with whom he had an £8000 portion in his marriage settlement, had a power by deed or writing by him subscribed and sealed in the presence of three or more credible witnesses or by his last will in writing signed, sealed, and published in the presence of the like number of witnesses to charge by way of mortgage or otherwise £7000 for the portions of younger children. He, by reason of illness, was forced to remove from his own house to Kensington, where, being desirous to provide for his younger children but not having the deed of settlement to see what directions were there given for the execution of the power, yet knowing that had a power to charge his land, makes his will and therein recites that, in pursuance of a power given to him in certain articles or deed of settlement on such a marriage between him and his then wife for raising the sum of £8000 or thereabouts, he did by will give to his children, naming all the younger, the sum of £8000 to be divided among them, which will was executed only in the presence of two witnesses.

And it was decreed that this being a provision for younger children, who were otherwise unprovided for and the defect of the execution of the power being occasioned by a sudden and extreme illness of the testator, it was a good charge for £7000 and that it should carry interest until the fortunes became payable equal to the power the testator had of appointing a maintenance and, therefore, directed the £300 *per annum* should be raised and paid as interest for the £7000 until the principal should be raised.

Lincoln's Inn MS. Misc. 11, p. 51

15 June 1714.

Mr. Parker, having six younger children and there being a power in his marriage settlement by deed or will executed in the presence of three witnesses to charge the lands by way of mortgage, lease for years, or otherwise with the following sums for his younger children, *viz.* if but one, then with £2000 and £100 a year maintenance; if two only, then with £4000 and £200 a year maintenance; if three or more, then with any sum not exceeding £7000 and with maintenance not exceeding £300 a year. Mr. Parker, whilst he was at Kensington dangerously ill of the sickness whereof he died and not having his settlement with him, makes his will. And, taking notice that he had a power to raise £8000 or thereabouts for his younger children, he does thereby limit £8000 for all his younger children, to be equally divided between them. And this will was executed in the presence of two witnesses only. And there was no time limited by the will when the portions should be paid, nor any appointment as to maintenance.

And to supply the defective execution of this power and to have £7000 raised for the plaintiffs' portions, who are the younger children, and £300 a year for maintenance was the end of the bill.

Mr. *Vernon*: Where it is a power coupled with an interest, this court has always supplied defective executions of powers. Where it is a bare power indeed, it may perhaps be otherwise.

He cited the Case of Lady Clifford and Lord Burlington,[1] which was thus. Lord Clifford had a power to limit a sum not exceeding £1000 a year for a jointure for any wife he should marry. Upon his marriage with the plaintiff, he agrees to settle £1000 a year out of his Irish estate for her jointure. And in order thereunto, he sends to his steward in Ireland to send him a particular of lands of that value, which he did. And Lord Clifford, pursuant to his power, settles those lands for the plaintiff's jointure. After his death, it appeared that the jointure lands at the time of the settlement were but £800 a year. And she brought her bill to supply this defective appointment and had a decree to make up her jointure full £1000 a year.

Lord Chancellor [LORD HARCOURT]: The case of Lady Clifford goes a great deal farther than this case. Defective executions of powers for the payment of debts etc. for the provision for younger children are always aided in this court and ought to be so in this case.

I think the charge in the will of £8000 is a good charge for £7000 and that, therefore, the plaintiffs are entitled to that sum.

He decreed £7000 to be raised with interest at £5 percent and the Master to settle the plaintiffs' maintenance and what could be laid up out of the interest above their maintenance to be paid them as they come of age.

Note he first directed £300 a year to be paid for the plaintiffs' maintenance according to the settlement, which he said was less than the interest of £7000. But, afterwards, he varied that direction and decreed *ut supra*.

1 Strange 604, 93 E.R. 727,
Gilbert Rep. 168, 25 E.R. 118

15 June 1714.

Mr. Parker had a power to raise £7000 for younger children by deed or will executed in the presence of three witnesses. Afterwards, by will executed in the presence of two witnesses, he charged the premises with £8000 for his younger children.

And it was decreed good for the £7000.

[1] *Lady Clifford v. Lord Burlington* (1700), 2 Vernon 379, 23 E.R. 841, Lincoln's Inn MS. Misc. 11, p. 51, pl. 2.

## 626

## Wheatly v. Wheatly

(Ch. 1714)

*The question in this case was whether a mortgage which had been forfeited many years beforehand but the equity of redemption neither released nor foreclosed should be considered as a real or a personal estate of the mortgagee.*

British Library MS. Hargrave 80, f. 184, pl. 1

In this case, the Master of the Rolls [Trevor] was of opinion and, as he said, agreeable to the opinion of Serjeant Maynard, that a mortgage in fee which had been forfeited in the year 1688 and the mortgagor[1] being in possession ever since ought to be looked upon as the real, not the personal, estate of the mortgagee though the equity of redemption was never released or foreclosed. But he suspended decreeing it to be so until, upon an account directed in the cause, it shall appear whether his younger children will be sufficiently provided for without making it part of his personal estate.

[Other copies of this report: Lincoln's Inn MS. Misc. 383, p. 303, Lincoln's Inn MS. Misc. 107, f. 21, pl. 1.]

## 627

## Wilcocks v. Gore

(Ch. 1714)

*The question in this case was whether a widow can retain the jewels that she usually wore against the deceased husband's devisee.*

British Library MS. Hargrave 80, f. 184, pl. 2

In this case, one question was whether the wife should retains jewels that she usually wore against the devisee of the husband.

The Attorney General [*Northey*] said that a woman shall hold her paraphernalia against a bare executor of the husband, but that there is no authority in the book that she should hold them against an express devise of the husband, that, in most of the great families, the jewels were commonly devised to the wife for her life only and then over, and that the ladies always submitted to those devises, and that a resolution to the contrary might be of fatal consequence.

On the other side, *Jekyll* insisted that there was no ground for making any distinction between an executor and a devisee, that, before the Case of Foster and

---

[1] Sic in MS.

Munt,[1] the law knew no difference between them, but that making a man executor always implied a bequest to him of his personal estate, and that, therefore, a wife ought to retain the paraphernalia against a devisee as well as against an executor. The case of Lord Hastings and Sir Archibald Douglass, Cro. Cha. 343,[2] was cited, where the four judges seem to agree that the husband may dispose of them by his deed in his lifetime, that the wife cannot retain them against the creditors of the husband unless there are assets besides, and that she may retain against an executor, but, [whether] the husband could dispose of them by his will or not, they were equally divided.

Lord Chancellor [Lord Harcourt] reserved the consideration of this point, as he had of the like in the Case of Captain Dorrell, which is not yet determined.

[Other copies of this report: Lincoln's Inn MS. Misc. 383, p. 304, pl. 1, Lincoln's Inn MS. Misc. 107, f. 21, pl. 2.]

2 Eq. Cas. Abr. 626, 22 E.R. 526

Trinity 13 Ann. [1714].

The question was, if the husband can devise the paraphernalia of the wife to any other than the wife.

Lord Chancellor Harcourt said that this is a point of consequence, and he would reserve the consideration of it until after the Master's report upon the account. *Curia advisare vult.*

*Sir Joseph Jekyll* said creditors may come in against the wife to have her paraphernalia, but not a devisee under the husband's will. And there is not one case in the law to warrant such a devise. And it is no argument to say that the husband may dispose of them in his lifetime, therefore, he may give them away by will, for he may dispose of his wife's wearing apparel or a term in the wife in her lifetime, but he can dispose of neither by his will.

A., the relict of B. did claim her paraphernalia against the devisee of her husband, but he said he believed the matter was made up between the parties, for he did not remember that any judgment was given in that case. See Cro. Car. 343.

*Per Northey*, Attorney General: There is not one authority in the law that the husband cannot devise the paraphernalia of his wife. It is true the husband's executor shall not take the paraphernalia of the wife from her. And the case in Cro. Car. 343, goes no further.

---

[1] *Foster v. Munt* (1687–1689), 1 Vernon 473, 23 E.R. 598, 1 Eq. Cas. Abr. 243, 21 E.R. 1020, 2 Eq. Cas. Abr. 433, 443, 22 E.R. 368, 378, Dodd 78, Chancery Repts. *tempore* Jac. II, 368.

[2] *Lord Hastings v. Douglas* (1634), Croke Car. 343, 79 E.R. 901, also W. Jones 332, 82 E.R. 175.

It is the constant practice in great families to give the family jewels to the wife for her life and, after her death, to the eldest son. And he said he never knew such a devise called in question, but always submitted to.

## 628

## Anwell v. Brereton

(Ch. 1714)

*A bill of review can be grounded upon the errors shown by the defendant in his plea to the bill of review.*

British Library MS. Hargrave 80, f. 187v

The plaintiff, by his bill of review, set out the decree wrongly; the defendant, by his plea, set it out rightly.

*Sir Joseph Jekyll* [said] that the plaintiffs had assigned their errors in the decree as set out by them and that the defendant had pleaded *nul tiel record* and that the plaintiff ought not to be admitted to show errors in the decree set out by the defendant.

*Vernon*: It is not necessary for the plaintiff to set out the decree *in haec verba* but, if the plaintiff makes any mistake in setting it out, the defendant may set it right by a plea, but, then indeed, the plaintiff must be confined, as we submit to be here, to show errors in the decree as set out by the defendant.

Upon showing errors, Lord Chancellor [Lord Harcourt] overruled the plea.

[Other copies of this report: Lincoln's Inn MS. Misc. 383, p. 306, pl. 2, Lincoln's Inn MS. Misc. 107, f. 26, pl. 1.]

## 629

## Frith v. Ravenhill

(Ch. 1714)

*The question in this case was whether, where a mortgagee has sued to foreclose, can the mortgagor then enter into a statute to a third party and the creditor by the statute redeem the statute against the first mortgagee pendente lite.*

British Library MS. Hargrave 80, f. 188

The plaintiff was a creditor by a statute of the mortgagor and brought his bill to redeem against the defendant, who was a mortgagee and had obtained a decree of foreclosure. The statute was acknowledged a few days after the filing of the defendant's bill to foreclose.

To this, the defendant pleaded the proceedings in his cause and the decree and that he had no notice of the plaintiff's demand.

*Vernon*, for the defendant, cited a case before Lord Cowper, but did not name it, where a mortgagee brought a bill against the mortgagor and all parties that he then knew to have any interest in the equity of redemption to foreclose and obtained a decree. An incumbrancer who was no party, afterwards, brought his bill to redeem, to which the mortgagee pleaded the former decree and that he had no notice of this encumbrance. Lord Cowper would not cut the plaintiff out of his security, but, in regard that he had lain by while the former suit depended, he would not permit him to break in upon the account taken in that cause any further than to surcharge or falsify.

*Vernon* said the present case was much stronger. Here, the plaintiff came in *pendente lite* and that, if any countenance should be given to a demand of this nature, every mortgagor would make encumbrances pending a suit against him to foreclose and, by that means, it would be impossible ever to obtain a foreclosure.

*Jekyll*, for the plaintiff, insisted that he was a just creditor, that the foreclosure was recent in 1712 and then barely upon the foot of the decretal order upon the expiration of six months after the report without any new order to make the foreclosure absolute, which is much, though perhaps not necessary or without the times having every been enlarged, and that the security was of a much greater value than the money due to the defendant.

Lord Chancellor [Lord Harcourt] saved the benefit of the plea to the hearing, but particularly directed that they should not except to any matters of account, which he seemed determined not to unravel.

[Other copies of this report: Lincoln's Inn MS. Misc. 383, p. 307, pl. 1, Lincoln's Inn MS. Misc. 107, f. 26, pl. 2.]

## 630

## Anonymous

(Ch. 1714)

*Contracts between private persons as to prizes taken in war are enforced in the common law courts, but such contracts as to prizes taken by royal ships are enforced in the Court of Admiralty.*

British Library MS. Hargrave 80, f. 190v, pl. 1

*Mead*: The American Act[1] vesting the ownership of prizes taken by private ships in the owners according to their agreements among themselves, it has been often adjudged that the Admiralty has no jurisdiction in the distribution of those priz-

[1] Stat. 6 Ann., c. 64 (*SR*, VIII, 804–809).

es which is to be regulated by the articles between the owners. But, in the distribution of prizes taken by the queen's ships, the jurisdiction of the Admiralty still remains, the queen by the proclamation issued pursuant to that Act having referred it to the Admiralty.

[Other copies of this report: Lincoln's Inn MS. Misc. 383, p. 309, pl. 1, Lincoln's Inn MS. Misc. 107, f. 30, pl. 1.]

## 631

## Anonymous

(Ch. 1714)

*An annuity by a devise is assets of the testator's estate available to pay his debts.*

British Library MS. Hargrave 80, f. 190v, pl. 2

The Case of Lord Pembroke's creditors[1] was cited thus. Lord Pembroke created an annuity by a devise to the annuitant for ninety-nine years and re-demised to him. Though the term was created for a particular purpose, yet, it being assets at law and equity assisting, not defeating, creditors, it was, therefore, decreed to be assets in favor of the creditors.

[Other copies of this report: Lincoln's Inn MS. Misc. 383, p. 309, pl. 2, Lincoln's Inn MS. Misc. 107, f. 30, pl. 2.]

## 632

## Atkyns v. Atkyns

(Ch. 1714)

*Where there is an incomplete settlement of lands, the court will presume a last remainder to the right heir of the husband.*

*The connection between something devised as an heirloom and the real estate ends when they come to the hands of a person who has a power over the estate.*

British Library MS. Hargrave 80, f. 191, pl. 1

£1500 of the wife's and as much of the husband's [was] settled to them for their lives, remainder to the issue of the marriage without any further limitations expressed. Jeffreys looked upon it as a real estate and, upon a presumption that, if the lands [were] settled, the last remainder would have been for the right heirs of the husband.

[1] *Baden v. Earl of Pembroke* (1688–1690), 2 Vernon 52, 213, 23 E.R. 644, 739, 3 Chancery Reports 217, 21 E.R. 771, 1 Eq. Cas. Abr. 241, 265, 21 E.R. 1019, 1035.

[It was] decreed in favor of the heir against the executors.

Note here, both were volunteers.

The connection between a thing devised as an heirloom and the real estate determines when they come to the hands of a person who has a power over the estate, and not sooner.

[Other copies of this report: Lincoln's Inn MS. Misc. 383, p. 309, pl. 4, Lincoln's Inn MS. Misc. 107, f. 31, pl. 2.]

633

## Erby v. Erby

(Ch. 1714)

*A judgment creditor has priority over a creditor who has only sued out an outlawry.*

*A judgment creditor has priority according to the date of his first judgment.*

Lincoln's Inn MS. Misc. 10, p. 161

22 June 1714. Irby v. Irby.

Upon a petition, the decree was that an estate should be sold and the creditors paid according to the priority of their respective debts.

It appeared by the Master's report that some of the creditors had sued the defendant to an outlawry and had taken out a [writ of] *capias utlagatum* against him and delivered it to the sheriff but proceeded no farther and others of them had judgments subsequent. And the question was which should have the preference.

Lord Chancellor [Lord Harcourt]: The outlawry is only in the nature of mesne process to compel the party to appear. And, therefore, though prior in time to the judgment, I do not think they ought to have a precedency.

The second question was whether a judgment creditor who had brought an action on his judgment and recovered a second judgment should be reputed a creditor from the time of his first judgment in regard it was said he could not now take out a [writ of] *elegit* upon his first judgment and, if he takes out one upon his second judgment, the inquisition must be to enquire what lands the defendant was seised of at the time of the second judgment.

Lord Chancellor [Lord Harcourt] was clear of the opinion that such judgment creditor ought to be considered as a judgment creditor and have a preference from the time of his first judgment.

1 Salkeld 80, 91 E.R. 75

Trinity 1714.

The creditors of J.S. brought a bill for debts, which debts were mortgages, judgments, and bonds. Upon one of the bonds, the defendant was outlawed, and, upon one of the judgments, the recoveror had brought an action of debt.

And the question being concerning priority of payment, it was objected, first, that the judgments were by confession and it was not equitable that it should be in the power of the party to prefer one creditor to another.

But that seemed to be overruled.

And, as to the outlawry, the court ruled that, being only upon mesne process before judgment, it did not alter the nature of the debt nor create a lien upon the land in this case but that, where there is an outlawry and a seizure thereupon, the debt attaches upon the land and shall be preferred to a judgment though prior to the outlawry, but that it is the seizure that gives the preference.

It was also objected that bringing [an action of] debt upon the judgment was a waiver of the lien created by that judgment, for he can only extend the land that the party had at the time of the latter judgment.

But the court held that bringing [an action of] debt upon a judgment did not postpone this to other judgments and that it was the act of the attorney and that it would be no waiver because there was no other remedy after the year and day at common law.

## 634

## Aylesworth v. Lady Lempster

(Ch. 1714)

*A bond to resign from a rectory or a vicarage will be relieved against in a court of equity unless some good cause for having entered into it has been shown.*

Lincoln's Inn MS. Misc. 10, p. 162, pl. 1

1 July 1714.

The plaintiff, having entered into a bond of resignation [of a church], brought his bill to be relieved against it.

The Master of the Rolls [Trevor] decreed a perpetual injunction. He allowed such bonds to be good in law, but he said this court had always restrained them from being put in suit unless some very good cause could be assigned.

# 635

## Arnold v. Wilkinson

(Ch. 1714)

*Where there is a serious likelihood that an executor will alienate the assets of a decedent's estate, a court of equity will order the assets to be brought into the court for safe keeping pendente lite.*

British Library MS. Hargrave 81, f. 122, pl. 2

2 July 1714.

The defendant was executor of the plaintiff's father, who left a considerable personal estate in money, stock, and security and devised them to his executor in trust for the plaintiff, an infant. The bill was brought for a discovery and satisfaction of this estate, suggesting that the executor had withdrawn himself[1] and called in most part of the testator's estate, which was confessed by his answer. And it was proved that he intended to apply it in satisfaction of his own debts.

Therefore, it was prayed by Serjeant *Hooper* that an account may be decreed and the consideration of the interests and costs reserved until after the report.

And it was ordered accordingly.

It was also prayed that, this being in the case of an infant's estate and there being great reason to believe that the estate is in danger, the court would order that, in the meantime, the testator's estate and effects might be brought before the Master for the infant's security to remain until a report and further order and that this was most reasonable being at hearing and that the like had been done before the hearing upon an interlocutory order to secure the estate in all events for the party who should appear entitled though there were no suspicions either as to the integrity or sufficiency of the creditor, as in the case of Lyon and Lyon, by Lord Cowper, and in other cases where there was a doubt of the executor.

The Court ordered the securities confessed in the answer to be brought before the Master.

[Other copies of this report: British Library MS. Hargrave 82, f. 136, British Library MS. Hargrave 77, f. 34, pl. 1, British Library MS. Hargrave 303, f. 661v, pl. 1.]

# 636

## Hatley v. Hatley

(Ch. 1714)

*A court of equity will order a copyhold to be surrendered for the benefit of a younger child where a testator has neglected to do so.*

---

[1] *I.e.* absconded from his creditors.

Lincoln's Inn MS. Misc. 10, p. 162, pl. 2

2 July 1714. Hutley v. Hutley.

The defect of a surrender of copyhold land to the use of a will [was] supplied in favor of a younger son though he had other freehold lands given him by the will.

British Library MS. Hargrave 81, f. 124

*Eodem die [2 July 1714].*

The father of the plaintiff and defendant had freehold and copyhold in Essex. And he devises all his freehold lands in A. and B. to his oldest son John, the defendant, in fee and other freehold and copyhold lands to the plaintiff, his second son. But he made no surrender to the use of his will. After the testator's death, the plaintiff desired to be admitted, but the lord refused because there was no surrender. The two brothers were both infants.

The plaintiff brings a bill to have the want of surrender supplied, it being a provision for a younger child and the defendant [was] well provided for by the devise to him in fee and absolute without any manner of restraint or condition.

The Court decreed accordingly and that the plaintiff should hold and enjoy against the defendant, his brother, and all claiming under him and that the defendant the lord of the manor should admit the plaintiff, paying the usual fine, and that the defendant, the heir at law, when at full age, should, if required, surrender a release to the plaintiff and his heirs and, if so required, the defendant to have his costs to be taxed at 40s. only, for the procuring of the bill was not for the benefit of the defendant, the eldest son, who looks for nothing nor did desire anything by the bill, but it was purely for the plaintiff's benefit.

[Other copies of this report: British Library MS. Hargrave 82, f. 137, British Library MS. Hargrave 77, f. 34, pl. 2, British Library MS. Hargrave 303, f. 61v, pl. 2.]

## 637

## Fulham v. Jones

(Ch. 1714)

*Money contracted to be invested in land and settled is considered to be real estate for all purposes.*

Lincoln's Inn MS. Misc. 384, p. 13, pl. 3

13 July 1714.

Dr. Fulham, by his will, gives all his real estate to the plaintiff, his son, and directs that his personal estate should be applied by the defendant, his executor, to pay all his debts. The question was whether £4000, which was covenanted by the testator to be laid out in land, should be taken as a real or a personal estate.

*Vernon*, for the plaintiff: In the Case of Whitlock v. Jermin,[1] it was taken as land. But that was between the heir and the executor. There has been dower and tenancy by the curtesy allowed in such a case. Atkyns v. Atkyns, in Lord Jeffreys' time.[2] That was no limitation of the remainder in fee, it was decreed to the heir as land.

Lord Harcourt: None of these cases comes up to this, for they were between the heir and the executor. But here are creditors and a charity concerned, for the testator gives all the residue of his personal estate to charity. I cannot give my opinion until the Master has stated the debts.

British Library MS. Hargrave 80, f. 190v, pl. 3

Whittick v. Germin [was] cited per *Vernon*. Money was agreed by marriage articles to be invested in land and settled. Upon a question between the creditors and the issue of the marriage, it was ruled with the assistance of Lord Hale that it was to be considered to all intents as a real estate and that the creditors were bound as well as others. Note that the issue were purchasers and equally entitled to favor with the creditors.

[Other copies of this report: Lincoln's Inn MS. Misc. 383, p. 309, pl. 3, Lincoln's Inn MS. Misc. 107, f. 31, pl. 1.]

[Other reports of this case: 2 Eq. Cas. Abr. 250, 296, 298, 22 E.R. 212, 249, 250.]

## 638

## Parrie v. Sims

(Ch. 1714)

*The question in this case was whether a court of equity will cure a defective appointment of a bequest to younger children.*

British Library MS. Hargrave 81, f. 160

At Westminster, Lord Chancellor.

Sims, the grandfather of the defendant's son, by settlement on his son's marriage, limited a term to trustees to raise £1000 to be paid among the younger children of his son by the intended marriage as the son should appoint. The marriage was had. And there were children of that marriage, a son and other children. The son died without making any appointment. The younger children were ignorant as to the settlement and provision made for them until being concerned

[1] *Whitwick v. Jermy* (Ch. 1685), Chancery Repts. *tempore* Jac. II, 168.

[2] Perhaps *Knight v. Atkyns* (Ch. 1686–1687), 2 Chancery Reports 400, 21 E.R. 699, 2 Vernon 20, 23 E.R. 624, 1 Eq. Cas. Abr. 274, 21 E.R. 1041, Chancery Repts. *tempore* Jac. II, 274.

in another cause and accidentally in court when the deed was read, they became acquainted with it. And, thereupon, they brought their bill for the £1000.

For the plaintiffs, it was said by *Peere Williams* that this charge did arise, though there was not any appointment and though, strictly it might be otherwise, yet, in equity, it should be so considered, it being in the case of a provision for younger children. The question was whether, in this case, the charge did arise or not; if not, equity should aid the defect where the intention was clear and manifest.

Against this was cited Doctor Garth's Case and Lady Beaufoy, Sir Seymor Pyle's wife and children, a sum not exceeding £1000 to such of his children's portions as he should appoint [and] no agreement in what proportion the money should be paid.[1]

Curia: The charge here does not arise, and here is no proper bill nor proper parties. He dismissed the bill but without prejudice to a proper bill to be brought.

[Other copies of this report: British Library MS. Hargrave 82, f. 170, British Library MS. Hargrave 303, f. 74.]

## 639

## Done's Case

(Ch. 1714)

*A writ of ne exeat regno lies to prevent a party from leaving the jurisdiction of the court.*

1 Peere Williams 263, 24 E.R. 380

On an application made to the court for a [writ of] *ne exeat regnum* to stop the defendant from going to Scotland, it was objected that, since the Union, Scotland was part of this kingdom and, consequently, that going to Scotland could not be construed going out of the kingdom, nor any breach of the condition of the security given on such writ.

Lord Chancellor [Lord Harcourt]: Scotland being out of the jurisdiction of this court and, consequently, out, of the reach of the process thereof, the defendant's going into Scotland is equally mischievous to the suitor here as if he went actually out of the kingdom, wherefore take a *ne exeat regnum*. And though, in this case, the party moving for the writ be also a defendant, yet, forasmuch as it is a matter of account, in which both parties are actors and money being sworn due from the party, against whom the writ is prayed, to the other, the motion is proper.

[1] *Garth v. Lady Blanfrey* (1695), Gilbert Rep. 166, 25 E.R. 117, 2 Eq. Cas. Abr. 659, 22 E.R. 554.

Note: Where the party is to be restrained from going to Scotland, the condition must be not to go out of the realm or to Scotland, for, if it be only not to go out of the realm, the parties going to Scotland will not forfeit the bond or recognizance.

2 Salkeld 702, 91 E.R. 593

Trinity 13 Anne.

A [writ of] *ne exeat regno* was granted to stay the defendant from going to Scotland, for, though that is not out of the kingdom, yet it is out of the reach of the process of this court and within the same mischief.

## 640

## Sands and Lloyd v. Price

(Ch. 1710–1714)

*A court of equity can set aside a deed that was obtained by fraud but not a will, the latter being within the jurisdiction of the ecclesiastical courts.*

Harvard Law Sch. MS. 1105, p. 1

In Chancery, before Lord Harcourt.

A bill [was brought] to set aside a will and also some deeds unduly obtained, and, though there was plain proof of fraud used in obtaining both, the deeds only were set aside, but the will was sent by him into the Prerogative Court to remain there during the testator's life, and, after his death, it was set aside by the [Court of] Delegates,[1] which case is contrary to that of Herbert v. Lowndes.[2]

---

[1] *Sands and Lloyd v. Pearce* (Del. 1715), Misc. Delegates Repts. 114.

[2] *Herbert v. Lowndes* (Ch. 1628), 1 Chancery Reports 22, 21 E.R. 495, 118 Selden Soc. 578, Chancery Repts. *tempore* Coventry 71.

# Index of Names

[These references are to case numbers, not page numbers.]

# Subject Index

[These references are to case numbers, not page numbers.]